The Complete Book of
Knitting Crochet & Embroidery

Marshall Cavendish London & New York

Published by Marshall Cavendish Books Limited
58 Old Compton Street
London W1V 5PA

© Marshall Cavendish Limited 1972, 1973, 1974, 1975, 1976, 1977

This material was first published by Marshall Cavendish Limited
in the publications Golden Hands Monthly, Encyclopedia of
Crafts and Fashion Maker.

First printed 1976
Reprinted 1977

Printed in Great Britain by Ben Johnson and Company Ltd., York

ISBN 0 85685 198 1

CONTENTS

AN INTRODUCTION TO KNITTING

In presenting this book my genuine hope is that I can communicate some of my enthusiasm for this most beautiful craft to the reader and whether you approach it as a complete beginner or knowledgeable knitter, arouse your interest in its almost limitless possibilities.

For the first half of this century, knitting was tagged with the fuddy-duddy image it had acquired during the Victorian era and suffered an undeserved decline in popularity. Today it has rightly taken its place as a unique and practical way of interpreting fashion but, even now, most knitters are still not aware of its tremendous scope. In no other field of fashion or craft, other than the allied craft of crochet, do you have such complete control not only over the shape of the ultimate design, but the texture and colour of the fabric. In this craft, you as the knitter, combine both the skill of a weaver and the practical knowledge of a dressmaker – and all for the price of a pair of needles and a few balls of yarn. Of all the crafts and skills acquired by man – and I use the word 'man' advisedly, in that women's skill in this field is only recent in terms of history – knitting has proved to be one of the most fascinating and enduring. It has survived, sometimes through countless centuries without any record, either written or visual, and has developed and evolved by word of mouth from one generation to the next.

The first steps in knitting are as simple as those required for basic cookery, but its ultimate variety is akin to the art of cordon bleu cooking, where nothing that individual taste, ability and imagination can devise is impossible. The only manufactured materials required are a pair of needles and a ball of spun thread but, with sufficient knowledge and time to experiment, even these are comparatively easy to produce by hand. The simple talents needed to encompass its full range are a willing pair of hands, an eye for colour and fabric, some simple mathematical skill and basic dressmaking knowledge. Armed with these attributes the world of knitting is your oyster and you can begin to design garments to suit your own individual shape and taste, without being tied to existing patterns.

The main purpose of this book is to take the technical knowledge it contains and apply this to the basic guide to designing, which is also explained. You can, of course, accept it as it stands and still acquire the necessary skill to become a proficient knitter, but taking the step from knitter to designer is a relatively small one and out of all proportion to the exciting and creative field it opens up for you.

With the present necessity to conserve all natural resources and survive an unhealthy economic period, it is important to know how to make warm, wearable and fashionable garments for the minimum of outlay, both in costs and materials. Knitting is the most practical and satisfying solution to these problems and has the added bonus of extending your own latent creative talents and the therapeutic benefit of making something beautiful with your own hands.

Pam Dawson

HISTORY OF KNITTING

Knitting is an ancient craft, first developed in the deserts of Arabia among the nomadic tribes who lived there 3,000 years ago. It may even have been a familiar technique in pre-biblical times, for knitting of high quality, well advanced in both technique and design, was certainly being produced in Arabia 1,000 years before the death of Christ. No one can date the birth of knitting exactly. It has grown up with civilization. The early knitters were the men of the tribes, and they were very skilled at their craft. As these people kept straggling herds of sheep and goats there was no shortage of material. The women gathered wool from the animals and spun it into yarn for the men, who would sit for hours, tending the flocks and knitting. The articles they produced were simple scarves, robes and socks to wear with sandals.

Ancient knitting

Very few examples of really early knitting are still in existence, but a pair of red sandal socks, pre-Christian in origin, still survive. They are beautifully made, with expertly turned heels. It is interesting to note that stitches have been carefully divided for the big toe, so that the socks were comfortable to wear with sandals.

The socks were knitted in the round on a circular frame, probably made of thin wire. Pins were inserted all round the edge of the circle, and loops were made on the pins. When the wool was wound around the outside of the pins and the loops drawn over it, circular knitting of a rather loose tension was produced.

A spectacular fragment

Twin needles, hooked at the ends rather like today's crochet hooks, were used to make another surviving fragment of Arabic knitting. This piece of work was discovered at Fustat, an ancient ruined city near Cairo in Egypt, and it has been dated at between the 7th and the 9th centuries. From beneath the sand and dust of centuries a fragile piece of knitted silk fabric was retrieved. Worked with exquisite care on a pair of fine wire needles, to an easily-checked tension of 36 stitches to the inch, the fragment reveals an elaborate design in maroon and gold.

Between the years AD 1000 and 1200 little round knitted caps called Coptic caps were being made in Egypt. They were worn by monks and missionaries and it is possible that these men carried the knowledge of knitting with them out of Egypt. Craftsmen in Spain, then in Italy and France and eventually in England and the New World, were fascinated by this new kind of fabric weaving. Knowledge of the craft quickly spread, each nation adding its own ideas and patterns. By the Middle Ages knitting was a common craft form all over Europe. Italy and France were the great medieval homes of fine knitting, and there the knitters soon formed themselves, under Church patronage, into organized guilds.

The Knitters' Guilds

The Knitters' Guild of Paris was a typical example. Young boys of intelligence and manual ability were carefully selected as apprentices. They were bound for six years, three of which were spent working with a master-knitter at home and three learning new techniques in a foreign country. At the end of this time the apprentice was required to demonstrate his skill to his elders. The test was prodigious. In only thirteen weeks the apprentice had to knit an elaborate carpet eight feet by twelve, with extremely intricate designs incorporating flowers, birds, foliage and animals in natural colours, using between twenty and thirty different coloured wools; a beret, sometimes to be felted and blocked after knitting; a woollen shirt; and a pair of socks with Spanish clocks.

No apprentice was accepted who did not produce masterpieces in all these categories, and when he became a master-knitter he knew that shoddy or skimped work would result in heavy fines and even expulsion from the guild, which meant loss of livelihood. The only women admitted to these guilds were the widows of master-knitters. For the most part, the women still sat at home spinning the wool for the men to knit up.

Knitting in England

By the time of Queen Elizabeth I, England was the world leader in knitting. Fine work was being produced by the master-craftsmen, and, in addition, many poor people were knitting up fabrics for felting into leggings, topcoats and caps. Hand knitting gradually became widespread as an important village industry, particularly in the dales of Yorkshire where the finest wool was always available.

Apart from the domestic and commercial work being produced in England, much exquisite decorative knitting was done in the seclusion of the monasteries and the nunneries. The religious influence on the beautiful silk knitting of the 16th and 17th centuries is very marked.

The hand knitting tradition continued to be strong in England until the Industrial Revolution in the 19th century, the age of mass production when interest in handicrafts declined.

Individuality still flourished, however, notably in

Scotland and the Channel Islands, where traditional jumpers (sweaters) and jerseys were made. The 'guernsey', produced on the Channel Island of Guernsey for centuries, took two forms. The everyday one, in plain stocking stitch, was the one most often seen, but on special occasions the men wore guernseys in heavy cable and bobble patterns, each family or village having its own distinctive design. They were called 'bridal shirts' because a courting girl would start to knit one for her sweetheart's wedding day.

The word 'knitting' comes from an old English word meaning 'a knot', and basic techniques have altered little over the centuries. Today, interest in the craft has revived after its Victorian decline. Machine knitting techniques have gained popularity, but most knitters still practice the craft using needles very little different from those used by the Arab pioneer knitters. Knitting or Knotting, the ancient craft is more popular now than it has ever been before.

Right: An English apron, knitted in multi-coloured wool in the early nineteenth century.
Below: A sandal sock knitted in wool. It is Egyptian in origin and dates from the fifth century AD. However, it is thought that knitting probably originated centuries before this, possibly as much as 1000 years before the birth of Christ.

BASIC SKILLS
THE FIRST STEPS

Knitting needles

Modern needles are usually made of lightweight coated metal or plastic and are supplied in a comprehensive range of sizes, both in diameter and length. For British needles, the gauge or diameter of the needle is given as a figure, such as No. 11, No. 10, No. 9 and so on, and the higher the number the smaller the diameter of the needle. The length of the needle is also given and the choice of length will depend on the size and type of garment to be knitted. French and American needle sizes use the reverse of the British system and the highest number is used to denote the largest needle.

For 'flat' knitting – that is, working forwards and backwards on two needles in rows – needles are manufactured in pairs and each needle has a knob at one end to prevent the stitches slipping off.

For 'circular' knitting – that is, working in rounds without a seam – needles are manufactured in sets of four and each needle is pointed at both ends. A flexible, circular needle is also manufactured and the effect is the same as dividing the work between three needles and working with the fourth, but a larger number of stitches may be used.

Holding yarn and needles

Until the art of holding both the yarn and needles comfortably has been mastered, it is impossible to begin to knit. For a right handed person the yarn will be looped around the fingers of the right hand to achieve firm, even knitting. The needle which is used to make the stitches is held in the right hand and the left hand holds the needle with the made stitches ready for working. The reverse of these positions would be adopted by a left handed person.

To hold the yarn correctly, loop the yarn from the ball across the palm of the right hand between the 4th and 3rd fingers, round the 4th finger and back between the 4th and 3rd fingers, over the 3rd finger, between the 3rd and 2nd fingers, under the 2nd finger then over the index finger, leaving the end of the ball of yarn free, in which a slip loop will be made to begin casting on.

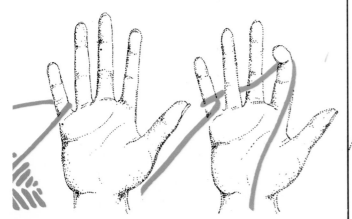

Casting on

This is the first step in hand knitting and it provides the first row of loops on the needle. Different methods of casting on produce different types of edges, each with its own appropriate use, and it is advisable to practise all these variations at some stage.

The thumb method is an excellent way to begin most garments where an edge with some elasticity is required, such as the welt of a jersey, but the two needle method is necessary where extra stitches need to be made during the actual knitting of a garment, such as for buttonholes and pockets. Beginners should practise these two methods. The invisible method gives the appearance of a machine-made edge and is very flexible and neat. The circular method is required for knitting in rounds to produce seamless garments, such as gloves and socks. Experienced knitters will find these methods of interest.

Two needle method of casting on

Make a slip loop in the end of the ball of yarn and put this loop on to the left hand needle. Holding the yarn in the right hand, insert the point of the right hand needle into the slip loop, wind the yarn under and over the point of the right hand needle and draw a new loop through the slip loop. Put the newly made stitch on to the left hand needle. Place the point of the right hand needle between the 2 loops on the left hand needle and wind the yarn under and over the point of the right hand needle again and draw through a new loop. Put the newly made stitch on to the left hand needle. Place the point of the right hand needle between the last 2 loops on the left hand needle and wind the yarn under and over the point of the right hand needle again and draw through a new loop. Put the newly made stitch on to the left hand needle. Continue repeating the last action until the required number of stitches are formed on the left hand needle. This method produces a firm edge and is also used as an intermediate stage in increasing.

Two needle method stage 1

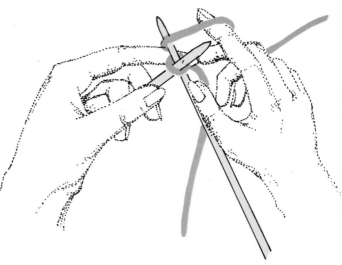

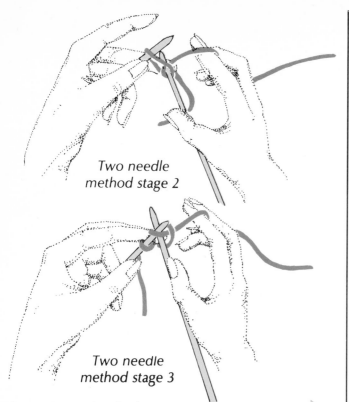

*Two needle
method stage 2*

*Two needle
method stage 3*

Thumb method of casting on using one needle

Make a slip loop in the ball of yarn about 91.5 centimetres *(one yard)* from the end. This length will vary with the number of stitches to be cast on but 91.5 centimetres *(one yard)* will be sufficient for about one hundred stitches.

Put the slip loop on to the needle, which should be held in the right hand. Working with the short length of yarn in the left hand, pass this between the index finger and thumb, round the thumb and hold it across the palm of the hand. Insert the point of the needle under the loop on the thumb and bring forward the long end of yarn from the ball. Wind the long end of yarn under and over the point of the needle and draw through a loop on the thumb, leaving the newly formed stitch on the needle. Tighten the stitch on the needle by pulling the short end of yarn, noting that the yarn is then wound round the left thumb ready for the next stitch. Continue in this way until the required number of stitches are formed on the needle. This method produces **an elastic edge** which is very hardwearing.

*Thumb method stage 1 –
making a slip loop*

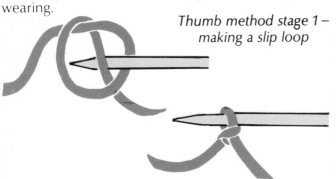

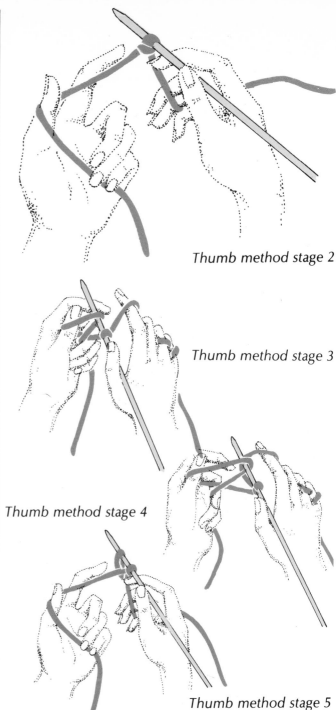

Thumb method stage 2

Thumb method stage 3

Thumb method stage 4

Thumb method stage 5

Invisible method of casting on

Using a length of yarn in a contrast colour which is later removed and the thumb method, cast on half the number of stitches required plus one extra. Using the correct yarn and two needles, begin the double fabric which forms the invisible method.

1st row Holding the yarn in the right hand and the needle with the cast on stitches in the left hand, insert the point of the right hand needle into the first stitch from front to back, wind the yarn under and over the point of the right hand needle and draw through a loop which is kept on the right hand needle – this is a knitted stitch and is called 'K1' –, *bring the yarn forward between the two needles and back over the top of the right hand needle to make a stitch on this row only – this is called 'yarn forward' or 'yfwd' –, K1, repeat from the point marked with a * to the end of the row.

2nd row K1, *yfwd and keep at front of work without taking it back over the right hand needle insert the point of the right hand needle into the front of the next stitch on the left hand needle from right to left, and lift it off the left hand needle on to the right hand needle without working it – this is a slipped stitch and is called 'sl 1' –, bring the yarn across in front of the sl 1 and back between the two needles again – this is called 'yarn back' or 'yb' –, K1, repeat from the point marked with a * to the end of the row.

3rd row Sl 1, *ybk, K1, yfwd, sl 1, repeat from the point marked with a * to the end of the row. Repeat the 2nd and 3rd rows once more. Now continue with the single ribbing which completes this method.

6th row K1, *bring the yarn forward between the two needles, insert the point of the right hand needle into the front of the next stitch on the left hand needle from right to left, wind the yarn over the top of the needle and round to the front and draw through a loop which is kept on the right hand needle – this is a purled stitch and is called 'P1' –, put the yarn back between the two needles, K1, repeat from the point marked with a * to the end of the row.

7th row P1, *put the yarn back between the two needles, K1, bring the yarn forward between the two needles, P1, repeat from the point marked with a * to the end of the row.

Continue repeating the 6th and 7th rows until the rib is the required length, then unpick the contrast yarn used for casting on. This method gives the appearance of the ribbing running right round the edge with no visible cast on stitches.

Increasing on 1st row of invisible casting on

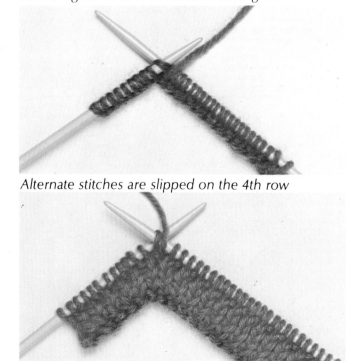

Alternate stitches are slipped on the 4th row

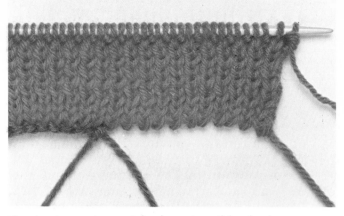

Contrast yarn is unpicked to give ribbed edge

Circular method of casting on using four needles

When working with sets of four needles, one is used for making the stitches and the total number of stitches required is divided between the remaining three needles. Use the two needle method of casting on and either cast on the total number of stitches on to one needle and then divide them on to the 2nd and 3rd needles, or cast on the required number of stitches on to the first needle, then proceed to the 2nd and 3rd needles, taking care that the stitches do not become twisted. Form the three needles containing the stitches into a triangle shape and the fourth needle is then ready to knit the first stitch on the first needle. This method produces a circular fabric without seams.

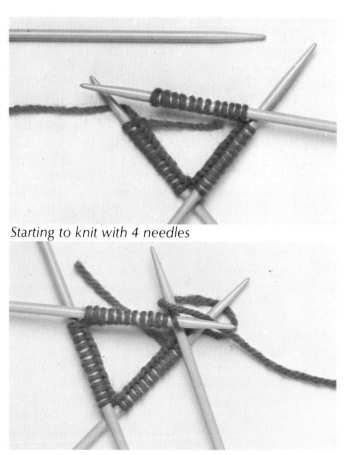

Starting to knit with 4 needles

Basic stitches

Once you have cast on your stitches and can hold the yarn and needles comfortably, you can begin to knit – it's as easy as that. All knitting stitches are based on just two methods – knitting and purling – and however complicated patterns may appear they are all achieved by simple, or intricate, arrangements of these two methods to produce an almost infinite variety of fabric and texture. Anything from the finest lace to the thickest carpet can be knitted. The advantages of knitted fabrics are almost too numerous to list and they have been used since time immemorial to achieve examples of exquisite beauty.

Tools of the trade
Before beginning to knit it is essential to ensure that you have all the tools you will require to hand, including yarn and needles. In addition you will need:–
A rigid metal or wooden centimetre/*inch* rule
Scissors
Blunt-ended sewing needles
Rustless steel pins
Stitch holders to hold stitches not in use
Knitting register for counting rows
Knitting needle gauge to check needle sizes
Cloth or polythene bag in which to keep work clean
Iron and ironing surface with felt pad or blanket
Cotton cloths suitable for use when pressing

The basic stitches
To work knitted stitches – hold the needle with the cast on stitches in the left hand and the yarn and other needle in the right hand. Insert the point of the right hand needle through the first stitch on the left hand needle from the front to the back. Keeping the yarn at the back of the work pass it under and over the top of the right hand needle and draw this loop through the stitch on the left hand needle. Keep this newly made stitch on the right hand needle and allow the stitch on the left hand needle to slip off. Repeat this action into each stitch on the left hand needle until all the stitches are transferred to the right hand needle. You have now knitted one row. To work the next row, change the needle holding the stitches to your left hand so that the yarn is again in position at the beginning of the row and hold the yarn and free needle in your right hand.

To work purled stitches – hold the needle with the cast on stitches in your left hand and the yarn and other needle in the right hand. Insert the point of the right hand needle through the first stitch on the left hand needle from right to left, keeping the yarn

at the front of the work pass it over and round the top of the right hand needle and draw this loop through the stitch on the left hand needle. Keep this newly made stitch on the right hand needle and allow the stitch on the left hand needle to slip off. Repeat this action into each stitch on the left hand needle until all the stitches are transferred to the right hand needle. You have now purled one row. To work the next row, change the needle holding the stitches to your left hand so that the yarn is again in position at the beginning of the row and hold the yarn and free needle in your right hand.

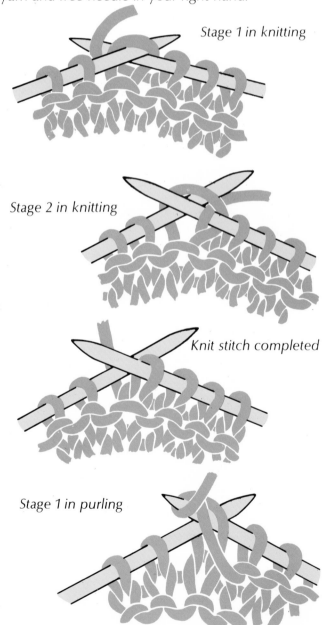

Stage 1 in knitting

Stage 2 in knitting

Knit stitch completed

Stage 1 in purling

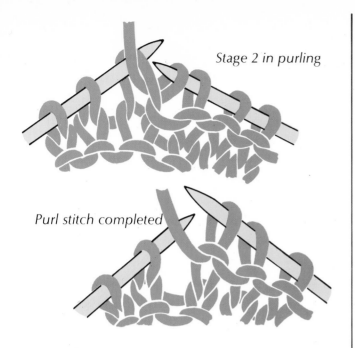

Stage 2 in purling

Purl stitch completed

Garter stitch

This is the simplest of all knitted stitches and is formed by working every row in the same stitch, either knit or purl. If you purl every row, however, you do not produce such a firm, even fabric and unless otherwise stated, wherever you see instructions referring to garter stitch, it is intended that every row should be knitted.

▲ *Purled garter stitch* ▼ *Knitted garter stitch*

Stocking stitch

This is the smoothest of all knitted stitches and is formed by working one row of knitted stitches and one row of purled stitches alternately. The smooth, knitted side of the fabric is usually called the right side of the work but where a pattern uses the purl side of stocking stitch as the fabric, it is referred to as reversed stocking stitch.

Stocking stitch

Single rib

This is one of the most useful of all knitted stitches and forms an elastic fabric, ideal for welts, cuffs and neckbands, since it always springs back into shape. It is formed by knitting the first stitch of the first row, bringing the yarn forward to the front of the work between the two needles, purling the next stitch and taking the yarn back between the two needles, ready to knit the next stitch again, then continuing in this way until all the stitches are transferred to the right hand needle. On the next row, all the stitches which were knitted on the first row must be purled and all the stitches which were purled must be knitted. It is essential to remember that the yarn must be brought forward after knitting a stitch so that it is in the correct position ready to purl the next stitch, and taken to the back again after purling a stitch so that it is in the correct position ready to knit the next stitch.

Single rib

Useful hints

Before beginning to knit any pattern, study the list of general abbreviations so that you become familiar with these.
Always wash your hands before beginning to knit and keep them soft and cool.
A bag pinned over the finished work and moved up as it grows will help to keep your knitting clean.
Never leave your knitting in the middle of a row, as this will spoil the line of the work.
Never stick knitting needles through a ball of yarn as this can split the yarn.
When measuring knitting, place it on a flat surface and measure it in the centre of the work, not at the edges.
Always join in a new ball of yarn at the beginning of a row, never in the centre of a row by means of a knot.

Casting off

Casting off is the final stage in knitting and it securely binds off any stitches which remain after all the shaping has been completed, or at the end of the work. It is also used as an intermediate step in decreasing, such as casting off the required number of stitches for an underarm or in the centre of a row for neck shaping.

Where stitches need to be cast off at each end of a row it is usual to do this over two rows by casting off the given number of stitches at the beginning of the first row then working to the end of the row, turning the work and casting off the same number of stitches at the beginning of the next row and then completing this row. If you cast off stitches at the beginning and end of the same row the yarn must then be broken off and rejoined to commence the next row. This is necessary in some designs but the pattern will always clearly state where this method is to be used.

Care must be taken in casting off to keep the stitches regular and even, otherwise the edge will either be too tight or too loose and can pull the whole garment out of shape. In some patterns you will come across the phrase, 'cast off loosely' and, in this case, it is advisable to use one size larger needle in the right hand and work the stitches with this needle, before casting them off.

The normal method of casting off produces a very firm, neat edge, which is not always suitable for some designs, such as the toe of a sock where this line would cause an uncomfortable ridge. In this case, the stitches can be grafted together to give an almost invisible seam. Similarly, a ribbed neckband can be cast off by the invisible method to give a very elastic edge with the appearance of a machine-made garment.

Two needle method of casting off

To cast off on a knit row, knit the first two stitches in the usual way and leave them on the right hand needle, *with the point of the left hand needle lift the first stitch on the right hand needle over the top of the second stitch and off the needle, leaving one stitch on the right hand needle, knit the next stitch and leave it on the right hand needle, repeat from the point marked with a * until the required number of stitches have been cast off and one stitch remains on the right hand needle. If this is at the end of the work, break off the yarn, draw it through the last stitch and pull it up tightly. If stitches have been cast off as a means of shaping, continue working to the end of the row noting that the stitch on the right hand needle will be counted as one of the remaining stitches.

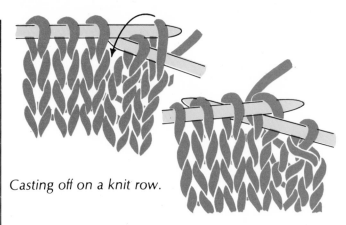

Casting off on a knit row.

To cast off on a purl row, work in exactly the same way but purl each stitch instead of knitting it.

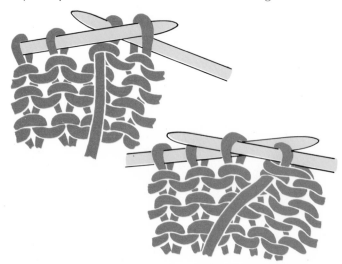

Circular method of casting off using 4 needles
Cast off the stitches on each needle as given for the two needle method of casting off.

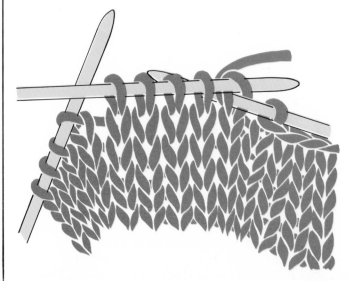

Invisible method of casting off

These instructions are for casting off in single rib when an odd number of stitches has been used and the right side rows begin with K1. Work in ribbing until only two more rows are required to give the finished depth, ending with a wrong side row.

1st row K1, *yfwd, sl 1, ybk, K1, repeat from the point marked with a * to the end of the row.

2nd row Sl 1, *ybk, K1, yfwd, sl 1, repeat from the point marked with a * to the end of the row. Break off the yarn, leaving an end three times the length of the edge to be cast off and thread this into a blunt-ended sewing needle. Hold the sewing needle in the right hand and the stitches to be cast off in the left hand, working throughout from right to left along the row.

1. Insert the sewing needle into the first knit stitch as if to purl it and pull the yarn through, then into the next purl stitch as if to knit it and pull the yarn through, leaving both of the stitches on the left hand needle.

2. *First work two of the knit stitches. Go back and insert the sewing needle into the first knit stitch as if to knit it, pull the yarn through and slip this stitch off the left hand needle, pass the sewing needle in front of the next purl stitch and into the following knit stitch as if to purl it, pull the yarn through.

3. Now work two of the purl stitches. Go back and insert the sewing needle into the purl stitch at the end of the row as if to purl it, pull the yarn through and slip this stitch off the left hand needle, pass the sewing needle behind the next knit stitch and into the following purl stitch as if to knit it, pull the yarn through.

Repeat from the point marked with a * until all the stitches have been worked off. Fasten off the end of yarn.

Grafting stitches

To graft two stocking stitch, or knit edges together have the stitches on two needles, one behind the other, with the same number of stitches on each needle. Break off the yarn, leaving an end three times the length of the edge to be grafted and thread this into a blunt-ended sewing needle. Have the wrong sides of each piece facing each other, with the knitting needle points facing to the right.

*Insert the sewing needle through the first stitch on the <u>front</u> needle as if to <u>knit</u> it, draw the yarn through and slip the stitch <u>off</u> the knitting needle, insert the sewing needle through the next stitch on the <u>front</u> needle as if to <u>purl</u> it, draw the yarn through and leave the stitch <u>on</u> the knitting needle, insert the sewing needle through the first stitch on the <u>back</u> needle as if to <u>purl</u> it, draw the yarn through and slip the stitch <u>off</u> the knitting needle, insert the sewing needle through the next stitch on the <u>back</u> needle as if to <u>knit</u> it, draw the yarn through and leave the stitch <u>on</u> the knitting needle, repeat from the point marked with a * until all the stitches have been worked off both needles.

To graft two edges of purl fabric together, work in the same way as given for stocking stitch, reading knit for purl and purl for knit. It is possible, however, to graft purl edges by turning the work to the wrong side and grafting as given for the stocking stitch method, then turn the work to the right side when the grafting is completed.

To graft two garter stitch edges together, first make certain that the last row knitted on the front needle leaves a ridge on the right side, or outside, of the work and that the last row on the back needle leaves a ridge on the wrong side, or inside, of the work. Work as stocking stitch method, working both needles as given for front needle.

To graft two ribbed edges together. Join each stocking stitch or knit rib to each stocking stitch or knit rib, using the stocking stitch method, and each purl rib to each purl rib, using the purl method.

Variations

The ways of using simple knit and purl stitches to form interesting fabrics are numerous. These basic stitches are simple to work and each one gives a different texture. Use a double knitting yarn and No. 8 needles to practise these stitches.

Reversed stocking stitch
This variation of stocking stitch uses the wrong side, or purl side of the work to form the fabric.
Cast on any number of stitches.
1st row (right side) P to end.
2nd row K to end.
These 2 rows form the pattern.

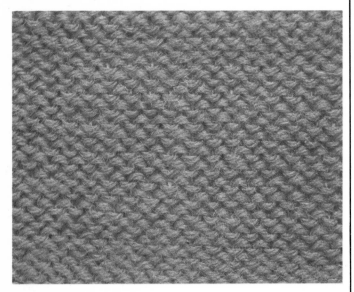

Twisted stocking stitch
This variation of simple stocking stitch has a twisted effect added on every knitted row by working into the back of every stitch.
Cast on any number of stitches.
1st row K into the back of each stitch to end.
2nd row P to end.
These 2 rows form the pattern.

Broken rib
Cast on a number of stitches divisible by 2+1.
1st row K1, *P1, K1, rep from * to end.
2nd row P1, *K1, P1, rep from * to end.
3rd row K to end.
4th row As 3rd.
These 4 rows form the pattern.

Rice stitch
Cast on a number of stitches divisible by 2+1.
1st row K to end.
2nd row P1, *K1, P1, rep from * to end.
These 2 rows form the pattern.

Moss stitch
Cast on a number of stitches divisible by 2+1.
1st row K1, *P1, K1, rep from * to end.
This row forms the pattern.
Where an even number of stitches are cast on, moss stitch is worked as follows:
1st row *K1, P1, rep from * to end.
2nd row *P1, K1, rep from * to end.
These 2 rows form the pattern.

Irish moss stitch

Cast on a number of stitches divisible by 2+1.
1st row K1, *P1, K1, rep from * to end.
2nd row P1, *K1, P1, rep from * to end.
3rd row As 2nd.
4th row As 1st.
These 4 rows form the pattern.

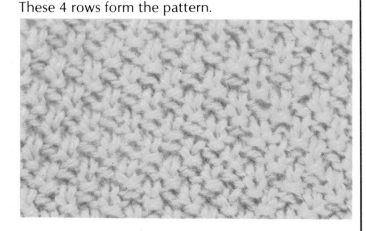

Woven stitch

Cast on a number of stitches divisible by 2+1.
1st row K1, *yfwd, sl 1 P-wise, ybk, K1, rep from * to end.
2nd row P to end.
3rd row K2, *yfwd, sl 1, P-wise, ybk, K1, rep from * to last st, K1.
4th row As 2nd.
These 4 rows form the pattern.

Honeycomb slip stitch

Cast on a number of stitches divisible by 2+1.
1st row P1, *sl 1 P-wise, P1, rep from * to end.
2nd row P to end.
3rd row P2, *sl 1 P-wise, P1, rep from * to last st, P1.
4th row As 2nd.
These 4 rows form the pattern.

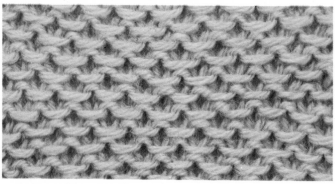

Bright and easy knits

When learning a new skill, there is nothing more encouraging than seeing simple articles you make yourself. For each of these ideas you only need to know how to cast on, how to work the basic stitches and how to cast off!

Muffler
Materials
5 × 50grm balls of any Double Knitting yarn
A pair of No.4 needles
To make
Cast on 60 stitches. Work in garter stitch until scarf measures 178.0cm (*70in*). Cast off.

Evening belt
Materials
1 × 50grm ball of any glitter yarn
A pair of No.9 needles
A 5.0cm (*2in*) buckle
To make
Cast on 16 stitches. Work in single rib until belt measures required length to go round waist plus approximately 20.5cm (*8in*). Cast off. Sew on buckle to one end.

Shoulder bag
Materials
2 × 50grm balls of any Double Knitting yarn
A pair of No.8 needles
To make
Cast on 50 stitches. Work in stocking stitch until bag measures approximately 61.0cm (*24in*). Cast off. Fold bag in half with right sides facing and join side edges. Fold over 5.0cm (*2in*) at top edge and sew down. Turn bag right side out. Embroider each side or sew on motifs.
Cut remaining yarn into 152·5cm (*60in*) lengths and plait together, knotting each end of plait. Stitch each end of plait along sides of bag, leaving centre of plait free as shoulder strap.

TENSION

Now that you have mastered the basic steps in knitting, the next stage is to fully understand the significance of achieving the correct tension. It is of such vital importance that it cannot be stressed too often and must not be overlooked, either by the beginner or by the more experienced knitter. It is the simple key to success and no amount of careful knitting will produce a perfect garment unless it is observed.

Tension

Quite simply, the word 'tension' means the number of rows and stitches to a given measurement, which has been achieved by the designer of the garment, using the yarn and needle size stated. As a beginner, it is vital to keep on practising and trying to obtain the correct tension given in a pattern. If it is impossible to hold the yarn and needles comfortably, without pulling the yarn too tightly or leaving it too loose and at the same time obtain the correct tension, then change the needle size. If there are too many stitches to the centimetre (inch), try using one size larger needles; if there are too few stitches to the centimetre (inch), try using one size smaller needles. Too many stitches mean that the tension is too tight and too few stitches mean that the tension is too loose.

This advice applies not only to the beginner but to all knitters beginning a new design. It is so often overlooked on the assumption that the knitter's tension is 'average' and therefore accurate. The point to stress is that although all knitting patterns are carefully checked, the designer of a garment may have produced a tighter or looser tension than average and all the measurements of the garment will have been based on calculations obtained from her tension. With this in mind, it will be readily appreciated that even a quarter of a stitch too many or too few can result in the measurements of the garment being completely inaccurate – through no fault of the designer. It doesn't matter how many times you have to change the needle size – what is important is to obtain the correct tension given in a pattern, before commencing to knit it. Most instructions give the number of stitches in width and the number of rows in depth and if you have to choose between obtaining one and not the other, then the width tension is the most important. Length can usually be adjusted by working more or less rows, as required, but check that the pattern is not based on an exact number of rows but is measured in centimetres (inches).

How to check tension

Before commencing to knit any garment, always work a tension sample at least 10 centimetres (3.9 inches) square, using the yarn, needle size and stitch quoted. Lay this sample on a flat surface and pin it down. Place a firm rule over the knitting and mark out 10 centimetres (3.9 inches) in width with pins. Count the number of stitches between the pins very carefully and make sure that you have the same number as given in the tension. Pin out and count the number of rows in the same way. If there are too many stitches to the given tension measurement then your tension is too tight and you need to use one, or more, size larger needles. If there are too few stitches, then your tension is too loose and you need to use one, or more, size smaller needles.

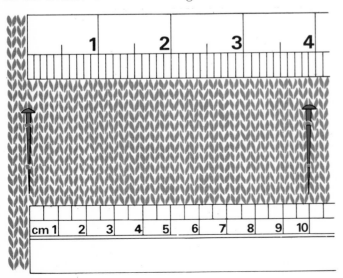

Here the tension is correct

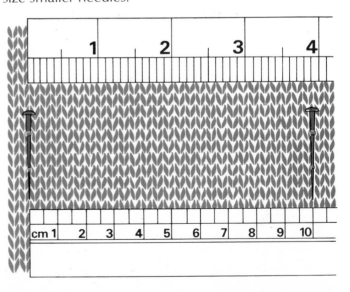

Here the tension is too loose

A decorative cushion cover

An afghan, made from tension samples, is a delightful mixture of colours, patterns and textures

Substituting yarns

Each design has been worked out for the knitting yarn which is quoted in the instructions and this should always be obtained, if possible. If it is impossible to buy the correct yarn, then a substitute may be used but, in this event, it is even more vital to check your tension before beginning the pattern.

To make an afghan or cushion cover

A few minutes spent in the preparation of a tension sample need not be wasted. Similarly, samples of the stitches which interest you can be utilized. As each one is finished it can be laid aside and when you have collected enough, they can be joined together to make a colourful and original afghan or cushion cover. The only requirement is that each sample must be worked to the same size and 10 centimetres *(3.9 inches)* square would be an ideal measurement. In this way you can keep a lasting record of your progress as a

knitter, which will eventually serve a very useful purpose.

Afghan

You will require a minimum of 120 squares. Join 10 squares together to form one row, having a total of 12 rows. Bind round all the edges with wool braid or work blanket stitch round all the edges to neaten them.

Cushion cover

You will require 32 squares and a cushion pad or kapok for stuffing. Join 4 squares together to form one row, then 4 rows together to form one side of the cushion. Work the second side in the same way, Place the right sides of each piece facing each other and join 3 sides together. Turn the cover right side out. Insert the cushion pad or stuffing and join the remaining edge, inserting a zip fastener if required.

YARNS

Success in knitting designs is the result of combining two skills in one – those of a weaver and those of a dressmaker – as the fabric and the shape of the garment are produced at the same time. All knitters need to know something about the construction of the many colourful and interesting yarns which are now available. This knowledge, combined with the needle size to be used and the tension obtained, will enable knitters to understand how the right fabric for any garment is achieved. To produce a hard-wearing, textured fabric, using variations of cable stitches, you cannot select a fine baby yarn for the garment, similarly, a thick, chunky yarn would not be suitable for a lacy evening top.

Yarns and ply

'Yarn' is the word used to describe any spun thread, fine or thick, in natural fibres such as wool, cotton, linen, silk, angora or mohair, or in man-made fibres such as Acrilan, Orlon, Nylon or Courtelle. These fibres can be blended together, as with wool and Nylon or Tricel and Nylon, to produce extra hard-wearing yarns which are not too thick.

The word 'ply' indicates a single spun thread of any thickness. Before this thread can be used it must be twisted together to make two or more plys to produce a specific yarn and this process is called 'doubling'. Because each single thread can be spun to any thickness, reference to the number of plys does not necessarily determine the thickness of the finished yarn. Some Shetland yarns, for instance, use only two ply very lightly twisted together to produce a yarn almost comparable to a double knitting quality but, generally speaking, the terms 2 ply, 3 ply, 4 ply and double knitting are used to describe yarn of a recognised thickness.

The following ply classification is applicable to the majority of hand knitting yarns, whether made from natural fibres, man-made fibres or a blend of both.

Baby yarns are usually made from the highest quality fibres and are available in 2 ply, 3 ply, 4 ply and double knitting weights.

Baby Quickerknit yarns are generally equivalent to a 4 ply but as they are very softly twisted, they are light in weight.

2 ply, 3 ply and 4 ply yarns are available in numerous fibres and are usually produced by twisting two or more single spun threads together.

Double Knitting yarns are usually made from four single spun threads – although there are exceptions to this – twisted together to produce yarns virtually double the thickness of 4 ply yarns.

Chunky and Double Double Knitting yarns are extra thick yarns which vary considerably in their construction. They are ideal for outer garments and some are oiled to give greater warmth and protection.

Crepe yarns are usually available in 4 ply qualities – sometimes called 'single crepe' – and Double Knitting weights – called 'double crepe' – and are more tightly twisted than normal yarns. They produce a smooth, firm fabric which is particularly hard-wearing.

Weights and measures

Since there is no official standardisation, yarns marketed by the various Spinners often vary in thickness and in yardage. As most yarns are marketed by weight, rather than length, even the density of dye used to produce certain colours in each range can result in more or less yarn in each ball, although the

structure of the yarn is exactly the same. Although all knitting designs are carefully checked, it would be impossible to make up a separate garment for each colour in the range of yarn quoted and you may sometimes find that you need one ball more or less than given in the instructions because of this difference in dye.

If it is impossible to obtain the correct yarn quoted in the instructions then another comparable yarn may be used, provided the same tension as that given in the pattern is obtained.

Equivalent yarns will knit up to the appropriate tension but do remember that the quantity given will not necessarily apply to another yarn.

Always buy sufficient yarn at one time to ensure that all the yarn used is from the same dye lot. Yarn from a different dye lot may vary slightly in colour, although this may not be noticeable until you have started to knit with it.

Yarns and metrication

When purchasing yarn it is advisable to check the weight of each ball as they now vary considerably, due to the intended introduction of the metric system. Metrication has already been adopted by some Spinners, while others are still in the process of changing over. Also, large stocks of yarns in standard ounces will take some time to run out, so this confused situation will be with us for some time.

Measurements and metrication

The next step in the metric system will be the changeover from imperial measurements in inches and yards to metric measurements in centimetres and metres. To allow readers time to become accustomed to this new system, all measurements will be given in metric sizes followed by the nearest accurate measurements in imperial sizes.

More simple knits

To illustrate how the same stitch worked in a different yarn can produce a variety of fabrics, try making the muffler given earlier in a mohair yarn, to give a lighter, softer version. Or use a yarn which combines a lurex thread to give a glitter effect to make an evening stole. The evening belt also given earlier could equally well be worked in a crisp cotton to make a useful summer accessory. The more you experiment, the more you will be delighted with the fabrics which can be produced.

Shawl

You will need 6 × 25grm balls of 2 ply Baby quality, or super-soft 2 ply, and a pair of No. 9 needles, also 144.0 centimetres (57in) of narrow lace.

Cast on 288 stitches. Work in garter stitch until shawl measures 91.5 centimetres (36in). Cast off loosely. Sew on lace all round edges, gathering it slightly round corners.

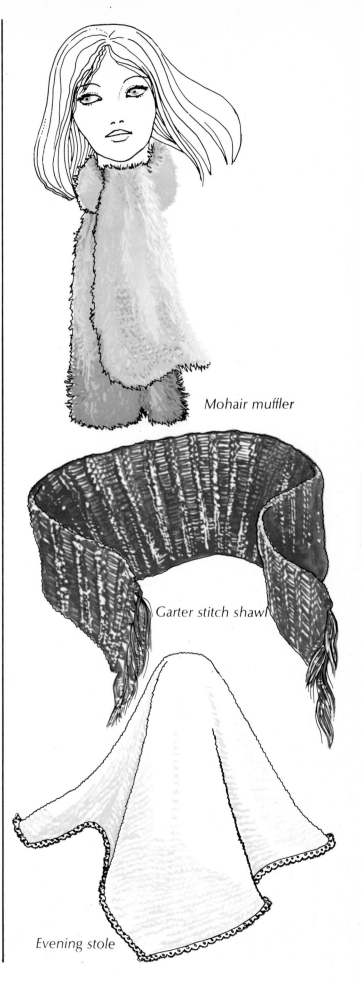

Mohair muffler

Garter stitch shawl

Evening stole

WORKING A PATTERN

A finished knitted garment should look just as attractive and well-fitting as in the illustration and a great deal of care is taken in compiling knitting patterns to ensure that this is possible. The secret lies in being completely objective about the design you choose, just as you would when selecting ready-to-wear clothes. The range of knitting patterns which are available cater for every type of garment in varying sizes. Where a design is only given in smaller sizes, such as a 81.5 (32) or 86.5cm (34 inch) bust, it is usually because the designer feels that it would not be suitable for a more generous figure. Similarly, if only one size is given it is probably because the pattern used for the design covers a large multiple of stitches and another whole repeat of the pattern, to give a larger size, would not be practical.

When you find a design which incorporates all the details you require make sure you read right through all the instructions before beginning to knit. Beginners and experts alike should pay particular attention to the making up section – a deceptively simple shape may require a crochet edging to give it that couture look, or an unusual trimming effect such as a twisted cord belt.

Knitting patterns

Knitting publication styles vary considerably but generally, all instructions fall into three sections:–

1 Materials required, tension, finished sizes and abbreviations.
2 Working instructions for each section.
3 Making up details, edges and trimmings.

Sizes

Check that the size range given in the instructions provides the size you require. If the skirt or sleeve lengths need altering to suit your requirements, read through the working instructions to see if the design allows for these amendments. Some designs are based on an exact number of rows which cannot be altered. After the actual measurements of the design are given, take note that the instructions for the smallest size are given as the first set of figures and that the figures for any other sizes follow in order and are usually shown in brackets. Go through the instructions and underline all the figures which are applicable to the size required, noting that where only one set of figures is given, it applies to all the sizes.

Tension

This section must not be overlooked as it is the vital key to success. Never begin any design without first checking that you can obtain the correct tension.

Materials

Each design will have been worked out for the knitting yarn which is quoted and this should be obtained, if possible. If for any reason it is quite impossible to obtain the correct yarn, you may select a substitute as long as you gain the correct tension but remember that the quantity given will only apply to the original yarn and if a substitute is used, you may require more or less yarn.

Abbreviations

All knitting patterns are abbreviated into a form of shorthand and every knitter soon comes to recognize the terms, 'K2 tog' or 'sl 1, K1, psso' and their meanings. A list of general knitting abbreviations has already been given in the introductory pages of this book but the same terms may not be abbreviated in the same way by other publications and this can sometimes lead to confusion. It is therefore essential to read through any list of abbreviations before beginning a pattern, to make sure you understand them. This is particularly important when they refer to increasing, as the terms, 'make 1' and 'increase 1' can mean two different methods.

In this course, where a specific stitch or technique is given in a pattern, the working method is given out in full for the first time it is used in a row and its abbreviated form given at the end of the working instructions. From that point on, each time the same stitch or technique is used, its abbreviated term will be given.

Working instructions

Each section will be given separately under an appropriate heading, such as, 'Back', 'Front', 'Sleeves' and so on. Each section should be worked in the correct order as it may be necessary to join parts of the garment together at a given point, before you can proceed with the next stage. When measuring knitting

it is necessary to lay it on a flat surface and use a rigid rule. Never measure round a curve but on an armhole or sleeve, measure the depth in a straight line.

Where an asterisk, *, is used in a pattern row it means repeat from that point, as directed. This symbol is also used at the beginning of a section, sometimes as a double asterisk, **, or triple asterisk, ***, to denote a part which is to be repeated later on in the instructions.

When working in rows, always join in a new ball of yarn at the beginning of a row. You can easily gauge whether you have sufficient yarn for another row by spreading out your work and checking whether the remaining yarn will cover its width four times. Any odd lengths of yarn can always be used later for seaming.

If the yarn has to be joined in the middle of the work, which is necessary when working in rounds, then the ends of the old ball of yarn and the new ball should be spliced together. To do this, unravel the end of the new ball and cut away one or two strands from each end. Overlay the two ends from opposite directions and twist them together until they hold. The twisted ends should be of the same thickness as the original yarn. As the join will not be very strong, knit very carefully with the newly twisted yarn for a few stitches. Then carefully trim away any odd ends with a pair of sharp scissors.

Never join in new yarn by means of a knot in the middle of your work, whether working in rows or rounds.

Making up

Most knitters give a sigh of relief when they have cast off the very last stitch and look forward to wearing their new creation. If the finished garment is to be a success however the making up of the separate pieces must be looked upon as an exercise in dressmaking. Details are always given in the instructions as to the order in which the sections are to be assembled, together with any final instructions for edgings or trimmings. Pressing instructions will also be given in this section and if a substitute yarn has been used, it is essential to check whether or not it requires pressing.

Mistakes!

These can happen – a dropped stitch, an interruption in a pattern row which has then been misread and needs unpicking – but don't be tempted to pull the stitches off the needle until you have tried other ways of rectifying the error.

To pick up a dropped stitch on a knit row Insert a crochet hook into the dropped stitch from the front to

the back, put the hook under the thread which lies between the two stitches above the dropped stitch and pull this thread through the dropped stitch. Continue in this way until the dropped stitch is level with the last row worked and transfer the stitch to the left hand needle, then continue knitting in the usual way.

To pick up a dropped stitch on a purl row Insert a crochet hook into the dropped stitch from the back to the front, put the hook over the thread which lies between the two stitches above the dropped stitch and pull this thread through the dropped stitch. Slip the stitch on to a spare needle and remove the hook, ready to insert it into the dropped stitch from the back to the front again. Continue in this way until the dropped stitch is level with the last row worked and transfer the stitch to the left hand needle, then continue purling in the usual way.

To take back stitches on a knit row Insert the left hand needle from the front to the back into the stitch below the next stitch on the right hand needle, then withdraw the right hand needle from the stitch above and pull the yarn with the right hand to unravel this stitch, keeping the yarn at the back of the work. Continue in this way until the required number of stitches have been unpicked.

To take back stitches on a purl row Insert the left hand needle from the front to the back into the stitch below the next stitch on the right hand needle, then withdraw the right hand needle from the stitch above and pull the yarn with the right hand to unravel this stitch, keeping the yarn at the front of the work. Continue in this way until the required number of stitches have been unpicked.

Shaping stitches

Knitting may be perfectly straight, as in a scarf, or intricately shaped as in a tailored jacket. This shaping is achieved by means of increasing the number of stitches in a row to make the work wider, or decreasing the stitches in a row to make the work narrower. This is usually done by making two stitches out of one, or by working two stitches together to make one stitch, at a given point in the pattern. Sometimes the shaping forms an integral part of the design and decorative methods of increasing and decreasing are used to highlight the shaping, such as fully-fashioned seams on a raglan jersey.

By means of an eyelet hole method of increasing stitches, carrying the yarn over or round the needle in a given sequence and compensating for these made stitches later on in the row, beautiful lace patterns are produced.

How to increase

The simplest way is to make an extra stitch at the beginning or end of the row, but a pattern will always give exact details where more intricate shaping is required, such as skirt darts.

To make a stitch at the beginning of a row, knit or purl the first stitch in the usual way but do not slip it off the left hand needle. Instead, place the point of the right hand needle into the back of the same stitch and purl or knit into the stitch again. One stitch has been increased.

To make a stitch at the end of a row, work until two stitches remain on the left hand needle, increase into the next stitch and work the last stitch in the usual way. One stitch has been increased.

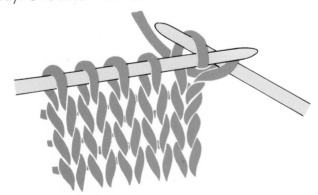

Invisible increasing

Insert the right hand needle into the front of the stitch on the row below the next stitch on the left hand needle and knit a new stitch in the usual way, then knit the next stitch on the left hand needle. One stitch has been increased.

If the increase is on a purl row, insert the right hand needle in the same way and purl a stitch in the usual way, then purl the next stitch on the left hand needle.

Increasing between stitches

With the right hand needle pick up the yarn which lies between the stitch just worked and the next stitch on the left hand needle and place this loop on the left hand needle. Knit into the back of this loop so that the new stitch is twisted and does not leave a hole in the work and place the new stitch on the right hand needle. One stitch has been increased.

If the increase is on a purl row, pick up the yarn between the stitches in the same way and purl into it from the back, then place the new stitch on the right hand needle.

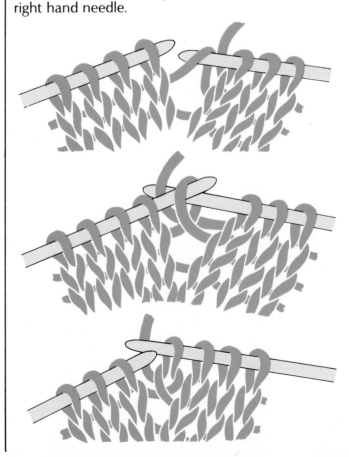

Decorative increasing

To make a stitch between two knit stitches, bring the yarn forward between the needles then back over the top of the right hand needle, ready to knit the next stitch. The abbreviation for this is 'yfwd'.

To make a stitch between a purl and a knit stitch, the yarn is already at the front of the work and is carried over the top of the right hand needle ready to knit the next stitch. The abbreviation for this is 'yon'.

To make a stitch between two purl stitches, take the yarn over the top of the right hand needle and round between the two needles to the front again ready to purl the next stitch. The abbreviation for this is 'yrn'.

To make a stitch between a knit and a purl stitch, bring the yarn forward between the two needles, over the top of the right hand needle then round between the two needles to the front again ready to purl the next stitch. The abbreviation for this is also 'yrn'.

How to decrease

The way to make a simple decrease is by working two stitches together, either at the ends of the row or at any given point. To do this on a knit row, insert the point of the right hand needle through two stitches instead of one and knit them both together in the usual way. This stitch will slant to the right and the abbreviation is 'K2 tog'. One stitch has been decreased.

If the decrease is on a purl row, purl the two stitches together in the same way. This stitch will slant to the left and the abbreviation is 'P2 tog'.

▲*Decreasing on a knit row* ▼*Decreasing on a purl row*

Decreasing by means of a slipped stitch

This method is most commonly used where the decreases are worked in pairs, one slanting to the left and one slanting to the right, as on a raglan sleeve. Slip the stitch to be decreased from the left hand needle on to the right hand needle without working it, then knit the next stitch on the left hand needle. With the point of the left hand needle lift the slipped stitch over the knit stitch and off the needle. This stitch will slant to the left and the abbreviation is 'sl

1, K 1, psso'.

If the decrease is on a purl row, purl the two stitches together through the back of the stitches. This stitch will slant to the right and the abbreviation is 'P2 tog tbl'.

Decorative decreasing

The decorative use of decreasing can be accentuated by twisting the stitches round the decreased stitches to give them greater emphasis. This example shows a decrease which has been twisted and lies in the opposite direction to the line of the seam. The decrease is worked at the end of a knit row for the left hand side and at the end of a purl row for the right hand side.

Knit to the last six stitches, pass the right hand needle behind the first stitch on the left hand needle and knit the next two stitches together through the back of the stitches, then knit the first missed stitch and slip both stitches off the left hand needle and knit the last three stitches in the usual way.

On a purl row, purl to the last six stitches, pass the right hand needle across the front of the first stitch on the left hand needle and purl the next two stitches together, then purl the first missed stitch and slip both stitches off the left hand needle and purl the last three stitches in the usual way.

Decorative decreasing on knit and purl rows

More about shaping

Even the most basic stocking stitch jersey needs careful shaping at the underarm, back and front neck and shoulders, sleeves and top of the sleeves, if it is to fit together correctly. The correct proportions for all these measurements will have been taken into account in every knitting design and the instructions will clearly state where and when the shaping is to be worked.

Where so many knitters come to grief however is in the accurate measuring of each section, so that when a garment is assembled it all fits together without stretching or easing one piece to fit another. The easiest way to overcome this problem is to use a row counter to ensure that the back and front of a garment have exactly the same number of rows before beginning any shaping and that both sleeves match. Many professional knitters prefer to knit both sleeves at the same time, using two separate balls of yarn, to make sure that the shaping for each sleeve is worked on the same row. Another useful tip is to make a note of the number of rows which have been worked for any section, such as the ribbing on the welt of a jersey, before beginning any pattern rows, so that when you come to do the next piece you do not even have to measure the length but can work to the same number of rows.

Whichever method you adopt it is essential to know how to take accurate measurements, if you are to achieve satisfactory results.

Taking measurements

Before taking any measurements it is necessary to lay the section of knitting on a flat surface. If you are sitting comfortably in a chair, it is tempting to try and measure it across your knees, or on the arm of the chair, but this will not give an accurate figure.

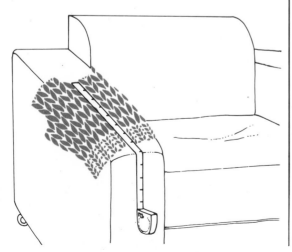

Always measure with a firm rule and not a tape measure and never be tempted to stretch the section to the required length to avoid working a few extra rows before the next stage.

Never measure round a curve but always on the straight of the fabric – a curved measurement is obviously greater and will result in an incorrect depth on armholes or sleeve seams. When measuring an armhole, sleeve or side edge of a section which has been shaped, place the rule on the fabric in a straight line from the commencement of the section to the point you have reached.

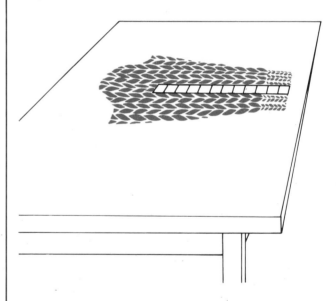

Measurements and tension

It cannot be stressed too often that every design you knit has been calculated on the tension achieved by the designer of the garment and based on the correct proportions for each size. The normal ratio of 5cm (*2 in*) difference between the bust and hip measurements will have been taken into account, also an allowance of 2.5cm (*1 in*) or 5.0cm (*2 in*) for movement, or what is known as tolerance. The width tension, or number of stitches to a given measurement, is vital if you are to obtain an accurate fit. The length tension, or number of rows to a given measurement, is not so important and can be adjusted where a pattern is not given over an exact number of rows and provided you remember that it is even more essential to measure each section accurately. The designer may have achieved more rows to the centimetre (*inch*) than you are obtaining and her shaping on the sleeves, for instance, will have been calculated to ensure that this is completed well before the point has been reached to shape the head of the sleeve. Where she is increasing on every 6th row in order to complete the shaping inside a certain measurement, you may be working to a looser row tension and will need to increase on every 5th row, in order to end up with the correct number of stitches within the same length. Similarly, if you are working to a tighter row tension, you may need to adjust the shaping and work it on every 7th row, otherwise all the shaping may well be completed before reaching the elbow level and the whole sleeve will be out of shape.

Shaping in rows

Details of casting on or casting off stitches to achieve the correct shape, such as for the underarm, neck or shoulders, will be given in a pattern in detail.

When shaping is required on both side edges of a section, the pattern may simply say, 'decrease one stitch at each end of the next knitted row' and will leave the knitter to adopt whichever method she prefers. In this case, if you use the slip one, knit one, pass slipped stitch over method at the beginning of the row, producing a decreased stitch which slants to the left, when the fabric is facing you, use the knit two together method at the end of the row to make a stitch which slants to the right.

When increasing in a row, whether it is at each end to increase two stitches, or across the row to increase a greater number of stitches, when working twice into a stitch the last stitch made is the increased stitch. If you increase in the first stitch at the beginning of a row, the made stitch will lie inside the first knitted stitch. At the end of the row you should increase in the last but one stitch, so that the made stitch again lies inside the last stitch, which is then knitted in the usual way. Sometimes a pattern will tell you to increase a given number of stitches across a row, without giving exact instructions. To do this you must first work out the exact position for each increased stitch. As an example, say a pattern has commenced

with 80 stitches and at a given point you are required to increase 8 stitches evenly across a row. The accurate way to achieve this would be to increase in the 5th stitch and then into every following 10th stitch 7 times more and knit the last 5 stitches. In this way, each made stitch is evenly spaced across the row.

Shaping in rounds

The same principles apply, whether working in rows or in rounds. A skirt may be worked from the hem to waist in rounds and will need to be shaped by means of decreasing, to lose the extra width at the hem. As an example, if you are working a pattern in wide panels of stocking stitch and narrow panels of reversed stocking stitch, the shaping needs to be worked on the stocking stitch panels to eventually bring them down to the same width as the reversed stocking stitch panels. The pattern may simply say, 'decrease one stitch at each end of every stocking stitch panel' and you should use the slip one, knit one, pass slipped stitch over method at the beginning of each panel and the knit two together method at the end of each panel. In this way, each decreased stitch lies in the same direction as the line of the stocking stitch panels.

Using the same example, when increasing in rounds remember that if you increase in the first stitch of each panel you must increase in the last but one stitch and not in the last stitch.

Casting off and selvedges

Each piece of knitted fabric has selvedge edges which are formed as the work progresses and these edges must be suitable for the fabric produced. Every section of flat knitting has a cast on selvedge, the right and left hand side edges and the cast off edge. Round knitting has only a cast on and cast off selvedge.

Various methods of casting on and off have already been given but the following methods are not so well known. The ways of forming side edge selvedges are also important, as an edge which is too tight or too loose will present difficulties in making up, pulling the garment out of shape.

Double casting on

Two needles are required for this method, which are both held together in the right hand. Make a slip loop in the ball of yarn as given for the thumb method and place this on both needles. Take both ends of the yarn, that is, the end of the yarn from the slip loop and the end from the ball and hold them together in the palm of the left hand, putting the slip loop end round the thumb and the ball end round the forefinger. Using both needles put them up under the first loop on the thumb and over and down through the loop on the forefinger, then through the thumb loop. Release the thumb loop and tighten the stitch on the needles with an upward movement of the right hand, without releasing either end of the yarn held in the palm of the hand. Continue in this way until the required number of stitches are formed on the needles, then withdraw the second needle, transfer the needle holding the stitches to the left hand and have the second needle in the right hand, ready to knit. This forms a very strong yet elastic edge.

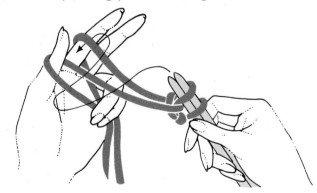

Picot casting on

Two needles are required for this method, one held in each hand. Make a slip loop and place this on the left hand needle then cast on one stitch by the two needle method. Using these two loops make a strip long enough for the number of stitches required by

bringing the yarn forward and ready to take over the top of the right hand needle to make a stitch, slip the first stitch on the left hand needle purlwise, knit the second stitch on the left hand needle and lift the slipped stitch over the knitted stitch and off the right hand needle. Turn and repeat this row until the required number of picot loops are formed by the yarn forward. Pick up these picot loops along one edge with a needle and then continue knitting in the usual way. The other side of the picot edge forms a dainty selvedge ideal for baby garments.

Suspended casting off

Knit the first two stitches in the usual way, then lift the first stitch over the second stitch but instead of allowing it to drop off the right hand needle, retain it on the point of the left hand needle. Pass the right hand needle in front of the held stitch and knit the next stitch on the left hand needle in the usual way, slipping the stitch and the held stitch off the left hand needle together, leaving two stitches on the right hand needle. Continue in this way until all stitches are cast off. This method avoids any tendency to cast off too tightly.

Shaped casting off

Preparation for this method must be made before the final casting off by means of turning the last few rows of knitting without completing them to form a shaped angle, then all the stitches are cast off at once on the final row. It is an ideal way of working shoulder shaping as it does not produce the stepped effect of normal casting off and makes seaming that much easier.

On a right back shoulder edge when the point has been reached for the shoulder shaping, instead of casting off the required number of stitches at the beginning of the next knit row, on the previous purl row work to within this number of stitches then turn the work, slip the first stitch on the left hand needle then knit to the end of the row. Repeat this action the required number of times, then purl across all the stitches. Cast them off on the next knit row in the usual way. Reverse this for a left back shoulder edge by beginning the shaping on a knit row.

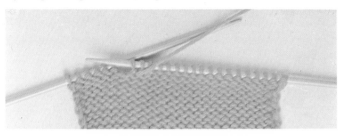

Three stages of shaped casting off

Side selvedges
Where side edges are to be joined together in making up they need to be firm to give a neat edge for seaming. When both edges must show, as in a scarf, they need to be tidy without pulling the sides out of shape.

To work a selvedge for seaming. Slip the first stitch purlwise and knit the last stitch on every row, when working in stocking stitch. On garter stitch, bring the yarn to the front of the work, slip the first stitch on every row purlwise, then take the yarn back between the needles and knit to the end in the usual way.

To work an open selvedge. When working in stocking stitch, slip the first and last stitch on every knit row

knitwise, to form a chain effect, then purl each stitch on the following row in the usual way.

Slipped stitches
Stitches which are slipped from one needle to the other without being worked are used in various ways – as edge stitches, as a means of decreasing and to form part of a pattern. When a slip stitch forms part of a decrease on a knit row, the stitch must be slipped knitwise, otherwise it will become crossed. On a purl row, the stitch must be slipped purlwise, when decreasing. In working a pattern, however, where the slip stitch is not part of a decrease it must be slipped purlwise on a knit row to prevent it becoming crossed when it is purled in the following row.

Slip stitch knitwise on a knit row. Hold the yarn behind the work as if to knit the next stitch, insert the point of the right hand needle into the next stitch from front to back as if to knit it and slip it on to the right hand needle without working it.

Slip stitch purlwise on a knit row. Hold the yarn behind the work as if to knit the next stitch, insert the point of the right hand needle into the next stitch from back to front as if to purl it and slip it on to the right hand needle without working it.

Slip stitch purlwise on a purl row. Hold the yarn at the front of the work as if to purl the next stitch, insert the point of the right hand needle into the next stitch from back to front as if to purl it and slip it on to the right hand needle without working it.

FINISHING TOUCHES
Buttonholes

Details for working buttonholes will always be given in the instructions for a garment but unless they are neatly finished they can spoil the appearance of the garment. Various methods may be used, largely depending on the size of the button required and the overall width of the buttonhole band or border. The buttonholes can be horizontal, vertical or, on a baby garment where a small button is required, simply worked by means of an eyelet hole.

Simple eyelet buttonholes

If the buttonhole is being incorporated in the main fabric, or the buttonhole band, work the front of the garment until the position for the first buttonhole is reached, ending with a wrong side row. On the next row work the first few stitches in the row to the position for the buttonhole, then pass the yarn forward, over or round the needle, depending on the stitch being worked, to make an eyelet hole, work the next two stitches on the left hand needle together to compensate for the made stitch, then work in pattern to the end of the row. On the next row, work across all the stitches in pattern, counting the made stitch as one stitch. Repeat this action for as many buttonholes as are required.

Horizontal buttonholes

These can either be worked as part of the main fabric or on a separate buttonhole band.

Buttonholes worked in one with the main fabric In this case provision will already have been made for a turned under hem and buttonholes will have to be made in the hem and in the main fabric, to form a double buttonhole, which is then neatened with buttonhole stitch on completion. Work until the position for the buttonhole is reached ending at the centre front edge. On the next row work a few

stitches across the hem, cast off the number of stitches required for the buttonhole by the two needle method then continue across the remainder of the hem, work the same number of stitches on the main fabric as were worked on the hem then cast off the same number of buttonhole stitches and work in pattern to the end of the row. On the next row you

need to replace the same number of stitches as were cast off for each buttonhole on the previous row but to avoid spoiling the buttonhole by a loose loop of yarn at one end, which would be the result by merely casting on the same number of stitches, work to the last stitch before the cast off stitches and increase in this last stitch by working into the front and back of it, then cast on one stitch less than was cast off in the previous row. Repeat this action for as many buttonholes as are required. If a turned under hem is not being worked in one with the main fabric, then only a single buttonhole is required.

Buttonholes worked in a separate border Here again, only a single buttonhole is required. Work the band until the position for the buttonhole is reached, ending at the centre front edge. On the next row work a few stitches until the position for the buttonhole is reached, cast off the required number of stitches for the buttonhole and pattern to the end of the row. On the next row, cast on the number of stitches needed to complete the buttonhole as given for working buttonholes in one with the main fabric. Repeat this action for as many buttonholes as are required.

Vertical buttonholes

This method of working buttonholes is ideal when only a narrow band is required and they can also be worked in one with the main fabric. The working instructions are the same for a separate band or when incorporated in the main fabric, remembering to make provision for a double buttonhole if a turned under hem is being worked with the main fabric. Work until the position for the buttonhole is reached, ending at the centre front edge. On the next row

work across a few stitches to the buttonhole opening then turn the work at this point and continue across these stitches only for the required number of rows to take the size of button, ending at the buttonhole opening edge. Break off the yarn and leave these stitches for the time being. Rejoin the yarn to the remaining stitches and work the same number of rows over these stitches, ending at the side edge away from the buttonhole opening. On the next row work across all the stitches to close the buttonhole. Repeat this action for the number of buttonholes required.

Finishing buttonholes

All buttonholes need to be neatened and reinforced when they are completed. This can either be done by working round them in buttonhole stitch, using the same yarn or a matching silk thread, or by means of a ribbon facing.

Buttonhole stitch Work along both sides of the buttonhole opening in buttonhole stitch for a horizontal or vertical buttonhole, neatening each end with three straight stitches. Take care not to work too many stitches round the buttonhole so that the edges become stretched or too few stitches, which would make the hole smaller than intended. Eyelet buttonholes need to be neatened with several evenly spaced buttonhole stitches round the hole, keeping the loops lying towards the centre.

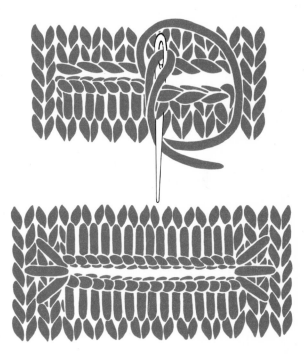

Ribbon facing The ribbon should be straight grained and wide enough to cover the buttonholes with an extra 1.5cm ($\frac{1}{2}$ *inch*) on either side and at each end of the band. Take care not to stretch the fabric when measuring the ribbon length and cut the buttonhole and button band facings together so that they match. Fold in the turnings on the ribbon and pin in place on the wrong side of the knitting, easing the fabric evenly and checking that the buttonholes are correctly spaced. Pin the ribbon on each side of every buttonhole to hold it in place. Slip stitch neatly round the edges of the ribbon then cut through the buttonholes in the ribbon making sure that they are exactly the same size as the knitted buttonholes. Work round the knitting and ribbon with buttonhole stitch to neaten the edges.

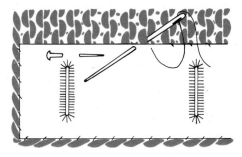

Hems and waistbands

Neat hems and waistbands are very important, particularly on babies' and children's garments where any unnecessary bulk produces an unsightly and uncomfortable edging.

Hems on skirts and dresses may be worked in one with the main fabric, then turned in and slip stitched into place when the garment is completed, or the hem may be knitted in to avoid seaming. Waist bands should be neatly ribbed and either folded in half to form a casing for the elastic, or the elastic may be directly applied to the wrong side of the fabric by means of casing, or herringbone stitch.

Turned under stocking stitch hem

Using one size smaller needles than given for the main fabric, cast on the required number of stitches. Beginning with a knitted row work an odd number of rows in stocking stitch, then change to the correct needle size. On the next row, instead of purling to the end, knit into the back of each stitch to form a ridge which marks the hemline. Beginning with a knitted row again, work one row less in stocking stitch than was worked for the hem, thus ending with a purl row to complete the hem. **. When the garment is completed and the side seams have been joined, turn the hem to the wrong side of the work at the hemline and slip stitch in place.

Knitted in hem in stocking stitch

Work as given for the turned under hem to ** Before continuing with the pattern, use an extra needle and pick up the loops from the cast on edge from left to right, so that the needle point is facing the same way as the main needle. Hold this needle behind the stitches already on the left hand needle and knit to the end of the row, working one stitch from the left hand needle together with one stitch from the extra needle. When the garment is completed, join the side seams working through the double fabric of the hem.

Picot hem

Using one size smaller needles than given for the main fabric cast on an odd number of stitches. Beginning with a knitted row work an even number of rows in stocking stitch. Change to the correct needle size.

Next row (eyelet hole row) *K2 tog, yfwd, rep from * to last st, K1.

Beginning with a purl row work one more row in stocking stitch than was worked for the hem, thus ending with a purl row to complete the hem. When the garment is completed and the side seams have been joined, turn the hem to the wrong side at the eyelet hole row and slip stitch in place.

Ribbed waistband

Using one size smaller needles than those given for the main fabric, work in K1, P1 rib for twice the width of the elastic, plus a few extra rows. If 2.5cm(1in) elastic is being used, work 5cm (2in) plus 2 extra rows, then cast off in rib. When the garment is completed and the side seams have been joined, turn in the waistband to the wrong side and slip stitch in place leaving an opening at one side to thread the elastic through. Insert the elastic and fasten off securely, then neaten the opening.

Casing stitch waistband

When the garment is completed join the side seams. Cut the elastic to the required waist length, allowing 2.5cm (1in) extra for an overlap, and secure the 2 ends to form a circle. Using pins mark off the waistband and elastic into equal sections. Pin the elastic into place on the wrong side of the fabric. Thread a blunt ended sewing needle with matching yarn and secure to the side seam of the waistband. Hold the waistband and elastic, slightly stretched, over the fingers of the left hand then take the sewing needle over the elastic and lightly insert it through the top of the waistband from right to left and pull the yarn through. Take the sewing needle over the elastic again and lightly insert it through the fabric below the elastic from right to left about 2 stitches along to the right and pull the yarn through. Take the sewing needle back over the top of the elastic to the top edge about 2 stitches along to the right, insert the needle lightly through the fabric from right to left and pull the yarn through. Continue in this way right round the waistband until the elastic is secured, taking great care to distribute the knitting evenly, then fasten off.

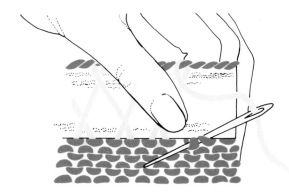

Baby's pants

Size

To fit 51[56:61]cm (20[22:24]in) hips
Length at side, 18[20.5:23]cm (7[8:9]in)
The figures in brackets [ ] refer to the 56 (22) and 61cm (24in) sizes respectively

Tension

30 sts and 40 rows to 10cm (3.9in) over st st worked on No.11 needles

Materials

2[2:3] × 25grm balls of Robin Tricel-Nylon Perle 4 ply
One pair No.11 needles
One pair No.12 needles
Waist length of 2.5cm (1in) wide elastic
Leg lengths of 1.5cm ($\frac{1}{2}$in) wide elastic

Pants left side

Using No.11 needles cast on 93[99:105]sts. Beg with a K row work 2 rows st st.

Shape crotch

Cont in st st, cast off for back edge 3 sts at beg of next and foll alt row then dec one st at same edge on every foll 4th row 4 times in all, *at the same time* cast off 2 sts for front edge on foll alt row and dec one st at same edge on every alt row 8 times in all. 73[79:85]sts. Cont without shaping until work measures 15[18:20.5]cm (6[7:8]in) from beg, ending with a P row.

Shape back

Next row K to last 24 sts, turn.
Next row Sl 1, P to end.
Next row K to last 32 sts, turn.
Next row Sl 1, P to end.
Cont working 8 sts less in this way on next and every alt row 4[5:6] times more. Change to No.12 needles.

Waistband

Next row K1, *P1, K1, rep from * to end.
Next row P1, *K1, P1, rep from * to end.
Rep last 2 rows 4 times more. Cast off in rib.

Pants right side

Work as given for left side, reversing all shaping.

Leg bands

Using No.12 needles and with RS of work facing, K up 93[99:105]sts round leg. Work 2.5cm (1in) K1, P1 rib as given for waistband. Cast off in rib.

To make up

Press each piece under a dry cloth with a cool iron. Join front, back and leg seams. Sew elastic inside waistband using casing st. Fold leg bands in half to WS and sl st down. Thread elastic through leg bands and fasten off. Press seams.

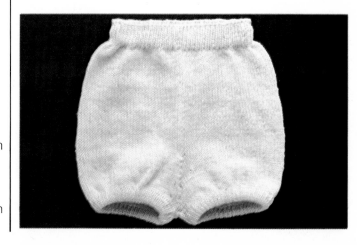

Pockets

Pockets are always a practical addition, particularly on men's and children's garments. They can be easily added to any chosen design, and inserted horizontally or vertically, as part of the main fabric, or applied as patch pockets when the garment is completed. In each case, a certain amount of planning is required before beginning the garment, to work out the exact positioning for each pocket. It must also be remembered that they will use extra yarn, so it would be as well to buy an extra ball.

If you have, for example, a favourite cardigan pattern for a man but would like to add inserted horizontal pockets above the welt, first check the given length to the underarm and work out the depth of pocket required. About 10cm (*4in*) by 10cm (*4in*) would be a reasonable size and this should be calculated to allow the pocket lining to come above any ribbed welts or inside any front edges. The same measurements apply to a patch pocket.

For an inserted vertical pocket, the same calculations must be made to ensure that the opening is correctly positioned and that the pocket lining has sufficient room to lie flat inside any front edges.

Patch pockets are the simplest to work and easy to apply, see later. They can be used as breast pockets on an otherwise plain jersey, applied to the sleeves above elbow level on a teenage jacket, or on the skirt of a dress at hip level. A straight turned down, buttoned flap can be added, or a plain square pocket can be given a highly individual touch if it is worked in a contrasting stitch or finished with embroidery.

Inserted horizontal pockets

First check the number of stitches you need to make the size of pocket required – on a tension of 6 stitches

to 2.5cm (*1in*), a 10cm (*4in*) pocket would need 24 stitches. Cast on this number of stitches and make the inside pocket flap first, working in stocking stitch until it is the required depth, ending with a wrong side row, then leave these stitches on a holder. Now work the main fabric of the garment until the required depth for the pocket has been reached, ending with the right side of the work facing you. On the next row work until the position for the pocket opening is reached, slip the required number of stitches for the pocket top on to a holder, with the right side of the pocket lining stitches facing the wrong side of the main fabric, work across the pocket lining stitches, then work to the end of the row across the main fabric. Complete the section as given in the instructions. With the right side of the work facing, rejoin the yarn to the pocket top stitches on the holder and work 1.5cm ($\frac{1}{2}$*in*) to 2.5cm (*1in*) in rib or garter stitch

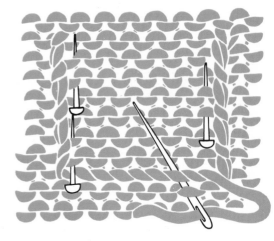

to complete the pocket. To make up the pocket, stitch the lining in place on the wrong side and neaten the side edges of the pocket top by slip stitching the edges to the main fabric.

Inserted vertical pockets

First check the number of rows you need to make the size of pocket required – if a tension of 8 rows to 2.5cm (*1in*) is given, a 10cm (*4in*) pocket will require 32 stitches. Cast on this number of stitches and make the inside pocket flap first, working in stocking stitch until it is the required depth, then leave these stitches on a holder. Work the main fabric of the garment until the required position for the pocket opening has been reached, ending with the right side of the work facing you. On the next row work until the position for the pocket opening is reached, turn at this point and work the required number of rows on

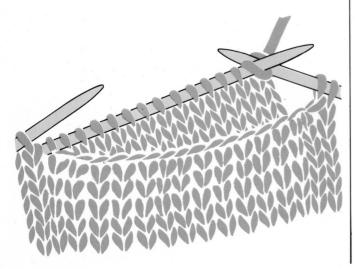

this section only, ending with a wrong side row. Break off the yarn. Return to where the work was divided, rejoin the yarn to the remaining stitches and work the same number of rows on this section, ending with a

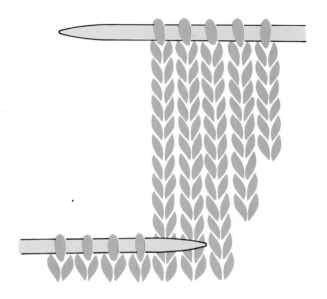

wrong side row. Break off the yarn. Return to the first section, rejoin the yarn and work across all the stitches to close the pocket opening, then complete the section as given in the instructions. With the right side of the work facing you, rejoin the yarn along the edge of the first pocket section worked on the right front of a garment, or along the second pocket section worked on the left front of a garment, and

pick up the required number of stitches. Work 1.5cm ($\frac{1}{2}in$) to 2.5cm (1in) rib or garter stitch to complete the pocket opening. With the right side of the pocket flap against the wrong side of the main fabric, join the flap to the other edge of the pocket opening and sew round the other 3 edges. Neaten the pocket opening by slip stitching the edges to the main fabric.

Patch pocket

Check the number of stitches and rows required to give the correct size for the pocket. If using a patterned stitch, such as cable, make sure that the pattern will work out exactly over the number of stitches and adjust them accordingly – it is better to have a slightly smaller or larger pocket than an incorrect pattern repeat. Cast on the stitches and work the number of rows to give the required depth, then cast off. With the wrong side of the patch pocket facing the right side of the main fabric, sew round 3 sides of the pocket.

Patch pocket with flap

Work as given for patch pocket until the required depth has been reached but do not cast off. Unless a completely reversible stitch, such as ribbing or garter stitch, has been used for the pocket, the pattern must now be reversed so that when the flap is turned down, the right side of the fabric will be showing. To do this if you have ended with a wrong side row, simply work another wrong side row for the first row of the flap, then continue in pattern for the required depth of the flap and cast off. Similarly, if you have ended with a right side row, work another right side row and complete in the same way. Sew on the pocket as given for patch pockets, turn the flap over to the right side and trim with one button at each end, if required.

Patch pockets with cable trim on a slip-over and patch pockets with flaps on a plain sweater

Neckbands and collars

Neckbands and collars

The neck opening on any garment, where the necessary shaping to give a good fit has been worked as part of the main fabric, will require neatening, either by means of a neckband or a collar. The most usual method of working a neckband on a round-necked jersey is to pick up the required number of stitches round the neck opening and work a few rows, or rounds, in single or double rib. This forms a neat edge with sufficient elasticity to hold its shape when it is pulled on or off over the head.

Collars may be added to a jersey or cardigan, either by picking up stitches round the neck edge or by making a separate section, which is then sewn round the neck edge to complete the garment. When working either a neckband or collar where the stitches must be picked up, see section on Making Up to ensure that stitches are picked up neatly and evenly round the opening.

Neckbands

To complete a round neck on a jersey, provision for an opening must be made if the neckband is to be worked on two needles. If a back or front neck opening has not been worked as part of the main fabric, only one shoulder seam should be joined, leaving the other seam open until the neckband has been completed. When a round neckband is worked on 4 needles, no opening is required and the stitches are simply picked up and worked in rounds to the required depth. When working a ribbed neckband, the depth can quite easily be adjusted to suit personal taste, to form either a round, crew or polo neck. If a polo neck is required, however, it must be remembered that this will take extra yarn and provision should be made for this when purchasing the yarn.

To complete a square neck on a jersey or cardigan, each corner must be mitred to continue the square shape and allow the neckband to lie flat. The neatest way to do this is to pick up the required number of stitches and mark each corner stitch with coloured thread. Keep these marked stitches as knitted stitches on the right side of the work, whether working in rows or rounds, and decrease one stitch on either side of each marked stitch on every row or round, making sure that the decreased stitches slant towards the corner stitch. As an example, when working in rows of garter stitch with the right side of the work facing, work to within 2 stitches of the corner stitch, sl 1, K1, psso, K corner st, K2 tog, then K to within 2 stitches of the next corner. On the following row, the decreased stitches will be worked in the same way but the corner stitch must be purled.

Collars

Collars come in all styles and sizes but to sit correctly round the neck, they must be carefully shaped. They can be worked in 2 sections to form a divided collar, where a jersey has a centre back neck opening, or in one piece to complete a jersey or a cardigan. Where the fabric used for the collar is reversible, such as garter stitch or ribbing, the stitches should be picked up round the neck in the usual way with the right side of the work facing. Where a fabric such as stocking stitch is used for a collar, however, the stitches must be picked up with the wrong side of the work facing, to ensure that the correct side of the fabric is shown when the collar is turned down.

Jersey with ribbed neckband or shirt collar

Sizes

To fit 86.5[91.5:96.5]cm (34[36:38]in) bust
Length to shoulder, 58.5[59.5:61]cm (23[23½:24]in)
Sleeve seam, 43[44.5:45.5]cm (17[17½:18]in)
The figures in brackets [] refer to the 91.5 (36) and 96.5cm (38in) sizes respectively

Tension

30 sts and 38 rows to 10cm (3.9in) over st st worked on No.11 needles

Materials

7[7:8] × 50 grm balls of any 4 ply plus 1 extra ball if collar is required
One pair No.11 needles
One pair No.12 needles
5 buttons

Back

Using No.12 needles cast on 134[142:150] sts. Work 5cm (2in) K1, P1 rib. Change to No.11 needles. Beg with a P row cont in reversed st st until work measures 40.5cm (16in) from beg, ending with a K row.
Shape armholes
Cast off 5[6:7] sts at beg of next 2 rows. Dec one st at each end of next and every alt row until 102[108:114] sts rem. Cont without shaping until armholes measure 18[19:20.5]cm (7[7½:8]in) from beg, ending with a K row.
Shape shoulders
Cast off at beg of next and every row 12 [12:13] sts twice, 12[13:13] sts twice and 12[13:14] sts twice. Leave rem 30[32:34] sts on holder.

Front

Work as given for back until front measures 39.5cm (15½in) from beg, ending with a P row.
Divide for front opening
Next row K62[66:70] sts, cast off 10 sts, K to end.
Complete this side first. Cont in reversed st st until work measures same as back to underarm, ending at armhole edge.
Shape armhole
Cast off 5[6:7] sts at beg of next row. Dec one st at armhole edge on every alt row until 46[49:52] sts rem. Cont without shaping until armhole measures 14cm (5½in) from beg, ending at centre front edge.

Shape neck

Cast off 3[4:5] sts at beg of next row. Dec one st at neck edge on every alt row until 36[38:40] sts rem. Cont without shaping until armhole measures same as back to shoulder, ending at armhole edge.

Shape shoulder

Cast off at beg of next and every alt row 12[12:13] sts once, 12[13:13] sts once and 12[13:14] sts once.

With RS of work facing, rejoin yarn to rem sts and complete to match first side, reversing shaping.

Sleeves

Using No.12 needles cast on 64[68:72] sts. Work 7.5cm (3in) K1, P1 rib. Change to No.11 needles. Beg with a P row cont in reversed st st, inc one st at each end of 7th and every foll 8th row, until there are 96[100:104] sts. Cont without shaping until sleeve measures 43[44.5:45.5]cm (17[17½:18]in) from beg, ending with a K row.

Shape top

Cast off 5[6:7] sts at beg of next 2 rows. Dec one st at each end of next and every alt row until 60 sts rem, ending with a K row. Cast off 4 sts at beg of next 10 rows. Cast off rem 20 sts.

Button band

Using No.12 needles cast on 12 sts. Beg 1st row with P1, work in P1, K1 rib until band fits up left front edge to beg of neck shaping, when slightly stretched. Leave sts on holder. Mark positions for 4 buttons with 5th to come in neckband.

Buttonhole band

Work as given for button band, beg 1st row with K1 and making buttonholes as markers are reached, as foll:

Next row (buttonhole row) Rib 5, cast off 2, rib 5.

Next row Rib to end, casting on 2 sts above those cast off in previous row.

Ribbed neckband

Join shoulder seams. Sew on button and buttonhole bands, making sure that next row will beg and end with K1. Using No.12 needles and with RS of work facing, rib across buttonhole band, K up 28[30:32] sts up right side of neck, K across back neck sts inc 5 sts evenly across sts and K up 28[30:32] sts up left front neck, then rib across button band. 115[119:123] sts. Work 9 rows K1, P1 rib, making buttonhole as before on 5th and 6th rows. **. Cast off.

Collar

Work as given for neckband to **.

Next row Cast off 6 sts, rib 5 sts and leave on holder, rib to last 11 sts, rib 5 sts and leave on holder, cast off 6 sts. Break off yarn.

Change to No.11 needles. Using 2 strands of yarn, work 15 more rows rib, inc one st at each end of every row. Dec one st at each end of next 6 rows. Cast off 3 sts at beg of next 6 rows. Cast off rem sts.

Edging

Using No.12 needles and one strand of yarn, rejoin yarn to WS of first set of 5 sts. Work in rib until edging fits round outer edge of collar to centre back. Cast off. Work other side in same way. Sew edging round collar, joining at centre back.

To make up

Press as required. Join side and sleeve seams. Set in sleeves. Sew on buttons.

MAKING UP
YARNS AND SEAMS

The making up of a garment requires as much care and skill as the actual knitting of each section. The technical knowledge which has been involved in producing an interesting fabric and the correct shape and proportions of the garment will be of no avail if the pieces are hurriedly assembled, or if scant attention is paid to the specific instructions for handling the yarn used. Some yarns do not require pressing, in fact, they lose their character if they are pressed and the texture of certain stitches, such as Aran patterns, can be completely ruined by over-pressing. Read the instructions carefully before beginning any making up and if you have not used the yarn specified, check whether or not the substitute requires pressing by referring to the instructions given on the ball band.

Handling yarns

Each yarn, whether it is made from natural fibres, man-made fibres, or various blends of both, requires a different method of handling in making up. The Home Laundering Consultative Council has compiled an ironing and dry-cleaning code in respect of hand knitting yarns and the relative symbols are shown on most ball bands. The following list gives a guide to the correct method of handling various qualities but with so many new and exciting yarns becoming available, it is even more essential to check the specific requirements of each yarn.

Pure wool This quality should be pressed under a damp cloth with a warm iron.

Blends of wool and nylon fibres Provided the wool content is greater than the nylon content, such as 60% wool and 40% nylon, these qualities should be pressed lightly under a damp cloth with a warm iron.

Blends of wool and acrylic fibres Do not press.

Nylon Press under a dry cloth with a cool iron.

Courtelle Do not press.

Acrylic fibres Do not press.

Cotton Press under a damp cloth with a fairly hot iron.

Mohair Press very lightly under a damp cloth with a warm iron.

Blends of mohair and acrylic fibres Do not press.

Blends of tricel and nylon Press lightly under a dry cloth with a warm iron.

Glitter yarns Do not press, unless otherwise clearly stated on the ball band.

Angora Steam press under a very damp cloth with a warm iron, by holding the iron over the cloth to make steam but not applying any pressure.

Embossed stitches Heavy cables, Aran patterns and any fabric with a raised texture should be steam pressed. This will neaten the fabric without flattening the pattern.

Warning! If in doubt, do not press.

Blocking

As so many yarns now available do not require pressing, it is not always necessary to block out each piece to the correct size and shape. If pressing is required however place each piece right side down on an ironing pad and pin it evenly round the edges to the pad. Use rustless tailor's pins and never stretch the knitting, or the pins will tend to make a fluted edge.

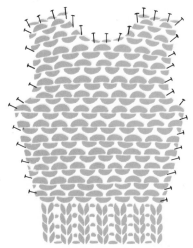

Take care to see that the stitches and rows run in straight lines and that the fabric is not pulled out of shape. Once the pieces are pinned into place, check with a firm rule that the width and length are the same as those given in the instructions.

	HOT	WARM	COOL	DO NOT IRON
IRONING				
DRYCLEAN	(A)	(P)	(F)	(X)
	Usual dry cleaning	Normally drycleanable in most solvents. If drycleaned inform cleaner of composition of yarn.	Drycleanable in some solvents It is important that the cleaner is informed of the composition of the yarn if dry-cleaning is to be undertaken.	DO NOT DRYCLEAN

Pressing

Use a clean cloth and place it over the piece to be pressed, then press the iron down on top of the cloth and lift it up again, without moving it over the surface of the cloth as you would if you were actually ironing. Each area should be pressed evenly but not too heavily before lifting the iron to go on to the next area. Ribbed or garter stitch edges on any piece do not require pressing, or they will lose their elasticity.

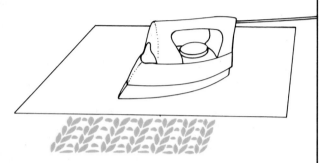

Seams

The choice of seaming method will largely depend on the type of garment being assembled. A baby's vest needs invisible seams without any hard edges and the flat seam method is normally used to join any ribbed edges where a neat, flat edge is required. Use a blunt ended wool needle and the original yarn for joining pieces together. If the yarn is not suitable for sewing purposes, as with mohair, use a finer quality such as 3 ply in the same shade.

Invisible seam Secure the sewing yarn to one side of the pieces to be joined. With the right sides of both pieces facing you, pass the needle across to the other side of the work, pick up one stitch and pull the yarn through. Pass the needle across the back to the first side of the work, pick up one stitch and pull the yarn through. Continue working in this way, making rungs across from one piece to the other and pulling each stitch up tightly so that it is not seen on the right side of the work when the seam is completed.

Back stitch seam Place the right sides of each piece to be joined together and work along the wrong side of the fabric about one stitch in from the edge. Keep checking the other side of the seam to make sure that you are working in a straight line. Begin by securing the sewing yarn, making two or three small running stitches one on top of the other, *with the needle at the back of the work move along to the left and bring the needle through to the front of the work the width

of one stitch from the end of the last stitch, and pull the yarn through, take the needle back across the front of the work to the right and put it through to the back of the work at the end of the last stitch and pull the yarn through. Continue in this way repeating from * until the seam is completed, taking care to pull each sewing stitch firmly through the knitting, without stretching the pieces or drawing up the seaming stitches too tightly.

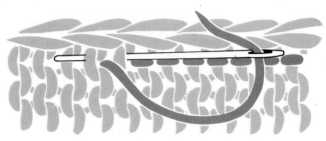

Flat seam Place the right sides of each piece to be joined together and place your forefinger between the two pieces. Secure the sewing yarn to one side of the pieces to be joined then pass the needle through the edge stitch on the underside piece directly across to the matching stitch on the upper-side piece and pull the yarn through. Turn the needle and work back through the next stitch on the upper-side piece directly across to the matching stitch on the underside piece, again pulling the yarn through. Continue in this way until the seam is completed.

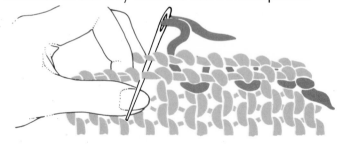

Slip stitch seam This is required for turning in hems and facings to the wrong side of the work. Turn in the hem or facing so that the wrong side of the main fabric is towards you. Secure the sewing yarn at a seam then insert the needle and lightly pick up one stitch from the main fabric and pull the yarn through, move along to the left the width of one stitch, insert the needle into the edge stitch of the hem or facing and pick up one stitch, then pull the yarn through. Move along to the left the width of one stitch and continue in this way until the seam is completed.

SETTING IN

More about making up! As we have already explained in the previous chapter, the care and attention to detail required in making up are as essential as in knitting the actual pieces. The correct seaming method, the correct handling and pressing of yarns, the correct method of finishing hems, applying pockets, completing edgings – all these techniques mean the difference between a hand-made garment and a couture design. Here are more tricks of the trade which will enable you to give all your garments the finish and flair of a ready-to-wear design.

Sewn on bands

Where bands are worked separately and are not incorporated in the working instructions for the main sections, such as button and buttonhole bands, use a flat seam to apply the bands. Each band should be slightly less than the finished length of the main fabric and should be slightly stretched and pinned into position before seaming.

Sewn on pockets

Use a slip stitch seam to apply the pocket, taking care to keep the line of the pocket and main fabric straight. A useful tip is to use a fine knitting needle, pointed at both ends, to pick up every alternate stitch along the line of the main fabric, then catch one stitch from the edge of the pocket and one stitch from the needle alternately. Make sure that the lower edge of the pocket lies in a straight line across a row of the main fabric.

Applying the pocket

Shoulder seams

Use a firm back stitch seam, taking the stitches across the steps of shaping in a straight line. On heavy outer garments, school or sports jerseys, or any garment where extra strength is needed, re-inforce these seams with ribbon or tape.

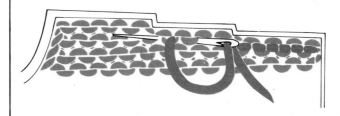

Set-in sleeves

Mark the centre top of the sleeve head and pin this to the shoulder seam, then pin the cast off underarm stitches to the underarm stitches of the body. Use a back stitch seam, working in a smooth line around the curve of the armhole and taking care not to pull the stitches too tightly.

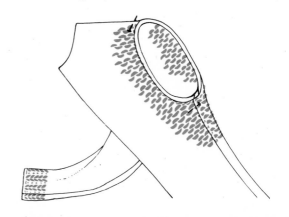

Side and sleeve seams

Use a back stitch seam and join in one piece, working extra stitches across the underarm join to secure it firmly.

Sewing in zip fasteners

Pin the zip fastener into the required opening, taking care not to stretch the knitting. With the right side of the work facing, sew in the zip using a back stitch seam and keeping as close to the edge of the knitting as possible. On something like a back neck opening or skirt side seam, work in a straight line down the zip from top to bottom, then work extra stitches across the end of the zip to secure it and continue up the other side of the zip.

When inserting an open-ended zip, keep the fastener closed and insert it as for an opening from top to lower edge, fastening off securely at the end. Break off the yarn and work along the other side in the same way. This ensures that both sides match and that one side is not pulled out of shape, making it difficult to operate the zip smoothly.

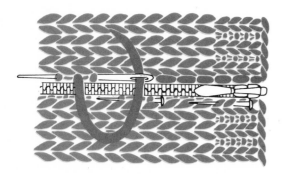

Knitting up edges

You will frequently come across the phrase, 'knit up stitches', such as round a neckline, along a front edge or pocket top, as a means of neatening an unfinished edge. This is usually worked with the right side of the garment facing you. The instructions will always clearly state where stitches are required to be picked up with the wrong side facing you, such as would be needed for a stocking stitch collar, where the turned down collar fabric must match the main fabric. You can either pick up these stitches directly on to a knitting needle, or use a crochet hook to pick up the stitches and then transfer them to a knitting needle.

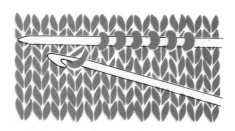

Knitting up stitches across the line of main fabric

Knitting up stitches across the line of main fabric

Have the right side of the fabric facing you and hold the yarn at the back of the work. Use a crochet hook and put this through the work from the right side to the wrong side and pick up a loop of yarn from the back, bring this loop through to the right side and transfer the stitch to a knitting needle. Continue in this way until the required number of stitches have been picked up.

Knitting up stitches round a curved edge This could be a neckband or armhole band. Have the yarn at the back of the work and the right side of the fabric facing you. Put a knitting needle through from the front to the back of the fabric and pick up a loop of yarn, bring this loop through to the right side of the work and leave the stitch on the needle. If a crochet hook is used, pick up the loop in the same way with the hook then transfer the stitch to a knitting needle. Continue in this way until the required number of stitches have been picked up.

An easy way to ensure that stitches are picked up evenly is to pin out the main section of fabric at regular intervals of, say, 5cm (*2in*) and pick up the same number of stitches inside each pin. As a guide, make sure that where you are picking up stitches across stitches you pick up one loop for each stitch and across rows, approximately one stitch for every two rows.

Knitting up front bands Count the number of rows on the main fabric then check this against the number of stitches to be picked up and make sure that you knit them up evenly. Pin out sections as given for knitting up stitches round a curved edge and pick up the same number of stitches between each pin. Unless otherwise stated in the instructions, always work the button band first so that you can mark the exact position for each button and then work the appropriate buttonhole on the buttonhole band, as these markers are reached.

TAKING CARE

The correct after-care of all knitted garments is extremely important if they are to retain their original texture and shape. Many of the yarns available today are machine-washable and the ball band will clearly indicate where this is applicable. If you are in any doubt at all, however, always hand wash rather than risk ruining the garment. Similarly, check whether the yarn can be dry cleaned from the ball band, referring to the Home Laundering chart earlier for details.

Care in washing
Whether you are machine washing or hand washing a garment, it is essential that the minimum amount of handling occurs when the fabric is wet. Before washing, turn the garment inside out. Never lift the garment by the shoulders, thus allowing the weight of the water to pull the design out of shape. Squeeze out any excess moisture very gently but never wring the garment, supporting the whole weight with both hands.

Always rinse two or three times, making sure that all soap or detergent deposits have been thoroughly removed, using a fabric conditioner if required. Once the garment has been rinsed, gently lift it on to a draining board, again supporting the weight, while you prepare a drying area.

Care in drying
Very few yarns take kindly to contact with direct heat or sunlight and the garment should always be allowed to dry out naturally. You also run the risk of pulling the whole garment out of shape if you peg it on to a line while it is still wet, however carefully. The best possible way of drying any garment, whatever the composition of the yarn used, is on a flat surface – a kitchen table top is ideal.

First place 3 or 4 old newspapers over the surface which is to be used for drying, spreading them out well beyond the full extent of the garment. Cover the newspapers completely with one or two clean towels which are colour-fast – a white garment placed on a red towel which is not completely colour-fast could result in some unsightly pink patches! Gently lift the garment on to the centre of the towel. Spread it into its original size and shape and gently pat it flat on to the towel, smoothing out any creases. Leave the garment until all the excess moisture has been absorbed by the towels and newspapers. Then – and only then – should it be carefully lifted and placed over a line for the final airing, pegging the

garment at the underarms only and never from the shoulders.

Care in pressing
If the garment has been well smoothed out and allowed to dry in shape it should not require any pressing. If it does need ironing, however, first check the instructions given on the ball band, then refer to the beginning of this section for handling details.

Care in wear
However careful you are, a garment may become snagged or the yarn may 'pill' into little balls of fluff. It is a simple matter to remedy these faults before too much damage is done.

To prevent the risk of snagging, do not put on a garment while you are wearing any jewellery which could catch in the yarn and pull a thread. Should you discover a snag in a garment, however, never cut it off or you will run the risk of the fabric unravelling. Using a blunt ended sewing needle, push the snagged end of yarn through to the wrong side of the fabric and gently tighten the yarn until the stitch is the correct size, then knot the end of yarn and leave it on the wrong side.

Where pilling occurs in the yarn, gently pull off these

little balls of fluff, taking care not to snag the yarn. If the pilling is excessive, the fabric should be gently brushed over with a teasel to remove the fluff.

Make do and mend

Hand knitting need never be wasted, even if the original garment has outgrown its use. Unpick the seams of the garment, taking great care not to cut the fabric, and unravel each section winding the yarn into hanks by passing it round the backs of two chairs. To remove any crinkles from the yarn, either hand wash each hank and hang out to dry, or hold them taut in front of the spout of a gently steaming kettle, moving them backwards and forwards through the steam until the kinks have disappeared. Some areas of knitting may wear thin in use particularly on children's garments. These can easily be re-inforced by means of Swiss darning. It doesn't matter if you cannot match the original yarn – a contrasting colour darned into a motif will give an interesting new lease of life to the design.

Elbows which are worn through can easily be covered with a patch of leather or suede, applied to the right side of the fabric. To disguise the fact that these are patches, add new interest to the garment by making leather patch pockets to match.

KNITTING IN ROUNDS
BASIC TECHNIQUES

Knitting in rounds, as opposed to knitting in rows to produce flat knitting, literally means producing a seamless, tubular piece of fabric. This method may be worked on sets of needles, usually 4, which are pointed at both ends and manufactured in varying lengths and the length of needle will be determined by the total number of stitches required.

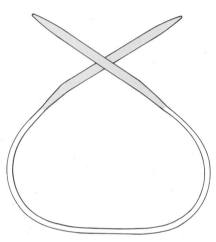

Circular needles are also obtainable and those manufactured by Aero, called Twin-Pins, comprise two rigid, shaped needle sections pointed at one end, with the other end of each section being joined into one continuous length by a light-weight, flexible strip of nylon. Before using Twin-Pins the twist which the nylon strip may develop through packing may be removed by immersing it in fairly warm water and then drawing it between the fingers until it lies in a gradual curve. These are also manufactured in varying lengths and the chart gives a guide to the minimum number of stitches required for each length, to reach from needle point to needle point without stretching. The advantage of circular needles over sets of needles is that they may also be used as an ordinary pair of needles for working to and fro in rows.

As knitting in rounds dispenses with seaming, it is the ideal way of making socks and stockings, gloves and mittens, hats, skirts and even jerseys. The minimum of seaming on a jersey is possible by working the body in one piece to a point where the work can be divided and continued in rows.

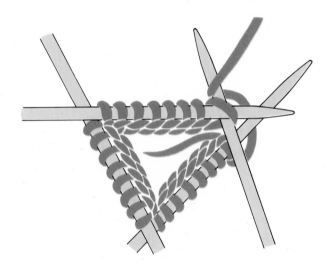

Casting on
Details of casting on with more than two needles have already been given in Chapter 1. The total number of stitches required can either be cast on to one needle and then divided between three of the needles, leaving the fourth needle to knit with, or can be cast on to each of the three needles separately.

When casting on with a circular needle, simply use each shaped section as a pair of needles, having one section in the left hand and one in the right.

Whether using sets of needles or a circular needle, the important point to remember is that the cast on stitches must not become twisted before joining them into a round.

Knitting in rounds
Once you have cast on the required number of stitches, using sets of needles, form them into a circle by putting the spare needle into the first stitch on the left hand needle and knit this stitch in the usual way. Continue to knit all the stitches on the first needle and once this is free use it to knit the stitches of the second needle, then use the second needle to knit the stitches of the third needle. Always pull the yarn tightly across to the first stitch of each needle to avoid a loose stitch.

With a circular needle, simply continue knitting each stitch until you come to the beginning of the round again.

TENSION	LENGTHS OF AERO CIRCULAR TWIN-PIN NEEDLES AVAILABLE AND MINIMUM NUMBER OF STITCHES REQUIRED						
Stitches to 2.5cm(1in.)	40.5cm 16"	51.0cm 20"	61.0cm 24"	68.5cm 27"	70.6 cm 30"	91.5cm 36"	106.5cm 42"
5	80	100	120	135	150	180	210
5½	88	110	132	148	165	198	230
6	96	120	144	162	180	216	250
6½	104	130	156	175	195	234	270
7 ·	112	140	168	189	210	252	294
7½	120	150	180	202	225	270	315
8	128	160	192	216	240	288	336
8½	136	170	204	220	255	306	357
9	144	180	216	243	270	324	378

As it is easy to lose track of where each round of knitting begins, mark the beginning of the round with a knotted loop of contrast yarn on the needle before the first stitch of every round and slip this loop from the left hand needle to the right hand needle without knitting it.

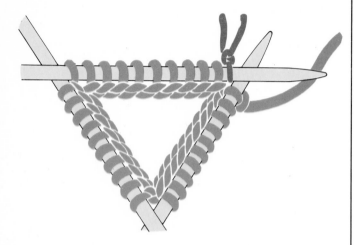

Stocking stitch in rounds

Since the right side of the fabric is always facing the knitter and the work is not turned at the end of each row as in flat knitting, stocking stitch in rounds is produced by knitting every round. This has a great advantage when working complicated, multi-coloured patterns.

Garter stitch in rounds

Because the work is not turned, to produce garter stitch in rounds the first round must be knitted and the second round purled, to form the ridged effect.

Ribbing in rounds

Here again, the right side of the fabric is facing so each knit stitch must be knitted on every round and each purl stitch purled on every round. When working in rounds of ribbing, remember that if you begin a round with one or more knitted stitches, you must end with one or more purled stitches to complete the round exactly.

Socks without heel shaping

This practical way of producing socks without heel shaping must be worked on sets of needles.

Size

Round top of sock, 20.5cm (8in)
Length to toe, 58.5cm (23in), adjustable

Tension

32 sts and 36 rows to 10.0cm (3.9in) over patt worked on No.12 needles

Materials

5 × 1oz balls of Patons Nylox 4 ply
Set of 4 No.12 needles pointed at both ends

Socks

Using set of 4 No.12 needles cast on 80 sts, 26 each on 1st and 2nd needles and 28 on 3rd needle. Mark beginning of round with coloured thread.
1st round *K1, P1, rep from * to end.
Rep 1st round for single ribbing until work measures 10.0cm (4in) from beg. Commence patt.
1st patt round *K3, P2, rep from * to end.
Rep 1st patt round 3 times more.
5th patt round P1, *K3, P2, rep from * to last 4 sts, K3, P1.
Rep 5th patt round 3 times more.
9th patt round *P2, K3, rep from * to end.
Rep 9th patt round 3 times more.
13th patt round K1, *P2, K3, rep from * to last 4 sts, P2, K2.
Rep 13th patt round 3 times more.
17th patt round K2, *P2, K3, rep from * to last 3 sts, P2, K1.
Rep 17th patt round 3 times more. These 20 rounds form patt. Cont in patt until work measures 52.0cm (20½in) from beg, or required length less 6.5cm (2½in). Cont in st st, K each round.
Shape toe
1st round *K8 sts, K2 tog, rep from * to end.
Work 2 rounds st st without shaping.
4th round *K7 sts, K2 tog, rep from * to end.
Work 2 rounds st st without shaping.
7th round *K6 sts, K2 tog, rep from * to end.
Work 2 rounds st st without shaping.
10th round *K5 sts, K2 tog, rep from * to end.
Work 2 rounds st st without shaping.
13th round *K4 sts, K2 tog, rep from * to end.
Work 2 rounds st st without shaping.
16th round *K3 sts, K2 tog, rep from * to end.
Work 2 rounds st st without shaping.
19th round *K2 sts, K2 tog, rep from * to end.
Work 2 rounds st st without shaping.
22nd round *K1 st, K2 tog, rep from * to end.
23rd round *K2 tog, rep from * to end.
Break off yarn, thread through rem sts, draw up and fasten off securely.

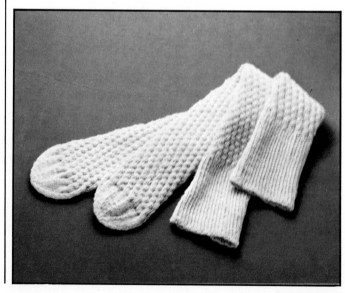

DOUBLE FABRICS

A double stocking stitch fabric can quite easily be produced by working in rounds and using this tube of material as a double sided fabric. Alternatively, double fabric can also be worked in rows on two needles by the simple means of a slipped stitch and this method is most effective when two different yarns, giving the same tension, are used for each side of the material.

The ideas shown here will enable you to practise both these methods to make a warm scarf or a glamorous evening hood.

Scarf

We have made our scarf in stocking stitch, knitting every round, in wide stripes. You can just as easily work narrow stripes in more than two colours or a simple, all-over patterned stitch in one colour, provided you check the multiples of stitches required for the pattern and amend the number of stitches cast on accordingly. The total quantity of yarn given will be a guide to the amount required but remember that a patterned stitch may need more yarn.

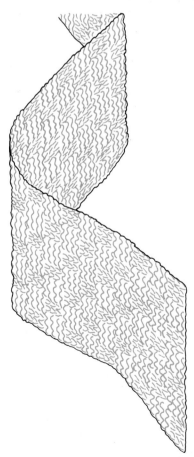

Scarf knitted in all-over patterned stitch.

Size

23cm (9in) wide by 152.5cm (60in) long

Tension

22 sts and 28 rows to 10cm (3.9in) over st st worked on No.8 needles.

Materials

4 × 50 grm balls of Jaeger Spiral-Spun in main shade, A
4 balls of same in contrast colour, B
Set of 4 No.8 needles pointed at both ends *or*
One No.8 circular Twin-Pin

Scarf

Using set of 4 No.8 needles or No.8 circular Twin-Pin and A, cast on 100 sts. Work in rounds of st st, every round K, until work measures 10cm (4in) from beg. Break off A and join in B. Work a further 10cm (4in) st st. Cont working stripes in this way until work measures 152.5cm (60in) from beg. Cast off.

To make up

Press under a damp cloth with a warm iron. Cut rem yarn into 30.5cm (12in) lengths and knot fringe along each short end, working through double fabric and using A and B alternately. Trim fringe.

Evening hood

We have used a glitter yarn and mohair to make this double sided hood for evening. Using a plain yarn and repeating the first pattern row only, a snug, day-time version can quite easily be made. The total quantity of yarn given will be a guide to the amount required but make sure that you can achieve the same tension.

Size
28cm (11in) wide by 142cm (56in) long

Tension
16 sts and 28 rows to 10cm (3.9in) over double fabric worked on No.8 needles

Materials
5 × 1oz balls of Jaeger Mohair-Spun in main shade, A
5 × 25 grm balls of Jaeger Astral-Spun in contrast colour, B
One pair No.8 needles pointed at both ends
One pair No.10 needles

Evening hood
Using No.10 needles and A, cast on 88 sts. Change to No.8 needles.
1st row (RS) Using A, *K1, yfwd, sl 1 P-wise, ybk, rep from * to end. Join in B.
(**Note:** When using one colour, turn and rep this row throughout.)

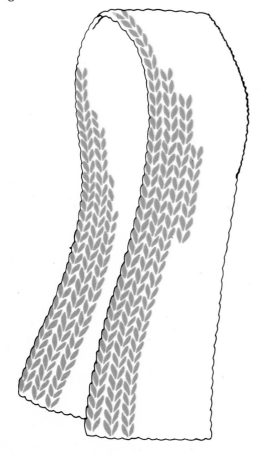

Hood worked in same yarn and colour throughout

2nd row Do not turn work but return to beg of row, using B, *sl 1 P-wise, yfwd, P1, ybk, rep from * to end. 44 sts each in A and B.
3rd row Turn work and cross A and B to close side edge, using B, *K1, yfwd, sl 1 P-wise, ybk, rep from * to end.
4th row Do not turn work but return to beg of row, using A, *sl 1 P-wise, yfwd, P1, ybk, rep from * to end. Turn and cross A and B to close side edge.
These 4 rows form the patt. Cont in patt until work measures 61cm (24in) from beg, ending with a 2nd or 4th patt row.
Shape top
Next row Dec one st at beg of row in A and B by using both strands tog and (K2 tog) twice, patt to end.
Next 3 rows Patt to end.
Rep last 4 rows 13 times more. 30 sts each in A and B.
Next row Using A and B tog, (inc in next st) twice, patt to end.
Next 3 rows Patt to end.
Rep last 4 rows 13 times more. 44 sts each in A and B. Cont in patt without shaping until work measures 61cm (24in) from last inc row. Cast off K2 tog along row.

To make up
Do not press. Join back shaping seam and 15cm (6in) of straight edges.

GLOVES AND MITTENS

When knitting in rounds to produce gloves, mittens, socks and stockings, the most difficult part to master is the shaping required to give a perfect fit to fingers and thumbs or heels and toes. To do this correctly, at a given point in the pattern some of the stitches will be left unworked and held in abeyance on a stitch holder, while the first section is completed. then the unworked stitches will be picked up, together with additional stitches in some instances, to complete the work.

All these shaping details will be given out in full in any pattern and in the sequence in which they are to be worked. This chapter deals with gloves and mittens, which can be worked entirely in rounds without seaming, and includes a pair of mittens for a baby – ideal for a first attempt.

Both the designs given here begin at the wrist, where a firm ribbed edge is required to give a snug fit, and stocking stitch has been used for the main sections. They can both be made in one colour only but, as a way of using up oddments of the same quality yarn, we have worked the wrist and thumb of the mittens in a contrasting colour, and the wrist, thumb, and each finger of the gloves in a different colour, for a really jazzy, fun effect.

Babies' mittens
Size
To fit 9/18 months

Tension
28 sts and 36 rows to 10cm (*3.9in*) over st st worked on No.10 needles

Materials
1 × 25 grm ball of 4 ply yarn in main shade, A
Oddment of contrast colour, B
Set of 4 No.10 needles pointed at both ends
Set of 4 No.12 needles pointed at both ends

Mittens
Using set of 4 No.12 needles and B, cast on 36 sts, 12 on each of 3 needles. Mark beg of round with coloured thread.
1st round *K1, P1, rep from * to end.
Rep this round until work measures 2.5cm (*1in*) from beg. Break off B. Join in A. Change to set of 4 No.10 needles. Beg with a K round work in rounds of st st until work measures 4cm (*1½in*) from beg.
Shape thumb
Next round K17, pick up loop lying between sts and K tbl – called inc 1 –, K2, inc 1, K17.
Next round K to end.

Next round K17, inc 1, K4, inc 1, K17. 40 sts.
Next round K to end.
Cont inc in this way on next and every alt round until there are 46 sts.
Divide for thumb
Next round K18, sl next 10 sts on to holder and leave for thumb, turn and cast on 2 sts, turn and K18. 38 sts.
Cont in rounds of st st until work measures 10.5cm (*4¼in*) from beg.
Shape top
Next round K1, sl 1, K1, psso, K13, K2 tog, K2, sl 1, K1, psso, K13, K2 tog, K1. 34 sts.
Next round K to end.
Next round K1, sl 1, K1, psso, K11, K2 tog, K2, sl 1, K1, psso, K11, K2 tog, K1. 30 sts.
Cont dec 4 sts in this way on every alt round until 14 sts rem. Arrange sts on 2 needles and cast off tog or graft sts.
Thumb
Using set of 4 No.10 needles, B and with RS of work facing, arrange 10 thumb sts on 3 needles, then K up 2 sts from base of cast on sts. 12 sts. Cont in rounds of st st until thumb measures 2cm (*¾in*) from beg.
Shape top
Next round *K2 tog, rep from * to end. 6 sts.
Rep last round once more. Break off yarn, thread through rem sts, draw up and fasten off.

Children's gloves
Size
To fit 15.5cm (6¼in) all round hand

Tension
30 sts and 38 rows to 10cm (3.9in) over st st worked on No.11 needles.

Materials
1 × 25 grm ball of 4 ply in main shade, A
1 ball each, or oddments of contrast colours, B, C, D, E and F.
Set of 4 No.11 needles pointed at both ends
Set of 4 No.12 needles pointed at both ends

Gloves
Using set of 4 No.12 needles and B, cast on 48 sts and arrange on 3 needles. Mark beg of round with coloured thread. Work 6.5cm (2½in) rib as given for mittens. Break off B. Join in A. Change to set of 4 No.11 needles. Work 4 rounds st st.
Shape thumb
Next round K23, inc 1 as given for mittens, K2, inc 1, K23.
Work 3 rounds st st without shaping.
Next round K23, inc 1, K4, inc 1, K23.
Cont inc in this way on every foll 4th round until there are 60 sts, ending with 3 rounds st st after last inc round.

Divide for thumb
Next round K24, sl next 12 sts on to holder and leave for thumb, turn and cast on 2 sts, turn and K24. 50 sts.
Cont in st st until work measures 15cm (6in) from beg.
First finger
Next round Sl first 18 sts of round on to holder, join C to next st and K14, turn and cast on 2 sts, leave rem 18 sts on 2nd holder.
Cont in st st on these 16 sts until finger measures 5.5cm (2¼in) from beg.
Shape top
Next round K1, *K2 tog, K1, rep from * to end. 11 sts.
Next round K to end.
Next round K1, *K2 tog, rep from * to end. 6 sts.
Break off yarn, thread through rem sts, draw up and fasten off.
Second finger
Next round Using D and with RS of work facing, leave first 11 sts on holder and K across last 7 sts on first holder, K up 2 sts from base of first finger, K across next 7 sts on 2nd holder, turn and cast on 2 sts. 18 sts.
Cont in st st until finger measures 6.5cm (2½in) from beg.
Shape top
Next round *K1, K2 tog, rep from * to end. 12 sts.
Next round K to end.
Next round *K2 tog, rep from * to end. Complete as given for first finger.
Third finger
Next round Using E and with RS of work facing, leave first 6 sts on holder and K across last 5 sts on first holder, K up 2 sts from base of 2nd finger, K across next 5 sts on 2nd holder, turn and cast on 2 sts. 14 sts.
Cont in st st until finger measures 5.5cm (2¼in) from beg.
Shape top
Next round K1, *K2 tog, K1, rep from * to last st, K1. 10 sts.
Complete as given for 2nd finger.
Fourth finger
Next round Using F and with RS of work facing, K across rem 6 sts on first holder, K up 2 sts from base of 3rd finger, K across rem 6 sts on 2nd holder. 14 sts.
Cont in st st until finger measures 5cm (2in) from beg.
Shape top
Work as given for 3rd finger.
Thumb
Next round Using B and with RS of work facing, K across 12 thumb sts, then K up 4 sts from base of cast on sts. 16 sts.
Cont in st st until thumb measures 4.5cm (1¾in) from beg.
Shape top
Work as given for 1st finger.

SOCKS AND STOCKINGS

The previous chapter dealt with knitting in rounds to produce gloves and mittens, where the complete design can be worked without seaming. This chapter shows how simple it is to make socks and stockings, where the leg and foot can be worked in rounds and the stitches are divided at the heel and worked in rows, to produce the heel gusset shaping.

A plain basic sock design can be adapted in a variety of ways, either by using stripes for the leg and instep, keeping the top, heel and sole in a plain colour, or by introducing a patterned stitch for the leg and instep but, in this event, make sure that the pattern chosen will divide evenly into the total number of stitches cast on. Alternatively, men's socks look most effective when a small, two-colour motif is used as a clock on either side of the leg.

Here we give instructions for a pair of hard-wearing socks for children and a pair of beautiful, lacy stockings as a fashion accessory.

Socks
Sizes
To fit 18cm (*7in*) foot
Length of leg from top of heel, 20.5cm (*8in*)

Tension
32 sts and 40 rows to 10cm (*3.9in*) over st st worked on No.12 needles

Materials
4 × 25 grm balls of Wendy 4 ply Nylonised
Set of 4 No.12 needles pointed at both ends

Socks
Using set of 4 No.12 needles cast on 56 sts and arrange on 3 needles. Mark end of round.
1st round *K1, P1, rep from * to end.
Rep this round until work measures 4cm (*1½in*) from beg. Beg with a K round cont in rounds of st st until work measures 7.5cm (*3in*) from beg.
Shape leg
Next round K1, sl 1, K1, psso, K to last 3 sts, K2 tog, K1.
Work 4 rounds st st without shaping. Rep last 5 rounds until 42 sts rem. Cont without shaping until work measures 20.5cm (*8in*) from beg. Break off yarn.
Divide for heel
Next row Sl first and last 11 sts of round on to one needle, rejoin yarn and P to end. 22 sts.
Beg with a K row work 16 rows st st, ending with a P row.

Turn heel
Next row K14 sts, sl 1, K1, psso, turn.
Next row P7 sts, P2 tog, turn.
Next row K7 sts, sl 1, K1, psso, turn.
Next row P7 sts, P2 tog, turn.
Rep last 2 rows until all sts are on one needle.
Next round K4 sts, using 2nd needle K rem 4 heel sts, K up 10 sts down side of heel, using 3rd needle K across 20 sts of instep, using 4th needle K up 10 sts up other side of heel then K the first 4 sts on to this needle.

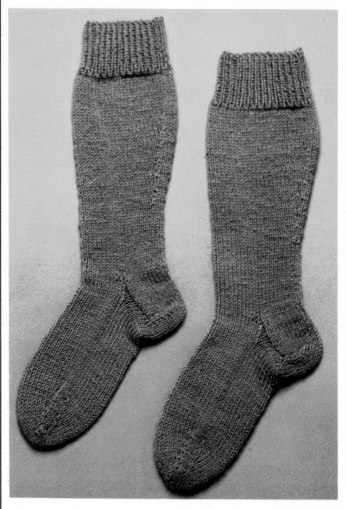

Shape instep
1st round K to end.
2nd round 1st needle K to last 3 sts, K2 tog, K1; 2nd needle K to end; 3rd needle K1, sl 1, K1, psso, K to end.
Rep last 2 rounds until 42 sts rem. Cont without shaping until work measures 10cm (*4in*) from where sts were picked up at heel.

Shape toe

1st round 1st needle K to last 3 sts, K2 tog, K1; 2nd needle K1, sl 1, K1, psso, K to last 3 sts, K2 tog, K1; 3rd needle K1, sl 1, K1, psso, K to end. Work 2 rounds st st without shaping. Rep last 3 rounds until 22 sts rem, then K across sts on 1st needle. Cast off sts tog or graft sts.

Lacy stockings
Sizes

To fit 21.5[24]cm ($8\frac{1}{2}$[$9\frac{1}{2}$]in) foot
Leg length to top of heel, 71cm (28in), adjustable
The figures in brackets [ ] refer to the 24cm ($9\frac{1}{2}$in) size only

Tension

28 sts and 30 rows to 10cm (3.9in) over patt worked on No.5 needles

Materials

3 × 1 oz balls Jaeger Faerie-Spun 2 ply
Set of 4 No.6 needles pointed at both ends
Set of 4 No.7 needles pointed at both ends
Set of 4 No.9 needles pointed at both ends
Set of 4 No.10 needles pointed at both ends

Stockings

Using set of 4 No.6 needles cast on 68 sts very loosely and arrange on 3 needles. Mark beg of round with coloured thread. Work 8 rounds K1, P1 rib. Commence patt.
1st round *(K2 tog) 3 times, yfwd, (K1, yfwd) 5 times, (K2 tog tbl) 3 times, rep from * to end.
2nd and 3rd rounds K to end.
4th round P to end.
These 4 rounds form patt, noting that sts should be arranged on needles as required. Rep 4 patt rounds 17 times more, adjusting length at this point and noting that work will stretch to 81.5cm (32in). Change to set of 4 No.7 needles and rep patt rounds 16 times. Change to set of 4 No.9 needles and rep patt rounds 16 times. Change to set of 4 No.10 needles and rep patt rounds 8 times.

Shape heel

Next round K15, K into front and back of next st – called inc 1 –, K1, patt 34 sts, inc 1, K16.
Next round K18, patt 34, K18.
Next round K16, inc 1, K1, patt 34, inc 1, K17.
Next round K19, patt 34, K19.
Keeping heel sts in st st and centre 34 sts in patt, cont to inc in this way on next and every alt round until there are 80 sts, then work 4 rounds without shaping.
Next round Still keeping centre 34 sts in patt, K21, K2 tog, patt 34, sl 1, K1, psso, K21.
Next round K22, patt 34, K22.
Next round K20, K2 tog, patt 34, sl 1, K1, psso, K20.
Next round K21, patt 34, K21.
Cont dec in this way on next and every alt round until 56 sts rem, then cont without shaping until foot measures 18[20.5]cm (7[8]in) from centre of heel, or required length less 4cm ($1\frac{1}{2}$in).

Shape toe

Next round K12, K2 tog, sl 1, K1, psso, K24, K2 tog, sl 1, K1, psso, K12.
Next round K to end.
Next round K11, K2 tog, sl 1, K1, psso, K22, K2 tog, sl 1, K1, psso, K11.
Next round K to end.
Cont dec in this way on next and every alt round until 20 sts rem. K sts from 3rd needle on to 1st needle and graft sts.

MOTIFS IN ROUNDS

We have already explained earlier how knitting in rounds produces seamless, tubular fabric. This section deals with knitting in rounds to form flat, circular medallion shapes, which have a variety of uses.

Fine cotton yarn and lacy stitches can be used to make delicate table mats, or a thick cotton yarn and a simple stitch can be used for a hard-wearing rug. Oddments of double knitting yarns can also be utilized for colourful, circular cushions or afghans.

Tension

24 sts and 32 rows to 10cm (3.9in) over st st worked on No.8 needles

Materials

1 × 50grm ball each of Jaeger Spiral Spun in 4 contrast colours, A, B, C and D
Set of 4 No.8 needles
One No.8 circular Twin Pin
40·5cm (16in) diameter circular cushion pad

Cover

Work as given for hexagonal medallion, working 2 rounds each in A, B, C and D throughout and changing to circular Twin Pin when required, until work measures 40.5cm (16in) diameter. Cast off loosely. Make another hexagonal medallion in same way.

To make up

Press each piece under a damp cloth with a warm iron. With RS facing, join medallions tog leaving an opening large enough to insert cushion pad. Turn RS out. Insert pad and complete seam. Sew one button to centre of each side, if required.

To make a circular lace table mat
Size

25.5cm (10in) in diameter

Materials

1 × 20grm ball of Twilley's Twenty
Set of 4 No.12 needles

Simple hexagonal medallion

Using set of 4 needles cast on 6 sts, having 2 sts on each of 3 needles. Join needles into a round and K all sts tbl to keep centre flat. Commence patt.

1st round *K into front then into back of next st — called inc 1 —, rep from * to end. 12 sts.
2nd round *Inc 1, K1, rep from * to end. 18 sts.
3rd round *Inc 1, K2, rep from * to end. 24 sts.
4th round *Inc 1, K3, rep from * to end. 30 sts.
5th round *Inc 1, K4, rep from * to end. 36 sts.
6th round *Inc 1, K5, rep from * to end. 42 sts.
Cont inc 6 sts in this way on every round until medallion is required size. Cast off loosely.

To make a cushion cover
Size

40.5cm (16in) diameter

Table mat

Using set of 4 No.12 needles cast on 8 sts, having 2 sts on 1st needle and 3 sts each on 2nd and 3rd needles. Join needles into a round and K all sts tbl to keep centre flat. Commence patt.

1st round *Yfwd, K1, rep from * to end. 16 sts.
2nd and every alt round K to end.
3rd round *Yfwd, K2, rep from * to end. 24 sts.
5th round *Yfwd, K3, rep from * to end. 32 sts.
7th round *Yfwd, K4, rep from * to end. 40 sts.
9th round *Yfwd, K5, rep from * to end. 48 sts.
11th round *Yfwd, K6, rep from* to end. 56 sts.
13th round *Yfwd, K1, K2 tog, y2rn, K2 tog, K2, rep from * to end.
Note that on next and subsequent rounds where y2rn has been worked on previous round, you must K1 then P1 into y2rn.
15th round *Yfwd, K8, rep from * to end.
17th round *Yfwd, K9, rep from * to end.

19th round *Yfwd, K1, K2 tog, y2rn, (K2 tog) twice, y2rn, K2 tog, K1, rep from * to end.
21st round *Yfwd, K11, rep from * to end.
23rd round *Yfwd, K12, rep from * to end.
25th round *Yfwd, K5, K2 tog, y2rn, K2 tog, K4, rep from * to end.
27th round *Yfwd, K4, K2 tog, y2rn, (K2 tog) twice, y2rn, K2 tog, K2, rep from * to end.
29th round *Yfwd, K7, K2 tog, y2rn, K2 tog, K4, rep from * to end.
31st round *Yfwd, K1, yfwd, K2 tog, K3, K2 tog, y2rn, (K2 tog) twice, y2rn, K2 tog, K2, rep from * to end.
33rd round *Yfwd, K1, K2 tog, yfwd, K2 tog, K4, K2 tog, y2rn, K2 tog, K4, rep from * to end.
35th round *Yfwd, K1, yfwd, K2, yfwd, K1, yfwd, K2 tog, K11, rep from * to end.
37th round *Yfwd, K2, yfwd, K1, K2 tog, yfwd, K1, K2 tog, yfwd, K2 tog, K10, rep from * to end.
39th round *Yfwd, K1, yfwd, K2 tog, K1, yfwd, K2 tog, K1, yfwd, K2 tog, yfwd, K1, yfwd, (K2 tog) twice, y2rn, (K2 tog) twice, y2rn, K2 tog, K1, rep from * to end.
41st round *Yfwd, K2 tog, K1, yfwd, K1, K2 tog, yfwd, K2 tog, K1, yfwd, (K2 tog) twice, yfwd, K2 tog, K8, rep from * to end.
43rd round *Yfwd, K1, K2 tog, yfwd, (K2 tog) twice, yfwd, K1, K2 tog, yfwd, K1, K2 tog, yfwd, K2 tog, K7, rep from * to end.
45th round *Yfwd, K1, yfwd, K2 tog, K1, yfwd, K2 tog, K1, yfwd, K2 tog, K1, yfwd, K2 tog, yfwd, K1, yfwd, (K2 tog) twice, y2rn, K2 tog, K2, rep from * to end.
47th round *(Yfwd, K2 tog, K1) 3 times, yfwd, K1, K2 tog, yfwd, K2, yfwd, K2 tog, yfwd, K2 tog, K5, rep from

* to end.
49th round *Yfwd, (K2 tog) twice, yfwd, K2 tog, (K1, yfwd, K2 tog) 3 times, K1, yfwd, K2, yfwd, K2 tog, K4, rep from * to end.
51st round *Yfwd, (K2 tog) twice, (yfwd, K2 tog, K1) 5 times, yfwd, K2 tog, K3, rep from * to end.
53rd round *Yfwd, (K2 tog) twice, (yfwd, K2 tog, K1) 5 times, yfwd, K2 tog, K2, rep from * to end.
55th round *Yfwd, K3 tog, K1, (yfwd, K2 tog, K1) 5 times, yfwd, K2 tog, K1, rep from * to end.
57th round *Yfwd, (K2 tog) twice, (yfwd, K2 tog, K1) 5 times, yfwd, K2 tog, rep from * to end.
58th round As 2nd.
Cast off loosely.

Edging
Using 2 No.12 needles cast on 9 sts.
1st row Sl 1, K1, yfwd, K2 tog, K1, yfwd, K2 tog, yfwd, K2.
2nd and every alt row K to end.
3rd row Sl 1, K1, yfwd, K2 tog, K2, yfwd, K2 tog, yfwd, K2.
5th row Sl 1, K1, yfwd, K2 tog, K3, yfwd, K2 tog, yfwd, K2.
7th row Sl 1, K1, yfwd, K2 tog, K1, yfwd, K2 tog, K1, yfwd, K2 tog, yfwd, K2.
9th row Sl 1, K1, yfwd, K2 tog, K2, yfwd, K2 tog, K5.
10th row Cast off 4 sts, K to end.
Rep 1st to 10th rows until edging fits round table mat. Cast off.

To make up
Press under a damp cloth with a warm iron. Sew cast on edge of edging to cast off edge. Sew round table mat. Press.

More motifs

The same technique which produces flat, circular shapes can be used to form other geometric medallions, such as triangles, squares and octagons. It is simply a matter of working out how many sides you need and spacing the shaping on each side to increase the size of the medallion.

Because you are working on 3 needles with numbers of stitches which will not always divide by 3, the number of stitches cast on to each needle will not always be equal. When the number of stitches become too many to hold comfortably on 3 needles, change to a circular Twin Pin. Always mark the beginning of the round with a coloured marker and, if you find it easier, cast on the full number of stitches on to one needle and knit each stitch through the back of the loop, before dividing them on to 3 needles.

Triangular medallion

Using set of 4 needles cast on 6 sts, having 2 sts on each needle. Join needles into a round and K all sts tbl to keep centre flat.

1st round *K into front then into back of next st – called inc 1 –, rep from * to end. 12 sts.

2nd round *Inc 1, K2, inc 1, rep from * to end. 18 sts.

3rd round * Inc 1, K4, inc 1, rep from * to end. 24 sts.

4th round *Inc 1, K6, inc 1, rep from * to end. 30 sts.

5th round *Inc 1, K8, inc 1, rep from * to end. 36 sts. Cont inc 6 sts in this way on every round until medallion is required size. Cast off loosely.

Square medallion

Using set of 4 needles cast on 8 sts, having 2 sts on 1st needle and 3 sts each on 2nd and 3rd needles. Join needles into a round and K all sts tbl to keep centre flat. Commence patt.

1st round *K into front then into back of next st – called inc 1 –, rep from * to end. 16 sts.

2nd and every alt round K to end.

3rd round *Inc 1, K2, inc 1, rep from * to end. 24 sts.

5th round *Inc 1, K4, inc 1, rep from * to end. 32 sts.

7th round *Inc 1, K6, inc 1, rep from * to end. 40 sts.

8th round K to end.

Cont inc 8 sts in this way on next and every alt round until medallion is required size. Cast off loosely.

Octagonal medallion

Cast on and work 1st and 2nd rounds as given for square medallion.

3rd round As 1st. 32 sts.

4th and 5th rounds K to end.

6th round *Inc 1, K2, inc 1, rep from * to end. 48 sts.

7th and 8th rounds K to end.

9th round *Inc 1, K4, inc 1, rep from * to end. 64 sts.

10th and 11th rounds K to end.

12th round *Inc 1, K6, inc 1, rep from * to end. 80 sts.
13th and 14th rounds K to end.
Cont inc 16 sts in this way on next and every foll 3rd round until medallion is required size. Cast off loosely.

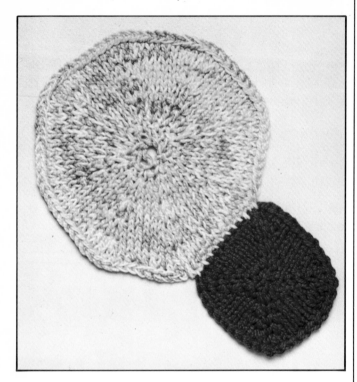

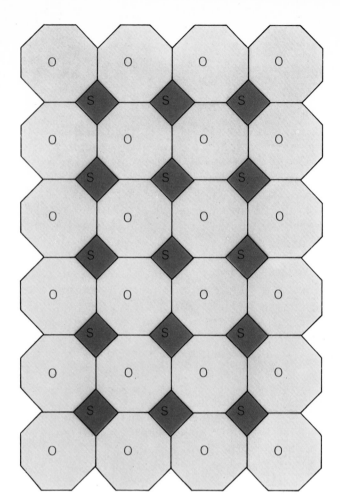

24 octagonal medallions = O
15 square medallions = S

Bath mat
Size
51cm (*20in*) wide by 76cm (*30in*) long

Tension
Each octagonal medallion measures 12.5cm (*5in*) diameter worked on No.8 needles and using 2 strands of yarn

Materials
6 × 50grm balls of Twilley's Stalite in main shade, A
2 × 50grm balls of contrast colour, B
Set of 4 No.8 needles

Note
Yarn is used double throughout

Bath mat
Using set of 4 No.8 needles and A, make 24 octagonal medallions, working 14 rounds only for each one.
Using set of 4 No.8 needles and B, make 15 square medallions, working 8 rounds only for each one.

To make up
Press each piece under a damp cloth with a warm iron. Join medallions as shown in diagram. Press.

Another way of using instructions for the bath mat would be to use up oddments of double knitting yarn in as many colours as possible to make a cheerful and practical pram rug.

ACHIEVING EXPERTISE
ADJUSTING PATTERNS

Making amendments to an existing pattern is quite an easy matter, provided you take the time to work out the correct positioning of these alterations before commencing any knitting. A plain cardigan can be given an entirely different look by the addition of picot edgings instead of ribbed edges. Slimming bust darts may be incorporated into a basic jersey to achieve a better fit for the fuller figure. With a little care even the proportions of armholes and shoulders may be altered to suit your own individual requirements. Once you have the know-how, it is a simple matter to apply it and so gain even greater satisfaction from your knitting.

Edges
With knitting, the same basic shape can always be worked in a variety of stitches (see Bobble Stitches). Similarly, an existing pattern for a plain jersey or cardigan does not always need to have ribbed edges. Instead, try a picot edging on the welt, cuffs and neckband of a jersey, or even the front bands of a cardigan. On a straight edge first check the number of stitches for each piece of the original pattern, after the ribbing has been completed. This will be the correct number of stitches to cast on to begin the picot edging. Beginning with a knit row work the required depth for a turned-under hem, say 2.5cm (*1 inch*), ending with a purl row. On the next row make a picot edge by knitting two stitches together, then bring the yarn forward and over the needle to make a stitch and continue in this way to the end of the row, making sure that you end with the correct number of stitches. Beginning with a purl row work one row less than the hemline to complete the edging, then either continue in stocking stitch or pattern as directed in the instructions, remembering to adjust the total length which will have taken the ribbing into account.

Where these picot edges need to be joined at right angles, such as the corner where the hem or neckband

meet the front bands on a cardigan, these edges must be mitred to fit correctly. To do this simply increase one stitch at the joining edge on the 2nd and every following row, work the picot row, then decrease one stitch at the same edge on every row for the completion of the edging, until the original number of cast on stitches remains.

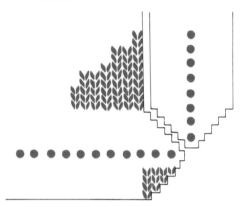

Another alternative is to work turned-under stocking stitch hems or facing in place of ribbing. To do this on a straight hem, work as for the picot edging but end with a knit row, then instead of working the next row as a picot row, knit each stitch through the back of the loop to form the hemline. From this point you can continue in stocking stitch or pattern as required.

To use this method for edges which need to be joined at right angles, you must again mitre the corners where the hem or neckband meet the front band.

As an example, say the original number of cast on stitches for the main section is 54 and an additional 8 stitches are needed for the front band, making a total of 62 stitches for the full width. If you are working a turned-under hem of 9 rows and are increasing one stitch at the front edge for the mitred corner on the 2nd and every following row, you will increase

lower front edge

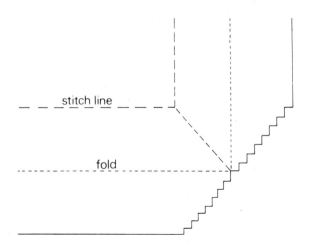

stitch line

fold

8 stitches on this edge and therefore need to cast on 8 stitches less than the total given number, in this case 54 stitches in place of 62 stitches. Work the turned-under hem and the hemline row, increasing as shown, then continue increasing one stitch at the same edge on every row until you have a total of 70 stitches, which will give 8 extra stitches for the turned-under facing. Slip the last stitch of the main fabric on every right side row to form a fold line. When turned in the increased stitches on the hems and front facing will join into a neat mitred corner.

Bust darts

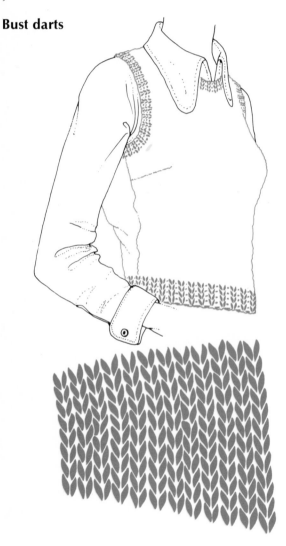

For the fuller figure, slimming bust darts can be incorporated into a plain stocking stitch jersey, to give extra depth across the bust without altering the underarm length of the garment.

Measure the exact underarm position for the darts, which should commence between 4.0cm (1½ inch) and 6.5cm (2½ inch) below the beginning of the armhole shaping. The fuller the figure the greater the number of rows required for shaping the darts and the 12 row example given here is suitable for a 96.5/101.5cm (38/40 inch) bust size. Work the front of the jersey until the position for the bust darts is reached, ending with a knit row, then commence the dart shaping.

1st row P to last 5 sts, turn.
2nd row Sl 1, K to last 5 sts, turn.
3rd row Sl 1, P to last 10 sts, turn.
4th row Sl 1, K to last 10 sts, turn.
5th row Sl 1, P to last 15 sts, turn.
6th row Sl 1, K to last 15 sts, turn.
7th row Sl 1, P to last 20 sts, turn.
8th row Sl 1, K to last 20 sts, turn.
9th row Sl 1, P to last 25 sts, turn.
10th row Sl 1, K to last 25 sts, turn.
11th row Sl 1, P to end of row.
12th row K to end of row, closing holes between groups of 5 sts by picking up loop under the 5th st of each group and K this loop tog with next st on left hand needle.

This completes the dart shaping. Continue until the position for the armhole shaping is reached, remembering to measure on the side seam and not over the bust darts.

Amending proportions of armholes and shoulders

For a narrow shouldered figure it is a simple matter to amend underarm and shoulder shaping. If this is required, first work out the exact number of extra stitches which need to be decreased, based on the tension given. Mark these alterations on the pattern so that you can work the complete armhole and shoulder section without further calculations.

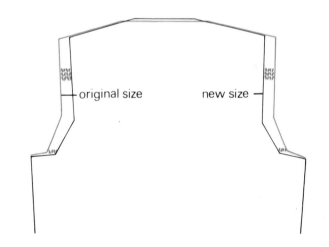

original size   new size

As an example, say you need to lose a further 8 stitches on the back of a jersey, to achieve a narrower fit. Decrease half of this total at the underarm point, casting off 2 extra stitches at each side, then work 2 more decreasing rows to lose the remaining 4 stitches, thus arriving at the required total. At the shoulder line, cast off 3 stitches less than the given number on the last 2 rows and allow for 2 stitches less than the given number in the remaining centre back neck stitches. When working the front remember to make the same adjustments at the underarm and shoulder line and allow for 2 stitches less than the given number in the remaining centre front neck stitches. The top of the sleeve shaping must also be amended to match the underarm shaping.

ADJUSTING LENGTHS

With a little care and patience, horizontal hems can quite easily be lengthened or shortened, to contend with fashion changes or a growing family. Skirt, bodice or cuff lengths can be altered in this way and when making children's garments, it is always useful to buy one or two extra balls of yarn in the same dye lot to put aside for the day when such adjustments can be made quickly and cheaply instead of wasting a whole garment.

When shortening a garment no extra yarn is required – in fact, a quantity of the original yarn will become available. Instead of wasting this, it can be wound into

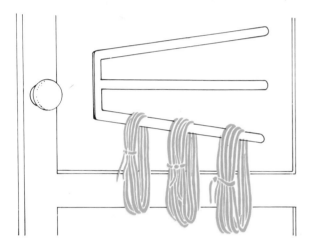

hanks and hand washed, then hung up to dry to remove the kinks. If a design needs to be lengthened, however, extra yarn is needed but it does not necessarily have to be the original yarn. Oddments of the same ply can be used to add a striped hem to a skirt or welt of a jersey and if the neckband is also unpicked and re-knitted in the same stripes, the whole

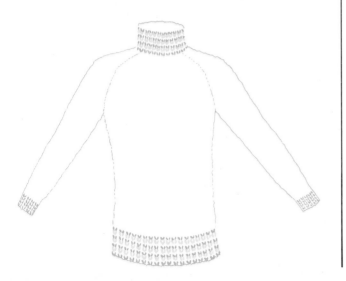

effect will give a completely new look to the garment. Before beginning any adjustment, check the garment to find the best position for the lengthening or shortening. As an example, if the body or sleeves of a jersey need lengthening and it already has a ribbed welt or cuff 5cm (2in) long, then the work must be picked up and re-knitted above the welt or cuff. If a skirt needs shortening and it has a turned under hem, the adjustment must be made above the existing hemline. It is not advisable to attempt these alterations on a fabric which has used a very complicated stitch unless you are quite certain that you will be able to pick up the original number of stitches in their correct sequence but stocking stitch, garter stitch or any simple pattern can be altered quite easily in this way.

Lengthening a garment
Make sure that you have some additional yarn to hand. Check the garment and mark both the position where the garment is to be unpicked and a further point 2·5cm (1in) above this, then count the exact

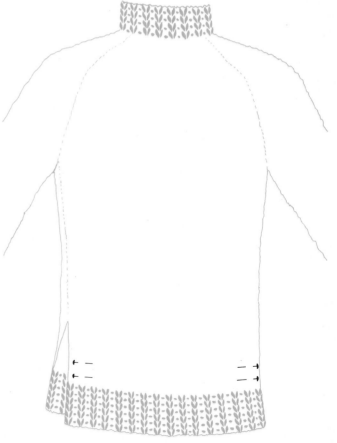

number of rows between each point. Prepare the work by unpicking any hems and side seams to approximately 5cm (*2in*) above the last marked point, to allow for freedom in manipulating the needles when re-knitting, taking great care not to cut the fabric.

With the right side of the fabric facing and the correct needle size, pick up a loop with a needle at the marked

point above the required adjustment point, and pull this up tightly. Cut through this loop and carefully pull the fabric apart until two sets of stitches are

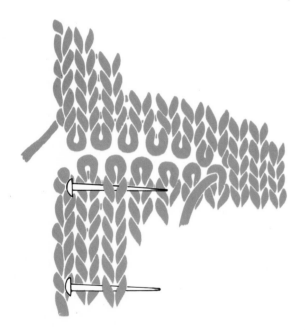

exposed. Pull the cut end of yarn again tightly and cut it, easing the fabric apart. Continue in this way until the fabric is in two separate sections, then pick up the stitches of the main section with a knitting needle, making sure that the original number of stitches are on the needle and that each stitch is lying in the correct direction and has not become twisted.

Unravel the remaining yarn, winding it into a neat ball ready to use for re-knitting. **. Join in the yarn at the beginning of the row and continue knitting for the required number of rows calculated between the two marked points, then continue knitting to give the extra length required. Complete the garment by working the original number of rows in ribbing for a welt or cuff, or by working the exact number of rows used for the original hem on a skirt. Cast off very loosely then work any other sections in the same way. Re-seam any edges or hems and check whether the yarn used can be pressed and proceed accordingly.

Shortening a garment

Check and prepare the garment and work as given for lengthening to **. Join in the yarn at the beginning of the row and continue knitting for the required number of rows calculated between the two marked points. Cast off very loosely and finish the garment as given for lengthening.

Words of warning!

When unpicking seams great care must be taken not to cut the actual fabric but only the yarn used for sewing. Never rush this stage but gently ease the seam apart until you are quite sure which is the exact strand to be cut.

Once the fabric has been divided into two separate sections, check at which end of the work the un-picked yarn finishes, to ascertain whether the next row to be knitted is a right or wrong side row. Only then pick up the stitches with a knitting needle, making sure that each stitch lies in the correct position and that the needle point is facing the correct end, ready to rejoin the yarn. Using a double ended needle can help at this stage. Don't panic if a few of the stitches begin to run! These can quite easily be picked up to the correct depth, using a crochet hook. Because the yarn has already been knitted up once, it will not re-knit to such an even fabric as the original. If the yarn does not require pressing but looks rather uneven, simply wash and dry the garment when it is completed in the recommended way, to even out the fabric.

TUCKS AND TRIMS

The more you know about knitting, the more fascinating it becomes. Once you have mastered the basic techniques, it is the small, finishing touches which make all the difference to any design.

This chapter deals with four ideas which can be applied to almost any basic design – and they are fun to work. Two of these trimmings are worked in with the actual knitting, one is worked as part of the making up and the last can be applied when the garment is completed.

Try incorporating one of these suggestions to lift your knitting from the mundane to the couture class, setting your own individual stamp on any design.

Tucks

Horizontal tucks are easy to work and can be incorporated into the skirt or bodice of almost any plain garment. They look their most effective when worked in stocking stitch with a picot edge – imagine the skirt of a litle girl's dress embellished with two or three layers of tucks, or the yoke of a plain jersey finished with two rows of tucking at underarm level. Remember that these will use extra yarn over and above the quantity stated and allow for one or two more balls before beginning any design.

To work horizontal tucks Mark the position on the pattern where the tucks are to be incorporated and work to this point, ending with a purl row. Mark each end of the last row with a coloured thread. Depending on the depth of tuck required, work a further 5 to 9 rows in stocking stitch, ending with a knit row. On the next row either knit all the stitches through the back of the loops to mark the foldline of the tuck, or work a row of eyelet holes by knitting 2 together, then bringing the yarn forward to make a stitch, all along the row. Beginning with a knit row work a further 4 to 8 rows stocking stitch, ending with a purl row. Using a spare needle, go back to the row marked with coloured thread and pick up the correct number of stitches all along the row on the wrong side of the work, so that the points of the spare needle and the left hand needle holding the stitches are both facing in the same direction. Hold the spare needle behind the left hand needle and knit to the end of the row, working one stitch from the left hand needle together with one stitch from the spare needle. This forms one tuck and can be repeated as required.

To work vertical tucks These can be used to highlight any dart shapings on a design and, again, look their best against a plain stocking stitch background. The continuity of the tucks must be kept throughout the whole length of the design and an additional 2 stitches should be cast on at the beginning for each tuck required. As an example, if the front of a skirt has two dart shapings which begin below hip level, read through the pattern to ascertain the place in the row where these shapings are first worked and allow 2 extra stitches on the right hand side of the first dart and 2 extra stitches on the left hand side of the second dart. Cast on 4 extra stitches at the beginning of the skirt and work as follows:–

1st row K to within 2 sts of the position for the first dart, sl the next 2 sts P-wise keeping the yarn at the back of the work, work the first dart shaping, K to and then work the second dart shaping, sl the next 2 sts P-wise keeping the yarn at the back of the work, K to end.

2nd row P to end.

These 2 rows form the pattern and are repeated throughout, even when the dart shaping has been completed.

Lapped seams

These are worked at the making up stage and are referred to in dressmaking as run and fell seams, such as you would see on a man's shirt. To look most effective they should be worked on a smooth fabric, such as stocking stitch. As an example, a plain raglan sleeved jersey would look highly original where lapped seams are used to join the side, sleeve and raglan seams.

To work lapped seams Depending on the position of the seam and the yarn being used, cast on an additional 2 or 3 stitches for each vertical seam and work a further 3 or 4 rows for each horizontal seam. When the pieces are completed, press as given in the instructions. Now place the two pieces to be joined with right sides together, with the underneath piece extending about 1.5cm ($\frac{1}{2}$in) beyond the edge of the upper piece. Work a firm back stitch seam along this edge. Turn the pieces to the right side and carefully back stitch the loose edge of the seam through both thicknesses of the fabric, about 1.5cm ($\frac{1}{2}$in) from the first seam. Press seam.

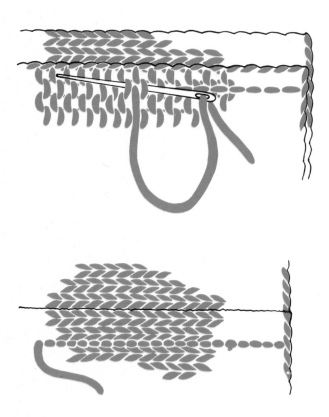

Piping cords

As children, most knitters will have experimented with French knitting, or 'dolly' knitting. The round piping produced by this method can be thick or thin, depending on the yarn used and looks most attractive as a straight length of trimming sewn round the neck of a jersey, or on either side of the front bands of a cardigan. Alternatively, separate lengths can be worked, then wound round and stitched to form flat, circular motifs. These motifs could be stitched at

random on the bodice of a child's dress or used in a band above the welt and cuffs on a plain jersey. Any oddments of yarn will do – but think how colourful this piping would look in random yarn. The possibilities are endless and fun to work.

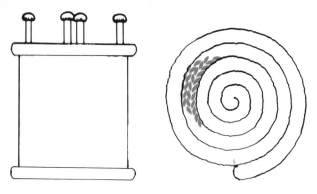

How to work piping cord Either purchase a 'dolly' bobbin or use a wooden cotton reel to make a bobbin, spacing 4 panel pins with heads evenly and firmly round the centre hole at one end of the reel. Thread the yarn to be used through the centre hole of the bobbin or reel, from the opposite end to the panel pins, leaving an end free. Working in a clockwise direction throughout, wind the yarn round each of the 4 pins and work as follows:–

1st round Take the yarn once more round all 4 pins without looping it round the pins and placing the yarn above the first round, using a fine crochet hook lift the first loop over the second strand of yarn from the outside to the centre and over the pin head, repeat on all 4 pins.

Continue repeating this round until the piping is the required length, pulling the cord down through the centre hole of the bobbin or reel as it is formed. When the cord is the required length, break off the yarn leaving an end, thread this end through a blunt ended wool needle, insert needle through loop on pin and lift loop off pin, repeat on all 4 pins, pull up yarn and fasten off securely.

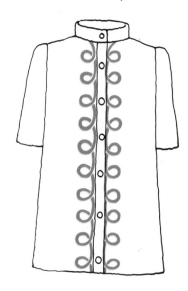

PLEATS

A swirling, pleated skirt is a most useful and adaptable knitted garment, which can form the basis of a mix-and-match wardrobe of skirt, jersey, jacket and hat all worked in toning colours and contrasting patterns or stitch textures.

The method of working the pleats can be a simple, mock version or the inverted type, both of which give such a graceful swing to any skirt. They can be knitted vertically in stripes to form an even more striking variation and this is another ideal way of using up oddments of the same thickness of yarn, to make a warm and practical skirt for a toddler. Use a yarn which will retain its shape without dropping, such as a pure wool crepe, for all versions.

Planning pleats

The mock version is the most economical and is based on the width which is required round the hem of the skirt. Use this measurement and the tension obtained with the yarn chosen to calculate the number of stitches which must be cast on. This number must be divisible by 8, so adjust the total if necessary by adding a few more stitches.

For inverted pleats, work out the required waist measurement and multiply this by three, to arrive at the correct hem measurement. Use this measurement to determine the number of stitches to be cast on at the hem, again based on the tension obtained. This number must be divisible by 12, plus 8, and the total can be adjusted by adding a few more stitches.

For vertical pleats you must measure the length required from waist to hem, plus an allowance of approximately 2.5cm (1in) for a turned under hem. Use this measurement and the tension obtained to arrive at how many stitches must be cast on, having an even number of stitches, and work from side edge to side edge.

Mock pleats

These can be worked on two needles, either in two separate sections to form the back and the front of the skirt with a seam at each side, or in one piece to give the total width, having a centre back seam.
Cast on the required number of stitches.
1st row (RS) *K7, P1, rep from * to end.
2nd row K4, *P1, K7, rep from * to last 4 sts, P1, K3.
These 2 rows form the pattern and are repeated for the required length. Cast off.
To work mock pleats without a seam, use a circular needle and cast on the required number of stitches.
1st round *K7, P1, rep from * to end of round.
2nd round P3, K1, *P7, K1, rep from * to last 4 sts, P4.
These 2 rounds form the pattern and are repeated for

the required length. Cast off.
To complete the skirt, cut a waist length of elastic and

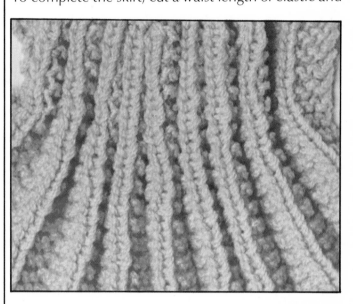

sew inside the waist edge, using casing stitch. As an alternative, cast on the required number of stitches to form a separate waistband, allowing sufficient extra stitches for ease in pulling the skirt on and off, and work 5.5cm ($2\frac{1}{4}$in) st st. Cast off. Sew waistband to waist edge of skirt, fold in half to WS and sl st down. Thread elastic through waistband and fasten off.

Inverted pleats

This method requires a set of 4 needles pointed at both ends to close the pleats. Because of the total number of stitches required, it is easier to work the skirt in two separate sections, having a seam at each side.

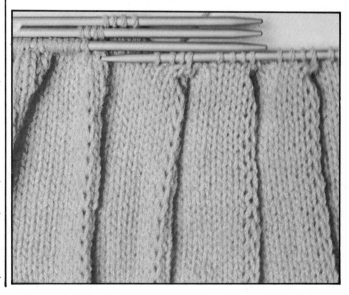

Using two of the needles, cast on the required number of stitches.
1st row (RS) *K8, P1, K2, sl 1 P-wise, rep from * to last 8 sts, K8.
2nd row *P11, K1, rep from * to last 8 sts, P8.
These 2 rows form the pattern and are repeated for the required length, less 5cm (*2in*) for the waistband. To close the pleats you will need to use all 4 needles.
Last row (waist edge) K4, *sl next 4 sts on to first extra needle, sl next 4 sts on to 2nd extra needle, place first extra needle behind 2nd extra needle and hold both extra needles behind the left hand needle, (K tog one st from all 3 needles) 4 times, rep from * to last 4 sts, K4.
Cast off.
To complete the skirt join seams, overlapping 4 sts at beg of row over 4 sts at end of row to complete pleating. Make a separate waistband and complete as given for mock pleats.

Vertical pleats

This method is worked on two needles to a length which will give twice the required waist measurement, having one seam at the centre-back. If you are working in stripes, carry the yarn not in use loosely up the side edge until it is required again. For neatness, this edge will become the waist edge, so that the strands of yarn can be sewn inside the waistband when the skirt is completed. Cast on the required number of stitches, allowing approximately 2.5cm (*1in*) extra for the hem.
1st row (RS) K to end.
2nd row P to end.
Rep 1st and 2nd rows 5 times more, then 1st row once more.
14th row P across sts for hem, *yrn, P2 tog, rep from * to end.
Rep 1st and 2nd rows twice more, then 1st row once more.
20th row P across sts for hem, K tbl all sts to end.
These 20 rows form the pattern. Continue until work measures twice the required waist measurement, ending with a 20th row. Cast off.
To complete the skirt, join cast on edge to cast off edge to form centre back seam. Turn hem at lower edge to WS and sl st down. Tack pleats in position along waist edge, folding each pleat at picot row to form inner fold and at knit row to form outer fold. Make separate waistband and complete as given for mock pleats.

Toddler's striped skirt
Size
To fit 51cm (*20in*) waist, adjustable
Length, 25cm (*10in*)

Tension
30 sts and 36 rows to 10cm (*3.9in*) over st st worked on No.10 needles

Materials
4 × 25grm balls of 4 ply Crepe in main shade, A
2 balls of contrast colour, B
One pair No.10 needles
Waist length of elastic

Skirt
Using No.10 needles and A, cast on 76 sts. Keeping 8 sts at lower edge for hem, work as given for vertical pleats, working first 14 patt rows in A and next 6 rows in B throughout, until work measures 101.5cm (*40in*) from beg, or required length. Cast off.
Waistband
Using No.10 needles and A, cast on 180 sts. Work 5cm (*2in*) st st. Cast off.

To make up
Press as directed on ball band. Complete as given for vertical pleats.

DESIGNING
BASIC TECHNIQUES

Designing your own clothes can be the most rewarding of all aspects of hand knitting. Details have already been given in previous chapters of the important part tension plays in any designing, together with the compositions of various yarns and the structure of numerous stitches. These three factors form the basis of all successful hand knitting designs.

Before you can begin any design you need to know the exact measurements of the garment you have in mind. Don't tackle anything too complicated for a first attempt – something as simple as the skirt shown here would be ideal, as it does not entail a great deal of shaping.

Each section must be calculated exactly to the required width and length, based on the tension obtained with any given yarn and needle size. To these measurements you must then add an additional number of stitches which will give sufficient tolerance for ease of movement and also provide multiples of stitches which will work out correctly over the pattern which has been chosen. An overall tolerance of 5cm (2 in) is sufficient for most garments, although something as bulky as a casual jacket which is intended to be worn over another garment will obviously require more tolerance than a sleekly-fitting fine ply jersey.

Measurements

For something as simple as a skirt, five accurate measurements are required.

a The actual waist measurement in width.
b The actual hip measurement in width.
c The actual measurement from waist to hip in depth.
d The actual measurement from hipline to hemline in depth.
e The actual width of hemline at lowest point.

The exact shape of the required skirt must then be determined. It can have almost straight sides, with the hem and hip measurement being almost the same, then gently curving from the hipline into the waist. If a flared hemline is required, this must be shaped into the hips, before shaping from the hips to the waist. Whatever the style of skirt you choose, it can be worked in two separate sections, the back and front being exactly the same. To this actual measurement you must now add the overall tolerance required to give an easy-fitting garment, allowing half this additional measurement for the front and half for the back.

At this stage, decide whether you want a separate waistband or the waist edge knitted in with the main fabric and finished with casing stitch worked over

elastic. If the skirt is to be very slim-fitting you will also need to make provision for a zip fastener on the side seam. Plan the sort of hem you require and take this into your calculations – most skirts hang better with a turned under hem, so you will need to add an additional 2.5cm (1 in) to the length.

Tension

You must now decide on the type of yarn you wish to use and the tension obtained on needles of your choice, which will produce a smooth, even fabric, neither too hard and tight nor too loose and open. Work a sample swatch, using a basic stitch such as stocking stitch to begin with, and measure this accurately. If you do not measure this sample exactly, or feel that half a stitch difference to 2.5cm (1 in) is unimportant, you will not be able to produce the exact shape you require. In printed patterns this procedure has already been overcome, as the yarn is specified and a guide to the needle size has been given. When designing for yourself, however, you are no longer limited to the tension which has been obtained by the original designer but can decide for yourself what tension will produce the effect you require.

Making a diagram

Now that you have established the measurements needed and the tension which will produce the type of fabric you have in mind, you must put all this information down on paper in the form of a diagram.

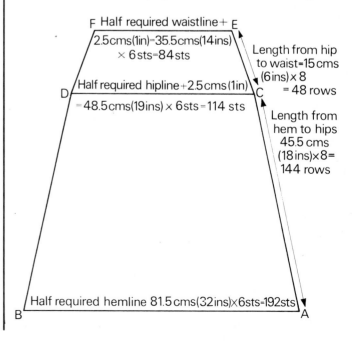

F Half required waistline+
2.5cms(1in)=35.5cms(14ins)
× 6sts=84sts   E

Length from hip
to waist=15cms
(6ins) x 8
= 48 rows

D Half required hipline+2.5cms(1in)
=48.5cms(19ins) × 6sts=114 sts C

Length from hem to hips
45.5 cms
(18ins)×8=
144 rows

Half required hemline 81.5cms(32ins)×6sts=192sts
B   A

This does not have to be drawn to scale, as with a dressmaking pattern, but is simply used as a guide. The diagram shown here has been based on measurements to give a 91.5cm (36 in) hip size and has been calculated on a tension of 6 stitches and 8 rows to 2.5cm (1 in), worked in double knitting yarn on No.8 needles.

Remember that with most knitted stitches the right side of the work is facing you, therefore your first knitted row will be worked from the right hand edge to the left hand edge. Our example has been worked in rice stitch, where the first, or right side row is knitted and the second, or wrong side row is worked in single rib. It has also been worked from the hemline to the waist edge, decreasing as required to give the final waist measurement.

Hemline This is the point marked A–B on the diagram.
Hipline This is the point marked C–D on the diagram.
Waist This is the point marked E–F on the diagram.

Calculating the number of stitches and rows

The measurements shown in the diagram given here now have to be multiplied by the number of stitches and rows to 2.5cm (1 in) which have been obtained in your tension sample. The hemline width is 81.5cm (32 in) and when multiplied by 6 stitches, this gives a total of 192 stitches. Before the hipline point is reached, this width must be decreased to give 45.5cm (18 in) plus 2.5cm (1 in) tolerance, multiplied by 6 stitches to give a total of 114 stitches. Similarly, the depth from the hipline to the waist must be decreased to give 33cm (13 in) plus 2.5cm (1 in) tolerance, multiplied by 6 stitches to give a total of 84 stitches.

If you are working a straight skirt, the required number of stitches can be decreased at the side edges only. A flared skirt, however, has considerably more stitches to begin with and these will need to be decreased as carefully spaced darts as well as at the side edges. Calculate the number of rows which will be worked to give the required length from the hemline to the hipline, then work out how many decrease rows are needed to arrive at the correct number of stitches for the hip measurement, then how many rows are required between each set of decreases to give the correct length.

Skirt
Sizes
To fit 91.5cm (36in) hips
Length, 63.5cm (25in)

Tension
24 sts and 32 rows to 10cm (3.9in) over st st worked on No.8 needles

Materials
18 × 25grm balls of Robin Bernat Klein Shetland No.2
One pair No.8 needles

One pair No.9 needles
Waist length of 2.5cm (1in) wide elastic

Back
Using No.8 needles cast on 192 sts. Beg with a K row work 7 rows st st.
Next row K all sts tbl to form hemline.
Next row K to end.
Next row *K1, P1, rep from * to end.
The last 2 rows form patt. Cont in patt until work measures 15cm (6in) from hemline, ending with a WS row.
Shape darts
Next row Sl 1, K1, psso, K61, sl 1, K2 tog, psso, K60, sl 1, K2 tog, psso, K61, K2 tog. 186 sts.
Work 7 rows patt without shaping.
Next row Sl 1, K1, psso, K59, sl 1, K2 tog, psso, K58, sl 1, K2 tog, psso, K59, K2 tog. 180 sts.
Work 7 rows patt without shaping.
Cont dec in this way on next and every foll 8th row until 114 sts rem, then on every foll 6th row until 84 sts rem. Cont without shaping until work measures 61cm (24in) from hemline, ending with a WS row. Change to No.9 needles. Work 2.5cm (1in) K1, P1 rib. Cast off in rib.

Front
Work as given for back.

To make up
Join side seams. Turn hem at lower edge to WS and sl st down. Sew elastic inside waistband using casing st.

MORE ABOUT DESIGNING

This chapter continues with the necessary know-how required for designing your own clothes. As explained in the previous chapter, you need to know the exact measurements plus tolerance allowance for each section of the garment and the tension obtained with the yarn and needle size of your choice.

To plan the shape of the garment you can either make a diagram of each section and use this as a guide or, if the design you have in mind is rather complicated, you may find it easier to draft the garment out on squared graph paper, where each square represents one stitch and each line of squares shows a complete row of knitting. Most professional designers use the last method as it forms a detailed record of the design which can be checked against the written instructions.

Neither of these methods will be to the exact scale of the completed garment.

The jersey shown here has been worked to the same tension as the skirt featured in the previous chapter, that is, 6 stitches and 8 rows to 2.5cm (*1 inch*) over stocking stitch worked on No.8 needles. With this knowledge you can make a diagram or knitting chart which will give you the exact measurements you require but if you alter the yarn or needle size, you must first determine the tension you will achieve before you can begin your design.

Basic jersey measurements

The diagrams and charts shown here represent the measurements and details of the shaping required for the body and sleeves of a plain, round-necked jersey.

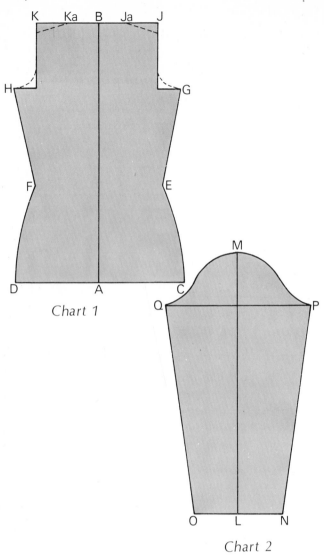

Chart 1

Chart 2

shaping on the body is not always essential and has been omitted on the jersey shown here. However, it is easier to show details of the graduated shaping required for each section on squared graph paper. The symbols used are a form of shorthand and are in standard use throughout all knitting charts.

Armhole shaping Where a set in sleeve is required, the shaping takes place in the first 5/7.5cm (*2/3 inches*)

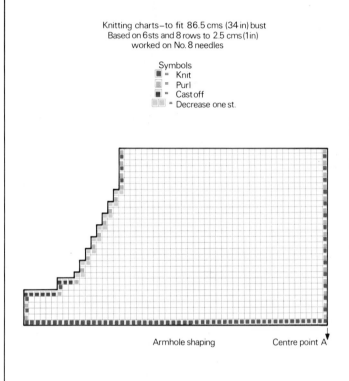

Knitting charts – to fit 86.5 cms (34 in) bust
Based on 6 sts and 8 rows to 2.5 cms (1 in)
worked on No. 8 needles

Symbols
■ = Knit
▨ = Purl
■ = Cast off
▨▨ = Decrease one st.

Armhole shaping   Centre point A

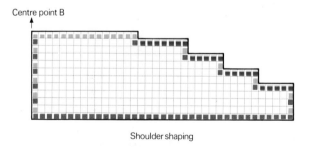

Centre point B

Shoulder shaping

The centre line on Chart 1, from the points marked A–B, represent the total length required from the lower edge to the back neck on the back of the jersey. The points marked C–D give the hemline measurements, E–F the waist measurements, G–H the bust measurement before shaping the armholes and J–K the shoulders and back neck width.

The centre line on Chart 2, from the points marked L–M, show the outside sleeve measurement from the wrist to the shoulder line. The points marked N–O represent the total wrist measurement and P–Q, the underarm sleeve width before shaping the head of the sleeve.

Calculate the number of stitches and rows needed to give these measurements by multiplying the total number of centimetres (*inches*) from point to point by the number of stitches and rows obtained from your tension sample.

Using graph paper
Charts 1 and 2 show the basic measurements needed when planning a jersey design, although the waist

above the points marked G–H on Chart 1 in a gradual curve, which is more acute at the beginning to give a neat underarm shape. On a raglan sleeve, the same underarm shaping is required but the remaining stitches are then steadily decreased until only the number needed to form the back neck remain.

Shoulder shaping For a set in sleeve, measure the shoulder seam length required from the points marked J–Ja and K–Ka on Chart 1 and commence the shoulder shaping approximately 2.5cm (*1 inch*) below the total length given from points marked A–B

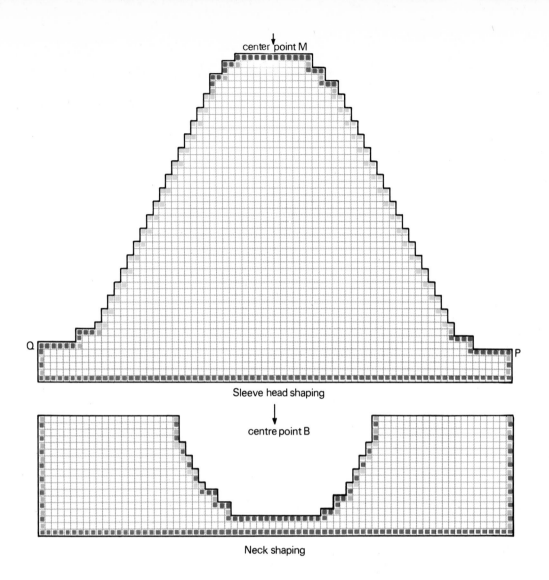

center point M

Sleeve head shaping

Q

P

centre point B

Neck shaping

on Chart 1. A raglan sleeve does not require shoulder shaping, as the head of the sleeve is continued to form the shoulder line.

Sleeve shaping All sleeves whether long, short, set in or raglan, need to be shaped from the lower edge to the underarm to give a good fit. For a set in sleeve the head must be shaped in a gradual curve, which is again more acute at the beginning to match the underarm shaping on the body. The number of remaining stitches on the last row of the sleeve head should not be less than 7.5cm (3 inches) in width, to fit neatly across the shoulder line, and the final shape will depend on how the stitches are decreased to leave the correct number on the last row. After shaping the underarm, one stitch should be decreased at each end of the next 4−8 rows, depending on the row tension being worked, and then on every alternate row to soften the curve until the sleeve is approximately 2.5cm (1 inch) less than the total length from points marked L−M on Chart 2. The remaining stitches can then be cast off evenly at the beginning of the last few rows until the correct number remain for the final row.

Raglan sleeves should be shaped at the underarm,

then decreased until sufficient stitches remain to form the side neck edge.

Neck shaping For a round neck the back and front body sections are exactly the same, except for the shaping of the front neck. This point should be approximately 5cm (2 inches) lower than the back neck and the stitches need to be divided at this point and each shoulder worked separately. You will have established how many stitches are required to work each shoulder on the back and this total should be deducted from the stitches which remain after the armhole shaping has been completed. The remaining stitches are used to shape the neck in a gradual curve before the shoulder shaping is commenced.

A V-neck will be divided at a lower point, either at the same time as the armhole shaping is commenced or after this section has been completed, depending on the final depth required. Each shoulder is again completed separately, decreasing evenly at the front neck edge until the number of stitches needed to complete the shoulder remain.

The neckband can be completed in a variety of ways, either as a crew neck, polo collar or neat ribbed V-neck.

A BASIC DESIGN PROJECT

The two previous chapters have explained how easy it is to design your own basic garments to a required shape and size. With this knowledge you can begin to combine all the skills and techniques which have been given in this Course, to make the most exciting and original designs – all to your own personal taste. Once you know how to plan a basic shape, you can begin to experiment with different patterns and textures. If you keep to coloured patterns, this need not be an expensive trial run as you can use up all sorts of oddments of the same thickness of yarn in a variety of ways. Keep to a fairly simple shape to begin with but use as many colours and patterns as you like, so that all the interest of the design is in the fabric and not in the shape. Remember to check the multiples of stitches which are required for each pattern and, if necessary, adjust the row beginnings and endings to ensure that each pattern works out correctly over the total number of stitches.

All the stitches, methods and techniques used for the jersey shown here are given throughout the book.

Rainbow jersey

Sizes
To fit 86.5/91.5cm (*34/36in*) bust
Length to shoulder, 63.5cm (*25in*)
Sleeve seam, 43cm (*17in*)

Tension
24 sts and 32 rows to 10cm (*3.9in*) over st st worked on No. 8 needles

Materials
Total of 30 × 25grm balls of Wendy Double Knitting in 12 contrast colours, or as required
One pair No.8 needles

Note
Colours may be used in any sequence and are not coded

Jersey body
Using No.8 needles and any colour, cast on 112 sts for lower edge. K 9 rows g st.
Work 22 rows Greek key pattern, working one extra st at each end of row (see Mosaic patterns later), K6 rows g st.
Work in stripes of 2 rows, 1 row, 3 rows, 1 row, 4 rows, 1 row, 3 rows, 1 row and 2 rows. K 6 rows g st.

Cast off loosely. Make another section in same way, working same colour sequence.
Using No. 8 needles and any colour, cast on 112 sts for main body. K 6 rows g st.
Work in diagonal stripes of 2 sts in each of 2 colours for 10 rows, see horizontal stripes later. K6 rows g st.
Work in chevron pattern for 20 rows, having multiples of 11 sts plus 2 not 13 stitches plus 2, keeping 3 sts at each side of shaping, see chevron stripes later. K6 rows g stitch.
Work in patchwork pattern across 2nd, 1st, 5th and 3rd patches, or 4 complete patches of 28 sts, for 30 rows, see patchwork later. K6 rows g st.
Work in lattice stitch, omitting 1st row and working one extra st at each end of row for 32 rows, see lattice stitch later.

Shape shoulders
Cont in g st only, cast off at beg of next and every row 10 sts 6 times. K 3 rows g st on rem sts.
Cast off loosely. Make another section in same way, working same colour sequence.

Diamond panel
**Using No.8 needles and any colour, cast on 2 sts. K 1 row. Cont in g st, inc one st at each end of next and every alt row until there are 28 sts. K 3 rows g st. **.
Dec one st at each end of next and every alt row until 2 sts rem. K 1 row. Cast off. Make 7 more diamonds in same way, varying colours.
Make 16 half diamonds as given from ** to **, varying colours. Cast off.

Sleeves
Using No.8 needles and any colour, cast on 49 sts. K 9 rows g st, inc one st in every st on last row. 98 sts. Omitting diamond panel and chevron pattern, work in patterns as given for body, with 6 rows g st between each pattern, ending with 6 rows g st. Cast off loosely.

To make up
Press each section under a damp cloth with a warm iron. Join shoulder seams of main sections and side seams of lower sections. Join side seams of main body leaving 20.5cm (*8in*) open at top for armholes. Join diamonds and half diamonds as shown in diagram. Sew cast off edge of lower edge of body to lower edge of diamond panel, then sew cast on edge of main body to top edge of diamond panel. Sew in sleeves. Join sleeve seams. Press seams.

join to
other
end to
form circle

FINISHING TOUCHES

Unusual trimmings and finishing touches on a garment are the easiest way of achieving fashion flair and turning a simple, straightforward design into an original which no-one else will have. It may just mean the addition of a belt to a dress or tunic, or your own initials embroidered on the shoulder of a plain jersey. These know-how ideas are invaluable and you will have great fun both in trying them out and applying them.

Twisted cords

These are simple to make and have a variety of uses, depending on their thickness and length. They can be used instead of ribbon on a baby garment – saving additional expense as well as using up any oddments of yarn left over. A thick cord trimmed with tassels makes a most attractive belt and avoids the problem of trying to match colours.

The number of strands of yarn required will vary according to the thickness of the cord needed and the yarn being used. As a guide, try using 4 strands for a baby garment and up to 12 strands for a thick belt. Take the required number of strands and cut them into lengths 3 times the length of the finished cord. As an example, for a cord 51cm (20in) long you will need lengths of 152.5cm (60in). Enlist the aid of another person but if this is not possible, then one end of the strands may be fastened over a convenient hook. Knot each end of the strands together before beginning. If working with another person, each should insert a knitting needle into the knot and twist the strands in a clockwise direction, until they are tightly twisted. Do not let go of the strands but holding them taut, fold them in half at the centre and knot the 2 ends together. Holding the knot, let go of the folded end and give the cord a sharp shake, then smooth it down from the knot to the folded end to even out the twists. Make another knot at the folded end, cut through the folded loops and ease out the ends.

Plaited belt

Here is another idea for a highly original belt. In addition to the yarn you will need 12 small wooden beads. Cut 12 lengths of yarn, preferably double knitting, 228.5cm (90in) long. Take 2 ends together at a time and knot at one end, then slide a bead down to the knot, and make 6 strands in this way. Tie these strands together about 25.5cm (10in) above the beaded ends. Form into 3 strands having 4 lengths in each strand and plait together, taking the left hand strands over the centre strands, then the right hand strands over the centre strands and continuing in this way to within 40.5cm (16in) of the other end. Knot all 12 strands together at this point. Now take 2 ends together and thread a bead on to them, then knot them at the end to hold the bead. Make 5 more strands in this way. Trim ends.

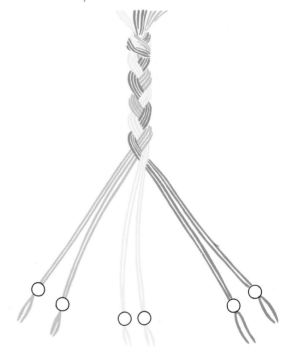

Pompons

These are a most attractive way of trimming a hat, with 2 or more in contrasting colours placed just above the brim, or one enormous loopy pompon placed on the top of a beret.

Round pompon Cut 2 circles of cardboard the size required for the finished pompon, then cut out a circle from the centre of each. Place the 2 pieces of card together and wind the yarn evenly round them and through the centre hole until the hole is nearly filled. Break off the yarn leaving a long end, thread this through a blunt ended wool needle and use this to thread the last turns through the hole until it is completely filled. Cut through the yarn round the outer edge of the circles, working between the 2 pieces of cardboard. Take a double length of yarn and tie very securely round the centre of the pompon, between the 2 pieces of card, leaving an end long enough to sew to the garment. Pull away the card, then tease out the pompon and trim into shape.

Loopy pompon Cut a strip of very thin card about 20.5cm (*8in*) long by 10cm (*4in*) wide, depending on the size of pompon required. Leave a short end of yarn free, then wind the yarn very loosely along the length of card for the thickness required. **. Cut the yarn leaving an end about 30.5cm (*12in*) and thread this into a blunt-ended wool needle. Insert the needle under the loops at one edge of the card, going under 3 or 4 loops at a time, then bring the needle up and back over these loops to form a firm back stitch. Continue along the length of the card until all the loops are secured in this way, then work another row of back stitch if required. Bend the card slightly and remove from the loops, then insert the needle through all the loops at once but do not pull up too tightly. Now bring one end of the secured loops round in a circle to meet the other end and fasten off securely, tying the first short end of yarn to secure and using the remainder of the yarn to sew on the pompon.

Tassels

Work as given for the loopy pompon to **, then cut the yarn. Using a blunt ended wool needle threaded with yarn, insert the needle at one edge of the card under all the strands and fasten off securely. Cut through the strands of yarn at the other untied edge of the card. Finish the tassel by winding an end of yarn several times round the top, folded ends, about 1.5cm ($\frac{1}{2}$*in*) down and fasten off securely, leaving an end long enough to sew on the tassel.

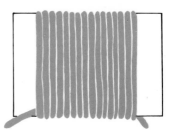

Swiss darning

For this type of embroidery it is advisable to use yarn of the same thickness as the knitted fabric – if the embroidery yarn is too thin the knitting will show through and if it is too thick, it will look clumsy.

Working from the chart, use a blunt ended wool needle threaded with the embroidery yarn and begin at the lower right hand corner of the design to be applied, working from right to left. Bring the needle through from the back to the front at the base of the first stitch to be embroidered and draw yarn through; insert the needle from right to left under the 2 loops of the same stitch one row above and draw yarn through; insert the needle back into the base of this stitch, along the back of the work then into the base of the next stitch to the left from the back to the front and draw the yarn through. Take great care to keep the loops at the same tension as the knitting. Continue along the row in this way. At the end of the row, insert the needle into the base of the last stitch worked, then up in the centre of this same stitch, which will form the base of the same stitch on the next row above. Now insert the needle from left to right under the 2 loops of this stitch on the row above, and continue working as before from left to right.

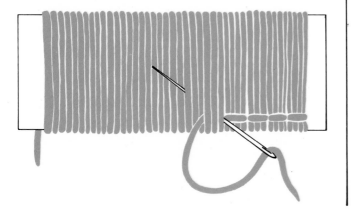

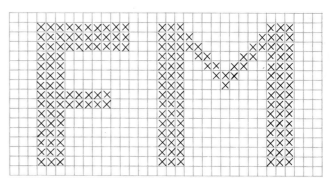

APPLIED EMBROIDERY

Embroidery can quite easily be applied to knitting without the need for charts or transfers. Quite apart from Swiss darning which gives a jacquard effect and is worked from a chart (as described on the previous page), simple embroidery stitches such as cross stitch and chain stitch can be used to highlight a seam or as a border pattern. Because of the amount of give in most knitted fabrics, smocking, either knitted in as part of the main fabric or applied when the garment is completed, is particularly effective.

The following suggestions can be incorporated in a variety of ways but a certain amount of planning is required before beginning any garment. With the exception of smocking, they can all be worked on a plain stocking stitch background but care must be taken in working out the exact position for each stitch. Smocking, worked in one with the fabric or applied, needs a ribbed background and the pattern for any garment using these methods will give detailed instructions for the correct placing. However, if you wish to try some smocking – perhaps on the bodice of a little girl's dress or round the cuffs of a plain jersey – remember to check and make sure that the number of stitches at the required point will allow for the correct multiples of stitches.

Smocking knitted-in

Worked in one with the main fabric over P3, K1 rib. The background colour will be used for the main fabric, coded as A, and a contrast colour in the same quality used to work the smocking, coded as B.

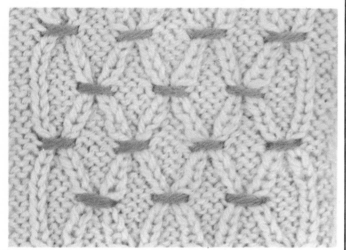

Either cast on or make sure that you have a number of stitches divisible by 8+3. This allows for the knit stitches of the rib to be drawn together with the contrast colour, alternating the position to give the smocked effect.

1st row (RS) Using A, *P3, K1, rep from * to last 3 sts, P3.
2nd row *K3, P1, rep from * to last 3 sts, K3.
Rep 1st and 2nd rows once more.
5th row Using A, P3, *K1, P3, K1, sl these last 5 sts on to a cable needle and hold at front of work, join in B at back of work, pass B in front of sts on cable needle to back of work then round to front and back again in an anti-clockwise direction, leaving B at back sl 5 sts on to right hand needle – called S5 –, P3 A, rep from * to end. Do not break off B.
6th row As 2nd.
Rep 1st and 2nd rows once, then 1st row once more.
10th row Using A, K3, P1, *K3, S5 by P1, K3, P1, holding cable needle at back of work and winding yarn round in a clockwise direction, rep from * to last 7 sts, K3, P1, K3. Do not break off B.
These 10 rows form the pattern.

Smocking applied

Work the background rib as given for knitted-in smocking until the garment or section is completed. Using a blunt ended wool needle threaded with B, *insert needle from back to front of the work after the 2nd knitted st of the 5th row, pass the needle across the front of the knit st, the next 3 purl sts and the next knit st, Insert it from front to back after this knit st and pull yarn through, carry the yarn across the back of the work through to the front and round the 5 sts again through to the back, carry the yarn across the back of the work, miss (P3, K1) twice, rep from * to end. On the 10th row with the WS of the work facing, * work round the 2nd knit st of the first smocked sts, the next 3 purl sts and the first knit st of next smocked sts, then miss (K3, P1) twice, rep from * to the end. Continue in this way for the required depth of smocking.

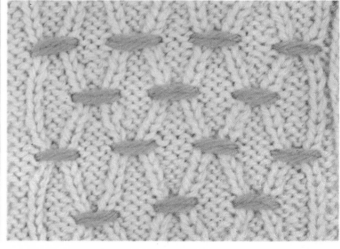

Applied bows

Work the stocking stitch background and mark the positions for the bows on the RS of the work, allowing 5 sts and 5 rows for each bow and a further 5 sts between each bow. Using a blunt ended wool needle threaded with contrast yarn, *insert the needle from back to front at the first marked st of the 1st row and pull yarn through, working from right to left insert the needle under the 3rd st of the 3rd row and pull yarn through, insert the needle from front to back after the 5th st of the 1st row and pull yarn through; carry yarn across back of work, insert needle from back to front at first marked st of 2nd row and pull yarn through, insert needle under same 3rd st of 3rd row and pull yarn through, insert needle from front to back after 5th st of 2nd row and pull yarn through; carry yarn across back, insert needle from back to front at first marked st of 3rd row and pull yarn through, under the same 3rd st of 3rd row and pull yarn through, insert needle from front to back after 5th st of 3rd row and pull yarn through; carry yarn across back, insert needle from back to front at first marked st of 4th row and pull yarn through, under same 3rd st of 3rd row and pull yarn through, insert needle from front to back after 5th st of 4th row and pull yarn through; carry yarn across back, insert needle from back to front at first marked st of 5th row and pull yarn through, under same 3rd st of 3rd row and pull yarn through, insert needle from front to back after 5th st of 5th row and pull yarn through, carry yarn across back to next position and rep from * to end.

The next time the bows are worked on 5 rows above, work them over 5 sts in between each bow of previous row.

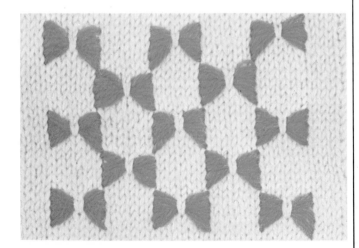

Applied chain stitch

This looks most effective if it is worked in a contrast colour on a stocking stitch background, where wide stripes of the main colour and narrow stripes of the contrast colour have been used, to give a checked effect. Mark the positions for vertical chains depending on the size of check required and allowing one stitch, one above the other, on every row.

Using a blunt ended wool needle threaded with contrast colour, begin at lower edge of first marked position and insert needle from back to front in centre of marked st and pull yarn through, *hold the yarn down with the thumb of the left hand, insert the needle into the same st and up into the next st above pulling the yarn through, rep from * to end and fasten off. Repeat on each marked st as required.

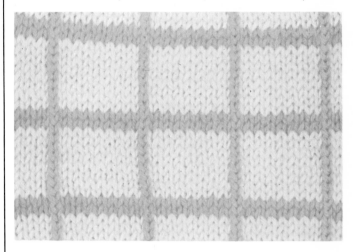

Applied cross stitch

Work the stocking stitch background and mark positions for the cross sts on the RS of work, allowing 3 sts and 4 rows for each cross st, with a further 3 sts between each cross st. Using a blunt ended wool needle threaded with one or two thicknesses of contrast colour begin at lower edge, *insert needle from back to front at side of first marked st and pull yarn through, working from right to left insert needle from front to back after 3rd st on 4th row above and pull yarn through, carry yarn across back of work, insert needle from back to front after first st on 4th row and pull yarn through, insert needle from front to back after 3rd st of 1st row and pull yarn through, carry yarn across back to next position and rep from * to end. The next time the cross sts are worked on 4 rows above, work them over 3 sts in between each cross st of previous row.

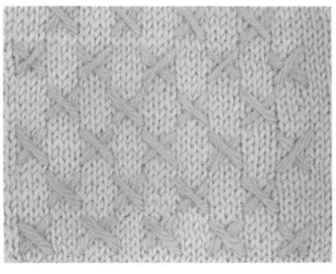

COVERED BUTTONS

Just as untidy buttonholes can mar the effect of an otherwise perfect garment, buttons which do not match exactly or tone in with the yarn used for a design can spoil the whole appearance.

Sometimes it is impossible to find suitable buttons and the cheap and simple answer to this problem is to cover button moulds, such as Trims, with knitting to achieve a perfect match.

Here we give a selection of buttons to suit all garments.

Bouclé yarn button

Using No.14 needles cast on 4 sts. Work in st st, inc one st at each end of every row until there are 12 sts. Work 6 rows without shaping. Dec one st at each end of every row until 4 sts rem. Cast off. Gather over wooden mould.

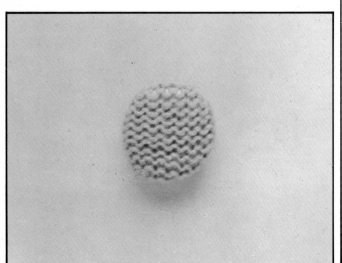

Reversed stocking stitch button

Using No.14 needles and 4 ply, work as given for bouclé yarn button, beg with a P row. Cover 2cm ($\frac{7}{8}$in) Trim.

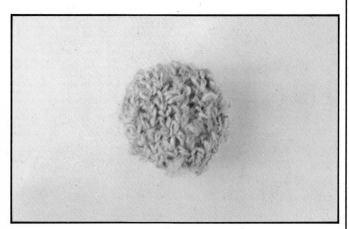

Single rib button

Using No.14 needles and 4 ply, work in K1, P1 rib as given for reversed st st button. Cover 2cm ($\frac{7}{8}$ inch) Trim.

Bobble button

Using No.14 needles and 4 ply, cast on 3 sts. Work in st st, inc one st at each end of every row until there are 11 sts. Work 3 rows without shaping.

Next row K5, K into front and back of next st 5 times, K5.

Next row P5, K5 tog, P5.

Work 2 rows without shaping. Dec one st at each end of every row until 3 sts rem. Cast off. Cover 2cm ($\frac{7}{8}$in) Trim.

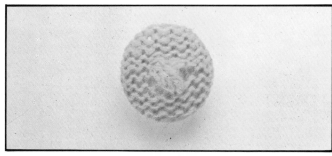

Continental stocking stitch button

Using No.14 needles and 4 ply, cast on and work as given for reversed st st button, working in foll patt:

1st row K into back of each st to end.

2nd row P to end.

Cast off. Cover 2cm ($\frac{7}{8}$ in) Trim.

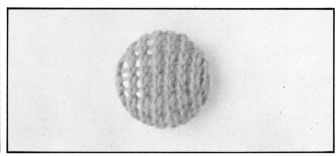

Tweed stitch button

Using No.14 needles and 4 ply, cast on and work as given for reversed st st button, working in foll patt:
1st row *K1, yfwd, sl 1 P-wise, ybk, rep from * to end.
2nd row P to end.
3rd row *Yfwd, sl 1 P-wise, ybk, K1, rep from * to end.
4th row P to end.
Cast off. Cover 2cm ($\frac{7}{8}$in) Trim.

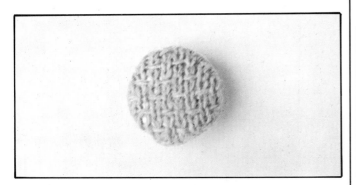

Two-colour button

Using No.14 needles and 4 ply in 2 colours, A and B, cast on and work as given for reversed st st button, working in foll patt:
1st row (WS) Using A, *P1, sl 1 P-wise, rep from * to end.
2nd row Using A, K to end.
3rd row Using B, as 1st.
4th row Using B, as 2nd.
Cast off. Cover 2cm ($\frac{7}{8}$in) Trim.

Embroidered button

Using No.14 needles and 4 ply, cast on 6 sts. Work in st st inc one at each end of every row until there are 16 sts. Work 8 rows without shaping.
Dec one st at each end of every row until 6 sts rem. Cast off. Using 3 colours of stranded embroidery cotton and chain st, work flower motif in centre of button. Gather over wooden mould.

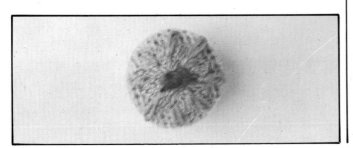

Basket stitch button

Using No.11 needles and double knitting, cast on and work as given for bouclé yarn button, working in foll patt:
1st row *K2, P2, rep from * to end.
2nd row As 1st.
3rd row *P2, K2, rep from * to end.
4th row As 3rd.
Cast off. Gather over wooden mould.

Woven basket stitch button

Using No.11 needles and double knitting, cast on and work as given for Basket stitch button, working in foll patt:
1st row *Pass right hand needle behind first st on left hand needle and K second st, then K first st in usual way, dropping both sts off needle tog, rep from * to end.
2nd row P1, *P second st on left hand needle then P first st and sl both sts off needle tog, rep from * to last st, P1.
Cast off. Gather over wooden mould.

Beret button

Using No.12 needles and double knitting, cast on 11 sts.
1st and every alt row (WS) P to end.
2nd row K1, (K twice into next st, K1) 5 times. 16 sts.
4th row (K2, K twice into next st) 5 times, K1. 21 sts.
6th row (K2, K2 tog) 5 times, K1. 16 sts.
8th row (K1, K2 tog) 5 times, K1. 11 sts.
10th row (K2 tog) 5 times, K1. 5 sts.
Break off yarn, thread through rem sts, insert 3cm ($1\frac{1}{4}$in) wooden mould, draw up and fasten off.

APPLIED EDGINGS

Knitted edgings

Although many beautiful and interesting forms of edgings are given in crochet patterns, reference is seldom made to the equally effective variations of knitted borders. These may be used to trim anything from baby clothes and fashion garments to household linens.

The correct choice of yarn for these borders is very important, depending upon the use to which they will be put. Something as fine as a 2 or 3 ply would produce a delicate edging for a baby dress or shawl, a double knitting quality would give a firm, textured border for a fashion garment, or a crisp cotton would be ideal for household linens. All of the examples shown here are worked separately to the required length, then sewn in place when the item is completed.

Simple lace edging

Cast on a number of stitches divisible by 5 plus 2.
1st row K1, yfwd and over needle to make one st, * K5, turn, lift 2nd, 3rd, 4th and 5th sts over the first st and off the needle, turn, yfwd, rep from * to last st, K1.
2nd row K1, *(P1, yon to make one st, K1 tbl) all into

next st, P1, rep from * to end.
3rd row K2, K1 tbl, *K3, K1 tbl, rep from * to last 2 sts, K2.
Work 3 rows g st. Cast off.

Shell edging

Using thumb method, cast on a number of stitches divisible by 11 plus 2.
1st row P to end.
2nd row K2, *K1, sl this st back on to left hand needle and lift the next 8 sts on left hand needle over this st and off the needle, yfwd and round right hand needle twice to make 2 sts, then K first st again, K2, rep from * to end.
3rd row K1, *P2 tog, drop extra loop of 2 made sts on previous row and into this long loop work (K1, K1 tbl) twice, P1, rep from * to last st, K1.
Work 5 rows g st. Cast off.

Leaf edging

Cast on a number of stitches divisible by 13 plus 2.
1st row K1, *K2, sl 1, K1, psso, sl 2, K3 tog, p2sso, K2 tog, K2, rep from * to last st, K1.

2nd row P4, *yrn, P1, yrn, P6, rep from * ending last rep with P4 instead of P6.

3rd row K1, yfwd, *K2, sl 1, K1, psso, K1, K2 tog, K2, yfwd, rep from * to last st, K1.

4th row P2, *yrn, P2, yrn, P3, yrn, P2, yrn, P1, rep from * to last st, P1.

5th row K2, *yfwd, K1, yfwd, sl 1, K1, psso, K1, sl 1, K2 tog, psso, K1, K2 tog, yfwd, K1, yfwd, K1, rep from * to last st, K1.

6th row P to end.

7th row K5, *yfwd, sl 2, K3 tog, p2sso, yfwd, K7, rep from * ending last rep with K5 instead of K7.
Work 4 rows g st. Cast off.

Chain edging

Using 2 needle method and working into each st instead of between sts, cast on a number of stitches divisible by 29.

1st row *K3 tbl, (pick up loop lying between sts and K tbl – called inc 1 –, drop 3 sts off left hand needle, K2 tog tbl) 4 times, inc 1, drop 3 sts off left hand needle, K3, rep from * to end.

2nd row P to end.

3rd row *K2 tbl, (sl 1, K1, psso) twice, sl 1, K2 tog, psso, (K2 tog) twice, K2, rep from * to end.

4th row P to end.
Work 3 rows g st. Cast off.

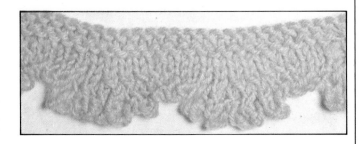

Serrated edging

Cast on 8 sts loosely.

1st row K to last 2 sts, K twice into next st, yfwd and hold at front of work, sl 1 P-wise. 9 sts.

2nd row K1 tbl, K1, (yfwd and over needle – called M1 –, sl 1, K1, psso, K1) twice, yfwd, sl 1 P-wise.

3rd row K1 tbl, K to end, turn and cast on 3 sts.

4th row K1, K twice into next st, K2, (M1, sl 1, K1, psso, K1) twice, M1, K1, yfwd, sl 1 P-wise.

5th row K1 tbl, K to last 2 sts, K twice into next st, yfwd, sl 1 P-wise.

6th row K1 tbl, K twice into next st, K2, (M1, sl 1, K1,

psso, K1) 3 times, K1, yfwd, sl 1 P-wise.

7th row K1 tbl, K to last 2 sts, K2 tog.

8th row Sl 1 P-wise, ybk, K1, psso, sl 1, K1, psso, K4, (M1, sl 1, K1, psso, K1) twice, yfwd, sl 1 P-wise.

9th row K1 tbl, K to last 2 sts, K2 tog.

10th row Cast off 3 sts, K2, M1, sl 1, K1, psso, K1, M1, sl 1, K1, psso, yfwd, sl 1 P-wise. 9 sts.
Rows 3 to 10 inclusive form pattern. Repeat pattern rows until edging is required length. Cast off.

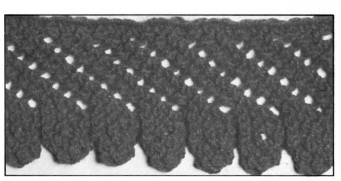

Fan edging

Cast on 13 sts loosely.

1st row (RS) Sl 1, K1, yfwd, K2 tog, K5, yfwd, K2 tog, yfwd, K2.

2nd and every alt row Yrn to inc 1, K2 tog, K to end.

3rd row Sl 1, K1, yfwd, K2 tog, K4, (yfwd, K2 tog) twice, yfwd, K2.

5th row Sl 1, K1, yfwd, K2 tog, K3, (yfwd, K2 tog) 3 times, yfwd, K2.

7th row Sl 1, K1, yfwd, K2 tog, K2, (yfwd, K2 tog) 4 times, yfwd, K2.

9th row Sl 1, K1, yfwd, K2 tog, K1, (yfwd, K2 tog) 5 times, yfwd, K2.

11th row Sl 1, K1, yfwd, K2 tog, K1, K2 tog, (yfwd, K2 tog) 5 times, K1.

13th row Sl 1, K1, yfwd, K2 tog, K2, K2 tog, (yfwd, K2 tog) 4 times, K1.

15th row Sl 1, K1, yfwd, K2 tog, K3, K2 tog, (yfwd, K2 tog) 3 times, K1.

17th row Sl 1, K1, yfwd, K2 tog, K4, K2 tog, (yfwd, K2 tog) twice, K1.

19th row Sl 1, K1, yfwd, K2 tog, K5, K2 tog, yfwd, K2 tog, K1.

20th row Yrn, K2 tog, K11.
These 20 rows form the pattern. Repeat pattern rows until edging is required length. Cast off.

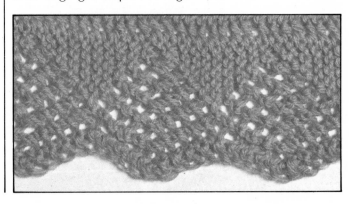

SHAPED EDGINGS

Knitted borders

The last chapter dealt with straight knitted edgings, either worked over multiples of stitches in rows to give the required length, or from side edge to side edge over a set number of stitches for the desired length. Where a border is required to fit a rectangular, square or circular shape, however, provision must be made for working corners or shaping the border so that the outer edge is wider than the inner edge.

The circular border given here is used to trim a baby's shawl, where the centre is knitted in stocking stitch to a circular shape, but if it is worked in a fine cotton yarn, the same border would most effectively trim a circular fabric tablecloth.

The border with corner shaping, used here to trim a fabric traycloth, would also be ideal for trimming pillow cases, tablecloths or a delicate evening stole.

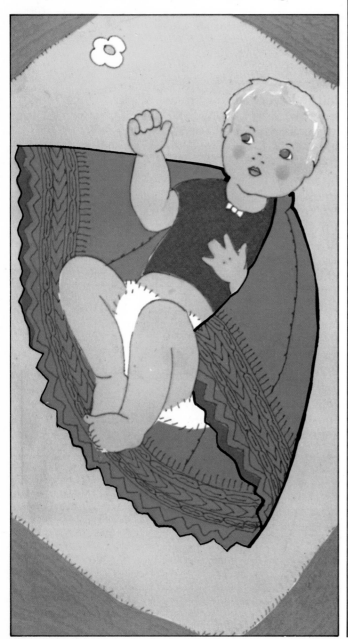

Shawl centre

Using set of 4 needles pointed at both ends, cast on 6 sts.

1st round *K into front then into back of next st, rep from * to end. 12 sts.

2nd round K1, *yfwd to make one, K2, rep from * to last st, yfwd, K1. 18 sts.

3rd round K1, *K into front then into back of yfwd of previous round, K2, rep from * to last 2 sts, K into front then into back of yfwd, K1. 24 sts.

4th round K2, *yfwd, K4, rep from * to last 2 sts, yfwd, K2. 30 sts.

5th round K2, *K into front then into back of yfwd, K4, rep from * to last 3 sts, K into front then into back of yfwd, K2. 36 sts.

6th round K3, *yfwd, K6, rep from * to last 3 sts, yfwd, K3. 42 sts.

7th round K3, *K into front then into back of yfwd, K6, rep from * to last 4 sts, K into front then into back of yfwd, K3.

Cont inc 6 sts on every round in this way until centre is required diameter. Cast off very loosely.

Shawl border

Cast on 52 sts loosely.

1st row K2, (K2 tog, yfwd to make one – called M1 –, K2) 3 times, K2 tog, K11, K2 tog, (K2 tog, M1, K2) 3 times, K2 tog, (M1, K2 tog) 4 times. 49 sts.

2nd row P10, turn and leave 39 sts unworked.

3rd row K2 tog, (M1, K2 tog) 4 times.

4th row P8, (K2 tog, M1, K2) 3 times, P13, (K2 tog, M1, K2) 3 times, K3.

5th row K3, (K2 tog, M1, K2) 3 times, (K2 tog) twice, (M1, K1) 5 times, M1, (K2 tog) twice, (K2 tog, M1, K2) 3 times, K1, (M1, K2 tog) 3 times, M1, K1.

6th row P9, (K2 tog, M1, K2) 3 times, P15, (K2 tog, M1, K2) 3 times, K3.

7th row K3, (K2 tog, M1, K2) 3 times, K2 tog, K11, K2 tog, (K2 tog, M1, K2) 3 times, K2, (M1, K2 tog) 3 times, M1, K1.

8th row P10, (K2 tog, M1, K2) 3 times, P12, turn and leave 16 sts unworked.

9th row K1, K2 tog, (M1, K1) 5 times, M1, (K2 tog) twice, (K2 tog, M1, K2) 3 times, K3, (M1, K2 tog) 3 times, M1, K1.

10th row P11, (K2 tog, M1, K2) 3 times, P14, P2 tog,

(K2 tog, M1, K2) 3 times, K3.

11th row K3, *K2 tog, M1, K1, s1 next 3 sts on to cable needle and hold at back of work, K1, K2 tog from left hand needle, M1, K2 from cable needle, K next st on left hand needle and last st on cable needle tog, M1, K2, *, K2 tog, K11, K2 tog, rep from * to *, K4, (M1, K2 tog) 3 times, M1, K1.

12th row P13, turn and leave 39 sts unworked.

13th row K6, (M1, K2 tog) 3 times, M1, K1.

14th row *P13, (K2 tog, M1, K2) 3 times, rep from * once more, K3.

15th row K3, (K2 tog, M1, K2) 3 times, (K2 tog) twice, (M1, K1) 5 times, M1 (K2 tog) twice, (K2 tog, M1, K2) 3 times, K3, K2 tog, (M1, K2 tog) 4 times.

16th row P12, (K2 tog, M1, K2) 3 times, P15, (K2 tog, M1, K2) 3 times, K3.

17th row K3, (K2 tog, M1, K2) 3 times, K2 tog, K11, K2 tog, (K2 tog, M1, K2) 3 times, K2, K2 tog, (M1, K2 tog) 4 times.

18th row P11, (K2 tog, M1, K2) 3 times, P12, turn and leave 16 sts unworked.

19th row K1, K2 tog, (M1, K1) 5 times, M1, (K2 tog) twice, (K2 tog, M1, K2) 3 times, K1, K2 tog, (M1, K2 tog) 4 times.

20th row P10, (K2 tog, M1, K2) 3 times, P14, P2 tog, (K2 tog, M1, K2) 3 times, K3.

These 20 rows form patt. Cont in patt until inner edge of border fits round outer edge of centre. Sew in place.

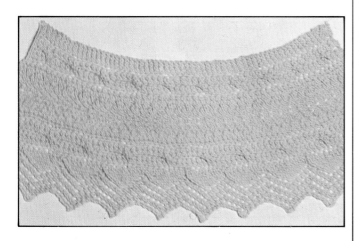

Traycloth

Cut fabric to required size and hem round all edges.

Border

Cast on 9sts. Commence patt.

1st row (RS) K to end.

2nd row K3, K2 tog, yfwd to make one, K2 tog, yfwd, K1, yfwd, K1. 10 sts.

3rd and every alt row K to end.

4th row K2, K2 tog, yfwd, K2 tog, yfwd, K3, yfwd, K1. 11 sts.

6th row K1, K2 tog, yfwd, K2 tog, yfwd, K5, yfwd, K1. 12 sts.

8th row K3, yfwd, K2 tog, yfwd, K2 tog, K1, K2 tog, yfwd, K2 tog. 11 sts.

10th row K4, yfwd, K2 tog, yfwd, K3 tog, yfwd, K2 tog. 10 sts.

12th row K5, yfwd, K3 tog, yfwd, K2 tog. 9 sts.

These 12 rows form patt. Cont in patt until border is required length to first corner, ending with a 6th row.

Shape corner

1st row K10, turn.

2nd row Sl 1 K-wise, yfwd, K2 tog, yfwd, K2 tog, K1, K2 tog, yfwd, K2 tog. 11 sts.

3rd row K8, turn.

4th row Sl 1 K-wise, yfwd, K2 tog, yfwd, K3 tog, yfwd, K2 tog. 10 sts.

5th row K6, turn.

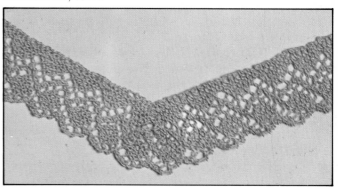

6th row Sl 1 K-wise, yfwd, K3 tog, yfwd, K2 tog. 9 sts.

7th row K6, turn.

8th row K2 tog, yfwd, K2 tog, yfwd, K1, yfwd, K1. 10 sts.

9th row K8, turn.

10th row K2 tog, yfwd, K2 tog, yfwd, K3, yfwd, K1. 11 sts.

11th row K10, turn.

12th row K2 tog, yfwd, K2 tog, yfwd, K5, yfwd, K1. 12 sts.

13th row K to end.

This completes corner shaping. Beg with an 8th patt row, cont in patt to next corner, then rep shaping rows. Cont in this way until border is completed. Sew in place round traycloth.

EDGINGS AND INSERTIONS

Knitted edgings and insertions can be used most effectively as a trim for fabric garments, or household linens. They look their best when worked in a fine cotton, such as No.20, which will also stand up to laundering without losing its shape.

The insertion pattern given here may be used on its own to form a delicate panel on each side of the front of a fabric blouse, or it could be combined with any one of the edgings to form the yoke of a demure nightgown.

Alternatively, the insertion could be applied across the top of a sheet, which could then be finished off with one of the edgings to transform plain household linen into a family heirloom.

7th row K4, P2, K1, P4, K2, (yrn, P2 tog) twice, K1.
8th row K3, (yrn, P2 tog) twice, yon, K1 tbl, K1, K1 tbl, yfwd, sl 1, K2 tog, psso, yfwd, K5.
9th row K5, P7, K2, (yrn, P2 tog) twice, K1.
10th row K3, (yrn, P2 tog) twice, yon, K1 tbl, K3, K1 tbl, yfwd, K7.
11th row Cast off 4 sts, K2, P7, K2, (yrn, P2 tog) twice, K1.
The 2nd to 11th rows form the pattern.

Shell edging
Cast on 13 sts.
1st row (WS) P to end.
2nd row Sl 1, K1, yrn, P2 tog, K1, (yfwd, sl1, K1, psso) 3 times, y2rn, K2 tog.

Leaf edging
Cast on 17 sts.
1st row (WS) K to end.
2nd row K3, (yrn, P2 tog) twice, yon, K1 tbl, K2 tog, P1, sl 1, K1, psso, K1 tbl, yfwd, K3.
3rd row K3, P3, K1, P3, K2, (yrn, P2 tog) twice, K1.
4th row As 2nd.
5th row As 3rd.
6th row K3, (yrn, P2 tog) twice, yon, K1 tbl, yfwd, K2 tog, P1, sl 1, K1, psso, yfwd, K4.

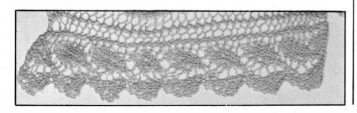

3rd row Yfwd to make 1, K2 tog, P9, yrn, P2 tog, K1, noting that the first K2 tog includes the first loop of

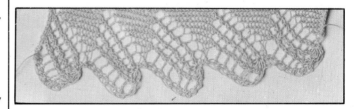

y2rn and the second loop forms the first P st.
4th row Sl 1, K1, yrn, P2 tog, K2, (yfwd, sl 1, K1, psso) 3 times, y2rn, K2 tog.
5th row Yfwd, K2 tog, P10, yrn, P2 tog, K1.
6th row Sl 1, K1, yrn, P2 tog, K3, (yfwd, sl 1, K1, psso) 3 times, y2rn, K2 tog.
7th row Yfwd, K2 tog, P11, yrn, P2 tog, K1.

8th row Sl 1, K1, yrn, P2 tog, K4, (yfwd, sl 1, K1, psso) 3 times, y2rn, K2 tog.

9th row Yfwd, K2 tog, P12, yrn, P2 tog, K1.

10th row Sl 1, K1, yrn, P2 tog, K5, (yfwd, sl 1, K1, psso) 3 times, y2rn, K2 tog.

11th row Yfwd, K2 tog, P13, yrn, P2 tog, K1.

12th row Sl 1, K1, yrn, P2 tog, K6, (yfwd, sl 1, K1, psso) 3 times, y2rn, K2 tog.

13th row Yfwd, K2 tog, P14, yrn, P2 tog, K1.

14th row Sl 1, K1, yrn, P2 tog, K7, (yfwd, sl 1, K1, psso) 3 times, y2rn, K2 tog.

15th row Yfwd, K2 tog, P15, yrn, P2 tog, K1.

16th row Sl 1, K1, yrn, P2 tog, K8, yfwd, K1, return last st to left hand needle and with point of right hand needle lift the next 7 sts one at a time over this st and off needle, then sl st back on to right hand needle.

17th row P2 tog, P9, yrn, P2 tog, K1.

The 2nd to 17th rows form the pattern.

Cockleshell edging

Cast on 16 sts.

1st row K to end.

2nd row Yfwd to make 1, K2 tog, K1, yfwd, K10, yfwd, K2 tog, K1.

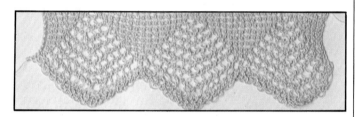

3rd row K2, yfwd, K2 tog, K12, P1.

4th row Yfwd, K2 tog, K1, yfwd, K2 tog, yfwd, K9, yfwd, K2 tog, K1.

5th row K2, yfwd, K2 tog, K13, P1.

6th row Yfwd, K2 tog, K1, (yfwd, K2 tog) twice, yfwd, K8, yfwd, K2 tog, K1.

7th row K2, yfwd, K2 tog, K14, P1.

8th row Yfwd, K2 tog, K1, (yfwd, K2 tog) 3 times, yfwd, K7, yfwd, K2 tog, K1.

9th row K2, yfwd, K2 tog, K15, P1.

10th row Yfwd, K2 tog, K1, (yfwd, K2 tog) 4 times, yfwd, K6, yfwd, K2 tog, K1.

11th row K2, yfwd, K2 tog, K16, P1.

12th row Yfwd, K2 tog, K1, (yfwd, K2 tog) 5 times, yfwd, K5, yfwd, K2 tog, K1.

13th row K2, yfwd, K2 tog, K17, P1.

14th row Yfwd, K2 tog, K1, (yfwd, K2 tog) 6 times, yfwd, K4, yfwd, K2 tog, K1.

15th row K2, yfwd, K2 tog, K18, P1.

16th row Yfwd, K2 tog, K1, (yfwd, K2 tog) 7 times, yfwd, K3, yfwd, K2 tog, K1.

17th row K2, yfwd, K2 tog, K19, P1.

18th row Yfwd, (K2 tog) twice, (yfwd, K2 tog) 7 times, K3, yfwd, K2 tog, K1.

19th row As 15th.

20th row Yfwd, (K2 tog) twice, (yfwd, K2 tog) 6 times, K4, yfwd, K2 tog, K1.

21st row As 13th.

22nd row Yfwd, (K2 tog) twice, (yfwd, K2 tog) 5 times, K5, yfwd, K2 tog, K1.

23rd row As 11th.

24th row Yfwd, (K2 tog) twice, (yfwd, K2 tog) 4 times, K6, yfwd, K2 tog, K1.

25th row As 9th.

26th row Yfwd, (K2 tog) twice, (yfwd, K2 tog) 3 times, K7, yfwd, K2 tog, K1.

27th row As 7th.

28th row Yfwd, (K2 tog) twice, (yfwd, K2 tog) twice, K8, yfwd, K2 tog, K1.

29th row As 5th.

30th row Yfwd, (K2 tog) twice, yfwd, K2 tog, K9, yfwd, K2 tog, K1.

31st row As 3rd.

32nd row Yfwd, (K2 tog) twice, K10, yfwd, K2 tog, K1.

33rd row K2, yfwd, K2 tog, K11, P1.

The 2nd to 33rd rows form the pattern.

Diamond insertion panel

Cast on 21 sts.

1st and every alt row (WS) P to end.

2nd row K2, yfwd, sl 1, K1, psso, K1, yfwd, sl 1, K1, psso, K3, K2 tog, yfwd, K1, yfwd, sl 1, K1, psso, K6.

4th row K3, (yfwd, sl 1, K1, psso, K1) twice, K2 tog, yfwd, K3, yfwd, sl 1, K1, psso, K5.

6th row K4, yfwd, sl 1, K1, psso, K1, yfwd, K3 tog, yfwd, K2, yfwd, sl 1, K1, psso, K1, yfwd, sl 1, K1, psso, K4.

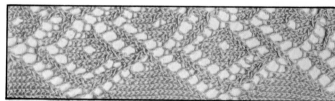

8th row K5, yfwd, sl 1, K1, psso, (K2 tog, yfwd, K1) twice, yfwd, sl 1, K1, psso, K1, yfwd, sl 1, K1, psso, K3.

10th row K6, yfwd, sl 1, K1, psso, K1, K2 tog, yfwd, K3, yfwd, sl 1, K1, psso, K1, yfwd, sl 1, K1, psso, K2.

12th row K7, yfwd, K3 tog, yfwd, K5, (yfwd, sl 1, K1, psso, K1) twice.

14th row K7, K2 tog, yfwd, K3, yfwd, sl 1, K1, psso, K2, yfwd, sl 1, K1, psso, K1, yfwd, sl 1, K1, psso.

16th row K6, K2 tog, yfwd, K1, yfwd, sl 1, K1, psso, K3, K2 tog, yfwd, K1, K2 tog, yfwd, K2.

18th row K5, K2 tog, yfwd, K3, yfwd, sl 1, K1, psso, (K1, K2 tog, yfwd) twice, K3.

20th row K4, K2 tog, yfwd, K1, K2 tog, yfwd, K2, yfwd, sl 1, K2 tog, psso, yfwd, K1, K2 tog, yfwd, K4.

22nd row K3, (K2 tog, yfwd, K1) twice, yfwd, sl 1, K1, psso, K1, yfwd, sl 1, K1, psso, K2 tog, yfwd, K5.

24th row K2, K2 tog, yfwd, K1, K2 tog, yfwd, K3, yfwd, sl 1, K1, psso, K1, K2 tog, yfwd, K6.

26th row (K1, K2 tog, yfwd) twice, K5, yfwd, sl 1, K2 tog, psso, yfwd, K7.

28th row K2 tog, yfwd, K1, K2 tog, yfwd, K2, K2 tog, yfwd, K3, yfwd, sl 1, K1, psso, K7.

These 28 rows form the pattern.

SEQUINS AND BEADS

Beaded and sequinned tops and jackets make glamorous and dazzling garments for evening wear and this technique is very simple to work. The beads or sequins are knitted in with the fabric and they can be used to form an all-over design, or as a most effective trimming.

Most large departmental stores sell packets of beads and sequins which will prove suitable for this type of knitting.

If you are using beads, they should not be too large or heavy, as this will pull the fabric out of shape – small pearl beads are ideal. The hole in the centre of the bead must be large enough to thread over the yarn being used.

Sequins also come in various sizes and shapes and must also have a hole large enough to be threaded over the yarn. This hole should be at the top of the sequin and not in the centre, so that the sequins do not stick out but hang flat against the knitted background.

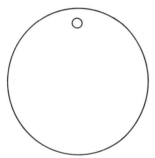

To thread beads or sequins on to a ball of yarn

Cut a 25.5cm (10in) length of ordinary sewing thread and fold this in half. Thread both cut ends through a fine sewing needle, leaving a loop of cotton as shown in diagram 1.

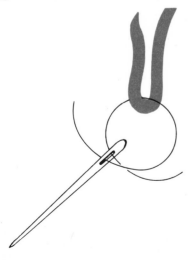

Thread the required number of beads or sequins on to the ball of yarn with which you are going to knit by passing approximately 15cm (6in) of the end of this ball through the loop of sewing cotton. Thread the beads or sequins on to the needle, then slide them down the cotton and on to the ball of yarn, as shown in diagram 2.

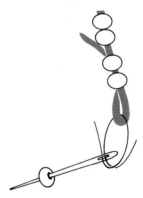

To knit in beads or sequins

Prepare a ball of yarn by threading on the required number of beads or sequins. These should be knitted in on a right side row against a stocking stitch background, although they can be worked in panels and interspersed with a lace pattern, as shown in the evening top given here.

Knit until the position for the bead or sequin is reached, push one bead or sequin up the ball of yarn close to the back of the work, knit the next stitch through the back of the loop in the usual way, pushing the bead or sequin through to the front of the work with the loop of the stitch, taking care not to split the yarn. This allows the bead or sequin to lie flat against the fabric.

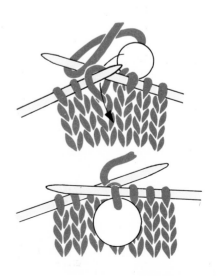

Evening top
Sizes
To fit 81.5[86.5:91.5:96.5:101.5]cm (32[34:36:38:40]in) bust
Length to centre back, 35.5cm (14in)
The figures in brackets [] refer to the 86.5 (34), 91.5 (36), 96.5 (38) and 101.5cm (40in) sizes respectively

Tension
24 sts and 36 rows to 10cm (3.9in) over patt worked on No.9 needles

Materials
4 × 25grm balls of Jaeger 3 ply Botany wool
Approx 700 sequins with hole at top
One pair No.9 needles
One pair No.10 needles

Note
Thread approx 350 sequins on to each of 2 balls of yarn

Back
Using No.10 needles and ball of yarn which has not been threaded with sequins, cast on 94[100:106:112: 118] sts. Work 15cm (6in) K1, P1 rib. Break off yarn. Change to No.9 needles. Join in ball threaded with sequins. Commence patt.

1st row (RS) K1, *K2, K2 tog, y2rn, K2 tog tbl, rep from * to last 3 sts, K3.
2nd row *P4, P into front then into back of y2rn, rep from * to last 4 sts, P4.
3rd row K1, *K1, K sequin in with next st tbl – called K1S –, K2 tog, y2rn, K2 tog tbl, rep from * to last 3 sts, K1, K1S, K1.
4th row As 2nd.
5th row As 1st.
6th row As 2nd.
7th row K1, *K1S, K1, K2 tog, y2rn, K2 tog tbl, rep from * to last 3 sts, K1S, K2.
8th row As 2nd.
These 8 rows form patt. Cont in patt until work measures 30.5cm (12in) from beg, ending with a WS row.

Shape armholes
Keeping patt correct, cast off 5[6:7:8:9] sts at beg of next 2 rows. Dec one st at each end of next and every alt row 8 times in all, ending with a WS row. 68[72: 76:80:84] sts.

Shape neck
Next row Dec one st, patt 20[21:22:23:24] sts, cast off 24[26:28:30:32] sts, patt to last 2 sts, dec one st.
Complete left shoulder first.
Next row Patt to end.
Next row Dec one st, patt to last 2 sts, dec one st.
Rep last 2 rows until 3[2:3:2:3] sts rem. K3[2:3:2:3] tog. Fasten off.
With WS of work facing, rejoin yarn to rem sts and complete right shoulder to match left shoulder.

Front
Work as given for back.

Shoulder straps (make 2)
Using No.10 needles and ball of yarn which has not been threaded with sequins, cast on 11 sts.
1st row K1, *P1, K1, rep from * to end.
2nd row P1, *K1, P1, rep from * to end.
Rep these 2 rows until strap measures 51cm (20in) from beg, or required length to fit round armhole to shoulder. Cast off. Join cast on edge to cast off edge. Join side seams. Pin straps in place round armhole.

Neck edging (make 2)
Work as given for shoulder straps until edging fits down side of one shoulder strap, round centre neck edge and up side of other shoulder strap.
Cast off.

To make up
Do not press. Sew shoulder straps in place. Sew neck edging down inner edge of shoulder strap, round neck and along inner edge of other strap, then join shoulder seam. Fold straps and edging in half to WS and sl st down.

CHANGING COLOURS

SIMPLE STRIPES

Striped patterns, using simple stitches and subtle combinations of colours, are the easiest way of achieving a colourful knitted fabric. A plain, basic jersey can be adapted and given a completely new look by working regular or random stripes in three or four colours, and this is a very useful way of using up oddments of yarn in the same thickness.

Twisting yarns to change colour

When working any form of horizontal stripe, there is no problem about joining in a different ball of yarn. As one colour is finished with at the end of a row, the new one is brought in at the beginning of the next row. When each colour has been brought into use it is left until it is required again, then carried loosely up the side of the work and twisted once round the last colour used, before beginning to work with it again. Vertical or diagonal stripes are a little more difficult to work, as the colours must be changed at several points within the same row. When using narrow vertical or diagonal stripes it is best to twist each yarn with the last colour used as it is brought into use, then carry the yarn not in use across the back of the work until it is required again. For wider stripes however it is not advisable to use this method of carrying the yarn across the back of the work as, apart from the waste of yarn, there is a tendency to pull the yarn too tightly, which results in an unsightly bunching of the fabric and loss of tension. It is much better to divide each colour into small separate balls before beginning to work and then use one ball of yarn for each stripe, twisting one colour to the next at the back of the work when a change is made. It is important to remember that stripes worked by twisting the yarn on changing colours give a fabric of normal thickness, while stripes worked by carrying the yarn across the back of the work produce a fabric of double thickness.

Horizontal stripes

These are usually worked in stocking stitch and are achieved by changing colour at the beginning of a knit row. This gives an unbroken line of colour on the right side of the fabric. An even number of rows must be worked, either two, four, six and so on, and the same number of rows can be used for each colour or varied to give a random striped effect.

The purl side of this fabric can also be used as the right side of the work. Where each new colour is brought into use, it gives a broken line of colour on the purl side, which looks most effective.

Ribbed stitches can also be used to produce a striped fabric. Where an unbroken line of colour is required on the right side of the fabric, then the row where a change of colour is made needs to be knitted each time, and the other rows of each stripe worked in ribbing. An interesting fabric is produced by working in ribbing throughout, irrespective of the colour change to give a broken line of colour each time.

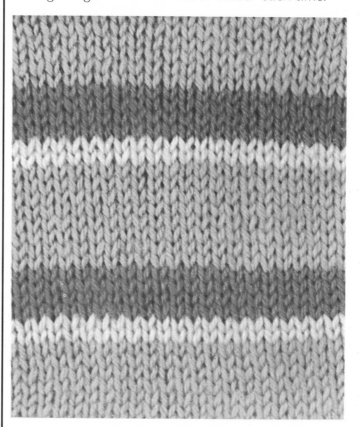

Fancy striped rib

Cast on a number of stitches divisible by 10 plus 5.
1st row P5, *K1, yfwd, sl 1, ybk, K1, yfwd, sl 1, ybk, K1, P5, rep from * to end.
2nd row K1, yfwd, sl 1, ybk, K1, yfwd, sl 1, ybk, K1, *P5, K1, yfwd, sl 1, ybk, K1, yfwd, sl 1, ybk, K1, rep from * to end.
These 2 rows form the pattern, changing colours as required.

Chevron stripes

Cast on a number of stitches divisible by 13 plus 2.
1st row *K2, pick up loop lying between needles and place it on the left hand needle then K this loop through the back – called inc 1 –, K4, sl 1 P-wise, K2 tog, psso, K4, inc 1, rep from * to last 2 sts, K2.

2nd row P to end.

These 2 rows form the pattern, changing colours as required on a 1st row.

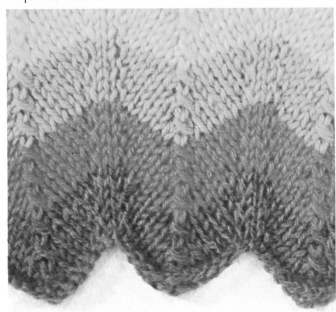

Vertical stripes

To work narrow or wide vertical stripes, the best effect is achieved in stocking stitch with the knit side of the fabric as the right side. The yarn must be carried across or twisted at the back of the fabric.

To work a wide stripe it is necessary to use a separate ball of yarn for each colour. Using two colours, the first colour used would be referred to as A and the second colour as B.

Wide vertical stripe

Cast on 6 stitches with B, 6 with A, 6 with B and 6 with A, making a total of 24 stitches.

1st row *Using A, K6 sts, hold A to the left at the back of the work, take up B and bring it towards the right at the back of the work and under the A thread no longer in use, K6 B, hold B to the left at the back of the work, take up A and bring it towards the right at the back of the work and under the B thread no longer in use, rep from * to end.

2nd row (WS) *Using B, P6 sts, hold B to the left at the front of the work, take up A and bring it towards the right at the front of the work and over the B thread no longer in use, P6 A, hold A to the left at the front of the work, take up B and bring it towards the right at the front of the work and over the A thread no longer in use, rep from * to end.

These 2 rows form the pattern.

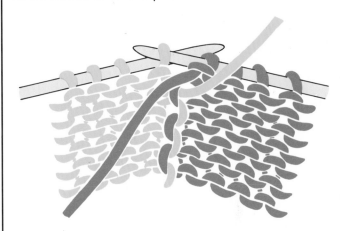

Diagonal stripes

Depending on the width of the stripes, the yarn can either be carried across the back of the work, or separate balls of yarn used for each colour as explained for wide vertical stripes.

Narrow diagonal stripes

Cast on a number of stitches divisible by 5 plus 3, using two colours, A and B.

1st row (RS) K3 A, *pick up B and K2, pick up A and K3, rep from * to end.

2nd row Pick up B and P1, *pick up A and P3, pick up B and P2, rep from * to last 2 sts, pick up A and P2.

3rd row K1 A, *pick up B and K2, pick up A and K3, rep from * to last 2 sts, pick up B and K2.

4th row Pick up A and P1, pick up B and P2, *pick up A and P3, pick up B and P2, rep from * to end.

Continue working in this way, moving the stripes one stitch to the right on K rows and one stitch to the left on P rows.

TWO COLOUR PATTERNS

By combining the working method for horizontal stripes with the clever use of slipped stitches colourful tweed fabrics can be achieved which are quick and easy to work. These stitches can be worked in two or more colours and on each change of colour, the yarn is merely carried up the side of the work and does not have to be carried across the back of the fabric as for the more difficult jacquard and Fair Isle patterns.

Bird's eye stitch

Using 2 colours coded as A and B, cast on multiples of 2 stitches.

1st row Using A, *sl 1 P-wise, K1, rep from * to end.
2nd row Using A, P to end.
3rd row Using B, *K1, sl 1 P-wise, rep from * to end.
4th row Using B, P to end.
These 4 rows form the pattern.

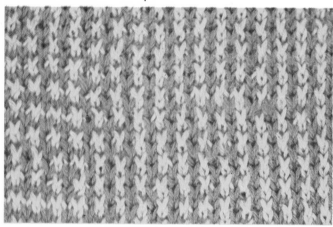

Mock houndstooth stitch

Using 2 colours coded as A and B, cast on multiples of 3 stitches.

1st row Using A, '*sl 1 P-wise, K2, rep from * to end.

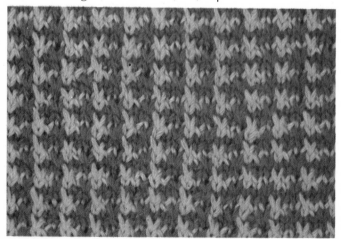

2nd row Using A, P to end.
3rd row Using B, *K2, sl 1 P-wise, rep from * to end.
4th row Using B, P to end.
These 4 rows form the pattern.

Crossed stitch

Using 2 colours coded as A and B, cast on multiples of 2 plus 1.

1st row Using A, K to end.
2nd row Using A, K to end.
3rd row Using B, *K1, sl 1 P-wise, rep from * to last st, K1.
4th row Using B, *K1, yfwd, sl 1 P-wise, ybk, rep from * to last st, K1.
5th row Using A, K to end.
6th row Using A, K to end.
7th row Using B, *sl 1 P-wise, K1, rep from * to last st, sl 1 P-wise.
8th row Using B, *sl 1 P-wise, ybk, K1, yfwd, rep from * to last st, sl 1 P-wise.
These 8 rows form the pattern.

Bee stitch

Using 2 colours coded as A and B, cast on multiples of 2 stitches.

1st row Using A, K to end.
2nd row Using A, K to end.
3rd row Using B, *insert right hand needle into next stitch on the row below and K in usual way – called K1B –, K next st on left hand needle, rep from * to end.
4th row Using B, K to end.
5th row Using A, *K1, K1B, rep from * to end.

6th row Using A, K to end.
Rows 3 to 6 form the pattern.

Two colour fuchsia stitch

Using 2 colours coded as A and B, cast on multiples of 4 stitches.

1st row Using A, K to end.
2nd row Using A, P to end.
Rep 1st and 2nd rows once more.
5th row Using B, *K3, insert right hand needle into next st in first row of A and draw through a loop, K1 and pass the loop over K1, rep from * to end.
6th row Using B, P to end.
7th row Using B, K to end.
8th row Using B, P to end.
9th row Using A, *K1, insert right hand needle into next st in first row of B and draw through a loop, K1 and pass the loop over K1, K2, rep from * to end.
Rows 2 to 9 form the pattern.

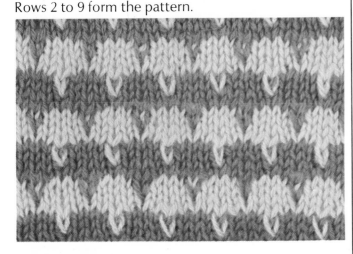

Ladder stitch

Using 2 colours coded as A and B, cast on multiples of 6 stitches plus 5.

1st row Using A, K2, *sl 1 P-wise, K5, rep from * to last 3 sts, sl 1 P-wise, K2.
2nd row Using A, P2, *sl 1 P-wise, P5, rep from * to last 3 sts, sl 1 P-wise, P2.
3rd row Using B, *K5, sl 1 P-wise, rep from * to last 5 sts, K5.

4th row Using B, *K5, yfwd, sl 1 P-wise, ybk, rep from * to last 5 sts, K5.
These 4 rows form the pattern.

Brick stitch

Using 2 colours coded as A and B, cast on multiples of 4 stitches.

1st row Using A, K to end.
2nd row Using A, K to end.
3rd row Using B, *K3, sl 1 P-wise, rep from * to end.
4th row Using B, *sl 1 P-wise, P3, rep from * to end.
5th row As 1st.
6th row As 2nd.
7th row Using B, K2, *sl 1 P-wise, K3, rep from * to last 2 sts, sl 1 P-wise, K1.
8th row Using B, P1, *sl 1 P-wise, P3, rep from * to last 3 sts, sl 1 P-wise, P2.
9th row As 1st.
10th row As 2nd.
11th row Using B, K1, *sl 1 P-wise, K3, rep from * to last 3 sts, sl 1 P-wise, K2.
12th row Using B, P2, *sl 1 P-wise, P3, rep from * to last 2 sts, sl 1 P-wise, P1.
13th row As 1st.
14th row As 2nd.
15th row Using B, *sl 1 P-wise, K3, rep from * to end.
16th row Using B, *P3, sl 1 P-wise, rep from * to end.
These 16 rows form the pattern.

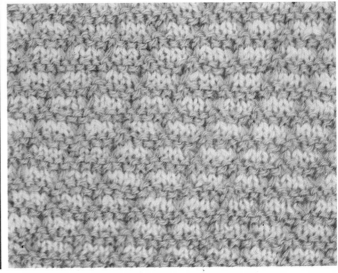

TEXTURED PATTERNS

Unlike patterns which produce a plain knitted fabric with colourful designs, such as Fair Isle (see later), patterns worked in stripes which also combine slipped stitches, form textured fabrics which are further enhanced by contrasting colours. Because these stitches do not need such careful regulation of the tension, they do not necessarily need contrasting yarns of the same thickness. A wool yarn can be combined with many different materials, such as macramé cord, cotton or metallic yarns to give an exciting and colourful effect.

All the stitches illustrated here are produced by working a set number of rows with one or more colours and, however complicated they may appear, the colours are changed at the end of the row just as for more usual striped patterns.

Ridged check stitch

Two colours of the same yarn have been used for this sample, coded as A and B. Cast on a number of stitches divisible by 4 plus 3 in A.

1st row (WS) Using A, P to end.
2nd row Using B, K3, *sl 1 P–wise keeping yarn at back of work – called sl 1B –, K3, rep from * to end.
3rd row Using B, P3, *sl 1 P-wise keeping yarn at front of work – called sl 1F –, P3, rep from * to end.
4th row As 2nd.
5th row Using B, P to end.
6th row Using A, as 2nd.
7th row Using A, as 3rd.
8th row Using A, as 4th.
These 8 rows form the pattern.

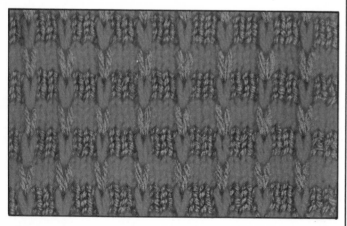

Fancy checked stitch

Two colours of contrasting yarn have been used for this sample, a plain yarn coded as A and a metallic yarn coded as B. Cast on a number of stitches divisible by 6 plus 5 in A.

1st row (RS) Using A, K to end.
2nd row Using A, P to end.
3rd row Using B, K2, *sl 1 P-wise keeping yarn at back of work – called sl 1B –, K1, rep from * to last st, K1.
4th row Using B, K1, *(K1, sl 1 P-wise keeping yarn at front of work – called sl 1F) twice, P1, sl 1F, rep from * to last 4 sts, K1, sl 1F, K2.
5th row Using A, K5, *sl 1B, K5, rep from * to end.
6th row Using A, P5, *sl 1F, P5, rep from * to end.
7th row As 5th.
8th row As 6th.
9th row Using A, as 1st.
10th row Using A, as 2nd.
11th row Using B, K1, *sl 1B, K1, rep from * to end.
12th row Using B, K1, *sl 1F, P1, (sl 1F, K1) twice, rep from * to last 4 sts, sl 1F, P1, s1 1F, K1.
13th row Using A, K2, *sl 1B, K5, rep from * to last 3 sts, sl 1B, K2.
14th row Using A, P2, *sl 1F, P5, rep from * to last 3 sts, sl 1F, P2.
15th row As 13th.
16th row As 14th.
These 16 rows form the pattern.

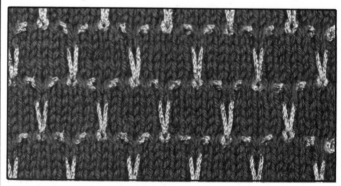

Ribbon stitch

Two colours of contrasting yarn have been used for this sample, a plain yarn coded as A and a macramé cord coded as B. Cast on a number of stitches divisible by 4 plus 3 in A.

1st row (WS) Using A, P to end.
2nd row Using B, K1, *sl 1 P-wise keeping yarn at back of work – called sl 1B –, K3, rep from * to last 2 sts, sl 1B, K1.
3rd row Using B, K1, *sl 1 P-wise keeping yarn at front of work – called sl 1F –, K1, K1 winding yarn 3 times round needle, K1, rep from * to last 2 sts, sl 1F, K1.
4th row Using A, K3, *sl 1B dropping extra loops, K3, rep from * to end.
5th row Using A, P3, *sl 1B, P3, rep from * to end.
6th row Using A, K3, *sl 1B, K3, rep from * to end.

7th row Using A, as 5th.
8th row Using A, as 6th.
These 8 rows form the pattern.

Tapestry stitch
Two colours of the same yarn have been used for this sample, coded as A and B. Cast on a number of stitches divisible by 4 plus 3 in A.

1st row (WS) Using A, P to end.
2nd row Using B, K1, sl 1 P-wise keeping yarn at front of work − called sl 1F −, K1, *sl 1 P-wise keeping yarn at back of work − called sl 1B −, K1, sl 1F, K1, rep from * to end.
3rd row Using B, P3, *sl 1F, P3, rep from * to end.
4th row Using A, K1, *sl 1B, K3, rep from * to last 2 sts, sl 1B, K1.
5th row Using A, P to end.
6th row Using B, K1, sl 1B, K1, *sl 1F, K1, sl 1B, K1, rep from * to end.
7th row Using B, P1, *sl 1F, P3, rep from * to last 2 sts, sl 1F, P1.
8th row Using A, K3, *sl 1B, K3, rep from * to end.
These 8 rows form the pattern.

Lattice stitch
Two colours of contrasting yarn have been used for this sample, a plain yarn coded as A and a metallic yarn coded as B. Cast on a number of stitches divisible by 6 plus 2 in A.

1st row (WS) Using A, K to end.
2nd row Using B, K1, sl 1 P-wise keeping yarn at back of work − called sl 1B −, *K4, sl 2B, rep from * to last 6 sts, K4, sl 1B, K1.
3rd row Using B, P1, sl 1 P-wise keeping yarn at front of work − called sl 1F −, *P4, sl 2F, rep from * to last 6 sts, P4, sl 1F, P1.
4th row Using A, as 2nd.
5th row Using A, K1, sl 1F, *K4, sl 2F, rep from * to last 6 sts, K4, sl 1F, K1.
6th row Using B, K3, *sl 2B, K4, rep from * to last 5 sts, sl 2B, K3.

7th row Using B, P3, *sl 2F, P4, rep from * to last 5 sts, sl 2F, P3.
8th row Using A, as 6th.
9th row Using A, K3, *sl 2F, K4, rep from * to last 5 sts, sl 2F, K3.
Rows 2 − 9 form the pattern.

Cushion

Size
40.5cm (*16in*) wide by 40.5cm (*16in*) deep

Tension
26 sts and 32 rows to 10cm (*3.9in*) over patt worked on No.8 needles

Materials
5 × 25grm balls of Wendy Double Knitting Nylonised in main shade, A
5 balls of contrast colour, B
One pair No.8 needles
40.5cm (*16in*) by 40.5cm (*16in*) cushion pad
1.95 metres (2yd) silk cord, optional
20.5cm (*8in*) zip fastener

Cushion
Using No.8 needles and A, cast on 103 sts. Cont in tapestry st until work measures 40.5cm (*16in*) from beg. Cast off. Make another piece in same way.

To make up
Press each piece under a damp cloth with a warm iron. With RS facing, join 3 sides. Turn RS out. Insert cushion pad. Join rem seam inserting zip in centre. Sew cord round edges, looping at each corner.

MOSAIC PATTERNS

Mosaic patterns are worked in two colours, using the slip-stitch method to form complex and unusual geometric shapes. Although the patterns may appear to be complicated, the working method is very simple and is based on knitting two rows with one colour and two rows with the second colour.

What makes these designs so interesting is that bands of different patterns which require the same multiples of stitches can be worked together to form an overall fabric, using as many different colours as you like. This is another way of using up oddments of yarn which are of the same thickness.

You could use a basic pattern which gives the correct multiples of stitches required for each mosaic pattern to form a colourful and original child's jersey, a cushion or a warm and practical pram or cot cover. Because the yarn is not carried across the back of the work as in Fair Isle knitting, the back of the fabric formed is not untidy and is of a single thickness.

Brick pattern

Two colours are used, coded as A and B. Using A, cast on a number of stitches divisible by 4 plus 3.

1st row (RS) Using A, K to end.
2nd row Using A, P to end.
3rd row Using B, K3, *sl 1, K3, rep from * to end.
4th row Using B, K3, *yfwd, sl 1, ybk, K3, rep from * to end.
5th row Using A, K2, *sl 1, K1, rep from * to last st, K1.
6th row Using A, P2, *sl 1, P1, rep from * to last st, P1.
7th row Using B, K1, *sl 1, K3, rep from * to last 2 sts, sl 1, K1.
8th row Using B, K1, *yfwd, sl 1, ybk, K3, rep from * to last 2 sts, yfwd, sl 1, ybk, K1.
9th and 10th rows As 1st and 2nd.
11th and 12th rows As 7th and 8th.
13th and 14th rows As 5th and 6th.
15th and 16th rows As 3rd and 4th.
These 16 rows form the pattern.

Double brick pattern

Two colours are used, coded as A and B. Using A, cast on a number of stitches divisible by 4 plus 3.

1st row (RS) Using A, K to end.
2nd row Using A, K to end.
3rd row Using B, K3, *sl 1, K3, rep from * to end.
4th row Using B, K3, *yfwd, sl 1, ybk, K3, rep from * to end.
5th row Using A, K1, *sl 1, K3, rep from * to last 2 sts, sl 1, K1.
6th row Using A, K1, *yfwd, sl 1, ybk, K3, rep from * to last 2 sts, yfwd, sl 1, ybk, K1.

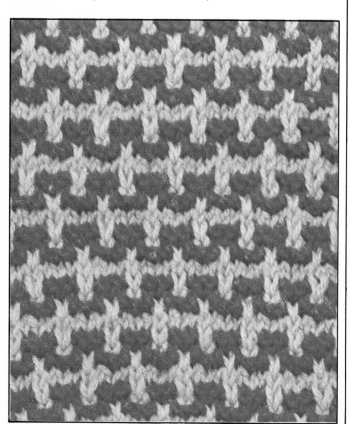

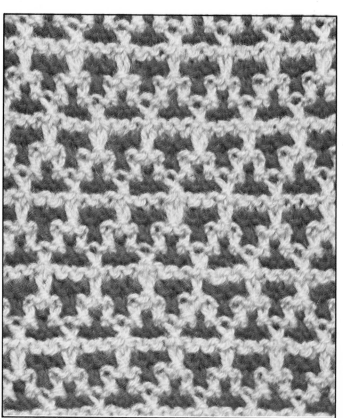

7th row Using B, K2, *sl 1, K1, rep from * to last st, K1.

8th row Using B, K2, *yfwd, sl 1, ybk, K1, rep from * to last st, K1.

9th and 10th rows Using A, as 3rd and 4th.

11th and 12th rows Using B, as 5th and 6th.

13th and 14th rows As 1st and 2nd.

15th and 16th rows As 11th and 12th.

17th and 18th rows As 9th and 10th.

19th and 20th rows As 7th and 8th.

21st and 22nd rows As 5th and 6th.

23rd and 24th rows As 3rd and 4th.

These 24 rows form the pattern.

Vertical chevron pattern

Two colours are used, coded as A and B. Using A, cast on a number of stitches divisible by 6 plus 2.

1st row (RS) Using A, *K5, sl 1, rep from * to last 2 sts, K2.

2nd and every alt row Using same colour as previous row, keep yarn at front of work and P all K sts of previous row and sl all sl sts.

3rd row Using B, K2, * sl 1, K3, sl 1, K1, rep from * to end.

5th row Using A, K3, *sl 1, K5, rep from * to last 5 sts, sl 1, K4.

7th row Using B, K4, *sl 1, K1, sl 1, K3, rep from * to last 4 sts, (sl 1, K1) twice.

9th row Using A, K1, *sl 1, K5, rep from * to last st, K1.

11th row Using B, K2, *sl 1, K1, sl 1, K3, rep from * to end.

13th, 15th, 17th, 19th and 21st rows Rep 1st, 3rd, 5th, 7th and 9th rows.

23rd, 25th, 27th and 29th rows Rep 7th, 5th, 3rd and 1st rows.

31st, 33rd, 35th, 37th and 39th rows Rep 11th, 9th, 7th, 5th and 3rd rows.

40th row As 2nd.

These 40 rows form the pattern.

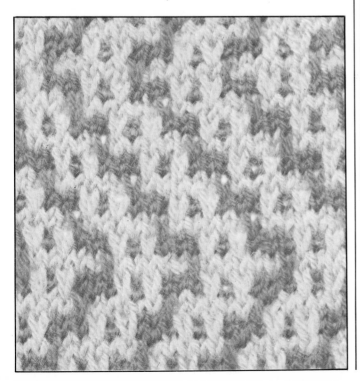

Greek key pattern

Two colours are used, coded as A and B. Using A, cast on a number of stitches divisible by 6 plus 2.

1st row (RS) Using A, K to end.

2nd row Using A, K to end.

3rd row Using B, K1, *sl 1, K5, rep from * to last st, K1.

4th and every alt row Using same colour as previous row, keep the yarn at front of work and K all K sts of previous row and sl all sl sts.

5th row Using A, K2, *sl 1, K3, sl 1, K1, rep from * to end.

7th row Using B, K1, *sl 1, K3, sl 1, K1, rep from * to last st, K1.

9th row Using A, K6, *sl 1, K5, rep from * to last 2 sts, sl 1, K1.

11th and 12th rows Using B, as 1st and 2nd.

13th row Using A, K4, *sl 1, K5, rep from * to last 4 sts, sl 1, K3.

15th row Using B, *K3, sl 1, K1, sl 1, rep from * to last 2 sts, K2.

17th row Using A, K2, *sl 1, K1, sl 1, K3, rep from * to end.

19th row Using B, K3, *sl 1, K5, rep from * to last 5 sts, sl 1, K4.

20th row As 4th.

These 20 rows form the pattern.

Maze pattern

Two colours are used, coded as A and B. Using A, cast on a number of stitches divisible by 12 plus 3.

1st row (RS) Using A, K to end.

2nd row Using A, P to end.

3rd row Using B, K1, *sl 1, K11, rep from * to last 2 sts, sl 1, K1.

4th and every alt row Using same colour as previous row, keep the yarn at front of work and P all K sts of previous row and sl all sl sts.

5th row Using A, K2, *sl 1, K9, sl 1, K1, rep from * to last st, K1.

7th row Using B, (K1, sl 1) twice, *K7, (sl 1, K1) twice, sl 1, rep from * to end omitting sl 1 at end of last rep.

9th row Using A, K2, sl 1, K1, sl 1, *K5, (sl 1, K1) 3 times, sl 1, rep from * to last 10 sts, K5, sl 1, K1, sl 1, K2.

11th row Using B, (K1, sl 1) 3 times, *K3, (sl 1, K1) 4 times, sl 1, rep from * to last 9 sts, K3, (sl 1, K1) 3 times.

13th row Using A, K2, *sl 1, K1, rep from * to last st, K1.

15th, 17th, 19th, 21st, 23rd and 25th rows Rep 11th, 9th, 7th, 5th, 3rd and 1st rows.

27th row Using B, K7, *sl 1, K11, rep from * to last 8 sts, sl 1, K7.

29th row Using A, K6, *sl 1, K1, sl 1, K9, rep from * to last 9 sts, sl 1, K1, sl 1, K6.

31st row Using B, K5, *(sl 1, K1) twice, sl 1, K7, rep from

* to last 10 sts, (sl 1, K1) twice, sl 1, K5.

33rd row Using A, K4, *(sl 1, K1) 3 times, sl 1, K5, rep from * to last 11 sts, (sl 1, K1) 3 times, sl 1, K4.

35th row Using B, K3, *(sl 1, K1) 4 times, sl 1, K3, rep from * to end.

37th row As 13th.

39th, 41st, 43rd, 45th and 47th rows Rep 35th, 33rd, 31st, 29th and 27th rows.

48th row As 4th.

These 48 rows form the pattern.

Lattice window pattern

Two colours are used, coded as A and B. Using A, cast on a number of stitches divisible by 12 plus 3. K 1 row.

1st row (RS) Using B, K1, *sl 1, K11, rep from * to last 2 sts, sl 1, K1.

2nd and every alt row Using same colour as previous row, keep the yarn at front of work and K all K sts of previous row and sl all sl sts.

3rd row Using A, K4, *(sl 1, K1) 3 times, sl 1, K5, rep from * to last 11 sts, (sl 1, K1) 3 times, sl 1, K4.

5th row Using B, K3, *sl 1, K7, sl 1, K3, rep from * to end.

7th row Using A, K2, *sl 1, K3, sl 1, K1, rep from * to last st, K1.

9th row Using B, K5, *sl 1, K3, sl 1, K7, rep from * to last 10 sts, sl 1, K3, sl 1, K5.

11th row Using A, K2, *sl 1, K1, sl 1, K5, (sl 1, K1) twice, rep from * to last st, K1.

13th row Using B, K7, *sl 1, K11, rep from * to last 8 sts, sl 1, K7.

15th and 16th rows As 11th and 12th.

17th and 18th rows As 9th and 10th.

19th and 20th rows As 7th and 8th.

21st and 22nd rows As 5th and 6th.

23rd and 24th rows As 3rd and 4th.

These 24 rows form the pattern.

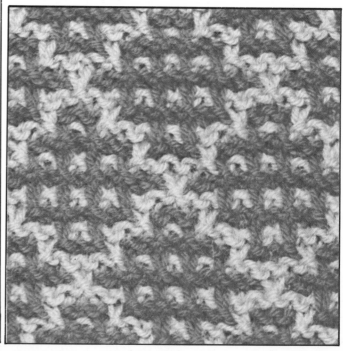

MOCK FAIR ISLE

Although they look rather complicated, Fair Isle patterns are quite simple to work as they rarely use more than two colours in one row at a time. The beautiful, multi-coloured effects are achieved by varying the two combinations of colours.

A form of 'mock' Fair Isle, however, is even simpler to work as this only requires two colours throughout – a plain background colour and a random yarn used for the contrast colour. As the random yarn is worked, it changes its colour sequence to give a most striking effect.

Unlike striped patterns, where the colour is changed at the end of a row, two yarns will be in use during the course of a row. As only a few stitches are worked in one colour, the yarn not in use can be carried loosely across the back off the work until it is required, then twisted round the last colour before it is brought into use again (see colour in knitting).

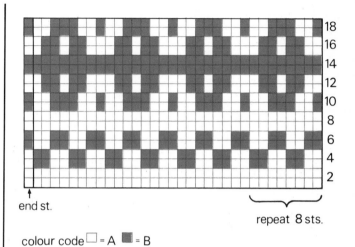

end st.

repeat 8 sts.

colour code ☐ = A ◼ = B

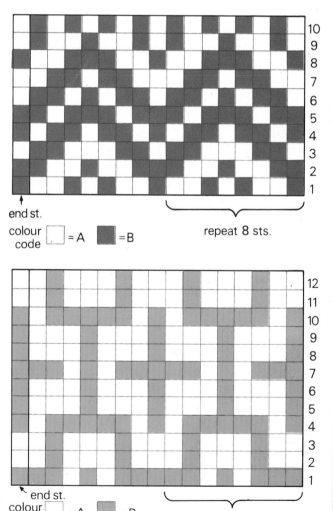

end st.

colour code ☐ = A ◼ = B

repeat 8 sts.

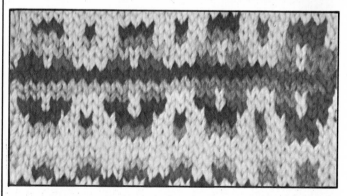

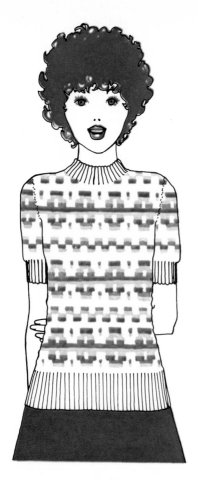

Three 'mock' Fair Isle patterns

We give three samples and charts here, any one of which can be used for the short sleeved jersey, as each pattern requires multiples of 8 stitches plus one.

Mock Fair Isle jersey
Sizes
To fit 86.5[91.5:96.5:101.5]cm (34[36:38:40]in) bust
Length to shoulder, 61[62:66:67.5]cm (24[24½:26:26½]in)
Sleeve seam, 10cm (4in)
The figures in brackets [] refer to the 91.5 (36), 96.5 (38) and 101.5cm (40in) sizes respectively

Tension
26 sts and 32 rows to 10cm (3.9in) over patt worked on No.9 needles

Materials
7[7:8:8] × 40grm balls of Wendy Marina Double Crepe in main shade, A
6[7:8:9] × 20grm balls of Wendy Random Courtelle Double Crepe in contrast colour, B
One pair No.9 needles
One pair No.11 needles

Back
Using No.11 needles and A, cast on 113[121:129:137] sts.
1st row K1, *P1, K1, rep from * to end.
2nd row P1, *K1, P1, rep from * to end.
Rep these 2 rows 11 times more. Change to No.9 needles. Beg with a K row cont in st st, working in any patt from chart, until work measures 43[43:45.5:45.5] cm (17[17:18:18]in) from beg, ending with a WS row.

Shape armholes
Keeping patt correct, cast off 6[7:8:9] sts at beg of next 2 rows. Dec one st at each end of next 8[9:10:11] rows. 85[89:93:97] sts. Cont in patt without shaping until armholes measure 18[19:20.5:21.5]cm (7[7½:8:8½] in) from beg, ending with a WS row.

Shape shoulders
Cast off at beg of next and every row 8[8:9:9] sts twice, 8[9:9:9] sts twice and 9[9:9:10] sts twice. Leave rem 35[37:39:41] sts on holder for back neck.

Front
Work as given for back until armhole shaping has been completed. 85[89:93:97] sts. Cont without shaping until armholes measure 14[15:16.5:18]cm (5½[6:6½:7]in) from beg, ending with a WS row.

Shape neck
Next row Patt 32[33:34:35], turn and leave rem sts on holder.
Complete this side first. Dec one st at neck edge on next and every row 7 times in all. 25[26:27:28] sts. Cont without shaping until front matches back to shoulder, ending at armhole edge.

Shape shoulder
Cast off at beg of next and every alt row 8[8:9:9] sts once, 8[9:9:9] sts once and 9[9:9:10] sts once.
With RS of work facing, sl first 21[23:25:27] sts on holder for front neck, rejoin yarn to rem sts and patt to end. Complete to match first side, reversing shaping.

Short sleeves
Using No.11 needles and A, cast on 81[89:89:97] sts. Work 12 rows rib as given for back. Change to No.9 needles. Beg with a K row cont in st st, working in any patt from chart and inc one st at each end of 3rd and every foll 6th row, until there are 87[95:95:103] sts. Cont without shaping until sleeve measures 10cm (4in) from beg, ending with a WS row.

Shape top
Cast off 6[7:8:9] sts at beg of next 2 rows. Dec one st at each end of next and every foll alt row until 47[55:47:49] sts rem. Patt one row. Cast off 2 sts at beg of next 16[18:14:14] rows. Cast off rem 15[17:19:21] sts.

Neckband
Join right shoulder seam. Using No.11 needles, A and with RS of work facing, K up 18 sts down left front neck, K across front neck sts on holder, K up 19 sts up right front neck and K across back neck sts on holder. 87[91:95:99] sts. Work 12 rows rib as given for back. Cast off loosely in rib.

To make up
Press under a dry cloth with a warm iron. Join left shoulder and neckband seam. Set in sleeves. Join side and sleeve seams. Press seams.

Toddler's dressing gown

The mock Fair Isle technique has been used for this trendy cardigan dressing gown for a toddler. An even more interesting pattern has been achieved, however, by using a plain background with a contrasting random yarn for the first pattern repeat, then reversing the pattern by using a second random yarn as the background and a second plain colour for the contrast for the next repeat.

Dressing gown
Sizes
To fit 56[61]cm (22[24]in) chest
Length to shoulder, 56[61]cm (22[24]in)

Sleeve seam, 16.5[20.5]cm (6½[8]in)
The figures in brackets [] refer to the 61cm (24in) size only

Tension
28 sts and 36 rows to 10cm (3.9in) over patt worked on No.10 needles

Materials
3[4] × 20grm balls of Sirdar Wash'n'wear 4 ply Crepe in 1st contrast, A
3[3] × 25grm balls of Sirdar Multi 4 ply in 2nd contrast, B
2[2] × 20grm balls of Sirdar Wash'n'Wear 4 ply Crepe in 3rd contrast, G

2[3] × 25grm balls of Sirdar Multi 4 ply in 4th contrast, D
One pair No.10 needles
One pair No.12 needles
8 buttons

Back and fronts

Using No.12 needles and A, cast on 162[175] sts and work in one piece to underarm. Beg with a K row work 9 rows st st.

Next row K all sts tbl to form hemline.

Change to No.10 needles. Beg with a K row cont in st st, join in B and work **22 rows from chart using A and B. Break off A and B. Join in C and D and work 22 rows from chart, using C for A and D for B. **. Cont in patt from ** to ** until work measures 43[47.5] cm (17[18¾]in) from hemline, ending with a WS row.

Divide for armholes

Next row Patt 37[39] sts, cast off 6[8] sts, patt 76[81] sts, cast off 6[8] sts, patt 37[39] sts.

Complete left front first. Keeping patt correct, dec one st at armhole edge on every row until 31[32] sts rem. Cont without shaping until armhole measures 9[9.5]cm (3½[3¾]in) from beg, ending at neck edge.

Shape neck

Cast off 5 sts at beg of next row. Dec one st at neck edge on every row until 20[20] sts rem. Cont without shaping until armhole measures 11.5[12]cm (4½[4¾]in) from beg, ending at armhole edge.

Shape shoulder

Cast off at beg of next and foll alt row 10 sts twice.

With WS of work facing, rejoin yarn to sts for back. Keeping patt correct, dec one st at each end of every row until 64[67] sts rem. Cont without shaping until armholes measure same as left front to shoulder, ending with a WS row.

Shape shoulders

Cast off at beg of next and every row 10 sts 4 times and 24[27] sts once.

With WS of work facing, rejoin yarn to rem sts and complete right front to match left front, reversing shaping.

Sleeves

Using No.12 needles and A, cast on 44[48] sts. Work 10 rows K1, P1 rib, inc 19[15] sts evenly across last row. 63[63] sts. Change to No.10 needles. Cont in patt as given for back until sleeve measures 16.5[20.5]cm (6½[8]in) from beg, taking care to beg with a patt row and colour which will enable sleeve seam to be completed on same row as back and fronts at underarm, ending with a WS row.

Shape top

Cast off 3[4] sts at beg of next 2 rows. Dec one st at each end of next and every alt row until 39[41] sts rem, then at each end of every row until 27 sts rem. Dec 2 sts at each end of every row until 11 sts rem. Cast off.

Button band

Using No.12 needles and A, cast on 12 sts. Work in

K1, P1 rib until band is long enough, when slightly stretched, to fit from hemline to beg of neck shaping. Leave sts on holder. St button band in place on left front for a girl and right front for a boy from hemline to neck. Mark positions for 8 buttons on button band, the first to come in neckband with 7 more evenly spaced at 5cm (2in) intervals, measured from base of previous buttonhole.

Buttonhole band

Work as given for button band, making buttonholes as markers are reached, as foll:

1st row (buttonhole row) Rib 5 sts, cast off 2, rib to end.
2nd row Rib to end, casting on 2 sts above those cast off in previous row.
Leave sts on holder.

Neckband

Join shoulder seams. St buttonhole band in place. Using No.12 needles, A and with RS of work facing, sl 12 sts of band on to needle, K up 59[63] sts evenly round neck then rib across rem sts on holder. Work 1 row K1, P1 rib. Make buttonhole as before on next 2 rows. Work 3 more rows rib. Cast off in rib.

To make up

Press each piece under a damp cloth with a warm iron. Join sleeve seams. Set in sleeves. Press seams. Turn hem to WS at lower edge and sl down. Sew on buttons.

2nd. size 1st.size 9 st. repeat for sleeves 1st.size 2nd.size
end   end   beg.   beg.

☐ =A–1st.contrast   ■ =B–2nd. contrast

TRADITIONAL FAIR ISLE
Simple patterns

Traditional Fair Isle patterns produce beautiful designs and fabrics, which are world-renowned for their subtle colour combinations. Ideally, they should be worked in the authentic, softly shaded yarn but they look just as effective when worked in bright, contrasting colours.

These patterns may be used to form an all-over fabric or as a border to highlight the welt and sleeves of a basic jersey or cardigan. When the pattern is small and is repeated as an all-over design, it is a fairly simple matter to work from a chart, where each colour in the pattern is shown as a separate symbol. Some knitters, however, experience difficulty in working from a chart when the pattern is large and fairly complex, particularly where shaping is required. In this event, it is preferable to work from a pattern which gives row-by-row instructions, where each separate colour is coded with a letter, such as A, B or C. To help you decide which method you wish to follow, the patterns here have been given with row by row instructions.

Fair Isle pattern No. 1

Cast on multiples of 12 stitches plus 6.

1st row *K3 A, 1 B, 5 A, 1 B, 2 A, rep from * to last 6 sts, 3 A, 1 B, 2 A.
2nd row *(P1 A, 1 B) twice, 2 A, rep from * to end.
3rd row *K1 A, 1 B, 3 A, 1 B, rep from * to end.
4th row As 2nd.
5th row *K1 B, 2 A, rep from * to end.
6th row *(P1 B, 1 A) twice, 2 B, rep from * to end.
7th row *K2 B, (1 A, 1 B) twice, rep from * to end.
Rep 6th and 7th rows once more.
10th row *P2 A, 1 B, rep from * to end.
11th row *K2 A, (1 B, 1 A) twice, rep from * to end.

12th row *P1 B, 3 A, 1 B, 1 A, rep from * to end.
13th row As 11th.
14th row *P2 A, 1 B, 5 A, 1 B, 3 A, rep from * to last 6 sts, 2 A, 1 B, 3 A.
15th row *K1 B, 5 A, rep from * to end.
16th row *P1 B, 3 A, 1 B, 1 A, rep from * to end.
17th row *K2 A, (1 B, 1 A) twice, rep from * to end.
18th row As 16th.
19th row *K1 B, 2 A, rep from * to end.
20th row *P1 A, 3 B, 1 A, 1 B, rep from * to end.
21st row *K1 B, 1 A, 3 B, 1 A, rep from * to end. Rep 20th and 21st rows once more.
24th row *P2 A, 1 B, rep from * to end.
25th row *K1 A, 1 B, 3 A, 1 B, rep from * to end.
26th row *(P1 A, 1 B) twice, 2 A, rep from * to end.
27th row As 25th.
28th row *P5 A, 1 B, rep from * to end.
These 28 rows form the pattern.

Fair Isle pattern No. 2

Cast on multiples of 18 stitches plus 1.
1st row *K1 B, 1 A, rep from * to last st, 1 B.
2nd row Using A, P to end.
3rd row Using A, K to end.
4th row *P1 C, 1 A, 1 C, 6 A, 1 C, 6 A, 1 C, 1 A, rep from * to last st, 1 C.
5th row *K2 C, 1 A, 1 C, 4 A, 3 C, 4 A, 1 C, 1 A, 1 C, rep from * to last st, 1 C.
6th row *P1 C, 3 A, 1 C, 2 A, 2 C, 1 A, 2 C, 2 A, 1 C, 3 A, rep from * to last st, 1 C.
7th row *K1 C, 4 A, 1 C, 1 A, 5 C, 1 A, 1 C, 4 A, rep from * to last st, 1 C.
8th row *P1 A, 1 C, 4 A, 3 C, 1 A, 3 C, 4 A, 1 C, rep from * to last st, 1 A.
9th row *K1 B, 3 A, 3 B, 2 A, 1 B, 2 A, 3 B, 3 A, rep from

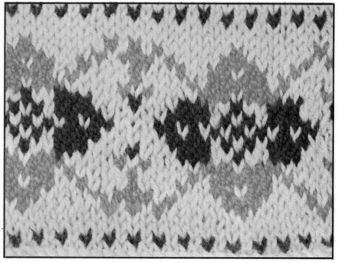

* to last st, 1 B.
10th row *P3 A, 4 B, (1 A, 1 B) twice, 1 A, 4 B, 2 A, rep from * to last st, 1 A.
11th row *K2 A, 2 B, (1 A, 1 B) 5 times, 1 A, 2 B, 1 A, rep from * to last st, 1 A.
Rep 10th to 1st rows. These 21 rows form border pattern, working 22nd row for all-over pattern.

Fair Isle pattern No. 3
Cast on multiples of 18 stitches plus 1.
1st row *K1 B, 1 A, rep from * to last st, 1 B.
2nd row *P1 A, 1 B, rep from * to last st, 1 A.
3rd row Using A, K to end.
4th row Using A, P to end.
5th row As 3rd.
6th row *P3 A, 1 C, 5 A, 1 C, 5 A, 1 C, 2 A, rep from * to last st, 1 A.
7th row *K2 A, 2 C, 4 A, 3 C, 4 A, 2 C, 1 A, rep from * to last st, 1 A.
8th row *P1 A, 3 C, 5 A, 1 C, 5 A, 3 C, rep from * to last st, 1 A.
9th row *K1 D, 2 C, 2 D, 3 C, 3 D, 3 C, 2 D, 2 C, rep from * to last st, 1 D.
10th row *P1 D, 1 C, 2 D, 3 C, 5 D, 3 C, 2 D, 1 C, rep from * to last st, 1 D.
11th row *K1 B, 2 E, 3 B, 3 E, 1 B, 3 E, 3 B, 2 E, rep from * to last st, 1 B.
12th row *P1 F, 2 B, 5 F, 3 B, 5 F, 2 B, rep from * to last st, 1 F.
Rep 11th to 3rd rows.
22nd row *P1 B, 1 A, rep from * to last st, 1 B.
23rd row *K1 A, 1 B, rep from * to last st, 1 A.
These 23 rows form border pattern, repeating 22 rows only for all-over pattern.

Fair Isle pattern No. 4
Cast on multiples of 28 stitches plus 1.
1st row *K2 B, 1 A, 1 B, rep from * to last st, 1 B.
2nd row *P1 B, 3 A, rep from * to last st, 1 B.
3rd row Using A, K to end.
4th row *P1 A, 2 C, 2 A, 2 C, 2 A, 2 C, 3 A, 1 C, 3 A, 2 C, 2 A, 2 C, 2 A, 2 C, rep from * to last st, 1 A.
5th row *K1 A, 1 C, (2 A, 2 C) twice, 3 A, 1 C, 1 A, 1 C, 3 A, (2 C, 2 A) twice, 1 C, rep from * to last st, 1 A.
6th row *P1 A, 1 C, 1 A, 2 C, 2 A, 2 C, 3 A, (1 C, 1 A) twice, 1 C, 3 A, 2 C, 2 A, 2 C, 1 A, 1 C, rep from * to last st, 1 A.
7th row *K1 A, 3 C, 2 A, 2 C, 3 A, 1 C, 1 A, 3 C, 1 A, 1 C, 3 A, 2 C, 2 A, 3 C, rep from * to last st, 1 A.
8th row *P1 A, 2 C, 2 A, 2 C, 3 A, 1 C, 2 A, 3 C, 2 A, 1 C, 3 A, 2 C, 2 A, 2 C, rep from * to last st, 1 A.
9th row *K1 A, 1 D, 2 A, 2 D, 3 A, 3 D, 2 A, 1 D, 2 A, 3 D, 3 A, 2 D, 2 A, 1 D, rep from * to last st, 1 A.
10th row *P1 A, 1 D, 1 A, 2 D, 3 A, 1 D, 2 A, 2 D, 1 A, 1 D, 1 A, 2 D, 2 A, 1 D, 3 A, 2 D, 1 A, 1 D, rep from *to last st, 1 A.
11th row *K1 A, 3 D, 3 A, 2 D, 3 A, 5 D, 3 A, 2 D, 3 A, 3 D, rep from * to last st, 1 A.
12th row *P1 A, 2 D, 3 A, 1 D, 1 A, 2 D, 3 A, 3 D, 3 A, 2 D, 1 A, 1 D, 3 A, 2 D, rep from * to last st, 1 A.
13th row *K1 A, 1 D, 3 A, 1 D, 3 A, 2 D, 3 A, 1 D, 3 A, 2 D, 3 A, 1 D, 3 A, 1 D, rep from * to last st, 1 A.
14th row *P1 A, 1 D, 2 A, 1 D, 1 A, 2 D, 2 A, 2 D, (1 A, 1 D) twice, 1 A, 2 D, 2 A, 2 D, 1 A, 1 D, 2 A, 1 D, rep from * to last st, 1 A.
15th row *K1 A, (1 B, 1 A) twice, 8 B, 1 A, 1 B, 1 A, 8 B, (1 A, 1 B) twice, rep from * to last st, 1 A.
Rep from 14th to 1st rows. These 29 rows form border pattern, working 30th row for all-over pattern.

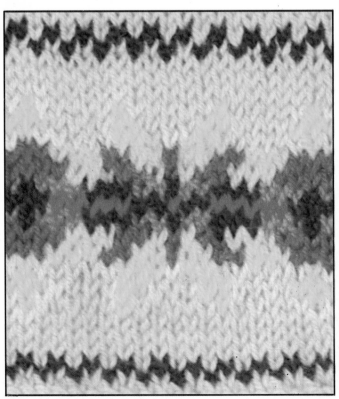

Snowflake patterns

The Scandinavian countries provide an endless source of what are loosely termed 'Fair Isle' designs, particularly variations of the delightful snowflake pattern. They are worked in the same way as the traditional Shetland designs but the patterns are usually bolder and the choice of colour is more distinctive.

From the middle European countries and further east, more intricate and colourful designs are introduced, often involving the use of three or more colours at a time. These beautiful fabrics, often based upon traditional carpet designs, feature floral or symmetrical patterns in rich, jewel colours.

To look most effective, the samples given here should not be used as over-all patterns but as borders, pockets, or cuff motifs.

Border pattern

This can either be worked as a horizontal or vertical

border. For a horizontal border cast on multiples of 20 stitches plus 7 and work the 7 pattern rows from the chart. To work the border vertically, turn the chart sideways and work over 7 stitches for 20 rows.

Star pattern

Another motif which can be used singly or as a horizontal border pattern.

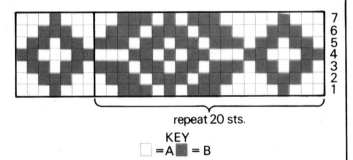

repeat 20 sts.

KEY
☐ = A ■ = B

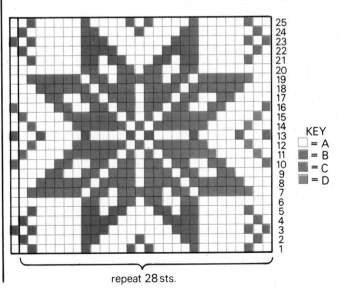

repeat 28 sts.

KEY
☐ = A
▨ = B
■ = C
▦ = D

JACQUARD KNITTING

Whereas traditional Fair Isle knitting normally uses only two colours in any one row, jacquard, collage and patchwork knitting are all forms of the same technique, where more than two colours are used at a time in any one pattern row. These designs are best worked in stocking stitch against a stocking stitch background, although collage knitting may also combine many different stitches to great effect.

Unlike Fair Isle knitting, this means that this method is very clumsy and untidy to work, when more than one strand has to be carried across the back of the work until required again. It is possible to work a small repeating jacquard design in this way, carrying the yarn not in use loosely across the back of the work but this does, inevitably, mean a variance in tension against the main fabric. When working in this way, it is therefore advisable to change to one size larger needles to work the jacquard pattern, reverting to the correct needle size to work the main pattern.

The correct method of working all large, multi-coloured patterns, motifs, wide vertical stripes and patchwork designs, is to use small, separate balls of yarn for each colour. In this way a fabric of single thickness is formed, without any strands of yarn across the back of the work. These patterns are usually worked from a chart, just as in Fair Isle knitting, with each different colour coded with a symbol.

Use of bobbins

Before beginning to knit, wind all the colours which are required into small, separate balls round a bobbin. These are easy to handle and hang at the back of the work, keeping each colour free from tangles.

To make a bobbin Use a stiff piece of cardboard and cut to shape as shown in the diagram, having a slit at the top of each bobbin. Wind the yarn round the centre of the bobbin with the working end passing through the slit as illustrated.

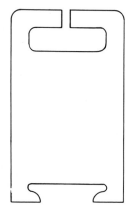
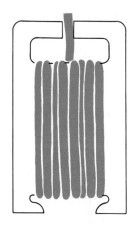

Joining in each new colour

The next important point to remember is that knitting patterns of a geometric or random shape, such as diamonds or flower motifs, as opposed to straight vertical stripes, require the colour to be changed by means of looping the two yarns round each other, on a right side row, to avoid gaps in the knitting. On the return purl row it is not so essential to loop the yarns round each other, as the purl stitch will probably encroach into the pattern sequence and the yarns will automatically be looped. Vertical bands of colour, however, must be looped on every row, as there will be no encroaching stitch to form a natural link in either direction.

To loop yarns on a knit row Keep each ball of yarn at the back of the work until it is required, knit the last stitch in the first colour, then take this end of yarn over the next colour to be used and drop it, pick up the next colour under this strand of yarn, take it over the strand ready to knit the next stitch.

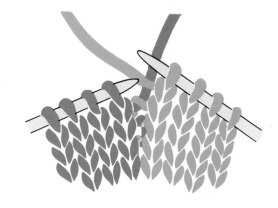

To loop yarns on a purl row Keep each ball of yarn at the front of the work until it is required, purl the last stitch in the first colour, then take this end of yarn over the next colour to be used and drop it, pick up the next colour under this strand of yarn, take it over the strand ready to purl the next stitch.

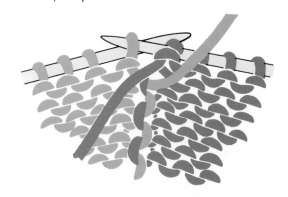

Jacquard borders

Begin by working something as simple as an all-over jacquard border pattern in three colours, stranding each colour across the back of the work until it is required again.

In these charts, the background, or main colour, is coded as A and shown as a blank square; the first contrast colour is coded as B and the 2nd contrast colour coded as C.

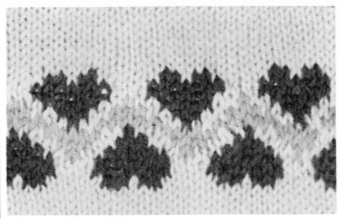

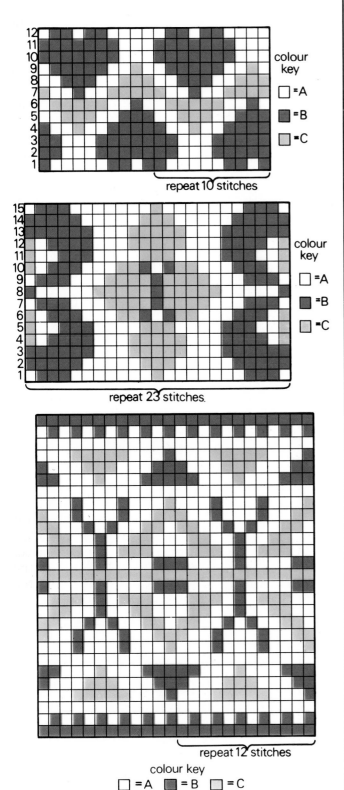

colour key

☐ =A

■ =B

☐ =C

repeat 10 stitches

colour key

☐ =A

■ =B

☐ =C

repeat 23 stitches.

repeat 12 stitches

colour key

☐ =A   ■ =B   ☐ =C

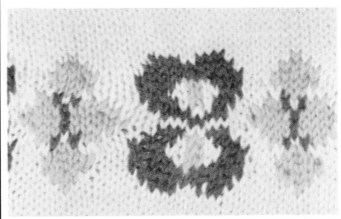

MOTIFS AND COLLAGE

As explained in the previous Chapter, jacquard and collage knitting provide tremendous scope for interesting all-over patterned fabrics, or as a single motif incorporated into an otherwise plain background.

The examples shown here should be worked with small, separate balls of yarn, twisting the yarns at the back of the work when changing colours.

Motifs

Almost any shape or design can be used as a separate jacquard motif, but if you are working out your own pattern it must be charted out on graph paper first, allowing one square for each stitch and one line of squares for each row. Code each different colour with a symbol and make a colour key of these symbols.

If you do not want to make up your own design, use an embroidery chart, such as given for cross stitch embroidery, and adapt this to suit your own colour scheme, again coding each different colour with a symbol.

Butterfly motif

This motif is worked in five contrasting colours against a plain background, making six colours in all. Each motif requires a total of 28 stitches and 34 rows to complete.

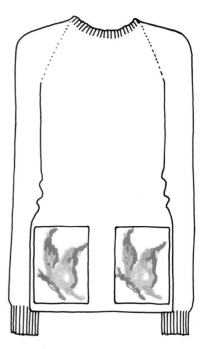

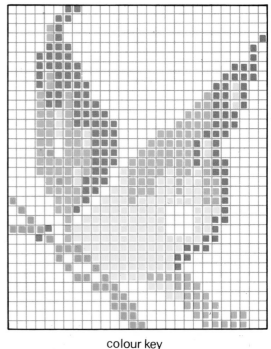

colour key

■=B ■=C □=D ■=E □=F

Heart motif

Here again, five contrasting colours have been used against a plain background, making a total of six. Each motif requires a total of 35 stitches and 32 rows to complete.

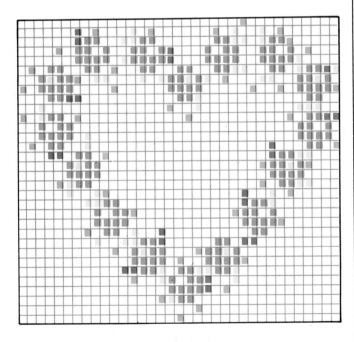

Multi-coloured collage pattern

This design can be worked with as many colours as you require, varying the sequence to ensure that you

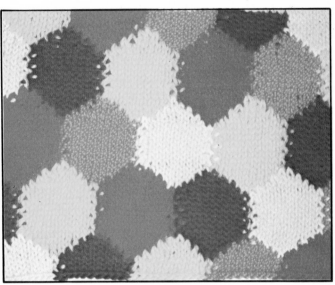

do not use the same colours next to each other.
Cast on a number of stitches divisible by 10, using the main colour. The sample shown here has been worked over 50 stitches with five colours.

1st row (RS) K10 sts in each of 5 colours.

2nd row Using same colours, P10 sts in each of 5 colours.

Rep 1st and 2nd rows once more.

5th row Varying colour sequence as required, K1 with contrast colour, K8 with original colour, *K2 with next contrast colour, K8 with original colour, rep from * to last st, K1 with last contrast colour.

6th row P2 with same contrast colour, *P6 with original colour, P4 with same contrast colour, rep from * to last 8 sts, P6 with original colour, P2 with same contrast colour.

7th row K3 with same contrast colour, *K4 with original colour, K6 with same contrast colour, rep from * to last 7 sts, K4 with original colour, K3 with same contrast colour.

8th row P4 with same contrast colour, *P2 with original colour, break off original colour, P8 with same contrast colour, rep from * to last 6 sts, P2 with original colour, break off original colour, P4 with same contrast colour.

9th row K5 with same contrast colour, keeping colour sequence correct as now set, K10 sts with each colour to last 5 sts, K5 sts with same colour.

10th row P as 9th row.

Rep 9th and 10th rows 3 times more.

17th row K4 sts with original colour as now set, *K2 sts with next contrast colour, K8 sts with original colour as now set, rep from * to last 6 sts, K2 with next contrast colour, K4 with original colour as now set.

18th row P3 sts with original colour, *P4 with same contrast colour, P6 with original colour, rep from * to last 7 sts, P4 with same contrast colour, P3 with

101

original colour.

19th row K2 with original colour, *K6 with same contrast colour, K4 with original colour, rep from * to last 8 sts, K6 with same contrast colour, K2 with original colour.

20th row P1 with original colour, break off original colour, *P8 with same contrast colour, P2 with original colour, break off original colour, rep from * to last 9 sts, P8 with same contrast colour, P1 with original colour, break off original colour.

21st row Keeping colour sequence correct as now set, work as given for 1st row.

22nd row As 2nd

23rd row As 1st.

24th row As 2nd.

These 24 rows form the pattern.

Collage pram cover
Size
56cm (*22in*) wide by 81.5cm (*32in*) long

Tension
18 sts and 22 rows to 10cm (*3.9in*) over st st worked on No.6 needles

Materials
5 × 50grm balls of Sirdar Pullman in main shade, A

1 ball each of 7 contrast colours, B, C, D, E, F, G and H
One pair No.6 needles

Pram cover centre
Using No.6 needles and A, cast on 80 sts. Work in multi-coloured collage pattern until work measures 71cm (*28in*) from beg, ending with a 12th patt row. Cast off.

Border
Using No.6 needles and A, cast on 100 sts. K 16 rows g st.

Next row K10 sts, cast off 80 sts, K10 sts.
Complete this side first. Cont in g st until band fits along side edge of cover, ending at inside edge. Break off yarn. Leave sts on holder.

With WS of work facing, rejoin yarn to rem 10 sts and complete to match first side, ending at outside edge. Do not break off yarn.

Next row K across first 10 sts, turn and cast on 80 sts, K across rem 10 sts on holder. 100 sts.
K16 rows g st. Cast off loosely.

To make up
Press centre only under a damp cloth with a warm iron. With RS facing, sew border round outer edge of centre. Press seams.

PATCHWORK KNITTING

Completely random patchwork fabrics are worked in the same way as collage patterns, using separate balls of yarn for each colour.

Each patch can be worked over any even number of stitches, or as many number of rows as required, and as each patch is completed it is not necessary to cast off, as you simply carry on with the next patch and colour sequence. The exciting part of this technique comes in arranging the sequence of patches, as no two knitters will work either the same colour or patch in identical order, so each sample has a completely original appearance.

The required number of stitches may be cast on to work two, three, or more patches side by side to give an overall fabric, or single patches can be worked in separate strips to the required length and then sewn together. The latter method means that shaping can be achieved on each side of the strips, to achieve a well-fitting skirt or the delightful patchwork dungarees shown here.

Patchwork samples

In all the examples given here the first, or main colour, is coded as A, the next colour as B, the next as C, and so on and a total of six colours have been used. Once you have decided which colours you would like to use, make a note of the sequence in which you are going to work them so that when you have to pick up contrast colour E you will know immediately to which colour this refers.

These samples have been worked over 28 stitches, allowing 30 rows for each patch. Cast on with A.

1st patch
1st row Using A, K to end.
2nd row Using A, P to end.
Rep these 2 rows 14 times more, using each colour in turn to form stripes. 30 rows.

2nd patch
1st row K14 B, 14 C.
2nd row P14 C, 14 B.
Rep these 2 rows 6 times more.
15th row Using D, K to end.
16th row Using D, P to end.
17th row K14 E, 14 F.
18th row P14 F, 14 E.
Rep last 2 rows 6 times more. 30 rows.

3rd patch
1st row Using A, K to end.
2nd row Using A, P to end.
Rep these 2 rows 4 times more.
11th row K10 B, 8 C, 10 D.
12th row P10 D, 8 C, 10 B.
Rep last 2 rows 9 times more. 30 rows.

4th patch
1st row Using E, K to end.
2nd row Using E, P to end.
Rep these 2 rows 14 times more. 30 rows.
Each time you work a repeat of this patch, use a different colour.

5th patch
1st row K12 F, 4 A, 12 B.
2nd row P12 B, 4 A, 12 F.
Rep these 2 rows 5 times more.
13th row Using C, K to end.
14th row Using C, P to end.
Rep last 2 rows twice more.
19th row K12 D, 4 E, 12 F.
20th row P12 F, 4 E, 12 D.
Rep last 2 rows 5 times more. 30 rows.

Dungarees

Size
Length to back waist, 45.5cm (*18in*)
Inside leg, 25.5cm (*10 in*)

Tension
30 sts and 38 rows to 10cm (*3.9in*) over st st worked on No.10 needles

Materials
2 × 25grm balls of Emu Scotch Superwash 4 ply in main shade, A
1 ball each of 5 contrast colours, B, C, D, E and F
One pair No.10 needles
2 buttons
Waist length of elastic

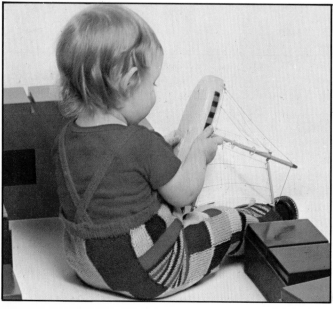

Right front leg
**Using No.10 needles and A, cast on 28 sts. Beg with a K row work 7 rows st st.
Next row Using A, K all sts tbl to form hemline. Work 1st, 2nd, 3rd, 4th and 5th patches, dec one st at beg of 9th and every foll 4th row 4 times in all, noting that less sts will be worked in first block of colour. 24 sts. Cont in patt without shaping until 60th patt row has been completed. **. Keeping patt correct, inc one st at beg of next and every foll 4th row 6 times in all, noting that extra sts will be worked in first block of colour. 30 sts. Cont without shaping until 82nd patt row has been completed.

Shape crotch
Cast off 2 sts at beg of next row. Work 1 row. Dec one st at beg of next and foll alt rows 4 times in all. 24 sts. Cont without shaping until 142nd patt row has been completed. Using A, work 8 rows K1, P1 rib. Cast off loosely in rib.

Right side leg
Using No.10 needles and A, cast on 32 sts. Work hem as given for right front leg. Work 4th, 5th, 2nd, 1st and 3rd patches, shaping dart on 9th row as foll:—

1st dec row Patt 14 sts, K2 tog, sl 1, K1, psso, patt 14 sts. Work 3 rows without shaping.
2nd dec row Patt 13 sts, K2 tog, sl 1, K1, psso, patt 13 sts. Work 3 rows without shaping. Cont dec in this way twice more. 24 sts. Cont in patt without shaping until 143rd row has been completed, ending with a K row.

Shape back
***Next 2 rows** Patt to last 8 sts, turn, patt to end.
Next 2 rows Patt to last 16 sts, turn, patt to end.
Next row Patt across all sts.
Using A, work 8 rows K1, P1 rib. Cast off loosely in rib.
***

Right back leg
Work as given for right front leg from ** to ** reversing shaping and working 3rd, 1st, 5th, 2nd and 4th patches. Inc one st at end of next and every alt row 10 times in all, noting that extra sts will be worked in last block of colour. 34 sts. Cont in patt without shaping until 83rd row has been completed, ending with a K row.

Shape crotch
Cast off 2 sts at beg of next row. Work 1 row. Dec one st at beg of next and every alt row 8 times in all. 24 sts. Cont in patt until 149th row has been completed, ending with a K row.

Shape back
Work as given for side from *** to ***, continuing 4th patch.

Left leg
Work 3 sections as given for right leg, reversing all shaping and sequence of patches, as required.

Bib
Using No.10 needles and A, cast on 44 sts.
1st row Using A, (K1, P1) 4 times, patt 28 sts as 1st row of 5th patch, using separate ball of A, (P1, K1) 4 times.
2nd row Using A, (P1, K1) 4 times, patt 28 sts as given for 2nd row of 5th patch, using A, (K1, P1) 4 times.
Cont in this way until 30th row of patch has been completed. Using A, work 8 rows K1, P1 rib across all sts.
Next row Rib 8, cast off 28 sts, rib to end.
Cont in rib on each set of 8 sts until strap is long enough to reach centre back of dungarees, making a buttonhole 2.5cm (*1 in*) before casting off as foll:—
Next row (buttonhole row) Rib 3 sts, yfwd to make 1, work 2 tog, rib 3 sts.

To make up
Press each part under a damp cloth with a warm iron. Join 3 right leg sections tog including hem and waistband. Join left leg in same way. Press seams. Join front, back and inner leg seams. Turn hems to WS at lower edge and sl st down. St bib in centre of front at top of waist ribbing. Sew elastic inside waistband from each side of bib using casing st. Sew on buttons inside back waist.

ADVANCED STITCHES
SIX STITCH PATTERNS

All patterns given here are made up of multiples of six stitches plus two edge stitches. Using the basic pattern which follows, which gives a tension of 24 stitches and 32 rows to 10cm (3.9in), you can use any of these stitches providing you make sure you achieve the correct tension over stocking stitch.

Cane basket stitch
Cast on a number of stitches divisible by 6 + 2.
1st row K2, *P4, K2, rep from * to end.
2nd row P2, *K4, P2, rep from * to end.
Rep these 2 rows once more.
5th row P3, *K2, P4, rep from * to last 5 sts, K2, P3.
6th row K3, *P2, K4, rep from * to last 5 sts, P2, K3.
Rep last 2 rows once more. These 8 rows form the pattern.

5th row P1, *sl next 2 sts on to cable needle and hold at back of work, K1 then P2 from cable needle – called C3B –, sl next st on to cable needle and hold at front of work, P2 then K1 from cable needle – called C3F –, rep from * to last st, P1.
6th row K1, P1, *K4, P2, rep from * to last 6 sts, K4, P1, K1.
7th row P1, K1, *P4, K2, rep from * to last 6 sts, P4, K1, P1.
Rep 6th and 7th rows once more, then 6th row once.
11th row P1, *C3F, C3B, rep from * to last st, P1.
12th row As 2nd.
These 12 rows form the pattern.

Stepped stitch
Cast on a number of stitches divisible by 6 + 2.
1st row P2, *K4, P2, rep from * to end.
2nd row K2, *P4, K2, rep from * to end.
Rep these 2 rows once more.
5th row P3, *K2, P4, rep from * to last 5 sts, K2, P3.
6th row K3, *P2, K4, rep from * to last 5 sts, P2, K3.
Rep last 2 rows once more.
9th row P to end.
10th row K to end.
These 10 rows form the pattern.

Trellis stitch
Cast on a number of stitches divisible by 6 + 2.
1st row P3, *K2, P4, rep from * to last 5 sts, K2, P3.
2nd row K3, *P2, K4, rep from * to last 5 sts, P2, K3.
Rep these 2 rows once more.

Stepped stitch

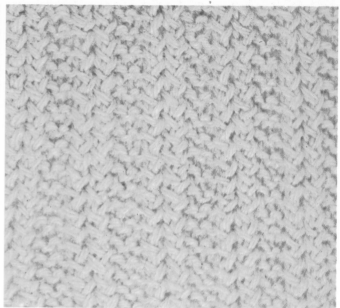

Corded rib

Spiral rib

Cast on a number of stitches divisible by 6 + 2.

1st row P2, *K4, P2, rep from * to end.

2nd and every alt row K2, *P4, K2, rep from * to end.

3rd row P2, *K 2nd st on left hand needle then first st and sl them both off needle tog – called Tw2 –, Tw2, P2, rep from * to end.

5th row P2, *K1, Tw2, K1, P2, rep from * to end.

6th row As 2nd.

The 3rd to 6th rows form the pattern.

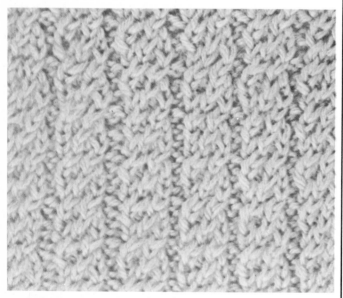

Corded rib

Cast on a number of stitches divisible by 6 + 2.

1st row P2, *K4, P2, rep from * to end.

2nd row P to end.

3rd row P2, *(sl 1, K1, yfwd, pass slip st over K1 and yfwd) twice, P2, rep from * to end.

4th row As 2nd.

The 3rd and 4th rows form the pattern.

Bobble rib

Cast on a number of stitches divisible by 6 + 2.

1st row P2, *K1, P2, rep from * to end.

2nd row K2, *P1, K2, rep from * to end.

3rd row P2, *K1, P2, (P1, K1, P1, K1) all into next st – called K4 from 1 –, P2, rep from * to end.

4th row K2, *P4, K2, P1, K2, rep from * to end.

5th row P2, *K1, P2, P4, turn and K4, turn and P4, P2, rep from * to end.

6th row K2, *P4 tog, K2, P1, K2, rep from * to end.

Rep 1st and 2nd rows once more.

9th row P2, *K4, from 1, P2, K1, P2, rep from * to end.

10th row K2, *P1, K2, P4, K2, rep from * to end.

11th row P2, *P4, turn and K4, turn and P4, P2, K1, P2, rep from * to end.

12th row K2, *P1, K2, P4 tog, K2, rep from * to end.

These 12 rows form the pattern.

A short sleeved sweater

This pretty bobble rib sweater (see opposite), illustrates the versatility of knitting. It can be made from any of the stitches shown on the previous two pages, providing that you can correctly gauge the tension before starting.

Sizes
To fit 86.5[91.5:96.5]cm (34[36:38]in) bust
Length to shoulder 56[57:58.5]cm (22[22½:23]in), adjustable
Sleeve seam, 10cm (4in)
The figures in brackets [] refer to the 91.5cm (36in) and 96.5cm (38in) sizes respectively

Tension
24 sts and 32 rows to 10cm (3.9in) over st st worked on No.9 needles

Materials
16[17:18] × 25grm balls of Lee Target Motoravia Double Knitting
One pair of No.9 needles
One pair of No.11 needles
Set of 4 No.11 needles pointed at both ends

Back
Using No. 11 needles, cast on 109[115:121]sts.
1st row K1, *P1, K1, rep from * to end.
    2nd row P1, *K1, P1, rep from * to end.
Rep these 2 rows for 4cm (1½in) ending with a 2nd row and inc one st in centre of last row. 110[116:122]sts. Change to No.9 needles. Work in patt as required from any of st patts in the previous chapter until work measures 37cm (14½in) from beg or required length to underarm, ending with a WS row.

Shape armholes
Cast off at beg of next and every row 4 sts twice and 2 sts twice. Dec one st at each end of next and foll 5[6:7] alt rows. 86[90:94]sts. Cont without shaping until armholes measure 19[20.5:21.5]cm (7½[8:8½]in) from beg, ending with a WS row.

Shape neck and shoulders
Next row Cast off 6[7:7]sts, patt 25[25:26]sts, turn and leave rem sts on holder.
Next row Cast off 2 sts, patt to end.
Next row Cast off 6[7:7]sts, patt to end.
Rep last 2 rows once more then first of them again. Cast off rem 7[5:6]sts.
With RS of work facing, sl first 24[26:28]sts onto holder, rejoin yarn to rem sts and patt to end.
Complete to match first side, reversing shaping.

Front
Work as given for back until armhole shaping is completed. Cont without shaping until armholes measure 14[15:16]cm (5½[6:6½]in) from beg, ending with a WS row.

Shape neck
Next row patt 35[36:37]sts, turn and leave rem sts on holder.
Cast off 2 sts at beg of next and foll 2 alt rows, then dec one st at neck edge on foll 4 alt rows.
Cont without shaping until armhole measures same as back shoulder, ending at armhole edge.

Shape shoulder
Cast off at beg of next and every alt row 6[7:7]sts 3 times and 7[5:6]sts once. With RS of work facing, sl first 16[18:20]sts on to holder, rejoin yarn to rem sts and patt to end. Complete to match first side, reversing shaping.

Sleeves
Using No.11 needles cast on 73[73:79]sts. Work 2.5cm (1in) rib as given for back, ending with a 2nd row and inc one st in centre of last row. 74[74:80]sts. Change to No.9 needles. Cont in patt as for back, inc one st at each end of 3rd and every foll 8th[6th:6th] row until there are 78[82:86]sts. Cont without shaping until sleeve measures 10cm (4in) from beg, ending with a WS row.

Shape top
Cast off 4 sts at beg of next 2 rows. Dec one st at each end of next and foll 11[12:13] alt rows, ending with a WS row. Cast off at beg of next and every row 2 sts 8[8:10] times, 3 sts 4 times, 4 sts twice and 10[12:10] sts once.

Neckband
Join shoulder seams. Using set of 4 No.11 needles and with RS of work facing, K up 8 sts down right back neck, K across back neck sts inc one st in centre, K up 8 sts up left back neck and 24 sts down left front neck, K across front neck sts inc one st in centre and K up 24 sts up right front neck. 106[110:114]sts. Cont in rounds of K1, P1 rib for 6.5cm (2½in). Cast off loosely in rib.

To make up
Press each piece under a damp cloth with a warm iron. Set in sleeves. Join side and sleeve seams. Press seams. Fold neckband in half to WS and sl st down.

TEXTURED PATTERNS

These fabric stitches are more complicated than the examples given in the previous chapter and use larger multiples of stitches and rows to form the pattern repeat. Each pattern is formed either by stitches which travel from one position to another in a row or by decreased stitches which are then compensated for by means of a made stitch without giving a lacy effect.

Pyramid pattern
Cast on a number of stitches divisible by 15 + 1.
1st row K to end.
2nd row P4, *K8, P7, rep from * to last 12 sts, K8, P4.
3rd row K1, *K up 1, K2, sl 1, K1, psso, P6, K2 tog, K2, K up 1, K1, rep from * to end.
4th row P5, *K6, P9, rep from * to last 11 sts, K6, P5.
5th row K2, *K up 1, K2, sl 1, K1, psso, P4, K2 tog, K2, K up 1, K3, rep from * to last 14 sts, K up 1, K2, sl 1, K1, psso, P4, K2 tog, K2, K up 1, K2.
6th row P6, *K4, P11, rep from * to last 10 sts, K4, P6.
7th row K3, *K up 1, K2, sl 1, K1, psso, P2, K2 tog, K2, K up 1, K5, rep from * to last 13 sts, K up 1, K2, sl 1, K1, psso, P4, K2 tog, K2, K up 1, K2.
8th row P7, *K2, P13, rep from * to last 9 sts, K2, P7.
9th row K4, *K up 1, K2, sl 1, K1, psso, K2 tog, K2, K up 1, K7, rep from * to last 12 sts, K up 1, K2, sl 1, K1, psso, K2 tog, K2, K up 1, K4.
10th row P to end.
These 10 rows form the pattern.

Leaf pattern
Cast on a number of stitches divisible by 24 + 1.
1st row K1, *K up 1, sl 1, K1, psso, K4, K2 tog, K3, K up 1, K1, K up 1, K3, sl 1, K1, psso, K4, K2 tog, K up 1, K1, rep from * to end.

2nd and every alt row P to end.
3rd row K1, *K up 1, K1, sl 1, K1, psso, K2, K2 tog, K4, K up 1, K1, K up 1, K4, sl 1, K1, psso, K2, K2 tog, K1, K up 1, K1, rep from * to end.
5th row K1, *K up 1, K2, sl 1, K1, psso, K2 tog, K5, K up 1, K1, K up 1, K5, sl 1, K1, psso, K2 tog, K2, K up 1, K1, rep from * to end.
7th row K1, *K up 1, K3, sl 1, K1, psso, K4, K2 tog, K up 1, K1, K up 1, sl 1, K1, psso, K4, K2 tog, K3, K up 1, K1, rep from * to end.
9th row K1, *K up 1, K4, sl 1, K1, psso, K2, K2 tog, K1, K up 1, K1, K up 1, K1, sl 1, K1, psso, K2, K2 tog, K4, K up 1, K1, rep from * to end.
11th row K1, *K up 1, K5, sl 1, K1, psso, K2 tog, K2, K up 1, K1, K up 1, K2, sl 1, K1, psso, K2 tog, K5, K up 1, K1, rep from * to end.
12th row P to end.
These 12 rows form the pattern.

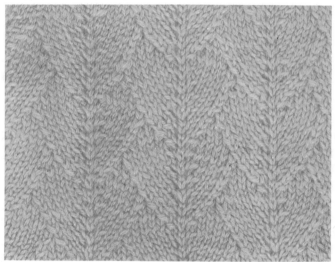

Seeded chevron pattern
Cast on a number of stitches divisible by 14 + 2.
1st row K14, *K second st on left hand needle then K first st and sl both sts off needle tog – called TwR –, K12, rep from * to last 2 sts, K2.
2nd row P1, *sl 1, P12, sl 1, rep from * to last st, P1.
3rd row K1, *put needle behind first st on left hand needle and K into back of second st then K first st and sl both sts off needle tog – called TwL –, K10, TwR, rep from * to last st K1.
4th row P1, K1, *sl 1, P10, sl 1, P1, K1, rep from * to end.
5th row K1, P1, *TwL, K8, TwR, K1, P1, rep from * to end.
6th row P1, K1, *P1, sl 1, P8, sl 1, K1, P1, K1, rep from * to end.
7th row K1, P1, *K1, TwL, K6, TwR, P1, K1, P1, rep from * to end.

8th row *(P1, K1) twice, sl 1, P6, sl 1, P1, K1, rep from * to last 2 sts, P1, K1.

9th row *(K1, P1) twice, TwL, K4, TwR, K1, P1, rep from * to last 2 sts, K1, P1.

10th row P1, *(K1, P1) twice, sl 1, P4, sl 1, (K1, P1) twice, rep from * to last st, K1.

11th row K1, *(P1, K1) twice, TwL, K2, TwR, (P1, K1) twice, rep from * to last st, P1.

12th row *(P1, K1) 3 times, sl 1, P2, sl 1, (P1, K1) twice, rep from * to last 2 sts, P1, K1.

13th row (K1, P1) 3 times, *TwL, TwR, (K1, P1) twice, TwR, (K1, P1) twice, rep from * to last 10 sts, TwL, TwR, (K1, P1) 3 times.

14th row P1, sl 1, *(P1, K1) 3 times, sl 1, K1, (P1, K1) twice, sl 2, rep from * to last 14 sts, (P1, K1) 3 times, sl 1, K1, (P1, K1) twice, sl 1, P1.

15th row K1, *TwL, (P1, K1) twice, TwL, (P1, K1) twice, TwR, rep from * to last st, K1.

16th row P2, *sl 1, (K1, P1) 5 times, sl 1, P2, rep from * to end.

17th row K2, *TwL, (K1, P1) 4 times, TwR, K2, rep from * to end.

18th row P3, *sl 1, (P1, K1) 4 times, sl 1, P4, rep from * to last 13 sts, sl 1, (P1, K1) 4 times, sl 1, P3.

19th row K3, *TwL, (P1, K1) 3 times, TwR, K4, rep from * to last 13 sts, TwL, (P1, K1) 3 times, TwR, K3.

20th row P4, *sl 1, (K1, P1) 3 times, sl 1, P6, rep from * to last 12 sts, sl 1, (K1, P1) 3 times, sl 1, P4.

21st row K4, *TwL, (K1, P1) twice, TwR, K6, rep from * to last 12 sts, TwL, (K1, P1) twice, TwR, K4.

22nd row P5, *sl 1, (P1, K1) twice, sl 1, P8, rep from * to last 11 sts, sl 1, (P1, K1) twice, sl 1, P5.

23rd row K5, *TwL, P1, K1, TwR, K8, rep from * to last 11 sts, TwL, P1, K1, TwR, K5.

24th row P6, *sl 1, K1, P1, sl 1, P10, rep from * to last 10 sts, sl 1, K1, P1, sl 1, P6.

25th row K6, *TwL, TwR, K10, rep from * to last 10 sts, TwL, TwR, K6.

26th row P8, *sl 1, P13, rep from * to last 8 sts, sl 1, P7.

27th row K7, *TwL, K12, rep from * to last 9 sts, TwL, K7.

28th row P to end.
These 28 rows form the pattern.

Travelling rib pattern

Cast on a number of stitches divisible by 12 + 2.

1st row P6, *K7, P5, rep from * to last 8 sts, K7, P1.

2nd row K1, *P7, K5, rep from * to last st, K1.

3rd row P5, *K second st on left hand needle then K first st and sl both sts off needle tog – called TwR –, K4, TwR, P4, rep from * to last 9 sts, TwR, K4, TwR, P1.

4th row K2, *P7, K5, rep from * to end.

5th row P4, *TwR, K4, TwR, P4, rep from * to last 10 sts, TwR, K4, TwR, P2.

6th row K3, *P7, K5, rep from * to last 11 sts, P7, K4.

7th row P3, *TwR, K4, TwR, P4, rep from * to last 11 sts, TwR, K4, TwR, P3.

8th row K4, *P7, K5, rep from * to last 10 sts, P7, K3.

9th row P2, *TwR, K4, TwR, P4, rep from * to end.

10th row K5, *P7, K5, rep from * to last 9 sts, P7, K2.

11th row P1, *TwR, K4, TwR, P4, rep from * to last st, P1.

12th row K6, *P7, K5, rep from * to last 8 sts, P7, K1.

13th row P1, *put needle behind first st on left hand needle and K into back of second st then K first st and sl both sts off needle tog – called TwL –, K4, TwL, P4, rep from * to last st, P1.

14th row As 10th.

15th row P2, *TwL, K4, TwL, P4, rep from * to end.

16th row As 8th.

17th row P3, *TwL, K4, TwL, P4, rep from * to last 11 sts, TwL, K4, TwL, P3.

18th row As 6th.

19th row P4, *TwL, K4, TwL, P4, rep from * to last 10 sts, TwL, K4, TwL, P2.

20th row As 4th.

21st row P5, *TwL, K4, TwL, P4, rep from * to last 9 sts, TwL, K4, TwL, P1.

22nd row As 2nd.
The 3rd to 22nd rows form the pattern.

WOVEN FABRIC STITCHES

Just as the yarn can be carried over the needle in a pattern sequence to form additional stitches, or carried across the back of the work to form stripes or multi-coloured patterns, it can also be held in front of a sequence of stitches to form a woven fabric. In many instances, this fabric as with Fair Isle and jacquard patterns, is double the thickness of ordinary knitting and may be used in a variety of ways.

If you use a very fine yarn and any of the all-over stitches given in this Chapter you will produce a very warm but light fabric, suitable for baby garments, bedjackets or lingerie, where extra warmth may be required but not extra weight. Using a double knitting quality yarn, the fabric will be firm and virtually windproof and most suitable for heavy outdoor garments, such as windcheaters, ski anoraks or chunky jackets.

All these stitches are simple to work as the patterns merely require a given sequence of stitches to be slipped from one needle to the other, carrying the yarn in front of these stitches ready to knit the next stitch. They do not have to be worked to produce an all-over fabric but can be worked at given intervals, as with cluster stitch and woven butterfly stitch, to add texture to an otherwise plain fabric. To keep the sides of the patterns neat and to avoid any 'fluting' effect, it is advisable to knit the first and last stitch on every row to form a firm, garter stitch edge.

Diagonal woven stitch
Cast on a number of stitches divisible by 4 + 2.
1st row K2, *yfwd, sl 2 P-wise, ybk, K2, rep from * to end.
2nd and every alt row K1, P to last st, K1.
3rd row Yfwd, sl 1 P-wise, ybk, *K2, yfwd, sl 2 P-wise, ybk, rep from * to last st, K1.

5th row Yfwd, sl 2 P-wise, ybk, *K2, yfwd, sl 2 P-wise, ybk, rep from * to end.
7th row K1, yfwd, sl 2 P-wise, ybk, *K2, yfwd, sl 2 P-wise, ybk, rep from * to last 3 sts, K2, yfwd, sl 1 P-wise, ybk.
8th row As 2nd.
These 8 rows form the pattern.

Woven bar stitch
Cast on a number of stitches divisible by 3 + 1.
1st row (RS) K to end.
2nd row *K1, keeping yarn at back of work sl 2 P-wise, rep from * to last st, K1.
These 2 rows form the pattern.

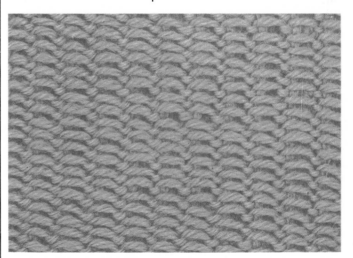

Woven ladder stitch
Cast on a number of stitches divisible by 8 + 1.
1st row *K5, yfwd, sl 3 P-wise, ybk, rep from * to last st, K1.

2nd row K1, *ybk, sl 3 P-wise, yfwd, P5, rep from * to end, ending last rep with K1.
3rd row As 1st.
4th row K1, P to last st, K1.
5th row K1, *yfwd, sl 3 P-wise, ybk, K5, rep from * to end.
6th row K1, *P4, ybk, sl 3 P-wise, yfwd, P1, rep from * to end, ending last rep K1.
7th row As 5th.
8th row As 4th.
These 8 rows form the pattern.

Woven chevron stitch
Cast on a number of stitches divisible by 10.
1st row *K1, yfwd, sl 3 P-wise, ybk, K2, yfwd, sl 3 P-wise, ybk, K1, rep from * to end.
2nd row *Ybk, sl 3 P-wise, yfwd, P2, rep from * to end, ending last rep K1.
3rd row Yfwd, *sl 1 P-wise, ybk, K2, yfwd, sl 3 P-wise, ybk, K2, yfwd, sl 2 P-wise, rep from * to end.
4th row Yfwd, *sl 1 P-wise, yfwd, P2, ybk, sl 3 P-wise, yfwd, P2, ybk, sl 2 P-wise, rep from * to end.
5th row *Yfwd, sl 3 P-wise, ybk, K2, rep from * to end.
6th row *P1, ybk, sl 3 P-wise, yfwd, P1, rep from * to end.
7th row As 5th.
8th row As 4th.
9th row As 3rd.

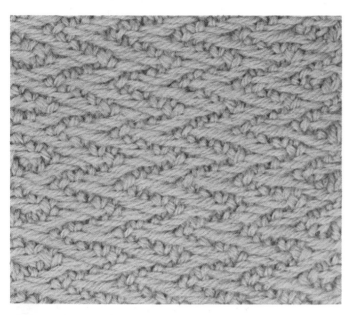

10th row As 2nd. These 10 rows form the pattern.

Cluster stitch
Cast on a number of stitches divisible by 8 + 5.
1st row K to end.
2nd row P to end.
3rd row *K5, sl next 3 sts on to cable needle and hold at front of work, pass the yarn across the back of these stitches and right round them 6 times in an anti-clockwise direction then K3 sts from cable needle – called 1CL, –, rep from * to last 5 sts, K5.
4th row P to end.
Rep 1st and 2nd rows once more.

7th row *K1, 1CL, K4, rep from * to last 5 sts, K1, 1CL, K1.
8th row P to end.
These 8 rows form the pattern.

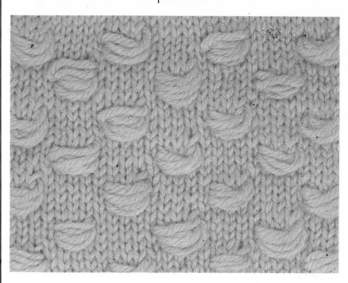

Woven butterfly stitch
Cast on a number of stitches divisible by 10 + 7.
1st row K6, *yfwd, sl 5 P-wise, ybk, K5, rep from * to last st, K1.
2nd row P to end.
Rep 1st and 2nd rows 3 times more.
9th row K8, *insert right hand needle under the 4 long loops, yarn round the needle and draw through a stitch, keeping this st on right hand needle K the next st on the left hand needle then pass the first st over the K1 – called B1 –, K9, rep from * to last 9 sts, B1, K8.
10th row As 2nd.
11th row K1, yfwd, sl 5 P-wise, ybk, *K5, yfwd, sl 5 P-wise, ybk, rep from * to last st, K1.
12th row As 2nd.
Rep 11th and 12th rows 3 times more.
19th row K3, B1, *K9, B1, rep from * to last 3 sts, K3.
20th row As 2nd.
These 20 rows form the pattern.

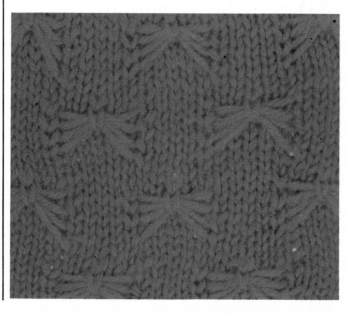

RAISED STITCHES

Bobble and cluster stitches

Although the overall heading refers to a cluster of raised stitches, which can be arranged to give an interesting and highly textured fabric, the size of a bobble or cluster can vary considerably.

There are various ways of working bobbles but the basic principle is always the same – working more than once into the stitch where the bobble is required and then decreasing again to the original stitch, either in the same row or several rows later.

Cluster stitches also are worked on this principle but they are not intended to be as dense as bobble stitches and once the cluster is formed, it is decreased more gradually over a number of rows until only the original stitch remains.

Both bobble and cluster stitches may be used most effectively to form an all-over pattern but, combined with other stitches such as cables, they produce some of the most beautiful variations of Aran patterns, which are renowned throughout the world.

Bobble patterns

The simplest forms of bobble stitches are small and easy to work. The working methods of the two samples given here differ slightly but both produce a small, berry type of stitch. Trinity stitch, which is used in Aran patterns, derives its name from the method of working 'three into one and one into three'.

Blackberry stitch

Cast on a number of stitches divisible by 4.
1st row *(K1, yfwd to make one st, K1) all into next st, P3, rep from * to end.
2nd row *P3 tog, K3, rep from * to end.
3rd row *P3, (K1, yfwd to make one st, K1) all into next st, rep from * to end.
4th row *K3, P3 tog, rep from * to end.
These 4 rows form the pattern.

Trinity stitch

Cast on a number of stitches divisible by 4.
1st row *(K1, P1, K1) all into next st, P3 tog, rep from * to end.

2nd row P to end.
3rd row *P3 tog, (K1, P1, K1) all into next st, rep from * to end.
4th row As 2nd.
These 4 rows form the pattern.

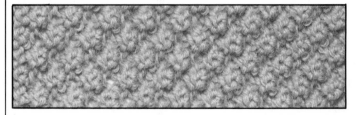

Small bobble stitch

Cast on a number of stitches divisible by 6 plus 5.
1st row (WS) P to end.
2nd row K2, (K1, P1, K1, P1, K1) all into next st then using point of left hand needle lift 2nd, 3rd, 4th and 5th sts over first st and off right hand needle – called B1 –, *K5, B1, rep from * to last 2 sts, K2.
3rd row P to end.
4th row *K5, B1, rep from * to last 5 sts, K5.
These 4 rows form the pattern.

Popcorn stitch

Cast on a number of stitches divisible by 6 plus 5.
1st row (WS) P to end.
2nd row K2, (K1, P1, K1, P1, K1) all into next st, turn and K these 5 sts, turn and P5 then using point of left hand needle lift 2nd, 3rd, 4th and 5th sts over first st and off right hand needle – called B1 –, *K5, B1, rep from * to last 2 sts, K2.
3rd row P to end.
4th row *K5, B1, rep from * to last 5 sts, K5.
These 4 rows form the pattern.

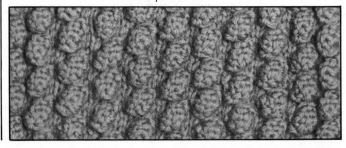

Currant stitch

Cast on a number of stitches divisible by 2 plus 1.
1st row (RS) K to end.
2nd row K1, *(P1, yrn to make one st, P1, yrn, P1) all into next st, K1, rep from * to end.
3rd row P to end.
4th row K1, *sl 2 P-wise keeping yarn at front of work – called sl 2F –, P3 tog, p2sso, K1, rep from * to end.
5th row K to end.
6th row K2, *(P1, yrn, P1, yrn, P1) all into next st, K1, rep from * to last st, K1.
7th row P to end.
8th row K2, *sl 2F, P3 tog, p2sso, K1, rep from * to last st, K1.
These 8 rows form the pattern.

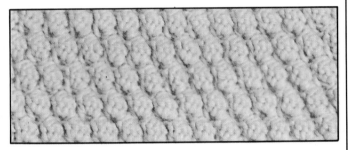

Long bobble stitch

Cast on a number of stitches divisible by 6 plus 3.
1st row (WS) P to end.
2nd row K1, *K3, (K1, yfwd to make one st, K1) all into next st, K1, (turn and P5, turn and K5) twice, K1, rep from * to last 2 sts, K2.
3rd row P1, *P2, P2 tog, P1, P2 tog tbl, P1, rep from * to last 2 sts, P2.
4th row K3, *K4, (K1, yfwd, K1) all into next st, K1, (turn and P5, turn and K5) twice, rep from * to last 6 sts, K6.
5th row P3, *P3, P2 tog, P1, P2 tog tbl, rep from * to last 6 sts, P6.
Rows 2–5 form the pattern.

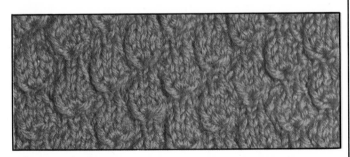

Cluster stitches

These patterns may be worked in two ways – either by increasing and shaping the cluster and working the stitches on either side row by row at the same time, or by working the cluster separately and then continuing to knit the background fabric until it has reached the same height as the cluster.

Bell cluster

Cast on a number of stitches divisible by 4 plus 4.
1st row (WS) K to end.

2nd row P4, *turn and cast on 8 sts – called C1 –, P4, rep from * to end.
3rd row *K4, P8, rep from * to last 4 sts, K4.
4th row P4, *K8, P4, rep from * to end.
5th row As 3rd.
6th row P4, *sl 1, K1, psso, K4, K2 tog, P4, rep from * to end.
7th row *K4, P6, rep from * to last 4 sts, K4.
8th row P4, *sl 1, K1, psso, K2, K2 tog, P4, rep from * to end.
9th row *K4, P4, rep from * to last 4 sts, K4.
10th row P4, *sl 1, K1, psso, K2 tog, P4, rep from * to end.
11th row *K4, P2, rep from * to last 4 sts, K4.
12th row P4, *K2 tog, P4, rep from * to end.
13th row *K4, P1, rep from * to last 4 sts, K4.
14th row P4, *K2 tog, P3, rep from * to end.
These 14 rows form the pattern.

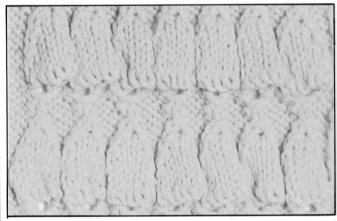

Detached cluster

Cast on a number of stitches divisible by 6 plus 5.
1st row (RS) P to end.
2nd row K to end.
3rd row *P5, (yfwd to make one st, K into next st) 3 times into same st to make 6 out of one, turn and P these 6 sts, turn and sl 1, K5, turn and sl 1, P5, turn and sl 1, K5, turn and (P2 tog) 3 times, turn and sl 1, K2 tog, psso – called C1 –, rep from * to last 5 sts, P5.
4th row K to end.
5th row P to end.
6th row K to end.
7th row P2, *C1, P5, rep from * to last 3 sts, C1, P2.
8th row K to end.
These 8 rows form the pattern.

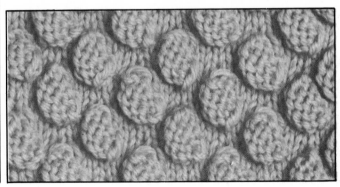

FUR FABRICS

Knitting patterns which have the appearance of fur fabrics are achieved by means of loops of yarn which are worked as the row is knitted on to the main background.

The usual method is to loop the yarn round the fingers or a strip of card for the required number of times, then to secure these loops to the knitted stitch so that they do not unravel. The fabric produced is warm and light and is most suitable for outer garments, trimmings such as collars and cuffs, pram and cot covers, or household items such as bath mats.

Another method given here combines a knitted background with lengths of crochet chains forming the fur effect, which gives a close, astrakan texture to the fabric. The loops achieved by this method will not catch or break as easily as the first method and this pattern is therefore most suitable for babies and childrens garments, where frequent washing, or rough-and-tumble use is required. Although it is not as quick or simple to work as the usual method, its appearance is so attractive that it is well worth a little time and trouble spent in practising this stitch.

Looped patterns

The density of these patterns may be varied as required, either by the number of times the yarn is looped round, or by the position of each loop on the background fabric. The samples given here have been worked in a double knitting yarn, alternating the position of the loops on every 4th row.

Single loop stitch

Here the loops are formed on a right side row when the work is facing you. Cast on a number of stitches divisible by 2 plus 1.

1st row (RS) K to end.
2nd row P to end.
3rd row *K1, K next st without letting it drop off left hand needle, yfwd, pass yarn over left thumb to make a loop approximately 4cm (1½in) long, ybk and K st rem on left hand needle letting it drop from the needle, return the 2 sts just worked to the left hand needle and K them tog tbl – called L1 –, rep from * to last st, K1.
4th row P to end.
Rep 1st and 2nd rows once more.
7th row K1, *K1, L1, rep from * to last 2 sts, K2.
8th row P to end.
These 8 rows form the pattern.

Double loop stitch

Here the loops are formed on the right side of the fabric when the wrong side of the work is facing you. Cast on a number of stitches divisible by 2 plus 1.

1st row (RS) K to end.
Rep 1st row twice more.
4th row (WS) K1, *insert right hand needle into next st on left hand needle as if to knit it, wind yarn over right hand needle point and round first and 2nd fingers of left hand twice, then over and round right hand needle point once more, draw all 3 loops through st and sl on to left hand needle, insert right hand needle through back of these 3 loops and through the original st and K tog tbl – called L1 –, K1, rep from * to end.
5th 6th and 7th rows K to end.

8th row K1, *K1, L1, rep from * to last 2 sts, K2. These 8 rows form the pattern.

Chain loop stitch

Here again, the density of the pattern can be altered by the position of each chain loop on the background fabric and by the number of rows worked between each pattern row. To work the sample given here you will require double knitting yarn, a pair of No.8 needles and a No.4.00 (ISR) crochet hook. Cast on a number of stitches divisible by 2 plus 1.

1st row (RS) K to end.
2nd row P to end.

3rd row K1, *K next st without letting it drop off left hand needle, insert crochet hook from front to back through loop on left hand needle, draw a loop through and leave on hook then drop st from left hand needle, wind yarn round left hand and make 12ch in the usual way, keeping ch at front of work and yarn at back of work sl loop on to right hand needle and remove hook, then lift last K st over loop – called L1 –, K1, rep from * to end.

4th row P to end.
Rep 1st and 2nd rows once more.
7th row K1, *K1, L1, rep from * to last 2 sts, K2.
8th row P to end.
These 8 rows form the pattern.

Cravat
Size

18cm (7in) wide at lower edge by 101.5cm (40in) long

Tension

22 sts and 30 rows to 10cm (3.9in) over st st worked on No.8 needles

Materials

4 × 50grm balls of Patons Bracken Tweed Double Knitting
One pair No.8 needles

Cravat

Using No.8 needles cast on 45 sts. K 3 rows g st. Commence patt.
1st row (RS) K2, work in any loop patt over next 41 sts, K2.
2nd row K2, patt 41 sts, K2.
Cont in patt, keeping 2 sts at each end in g st throughout, until work measures 12.5cm (5in) from beg, ending with a WS row.
Next row K2, sl 1, K1, psso, patt to last 4 sts, K2 tog, K2. Work 3 rows patt without shaping. Rep last 4 rows 8 times more. 27 sts. Cont without shaping until work measures 73.5cm (29in) from beg, ending with a WS row.
Next row K2, pick up loop lying between sts and K tbl – called inc 1 –, patt to last 2 sts, inc 1, K2.
Work 3 rows patt without shaping. Rep last 4 rows 8 times more. 45 sts. Cont without shaping until work measures 101cm (39¾in) from beg. K 3 rows g st. Cast off.

Loop fastening

Using No.8 needles cast on 6 sts. Work 10cm (4in) g st. Cast off.

To make up

Do not press. St loop fastening across back of one end approximately 18cm (7in) above lower end.
Slot other end through loop to secure.

FISHERMAN KNITTING

Fisherman knitting is the name given to seamless jerseys, knitted in a very closely woven fabric similar to a patterned brocade. Because of the fineness of the needles used for this type of knitting, sometimes on as fine a gauge as No.17, the textured patterns do not stand out in relief as with Aran stitches. The whole purpose is to make a fabric which is virtually wind-proof and a jersey which will stand up to the constant wear-and-tear of a fisherman's life.

As with many of the folk crafts which have been handed down to us through countless generations, these jerseys were often knitted by the fishermen themselves but were more often lovingly knitted by their womenfolk, in traditional patterns which varied from region to region.

The very name, 'jersey', originates from the island of that name. Another name in regular use is a 'guernsey', or 'gansey' as it became known, from the sister island in the same group.

Each port around the coastline of the British Isles has developed its own regional style of fisherman knitting. Some have patterned yokes, others have vertical panels of patterns, some have horizontal bands of patterns, but the original guernseys, which were made purely as hard-wearing working garments, were nearly always made in stocking stitch with very little decoration and always in the traditional colour, navy blue. The more elaborate examples which evolved were kept for Sunday best and in Cornwall they were often referred to as bridal shirts and were knitted by the young women for their betrothed.

A traditional guernsey is knitted entirely without seams, often worked on sets of 5, 6, or even more double pointed needles. The body is knitted in rounds to the armholes, then instead of dividing the work for the back and front at this point, the work is continued in rounds with the position of the armholes separated from the main sections of the guernsey by a series of loops wound round the needle on every round. These loops are dropped from the needle on the following round and the process is repeated until the guernsey is the required length. When this section is completed, a series of what look like the rungs of a ladder mark each armhole. These loops are cut in the middle and the ends carefully darned into the main fabric, then the sleeve stitches are picked up round the armholes and the sleeve is knitted in rounds down to the cuff. The shoulder stitches are grafted together to finish the garment without one sewn seam.

The shape of these garments is as distinctive as the patterns. They all feature a dropped shoulder line and crew neckline, with little, if any, shaping. Sometimes buttons and buttonholes would be added to one shoulder for ease in dressing and undressing, a gusset made before the armhole division and carried on into the top of the sleeve, or the neck would be continued to form a small collar but the simplicity of the basic design has never been bettered, to give the utmost warmth, freedom of movement and protection to the wearer.

Traditional guernsey

Sizes

To fit 96.5[101.5:106.5:112]cm (38[40:42:44]in) chest
Length to shoulder, 58.5[59.5:61:62]cm (23[23½:24:24½]in)
Sleeve seam, 45.5cm (18in), adjustable
The figures in brackets [] refer to the 101.5 (40), 106.5 (42) and 112cm (44in) sizes respectively

Tension

28 sts and 36 rows to 10cm (3.9in) over st st worked on No.10 needles

Materials

14[15:16:17] × 50grm balls of Double Knitting
Set of 4 No.10 needles pointed at both ends or No.10 circular Twin Pin
Set of 4 No.12 needles pointed at both ends or No.12 circular Twin Pin

Guernsey body

Using set of 4 No.12 needles cast on 264[276:288:300] sts. Mark beg of round with coloured thread. Cont in rounds of K1, P1 rib for 7.5cm (3in). Change to set of 4 No.10 needles. Cont in rounds of st st until work measures 33cm (13in) from beg. Commence yoke patt.
1st round P to end.
2nd round K to end.
Rep these 2 rounds twice more, then 1st round once more. **.
***Work 5 rounds st st.
Divide for armholes
1st round *K132[138:144:150] sts ,wind yarn 10 times round right hand needle – called loop 10 –, rep from * once more.
Rep last round once more, dropping extra loops from needle before loop 10.
3rd round *K6[9:0:3], (K6, P1, K11, P1, K5) 5[5:6:6] times, K6[9:0:3], drop extra loops, loop 10, rep from * once more.
4th round *K6[9:0:3], (K4, P1, K1, P1, K9, P1, K1, P1, K5) 5[5:6:6] times, K6[9:0:3], drop extra loops, loop 10, rep from * once more.
5th round *K6[9:0:3], (K4, P1, K3, P1, K7, P1, (K1, P1) twice, K3) 5[5:6:6] times, K6[9:0:3], drop extra loops, loop 10, rep from * once more.
6th round *K6[9:0:3], (K2, P1, (K1, P1) 3 times, (K5, P1) twice, K3) 5[5:6:6] times, K6[9:0:3], drop extra loops, loop 10, rep from * once more.
7th round *K6[9:0:3], (K2, P1, K7, P1, K3, P1, (K1, P1) 4 times, K1) 5[5:6:6] times, K6[9:0:3], drop extra loops, loop 10, rep from * once more.
8th round *K6[9:0:3], (P1, (K1, P1) 6 times, K9, P1, K1) 5 [5:6:6] times, K6[9:0:3], drop extra loops, loop 10, rep from * once more.
9th round *K6[9:0:3], (P1, K11, P12) 5[5:6:6] times, K6[9:0:3], drop extra loops, loop 10, rep from * once more.
10th round *K6[9:0:3], (P11, K1, P1, K9, P1, K1) 5[5:6:6] times, K6[9:0:3], drop extra loops, loop 10, rep from * once more.
11th round *K6[9:0:3], (K2, P1, K7, P1, K13) 5[5:6:6] times, K6[9:0:3], drop extra loops, loop 10, rep from * once more.
12th round *K6[9:0:3], (K14, P1, K5, P1, K3) 5[5:6:6] times, K6[9:0:3], drop extra loops, loop 10, rep from * once more.
13th round *K6[9:0:3], (K4, P1, K3, P1, K15) 5[5:6:6] times, K6[9:0:3], drop extra loops, loop 10, rep from * once more.
14th round *K6[9:0:3], (K16, P1, K1, P1, K5) 5[5:6:6] times, K6[9:0:3], drop extra loops, loop 10, rep from * once more.
15th and 16th rounds As 1st, dropping extra loops.
Keeping armhole loops correct, work 5 rounds st st, then rep from ** to ** once. ***. Rep from *** to *** once more. Beg with a 2nd row, cont working in patt from ** to ** until work measures 21.5[23:25:25.5]cm (8½[9:9½:10]in) from beg of loops, omitting loop 10 at end of last round. Break off yarn.
Divide for shoulders
Keeping patt correct, sl first and last 35[37:39:41] sts of back and front sections on to holders, knit across each set of 62[64:66:68] sts of neck separately for 6 rows. Cast off loosely. Graft shoulder sts from holders.

Sleeves

Cut loops of armholes and darn in ends. Using set of 4 No.10 needles and with RS of work facing, K up 110[114:118:122] sts round armhole. K 5 rounds st st, then rep from ** to ** as given for body.
Cont in rounds of st st, dec one st at beg and end of next and every foll 6th round until 74[80:84:88] sts rem. Cont without shaping until sleeve measures 40.5cm (16in) from beg, or required length less 5cm (2in). Change to set of 4 No.12 needles. Work 5cm (2in) K1, P1 rib. Cast off in rib.

MAXI KNITTING

Working a fabric on very large knitting needles can be both speedy and fun, as even the most basic stitches take on a completely different appearance. This particular type of knitting is often referred to as 'maxi-knitting' and needles of a special gauge are available in varying sizes.

The most popular needles are made from a special lightweight wood and are graded upwards from the smallest size 0, on to 00, 000, to the largest size 0000. Hollow jumbo sized needles are also available, to overcome the weight problem, and these are made from a plastic material and graded as sizes No.1 and No.2.

Great care must be taken in selecting a suitable yarn for this type of knitting, as two or more ends are used at the same time, which can produce a very heavy fabric. Any lightweight yarn, such as mohair, is ideal as this gives sufficient bulk to the fabric without being too heavy.

The stitch chosen also plays an important part, as the texture must be firm enough to avoid the knitting dropping but not so dense that it produces a thick, harsh fabric. Stocking stitch does not work too well with this method as it is very difficult to keep the smooth, even tension which is the main characteristic of this stitch. On the other hand, garter stitch, moss stitch and small, repeating lace or fabric patterns, such as given here, do produce interesting textures which will hold their shape.

When casting on and off, the stitches must be worked very loosely to avoid pulling the fabric out of shape.

Indian pillar stitch

Use two or more ends of yarn, depending upon the size of needle chosen. Cast on a number of stitches divisible by 4 plus 2.

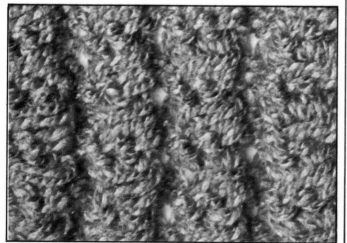

1st row P1, *insert needle purlwise into next 3 sts as if to purl them tog but instead (P1, K1, P1) into these 3 sts, K1, rep from * to last st, P1.
2nd row P to end.
These 2 rows form the pattern.

Waffle stitch

Use two or more ends of yarn and cast on a number of stitches divisible by 2.
1st row *K1 tbl, P1, rep from * to end.
2nd row *P1 tbl, K1, rep from * to end.
These 2 rows form the pattern.

Grecian plait stitch

This stitch requires one small and one large needle, the large needle being twice the size of the small needle. Use two ends of yarn and cast on an even number of stitches with the large needle.
1st row Using the small needle, K to end.
2nd row Using the large needle, P to end.
3rd row Using the small needle, lift the 2nd st over the first st and K it then K the first st, lift the 4th st over the 3rd st and K it then K the 3rd st, cont in this way all along the row.
4th row Using the large needle, P to end.
These 4 rows form the pattern.

Maxi-knit scarf

Size

Approx 23cm (9in) wide by 167.5cm (66in) long, excluding fringe

Tension

10 sts to 7.5cm (3in) over Indian pillar st worked on No.0000 needles

Materials

10 × 25grm balls of Hayfield DuBarry Double Knitting in each of 2 contrast colours, A and B
One pair No.0000 Milwards disc needles, or as required

Scarf

Using No.0000 needles if working in Indian pillar st or waffle st, or one No.0 and one No.0000 needle if working in Grecian plait st, and one strand each of A and B, cast on 30 sts loosely. Work in patt as required until scarf measures 167.5cm (66in) from beg. Cast off very loosely.

To make up

Do not press. Using 2 ends of A and B tog, make a fringe along each short end, knotting fringe into every alt st.
Trim fringe.

TRAVELLING STITCHES

Crossed stitches, which have a twisted appearance, are used extensively in Aran patterns and the same methods may be used to create effective miniature and mock cable patterns. Because only two, or at most three, stitches are crossed at any one time, it is not necessary to use a cable needle, so these patterns are simple to work.

Crossed stitches should be knitted against a purl background to show to their best advantage, but to produce an even tighter twist on the stitches, it is also necessary to know how to twist them on the wrong side, or on a purl row against a knitted background.

Knitted crossed stitches with back twist

The crossed stitches are worked over two knitted stitches and the twist lies to the left. Pass the right hand needle behind the first stitch on the left hand needle, knit into the back of the next stitch on the left hand needle then knit into the front of the first missed stitch and slip both stitches off the left hand needle together. The abbreviation for this is 'T2B'.

Mock cable

Cast on a number of stitches divisible by 5 + 3.
1st row P3, *K2, P3, rep from * to end.

2nd row K3, *P2, K3, rep from * to end.
Rep 1st and 2nd rows once more.
5th row P3, *T2B, P3, rep from * to end.
6th row As 2nd.
These 6 rows form the pattern.

Twisted rib

Cast on a number of stitches divisible by 14 + 2.
1st row P2, *T2B, P2, K4, P2, T2B, P2, rep from * to end.
2nd row K2, *P2, K2, P4, K2, P2, K2, rep from * to end.
Rep 1st and 2nd rows once more.
5th row P2, *T2B, P2, into 4th and 3rd sts on left hand needle work T2B leaving sts on needle then work T2B into 2nd and 1st sts and sl all 4 sts off needle tog, P2, T2B, P2, rep from * to end.
6th row As 2nd.
These 6 rows form the pattern.

Knitted crossed stitches with front twist

The crossed stitches are worked over two knitted stitches and the twist lies to the right. Pass the right hand needle in front of the first stitch on the left hand needle, knit into the front of the next stitch on the left hand needle then knit into the front of the first missed stitch and slip both stitches off the needle together. The abbreviation for this is 'T2F'.

Three stitches can be crossed in the same way by working into the 3rd stitch, then into the 2nd and then into the first, slipping all 3 stitches off the left hand needle together. The abbreviation for this is 'T3F'.

Twisted panels
Cast on a number of stitches divisible by 8 + 2.
1st row P2, *(T2F) 3 times, P2, rep from * to end.
2nd row K2, *P6, K2, rep from * to end.
3rd row P2, *(T3F) twice, P2, rep from * to end.
4th row As 2nd.
These 4 rows form the pattern.

Purled crossed stitches with front twist
The crossed stitches are worked over two purled stitches and form a crossed thread lying to the right on the knitted side of the work. Pass the right hand needle in front of the first stitch on the left hand needle and purl the next stitch on the left hand needle, purl the first missed stitch and slip both stitches off the left hand needle together. The abbreviation for this is 'T2PF'.

Purled crossed stitches with back twist
The crossed stitches are worked over two purled stitches and form a crossed thread lying to the left on the knitted side of the work. Pass the right hand

needle behind the first stitch on the left hand needle and purl the next stitch on the left hand needle through the back of the loop, purl the first missed stitch and slip both stitches off the left hand needle together. The abbreviation for this is 'T2PB'.

Crossing two knitted stitches to the right
Pass the right hand needle in front of the first stitch on the left hand needle and knit into the next stitch on the left hand needle, lift this stitch over the first missed stitch and off the needle then knit the first missed stitch. The abbreviation for this is 'C2R'.

Crossing two knitted stitches to the left
Slip the first stitch on to the right hand needle without knitting it, knit the next stitch on the left hand needle and slip it on to the right hand needle, using the left hand needle point pass the first slipped stitch over the knitted stitch, knitting into the slipped stitch at the same time. The abbreviation for this is 'C2L'.

Crossed cable
Cast on a number of stitches divisible by 7 + 3.
1st row P3, *K4, P3, rep from * to end.
2nd row K3, *P4, K3, rep from * to end.
3rd row P3, *C2R, C2L, P3, rep from * to end.
4th row As 2nd.
These 4 rows form the pattern.

CABLES
Basic stitches

Cable patterns, using variations of stitches, are among the most popular in knitting, since they are easy to work and give an interesting fabric with many uses – they can be thick and chunky for a sports sweater, or fine and lacy for baby garments. Twisting the cables in opposite directions can produce an all-over fabric, or simple panels of cables against the purl side of stocking stitch can give a special look to the most basic garment. All cable patterns are based on the method of moving a sequence of stitches from one position to another in a row, giving the effect of the twists you see in a rope – the more stitches moved, the thicker the rope.

The previous chapter dealt with the method of crossing two or three stitches to give a twisted effect but when altering the position of more than two stitches, it is easier to do so by means of a third needle, which is used to hold the stitches being moved until they are ready to be worked. For this purpose a special cable needle is the best, although any short, double pointed needle will do. Cable needles are very short and manoeuvrable and are made in the same sizes as knitting needles. If the cable needle is not the same thickness as the needles being used for the garment, then it should be finer and not thicker. A thicker needle is more difficult to use and, apart from this, it will stretch the stitches and spoil the appearance of the finished work.

Cable abbreviations

Although working instructions and abbreviations will usually be found in detail in any cable pattern, before beginning to knit it would be as well to study these, as they do vary considerably. As a general guide, the letter 'C' stands for the word 'cable', followed by the number of stitches to be cabled, then the letter 'B' for back, or 'F' for front, indicating the direction in which the stitches are to be moved. In this way a cable twist from right to left over 6 stitches is abbreviated as 'C6F' and a cable twist from left to right over 6 stitches is abbreviated as 'C6B'.

Cable twist from right to left

A simple cable worked over 6 knitted stitches against a purl background. To work this sample cast on 24 stitches.

1st row (RS) P9, K6, P9.
2nd row K9, P6, K9.
Rep 1st and 2nd rows twice more.
7th row P9, sl next 3 sts on to cable needle and hold at front of work, K next 3 sts from left hand needle then K3 sts from cable needle – called C6F –, P9.

8th row As 2nd.
These 8 rows form the pattern. Repeat pattern rows twice more. Cast off.

This sample produces a rope-like pattern in the centre, consisting of 6 knitted stitches twisted 3 times. Each twist lies in the same direction from the right to the left.

Cable twist from left to right

Cast on and work the first 6 rows as given for cable twist from right to left.

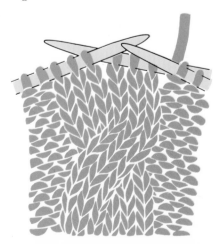

7th row P9, sl next 3 sts on to cable needle and hold at back of work, K next 3 sts from left hand needle then K3 sts from cable needle – called C6B –, P9.
8th row As 2nd.
These 8 rows form the pattern. Repeat pattern rows twice more. Cast off.
This sample will be similar to the first, but each twist will lie in the opposite direction from the left to the right.

Cable twist from right to left with row variations

The appearance of each cable twist is altered considerably by the number of rows worked between each twist. Cast on and work the first 4 rows as given for cable twist from right to left.
5th row P9, C6F, P9.
6th row As 2nd.
Rep 1st and 2nd rows twice more, then 5th and 6th rows once more.
Rep 1st and 2nd rows 4 times more, then 5th and 6th rows once more.
Rep 1st and 2nd rows 6 times more, then 5th and 6th rows once more.
Rep 1st and 2nd rows once more. Cast off.

This sample shows that the cable twist on every 4th row gives a very close, tight, rope look, whereas twisting on every 8th or 12th row gives a much softer look.

Alternating cables

This combines both the cable twist from right to left and cable twist from left to right, to produce a fabric with a completely different look although the methods used are exactly the same. Cast on and work the first 8 rows as given for cable twist from right to left.
9th row As 1st.
10th row As 2nd.
Rep 9th and 10th rows twice more.
15th row P9, C6B, P9.
16th row As 10th.
Rep 9th and 10th rows twice more. Cast off.
This sample shows the same 3 stitches being moved on each twist.

Panels of cable twist from right to left

This pattern is made up of panels of 4 knitted stitches, with one purl stitch between each panel, twisted from right to left on different rows to give a diagonal appearance. Cast on 31 stitches.
1st row P1, *K4, P1, rep from * to end.
2nd row K1, *P4, K1, rep from * to end.
3rd row P1, *K4, P1, sl next 2 sts on to cable needle and hold at front of work, K next 2 sts from left hand needle then K2 sts from cable needle – called C4F –, P1, rep from * to end.
4th row As 2nd.
Rep 1st and 2nd rows once more.
7th row P1, *C4F, P1, K4, P1, rep from * to end.
8th row As 2nd.
These 8 rows form the pattern. Repeat pattern rows 3 times more. Cast off.

More cable stitches

Based on combinations of the simple cable twists given in the previous chapter, the patterns which can be produced are numerous. All of the variations given here can be worked as all-over patterns or as separate panels against a purl background.

Try incorporating single plaited cable as an all-over pattern on a plain jersey design, or use a panel of link cables to highlight the front and centre of the sleeves on a basic cardigan. Another simple alternative would be to work two samples of honeycomb cable and use these as patch pockets on a stocking stitch cardigan, using the reverse side, or purl side as the right side of the cardigan fabric.

Link cable

The cable pattern is worked over 12 knitted stitches against a purl background. For this sample cast on 24 stitches.

1st row P6, K12, P6.
2nd row K6, P12, K6.
Rep 1st and 2nd rows twice more.
7th row P6, sl next 3 sts on to cable needle and hold at back of work, K next 3 sts from left hand needle then K3 sts from cable needle – called C6B –, sl next 3 sts on to cable needle and hold at front of work, K next 3 sts from left hand needle then K3 sts from cable needle – called C6F –, P6.
8th row As 2nd.
These 8 rows form the pattern. Repeat pattern rows twice more. Cast off.
This pattern gives the appearance of chain links, each link coming upwards out of the one below.

Inverted link cable

Cast on and work the first 6 rows as given for link cable.
7th row P6, C6F, C6B, P6.
8th row As 2nd.
These 8 rows form the pattern. Repeat pattern rows twice more. Cast off.
This pattern has the reverse appearance of link cables with each link joining and passing under the link above.

Honeycomb cable

This pattern combines the working methods of link cable and inverted link cable. For this sample cast on 24 stitches.
1st row P6, K12, P6.
2nd row K6, P12, K6.
Rep 1st and 2nd rows once more.

5th row P6, C6B, C6F, P6.
6th row As 2nd.
Rep 1st and 2nd rows twice more.
11th row P6, C6F, C6B, P6.
12th row As 2nd.
These 12 rows form the pattern. Repeat pattern rows twice more. Cast off.
This pattern forms a cable which appears to be superimposed on the fabric beneath.

Single plaited cable

This pattern is achieved by dividing the groups of stitches which are to be cabled into three sections instead of two and cabling each group alternately. For this sample cast on 30 stitches.
1st row P3, *K6, P3, rep from * to end.
2nd row K3, *P6, K3, rep from * to end.
3rd row P3, *sl next 2 sts on to cable needle and hold at back of work, K next 2 sts from left hand needle then K2 from cable needle – called C4B –, K2, P3, rep from * to end.
4th row As 2nd.
5th row P3, *K2, sl next 2 sts on to cable needle and hold at front of work, K next 2 sts from left hand needle then K2 from cable needle – called C4F –, P3, rep from * to end.
6th row As 2nd.
The 3rd to 6th rows form the pattern. Repeat pattern rows 6 times more. Cast off.

Double plaited cable

This pattern is even more textured than single plaited cable and is worked over 18 knitted stitches against a purl background. For this sample cast on 30 stitches.
1st row P6, K18, P6.
2nd row K6, P18, K6.
3rd row P6, (C6B) 3 times, P6.
4th row As 2nd.
Rep 1st and 2nd rows once more.

7th row P6, K3, (C6F) twice, K3, P6.
8th row As 2nd.
These 8 rows form the pattern. Repeat pattern rows twice more. Cast off.

Cable waves

Cable patterns have a completely different appearance when the stitches being moved are worked in knitting against a knitted background, instead of a purl fabric. For this sample cast on 24 stitches.
1st row K to end.
2nd and every alt row P to end.
3rd row *C6F, K6, rep from * to end.
5th row K to end.
7th row *K6, C6B, rep from * to end.
9th row K to end.
10th row As 2nd.
Rows 3 to 10 form the pattern. Repeat pattern rows twice more. Cast off.

Cables in rounds

Cable patterns are just as easy to work in rounds as in rows. Unless otherwise stated in a pattern, the cable twists are worked on the right side of the fabric and as the right side of the work is always facing you when knitting in rounds, it is quite a simple matter to combine both of these techniques.

This jaunty little hat has been specially designed so that the cable panels can be worked in any one of three variations. This will help you master the method of working cable stitches – at the same time resulting in a snug, warm, fashion extra!

Size
To fit an average head

Tension
22 sts and 30 rows to 10cm (*3·9in*) over st st worked on No.7 needles

Materials
3 × 25 grm balls of any Double Knitting quality
Set of 4 No.6 needles pointed at both ends
Set of 4 No. 7 needles pointed at both ends
Cable needle

Hat
Using set of 4 No.6 needles cast on 96 sts and arrange on 3 needles.
1st round *P2, K2, rep from * to end.
Rep this round for 10cm (*4in*), to form turned back brim. Change to set of 4 No.7 needles. Commence patt.

Cable patt 1
1st round *P2, K6, rep from * to end.
2nd round As 1st.
3rd round As 1st.
4th round *P2, sl next 3 sts on to cable needle and hold at front of work, K next 3 sts from left hand needle then K3 from cable needle – called C6F –, rep from * to end.
These 4 rounds form the patt.

Cable patt 2
1st round *P2, K6, rep from * to end.
2nd round As 1st.
3rd round As 1st.
4th round *P2, sl next 3 sts on to cable needle and hold at front of work, K next 3 sts from left hand needle then K3 from cable needle – called C6F –, rep from * to end.
5th round As 1st.
6th round As 1st.
7th round As 1st.
8th round *P2, sl next 3 sts on to cable needle and hold at back of work, K next 3 sts from left hand needle then K3 from cable needle – called C6B –, rep from * to end.
These 8 rounds form the patt.

Cable patt 3
1st round *P2, K6, rep from * to end.

2nd round As 1st.
3rd round As 1st.
4th round *P2, sl next 2 sts on to cable needle and hold at back of work, K next 2 sts from left hand needle then K2 from cable needle – called C4B –, K2, rep from * to end.
5th round As 1st.
6th round As 1st.
7th round As 1st.
8th round *P2, K2, sl next 2 sts on to cable needle and hold at front of work, K next 2 sts from left hand needle then K2 from cable needle – called C4F –, rep from * to end.
These 8 rounds form the patt.
Cont in patt as required until work measures 20cm (*8in*) from beg of patt, ending with a 4th or 8th patt round.

Shape top
Next round (dec round) *P2, sl 1, K1, psso, K2, K2 tog, rep from * to end. 72 sts.
Next round *P2, K4, rep from * to end.
Next round *P2, sl1, K1, psso, K2 tog, rep from * to end. 48 sts.
Next round *P2, K2, rep from * to end.
Next round *P2 tog, K2 tog, rep from * to end. 24 sts.
Next round *P1, K1, rep from * to end.
Next round *Sl 1, K1, psso, rep from * to end. 12 sts.
Break off yarn, thread through rem sts, draw up and fasten off.

To make up
Pressing on WS is required, omitting ribbing and taking care not to flatten patt. Turn RS out. Fold brim in half to outside then fold back again to form a double brim.

Cable panels

Panels of cable stitches are a most effective way of highlighting even a most basic jersey or cardigan design. They can be incorporated as separate bands spaced between panels of purl background stitches to form an all-over jersey fabric, or a single panel of cable stitches can be used as a border inside the ribbed front bands of a cardigan. Worked lengthways, they can be used as separate bands which can be sewn on to the lower edge or sleeves of a jersey, or as a headband on a snug little cap, as shown here.

Seeded cable

Cast on 12 stitches.

1st row (WS) K4, P4, K4.

2nd row P4, K4, P4.

3rd row K4, P1, sl next 2 sts keeping yarn at front of work, P1, K4.

4th row P2, sl next 3 sts on to cable needle and hold at back of work, K1 then K1, P1, K1 from cable needle, sl next st on to cable needle and hold at front of work, K1, P1, K1 then K1 from cable needle, P2.

5th row K2, (P1, K1) 3 times, P2, K2.

6th row P2, (K1, P1) 3 times, K2, P2.

Rep 5th and 6th rows twice more.

11th row K2, yfwd, sl 1 keeping yarn at front of work, ybk, (K1, P1) 3 times, sl 1 keeping yarn at front of work, ybk, K2.

12th row P2, sl next st on to cable needle and hold at front of work, P2, K1 then K1 from cable needle, sl next 3 sts on to cable needle and hold at back of work, K1 then K1, P2 from cable needle, P2.

Rep 1st and 2nd rows twice more. These 16 rows form the pattern.

Round linked cable

Cast on 12 sts.

1st row (WS) K2, yfwd, sl 1 keeping yarn at front of work, P6, sl 1 keeping yarn at front of work, ybk, K2.

2nd row P2, sl next st on to cable needle and hold at front of work, P3 then K1 from cable needle, sl next 3 sts on to cable needle and hold at back of work, K1 then P3 from cable needle, P2.

3rd row K5, P2, K5.

4th row P2, sl next 3 sts on to cable needle and hold at back of work, K1 then K3 from cable needle, sl next st on to cable needle and hold at front of work, K3 then K1 from cable needle, P2.

5th row K2, P8, K2.

6th row P2, K8, P2.

Rep 5th and 6th rows twice more. These 10 rows form the pattern.

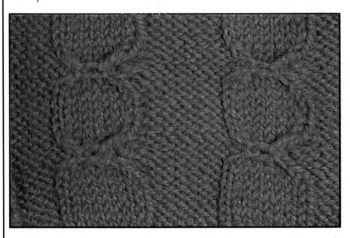

Wishbone cable

Cast on 12 sts.

1st row (RS) P2, sl next 3 sts on to cable needle and hold at back of work, K1 then P1, K1, P1 from cable needle, sl next st on to cable needle and hold at front of work, K1, P1, K1 then K1 from cable needle, P2.

2nd row K2, (P1, K1) 3 times, P2, K2.

3rd row P2, (K1, P1) 3 times, K2, P2.

Rep 2nd and 3rd rows once more.

6th row As 2nd.

7th row P2, K1, P1, K3, P1, K2, P2.

8th row K2, P1, K1, P3, K1, P2, K2.

These 8 rows form the pattern.

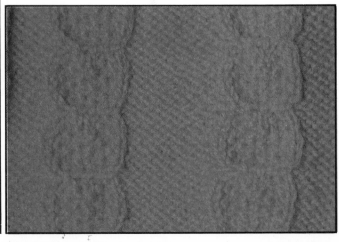

Cross cable

Cast on 12 sts.

1st row (RS) P3, K6, P3.

2nd row K3, P6, K3.

Rep 1st and 2nd rows twice more.

7th row P3, sl next 3 sts on to cable needle and hold at back of work, K3 then K3 from cable needle, P3.

8th row As 2nd.

9th row As 1st.

Rep 8th and 9th rows once more, then 8th row once more.

13th row P5, K2, P5.

14th row K5, P2, K5.

Rep 13th and 14th rows 3 times more. These 20 rows form the pattern.

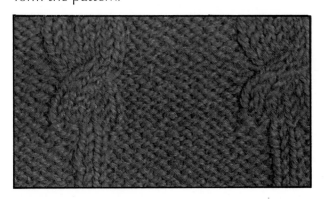

Diagonal link cable

Cast on 12 sts.

1st and every alt row (WS) K2, P8, K2.

2nd row P2, K2, sl next 2 sts on to cable needle and hold at front of work, K2 then K2 from cable needle, K2, P2.

4th row P2, K8, P2.

6th row As 2nd.

8th row As 4th.

10th row As 6th.

12th row P2, K2, K2 tog, sl 1, K1, psso, K2, P2.

13th row (WS) K2, P6, K2.

14th row P2, K1, sl1, K1, psso, K2 tog, K1, P2.

15th row K2, P4, K2.

16th row P2, sl next 2 sts on to cable needle and hold at back of work, K2 then K2 from cable needle, P2.

17th row As 15th.

18th row P2, K1, pick up loop lying between needles and K tbl – called M1 –, K2, M1, K1, P2.

19th row As 13th.

20th row P2, (K2, M1) twice, K2, P2.

These 20 rows form the pattern.

Pull-on cap

Size

To fit an average adult head

Tension

24 sts and 32 rows to 10cm (3.9*in*) over st st worked on No.8 needles

Materials

3 × 25 grm balls of any Double Knitting quality
One pair No.8 needles
Cable needle

Cap

Using No.8 needles cast on 96 sts. Beg with a P row cont in reversed st st until work measures 11.5cm ($4\frac{1}{2}$*in*) from beg, ending with a P row.

Shape top

Next row *K2 tog, K6, rep from * to end. 84 sts.

Next row P to end.

Next row *K2 tog, K5, rep from * to end. 72 sts.

Next row P to end.

Cont dec 12 sts in this way on next and every alt row until 12 sts rem. Break off yarn, thread through rem sts, draw up and fasten off.

Headband

Using No.8 needles cast on 24 sts. Work any cable patt as required.

1st row Patt 12 sts, K12.

2nd row P12, patt 12 sts.

Rep last 2 rows until band fits round lower edge of cap. Cast off.

To make up

Press as required. With RS tog, sew patt edge of head-band to lower edge of cap. Join centre back seam. Fold st st edge of headband in half to WS and sl st down.

Experiments
with cable stitch

More about cable patterns! There are so many variations of cable stitches and the fabric formed is so effective that it is well worth experimenting to see how best they can be included as for instance part of a basic jersey or cardigan design.

As already suggested in the preceding chapters, the cable patterns do not need to be worked as an all-over fabric, but panels can be incorporated in many interesting ways. The patterns shown here require a given number of stitches to form one panel, but if you wish to work more than one panel side by side, intersperse each panel with a few extra stitches, to give definition to each pattern.

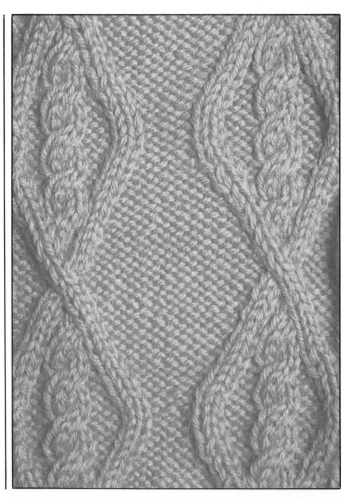

Diamond rope cable
This panel is worked over 18 stitches.
1st row (WS) K7, P4, K7.
2nd row P6, sl next st on to cable needle and hold at back of work, K2 then K1 from cable needle – called Cb3 –, sl next 2 sts on to cable needle and hold at front of work, K1 then K2 from cable needle – called Cf3 –, P6.
3rd and every alt row K all K sts and P all P sts.
4th row P5, Cb3, K2, Cf3, P5.
6th row P4, sl next st on to cable needle and hold at back of work, K2 then P1 from cable needle – called Bc3 –, sl next 2 sts on to cable needle and hold at back of work, K2 then K2 from cable needle – called Cb4 –, sl next 2 sts on to cable needle and hold at front of work, P1 then K2 from cable needle – called Fc3 –, P4.

8th row P3, Bc3, P1, K4, P1, Fc3, P3.
10th row P2, Bc3, P2, Cb4, P2, Fc3, P2.
12th row P1, Bc3, P3, K4, P3, Fc3, P1.
14th row P1, K2, P4, Cb4, P4, K2, P1.
16th row P1, Fc3, P3, K4, P3, Bc3, P1.
18th row P2, Fc3, P2, Cb4, P2, Bc3, P2.
20th row P3, Fc3, P1, K4, P1, Bc3, P3.
22nd row P4, Fc3, Cb4, Bc3, P4.
24th row P5, Fc3, K2, Bc3, P5.
26th row P6, Fc3, Bc3, P6.
28th row P7, sl next 2 sts on to cable needle and hold at front of work, K2 then K2 from cable needle, P7.
These 28 rows form the pattern.

Plaited braid cable
This panel is worked over 16 stitches.

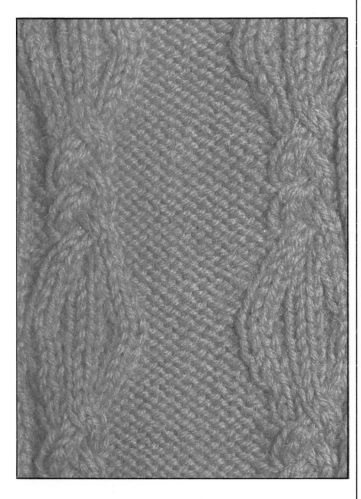

1st row (WS) K5, P6, K5.
2nd row P5, K2, sl next 2 sts on to cable needle and hold at back of work, K2 then K2 from cable needle – called Cb4 –, P5.
3rd and every alt row K all K sts and P all P sts.
4th row P5, sl next 2 sts on to cable needle and hold at front of work, K2 then K2 from cable needle – called Cf4 –, K2, P5.
6th row As 2nd.
8th row As 4th.
10th row As 2nd.
12th row As 4th.

14th row P4, sl next st on to cable needle and hold at back of work, K2 then P1 from cable needle – called Bc3 –, K2, sl next 2 sts on to cable needle and hold at front of work, P1 then K2 from cable needle – called Fc3 –, P4.
16th row P3, Bc3, P1, K2, P1, Fc3, P3.
18th row P2, Bc3, P2, K2, P2, Fc3, P2.
20th row P2, Fc3, P2, K2, P2, Bc3, P2.
22nd row P3, Fc3, P1, K2, P1, Bc3, P3.
24th row P4, Fc3, K2, Bc3, P4.
These 24 rows form the pattern.

Outlined cable
This panel is worked over 18 stitches.

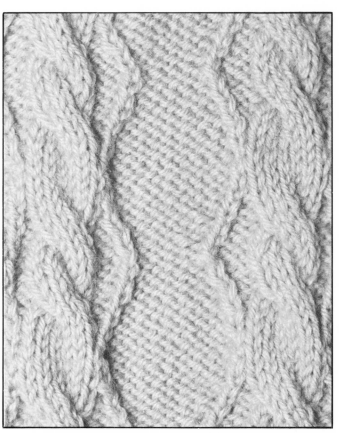

1st row (WS) K5, P8, K5.
2nd row P4, sl next st on to cable needle and hold at back of work, K1 tbl then P1 from cable needle – called Cb2 –, K6, sl next st on to cable needle and hold at front of work, P1 then K1 tbl from cable needle – called Cf2 –, P4.
3rd and every alt row K all K sts and P all P sts.
4th row P3, Cb2, P1, K6, P1, Cf2, P3.
6th row P2, Cb2, P2, sl next 3 sts on to cable needle and hold at front of work, K3 then K3 from cable needle – called Cf6 –, P2, Cf2, P2.
8th row P1, Cb2, P3, K6, P3, Cf2, P1.
10th row P1, Cf2, P3, K6, P3, Cb2, P1.
12th row P2, Cf2, P2, Cf6, P2, Cb2, P2.
14th row P3, Cf2, P1, K6, P1, Cb2, P3.
16th row P4, Cf2, K6, Cb2, P4.
These 16 rows form the pattern.

ARAN KNITTING
Basic stitches

The skilful and imaginative use of such patterns as cables, bobbles and crossed stitches, form the basis for a range of intricate and densely textured fabrics referred to as 'Aran' patterns. Most of the traditional stitches, with their highly evocative names, were originated in the remote Aran islands and derived their inspiration from the daily life of the islanders. The rocks are depicted by chunky bobble stitches, the cliff paths by zig-zag patterns, whilst the fishermen's ropes inspire a vast number of cable variations. The wealth of the sea around the islands, religious symbols and the ups and downs of married life all play a part in the formation of a rich tapestry of patterns, unique in knitting.

The Irish name for the thick, homespun yarn used for Aran knitting is 'bainin', which literally means 'natural'. These traditional stitches show to their best advantage in this light-coloured yarn but many vivid colours are now used with these stitches, to make fashion garments.

Practise the samples given here, using a Double Knitting yarn and No.8 needles, to form separate squares or panels, which can then be joined together to form cushions, afghans or even bedspreads.

Ladder of life

This simple design depicts man's eternal desire to climb upwards, the purl ridges forming the rungs of the ladder. Cast on a number of stitches divisible by 6 plus 1.

1st row (RS) P1, *K5, P1, rep from * to end.
2nd row K1, *P5, K1, rep from * to end.
3rd row P to end.
4th row As 2nd.
These 4 rows form the pattern.

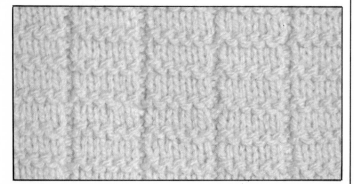

Lobster claw stitch

This represents the bounty of the sea. Cast on a number of stitches divisible by 9.

1st row (RS) *P1, K7, P1, rep from * to end.
2nd row *K1, P7, K1, rep from * to end.
3rd row *P1, sl next 2 sts on to cable needle and hold at back of work, K1 from left hand needle then K2 from cable needle, K1 from left hand needle, sl next st on to cable needle and hold at front of work, K2 from left hand needle then K1 from cable needle, P1, rep from * to end.
4th row As 2nd.
These 4 rows form the pattern.

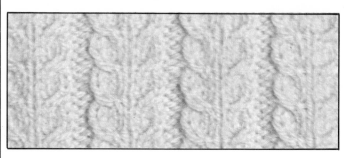

Tree of life

Narrow lines of travelling stitches branching out from a central stem form the basis for this traditional pattern. Cast on a number of stitches divisible by 15.
1st row (RS) *P7, K1, P7, rep from * to end.
2nd row *K7, P1, K7, rep from * to end.
3rd row *P5, sl next st on to cable needle and hold at back of work, K1 from left hand needle then P1 from cable needle – called C2B –, K1 from left hand needle, sl next st on to cable needle and hold at front of work, P1 from left hand needle then K1 from cable needle – called C2F –, P5, rep from * to end.
4th row *K5, sl 1 P-wise keeping yarn at front of work, K1, P1, K1, sl 1, K5, rep from * to end.
5th row *P4, C2B, P1, K1, P1, C2F, P4, rep from * to end.
6th row *K4, sl 1, K2, P1, K2, sl 1, K4, rep from * to end.
7th row *P3, C2B, P2, K1, P2, C2F, P3, rep from * to end.
8th row *K3, sl 1, K3, P1, K3, sl 1, K3, rep from * to end.

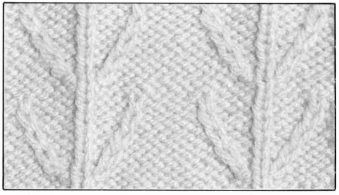

9th row *P2, C2B, P3, K1, P3, C2F, P2, rep from * to end.
10th row *K2, sl 1, K4, P1, K4, sl 1, K2, rep from * to end.
These 10 rows form the pattern.

Aran plaited cable
This simple cable depicts the interweaving of family life. Cast on a number of stitches divisible by 12.
1st row (WS) *K2, P8, K2, rep from * to end.
2nd row *P2, (sl next 2 sts on to cable needle and hold at back of work, K2 from left hand needle then K2 from cable needle) twice, P2, rep from * to end.
3rd row As 1st.
4th row *P2, K2, sl next 2 sts on to cable needle and hold at front of work, K2 from left hand needle then K2 from cable needle, K2, P2, rep from * to end.
These 4 rows form the pattern.

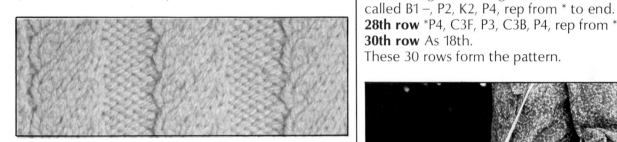

Aran diamond and bobble cable
The small diamond outlined with knitted stitches represents the small, walled fields of Ireland and the bobble depicts the stony nature of the ground. Cast on a number of stitches divisible by 17.
1st row (WS) *K6, P2, K1, P2, K6, rep from * to end.
2nd row *P6, sl next 3 sts on to cable needle and hold at back of work, K2 from left hand needle, sl P1 from end of cable needle back on to left hand needle and P1 then K2 from cable needle, P6, rep from * to end.
3rd row As 1st.
4th row *P5, sl next st on to cable needle and hold at back of work, K2 from left hand needle then P1 from cable needle – called C3B –, K1, sl next 2 sts on to cable needle and hold at front of work, P1 from left hand needle then K2 from cable needle – called C3F –, P5, rep from * to end.
5th and every alt row K all K sts and P all P sts.
6th row *P4, C3B, K1, P1, K1, C3F, P4, rep from * to end.

8th row *P3 C3B, (K1, P1) twice, K1, C3F, P3, rep from * to end.
10th row *P2, C3B, (K1, P1) 3 times, K1, C3F, P2, rep from * to end.
12th row *P2, C3F, (P1, K1) 3 times, P1, C3B, P2, rep from * to end.
14th row *P3, C3F, (P1, K1) twice, P1, C3B, P3, rep from * to end.
16th row *P4, C3F, P1, K1, P1, C3B, P4, rep from * to end.
18th row *P5, C3F, P1, C3B, P5, rep from * to end.
20th row As 2nd.
22nd row *P5, C3B, P1, C3F, P5, rep from * to end.
24th row *P4, C3B, P3, C3F, P4, rep from * to end.
26th row *P4, K2, P2, (K1, yfwd to make one st, K1, yfwd, K1) all into next st, turn and P5, turn and K5, turn and P2 tog, P1, P2 tog, turn and sl 1, K2 tog, psso – called B1 –, P2, K2, P4, rep from * to end.
28th row *P4, C3F, P3, C3B, P4, rep from * to end.
30th row As 18th.
These 30 rows form the pattern.

Shoulder bag
Size
30.5cm (*12in*) wide by 30.5cm (*12in*) deep

Tension
24 sts and 32 rows to 10cm (*3.9in*) over st st worked on No.8 needles

Materials
4 × 50grm balls of any Double Knitting
One pair No.8 needles

Bag
Using No.8 needles cast on 85 sts. Work in Aran diamond and bobble cable patt. Rep 30 patt rows 6 times in all, then first 20 rows once more. Cast off.

To make up
Fold work in half with RS facing. Join side seams and turn RS out. Turn in 1.5cm (*½in*) hem round top edge and sl st down. Make plait approx 152.5cm (*60in*) long, leaving tassels at both ends. Sew plait to side seams above tassels, leaving rest of plait free for strap.

Aran patterns

Aran panels

The variety and complexity of Aran stitches which may be formed give such scope for textured patterns that it is sometimes difficult to know where to begin a design and how best to combine these stitches to produce the most effective fabric. If each stitch is run on into the next, all definition will be lost and none of the stitches will show to their best advantage. Because these stitches nearly always have a raised texture, their beauty is enhanced if they are worked against a purled background. Similarly, if each panel of stitches is enclosed with a rope of twisted stitches and alternated with panels of either purl or moss stitches, each separate Aran panel stands out without detracting in any way from the next panel. The poncho design given here uses these techniques to full effect. It is made from two simple sections and the size can easily be adjusted by amending the number of stitches in each purl panel.

Poncho
Size
Approx 89cm (35in) square, excluding fringe

Tension
18 sts and 24 rows to 10cm (3.9in) over st st worked on No.7 needles

Materials
17 × 50grm balls Mahony Blarney Bainin wool
One pair No.7 needles
One pair No.8 needles
Set of 4 No.9 needles pointed at both ends
One No.7 circular Twin-Pin
One No.8 circular Twin-Pin
One cable needle

Poncho first section
Using No.8 circular Twin-Pin cast on 146 sts. K4 rows g st.
Next row (inc row) K3, pick up loop lying between needles and P tbl – called M1 –, K2, M1, *(K2, M1) twice, (K2, K into front and back of next st – called Kfb –) twice, K3, (M1, K2) twice, *, **(M1, K2) twice, (P1, M1, P1, P into front and back of next st – called Pfb –, P1, M1, P1, K2) twice, M1, K2, M1, **, ***K2, Pfb, K2, Kfb, K3, Pfb, K1, Pfb, K2, Kfb, K3, Pfb, K2, ***, rep from ** to **, then from *** to ***, then from ** to ** again, then rep from * to * once more, M1, K2, M1, K3. 204 sts.
Change to No.7 circular Twin-Pin. Commence patt.
1st row K2, P1, K1 tbl, P2, K1 tbl, *P2, sl next st on to cable needle and hold at front of work, P1, then K1 tbl from cable needle – called T2L –, P1, T2L, P9, sl next st on to cable needle and hold at back of work, K1 tbl, then P1 from cable needle – called T2R –, P1, T2R, P2, *, K1 tbl, P2, K1 tbl, **(P2, K8) twice, P2, K1 tbl, P2, K1 tbl, P2, K2, P3, into next st (K1, (yfwd, K1) twice, turn, P these 5 sts, turn, K5, turn, P5, turn, sl 2nd, 3rd and 4th sts over first st, then K first and last st tog tbl – called MB –) P3, sl next 3 sts on to cable needle and hold at back of work, K2, sl P st from cable needle onto left hand needle and hold cable needle at front of work, P1 from left hand needle, then K2 from cable needle – called Cr5 –, P3, MB, P3, K2, P2, K1 tbl, P2, K1 tbl, **, rep from ** to ** once more, (P2, K8) twice, P2, K1 tbl, P2, K1 tbl, rep from * to * once more, K1 tbl, P2, K1 tbl, P1, K2.
2nd row K3, *P1 tbl, K2, P1 tbl, K3, P1 tbl, K2, P1 tbl, K9, P1 tbl, K2, P1 tbl, K3, *, P1 tbl, K2, P1 tbl, **(K2, P8) twice, K2, P1 tbl, K2, P1 tbl, K2, (P2, K7, P2, K1) twice, K1, P1 tbl, K2, P1 tbl, **, rep from ** to ** once more, (K2, P8) twice, K2, rep from * to * once more, P1 tbl, K2, P1 tbl, K3.
3rd row K2, P1, *K1 tbl, P2, K1 tbl, P3, T2L, P1, T2L, P7, T2R, P1, T2R, P3, *, K1 tbl, P2, K1 tbl, **(P2, sl next 2 sts on to cable needle and hold at back of work, K2, then K2 from cable needle – called C4B –, sl next 2 sts on to cable needle and hold at front of work, K2, then K2 from cable needle – called C4F –) twice, P2, K1 tbl, P2, K1 tbl, P2, (sl next 2 sts on to cable needle and hold at front of work, P1, then K2 from cable needle – called C3L –, P5, sl next st on to cable needle and hold at back of work, K2, then P1 from cable needle – called C3R –, P1) twice, P1, K1 tbl, P2, K1 tbl, **, rep from ** to ** once more, (P2, C4B, C4F) twice, P2, rep from * to * once more, K1 tbl, P2, K1 tbl, P1, K2.
4th row K3, P1 tbl, K2, *P1 tbl, K4, P1 tbl, K2, P1 tbl, K7, P1 tbl, K2, P1 tbl, K4, *, P1 tbl, K2, P1 tbl, **(K2, P8) twice, K2, P1 tbl, K2, P1 tbl, (K3, P2, K5, P2) twice, K3, P1 tbl, K2, P1 tbl, **, rep from ** to ** once more, (K2, P8) twice, K2, P1 tbl, K2, rep from * to * once more, P1 tbl, K2, P1 tbl, K3.
5th row K2, P1, K1 tbl, *P2, K1 tbl, P4, T2L, P1, T2L, P5, T2R, P1, T2R, P4, *, K1 tbl, P2, K1 tbl, **(P2, K8) twice, P2, K1 tbl, P2, K1 tbl, (P3, C3L, P3, C3R) twice, P3, K1 tbl, P2, K1 tbl, **, rep from ** to ** once more, (P2, K8) twice, P2, K1 tbl, rep from * to * once more, K1 tbl, P2, K1 tbl, P1, K2.
6th row K3, P1 tbl, *K2, P1 tbl, (K5, P1 tbl, K2, P1 tbl) twice, K5, *, P1 tbl, K2, P1 tbl, **(K2, P8) twice, K2, P1 tbl, K2, P1 tbl, K4, P2, K3, P2, K5, P2, K3, P2, K4, P1 tbl, K2, P1 tbl, **, rep from ** to ** once more, (K2, P8) twice, K2, P1 tbl, rep from * to * once more, P1 tbl, K2, P1 tbl, K3.

T2L, P1, T2L, P5, *, K1 tbl, P2, K1 tbl, **(P2, K8) twice, P2, K1 tbl, P2, K1 tbl, P5, Cr5, P3, MB, P3, Cr5, P5, K1 tbl, P2, K1 tbl,**, rep from ** to ** once more, (P2, K8) twice, P2, K1 tbl, rep from * to * once more, K1 tbl, P2, K1 tbl, P1, K2.

10th row K3, P1 tbl, *K2, P1 tbl, (K5, P1 tbl, K2, P1 tbl) twice, K5, *, P1 tbl, K2, P1 tbl, **(K2, P8) twice, K2, P1 tbl, K2, P1 tbl, K5, P2, K1, P2, K7, P2, K1, P2, K5, P1 tbl, K2, P1 tbl, **, rep from ** to ** once more, (K2, P8) twice, K2, P1 tbl, rep from * to * once more, P1 tbl, K2, P1 tbl, K3.

11th row K2, P1, K1 tbl, *P2, K1 tbl, P4, T2R, P1, T2R, P5, T2L, P1, T2L, P4, *, K1 tbl, P2, K1 tbl, **(P2, C4F, C4B) twice, P2, K1 tbl, P2, K1 tbl, P4, C3R, P1, C3L, P5, C3R, P1, C3L, P4, K1 tbl, P2, K1 tbl, **, rep from ** to ** once more, (P2, C4F, C4B) twice, P2, K1 tbl, rep from * to * once more, K1 tbl, P2, K1 tbl, P1, K2.

12th row K3, P1 tbl, *K2, P1 tbl, K4, P1 tbl, K2, P1 tbl, K7, P1 tbl, K2, P1 tbl, K4, *, P1 tbl, K2, P1 tbl, **(K2, P8) twice, K2, P1 tbl, K2, P1 tbl, K4, P2, K3, P2, K5, P2, K3, P2, K4, P1 tbl, K2, P1 tbl, **, rep from ** to ** once more, (K2, P8) twice, K2, P1 tbl, rep from * to * once more, P1 tbl, K2, P1 tbl, K3.

13th row K2, P1, K1 tbl, *P2, K1 tbl, P3, T2R, P1, T2R, P7, T2L, P1, T2L, P3, *, K1 tbl, P2, K1 tbl, **(P2, K8) twice, P2, K1 tbl, P2, K1 tbl, (P3, C3R, P3, C3L) twice, P3, K1 tbl, P2, K1 tbl, **, rep from ** to ** once more, (P2, K8) twice, P2, K1 tbl, rep from * to * once more, K1 tbl, P2, K1 tbl, P1, K2.

14th row K3, P1 tbl, *K2, P1 tbl, K3, P1 tbl, K2, P1 tbl, K9, P1 tbl, K2, P1 tbl, K3, *, P1 tbl, K2, P1 tbl, **(K2, P8) twice, K2, P1 tbl, K2, P1 tbl, (K3, P2, K5, P2) twice, K3, P1 tbl, K2, P1 tbl,**, rep from ** to ** once more, (K2, P8) twice, K2, P1 tbl, rep from * to * once more, P1 tbl, K2, P1 tbl, K3.

15th row K2, P1, K1 tbl, *P2, K1 tbl, P2, T2R, P1, T2R, P9, T2L, P1, T2L, P2, *, K1 tbl, P2, K1 tbl, **(P2, C4F, C4B) twice, P2, K1 tbl, P2, K1 tbl, P2, (C3R, P5, C3L, P1) twice, P1, K1 tbl, P2, K1 tbl, **, rep from ** to ** once more, (P2, C4F, C4B) twice, P2, K1 tbl, rep from * to * once more, K1 tbl, P2, K1 tbl, P1, K2.

16th row K3, P1 tbl, *K2, P1 tbl, (K2, P1 tbl) twice, K11, (P1 tbl, K2) twice, *, P1 tbl, K2, P1 tbl, **(K2, P8) twice, K2, P1 tbl, K2, P1 tbl, K2, (P2, K7, P2, K1) twice, K1, P1 tbl, K2, P1 tbl, **, rep from ** to ** once more, (K2, P8) twice, K2, P1 tbl, rep from * to * once more, P1 tbl, K2, P1 tbl, K3.

These 16 rows form patt. Cont in patt until 8th row of 6th patt has been completed.

Shape neck

Next row Patt 93 sts, *(K2 tog, K1) twice, K2 tog, P2, (K2 tog, K1) twice, K2 tog, *, (P1, K2 tog) twice, **P5, K2 tog, P1, K2 tog, (P1, P2 tog) twice, (P1, K2 tog) twice, P5, **, (K2 tog tbl, P1) twice, rep from * to * once more, (P1, K2 tog) twice, P2, P2 tog, (P1, K2 tog) twice, P3, (K2 tog tbl, P1) twice, P2 tog, P2, K2 tog tbl, P1, K2 tog tbl, K2. 172 sts.

Next row Cast off 79 sts, patt to end. 93 sts.

7th row K2, P1, K1 tbl, *P2, K1 tbl, P5, T2L, P1, T2L, P3, T2R, P1, T2R, P5, *, K1 tbl, P2, K1 tbl, **(P2, C4B, C4F) twice, P2, K1 tbl, P2, K1 tbl, P4, C3L, P1, C3R, P5, C3L, P1, C3R, P4, K1 tbl, P2, K1 tbl, **, rep from ** to ** once more, (P2, C4B, C4F) twice, P2, K1 tbl, rep from * to * once more, K1 tbl, P2, K1 tbl, P1, K2.

8th row K3, P1 tbl, *K2, P1 tbl, K6, P1 tbl, K2, P1 tbl, K3, P1 tbl, K2, P1 tbl, K6, *, P1 tbl, K2, P1 tbl, **(K2, P8) twice, K2, P1 tbl, K2, P1 tbl, K5, P2, K1 P2, K7, P2, K1, P2 K5, P1 tbl, K2, P1 tbl, **, rep from ** to ** once more, (K2, P8) twice, K2, P1 tbl, rep from * to * once more, P1 tbl, K2, P1 tbl, K3.

9th row K2, P1, K1 tbl, *P2, K1 tbl, P5, T2R, P1, T2R, P3,

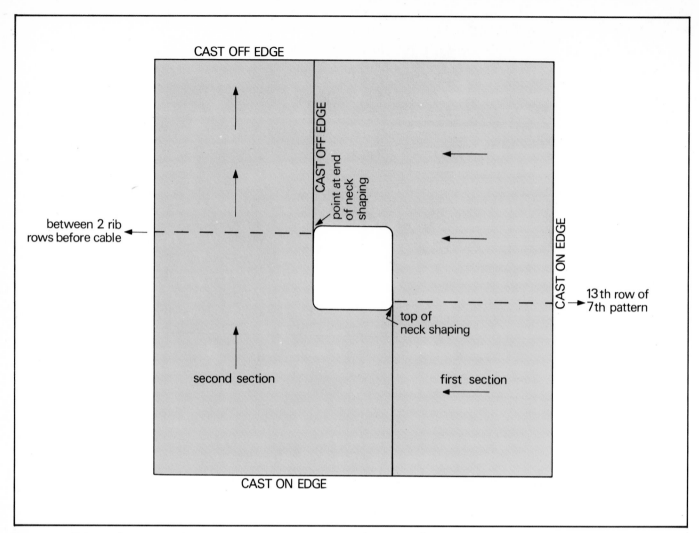

CAST OFF EDGE

CAST OFF EDGE

point at end
of neck
shaping

between 2 rib
rows before cable

CAST ON EDGE

13th row of
7th pattern

top of
neck shaping

second section

first section

CAST ON EDGE

Next row Patt to last 2 sts, P2 tog.

Keeping patt correct, cont dec one st at beg of next and every foll alt row 5 times in all. Work 8 rows without shaping. Inc one st at end of next and every alt row 6 times in all. 93 sts.

Next row K2, K2 tog, P1, K2 tog, P2, P2 tog, (P1, K2 tog tbl) twice, P3, (K2 tog, P1) twice, P2 tog, P2, (K2 tog tbl, P1) twice, rep from * to * of 1st shaping row, (P1, K2 tog) twice, rep from ** to ** of 1st shaping row, patt to end. 69 sts.

Cast off loosely.

Second section

Using No.8 needles cast on 83 sts. K 4 rows g st.

Next row (inc row) K3, M1, K2, M1, rep from * to * of inc row in first section, then from ** to ** in same row, then from *** to *** in same row, then from ** to ** again, omitting M1 at end of Row. 116 sts.

Change to No.7 needles. Commence patt.

1st row K1, P1, K1 tbl, (P2, K8) twice, P2, K1 tbl, P2, K1 tbl, P2, K2, P3, MB, P3, Cr5, P3, MB, P3, K2, P2, K1 tbl, P2, K1 tbl, (P2, K8) twice, P2, K1 tbl, P2, K1 tbl, P2, T2L, P1, T2L, P9, T2R, P1, T2R, P2, K1 tbl, P2, K1 tbl, P1, K2.

2nd row K3, P1 tbl, K2, P1 tbl, patt as now set to last 3 sts, P1 tbl, K2.

Cont in patt as now set until 8th row of 6th patt has been completed.

Shape neck

1st row K1, P1, K1 tbl, P2, (K2 tog, K1) twice, K2 tog, P2, (K2 tog, K1) twice, K2 tog, patt to end.

2nd row Patt 93 sts and leave these sts on a holder, cast off 12 sts, patt to end. 5 sts.

Dec one st at neck edge on foll 3 alt rows. Cast off. With RS of work facing, rejoin yarn to rem sts at neck edge, cont in patt dec one st at neck edge on foll 3 alt rows. 90 sts. Cont without shaping until 13th patt rep has been completed. Change to No.8 needles.

Next row K2, (K2 tog, K2, K2 tog, K1) 12 times, K2 tog, K2. 65 sts.

K 3 rows g st. Cast off.

To make up

Join both sections as shown in diagram, noting positions of top of neck shaping on second section and point at end of neck shaping on first section. Press seams on wrong side under a damp cloth with a warm iron.

Neckband Using set of 4 No.9 needles, K up 104 sts all round neck edge. Work 5 rounds K1, P1 rib. Cast off in rib, working K2 tog at each corner.

Fringe Cut yarn into lengths of 25.5cm (10in). Using 3 strands folded in half, draw centre of threads through edge of poncho and knot. Rep at 1.5cm ($\frac{1}{2}$in) intervals all round outer edge.

Aran shaping

Aran shaping

Where each Aran panel is combined with alternate panels of purl or moss stitches, it is simple to make provision for any shaping (see overleaf).

Because Aran stitches are rather complex, it is not advisable to try and combine them with any increasing or decreasing and most designs take this into account. The number of stitches required, say, for a raglan armhole and sleeve top shaping are carefully calculated to ensure that the correct number of stitches are decreased in a plain panel, without interfering with the Aran panels.

The variety of Aran designs available is sometimes restricted by this problem of shaping. This can be overcome, however, by the skilful use of shaping in each alternate plain panel and by the careful choice of a basic stitch, such as garter stitch or ribbing, to complete the shaped sections. The camisole top shown here perfectly illustrates these techniques.

Camisole top
Sizes
To fit 81.5[86.5:91.5]cm (32[34:36]in) bust
Length to shoulder, 47[49:51]cm (18[19$\frac{1}{4}$:20]in)
The figures in brackets [] refer to the 86.5 (34) and 91.5cm (36in) sizes respectively

Tension

32 sts and 40 rows to 10cm (3.9*in*) over rev st st worked on No.11 needles

Materials

4 × 50grm balls Mahony's Blarney Killowen 4 ply wool
One pair No.11 needles
One No. 11 circular Twin-Pin
One No.12 circular Twin-Pin
7 buttons

Camisole fronts and back

Using No.12 circular Twin-Pin cast on 237[253:269] sts and work in one piece, beg at lower edge.
1st row K1, *P1, K1, rep from * to end.
2nd row P1, *K1, P1, rep from * to end.
Rep last 2 rows 3 times more, then 1st row once more.
Next row P to end.
Next row P to end to form hemline.
Base row Cast on 7 sts for right front band, turn, K8, *P2, K15, P2, K8[10:12], P2, K3, P1, K2, P1, K8, P2, K8[10:12], rep from * 3 times more, P2, K15, P2, K1, turn and cast on 7 sts for left front band. 251[267:283] sts. Change to No.11 circular Twin-Pin. Commence patt.
1st row (RS) K7, P1, *K 2nd st on left hand needle, then first st − called T2 −, P7, K1, P7, T2, P8[10:12], T2, P7, K 2nd st on left hand needle, then P first st − called C2R−, P1, C2R, P3, T2, P8[10:12], T2, P2, K2, P7, K2, P2, T2, P8[10:12], T2, P7, C2R, P1, C2R, P3, T2, P8[10:12], rep from * once more, T2, P7, K1, P7, T2, P1, K7.
2nd row K8, *P2, K7, P1, K7, P2, K8[10:12], P2, K4, P1, K2, P1, K7, P2, K8[10:12], P2, K2, P3, K5, P3, K2, P2, K8[10:12], P2, K4, P1, K2, P1, K7, P2, K8[10:12], rep from * once more, P2, K7, P1, K7, P2, K8.
3rd row K7, P1, *T2, P6, K1, P1, K1, P6, T2, P8[10:12], T2, P6, C2R, P1, C2R, P4, T2, P8[10:12], T2, (P3, K3) twice, P3, T2, P8[10:12], T2, P6, C2R, P1, C2R, P4, T2, P8[10:12], rep from * once more, T2, P6, K1, P1, K1, P6, T2, P1, K7.
4th row K8, *P2, K6, P1, K1, P1, K6, P2, K8[10:12], P2, K5, P1, K2, P1, K6, P2, K8[10:12], P2, K4, P3, K1, P3, K4, P2, K8[10:12], P2, K5, P1, K2, P1, K6, P2, K8[10:12], rep from * once more, P2, K6, P1, K1, P1, K6, P2, K8.
5th row (buttonhole row) K2, K2 tog, (yrn) twice, sl 1, K1, psso, K1, P1, *T2, P5, (K1, P1) twice, K1, P5, T2, P8[10:12], T2, P5, C2R, P1, C2R, P5, T2, P8[10:12], T2, P5, K5, P5, T2, P8[10:12], T2, P5, C2R, P1, C2R, P5, T2, P8[10:12], rep from * once more, T2, P5, (K1, P1) twice, K1, P5, T2, P1, K7.
6th row K8, *P2, K5, (P1, K1) twice, P1, K5, P2, K8[10:12], P2, K6, P1, K2, P1, K5, P2, K8[10:12], P2, K6, P3, K6, P2, K8[10:12], P2, K6, P1, K2, P1, K5, P2, K8[10:12], rep from * once more, P2, K5, (P1, K1) twice, P1, K5, P2, K3, drop one loop of double loop to make long st and work K1, P1 into same st, K3.
Work 5 more buttonholes in same way with 18[20:22] rows between each buttonhole.
7th row K7, P1, *T2, P4, (K1, P1) 3 times, K1, P4, T2, P8[10:12], T2, P4, C2R, P1, C2R, P6, T2, P8[10:12], T2, P5, K5, P5, T2, P8[10:12], T2, P4, C2R, P1, C2R, P6, T2,

P8[10:12], rep from * once more, T2, P4, (K1, P1) 3 times, K1, P4, T2, P1, K7.
8th row K8, *P2, K4, (P1, K1) 3 times, P1, K4, P2, K8[10:12], P2, K7, P1, K2, P1, K4, P2, K8[10:12], P2, K4, P3, K1, P3, K4, P2, K8[10:12], P2, K7, P1, K2, P1, K4, P2, K8[10:12], rep from * once more, P2, K4, (P1, K1) 3 times, P1, K4, P2, K8.
9th row K7, P1, *T2, P3, (K1, P1) 4 times, K1, P3, T2, P8[10:12], T2, P3, C2R, P1, C2R, P7, T2, P8[10:12], T2, (P3, K3) twice, P3, T2, P8[10:12], T2, P3, C2R, P1, C2R, P7, T2, P8[10:12], rep from * once more, T2, P3, (K1, P1) 4 times, K1, P3, T2, P1, K7.
10th row K8, *P2, K3, (P1, K1) 4 times, P1, K3, P2, K8[10:12], P2, K8, P1, K2, P1, K3, P2, K8[10:12], P2, K2, P3, K5, P3, K2, P2, K8[10:12], P2, K8, P1, K2, P1, K3, P2, K8[10:12], rep from * once more, P2, K3, (P1, K1) 4 times, P1, K3, P2, K8.
11th row K7, P1, *T2, P2, (K1, P1) 5 times, K1, P2, T2, P8[10:12], T2, P3, K1, P2, K1, P8, T2, P8[10:12], T2, P2, K2, P7, K2, P2, T2, P8[10:12], T2, P3, K1, P2, K1, P8, T2, P8[10:12], rep from * once more, T2, P2, (K1, P1) 5 times, K1, P2, T2, P1, K7.
12th row K8, *P2, K2, (P1, K1) 5 times, P1, K2, P2, K8[10:12], P2, K8, P1, K2, P1, K3, P2, K8[10:12], P2, K15, P2, K8[10:12], P2, K8, P1, K2, P1, K3, P2, K8[10:12], rep from * once more, P2, K2, (P1, K1) 5 times, P1, K2, P2, K8.
13th row K7, P1, *T2, P3, (K1, P1) 4 times, K1, P3, T2, P8[10:12], T2, P3, P 2nd st on left hand needle, then K first st − called C2L −, P1, C2L, P7, T2, P8[10:12], T2, P6, K3, P6, T2, P8[10:12], T2, P3, C2L, P1, C2L, P7, T2, P8[10:12], rep from * once more, T2, P3, (K1, P1) 4 times, K1, P3, T2, P1, K7.

Shape waist

14th row K8, *P2, K3, (P1, K1) 4 times, P1, K3, P2, sl 1, K1, psso, K4[6:8], K2 tog, P2, K7, P1, K2, P1, K4, P2, sl 1, K1, psso, K4[6:8], K2 tog, P2, K5, P5, K5, P2, sl 1, K1, psso, K4[6:8], K2 tog, P2, K7, P1, K2, P1, K4, P2, sl 1, K1, psso, K4[6:8], K2 tog, rep from * once more, P2, K3, (P1, K1) 4 times, P1, K3, P2, K8. 235[251:267] sts.
15th row K7, P1, *T2, P4, (K1, P1) 3 times, K1, P4, T2, P6[8:10], T2, P4, C2L, P1, C2L, P6, T2, P6[8:10], T2, P4, K3, P1, K3, P4, T2, P6[8:10], T2, P4, C2L, P1, C2L, P6, T2, P6[8:10], rep from * once more, T2, P4, (K1, P1) 3 times, K1, P4, T2, P1, K7.
16th row K8, *P2, K4, (P1, K1) 3 times, P1, K4, P2, K6[8:10], P2, K6, P1, K2, P1, K5, P2, K6[8:10], P2, (K3, P3) twice, K3, P2, K6[8:10], P2, K6, P1, K2, P1, K5, P2, K6[8:10], rep from * once more, P2, K4, (P1, K1) 3 times, P1, K4, P2, K8.
17th row K7, P1, *T2, P5, (K1, P1) twice, K1, P5, T2, P6[8:10], T2, P5, C2L, P1, C2L, P5, T2, P6[8:10], T2, P2, K3, P5, K3, P2, T2, P6[8:10], T2, P5, C2L, P1, C2L, P5, T2, P6[8:10], rep from * once more, T2, P5, (K1, P1) twice, K1, P5, T2, P1, K7.
18th row K8, *P2, K5, (P1, K1) twice, P1, K5, P2, K6[8:10], P2, K5, P1, K2, P1, K6, P2, K6[8:10], P2, K2, P2, K7, P2, K2, P2, K6[8:10], P2, K5, P1, K2, P1, K6, P2, K6[8:10], rep from * once more, P2, K5, (P1, K1) twice, P1, K5, P2, K8.

19th row K7, P1, *T2, P6, K1, P1, K1, P6, T2, P6[8:10], T2, P6, C2L, P1, C2L, P4, T2, P6[8:10], T2, P2, K3, P5, K3, P2, T2, P6[8:10], T2, P6, C2L, P1, C2L, P4, T2, P6[8:10], rep from * once more, T2, P6, K1, P1, K1, P6, T2, P1, K7.

20th row K8, *P2, K6, P1, K1, P1, K6, P2, sl 1, K1, psso, K2[4:6], K2 tog, P2, K4, P1, K2, P1, K7, P2, sl 1, K1, psso, K2[4:6], K2 tog, P2, (K3, P3) twice, K3, P2, sl 1, K1, psso, K2[4:6], K2 tog, P2, K4, P1, K2, P1, K7, P2, sl 1, K1, psso, K2[4:6], K2 tog, rep from * once more, P2, K6, P1, K1, P1, K6, P2, K8. 219[235:251] sts.

21st row K7, P1, *T2, P7, K1, P7, T2, P4[6:8], T2, P7, C2L, P1, C2L, P3, T2, P4[6:8], T2, P4, K3, P1, K3, P4, T2, P4[6:8], T2, P7, C2L, P1, C2L, P3, T2, P4[6:8], rep from * once more, T2, P7, K1, P7, T2, P1, K7.

22nd row K8, *P2, K7, P1, K7, P2, K4[6:8], P2, K3, P1, K2, P1, K8, P2, K4[6:8], P2, K5, P5, K5, P2, K4[6:8], P2, K3, P1, K2, P1, K8, P2, K4[6:8], rep from * once more, P2, K7, P1, K7, P2, K8.

23rd row K7, P1, *T2, P15, T2, P4[6:8], T2, P8, K1, P2, K1, P3, T2, P4[6:8], T2, P6, K3, P6, T2, P4[6:8], T2, P8, K1, P2, K1, P3, T2, P4[6:8], rep from * once more, T2, P15, T2, P1, K7.

24th row K8, *P2, K15, P2, K4[6:8], P2, K3, P1, K2, P1, K8, P2, K4[6:8], P2, K15, P2, K4[6:8], P2, K3, P1, K2, P1, K8, P2, K4[6:8], rep from * once more, P2, K15, P2, K8.

These 24 rows set patt for Aran panels with rev st st between each one. Cont in patt as now set, dec 2 sts as before within each rev st st panel on foll alt row.

203[219:235] sts. Cont in patt until work measures 11.5[12:12.5]cm (4½[4¾:5]in) from hemline, ending with a RS row.

Next row K8, *P2, patt 15, P2, pick up loop lying between needles and K tbl – called M1 –, K2[4:6], M1, rep from * 7 times more, P2, patt 15, P2, K8.

Cont in patt, inc 2 sts as before within each rev st st panel on foll 20th row twice more. 251[267:283] sts. Cont in patt without shaping until work measures 28[29:30.5]cm (11[11½:12]in) from hemline, ending with a WS row.

Shape yoke

Next row K8, *K2 tog, K6, K2 tog, K7, K2 tog, K8[10:12], rep from * 7 times more, K2 tog, K6, K2 tog, K7, K2 tog, K8. 224[240:256] sts.

Beg with a K row, cont in g st until work measures 30.5[31.5:33]cm (12[12½:13]in) from hemline, ending with a WS row.

Divide for armholes

Change to No.11 needles.

Next row K55[58:61], turn and leave rem sts on holder. Complete right front first.

Shape armhole

Cast off at beg of next and every foll alt row 2 sts 3 times and one st 3[4:5] times, *at the same time* work 7th buttonhole 18[20:22] rows above previous buttonhole. K 2 rows, ending at front edge.

Shape neck

Cast off at beg of next and every foll alt row 23[24:25] sts once, 4 sts once, 2 sts 3 times and one st 3 times. 10[11:12] sts. Cont without shaping until work measures 47[49:51]cm (18[19¼:20]in) from hemline. Cast off.

With RS of work facing, rejoin yarn to back sts, cast off first 8[10:12] sts, K until there are 98[104:110] sts on right hand needle, turn and leave rem sts on holder for left front. Complete back first.

Shape armholes

Cast off 2 sts at beg of next 5 rows.

Shape back neck

Next row Cast off 2, K until there are 26[28:30] sts on right hand needle, cast off 34[36:38] sts for neck, K to end.

Dec one st at armhole edge on every alt row 3[4:5] times in all, *at the same time* cast off at neck edge on every alt row 4 sts once, 2 sts 3 times and one st 3 times. 10[11:12] sts. Cont without shaping until work measures 47[49:51]cm (18[19¼:20]in) from hemline. Cast off.

With WS of work facing, rejoin yarn to rem back sts and complete as given for first side, reversing shaping. With RS of work facing, rejoin yarn to rem left front sts, cast off 8[10:12] sts, K to end. 55[58:61] sts. Complete to match right front, reversing shaping and omitting buttonhole.

To make up

Press under a damp cloth with a warm iron. Join shoulder seams. Turn hem to WS at lower edge and sl st down. Press seams. Sew on buttons.

LACE STITCHES
Simple lace

Knitted lace stitches do not need to be **complicated** in order to produce openwork fabrics. Some of the most effective traditional patterns require only a few stitches and as little as two rows to form the pattern repeat.

The principle used for almost all lace stitches is that of decreasing one or more stitches at a given point in a row and compensating for these decreased stitches, either in the same row or a following row, by working more than once into a stitch or making one or more stitches by taking the yarn over or round the right hand needle the required number of times, as referred to earlier. Use a 4 ply yarn and No.10 needles to practice these simple lace stitches.

Laburnum stitch
Cast on a number of stitches divisible by 5 + 2.
1st row P2, *K3, P2, rep from * to end.
2nd row K2, *P3, K2, rep from * to end.
3rd row P2, *keeping yarn at front of work, sl 1, ybk, K2 tog, psso, bring yarn over top of needle from back to front then round needle again, P2, rep from * to end.
4th row K2, *P into the back of the first made st then into the front of the second made st, P1, K2, rep from * to end.
These 4 rows form the pattern.

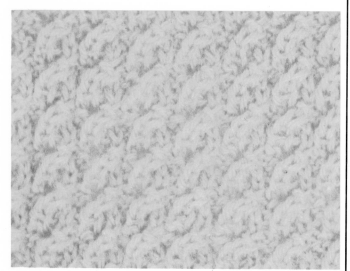

Indian pillar stitch
Cast on a number of stitches divisible by 4 + 3.
1st row (RS) P to end.
2nd row K2, *insert needle P-wise into the next 3 sts as if to P3 tog but instead work (P1, K1, P1) into these 3 sts, K1, rep from * to last st, K1. These 2 rows form the pattern.

Indian pillar stitch

Faggoting rib
Cast on a number of stitches divisible by 5 + 1.
1st row P1, *K2, yfwd, sl 1, K1, psso, P1, rep from * to end.
2nd row K1, *P2, yrn, P2 tog, K1, rep from * to end.
These 2 rows form the pattern.

Lace rib
Cast on a number of stitches divisible by 5 + 2.
1st row P2, *K1, yfwd, sl 1, K1, psso, P2, rep from * to end.
2nd row K2, *P3, K2, rep from * to end.
3rd row P2, *K2 tog, yfwd, K1, P2, rep from * to end.
4th row As 2nd.
These 4 rows form the pattern.

Eyelet cable rib

Cast on a number of stitches divisible by 5+2.

1st row P2, *K3, P2, rep from * to end.

2nd row K2, *P3, K2, rep from * to end.

3rd row P2, *sl 1, K2, psso the K2, P2, rep from * to end.

4th row K2, *P1, yrn, P1, K2, rep from * to end.

These 4 rows form the pattern.

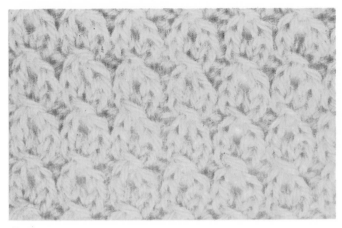

Cat's eye pattern

Cast on a number of stitches divisible by 4.

1st row K4, *yfwd over and round the needle again to make 2 sts, K4, rep from * to end.

2nd row P2, *P2 tog, P the first made st and K the second made st, P2 tog, rep from * to last 2 sts, P2.

3rd row K2, yfwd, *K4, yfwd over and round the needle again, rep from * to last 6 sts, K4, yfwd, K2.

4th row P3, *(P2 tog) twice, P the first made st and K the second made st, rep from * to last 7 sts, (P2 tog) twice, P3.

These 4 rows form the pattern.

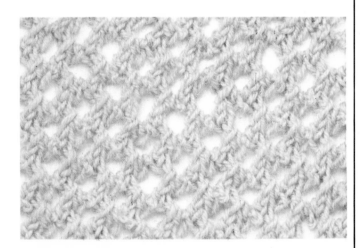

Open star stitch

Cast on a number of stitches divisible by 3.

1st row K2, *yfwd, K3 then pass the first of these 3 sts over the other 2 and off the right hand needle, rep from * to last st, K1.

2nd row P to end.

3rd row K1, *K3 then pass the first of these 3 sts over the other 2, yfwd, rep from * to last 2 sts, K2.

4th row P to end.

These 4 rows form the pattern.

Open star stitch

Hyacinth stitch

Cast on a number of stitches divisible by 6+3.

1st, 3rd and 5th rows P to end.

2nd row K1, *(K1, P1, K1, P1, K1) all into next st, K5 tog, rep from * to last 2 sts, (K1, P1, K1, P1, K1) into next st, K1.

4th row K1, *K5 tog, (K1, P1, K1, P1, K1) all into next st, rep from * to last 6 sts, K5 tog, K1.

6th row K to end winding yarn 3 times round right hand needle for each st.

7th row P to end dropping the extra loops.

The 2nd to 7th rows form the pattern.

Diagonal openwork stitch

Cast on a number of stitches divisible by 2+1.

1st row K1, *yfwd, K2 tog, rep from * to end.

2nd row P to end.

3rd row K2, *yfwd, K2 tog, rep from * to last st, K1.

4th row P to end.

These 4 rows form the pattern.

More simple lace

This chapter gives more simple lace patterns which are easy to work and produce most effective fabrics. Use a 3 or 4 ply yarn and No.11 or No.10 needles to practise these stitches.

Lace diamond pattern
Cast on a number of stitches divisible by 6 + 1.
1st row P1, *K5, P1, rep from * to end.
2nd row K1, *P5, K1, rep from * to end.
3rd row P1, *yon, sl 1, K1, psso, K1, K2 tog, yrn, P1, rep from * to end.
4th row K1, *K into back of next st – called K1B –, P3, K1B, K1, rep from * to end.
5th row P2, *yon, sl 1, K2, psso the 2 sts, yrn, P3, rep from * to last 5 sts, yon, sl 1, K2, psso the 2 sts, yrn, P2.
6th row K2, *K1B, P2, K1B, K3, rep from * to last 6 sts, K1B, P2, K1B, K2.
7th row P2, *K2 tog, yfwd, sl 1, K1, psso, P3, rep from * to last 6 sts, K2 tog, yfwd, sl 1, K1, psso, P2.
8th row K1, *P2 tog tbl, yrn, P1, yrn, P2 tog, K1, rep from * to end.
These 8 rows form the pattern.

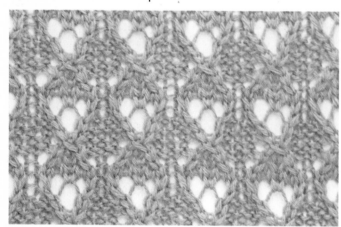

Embossed leaf pattern
Cast on a number of stitches divisible by 7.
1st row P to end.
2nd row K to end.
3rd row P3, *yon, K1, yrn, P6, rep from * to last 4 sts, yon, K1, yrn, P3.
4th row K3, *P3, K6, rep from * to last 6 sts, P3, K3.
5th row P3, *K1, (yfwd, K1) twice, P6, rep from * to last 6 sts, K1, (yfwd, K1) twice, P3.
6th row K3, *P5, K6, rep from * to last 8 sts, P5, K3.
7th row P3, *K2, yfwd, K1, yfwd, K2, P6, rep from * to last 8 sts, K2, yfwd, K1, yfwd, K2, P3.
8th row K3, *P7, K6, rep from * to last 10 sts, P7, K3.
9th row P3, *K3, yfwd, K1, yfwd, K3, P6, rep from * to last 10 sts, K3, yfwd, K1, yfwd, K3, P3.
10th row K3, *P9, K6, rep from * to last 12 sts, P9, K3.

11th row P3, *sl 1, K1, psso, K5, K2 tog, P6, rep from * to last 12 sts, sl 1, K1, psso, K5, K2 tog, P3.
12th row As 8th.
13th row P3, *sl 1, K1, psso, K3, K2 tog, P6, rep from * to last 10 sts, sl 1, K1, psso, K3, K2 tog, P3.
14th row As 6th.
15th row P3, *sl 1, K1, psso, K1, K2 tog, P6, rep from * to last 8 sts, sl 1, K1, psso, K1, K2 tog, P3.
16th row As 4th.
17th row P3, *sl 1, K2 tog, psso, P6, rep from * to last 6 sts, sl 1, K2 tog, psso, P3.
18th row As 2nd.
19th row As 1st.
20th row As 2nd.
These 20 rows form the pattern.

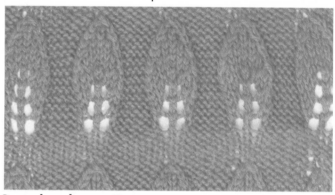

Snowdrop lace pattern
Cast on a number of stitches divisible by 8 + 3.
1st row K1, K2 tog, yfwd, *K5, yfwd, sl 1, K2 tog, psso, yfwd, rep from * to last 8 sts, K5, yfwd, sl 1, K1, psso, K1.
2nd and every alt row P to end.
3rd row As 1st.
5th row K3, *yfwd, sl 1, K1, psso, K1, K2 tog, yfwd, K3, rep from * to end.
7th row K1, K2 tog, yfwd, *K1, yfwd, sl 1, K2 tog, psso, yfwd, rep from * to last 4 sts, K1, yfwd, sl 1, K1, psso, K1.
8th row As 2nd.
These 8 rows form the pattern.

Falling leaf pattern

Cast on a number of stitches divisible by 10 + 1.

1st row K1, *yfwd, K3, sl 1, K2 tog, psso, K3, yfwd, K1, rep from * to end.

2nd and every alt row P to end.

3rd row K1, *K1, yfwd, K2, sl 1, K2 tog, psso, K2, yfwd, K2, rep from * to end.

5th row K1, *K2, yfwd, K1, sl 1, K2 tog, psso, K1, yfwd, K3, rep from * to end.

7th row K1, *K3, yfwd, sl 1, K2 tog, psso, yfwd, K4, rep from * to end.

9th row K2 tog, *K3, yfwd, K1, yfwd, K3, sl 1, K2 tog, psso, rep from * to last 9 sts, K3, yfwd, K1, yfwd, K3, sl 1, K1, psso.

11th row K2 tog, *K2, yfwd, K3, yfwd, K2, sl 1, K2 tog, psso, rep from * to last 9 sts, K2, yfwd, K3, yfwd, K2, sl 1, K1, psso.

13th row K2 tog, *K1, yfwd, K5, yfwd, K1, sl 1, K2 tog, psso, rep from * to last 9 sts, K1, yfwd, K5, yfwd, K1, sl 1, K1, psso.

15th row K2 tog, *yfwd, K7, yfwd, sl 1, K2 tog, psso, rep from * to last 9 sts, yfwd, K7, yfwd, sl 1, K1, psso.

16th row As 2nd.

These 16 rows form the pattern.

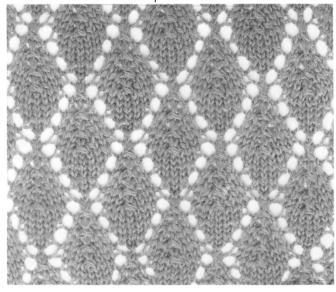

Cat's paw pattern

Cast on a number of stitches divisible by 12 + 1.

1st row K5, *yfwd, sl 1, K2 tog, psso, yfwd, K9, rep from * to last 8 sts, yfwd, sl 1, K2 tog, psso, yfwd, K5.

2nd and every alt row P to end.

3rd row K3, *K2 tog, yfwd, K3, yfwd, sl 1, K1, psso, K5, rep from * to last 10 sts, K2 tog, yfwd, K3, yfwd, sl 1, K1, psso, K3.

5th row As 1st.

7th row K to end.

9th row K2 tog, *yfwd, K9, yfwd, sl 1, K2 tog, psso, rep from * to last 11 sts, yfwd, K9, yfwd, sl 1, K1, psso.

11th row K2, *yfwd, sl 1, K1, psso, K5, K2 tog, yfwd, K3, rep from * to last 11 sts, yfwd, sl 1, K1, psso, K5, K2 tog, yfwd, K2.

13th row As 9th.

15th row As 7th.

16th row As 2nd.

These 16 rows form the pattern.

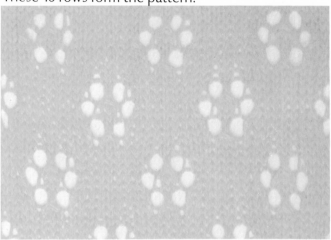

Gothic Pattern

Cast on a number of stitches divisible by 10 + 1.

1st row K1, *yfwd, sl 1, K1, psso, K5, K2 tog, yfwd, K1, rep from * to end.

2nd and every alt row P to end.

3rd row K2, *yfwd, sl 1, K1, psso, K3, K2 tog, yfwd, K3, rep from * to last 9 sts, yfwd, sl 1, K1, psso, K3, K2 tog, yfwd, K2.

5th row K3, *yfwd, sl 1, K1, psso, K1, K2 tog, yfwd, K5, rep from * to last 8 sts, yfwd, sl 1, K1, psso, K1, K2 tog, yfwd, K3.

7th row K4, *yfwd, sl 1, K2 tog, psso, yfwd, K7, rep from * to last 7 sts, yfwd, sl 1, K2 tog, psso, yfwd, K4.

9th row K1, *yfwd, sl 1, K1, psso, K2 tog, yfwd, K1, rep from * to end.

10th row As 2nd.

11th-18th rows Rep the 9th and 10th rows 4 times more.

19th row K2, *yfwd, sl 1, K1, psso, K3, K2 tog, yfwd, K3, rep from * to last 9 sts, yfwd, sl 1, K1, psso, K3, K2 tog, yfwd, K2.

21st row K3, *yfwd, sl 1, K1, psso, K1, K2 tog, yfwd, K5, rep from * to last 8 sts, yfwd, sl 1, K1, psso, K1, K2 tog, yfwd, K3.

23rd row K4, *yfwd, sl 1, K2 tog, psso, yfwd, K7, rep from * to last 7 sts, yfwd, sl 1, K2 tog, psso, yfwd, K4.

24th row As 2nd.

These 24 rows form the pattern.

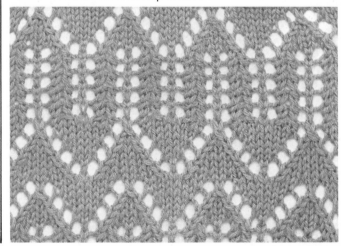

Traditional lace patterns

The history of lace stitches spans several centuries; many of the stitches, like those described in this chapter, have traditional names which are both beautiful and descriptive.

Shell and shower
Cast on a number of stitches divisible by 12 + 3.
1st row K2, *yfwd, K4, sl 1, K2 tog, psso, K4, yfwd, K1, rep from * to last st, K1.
2nd and every alt row P to end.
3rd row K3, *yfwd, K3, sl 1, K2 tog, psso, K3, yfwd, K3, rep from * to end.
5th row K1, K2 tog, *yfwd, K1, yfwd, K2, sl 1, K2 tog, psso, K2, yfwd, K1, yfwd, sl 1, K2 tog, psso, rep from * to last 12 sts, yfwd, K1, yfwd, K2, sl 1, K2 tog, psso, K2, yfwd, K1, yfwd, sl 1, K1, psso, K1.
7th row K1, *yfwd, sl 1, K1, psso, K2, yfwd, K1, sl 1, K2 tog, psso, K1, yfwd, K3, rep from * to last 2 sts, yfwd, K2 tog.
9th row K2, *yfwd, sl 1, K2 tog, psso, yfwd, K1, rep from * to last st, K1.
10th row As 2nd
These 10 rows form the pattern.

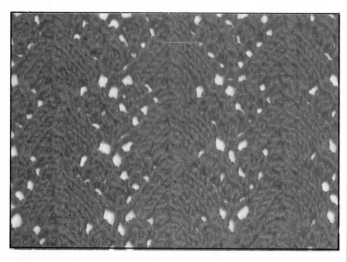

Ogee lace
Cast on a number of stitches divisible by 24 + 1.
1st row *K2, yfwd, K2 tog, K1, K2 tog, K3, yfwd, sl 1, K1, psso, yrn, P1, yon, K2, yfwd, sl 1, K1, psso, K1, sl 1, K1, psso, K1, sl 1, K1, psso, yfwd, K1, rep from * to last st, K1.
2nd row P1, *P7, yrn, P2 tog, P5, yrn, P2 tog, P8, rep from * to end.
3rd row *K1, yfwd, K2 tog, K1, K2 tog, K3, yfwd, sl 1, K1, psso, K1, yfwd, K1, yfwd, K3, yfwd, sl 1, K1, psso, K1, sl 1, K1, psso, K1, sl 1, K1, psso, yfwd, rep from * to last st, K1.

4th row P1, *P6, yrn, P2 tog, P7, yrn, P2 tog, P7, rep from * to end.
5th row *K3, K2 tog, K3, yfwd, sl 1, K1, psso, K1, yfwd, K3, yfwd, K3, yfwd, sl 1, K1, psso, K1, sl 1, K1, psso, K2, rep from * to last st, K1.
6th row P1, *P5, yrn, P2 tog, P9, yrn, P2 tog, P6, rep from * to end.
7th row *K2, K2 tog, K3, yfwd, sl 1, K1, psso, K3, yfwd, K1, yfwd, K5, yfwd, sl 1, K1, psso, K1, sl 1, K1, psso, K1, rep from * to last st, K1.
8th row P1, *P4, yrn, P2 tog, P11, yrn, P2 tog, P5, rep from * to end.
9th row *K1, K2 tog, K3, yfwd, sl 1, K1, psso, K3, yfwd, K3, yfwd, K5, yfwd, sl 1, K1, psso, K1, sl 1, K1, psso, rep from * to last st, K1.
10th row P1, *P3, yrn, P2 tog, P13, yrn, P2 tog, P4, rep from * to end.
11th row Sl 1, K1, psso, *K3, yfwd, sl 1, K1, psso, K1, sl 1, K1, psso, yfwd, K2, yfwd, K1, yfwd, K2, yfwd, K2 tog, K3, yfwd, sl 1, K1, psso, K1, sl 1, K2 tog, psso, rep from * to last 23 sts, K3, yfwd, sl 1, K1, psso, K1, sl 1, K1, psso, yfwd, K2, yfwd, K1, yfwd, K2, yfwd, K2 tog, K3, yfwd, sl 1, K1, psso, K1, sl 1, K1, psso.
12th row P1, *P2, yrn, P2 tog, P15, yrn, P2 tog, P3, rep from * to end.
13th row Sl 1, K1, psso, *K2, yfwd, sl 1, K1, psso, K5, yfwd, K3, yfwd, K7, yfwd, sl 1, K1, psso, sl 1, K2 tog, psso, rep from * to last 23 sts, K2, yfwd, sl 1, K1, psso, K5, yfwd, K3, yfwd, K7, yfwd, sl 1, K1, psso, sl 1, K1, psso.
14th row K1, *P1, yrn, P2 tog, P17, yrn, P2 tog, P1, K1, rep from * to end.
15th row *P1, yon, K2, yfwd, sl 1, K1, psso, K1, sl 1, K1, psso, K1, sl 1, K1, psso, yfwd, K3, yfwd, K2 tog, K1, K2 tog, K3, yfwd, sl 1, K1, psso, yrn, rep from * to last st, P1.
16th row As 12th.
17th row *K1, yfwd, K3, yfwd, sl 1, K1, psso, K1, sl 1, K1, psso, K1, sl 1, K1, psso, yfwd, K1, yfwd, K2 tog, K1, K2 tog, K3, yfwd, sl 1, K1, psso, K1, yfwd, rep from * to last st, K1.
18th row As 10th.
19th row *K2, yfwd, K3, yfwd, sl 1, K1, psso, K1, sl 1, K1, psso, K5, K2 tog, K3, yfwd, sl 1, K1, psso, K1, yfwd, K1, rep from * to last st, K1.
20th row As 8th.
21st row *K1, yfwd, K5, yfwd, sl 1, K1, psso, K1, sl 1, K1, psso, K3, K2 tog, K3, yfwd, sl 1, K1, psso, K3, yfwd, rep from * to last st, K1.
22nd row As 6th.
23rd row *K2, yfwd, K5, yfwd, sl 1, K1, psso, K1, sl 1, K1, psso, K1, K2 tog, K3, yfwd, sl 1, K1, psso, K3, yfwd, K1, rep from * to last st, K1.

24th row As 4th.

25th row *K1, yfwd, K2, yfwd, K2 tog, K3, yfwd, sl 1, K1, psso, K1, sl 1, K2 tog, psso, K3, yfwd, sl 1, K1, psso, K1, sl 1, K1, psso, yfwd, K2, yfwd, rep from * to last st, K1.

26th row As 2nd.

27th row *K2, yfwd, K7, yfwd, sl 1, K1, psso, sl 1, K2 tog, psso, K2, yfwd, sl 1, K1, psso, K5, yfwd, K1, rep from * to last st, K1.

28th row P1, *P8, yrn, P2 tog, P1, K1, P1, yrn, P2 tog, P9, rep from * to end.

These 28 rows form the pattern.

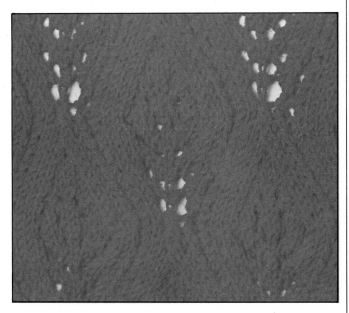

Spanish lace

Cast on a number of stitches divisible by 34 + 4.

1st row K2, *K3, K2 tog, K4, yrn, P2, (K2, yfwd, sl 1, K1, psso) 3 times, P2, yon, K4, sl 1, K1, psso, K3, rep from * to last 2 sts, K2.

2nd row P4, *P2 tog tbl, P4, yrn, P1, K2, (P2, yrn, P2 tog) 3 times, K2, P1, yrn, P4, P2 tog, P4, rep from * to end.

3rd row K3, *K2 tog, K4, yfwd, K2, P2, (K2, yfwd, sl 1, K1, psso) 3 times, P2, K2, yfwd, K4, sl 1, K1, psso, K2, rep from * to last st, K1.

4th row P2, *P2 tog tbl, P4, yrn, P3, K2, (P2, yrn, P2 tog) 3 times, K2, P3, yrn, P4, P2 tog, rep from * to last 2 sts, P2.

Rep the 1st to 4th rows twice more.

13th row *(K2, yfwd, sl 1, K1, psso) twice, P2, yon, K4, sl 1, K1, psso, K6, K2 tog, K4, yrn, P2, K2, yfwd, sl 1, K1, psso, rep from * to last 4 sts, K2, yfwd, sl 1, K1, psso.

14th row *(P2, yrn, P2 tog) twice, K2, P1, yrn, P4, P2 tog, P4, P2 tog tbl, P4, yrn, P1, K2, P2, yrn, P2 tog, rep from * to last 4 sts, P2, yrn, P2 tog.

15th row *(K2, yfwd, sl 1, K1, psso) twice, P2, K2, yfwd, K4, sl 1, K1, psso, K2, K2 tog, K4, yfwd, K2, P2, K2, yfwd, sl 1, K1, psso, rep from * to last 4 sts, K2, yfwd, sl 1, K1, psso.

16th row *(P2, yrn, P2 tog) twice, K2, P3, yrn, P4, P2 tog, P2 tog tbl, P4, yrn, P3, K2, P2, yrn, P2 tog, rep from * to last 4 sts, P2, yrn, P2 tog.

Rep the 13th to 16th rows twice more.
These 24 rows form the pattern.

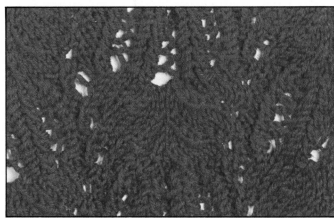

Candlelight lace

Cast on a number of stitches divisible by 12 + 1.

1st row K1, *yfwd, sl 1, K1, psso, K7, K2 tog, yfwd, K1, rep from * to end.

2nd and every alt row P to end.

3rd row K1, *yfwd, K1, sl 1, K1, psso, K5, K2 tog, K1, yfwd, K1, rep from * to end.

5th row K1, * yfwd, K2, sl 1, K1, psso, K3, K2 tog, K2, yfwd, K1, rep from * to end.

7th row K1, *yfwd, K3, sl 1, K1, psso, K1, K2 tog, K3, yfwd, K1, rep from * to end.

9th row K1, *yfwd, K4, sl 1, K2 tog, psso, K4, yfwd, K1, rep from * to end.

11th row *K4, K2 tog, yfwd, K1, yfwd, sl 1, K1, psso, K3, rep from * to last st, K1.

13th row *K3, K2 tog, K1, (yfwd, K1) twice, sl 1, K1, psso, K2, rep from * to last st, K1.

15th row *K2, K2 tog, K2, yfwd, K1, yfwd, K2, sl 1, K1, psso, K1, rep from * to last st, K1.

17th row *K1, K2 tog, K3, yfwd, K1, yfwd, K3, sl 1, K1, psso, rep from * to last st, K1.

19th row K2 tog, *K4, yfwd, K1, yfwd, K4, sl 1, K2 tog, psso, rep from * to last 11 sts, K4, yfwd, K1, yfwd, K4, sl 1, K1, psso.

20th row As 2nd.

These 20 rows form the pattern.

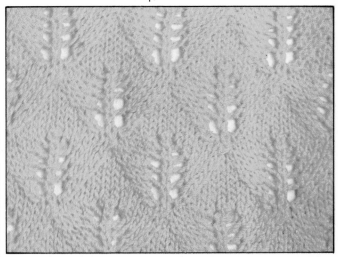

Larger lace patterns

The traditional lace stitches described here vary in complexity but each of them can be used to form a fabric of delicate beauty.

Wheatear pattern
Cast on a number of stitches divisible by 11.

1st row (RS) *K1, (K1, yfwd to make a st, K1, yfwd, K1) all into same st, turn and K5, turn and P5, turn and K1, sl 1, K2 tog, psso, K1, turn and P3 tog – called B1 –, K2, yfwd, K1, yfwd, K4, K2 tog, rep from * to end, noting that one extra st is inc in each rep on this and every RS row.

2nd, 4th, 6th, 8th and 10th rows *P2 tog, P10, rep from * to end.

3rd row *K5, yfwd, K1, yfwd, K3, K2 tog, rep from * to end.

5th row *K6, yfwd, K1, yfwd, K2, K2 tog, rep from * to end.

7th row *K7, (yfwd, K1) twice, K2 tog, rep from * to end.

9th·row *K8, yfwd, K1, yfwd, K2 tog, rep from * to end.

11th row *Sl 1, K1, psso, K4, yfwd, K1, yfwd, K2, B1, K1, rep from * to end.

12th, 14th, 16th and 18th rows *P10, P2 tog tbl, rep from * to end.

13th row *Sl 1, K1, psso, K3, yfwd, K1, yfwd, K5, rep from * to end.

15th row *Sl 1, K1, psso, K2, yfwd, K1, yfwd, K6, rep from * to end.

17th row *Sl 1, K1, psso, (K1, yfwd) twice, K7, rep from * to end.

19th row *Sl 1, K1, psso, yfwd, K1, yfwd, K8, rep from * to end.

20th row As 12th.
These 20 rows form the pattern.

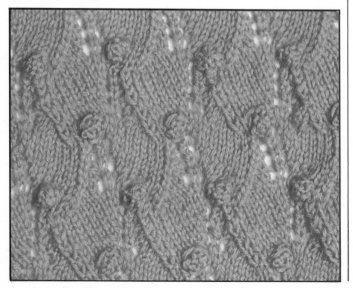

Fountain pattern
Cast on a number of stitches divisible by 16 plus 1.

1st row (WS) P to end.

2nd row Sl 1, K1, psso, *yfwd, K2, K2 tog, yfwd, K1, yfwd, sl 1, K2 tog, psso, yfwd, K1, yfwd, sl 1, K1, psso, K2, yfwd, sl 1, K2 tog, psso, rep from * ending last rep K2 tog instead of sl 1, K2 tog, psso.

3rd and every alt row P to end.

4th row Sl 1, K1, psso, *K3, yfwd, K2 tog, yfwd, K3, yfwd, sl 1, K1, psso, yfwd, K3, sl 1, K2 tog, psso, rep from * ending last rep as 2nd row.

6th row Sl 1, K1, psso, *(K2, yfwd) twice, K2 tog, K1, sl 1, K1, psso, (yfwd, K2) twice, sl 1, K2 tog, psso, rep from * ending last rep as 2nd row.

8th row Sl 1, K1, psso, *K1, yfwd, K3, yfwd, K2 tog, K1, sl 1, K1, psso, yfwd, K3, yfwd, K1, sl 1, K2 tog, psso, rep from * ending last rep as 2nd row.
These 8 rows form the pattern.

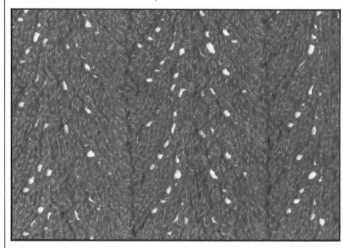

Oriel pattern
Cast on a number of stitches divisible by 12 plus 1.

1st row (RS) P1, *sl 1, K1, psso, K3, yrn, P1, yon, K3, K2 tog, P1, rep from * to end.

2nd row K1, *P5, K1, rep from * to end.
Rep 1st and 2nd rows twice more.

7th row P1, *yon, K3, K2 tog, P1, sl 1, K1, psso, K3, yrn, P1, rep from * to end.

8th row As 2nd.

9th row P2, *yon, K2, K2 tog, P1, sl 1, K1, psso, K2, yrn, P3, rep from * ending last rep P2 instead of P3.

10th row K2, *P4, K1, P4, K3, rep from * ending last rep K2 instead of K3.

11th row P3, *yon, K1, K2 tog, P1, sl 1, K1, psso, K1, yrn, P5, rep from * ending last rep P3 instead of P5.

12th row K3, *P3, K1, P3, K5, rep from * ending last rep K3 instead of K5.

13th row P4, *yon, K2 tog, P1, sl 1, K1, psso, yrn, P7, rep from * ending last rep P4 instead of P7.

14th row K4, *P2, K1, P2, K7, rep from * ending last rep K4 instead of K7.

15th row As 7th.

16th row As 2nd.

Rep 15th and 16th rows twice more.

21st row As 1st.

22nd row As 2nd.

23rd row P1, *sl 1, K1, psso, K2, yrn, P3, yon, K2, K2 tog, P1, rep from * to end.

24th row K1, *P4, K3, P4, K1, rep from * to end.

25th row P1, *sl 1, K1, psso, K1, yrn, P5, yon, K1, K2 tog, P1, rep from * to end.

26th row K1, *P3, K5, P3, K1, rep from * to end.

27th row P1, *sl 1, K1, psso, yrn, P7, yon, K2 tog, P1, rep from * to end.

28th row K1, *P2, K7, P2, K1, rep from * to end.

These 28 rows form the pattern.

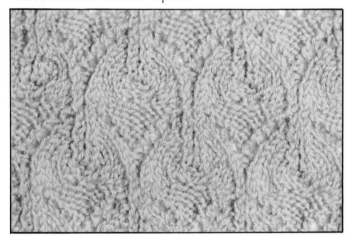

Bell pattern

Cast on a number of stitches divisible by 18 plus 1, noting that the number of stitches do not remain the same on every row but will revert to the original number on the 12th, 14th, 26th and 28th rows.

1st row (RS) K1, *(P2, K1) twice, yfwd, K2 tog, yfwd, K1, yfwd, sl 1, K1, psso, yfwd, (K1, P2) twice, K1, rep from * to end.

2nd row *(P1, K2) twice, P9, K2, P1, K2, rep from * to last st, P1.

3rd row K1, *(P2, K1) twice, yfwd, K2 tog, yfwd, K3, yfwd, sl 1, K1, psso, yfwd, (K1, P2) twice, K1, rep from * to end.

4th row *(P1, K2) twice, P11, K2, P1, K2, rep from * to last st, P1.

5th row K1, *(P2 tog, K1) twice, yfwd, K2 tog, yfwd, sl 1, K1, psso, K1, K2 tog, yfwd, sl 1, K1, psso, yfwd, (K1, P2 tog) twice, K1, rep from * to end.

6th row *(P1, K1) twice, P11, K1, P1, K1, rep from * to last st, P1.

7th row K1, *(P1, K1) twice, yfwd, K2 tog, yfwd, K1 tbl, yfwd, sl 1, K2 tog, psso, yfwd, K1, tbl, yfwd, sl 1, K1, psso, yfwd, (K1, P1) twice, K1, rep from * to end.

8th row *(P1, K1) twice, P13, K1, P1, K1, rep from * to last st, P1.

9th row K1, *(K2 tog) twice, yfwd, K2 tog, yfwd, K3, yfwd, K1, yfwd, K3, yfwd, sl 1, K1, psso, yfwd, (sl 1, K1, psso) twice, K1, rep from * to end.

10th, 12th and 14th rows P to end.

11th row K1, *(K2 tog, yfwd) twice, sl 1, K1, psso, K1, K2 tog, yfwd, K1, yfwd, sl 1, K1, psso, K1, K2 tog, (yfwd, sl 1, K1, psso) twice, K1, rep from * to end.

13th row K2 tog, *yfwd, K2 tog, yfwd, K1 tbl, yfwd, sl 1, K2 tog, psso, yfwd, K3, yfwd, sl 1, K2 tog, psso, yfwd, K1 tbl, yfwd, sl 1, K1, psso, yfwd, sl 1, K2 tog, psso, rep from * ending last rep sl 1, K1, psso, instead of sl 1, K2 tog, psso.

15th row K1, *yfwd, sl 1, K1, psso, yfwd, (K1, P2) 4 times, K1, yfwd, K2 tog, yfwd, K1, rep from * to end.

16th row P5, *(K2, P1) 3 times, K2, P9, rep from * ending last rep P5 instead of P9.

17th row K2, *yfwd, sl 1, K1, psso, yfwd, (K1, P2) 4 times, K1, yfwd, K2 tog, yfwd, K3, rep from * ending last rep K2 instead of K3.

18th row P6, *(K2, P1) 3 times, K2, P11, rep from * ending last rep P6 instead of P11.

19th row K1, *K2 tog, yfwd, sl 1, K1, psso, yfwd, (K1, P2 tog) 4 times, K1, yfwd, K2 tog, yfwd, sl 1, K1, psso, K1, rep from * to end.

20th row P6, *(K1, P1) 3 times, K1, P11, rep from * ending last rep P6 instead of P11.

21st row K2 tog, *yfwd, K1 tbl, yfwd, sl 1, K1, psso, yfwd, (K1, P1) 4 times, K1, yfwd, K2 tog, yfwd, K1 tbl, yfwd, sl 1, K2 tog, psso, rep from * ending last rep sl 1, K1, psso, instead of sl 1, K2 tog, psso.

22nd row P7, *(K1, P1) 3 times, K1, P13, rep from * ending last rep P7 instead of P13.

23rd row K1, *yfwd, K3, yfwd, sl 1, K1, psso, yfwd, (sl 1, K1, psso) twice, K1, (K2 tog) twice, yfwd, K2 tog, yfwd, K3, yfwd, K1, rep from * to end.

24th and 26th rows P to end.

25th row K1, *yfwd, sl 1, K1, psso, K1, K2 tog, (yfwd, sl 1, K1, psso) twice, K1, (K2 tog, yfwd) twice, sl 1, K1, psso, K1, K2 tog, yfwd, K1, rep from * to end.

27th row K2, *yfwd, sl 1, K2 tog, psso, yfwd, K1 tbl, yfwd, sl 1, K1, psso, yfwd, sl 1, K2 tog, psso, yfwd, K2 tog, yfwd, K1 tbl, yfwd, sl 1, K2 tog, psso, yfwd, K3, rep from * ending last rep K2 instead of K3.

28th row P to end.

These 28 rows form the pattern.

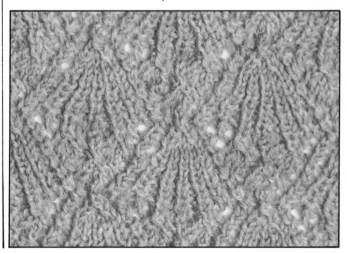

PATTERN SHAPES AND PICTURES

Patterned shapes and pictures can be achieved in knitting by means of different textures and stitches, using a single, overall colour. This technique can be incorporated into any plain, basic shape most effectively, either as a repeating border such as the fir trees and tulip stitches shown here, or as a single motif, such as the house pattern, centrally placed on the front of a jersey.

Before beginning to knit, work out the position for the border or motif, making sure that you have the correct multiples of stitches for the border repeat or that a motif is centrally placed.

Fir tree border

This pattern requires multiples of 12 stitches plus 1 and is worked against a reversed stocking stitch background.

1st row (RS) K1, *P1, K1, rep from * to end.
2nd row P1, *K1, P1, rep from * to end.
3rd row P6, *K1, P11, rep from * to last 7 sts, K1, P6.
4th row K6, *P1, K11, rep from * to last 7 sts, P1, K6.
Rep last 2 rows 3 times more.
11th row P2, *K1, P3, rep from * to last 3 sts, K1, P2.
12th row K2, *P1, K3, rep from * to last 3 sts, P1, K2.
13th row P2, *K2, P2, K1, P2, K2, P3, rep from * to last

11 sts, K2, P2, K1, P2, K2, P2.
14th row K2, *P2, K2, P1, K2, P2, K3, rep from * to last 11 sts, P2, K2, P1, K2, P2, K2.
15th row P2, *K3, P3, rep from * to last 5 sts, K3, P2.
16th row K2, *P3, K3, rep from * to last 5 sts, P3, K2.
17th row P2, *K4, P1, K4, P3, rep from * to last 11 sts, K4, P1, K4, P2.
18th row K2, *P4, K1, P4, K3, rep from * to last 11 sts, P4, K1, P4, K2.
19th row P3, *K7, P5, rep from * to last 10 sts, K7, P3.
20th row K3, *P7, K5, rep from * to last 10 sts, P7, K3.
21st row P4, *K5, P7, rep from * to last 9 sts, K5, P4.
22nd row K4, *P5, K7, rep from * to last 9 sts, P5, K4.
23rd row P5, *K3, P9, rep from * to last 8 sts, K3, P5.
24th row K5, *P3, K9, rep from * to last 8 sts, P3, K5.
25th row P6, *K1, P11, rep from * to last 7 sts, K1, P6.
26th row K6, *P1, K11, rep from * to last 7 sts, P1, K6.
These 26 rows complete the border pattern.

Tulip bed border

This pattern requires multiples of 20 stitches plus 1 and is worked against a stocking stitch background.
1st row (RS) K5, *K2 tog, yfwd, K1, yfwd, K2 tog, P1, sl 1, K1, psso, yfwd, K1, yfwd, sl 1, K1, psso, K9, rep from * ending last rep K5 instead of K9.

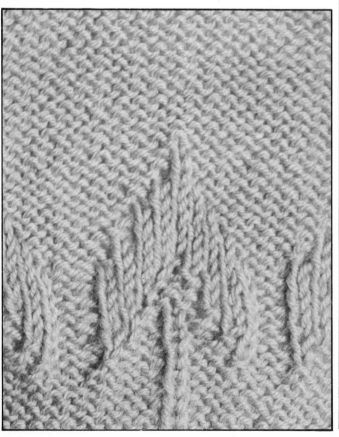

2nd and every alt row P to end.

3rd row K4, *K2 tog, yfwd, K2, yfwd, K2 tog, P1, sl 1, K1, psso, yfwd, K2, yfwd, sl 1, K1, psso, K7, rep from * ending last rep K4.

5th row K3, *K2 tog, yfwd, K3, yfwd, K2 tog, P1, sl 1, K1, psso, yfwd, K3, yfwd, sl 1, K1, psso, K5, rep from * ending last rep K3.

7th row K2, *K2 tog, yfwd, K4, yfwd, K2 tog, P1, sl 1, K1, psso, yfwd, K4, yfwd, sl 1, K1, psso, K3, rep from * ending last rep K2.

9th row K1, *K2 tog, yfwd, K5, yfwd, K2 tog, P1, sl 1, K1, psso, yfwd, K5, yfwd, sl 1, K1, psso, K1, rep from * to end.

11th row K2, *yfwd, K2 tog, K2, (K2 tog, yfwd) twice, K1, (yfwd, sl 1, K1, psso) twice, K2, sl 1, K1, psso, yfwd, K3, rep from * ending last rep K2.

13th row K2, *yfwd, K2 tog, K1, (K2 tog, yfwd) twice, K3, (yfwd, sl 1, K1, psso) twice, K1, sl 1, K1, psso, yfwd, K3, rep from * ending last rep K2.

15th row K2, *yfwd, (K2 tog) twice, yfwd, K2 tog, yfwd, K5, yfwd, sl 1, K1, psso, yfwd, (sl 1, K1, psso) twice, yfwd, K3, rep from * ending last rep K2.

17th row K2, *yfwd, sl 2, K1, p2sso, yfwd, K2 tog, yfwd, K7, yfwd, sl 1, K1, psso, yfwd, sl 2, K1, p2sso, yfwd, K3, rep from * ending last rep K2.

19th row K2, *K2 tog, yfwd, K2, yfwd, K2 tog, K5, sl 1, K1, psso, yfwd, K2, yfwd, sl 1, K1, psso, K3, rep from * ending last rep K2.

21st row K6, *yfwd, K2 tog, K5, sl 1, K1, psso, yfwd, K11, rep from * ending last rep K6.

23rd row K6, *yfwd, (K2 tog) twice, yfwd, K1, yfwd, (sl 1, K1, psso) twice, yfwd, K11, rep from * ending last rep K6.

25th row K6, *yfwd, sl 2, K1, p2sso, yfwd, K3, yfwd, sl 2, K1, p2sso, yfwd, K11, rep from * ending last rep K6.

26th row As 2nd.

These 26 rows complete the border pattern.

House motif

This pattern is worked over 28 stitches in all against a reversed stocking stitch background.

1st row (RS) P2, K7, K into front of 2nd st on left hand needle then into front of first st – called T2R –, P6, K into back of 2nd st on left hand needle then into front of first st – called T2L –, K7, P2.

2nd row K2, P9, K6, P9, K2.

Rep 1st and 2nd rows once more.

5th row P2, K2, (K2, yfwd, K2 tog for window), K1, T2R, P6, T2L, K1, (K2, yfwd, K2 tog), K2, P2.

6th row K2, P2, (P2, yrn, P2 tog), P3, K6, P3, (P2, yrn, P2 tog), P2, K2.

Rep 5th and 6th rows twice more.

11th row P2, K2, (K2, yfwd, K2 tog), K1, T2R, P1, (P1, K1, P1) all into next st, turn and K3, turn and P3 then lift 2nd and 3rd sts over first st to form door knob, P4, T2L, K1, (K2, yfwd, K2 tog), K2, P2.

12th row As 6th.

Rep 5th and 6th rows twice more.

17th row As 1st.

18th row As 2nd.

19th row P2, K8, T2R, P4, T2L, K8, P2.

20th row K2, P10, K4, P10, K2.

21st row P2, K9, T2R, P2, T2L, K9, P2.

22nd row K2, P11, K2, P11, K2.

23rd row P2, K10, T2R, T2L, K10, P2.

24th row K2, P24, K2.

25th row P2, K24, P2.

26th row As 24th.

27th row P2, K2, (K2, yfwd, K2 tog for window), K4, (K2, yfwd, K2 tog), K4, (K2, yfwd, K2 tog), K2, P2.

28th row K2, P2, (P2, yrn, P2 tog), P4, (P2, yrn, P2 tog), P4, (P2, yrn, P2 tog), P2, K2.

Rep 27th and 28th rows twice more, then 25th and 26th rows twice more.

37th row K to end.

38th row K to end.

39th row P1, K26, P1.

40th row K to end.

41st row P2, K24, P2.

42nd row K to end.

43rd row P3, K22, P3.

44th row K to end.

45th row P4, K20, P4.

46th row K to end.

47th row P5, K18, P5.

48th row K to end.

49th row P10, (K1, P1) twice, K1, P13.

50th row K13, (P1, K1) twice, P1, K10.

Rep 49th and 50th rows 3 times more.

These 56 rows complete motif.

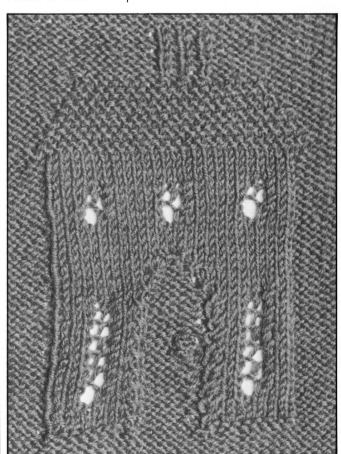

A simple patterned jersey

This chapter shows a simple jersey shape which incorporates the house motif given in the previous chapter on patterned shapes and motifs.

Jersey
Sizes
To fit 86 [91:96]cm (*34[36:38]in*) bust

Length to shoulder, 58.5[59:59.5]cm (*23[23¼:23½]in*)
Sleeve seam, 18cm (*7in*)
The figures in brackets [] refer to the 91 (*36*) and 96cm (*38in*) sizes respectively

Tension
28 sts and 36 rows to 10cm (*3.9in*) over st st worked on

No.10 needles

Materials
12[13:14] × 25grm balls Sirdar Superwash Wool 4 ply
One pair No.10 needles
One pair No.11 needles

Back
Using No.11 needles cast on 120[124:128]sts. Work 5cm (2in) K1, P1 rib. Change to No.10 needles. Beg with a P row work 4 rows reversed st st.

Next row P2, (patt 28 sts as given for 1st row of house motif, P16 [18:20] sts) twice, patt 28 sts as given for 1st row of house motif, P2.

Next row K2, (patt 28 sts as given for 2nd row of house motif, K16 [18:20] sts) twice, patt 28 sts as given for 2nd row of house motif, K2.

Cont in patt as now set until 56 patt rows have been completed. Beg with a P row work 4 rows reversed st st.

Next row P24 [25:26] sts, patt 28 sts as given for 1st row of house motif, P16 [18:20] sts, patt 28 sts as given for 1st row of house motif, P24 [25:26].

Next row K24 [25:26] sts, patt 28 sts as given for 2nd row of house motif, K16 [18:20] sts, patt 28 sts as given for 2nd row of house motif, K24 [25:26].

Cont in patt as now set until second 56 patt rows have been completed. Beg with a P row work 4 rows reversed st st.

Next row P46 [48:50] sts, patt 28 sts as given for 1st row of house motif, P46 [48:50].

Next row K46 [48:50] sts, patt 28 sts as given for 2nd row of house motif, K46 [48:50].

Cont in patt as now set until work measures 40.5cm (16in) from beg, ending with a K row.

Shape armholes
Keeping patt correct until third 56 patt rows have been completed, then cont in reversed st st across all sts, cast off at beg of next and every row 5 sts twice and 2 sts 4 times. Dec one st at each end of next and foll 5 alt rows. 90[94:98]sts. Cont without shaping until armholes measure 18[18.5:19]cm (7[7¼:7½]in) from beg, ending with a K row.

Shape shoulders
Cast off at beg of next and every row 7 sts 4 times and 11[12:13] sts twice. Leave rem 40[42:44] sts on holder for centre back neck.

Front
Work as given for back until armhole shaping is completed and third 56 patt rows have been worked. Cont without shaping in reversed st st until armholes measure 12.5[13:14]cm (5[5¼:5½]in) from beg, ending with a K row.

Shape neck
Next row P35[36:37] sts, cast off 20[22:24] sts, P to end. Complete this side first. K 1 row. Cast off at beg of next and every alt row 2 sts 3 times, then dec one st at neck edge on every alt row 4 times. 25[26:27] sts.

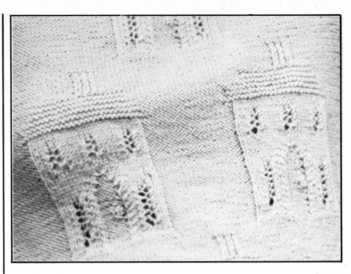

Cont without shaping until armhole measures same as back to shoulder, ending at armhole edge.

Shape shoulder
Cast off at beg of next and every alt row 7 sts twice and 11[12:13] sts once.

With WS of work facing, rejoin yarn to rem sts and complete to match first side, reversing shaping.

Sleeves
Using No.11 needles cast on 76[78:80] sts. Work 2.5cm (1in) K1, P1 rib. Change to No.10 needles. Beg with a P row work 4 rows reversed st st.

Next row P2, patt 28 sts as given for 1st row of house motif, P16[18:20] sts, patt 28 sts as given for 1st row of house motif, P2.

Next row K2, patt 28 sts as given for 2nd row of house motif, K16[18:20] sts, patt 28 sts as given for 2nd row of house motif, K2.

Cont in patt as now set, inc one st at each end of next and every foll 6th row until there are 86[90:94] sts, working extra sts into reversed st st, until 56 patt rows have been completed. Cont in reversed st st across all sts.

Shape top
Cast off 5 sts at beg of next 2 rows. Dec one st at each end of next and foll 10[11:12] alt rows, ending with a K row. Cast off at beg of next and every row 2 sts 6 times, 3 sts 6 times and 4 sts 4 times. Cast off rem 8[10:12] sts.

Neckband
Join right shoulder seam. Using No.11 needles and with RS of work facing, K up 20[21:22] sts down left front neck, K up 20[22:24] sts across front neck, K up 20[21:22] sts up right front neck and K across 40[42:44] back neck sts on holder. 100[106:112] sts. Work 5cm (2in) K1, P1 rib. Cast off in rib.

To make up
Press as directed on ball band. Join rem shoulder and neckband seam. Set in sleeves. Join side and sleeve seams. Fold neckband in half to WS and sl st down. Press seams.

SHETLAND LACE

Of all the traditional knitting techniques which have flourished in Britain, such as Aran and Fair Isle patterns, typical Shetland Isle lace stitches are among the most beautiful.

The finest examples come from Unst, the most northerly of all the Shetland Islands, where a few skilled knitters have carried on the tradition for many generations.

The stitches are few in number, only ten being truly native, and were inspired by examples of fine Spanish lace brought to the Shetland Isles as part of an exhibition in the early nineteenth century. Each stitch has been adapted to represent the natural beauty of the islands and carry such evocative names as 'Ears o'Grain', 'Print o'the Wave' and 'Fir Cones'.

Even today, the yarn used for the superb examples of this craft is hand spun to a single ply of such delicate fineness that few knitters would be able to work with it. However, a 2 ply yarn worked on No.12 needles can produce a reasonable facsimile of this most beautiful and rewarding method of knitting.

Casting on and off for lace knitting

Thick, harsh lines caused by casting on and off, or seaming, must be avoided or they will immediately detract from the delicate appearance of the lace.

Use the 2 needle method of casting on but instead of inserting the right hand needle between the last

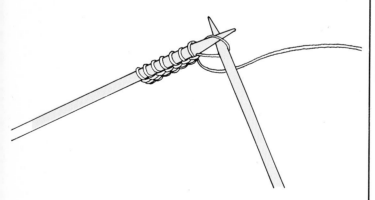

2 stitches on the left hand needle, insert it from front to back into the last stitch on the left hand needle and then draw a loop through to form the next stitch, transferring this to the left hand needle. This forms a loose, open edge.

Casting off should be worked in the usual way, using a needle 2 times larger to work the casting off than the size used for the main fabric.

Where the fabric has to be joined, it is best to use a spare length of yarn for casting on which can later be withdrawn, to allow the first and last rows to be grafted together for an invisible join.

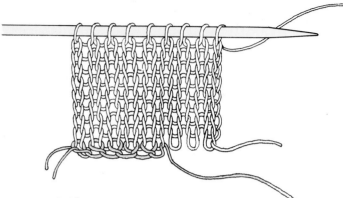

Crown of Glory pattern

This stitch is also known by the descriptive name of Cat's paw. Cast on a number of stitches divisible by 14 plus 5.

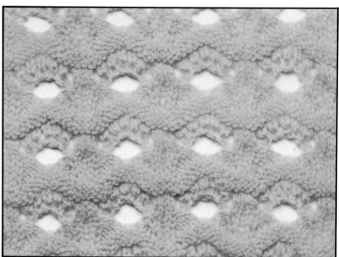

1st row (RS) K3, *sl 1, K1, psso, K9, K2 tog, K1, rep from * to last 2 sts, K2.

2nd row P2, *P1, P2 tog, P7, P2 tog tbl, rep from * to last 3 sts, P3.

3rd row K3, *sl 1, K1, psso, K2, yrn 3 times, K3, K2 tog, K1, rep from * to last 2 sts, K2.

4th row P2, *P1, P2 tog, P2, (K1, P1, K1, P1, K1) all into yrn 3 times making 5 sts, P1, P2 tog tbl, rep from * to last 3 sts, P3.

5th row K3, *sl 1, K1, psso, K6, K2 tog, K1, rep from * to last 2 sts, K2.

6th row P2, *P1, P2 tog, P6, rep from * ending last rep P3.

7th row K3, *K1, (yfwd, K1) 6 times, K1, rep from * to last 2 sts, K2.

8th row P to end.

9th and 10th rows K to end.

11th row P to end.

12th row K to end.

These 12 rows form the pattern.

Razor shell pattern

This stitch takes its name from the shells on the beach. It can be worked over multiples of 4, 6, 8, 10 or 12 stitches. For the sample shown here, cast on a number of stitches divisible by 6 plus 1.

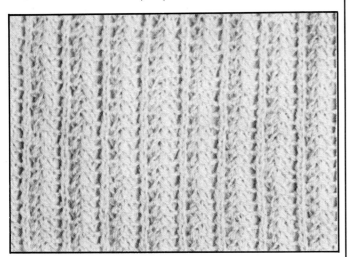

1st row (WS) P to end.

2nd row K1, *yfwd, K1, sl 1, K2 tog, psso, K1, yfwd, K1, rep from * to end.

These 2 rows form the pattern.

Horseshoe print pattern

Derived from the imprint of horseshoes on wet sand, this sample requires a number of stitches divisible by 10 plus 1.

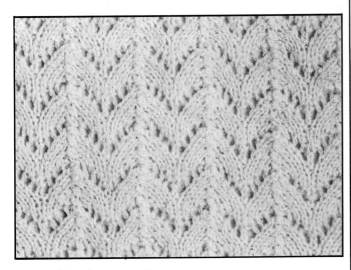

1st row (WS) P to end.

2nd row K1, *yfwd, K3, sl 1, K2 tog, psso, K3, yfwd, K1, rep from * to end.

3rd row As 1st.

4th row P1, *K1, yfwd, K2, sl 1, K2 tog, psso, K2, yfwd, K1, P1, rep from * to end.

5th row K1, *P9, K1, rep from * to end.

6th row P1, *K2, yfwd, K1, sl 1, K2 tog, psso, K1, yfwd, K2, P1, rep from * to end.

7th row As 5th.

8th row P1, *K3, yfwd, sl 1, K2 tog, psso, yfwd, K3, P1, rep from * to end.

These 8 rows form the pattern.

Fern pattern

This stitch is often used as a shawl border, as the shape of the lace motif allows for easy corner shaping. The size of the lace motif can vary but the working method remains the same. For the sample shown here, cast on a number of stitches divisible by 15.

1st row (RS) *K7, yfwd, sl 1 K-wise, K1, psso, K6, rep from * to end.

2nd row P to end.

3rd row *K5, K2 tog, yfwd, K1, yfwd, sl 1 K-wise, K1, psso, K5, rep from * to end.

4th row P to end.

5th row *K4, K2 tog, yfwd, K3, yfwd, sl 1 K-wise, K1, psso, K4, rep from * to end.

6th row P to end.

7th row *K4, yfwd, sl 1 K-wise, K1, psso, yfwd, sl 1, K2 tog, psso yfwd, K2 tog, yfwd, K4, and rep from * to end.

8th row P to end.

9th row *K2, K2 tog, yfwd, K1, yfwd, sl 1 K-wise, K1, psso, K1, K2 tog, yfwd, K1, yfwd, sl 1 K-wise, K1, psso, K2, rep from * to end.

10th row P to end.

11th row *K2, (yfwd, sl 1 K-wise, K1, psso) twice, K3, (K2 tog, yfwd) twice, K2, rep from * to end.

12th row *P3, (yrn, P2 tog) twice, P1, (P2 tog tbl, yrn) twice, P3, rep from * to end.

13th row *K4, yfwd, sl 1 K-wise, K1, psso, yfwd, sl 1, K2 tog, psso, yfwd, K2 tog, yfwd, K4, and rep from * to end.

14th row *P5, yrn, P2 tog, P1, P2 tog tbl, yrn, P5, rep from * to end.

15th row *K6, yfwd, sl 1, K2 tog, psso, yfwd, K6, rep from * to end.

16th row P to end.

These 16 rows form the pattern.

A Shetland lace shawl

The gossamer Shetland lace shawl shown here is a superb example of what is known as a 'wedding ring' shawl. It is so fine that it can easily be pulled through a wedding ring, hence its name, and it can be likened to a spider's web, having no beginning and no ending. This shawl is reproduced by kind permission of Highland Home Industries of Edinburgh, who still use a few highly skilled Shetland Islanders to make these garments in their own homes. Traditionally this would be made as a christening shawl but it could also be used as a beautiful winter wedding veil. As can be imagined, these shawls are in great demand but take so long to knit that they are literally worth their weight in gold. The yarn used has been homespun and is so fine that two strands together have been used to knit this shawl. It has been spun from the fine, soft wool which grows around the sheep's neck.

The needles used to knit this shawl are still called by their traditional name of 'wires' and, in all probability, the pattern has been passed from one generation to another by word of mouth and the instructions will never have been written down.

Once a shawl of this delicacy has been completed, it will be washed and then 'dressed', or stretched into shape. To dress the shawl in the traditional manner special wooden frames, as large as a bed, are needed. The shawl would be laced to this frame with lacing through every point along the edges of the border and left to dry naturally. In this way, the shawl is kept taut and square and each point, or scallop of the border is stretched out to its correct shape.

In this Chapter we give another two traditional lace stitches, to inspire you to experiment with this most beautiful craft.

Print o' the wave pattern

This beautiful, undulating pattern is a reminder that the sea is a constant part of life in the islands. To work this sample, cast on a number of stitches divisible by 22 plus 3 *very* loosely.

1st row (RS) K4, *K2 tog, K3, (yfwd, K2 tog) twice, yfwd, K13, rep from * to end, ending last rep with K12 instead of K13.

2nd and every alt row P to end.

3rd row K3, *K2 tog, K3, yfwd, K1, yfwd, (sl 1, K1, psso, yfwd) twice, K3, sl 1, K1, psso, K7, rep from * to end.

5th row K2, *K2 tog, (K3, yfwd) twice, (sl 1, K1, psso, yfwd) twice, K3, sl 1, K1, psso, K5, rep from * to last st, K1.

7th row K1, *K2 tog, K3, yfwd, K5, yfwd, (sl 1, K1, psso, yfwd) twice, K3, sl 1, K1, psso, K3, rep from * to last 2 sts, K2.

9th row *K12, yfwd, (sl 1, K1, psso, yfwd) twice, K3, sl 1, K1, psso, K1, rep from * to last 3 sts, K3.

11th row *K7, K2 tog, K3, (yfwd, K2 tog) twice, yfwd, K1, yfwd, K3, sl 1, K1, psso, rep from * to last 3 sts, K3.

13th row K6, *K2 tog, K3, (yfwd, K2 tog) twice, (yfwd, K3) twice, sl 1, K1, psso, K5, rep from * to end, ending last rep with K2 instead of K5.

15th row K5, *K2 tog, K3, (yfwd, K2 tog) twice, yfwd, K5, yfwd, K3, sl 1, K1, psso, K3, rep from * to end, ending last rep with K1 instead of K3.

16th row As 2nd.

These 16 rows form the pattern.

Fir cone pattern

As its name implies, this pattern represents the cones of fir trees and the number of times the pattern rows are repeated can be varied. For the sample shown here cast on a number of stitches divisible by 10 plus 1.

1st row (RS) K1, *yfwd, K3, sl 1, K2 tog, psso, K3, yfwd, K1, rep from * to end.

2nd row P to end.

Rep these 2 rows 3 times more.

9th row K2 tog, *K3, yfwd, K1, yfwd, K3, sl 1, K2 tog, psso, rep from * to last 9 sts, K3, yfwd, K1, yfwd, K3, sl 1, K1, psso.

10th row P to end.

Rep 9th and 10th rows 3 times more.

These 16 rows form the pattern.

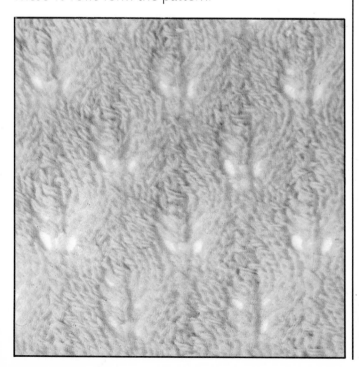

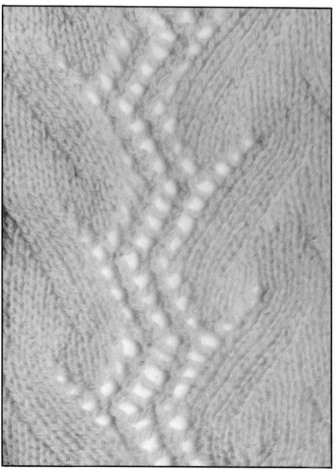

PICOT KNITTING

Picot knitting is an unusual technique which imitates Irish crochet, working with a pair of knitting needles instead of a crochet hook. It looks its best when it is worked in a very fine cotton, such as No.20, and on No.13 or 14 needles.

It has many applications and can be used as edgings, insertions, motifs or as an all-over background fabric. The dainty baby bonnet shown here is an example of how the various methods can be combined to form a garment.

To make a picot point

Make a slip loop in the usual way and place this on the left hand needle, *cast on 2 stitches, making 3 in all. Knit and cast off 2 of these 3 stitches, leaving one stitch on the needle. This forms one picot point. Transfer the remaining stitch to the left hand needle and repeat from * until the required length of picot points is completed. Fasten off.

The size of these picot points may be varied by casting on and off 3 stitches, 4 stitches or as many as required. This strip forms the basis of picot work and can be used to join medallions together, as flower centres, or as a simple edging.

It can also be used to form a dainty cast off edge on a garment, as follows:

Casting off row Insert the needle through the first st of the row to be cast off, *cast on 2 sts, knit and cast off 2 sts, knit the next st of the row, knit and cast off one st, transfer the rem st to the left hand needle, rep from * to end of row.

Fasten off.

Picot point crown

This method is worked across a number of stitches to give the width of edging required. Once this first section has been completed, it forms the basis for what is termed a 'lacis', or openwork fabric, and is referred to as a 'strip' and not a row. To continue working strips to build up a lacis, the last stitch is not fastened off.

Cast on a number of stitches divisible by 5 plus one.

1st row K to end.

2nd row Insert needle into the first st, *cast on 2 sts, cast off 2 sts, transfer rem st to left hand needle, *, rep from * to * 3 times more, (4 picot points formed), knit and cast off next 5 sts, transfer rem st to left hand needle, rep from * to end.

This completes first strip.

Next strip *Transfer rem st to left hand needle, make 4 picot points as given in 2nd row of first strip, join to centre of next picot crown in first strip by picking up and knitting a st between the 2 centre picot points, cast off one st, rep from * to end of strip.

Cont in this way until lacis is required depth. Fasten off.

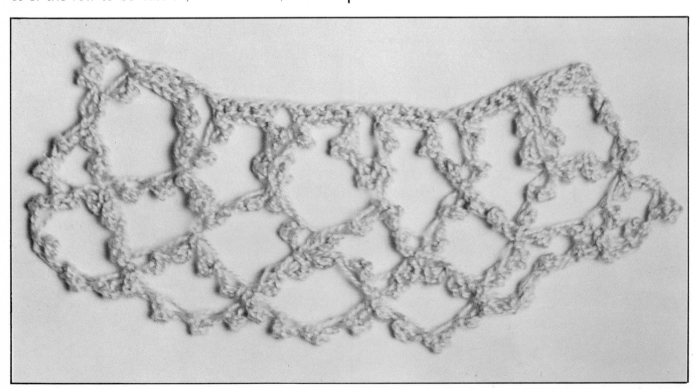

Picot point medallion

This simple motif can be used separately or to form the centre of a flower. Each separate motif can be stitched from the top of one point to the corresponding point of the next motif to form a daisy edging and a number of rows can be joined in the same way to form delicate shawls or interesting table linen, such as place mats and coasters.

However you wish to use these medallions, you can make as many picot points as you like, varying the size of each picot point as already explained. The example shown here has 6 picot points, using 3 stitches instead of 2 for each point.

Make a slip loop and place on left hand needle, *cast on 3 sts, making 4 in all, cast off 3 of these sts, transfer rem st to left hand needle, rep from * 5 times more. To join into a circle, insert needle into the first loop and draw up a st, cast off one st. Fasten off.

To continue making a flower motif, do not fasten off but transfer remaining stitch to left hand needle, ready to commence the first petal.

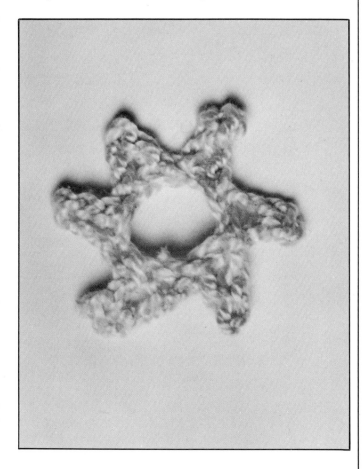

Picot point flower

Make a medallion as given above. Cast on one st, making 2 stitches on left hand needle.

1st row K1, K into front then into back of next st – called M1. 3 sts.
2nd and 4th rows K to end.
3rd row K2, M1.
5th row K3, M1. 5 sts.
K 4 rows g st.

10th row Cast off one st, K to end. 4 sts.
11th row K to end.
Rep last 2 rows twice more.
16th row Cast off one st, pick up and knit a loop between next 2 picot points, cast off one st, transfer rem st to left hand needle.
Cont in this way making 6 petals in all, or as required, joining last petal to same place as first petal, as given for picot point medallion.

Picot flower and lacis motif

Make a picot point flower and fasten off. Rejoin yarn to centre of any petal tip.

1st round *Make 4 picot points casting on and off 2 sts for each point, K up one st at tip of next petal, cast off one st, transfer rem st to left hand needle, rep from * all round flower.

2nd round Make 4 picot points and join between 2nd and 3rd picots of 1st round, make another 4 picot points and miss 2 picot points of 1st round, join between next 2 picot points of 1st round, cont in this way to end of round, joining last stitch to same place as first stitch. Fasten off.

3rd round Rejoin yarn between 2nd and 3rd of any picot points, *make 4 picot points and join between 2nd and 3rd of next 4 picot points, rep from * to end of round, joining as before. 12 loops. Fasten off.

4th round Rejoin yarn between 2nd and 3rd of any picot points, *make 3 picot points and join into same place to form a picot crest, make 4 picot points and join between 2nd and 3rd of next 4 picot points, rep from * to end of round, joining as before. Fasten off. Make as many more motifs as required, joining picot crests of each motif where they touch, to form a row.

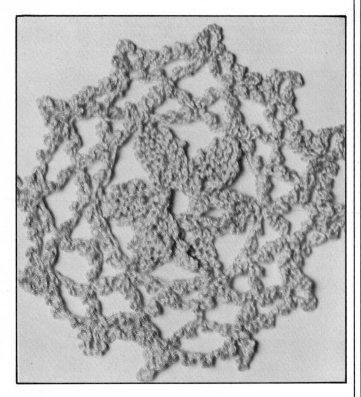

Baby bonnet
Size
To fit 0 to 3 months

Tension
32 sts and 60 rows to 10cm (*3.9in*) over g st worked on No.13 needles

Materials
1 × 25grm ball of Sunbeam St. Ives 3 ply
One pair No.13 needles
0.90 metre (*1yd*) ribbon for ties

Bonnet
Make one flower and lacis motif, omitting 4th round, to form centre of crown.
Make 11 picot point medallions and join into a row, joining the centre picots each side, leaving 2 free at top and bottom. Sew round edge of centre motif, joining 2 free points of each medallion to the centre 2 picots of each loop and leaving one loop free for bottom edge of bonnet.
Make a strip of 42 picots, mark the last picot with contrast thread and turn.
Next row Make 4 picots, join between 3rd and 4th picots after marker, *make 4 picots, miss 4 picots, join between 4th and 5th picots, rep from * to last 3 picots, make 4 picots, join to end of strip after last picot. Fasten off and turn.

Next row Rejoin yarn between 2nd and 3rd picots of first loop, *make 4 picots, join between 2nd and 3rd picots of next loop, rep from * to end. Do not fasten off but turn.
Next row Make 4 picots, join between 2nd and 3rd picots of first loop, *make 4 picots, join between 2nd and 3rd picots of next loop, rep from * to end, make 4 picots, join to beg of previous row where yarn was rejoined.
Rep last 2 rows once more. Fasten off.
Join the cast on edge of this strip to the centre piece, joining the first 2 picots to the 2 picots of first medallion, *miss 2 picots, join next 2 picots to 2 points of next medallion, rep from * to end.

To make up
Pin out and press under a damp cloth with a warm iron. Sew ribbon to each corner to tie at front.

FILET KNITTING

The word 'filet' means 'net', and this type of square mesh fabric can be produced in both knitting and crochet. Just as with crochet, patterns can be introduced into the mesh background, consisting of solid parts of the pattern, which are referred to as 'blocks', and open parts of the pattern which are called 'spaces'. The stitch used to produce filet lace fabric is garter stitch throughout, so it is a very simple method to work.

This fabric looks best when it is worked in a fine cotton on small size needles, to give a lace effect. It has many uses but is better used for insertions and edgings, rather than as an all-over fabric.

To knit filet lace
Working a block These comprise solid sections of garter stitch and each block consists of three knitted stitches in width and four rows in depth. Whether working an insertion or an edging, a number of extra stitches are required at the beginning and end of the rows and these are knitted throughout in the usual way.

Working a space These are the open sections of a design and each space is worked over three stitches. The third stitch of each space is knitted in the usual way and is either used as an edge stitch, or as a bridging stitch between spaces or between spaces and blocks. Each space is worked over two rows in depth:–

After completing a block of three knitted stitches or the edge stitches, as the case may be, bring the yarn forward between the needles, take it over the right hand needle and to the front again – called y2rn.

Over the next three stitches, slip the first stitch knitwise, then slip the 2nd stitch knitwise, using the point of the left hand needle lift the first stitch over the 2nd stitch and off the right hand needle.

Slip the 3rd stitch knitwise, using the point of the left hand needle lift the 2nd stitch over the 3rd stitch and off the right hand needle, return the 3rd stitch to the left hand needle and knit this in the usual way.

This working method is referred to as a space. There are now three loops on the right hand needle again, composed of the yarn twice round the needle and one knitted stitch. On the following row the first yarn round the needle is knitted and the 2nd yarn round the needle is purled, then the 3rd stitch is knitted, to complete the space.

Working basic filet net
This is worked entirely in spaces, plus one edge stitch at the beginning of the row. The 3rd stitch of

each space forms the bridging stitch between each space.

Working blocks and spaces
As each block requires four rows to complete it and a space only requires two rows, the pattern rows must be worked twice to give the necessary square shape to each block.

When a block changes to a space in a pattern, treat the three stitches of the block as a space, or when changing a space to a block, work the three stitches of the space as a block.

Filet lace insertion
This simple pattern can be used in many ways, either as centre front panels on a fabric or knitted blouse, as

an insertion on a dainty petticoat or on household linens.

It is worked over a total of five squares, each consisting of three stitches, plus three edge stitches at the beginning of the rows and two edge stitches at the end of the rows. Only two stitches are required to balance the end of the rows, as the last stitch of the last space is taken into this edge. The chart given here does not show the edge stitches.

Cast on a total of 20 stitches to work the insertion.

1st row (RS) K3 edge sts, work 2 spaces, K3 sts for a block, work 2 spaces, K2 edge sts.

2nd and every alt row K to end, purling the 2nd yarn round needle of every space.

Rep 1st and 2nd rows once more to complete the centre block.

5th row K3 edge sts, work 1 space, (K3 sts for a block, work 1 space) twice, K2 edge sts.

6th row As 2nd.

Rep 5th and 6th rows once more to complete the

blocks, then rep them twice more to complete another block.

13th row As 1st.

Chart for lace insertion

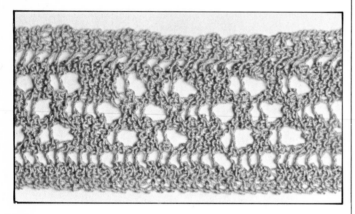

☐ = space

■ = block

rows 17–20
rows 13–16
rows 9–12
rows 5–8
rows 1–4

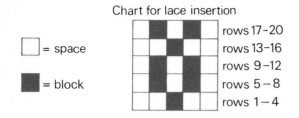

14th row As 2nd.
Rep 13th and 14th rows once more to complete the centre block.

17th row As 5th.
18th row As 6th.
Rep 17th and 18th rows once more to complete the blocks.
These 20 rows form the pattern and are repeated for the required length of the insertion.

Filet lace edging

This pattern has a serrated edge along one side and

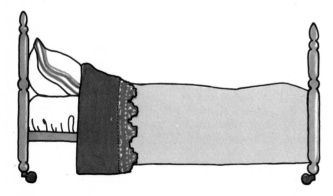

forms an ideal trimming for all types of household linens. The serrated edge is formed by casting on additional stitches two rows before they are taken into the pattern.

This pattern consists of three squares at the beginning, each comprising three stitches, plus one edge stitch at the beginning of the row only, the last edge stitch being formed by the last stitch of the last space. The chart given here does not show the edge stitch.

Cast on a total of 10 stitches to begin the edging.

1st row (RS) K1 edge st, work 1 space, K3 sts for a block, work 1 space.

2nd and every alt row K to end, purling the 2nd yarn round needle of every space.

3rd row As 1st, then turn and cast on 6 sts to form 2 extra spaces on the 5th row.

5th row K1 edge st, work 1 space, K3 sts for a block, work 3 spaces.

7th row As 5th, then turn and cast on 3 sts to form 1 extra space on the 9th row.

9th row K1 edge st, work 1 space, K3 sts for a block,

Chart for lace edging

☐ = space

■ = block

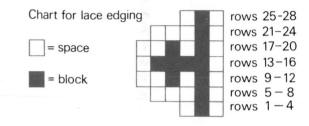

rows 25–28
rows 21–24
rows 17–20
rows 13–16
rows 9–12
rows 5–8
rows 1–4

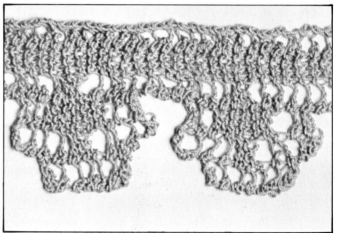

work 1 space, K3 sts for a block, work 2 spaces.

10th row As 2nd.
Rep 9th and 10th rows once more to complete blocks.

13th row K1 edge st, work 1 space, K12 sts to form 4 blocks, work 1 space.

14th row As 2nd.
Rep 13th and 14th rows once more to complete blocks.

17th row As 9th.
18th row As 2nd.
19th row As 17th.
20th row Cast off 3 sts to reduce one space, then work as 2nd row to end.

21st row As 5th.
22nd row As 2nd.
23rd row As 21st.
24th row Cast off 6 sts to reduce 2 spaces, then work as 2nd row to end.

25th row As 1st.
26th row As 2nd.
Rep 25th and 26th rows once more to complete block. These 28 rows form the pattern and are repeated for the required length of the edging.

AN INTRODUCTION TO CROCHET

This publication gives a new and completely different approach to crochet, which will be of interest both to beginners and experts alike. It guides the reader clearly and concisely through the very early stages to the more complicated techniques and gives a new dimension on the ways in which crochet can be applied and extended.

Very little is known about the early history of crochet. For many centuries it was worked mostly by nuns, to the extent that it was often referred to as 'nuns' work'. During the mid-nineteenth century, the beautiful fabric formed by Irish crochet became most popular and throughout Queen Victoria's reign, crochet was applied to everything from antimacassars to camisole tops. However, some of the examples produced were unbelievably ugly and did nothing to enhance the natural beauty of this delicate craft.

After many years of mis-use, crochet declined in popularity and for almost fifty years it remained virtually unknown, other than in areas such as Ireland, where the craft was most fortunately kept alive.

During the 1950s, a tremendous revival of interest in all crafts began in America and this revival spread rapidly to Britain and the continent. One of the first crafts to re-appear was crochet and the demand was so phenomenal that designers and publishers were inundated with requests for patterns. For the first time, it was realized that crochet could be used to form a complete fabric and was not limited to merely being used as an applied trimming or insertion. Interest quickly gathered momentum and all aspects of the craft were eagerly researched to cope with the demand for fashion garments, as well as household linens.

Today, crochet is rightly appreciated as a unique way of interpreting fashion. As with knitting, you have complete control over the texture and colour of the fabric and the ultimate shape of the design, combining both the skills of a weaver and a dressmaker. The fabric can be tough and sturdy, or gossamer-light lace and the shape can be casual and practical, or softly romantic.

Almost any type of spun thread can be used in crochet, from the very finest cotton to chunky, machine-washable yarns. Apart from its fashion appeal, crochet remains one of the most popular of all crafts when it is applied to household items. Nothing else lends itself quite so successfully to the delicate lace fabric which can be used to produce heirloom bedspreads and tablecloths, or to edge such items as sheets and pillow cases.

With the aid of this book, all you really need to begin exploring the exciting possibilities which this craft has to offer is a crochet hook, a ball of yarn and a willing pair of hands. With surprisingly little effort even a complete beginner can make simple 'granny squares', which will soon build up into a complete garment. The more experienced crochet worker will be delighted to discover ways in which she can extend her knowledge to combine leather with crochet, or apply crochet to a net material for a most original and attractive fabric.

Pam Dawson

HISTORY OF CROCHET

Nobody can really pinpoint the day or year someone picked up a bone or stick and some yarn and started knotting chains of fabric into what is now known as crochet. If you were to ask a sample of the millions of people all over the world who carry out this simple yet creative craft you would not find many who could tell you much about its history. That is not as surprising as it sounds. Its origins are very obscure, but archaeological finds lead us to believe that Arabia may have been the original area where wool was first worked with just one needle or hook.

Ancient crochet specimens have been found in Egypt and it can be presumed that the craft is of an age parallel with knitting, its sister craft. It goes back at least as far as the days of Solomon (around 950 BC) and some biblical historians credit its use even earlier – 1200 BC – when the Israelites fled Egypt during the Exodus. They were said to have worked wool this way during their long trek across the Sinai desert.

The evidence for this early use is quite substantial. Recorded civilization dates from the time when the Sumerians settled in the plain of Shinar in the area later called Babylon – now Iraq. Babylon became the centre for woollen crafts, in the same way that Egypt was known as the home of fine linen weaving.

Babylon's pleasant, hospitable climate certainly made sheep-rearing a good prospect, but that was not the only reason that woollen crafts flourished there. Unlike the Egyptians, who appeared to have loved clarity of line in everything, the Babylonians were fond of complicated, almost fussy, clothes made of heavy woollen fabric and covered with the most elaborate decoration. It is almost certain that crochet work was used for this purpose. Later in Babylonian history there was a revolt against the luxury of over-ornate clothes and people resorted to the simple wool 'sack', often knitted or worked in crochet.

Crochet and other wool crafts had a very profound place in the philosophy of the time. Creating fabric without any artificial aid was seen as a declaration of their link with a god. It was an acknowledgment that they owed their skill and intellect to some greater being.

Crochet patterns in use in India are very similar to Muslim patterns found in North Africa – giving strength to the theory that crochet has been a continuously-used craft in the Middle East for thousands of years.

Although it never quite died out over the centuries crochet did suffer an eclipse when more mechanical fabric-making methods were developed. However, it began to flourish again during the Renaissance period. Ecclesiastical crochet, in common with other fabrics of the time, acquired a high standard of technique and beauty. Much crochet work during that period was imitative of the more expensive lace or embroidery such as needlepoint, Richelieu, Guipure, Honiton or filet.

It is no wonder that crochet earned the rather derogatory nickname of 'nuns' work'. Woollen crafts such as crochet or knitting were a common occupation for the nuns of the time and, unlike weaving which ordinary people carried out in their own homes, these skills remained almost exclusively within the confines of the convent.

Later on, crochet was thought to be suitable for the richer young ladies of the parish to learn. Nuns established it as one of the main crafts learned in the 'finishing courses' of the day.

The word 'crochet' is probably derived from the French word *croc* – meaning hook – but has only really been in popular use in Britain since the early 1800s, when the production of fine cotton thread from the newly set-up mills made it easy to carry out the craft.

Paradoxically it took a disaster to make the craft a really widespread and popular pastime. It was the Irish potato famines of the 1840s and '50s which revived an almost forgotten skill and made it into a major cottage industry. Crop failures forced millions of farming families to look for an alternative method of earning much-needed cash. Making crochet collars, frills and other adornments was a simple if time-consuming method. It was just as well that fine crochet work was much in demand by the well-to-do ladies of the time.

There had been a history of crochet in Ireland since the end of the eighteenth century when it was probably introduced from France. One young Irish woman, Honoria Nagle, is often given much of the credit for this. She was lucky enough to be sent to Paris to be educated, and became aware of the vast gulf between the classes. The squalor of the poor compared with the ludicrous extravagance of the court and society people made her determined to do something worthwhile in her homeland.

When she returned home, she recruited four other young women who were sympathetic to her aims. They, too, went to learn the craft from the Carmelite nuns in France, so that the five of them would be in a strong position to pass on the skill to the poor of Cork. Anyone could learn the basic skills. Whenever there was a spare hour or two you would find these hard-working people busy with the hook. It was not just women's work either. Boys tending sheep or goats on the hills were expected to chip in, too. Many used the extra money to save for their passage to America, taking their skills with them. There were many happy immigrants well settled in the prosperous mid-West who could thank the humble crochet hook for deliverance from the starvation which killed thousands in their homeland.

Irish crochet became a craft in its own right. Its workers incorporated beautiful designs taken from their rural backgrounds. Motifs included farmyard animals, roses, wheels and, of course, the legendary shamrock leaf. It became a widespread cottage industry and was also included in the syllabus of the Church-run education system.

The main crochet centres were Cork and its surrounding district in the south, and Monaghan in the north. County Cork became a principal centre of the industry and by the 1870s it is estimated that there were from 12,000 to 20,000 women in the area producing crochet, using continental patterns adapted from original lace designs from France, Italy and Greece.

Prince Albert's brainchild, the Great Exhibition of 1851, did a great deal in promoting the craft. It brought it to the attention of designers and manufacturers from all over the world. The Victorians almost smothered the art with their enthusiasm for it. Ladies became addicted to the crochet needle, and made coverings to decorate everything imaginable. Nothing escaped them. Antimacassars, bedspreads, table-cloths, coasters – all were churned out with great enthusiasm. One wonders now whether these objects were made as useful household items or merely to indulge their passion for crochet. Even piano legs were discreetly covered with crochet frills!

Unfortunately, this over-indulgence helped to put following generations off the craft and it ceased to be fashionable for several decades. Luckily it did not disappear completely. It has a remarkable survival record, and was revived in the 1950s along with the new appreciation of all the well-known handcrafts. The present reaction to mass-production has meant that crochet has become widely popular, and is probably used more creatively now than at any time in its long history.

Below: An early example of one of the many exquisite Irish crochet designs.

FIRST STEPS
BASIC STITCHES

The crochet hook

There are a variety of hook sizes to choose from and these range from very fine to very thick, and are graded into an International Size Range, such as 6.00 (ISR) and up to 10.00 (ISR). An appropriately sized hook should be selected for working each thickness of yarn. For example, use a size 10.00 hook for thick rug yarn, a size 7.00 hook for Aran type yarns, a size 5.00 hook for Double Knitting yarn and a 1.00 or .60 hook for finer cotton yarns. The beginner will find it much easier to work with a fairly large hook, such as a 5.00 size and a Double Knitting yarn.

Unlike knitting, all crochet is made up from one working loop on the hook at any time and this first working loop begins as a slip loop. To make a slip loop, hold the cut end of yarn in the left hand and wrap the yarn around the first and second fingers. Place the hook under the first finger and draw yarn through loop on the fingers, removing loop from left hand. Draw the yarn tightly on the hook to keep in place. This first slip loop does not count as a stitch, but is merely a working loop throughout any pattern and is the last loop fastened off at the end of the work. The left hand holds the yarn to feed towards the hook and there are several ways of holding this to control the flow of yarn to achieve an even fabric.

It is important to keep the thumb and first finger of the left hand as close to the hook as possible and move up the work as each new stitch is completed.

To work chain stitches

Hold the hook in the right hand between the thumb and first finger, letting the hook rest against the second finger, and place the hook under the yarn between the first and second finger of the left hand from front to back. Let the hook catch the yarn and draw through a loop on the hook, thus replacing the stitch. One chain has now been completed and the abbreviation for this is 'ch'. Repeat this action to make the required length of chains.

An alternative to this method of foundation chain is the double chain. To work this, make 2 chain in the normal way, insert hook into the 2nd chain from hook, * yarn round hook and draw through a loop, yarn round hook and draw through both loops on hook, *, continue to make a length of double chain by inserting the hook into the 2nd or left hand loop of the 2 loops which have just been dropped from the hook and repeat from * to *. This gives a firm foundation and is easy to work.

Left hand workers should reverse the instructions, reading left for right and right for left. To follow the illustrations, the book should be propped up before a mirror where the reversed image is quite clearly seen.

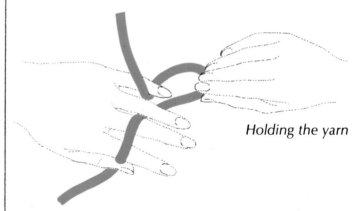

Holding the yarn

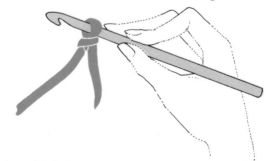

Position of hook to begin chain stitches

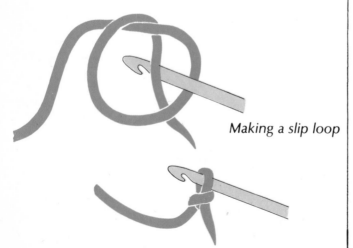

Making a slip loop

Basic stitches

Various stitches can now be worked into the foundation chain to form a crochet fabric. Each stitch gives a different texture and varies in depth, and every row gives a new chain line into which the next row is worked. Where stitches are worked backwards and forwards in rows there is no right or wrong side of the fabric, and the work is turned at the end of each row ready to begin the next row.

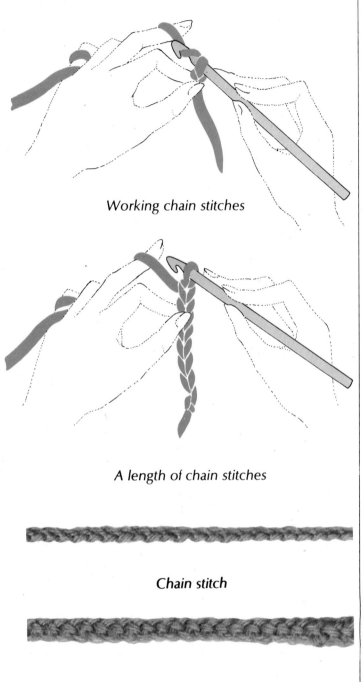

Working chain stitches

A length of chain stitches

Chain stitch

Double chain

Slip stitch. The first stitch with the smallest depth is the slip stitch and this is abbreviated as 'ss'. To work slip stitch into the foundation chain, work the desired length, say 10 chain, and place the hook into the last chain, place hook under the yarn in the left hand – this is called 'yarn round hook' and is abbreviated as 'yrh' –, and draw yarn through the chain and the loop on the hook. Repeat this action to the end of the chain.

Double crochet. The second stitch, which has a greater depth than slip stitch, is double crochet and this is abbreviated as 'dc'. To work this stitch make 10 foundation chain, but because this stitch is deeper than slip stitch, before working this row provision must be made to lift the working loop on the hook to the height of the double crochet stitches. For double crochet work one more chain than the required number of stitches, in this case 11 chain in all, and work the first double crochet into the 3rd chain from the hook. These extra chains are called 'turning chains' and the number of chains vary according to the depth of the stitch being worked. To work double crochet, place the hook under both loops of the chain or just under one loop of the chain, place yarn round hook and draw through a loop, place yarn round hook and draw yarn through both loops on hook.

One double crochet has been worked and this action is repeated to the end of the row. Check that 10 double crochet have been worked, noting that the first two turning chains count as the first double crochet on this row only. Turn the work, work one chain to count as the first double crochet of the next row, miss the first double crochet of the previous row which has been replaced by the turning chain, then work one double crochet into each stitch of the previous row, including the first turning chain at the beginning of the previous row.

Fastening off When you have achieved the required length of work, simply cut the yarn about 15cm (*6in*) from the work. Thread the end through the one remaining loop and pull tight. Darn the end in later.

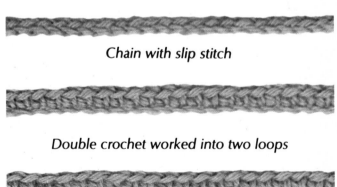

Chain with slip stitch

Double crochet worked into two loops

Double crochet worked into a single loop

Sample worked in double crochet

FABRIC STITCHES

There are numerous crochet stitches and by experimenting with different types of yarn, many effects can be achieved. Here we give instructions for working more basic stitches and several variations that may be formed from these. Work each sample on 10 stitches and these should be checked at the end of each row. Each stitch has a given depth and it is important that provision is made for these at the start of each row with 'turning chains'.

Half trebles

Work 10ch plus 1ch to be the turning chain. Place yarn round hook – this is abbreviated as 'yrh' –, insert hook into 3rd ch from hook, yrh and draw through a loop (3 loops on hook), yrh and draw through all 3 loops. One half treble has now been completed and this is abbreviated as 'htr'. Repeat this action into each ch to the end of the row. Turn work. Start a new row with 2ch to count as the first htr and work 1htr into each stitch to end, including the turning chain at the beginning of the previous row.

Trebles

Work 10ch plus 2ch to be the turning chain. Yrh and insert hook into 4th ch from hook, yrh and draw through a loop (3 loops on hook), yrh and draw through first 2 loops on hook, yrh and draw through remaining 2 loops. One treble has now been completed and this is abbreviated as 'tr'. Work 1tr into each ch to the end of the row. Turn work. Start a new row with 3ch to count as the first tr and work 1tr into each stitch to the end of the row, including the 3rd of the 3 turning chain of the previous row.

Double trebles

Work 10ch plus 3ch to be the turning chain. Yrh twice, insert hook into the 5th ch from hook, yrh and draw through a loop (4 loops on hook), (yrh and draw through first 2 loops on hook) twice, yrh and draw through remaining 2 loops. One double treble has now been completed and this is abbreviated as 'dtr'. Work 1dtr into each ch to the end of the row. Turn work. Start a new row with 4ch to count as first dtr and work 1dtr into each stitch to the end of the row, including the 4th ch of the 4 turning chain of the previous row.

Triple trebles

Work 10ch plus 4ch to be the turning chain. Yrh three times, insert hook into 6th ch from hook, yrh and draw through a loop (5 loops on hook), (yrh and draw through first 2 loops on hook) four times. One triple treble has now been completed and this is abbreviated as 'tr tr'. Start new rows with 5ch to count as first tr tr and work 1tr tr into each stitch to the end of the row, including the 5th ch of the 5 turning chain.

Ridged double crochet

This is produced by working in dc, but the hook is inserted into the back loop only of each stitch of every row. The unworked front loop of each stitch gives a pronounced ridge effect.

Russian stitch

This is another stitch that is formed by working in double crochet, but the work is not turned at the end of each row. Instead the yarn must be fastened off and cut when each row has been completed and the cut ends darned in. There is a definite right and wrong side to this stitch.

Raised double trebles

These are worked on the surface of a basic double crochet fabric to give a vertical ridged effect. Make 21ch and work 1dc into 3rd ch from hook, then work 1dc into each ch to the end of the row. Turn work. Working 1ch to count as the first dc at the beginning of every row, work 3 more rows in dc. Turn work. Start the pattern row with 1ch and 1dc into next dc, *yrh twice and insert hook into the horizontal loop of next dc in the third row below, yrh and complete the dtr in the normal way, 1dc into each of next 3dc, rep from * to the end of the row. Always working 3 rows of double crochet between the pattern rows, work subsequent pattern rows by inserting the hook under the vertical bar of the previous dtr and completing the dtr in the normal way.

Counterpane stitch

As the name implies counterpanes were made in this stitch. The fabric produced has a softness and elasticity suitable for the purpose. Work 11ch. Yrh, insert hook into 3rd ch from hook, yrh and draw a loop through this stitch and the first loop on the hook, yrh and draw through remaining 2 loops. Repeat this into each stitch throughout, always working 2ch to stand as the first stitch at the beginning of every row.

Trebles in relief

This is a more decorative stitch with a ridged effect. Make 12ch and work 1tr into 4th ch from hook, then work 1tr into each ch to the end of the row. Turn work. Start a new row with 3ch to count as the first tr and work across the row in tr by placing the hook between the first and second tr of the previous row horizontally, yrh and draw through a loop, yrh and complete the stitch. At the end of the row work 1tr into the 3rd of the 3 turning chain.

A selection of squares worked in the various stitches learnt so far may be made in Double Knitting yarn and a No. 5.00 (ISR) hook. Each will have a different texture and, made in a variety of colours, the squares will look most attractive. They can then be sewn together to make an attractive travelling rug.

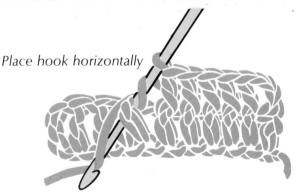

Place hook horizontally

167

First Projects

One of the most convenient ways of trying out new crochet stitches is to combine learning with making practical items. These two projects not only allow the beginner the opportunity to try out her new skills but also show the versatility of crochet when worked with unusual materials.

Mini cushions

These cushions, about 23cm *(9in)* square, are worked in half trebles but you could also use trebles and double crochet.

Materials

100grm *(4oz)* of tubular rayon macramé cord, raffia, or very narrow ribbon
One No. 7.00 (ISR) crochet hook
23cm *(9in)* square cushion pad made from calico and stuffed

Using No. 7.00 ISR hook make enough ch to make 23cm *(9in)*, about 22ch, which includes one extra chain to count as turning ch.
1st row Into third ch from hook work 1htr, then 1htr into each ch to end. Turn. If you had 22ch to start with you should now have 21htr.
2nd row 2ch to count as first htr, miss first htr, 1htr into each htr to end, working the last htr under the turning ch of the previous row. Rep second row until work measures 46cm *(18in)* from beg. Fasten off.

To make up

Fold work in half WS tog and join 2 side edges with a ss. Insert cushion pad and join the remaining edge.

Rag rug

This rug, measuring 2.6m by 1.3m *(8ft 8in by 4ft 4in)* is another example of using materials other than crochet wools. If you have a lot of scrap cotton fabric in a ragbag, you can tear it up into strips about 2cm *(¾in)* wide. Wind up the strips into balls, separating the colours. Work

two or three rows with one colour then change to another to build up a pleasing pattern. Because the rug is worked in strips it is easy to handle while working. If you don't feel like tackling a rug, use slightly thinner strips of fabric – about 1.5cm *(½in)* – to make country-style table mats.

Materials

Lengths of cotton fabric in 4 colours. The total amount of material will depend on the length of rug required and the way in which stripes of colours are arranged, 5.5m *(6yd)* of 90cm *(36in)* wide fabric

will work out at about 76cm *(30in)* in length.
One No. 7.00 (ISR) crochet hook
Button thread

1st strip Using No. 7.00 (ISR) hook and any colour, make enough ch to make 33cm *(13in)* width, about 27ch should be right, which includes one ch for turning.
1st row Into third ch from hook work 1dc, then 1dc into each ch to end. Turn. If you had 27ch to start with you should now have 26dc.
2nd row 1ch to count as first dc, 1dc into each dc to end, working the last dc under the turning ch of the previous row. Turn. Rep second row for required length, changing colours as required and working over the ends each time a new strip is joined in, to secure them.
2nd strip Make enough ch (about 19 should be right including 1ch for turning) to make 23cm *(9in)* width.
3rd strip Make enough ch (about 35 should be right including 1ch for turning) to make 43cm *(17in)* width.
4th strip Work as given for first strip to make 33cm *(13in)* width.

To make up

Sew strips together with button thread.

SHAPING
Increasing and decreasing

Crochet patterns can be increased or decreased in two ways – either at the side edges or in the course of a row. More than one stitch may be increased or decreased at a time and this is usually worked at the beginning and ending of a row. To increase several stitches extra chains are added and to decrease several stitches at the beginning of a row, the required number are worked across in slip stitch and then remain unworked on subsequent rows, and at the end of a row, the required number of stitches are simply left unworked.

In most designs the shaping required to ensure either a well-fitting garment or make provision for essential openings, such as armholes and neckbands, is achieved by means of increasing or decreasing at a given point in the pattern. Because of the depth of most crochet stitches, unless this shaping is worked neatly and evenly, an unsightly gap can be left in the pattern which can spoil the appearance of the finished garment. The methods given here will overcome this problem and wherever you are instructed to increase or decrease in a pattern, without being given specific details, choose the appropriate method which will give the best results.

Increasing
To increase one stitch in the course of a row, simply work twice into the same stitch. When working in trebles for example, continue along the row in the normal way until you reach the position for the increase, put yarn over hook, insert hook into next stitch and draw through yarn giving three loops on the hook, yarn over hook and draw through two loops on hook, yarn over hook and draw through last two loops on hook, yarn over hook and insert hook into the same stitch again and draw through yarn giving three loops on the hook, yarn over hook and draw through two loops on hook, yarn over hook and draw through last two loops on hook. One loop is now left on the hook and one treble has been increased. This method applies to all the various stitches.

To increase one stitch at each end of a row, work twice into the first and last stitch of the previous row. When using thick yarns, however, a smoother edge is formed if the increase is worked into the second stitch at the beginning of the row and into the last but one stitch at the end of the row. This method applies to all the various stitches.

To increase several stitches at the beginning of a row, make a chain equivalent to one less than the number of extra stitches required plus the required number of turning chains. If six stitches are to be increased when working in trebles, for example, make five chains plus three turning chains, the next treble for the new row being worked into the fourth chain from the hook and noting that the three turning chains count as the first stitch.

To increase several trebles at the end of a row, the neatest way is to make provision for these extra stitches at the beginning of the previous row. To do this make three chain to count as the turning chain then make the exact number of chains required for the increased stitches, say six, work in slip stitch along these first six chains then complete the row by working one treble into each stitch of the previous row, noting that the three turning chains have already been worked to count as the first stitch.

To increase several stitches at the beginning and end of the same row, combine the two previous methods, noting that the increase row will end by working one treble into the turning chain and each of the six slip stitches of the previous row.

Decreasing
To decrease one stitch in the course of a row when working in double crochet, simply miss one stitch of the previous row at the given point. Because double crochet is a short stitch, this missed stitch will not leave a noticeable hole.

To decrease one stitch when working in half trebles, work along the row until the position for the decrease is reached, yarn over hook and insert hook into next stitch, yarn over hook and draw through loop, yarn over hook and insert hook into next stitch, yarn over hook and draw through loop (five loops on hook), yarn over hook and draw through all loops on hook. One half treble has now been decreased by making one stitch out of two.

To decrease one stitch when working in trebles, work along the row until the position for the decrease is reached yarn over hook and insert hook into next stitch, yarn over hook and draw through loop, yarn over hook and draw through two loops on hook, yarn over hook and insert hook into next stitch, yarn over hook and draw through loop, yarn over hook and draw through two loops on hook, yarn over hook and draw through remaining three loops on hook. One treble has now been decreased by making one stitch out of two.

To decrease one stitch when working in double trebles, work along the row until the position for the decrease is reached, yarn over hook twice and insert hook into next stitch, yarn over hook and draw through loop, yarn over hook and draw through two loops on hook, yarn over hook and draw through two loops on hook (two loops on hook), yarn over hook twice, insert hook into next stitch, yarn over hook and draw through loop, yarn over hook and draw through two loops on hook, yarn over hook and draw through two loops on hook (three loops on hook), yarn over hook and draw through all loops

on hook. One double treble has now been decreased by making one stitch out of two.

To decrease one stitch at each end of a row when working in double crochet, make two turning chains at the beginning of the row, miss the first two double crochet of the previous row noting that the turning chain forms the first stitch, work one double crochet into the next stitch, continue in double crochet along the row until one double crochet and the turning chain of the previous row remain, miss the last double crochet and work one double crochet into the turning chain.

To decrease one stitch at each end of a row when working in half trebles, make one turning chain at the beginning of the row instead of two, miss the first half treble of the previous row noting that the turning chain forms this stitch, work in half trebles along the row until one half treble and the turning chain of the previous row remain, work the last half treble and the turning chain together to make one stitch. At the end of the next row, work one half treble into the last half treble and miss the turning chain.

To decrease one stitch at each end of a row when working in trebles and double trebles, work as given for half trebles noting that only two and three turning chains respectively are worked at the beginning of the decrease row.

To decrease several stitches at the beginning of a row slip stitch over the required number of stitches, make the required number of turning chains for the stitch being used and continue along the row.

To decrease several stitches at the end of a row, continue along the row within the number of stitches to be decreased and turn the work, noting that the turning chain of the previous row must be counted as one of the stitches.

How to make a belt or cushion

To practice the methods of increasing and decreasing, attractive triangle shapes can be made with oddments of Double Knitting yarn and a No. 5.50 (ISR) crochet hook.

To make a belt, begin with three chain and work in double crochet, increasing one stitch at the beginning and end of every row until the required size is reached, then fasten off. Continue making triangles in this way for the required length of the belt, then sew them together as shown. Finish one end of the belt with a buckle.

To make a cushion you will need eight large triangles, four for each side. Begin with 70 chain for each triangle and work in half trebles, decreasing one stitch at each end of every row until two stitches remain, then work these two stitches together to form a point. Sew four triangles together for each side, points to centre, then sew outside edges together, inserting a zip fastener in centre of last edge. Insert a cushion pad to complete cushion.

A pretty pull-on hat

Size
To fit an average head

Tension
24 sts and 16 rows to 10cm (3.9in) patt worked on No.3.50 (ISR) crochet hook

Materials
3 × 25 grm balls of any Bri-Nylon Double Knitting
One No.3.50 (ISR) crochet hook
90cm (1yd) narrow ribbon

Hat
Using No.3.50 (ISR) hook make 5ch. Join with a ss to first ch to form circle.
1st round 3ch to count as first htr and 1ch sp, (work 1htr into circle, 1ch) 7 times. Join with a ss to 2nd of first 3ch. 8 sps.
2nd round 3ch to count as first htr and 1ch sp, work 1htr into first ch sp, 1ch, *work 1htr, 1ch, 1htr all into next ch sp – called inc 1 –, 1ch, rep from * to end. Join with a ss to 2nd of first 3ch. 16 sps.
3rd round 3ch, work 1htr into first ch sp, 1ch, work 1htr into sp between htr groups, 1ch, *inc 1 into next inc 1, 1ch, 1htr into sp between htr groups, 1ch, rep from * to end. Join with a ss to 2nd of first 3ch. 24 sps.
4th round 3ch, miss first 1ch sp, *work 1htr into next 1ch sp, 1ch, rep from * to end. Join with a ss to 2nd of first 3ch. The 4th round forms patt and is rep throughout.
5th round 3 ch, work 1 htr into first ch sp, 1ch, (1htr into next 1ch sp, 1ch) twice, *inc 1, 1ch, (1htr into next 1ch sp, 1ch) twice, rep from * to end. Join with a ss to 2nd of first 3ch. 32 sps.
6th round As 4th.
7th round 3ch, work 1htr into first ch sp, 1ch, (1htr into next 1ch sp, 1ch) 3 times, *inc 1, 1ch, (1htr into next 1ch sp, 1ch) 3 times, rep from * to end. Join with a ss to 2nd of first 3ch. 40 sps.
8th round As 4th.
Cont inc 8 sps in this way on next and every alt round until there are 64 sps. Mark end of last round with coloured thread to show beg of rounds. Work 4th patt round 16 times more, without inc and without joining rounds.
Shape brim
Next round *Patt 7 sps, inc 1, rep from * to end.
Next round *Patt 8 sps, inc 1, rep from * to end.
Rep 4th patt round 4 times more, without inc and without joining rounds, or until brim is required depth. Fasten off.

To make up
Do not press. Thread ribbon through lower edge of crown to tie at back.

DECORATIVE FABRIC STITCHES

This chapter is about decorative fabric stitches, telling you how to work them and how they might be used. They are all variations of the basic stitches already described. Included with them are examples of cluster and bobble stitches, which look most effective used with basic stitches such as trebles and double crochet as they form a raised surface and add texture to the work.

Aligned stitch

Using No. 5.00 (ISR) hook and Double Knitting, make 22ch.

1st row (Yrh and insert into 4th ch from hook, yrh and draw through a loop, yrh and draw through first 2 loops on hook) twice, yrh and draw through remaining 3 loops – one aligned st has now been formed –, rep this action into every ch to the end of the row. Turn.

2nd row 3ch to count as first st, miss first aligned st, * yrh and insert into next aligned st, (yrh and draw through a loop, yrh and draw through first 2 loops on hook), yrh and rep this action into the same st, yrh and draw through 3 remaining loops on hook, rep from * to the end of the row, working last aligned st into 3rd of the 3ch. Turn.

The last row is repeated throughout to form the pattern.

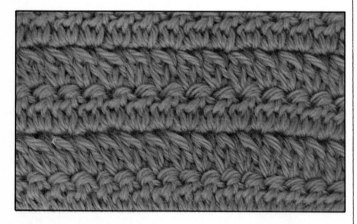

Crossed half trebles

Using No. 5.00 (ISR) hook and Double Knitting, make 21ch.

1st row Yrh and insert into 3rd ch from hook, yrh and draw through a loop, yrh and insert into next ch, yrh and draw through a loop, yrh and draw through all 5 loops on hook, 1ch, * yrh and insert into next ch, yrh and draw through a loop, yrh and insert into next ch, yrh and draw through a loop, yrh and draw through all 5 loops on hook, 1ch, rep from * to last ch, 1htr into last ch. Turn.

2nd row 3ch, yrh and insert into first 1ch space, yrh and draw through a loop, yrh and insert into next 1ch space, yrh and draw through a loop, yrh and draw through all 5 loops on hook, 1ch, * yrh and insert into 1ch space that was last worked into, yrh and draw through a loop, yrh and insert into next 1ch space, yrh and draw through a loop, yrh and draw through all 5 loops on hook, 1ch, rep from * to end, 1htr into 2nd of the 3ch. Turn.

The last row is repeated throughout to form the pattern.

Granite stitch

Using No. 5.00 (ISR) hook and Double Knitting, make 22ch.

1st row Into 3rd ch from hook work (1dc, 1ch and 1dc), miss next ch, * (1dc, 1ch and 1dc) into next ch, miss next ch, rep from * to last ch, 1dc into last ch. Turn.

2nd row 1ch, * (1dc, 1ch and 1dc) into 1ch space of next group, rep from * to end, 1dc into the turning ch. Turn.

The last row is repeated throughout to form the pattern.

Palm leaves

Using No. 5 00 (ISR) hook and Double Knitting, make 22ch.

1st row Into 4th ch from hook work 1dc, * 2ch, miss next 2ch, 1dc into next ch, rep from * to end. Turn.

2nd row 3ch to count as first tr, 1tr into first dc, * 3tr into next dc, rep from * to end, 2tr into first of the 3ch. Turn.

3rd row 3ch, 1dc into 2nd tr of the first 3tr group, * 2ch, 1dc into 2nd tr of next 3tr group, rep from * to end, working last dc into 3rd of the 3ch. Turn.

Repeat the 2nd and 3rd rows throughout to form the pattern.

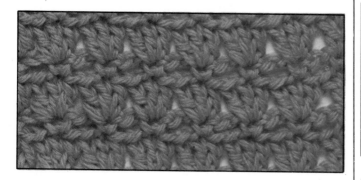

Cock's head trebles

Using No. 5.00 (ISR) hook and Double Knitting, make 22ch.

1st row Into 4th ch from hook work 1tr, * (yrh and insert into next ch, yrh and draw through a loop, yrh and draw through first 2 loops on hook) twice, yrh and draw through all 3 loops, 1ch, rep from * to end, omitting the 1ch at the end of the last rep.

2nd row 4ch, yrh and insert into first st, yrh and draw through a loop, yrh and draw through first 2 loops, miss next st, yrh and insert into next st, yrh and draw through a loop, yrh and draw through first 2 loops, yrh and draw through all 3 loops, * 1ch, yrh and insert into same st that last st was worked into, yrh and draw through a loop, yrh and draw through first 2 loops, miss next st, yrh and insert into next st, yrh and draw through a loop, yrh and draw through first 2 loops, yrh and draw through all 3 loops, rep from * to end, 1ch, 1tr into 3rd of the 3ch. Turn.

3rd row As 2nd, but note that the last st is worked into the 3rd of the 4ch. Turn.

The last row is repeated throughout to form the pattern.

Forget-me-not stitch

Using No. 5.00 (ISR) hook and Double Knitting, make 25ch.

1st row Into 4th ch from hook work (1tr, 2ch and 1dc), * miss next 2ch, (2tr, 2ch and 1dc) into next ch, rep from * to end. Turn.

2nd row 3ch, (1tr, 2ch and 1dc) into first 2ch space, * (2tr, 2ch and 1dc) into next 2ch space, rep from * to end. Turn.

The last row is repeated throughout to form the pattern. This stitch looks very attractive when two colours are used on alternate rows.

To design a dirndl skirt

One of these attractive stitches that you have just learnt, together with your knowledge of tension checking are the main ingredients you will need to design a lovely dirndl skirt.

For example, if you are a hip size 91.5 centimetres (36 inches), you will need 2.5 centimetres (one inch) ease. This means that each piece of your skirt will measure 47 centimetres (18½ inches) across. If your tension is 4 sts to 2.5 centimetres (one inch), then you will require $18\frac{1}{2} \times 4 = 74$ stitches for the basic pattern.

No shaping is required. You just work to the required length and gather the waist with rows of shirring elastic.

Wall hanging

Another use of the various stitches learnt so far is to make them into a wall hanging. This will look particularly attractive if you choose one colour and work each stitch in a different shade of this colour. A very stylish finishing touch would be to mount the hanging on a brass rail.

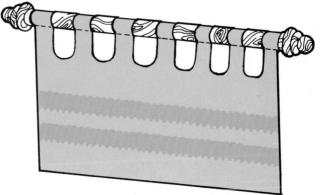

CLUSTER AND BOBBLE STITCHES

Cluster and bobble stitches

Edgings using either bobble or cluster stitch make ideal trimmings for the neckline or hemline of a dress and edgings for jackets, waistcoats and household linens. The same stitches can also be incorporated in making square or circular motifs for a bedspread or evening stole, or they can be used to replace stitches in a basic design and so add much more interest to the fabric.

Here three examples of cluster stitch are illustrated and explained in detail, but there are many other variations. For these samples a No. 4.50 (ISR) crochet hook and a Double Knitting yarn were used, but the hook size and type of yarn may vary depending on the final purpose of the work.

Cluster or pine stitch

Make 26ch.

1st row Into 3rd ch from hook work 1dc, 1dc into each ch to end. Turn.

2nd row 1ch to count as first dc, miss first dc, 1dc into each dc, ending with 1dc into the turning chain. Turn.

3rd row (cluster row) 4ch, miss first 2dc, ** yrh and insert into next dc, yrh and draw through a loop extending it for 1cm (⅜in), * yrh and insert it into same dc, yrh and draw through a loop extending it for 1cm (⅜in), rep from * 3 times, yrh and draw through all 11 loops on hook – called 1cl –, 1ch, miss next dc, rep from ** ending with 1tr into the turning chain. Turn.

4th and 5th rows Work in dc. Fasten off.

Using the cluster stitch practise making square motifs. Worked in one colour and a cotton yarn, they are ideal for a quilt or tablecloth, or worked in fine, multi-coloured yarns they make an attractive evening stole.

The instructions for the square motif are given using 4 colours which are referred to as A, B, C and D.

Square motif

With A, make 5ch. Join into circle with ss.

1st round 1ch to count as first dc, 15dc into circle, ending with ss into first ch. 16dc. Fasten off A and join in B.

2nd round 4ch to count as first tr and linking ch, * 1tr into next dc, 1ch, rep from * ending with ss into 3rd of the 4ch. Fasten off B and join in C.

3rd round Ss into next 1ch space, * 3ch, 1cl into same 1ch space, rep from * ending with 3ch, ss into top of first cl. Fasten off C and join in D.

4th round Ss into next 3ch space, 1ch, 2dc into same space, 3dc into each of next 2 spaces, * (1htr, 1tr, 2ch, 1tr, 1htr) into next space for corner, 3dc into each of next 3 spaces, rep from * twice more, 1 corner into next space, ss into first ch. Fasten off.

Raised clusters

By using the method of raising clusters on a basic fabric, many designs such as diagonals and zig-zags may be built up according to the position of the clusters. The instructions given below are for raised clusters on a double crochet fabric.

Make 25ch.

1st to 3rd rows Work in dc as given for basic cluster sample.

4th row 1ch to count as first dc, miss first dc, 1dc into each of next 3dc, * insert hook into next dc, yrh and draw through a loop, (yrh and insert into space on the 3rd row directly below this stitch position, yrh and draw through a loop, yrh and draw through first 2 loops on hook) 5 times, yrh and draw through all 6 loops on hook – called 1 raised cl – , 1dc into each of next 4dc, rep from * to end.

5th to 7th rows Work in dc.

8th row Repeat the raised cluster on every 5th stitch depending on the effect that you want to create.

You will see that diagonals or alternating clusters have been formed on our illustrations. Repeat rows 1 to 8 to achieve this effect.

Two more raised stitches are the bobble and the popcorn stitch. Here the instructions given are for an all-over bobble design and popcorn stitch that is worked into a braid.

Bobble stitch

Make 26ch.

1st row Into 3rd ch from hook work 1dc, 1dc into each ch to end. Turn.

2nd row 1ch to count as first dc, * 4ch, miss 2dc, leaving the last loop of each st on hook work 6tr tr into next dc, yrh and draw through all 7 loops on hook – called B1 – , 4ch, miss next 2dc, 1dc into next dc, rep from * ending with 1dc into turning chain. Turn.

3rd row 5ch to count as first tr and linking ch, 1dc into first B1, * 5ch, 1dc into next B1, rep from * ending with 2ch, 1tr into the turning chain. Turn.

4th row 5ch to count as first tr and linking ch, 1dc into next dc, * 4ch, B1 into next 5ch space, 4ch, 1dc into next dc, rep from * ending with 2ch, 1tr into 3rd of the turning chain. Turn.

5th row 1ch to count as first dc, * 5ch, 1dc into next Bl, rep from * ending with 5ch, 1dc into 3rd of the turning chain. Turn.

6th row 1ch to count as first dc, * 4ch, B1 into next 5ch space, 4ch, 1dc into next dc, rep from * ending with 1dc into the turning chain. Turn.

Repeat 3rd to 6th rows to form the pattern.

Bobble stitch

Popcorn stitch

Make 25ch.

1st row Into 4th ch from hook work 1tr, 1tr into each ch to end. Turn.

2nd row 3ch to count as first tr, miss first tr, 1tr into each tr, ending with 1tr into the turning chain.

3rd row 3ch to count as first tr, miss first tr, 1tr into next tr, * 1ch, 5tr into next tr, slip working st off the hook and pick up the ch st worked before the 5tr, pick up working loop and draw through the ch st – 1 popcorn st has now been worked – , 1tr into each of next 2tr, rep from * ending with 1tr into the turning chain. Turn.

4th and 5th rows Work in tr. Fasten off.

KNOW-HOW FOR PATTERNS

In the previous chapters, many stitches and ways of using them have been explained and a variety of materials have been used. This chapter is designed to give some useful hints on the treatment, pressing and making up of your work when finished and how these and various other interesting techniques can be applied to making useful and decorative bags.

Tension

Before commencing a piece of work that has a definite size requirement, for example, a jersey to fit a bust size 86.5cm (34in), it is important to make sure that the garment will measure the correct size when it is completed. A tension sample must be worked before you start. Follow the tension guide at the beginning of the pattern and, using the stated yarn and hook size, make a square. Place a rigid rule on the work and count how many stitches and rows there are to the centimetre (inch). If there are too many stitches, then your tension is too tight and you must practise with a larger hook until you gain the correct tension. Too few stitches mean that you are working too loosely and will have to use a smaller hook.

Pressing work

Part of the pleasing appearance of crochet is its textured surface and many people prefer not to press the work as they fear the effect of a warm iron and damp cloth will spoil this texture. Also with so many new and different kinds of yarn on the market, pressing could quite well be unnecessary. Always read the manufacturer's instructions on the yarn label to find if ironing is recommended and see the temperature advised.

As a general rule, most of the yarns containing a high percentage of natural fibres such as wool and cotton can be pressed under a damp cloth with a warm iron. Man-made yarns such as Nylon, Courtelle and Acrylics need a cool iron and dry cloth.

Blocking out

Most crochet, especially when it is very open in texture, should be blocked out on completion. Using a clean flat surface into which you can stick rustless dressmaking pins, pin the piece out to the correct measurements.

Cover with a damp cloth and leave until the cloth is absolutely dry.

Cotton crochet items such as delicate edgings or table cloths and tea cloths often look better for a light stiffening.

Use a starch solution (about two teaspoonfuls to a 600ml (1 pint) of hot water), or a gum arabic solution. Dab the solution over the article when it is blocked out.

Joining in new yarn

In crochet, it is better to avoid tying knots when joining in new yarn. Work until about 7.5cm (3in) of the yarn is left, lay it across the top of the previous row to the left, lay the beginning of the new yarn with it and work over both ends with the second ball of yarn.

If the join comes when chain is being worked, lay the

new thread alongside the first one, the ends pointing in opposite directions, and work with the double thickness until the first thread runs out.

Joining two pieces of crochet work

There are two methods of doing this – by sewing the pieces together or by using crochet stitches to join them.

Sewing Place the two pieces of work with right sides together and pin firmly. Oversew the edge using a matching yarn. When the seam is completed it may be necessary to press it.

Take care when joining stripes or patterns that the seams match exactly to ensure a professional finish.

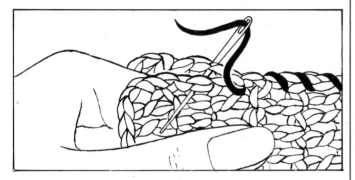

Crochet Joining work with crochet stitches can form part of the design and look very attractive. In the photograph you will see a section of a bag where the gusset has been joined to the main part with double crochet.

Methods of making a handbag

Generally there are two types of handbag, one with a gusset and one without. The gusset is a narrow piece of fabric between the two main sections to give the bag a three-dimensional effect.

Commercial handles for bags may be purchased from the needlework counters of most large stores. The

traditional wooden frames illustrated do not require a gusset. Simply work two pieces of crochet to the required size and join together either by sewing or crochet stitches, leaving a gap in the top edge for the handles to be inserted and hemmed into place.

If you have used crochet stitches to join your bag, then you could insert tassels through the joining stitches along the lower edge at whatever spacing you desired. Our sample illustration has been worked in different colours to clarify the various stages and the method of adding the tassels is shown clearly.

Other types of commercial handles available are the bamboo rings and various metal frames which have a screw-in bar and clasp fastening.

A firm handle may not be required and a gusset strip can be made to fit round the bag plus an extension which is left free for holding as in our illustration.

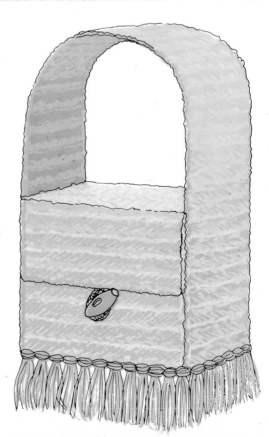

FIRST SIMPLE GARMENTS
Smart dress set

Sizes

To fit 81.5[86.5:91.5:96.5:101.5]cm (*32[34:36:38:40]in*) bust
86.5[91.5:96.5:101.5:106.5]cm (*34[36:38:40:42]in*) hips
Dress length to shoulder, 99[99:99.5:99.5:100.5]cm (*39[39:39$\frac{1}{4}$:39$\frac{1}{4}$:39$\frac{1}{2}$] in*)
Jacket length to shoulder, 59.5[59.5:59.5:61:61]cm (*23$\frac{1}{2}$[23$\frac{1}{2}$:23$\frac{1}{2}$:24:24]in*)
Sleeve seam 44.5cm (*17$\frac{1}{2}$in*)
The figures in brackets [] refer to the 86.5 (*34*), 91.5 (*36*), 96.5 (*38*) and 101.5cm (*40in*) bust sizes respectively

Tension

Dress and beret 19 sts and 24 rows to 10cm (*3.9in*) over patt worked on No.4.00 (ISR) crochet hook
Jacket 21 sts and 13 rows to 10cm (*3.9in*) over patt worked on No.4.00 (ISR) crochet hook

Materials

Dress 10[11:12:13:13] × 50grm balls Jaeger Donegal
Jacket 8[8:9:9:10] × 50grm balls of same
Beret 2 × 50grm balls of same
One No.4.00 (ISR) crochet hook
One 51cm (*20in*) zip for dress
3 buttons for jacket

Dress front

**Using No.4.00 (ISR) hook make 111[115:121:125:131]ch.
Base row (WS) Into 2nd ch from hook work 1dc, 1dc into each ch to end. Turn. 110[114:120:124:130] sts.
Commence patt.
1st row 1ch, 1dc into each st to end. Turn.
This row forms patt. Work 7 more rows patt.
Shape sides
Cont in patt, dec one st at each end of next and every foll 8th row until 88[92:98:102:108] sts rem. Work 7 rows without shaping. **
Shape waist darts
1st row Dec one st, 1dc into each of next 21[22:25:26:28] sts, dec one st, 1dc into each of next 38[40:40:42:44] sts, dec one st, 1dc into each st to last 2 sts, dec one st. Turn.
Work 7 rows without shaping.
9th row Dec one st by working 2dc tog, 1dc into each of next 20[21:24:25:27] sts, dec one st, 1dc into each of next 36[38: 38:40:42] sts, dec one st, 1dc into each st to last 2 sts, dec one st. Turn.
Work 7 rows without shaping. Cont dec in this way on next and every foll 8th row until 68[72:78:82:88] sts rem. Cont without shaping until work measures

62cm (*24$\frac{1}{2}$in*) from beg, ending with a WS row.
Shape bust darts
1st row 1ch, 1dc into same st, 1dc into each of next 17[18:21:22:24] sts, 2dc into next st, 1dc into each of next 30[32:32:34:36] sts, 2dc into next st, 1dc into each st to last st, 2dc into last st. Turn.
Work 7 rows without shaping.
9th row 1ch, 1dc into same st, 1dc into each of next 18[19:22:23:25] sts, 2dc into next st, 1dc into each of next 32[34:34:36:38] sts, 2dc into next st, 1dc into each st to last st, 2dc into last st. Turn.
Work 7 rows without shaping. Cont inc in this way on next and foll 8th row. 84[88:94:98:104] sts. Cont without shaping until front measures 80[80:80:82.5:82.5]cm (*31$\frac{1}{2}$[31$\frac{1}{2}$:31$\frac{1}{2}$: 32$\frac{1}{2}$:32$\frac{1}{2}$]in*) from beg, ending with a WS row.
Shape armholes
1st row Ss over first 5[5:6:7:8] sts, 1ch, patt to last 5[5:6:7:8] sts, turn.
Dec one st at each end of next and every foll alt row until 62[66:70:70:74] sts rem. Cont without shaping until armholes measure 14.5[14.5:15:15:15.5]cm (*5$\frac{3}{4}$[5$\frac{3}{4}$:6:6:6$\frac{1}{4}$]in*) from beg, ending with a WS row.
Shape neck
Next row Patt 25[27:28:28:30] sts, turn. Complete this side first. Keeping armhole edge straight, dec one st at neck edge on next 7 rows, ending at armhole edge.
Shape shoulder
1st row Ss over first 3[4:5:5:4] sts, 1ch, patt to end. Turn.
2nd row Patt to last 4[4:4:4:5] sts, turn.
3rd row Ss over first 4[4:4:4:5] sts, 1ch, patt to end. Turn.
4th row Patt 3[4:4:4:4] sts. Fasten off.
With RS of work facing, miss first 12[12:14:14:14] sts for centre front neck, rejoin yarn to next st, 1ch, 1dc into each st to end. Turn.
Dec one st at neck edge on next 7 rows, ending at neck edge.
Shape shoulder
1st row Patt to last 3[4:5:5:4] sts, turn.
2nd row Ss over first 4[4:4:4:5] sts, 1ch, patt to end. Turn.
3rd row Patt 7[8:8:8:9] sts. Turn.
4th row Ss over first 4[4:4:4:5] sts, 1ch, patt to end. Fasten off.

Dress back

Work as given for front from ** to **
Shape waist darts
1st row Dec one st, 1dc into each of next 21[22:25:26:28] sts, dec one st, 1dc into each of next 38[40:40:42:44] sts, dec

one st, 1dc into each st to last 2 sts, dec one st. Turn.
Work 3 rows without shaping.
5th row 1ch, 1dc into each of next 21[22:25:26:28] sts, dec one st, 1dc into each of next 36[38:38:40:42] sts, dec one st, 1dc into each st to end. Turn.
Work 3 rows without shaping.
9th row Dec one st, 1dc into each of next 20[21:24:25:27] sts, dec one st, 1dc into each of next 34[36:36:38:40] sts, dec one st, 1dc into each st to last 2 sts, dec one st. Turn.
Work 3 rows without shaping.
13th row 1ch, 1dc into each of next 20[21:24:25:27] sts, dec one st, 1dc into each of next 32[34:34:36:38] sts, dec one st, 1dc into each st to end. Turn. 76[80:86:90:96] sts.
Work one row without shaping.
Divide for back opening
Next row 1ch, 1dc into each of next 37[39:42:44:47] sts, turn.
Complete this side first.
1st row 1ch, 1dc into each st to end. Turn.
2nd row Dec one st, 1dc into each of next 19[20:23:24:26] sts, dec one st, 1dc into each st to end. Turn.
Work 3 rows without shaping.
6th row 1ch, 1dc into each of first 19[20:23:24:26] sts, dec one st, 1dc into each st to end. Turn.
Work 3 rows without shaping.
10th row Dec one st, 1dc into each of next 18[19:22:23:25] sts, dec one st, 1dc into each st to end. Turn.
Work 3 rows without shaping.
14th row 1ch, 1dc into each of first 18[19:22:23:25] sts, dec one st, 1dc into each st to end. Turn.
Work 3 rows without shaping.
18th row Dec one st, 1dc into each of next 17[18:21:22:24] sts, dec one st, 1dc into each st to end. Turn.
Work 3 rows without shaping.
22nd row 1ch, 1dc into each of first 17[18:21:22:24] sts, dec one st, 1dc into each st to end. Turn. 29[31:34:36:39] sts.
Cont without shaping until back measures 62cm (*24$\frac{1}{2}$in*) from beg, ending with a WS row.
Shape side edge and dart
1st row 1ch, 1dc into same st, 1dc into each of next 17[18:21:22:24] sts, 2dc into next st, 1dc into each st to end. Turn.
Work 3 rows without shaping.
5th row 1ch, 1dc into each of next 18[19:22:23:25] sts, 2dc into next st, 1dc into each st to end. Turn.
Work 3 rows without shaping.
9th row 1ch, 1dc into same st, 1dc into each of next 18[19:22:23:25] sts, 2dc into next st, 1dc into each st to end. Turn.
Cont inc at side edge in this way on every foll 8th row and for dart on every

4th row until there are 41[43:46:48:51] sts. Cont without shaping until back measures same as front to underarm, ending at side edge.

Shape armhole

1st row Ss over first 5[5:6:7:8] sts, 1ch, patt to end. Turn.
Dec one st at armhole edge on next and every alt row until 31[33:35:35:37] sts rem. Cont without shaping until armhole measures same as front to shoulder, ending at armhole edge.

Shape shoulder

1st row Ss over first 3[4:5:5:4] sts, 1ch, patt to end. Turn.
2nd row Patt to last 4[4:4:4:5] sts, turn.
3rd row Ss over first 4[4:4:4:5] sts, 1ch, patt 7[8:8:8:9] sts, turn.
4th row Patt 3[4:4:4:4] sts. Fasten off.
With RS of work facing, rejoin yarn to rem sts at back opening and complete to match first side, reversing shaping.

To make up

Press each piece lightly under a damp cloth with a warm iron. Join shoulder and side seams.

Neck and back opening edging Using No.4.00 (ISR) hook and with RS of work facing, rejoin yarn to left back neck edge at opening edge. Work one row dc round neck, down right back opening and up left back opening edge. Do not turn, but work one row of crab st, working in dc from left to right instead of from right to left.

Armhole edging Using No.4.00 (ISR) hook and with RS of work facing, work as given for neck and back edging.
Press seams lightly. Sew zip into back opening.

Jacket right front

**Using No.4.00 (ISR) hook make 44[47:50:53:56] ch.
Base row (WS) Into 2nd ch from hook work 1dc, *2ch, miss 2ch, 1dc into next ch, rep from * to end. Turn. 43[46:49:52:55] sts.
Commence patt.

1st row 2ch, 1tr into first dc, *miss 2ch, 3tr into next dc, rep from * ending with miss 2ch, 2tr into last dc. Turn.
2nd row 1ch, 1dc into first tr, *2ch, miss 2tr, 1dc into next tr, rep from * to end. Turn.
The last 2 rows form patt. Work 7 more rows patt, ending with a RS row.

Shape side edge

Keeping patt correct, dec one st at beg of next and at same edge on every foll 3rd row until 37[40:43:46:49] sts rem. Cont without shaping until front measures 25.5cm (*10in*) from beg, ending with a RS row. **.

Shape side and front edges

1st row Inc in first st, patt to last 2 sts, dec one st. Turn.
2nd and 3rd rows Patt to end. Turn.
4th row Dec one st, patt to end. Turn.
5th and 6th rows Patt to end. Turn.
Rep last 6 rows twice more. 34[37:40:43: 46] sts.

Shape armhole

Next row Ss over first 4[5:5:6:6] sts, 1ch, patt to last 2 sts, dec one st. Turn.
Cont dec at front edge as before, *at the*

same time dec one st at armhole edge on next 4[5:7:7:8] rows. Keeping armhole edge straight, cont dec at front edge on every 3rd row until 19[20:21:23:25] sts rem. Cont without shaping until armhole measures 18[18:18:19:19]cm (7[7:7:7½:7½]in) from beg, ending at armhole edge.

Shape shoulder

1st row Ss over first 4[5:5:5:7] sts, 1ch, patt to end. Turn.
2nd row Patt to last 5[5:5:6:6] sts, turn.

3rd row Ss over first 5[5:5:6:6] sts, 1ch, patt to end. Fasten off.

Left front
Work as given for right front from ** to **, reversing shaping.
Shape front and side edges
1st row Dec one st, patt to last st, inc in last st. Turn.
2nd and 3rd rows Patt to end. Turn.
4th row Patt to last 2 sts, dec one st. Turn.

5th and 6th rows Patt to end. Turn.
Rep last 6 rows twice more. Turn.
Shape armhole
Next row Dec one st, patt to last 4[5:5:6:6] sts, turn.
Complete armhole and front edge shaping as given for right front, reversing shaping. Cont without shaping until armhole measures 18[18:18:19:19]cm (7[7:7:7½:7½]in) from beg, ending at neck edge. Turn.
Shape shoulder
1st row Patt to last 4[5:5:5:7] sts, turn.
2nd row Ss over first 5[5:5:6:6] sts, 2ch, patt to end. Turn.
3rd row Patt 5[5:6:6:6] sts. Fasten off.

Back
Using No.4.00 (ISR) hook make 92[98:104: 110:116] ch. Work base row as given for right front. 91[97:103:109:115] sts. Work 9 rows patt as given for right front.
Shape sides
Dec one st at each end of next and every foll 3rd row until 79[85:91:97:103] sts rem. Cont without shaping until work measures 25.5cm (10in) from beg, ending with a RS row. Inc one st at each end of next and every foll 6th row 3 times in all. 85[91:97:103:109] sts.
Work 5 rows without shaping.
Shape armholes
Next row Ss over first 4[5:5:6:6] sts, 1ch, patt to last 4[5:5:6:6] sts, turn.
Dec one st at each end of next 4[5:7:7:8] rows. 69[71:73:77:81] sts.
Cont working in patt without shaping until armholes measure same as front to shoulder, ending with a RS row.
Shape shoulders
1st row Ss over first 4[5:5:5:7] sts, 1ch, patt to last 4[5:5:5:7] sts, turn.
2nd row Ss over first 5[5:5:6:6] sts, 2ch, patt to last 5[5:5:6:6] sts, turn.
3rd row Ss over first 5[5:5:6:6] sts, 1ch, patt over next 5[5:6:6:6] sts, ss over next 31 sts, patt over next 5[5:6:6:6] sts. Fasten off.

Sleeves
Using No.4.00 (ISR) hook make 41[44:44: 47:47] ch. Work base row as given for right front. 40[43:43:46:46] sts. Work 3 rows patt as given for right front. Keeping patt correct, inc one st at each end of next and every foll 3rd row until there are 50[53:55:62:64] sts, then inc one st at each end of every foll 4th row until there are 64[67:69:72:74] sts. Cont without shaping until sleeve measures 44.5cm (17½in) from beg, ending with a RS row.
Shape top
Next row Ss over first 4[5:5:6:6] sts, 1ch, patt to last 4[5:5:6:6] sts, turn.
Dec one st at each end of every row until

34[35:37:34:36] sts rem. Dec 2 sts at each end of next 4 rows. 18[19:21:18:20] sts. Fasten off.

To make up
Press each piece under a damp cloth with a warm iron. Join shoulder seams. Set in sleeves. Join side and sleeve seams.
Border Using No.4.00 (ISR) hook and with RS of work facing, rejoin yarn to right front at lower edge. Work one row dc up right front edge, working 3dc into each 2 row ends, cont across back neck, working into each st, then work down left front as given for right front. Turn.
Next row 1ch, 1dc into each st to end. Turn.
Rep last row once more. Mark position for 3 buttonholes on right front, first to come 1.5cm (½in) below first row of front edge shaping and last to come 6.5cm (2½in) from lower edge with 3rd evenly spaced between.
Next row (buttonhole row) Work in dc to end, making 3 buttonholes when markers are reached by working 3ch and missing 3 sts. Work 3 rows dc, working 3dc into 3ch buttonhole loop on first row. Fasten off. Press seams and border lightly. Sew on buttons.

Beret
Using No.4.00 (ISR) hook make 6ch. Join with a ss to first ch to form circle.
1st round 1ch, work 11dc into circle. Join with a ss to first ch. 12 sts.
2nd round 1ch, 1dc into same st, 1dc into next st, *2dc into next st, 1dc into next st, rep from * to end. Join with a ss to first 1ch. 18 sts.
3rd round 1ch, 1dc into same st, 1dc into each of next 2 sts, *2dc into next st, 1dc into each of next 2 sts, rep from * to end. Join with a ss to first 1ch. 24 sts.
4th round 1ch, 1dc into same st, 1dc into each of next 3 sts, *2dc into next st, 1dc into each of next 3 sts, rep from * to end. Join with a ss to first 1ch. 30 sts.
Cont inc in this way on every round until there are 132 sts. Work 10 rounds without shaping.
Shape headband
Next round *Dec one st, 1dc into each of next 20 sts, rep from * to end. Join with a ss to first st.
Next round *Dec one st, 1dc into each of next 19 sts, rep from * to end. Join with a ss to first st.
Cont dec in this way on every round until 84 sts rem. Turn.
Next round 1ch, 1dc into each dc to end. Join with a ss to first 1ch. Turn.
Rep last round 3 times more. Fasten off.

To make up
Press lightly as given for dress.

A simple lightweight dress

**

Sizes
To fit 86.5 [91.5:96.5:101.5]cm (34[36:38: 40]in) bust
Length to shoulder, 91.5[92:92.5:93]cm (36[36¼:36½:36¾]in)
Sleeve seam, 12.5cm (5in)
The figures in brackets [ ] refer to the 91.5 (36). 96.5 (38) and 101.5cm (40in) sizes respectively

Tension
20 sts and 9 rows to 10cm (3.9in) over tr worked on No.3.50 (ISR) crochet hook; 22 sts and 20 rows to 10cm (3.9in) over dc worked on No.3.50 (ISR) crochet hook

Materials
13[15:17:19] × 50 grm balls of Twilley's Stalite in main shade, A
1 ball each of contrast colours, B and C
One No.3.50 (ISR) crochet hook
51cm (20in) zip fastener

Skirt
Using No.3.50 (ISR) hook and A, make 111 ch and beg at waist, working from top to lower edge.

1st row (RS) Into 3rd ch from hook work 1dc, 1dc into each of next 18ch, 1htr into each of next 20ch, 1tr into each of next 70ch. Turn. 110 sts.

2nd row 3ch to count as first tr, 1tr into front loop only of next 69tr, 1htr into front loop only of next 20htr, 1dc into front loop only of next 19dc, 1dc into turning ch. Turn.

3rd row 1ch to count as first dc, 1dc into front loop only of next 19dc, 1htr into front loop only of next 20htr, 1tr into front loop only of next 69tr, 1tr into turning ch. Turn.

The 2nd and 3rd rows form patt and are rep throughout. Cont in patt until work measures 63.5[68.5:73.5:78.5]cm (25[27: 29:31]in) from beg, measured across dc waist edge. Fasten off.

Hem

Using No.3.50 (ISR) hook, B and with RS of work facing, rejoin yarn to lower edge of skirt.

Next row 2ch to count as first dc, (1tr, 1ch, 1tr, 1dc) into first row end, *1ch, 1dc into next row end, 1ch, (1dc, 1tr, 1ch, 1tr, 1dc) into next row end, rep from * to end. Break off B. Join in C. Do not turn.

Next row Rejoin yarn at beg of row, 2ch, (1tr, 1ch, 1tr, 1dc) into first ch sp between tr, *1ch, 1dc into next dc, 3ch, 1dc into same dc, 1ch, (1dc, 1tr, 1ch, 1tr, 1dc) into next 1ch sp between tr, rep from * to end. Fasten off.

Bodice

Using No.3.50 (ISR) hook, A and with RS of work facing, rejoin yarn and work 150 [162:174:186]dc across waist edge. Work 3 rows dc, working into front loop only of each dc throughout.

Shape darts

Next row 1ch, work 1dc into each of next 40[43:46:49]dc, (2dc into next dc) twice, 1dc into each of next 19[22:25:28] dc, (2dc into next dc) twice, 1dc into each of next 22dc, (2dc into next dc) twice, 1dc into each of next 19[22:25:28] dc, (2dc into next dc) twice, 1dc into each of next 41[44:47:50]dc. Turn. 158[170:182: 194]dc.

Work 3 rows without shaping.

Next row 1ch, work 1dc into each of next 41[44:47:50]dc, (2dc into next dc) twice, 1dc into each of next 21 [24:27: 30]dc, (2dc into next dc) twice, 1dc into each of next 24dc, (2dc into next dc) twice, 1dc into each of next 21[24:27:30] dc, (2dc into next dc) twice, 1dc into each of next 42[45:48:51]dc. Turn. 166 [178:190:202]dc.

Work 3 rows without shaping. Cont inc 8 sts in this way on next and every foll

4th row until there are 198[210:230: 242]sts. Cont without shaping until work measures 20.5cm (*8in*) from waist, or required length to underarm, ending with a WS row.

Divide for armholes

Next row Patt across 45[48:52:55] sts, turn.

Complete left back first. Dec one st at beg of next and at same edge on every row until 35[38:42:45] sts rem. Cont without shaping until armhole measures 14[14.5:15:15.5]cm (5½[5¾:6:6¼]in) from beg, ending at armhole edge.

Shape neck

Next row Patt across 20[22:24:26] sts, turn.

Dec one st at beg of next and at same edge on every row until 16[18:20:22] sts rem. Cont without shaping until armhole measures 18[18.5:19:19.5]cm (7[7¼:7½:7¾]in) from beg, ending at neck edge.

Shape shoulder

Next row Patt across 8[9:10:11] sts, turn and fasten off.

With RS of work facing, miss first 8[8:10:10] sts for underarm, rejoin yarn to next st and patt across 92[98:106:112] sts for front, turn.

Dec one st at each end of next 10 rows. 72[78:86:92] sts. Cont without shaping until armholes measure 9[9.5:10:10.5]cm (3½[3¾:4:4¼]in) from beg, ending with a WS row.

Shape neck

Next row Patt across 26[28:30:32] sts, turn.

Complete this side first. Dec one st at beg of next and at same edge on every row until 16[18:20:22] sts rem. Cont without shaping until armhole measures same as back to shoulder, ending at neck edge.

Shape shoulder

Next row Patt across 8[9:10:11] sts, turn and fasten off.

With RS of work facing, miss first 20[22: 26:28] sts for centre neck, rejoin yarn to rem sts and patt to end. Complete to match first side, reversing shaping. With RS of work facing, miss first 8[8: 10:10] sts for underarm, rejoin yarn to rem sts and patt to end. Complete right back to match left back, reversing shaping.

Sleeves

Using No.3.50 (ISR) hook and A, make 22 ch and work from side edge to side edge.

1st row (RS) Into 4th ch from hook work 1tr, 1tr into each ch to end. Turn. 20tr.

2nd row 3ch to count as first tr, *1tr into front loop only of next tr, rep from * ending with 1tr into turning ch. Turn.

Shape top

Next row 3ch, 1htr into 3rd of these 3 ch, *1tr into front loop only of next tr, rep from * ending with 1tr into turning ch. Turn. 22 sts.

Next row 3ch to count as first tr, 1tr into front loop only of next 19tr, 1htr into front loop only of next htr, 1htr into turning ch. Turn.

Next row 3ch, 1htr into 3rd of these 3 ch, 1htr into front loop only of next 2htr, 1tr into front loop only of each tr to end. Turn. 24 sts.

Next row 3ch to count as first tr, 1tr into front loop only of next 19tr, 1htr into front loop only of next 3htr, 1 htr into turning ch. Turn.

Cont inc in this way, rep last 2 rows 4[5:6:7] times more. 32[34:36:38] sts.

Next row 5ch, 1dc into 3rd of these 5ch, 1dc into each of next 2ch, 1htr into front loop only of each of next 14[16:18: 20] htr, 1tr into front loop only of each tr to end. Turn. 36[38:40:42] sts.

Next row 3ch, 1tr into front loop only of next 19tr, 1htr into front loop only of next 14[16:18:20] htr, 1dc into front loop only of next 3dc, 1dc into turning ch. Turn.

Rep last 2 rows 2[3:4:5] times more. 44 [50:56:62] sts. Work 12 rows patt as now set without shaping, ending at top edge.

Next row Ss over first 4dc and into next dc, 1ch to count as first dc, patt to end. Turn. 40[46:52:58] sts.

Next row Patt to end. Turn.

Rep last 2 rows 2[3:4:5] times more. 32[34:36:38] sts.

Next row Ss over first 2htr and into next htr, 2ch to count as first htr, patt to end, Turn. 30[32:34:36] sts.

Next row Patt to end. Turn.

Rep last 2 rows until 20tr rem. Work 1 row tr. Fasten off.

Cuff

Using No.3.50 (ISR) hook, B and with RS of work facing, work along lower edge of sleeve as given for hem. Fasten off.

Neckband

Join shoulder seams. Using No.3.50 (ISR) hook, B and with RS of work facing, work evenly round neck edge as given for hem. Fasten off.

To make up

Press each piece under a damp cloth with a warm iron. Join sleeve seams. Set in sleeves, easing in fullness at top. Join centre back seam leaving opening for zip fastener to come to top of neckband. Sew in zip. Press seams.

Using the remaining yarn, make a twisted cord or plaited belt.

CROCHET IN ROUNDS
CIRCULAR MOTIFS

Crochet may very easily and effectively be made into a circle or square instead of working to and fro in rows. Each piece is worked from the same side which means that there is a definite right and wrong side to the work.

Circular shapes are an important technique in crochet. Sun hats, berets, bags and doilys are amongst the many articles formed from this method.

Attractive shapes may be joined together to give a patchwork fabric that is useful for shawls, rugs, waistcoats and evening skirts.

Again try experimenting in various yarns to see the many effects that may be achieved.

1tr into base of the first 3ch. Join with a ss to the 3rd of the first 3ch. 64tr.

Continue in this way, working 1 extra tr on each round between increases, until the circle is the required size. To practise this method of making a circle and produce useful items for the home at the same time, make two circles to any desired size and use them to cover a cushion pad or, using three thicknesses of Dishcloth Cotton and a No. 10.00 (ISR) hook, make a bath mat. A fringed edging would add the final touch to both these items.

To work a circle in crochet

Using No. 5.00 (ISR) hook and Double Knitting, make 6ch. Join together to form a ring with a ss into the first ch.

1st round 3ch to count as the first tr, then work 15tr into the ring. Join with a ss to the 3rd of the first 3ch. 16tr.

2nd round 3ch, 2tr into each tr of the previous round, 1tr into the base of the first 3ch. Join with a ss to the 3rd of the first 3ch. 32tr.

3rd round 3ch, (1tr into next stitch, 2tr into next stitch) 15 times, 1tr into next stitch, 1tr into base of the first 3ch. Join with a ss into the 3rd of the first 3ch. 48tr.

4th round 3ch, (1tr into each of next 2 stitches, 2tr into next stitch) 15 times, 1tr into each of next 2 stitches,

Another way to make a circular motif

Make 6ch. Join with ss to first ch to form a circle.

1st round 2ch to count as first dc, work 7dc into circle. Do not join but cont working in rounds, working next 2dc into second of first 2ch.

2nd round Work 2dc into each dc to end. 16dc.

3rd round Work 1dc into each dc to end.

4th round Work 2dc into each dc to end. 32dc.

5th round Work 1dc into each dc to end.

6th round 2dc into first dc, 1dc into next dc, *2dc into next dc, 1dc into next dc, rep from * to end. 48dc.

7th round Work 1 round without shaping.

8th round 2dc into first dc, 1dc into each of next 2dc, *2dc into next dc, 1dc into each of next 2dc, rep from * to end. 64dc.

Cont inc 16dc on every other round until the motif is the required size.

To do this, the space between each 2dc into 1dc increases by one stitch every increasing round so, round 10, work 2dc into next dc, 1dc into next 3dc; round 12, work 2dc into next dc, 1dc into next 4dc. Cont increasing 16dc on every alternate round in this way until circle is required size. Ss into first st of previous round and fasten off.

String place mat (see page 184)

Size
A place mat 30cm (12in) diameter

Materials
1 ball of gardening twine (available from hardware and gardening stores)
No. 4.00 (ISR) crochet hook

Mat
Work as given for circular motif until 14 rounds have been worked, that is a total of 112dc, but do not fasten off.

Scallop edging
Next round 3ch to count as first dc and 1ch sp, miss first 2dc, 1dc into each of next 3dc, *1ch, miss 1dc, 1dc into each of next 3dc, rep from * to last 2dc, 1dc into each of last 2dc. Join with ss to second of first 3ch.

Next round Into each 1ch sp work (1dc, 3tr, 1dc). Join with ss to first dc. Fasten off.

Working circles to make a clown
The clown is made up of circles in various sizes. Oddments of any Double Knitting in red, yellow, orange and black and a No. 4.00 (ISR) hook are used.
For the main part make a total of 95 circles by working the first and second rounds of the circle motif. The black cuffs and ankle frills have the third round added, while the neck frill has the fourth round worked and the skirt has an additional fifth round.
Also make 2 small black circles for each hand and foot, join each pair of circles and stuff with cotton wool. Make the head in a similar way, but work 3 rounds of the circle motif and include a circle of stiff card with the stuffing.
Use elastic threaded through the centre of each circle and join them together in this way: each arm consists of 17 small circles and a cuff which is inserted 1 circle before the hand, the body has 11 circles plus the skirt, and the legs have 25 circles each plus a frill which again is inserted 1 circle before the foot.

Raffia belt

Size
To fit 58[63:68]cm (23[25:27]in) waist. Each motif measures 5.5cm (2¼in) diameter. The figures in [] refer to the 63cm (25in) and 68cm (27in) sizes respectively.

Materials
Total of 3[3:4] hanks of raffia in one colour or oddments.
No. 3.00 (ISR) crochet hook

Belt motifs
With No. 3.00 (ISR) hook and any colour work first 3 rounds as given for circular motif. Join next colour and work 2 more rounds as given for circular motif. Fasten off. Make 9 [10:11] more motifs in same way.

To make up
Join motifs tog where edges touch to form one row. Make 3 separate ch 122[127:132]cm (48[50:52]in) long. Working on wrong side, stitch one ch across back of top edge of motifs, one across centre and one across lower edge, to tie at centre front. Trim each end of ch with wooden beads to neaten ends if required.

WORKING WITH SQUARES

To work a square in crochet

Either make this square entirely in one colour or use a different colour for each round.

Using a No. 5.00 (ISR) hook and Double Knitting, make 6ch. Join together to form a ring with a ss into the first ch.

1st round 6ch, work (1tr and 3ch) 7 times into the ring. Join with a ss to the 3rd of the first 6ch.

2nd round Ss into the first 3ch space so that the next group of tr will be worked into a space and not into a stitch, work 3ch to count as the first tr, 3tr into this same space, (2ch and 4tr into the next space) 7 times, 2ch. Join with a ss to the 3rd of the first 3ch.

3rd round Ss into each of next 4 stitches to ensure that the next group of tr will be worked into a 2ch space, 3ch, 5tr into this same space, 1ch, (6tr and 3ch into next space, 6tr and 1ch into next space) 3 times, 6tr into next space, 3ch. Join with a ss to the 3rd of the first 3ch.

4th round Ss into each of next 6 stitches to ensure that the hook is over the next 1ch space, 4ch, (1dc into space between the 3rd and 4th tr of next 6tr group, 3ch, 2tr, 3ch, 2tr all into next 3ch space, 3ch, 1dc into space between 3rd and 4th tr of next 6tr group, 3ch, 1dc into next 1ch space, 3ch) 3 times, 1dc into space between 3rd and 4th tr of next 6tr group, 3ch, 2tr,

3ch, 2tr all into next 3ch space, 3ch, 1dc into space between 3rd and 4th tr of next 6tr group, 3ch. Join with a ss to 2nd of the first 4ch. Fasten off.

Granny squares using 2 or more colours

(Breaking off yarn at end of each round.) Make commencing ch and work first round as given for motif in one colour. Break off yarn and fasten off.

2nd round Join next colour to any 2ch sp with ss, 3ch to count as first tr, work 2tr into same ch sp, *1ch, work (3tr, 2ch, 3tr) into next 2ch sp to form corner, rep from * twice more, 1ch, 3tr into same 2ch sp as beginning of round, 2ch. Join with ss to third of first 3ch. Break off yarn and fasten off.

3rd round Join next colour to any 2ch sp with ss, 3ch to count as first tr, work 2tr into same ch sp, *1ch, 3tr into 1ch sp, 1ch, work (3tr, 2ch, 3tr) into 2ch sp, rep from * twice more, 1ch, 3tr into 1ch sp, 1ch, 3tr into same 2ch sp as beginning of round, 2ch. Join with ss to third of first 3ch. Break off yarn and fasten off.

4th round Join next colour to any 2ch sp with ss, 3ch to count as first tr work 2tr into same ch sp, *(1ch, 3tr into next 1ch sp) twice, 1ch, work (3tr, 2ch, 3tr) into 2ch sp, rep from * twice more, (1ch, 3tr into next 1ch sp) twice, 1ch, 3tr into same 2ch sp as beginning of round, 2ch. Join with ss to third of first 3ch. Break off yarn and fasten off. Darn in ends of yarn where colours were joined.

To make a half-square

Using one or more colours Each row must be started with a fresh strand of yarn from the same side at which the row was first begun.

Make 5ch. Join with ss to first ch to form circle.

1st row Using same colour, 4ch to count as first tr and 1ch sp, work (3tr, 2ch, 3tr) into circle, 1ch, 1tr into circle. Break off yarn and fasten off.

2nd row Join next colour to third of first 4ch with ss, 4ch, 3tr into first 1ch sp, 1ch, work (3tr, 2ch, 3tr) into 2ch sp, 1ch, 3tr into last 1ch sp, 1ch, 1tr into top of last tr in previous row. Break off yarn and fasten off.

3rd row Join next colour to third of first 4ch with ss, 4ch, 3tr into first 1ch sp, 1ch, 3tr into next 1ch sp, 1ch, work (3tr, 2ch, 3tr) into 2ch sp, (1ch, 3tr into next 1ch sp) twice, 1ch, 1tr into top of last tr in previous row. Break off yarn and fasten off.

4th row Join next colour to third of first 4ch with ss, 4ch, 3tr into first 1ch sp, 1ch, (3tr into next 1ch sp, 1ch) twice, work (3tr, 2ch, 3tr) into 2ch sp, (1ch, 3tr into next 1ch sp) 3 times, 1ch, 1tr into last tr. Break off yarn and fasten off.

Cushion

A cushion 40cm (*16in*) square

Materials

250grm (*8¾oz*) of Double Knitting in one colour; 50grm (*1¾oz*) in each of 7 contrasting colours, A, B, C, D, E, F and G
One No. 4.00 (ISR) crochet hook
Cushion pad 40cm (*16in*) square
20cm (*8in*) zip fastener

Large square

Using No. 4.00 (ISR) crochet hook and any colour, work first 4 rounds as for square, changing colour for each round.

5th round Join in any colour with ss to corner 2ch sp, 3ch to count as first tr, 2tr into same sp, *(1ch, 3tr into next 1ch sp) 3 times, 1ch, (3tr, 2ch, 3tr) into corner 2ch sp, rep from * twice more, (1ch, 3tr into next 1ch sp) 3 times, 1ch, 3tr into same sp as beg of round, 2ch. Join with ss to third of first 3ch. Break off yarn and fasten off.

Cont in this way changing the colour as shown and working one more group of 3tr and 1ch on each side on every round until work measures 40cm (*16in*) across. Fasten off. Darn in all ends. Make another square.

To make up

With RS of squares tog, join 3 edges. Turn RS out. Insert cushion pad. Join rem seam, leaving sp to insert zip in centre.

Edging Using No. 4.00 (ISR) hook and any colour, rejoin yarn with ss to any corner sp through both thicknesses. Into each ch sp round all edges work (1ss, 4tr, 1ss) working through both thicknesses, except across zip fastener opening, where you only work through one thickness. Join with ss to first ss. Fasten off. Sew in zip.

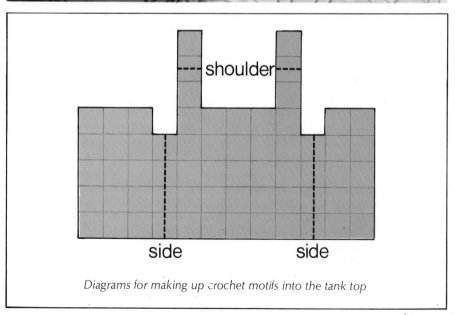

Diagrams for making up crochet motifs into the tank top

Crochet top

Sizes

86.5[91.5/96.5:99/101.5]cm (34[36/38: 39/40]in) bust
Length to shoulder, 49.5[53.5:57]cm (19½[21:22½]in)
The figures in brackets [ ] refer to the 91.5cm (36in), 96.5cm (38in) and 101.5cm (40in) sizes respectively

Tension

One square motif for first size measures 7.5cm × 7.5cm (3in × 3in) worked on No. 2.50 (ISR) hook; for second size measures 8cm × 8cm (3¼in × 3¼in) worked on No. 3.00 (ISR) hook; for third size measure 9cm × 9cm (3½in × 3½in) worked on No. 3.50 (ISR) hook

Materials

Wendy Double Knitting Nylonised 7[8:8] balls in main shade, A
contrast colour, B 6[8:8] balls of
One No. 2.50 [3.00:3.50] (ISR) crochet hook

Working the motifs

1st square motif (make 10)
Using No.2.50[3.00:3.50] (ISR) hook and B, make 4ch. Join with a ss into first ch to form a circle.
1st round 3ch to count as first tr, 2tr into circle, *1ch, 3tr into circle, rep from * twice more, 1ch. Join with a ss into 3rd of 3ch.
2nd round Ss into next ch sp, 3ch to count as first tr, 2tr into same sp, 1ch, 3tr into same sp, *1ch, into next ch sp work 3tr, 1ch and 3tr, rep from * twice more, 1ch. Join with a ss into 3rd of 3ch. Break off B.
3rd round Join in A. Ss into next ch sp, 3ch to count as first tr, 3tr into same sp, 1ch, 4tr into same sp, 1dc into next ch sp, *into next ch sp work 4tr, 1ch and 4tr, 1dc into next ch sp, rep from * twice more. Join with a ss into 3rd of 3ch.
4th round Ss into next ch sp, 3ch to count as first tr, 2tr into same sp, 1ch, 3tr into same sp, into next ch sp of 2 rounds below work 3dtr, 1ch and 3dtr, *into next ch sp of previous round work 3tr, 1ch and 3tr, into next ch sp of 2 rounds below work 3dtr, 1ch and 3dtr, rep from * twice more. Join with a ss into 3rd of 3ch. Fasten off.

2nd square motif (make 10)
As 1st square motif in colour sequence of 2 rounds A and 2 rounds B.

3rd square motif (make 11)
As 1st square motif in colour sequence of 1 round B, 2 rounds A and 1 round B.

4th square motif (make 10)
As 1st square motif in colour sequence of 1 round B, 1 round A, 1 round B and 1 round A.

5th square motif (make 11)
As 1st square motif in colour sequence of 1 round A, 2 rounds B and 1 round A.

6th square motif (make 12)
As 1st square motif in colour sequence of 1 round A, 1 round B, 1 round A and 1 round B.

64 square motifs should be worked in all to complete the top.

To make up

Press each square under a damp cloth with a warm iron. Using A, join squares as shown in diagram making a patchwork with the different colour combinations.

Edging Using No.2.50[3.00:3.50] (ISR) hook and A, work 1 row dc round each armhole, neck and shoulder edges and lower edge.

A bright bag
from Granny squares

Diagram for making up bag

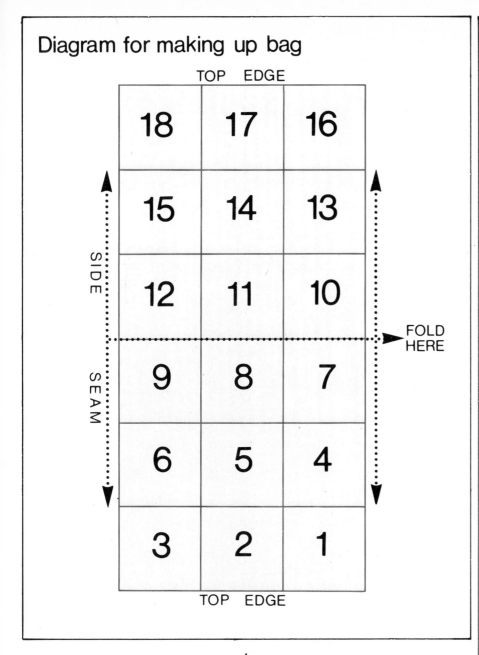

TOP EDGE

18	17	16
15	14	13
12	11	10
9	8	7
6	5	4
3	2	1

SIDE SEAM

FOLD HERE

TOP EDGE

Size
45.5cm (*18in*) wide by 45.5cm (*18in*) deep

Tension
Each motif measures 15cm (*6in*) by 15cm (*6in*) worked on No.5.00 (ISR) crochet hook

Materials
3 × 50 grm balls of Mahony Blarney Claude in main shade, A
1 ball each of 5 contrast colours, B, C, D, E and F
One No.5.00 (ISR) crochet hook
2 round wooden handles
Lining material 45.5cm (*18in*) wide by 91.5cm (*36in*) long

First motif
Using No.5.00 (ISR) hook and A, make

6ch. Join with a ss to first ch to form circle.

1st round Using A, 2ch to count as first dc, work 15dc into circle. Join with a ss to 2nd of first 2ch.

2nd round Using A, 5ch to count as first htr and 3ch, *miss 1dc, 1htr into next dc, 3ch, rep from * 6 times more. Join with a ss to 2nd of first 5ch. Break off A. Join in B.

3rd round Using B, work (1dc, 1htr, 1tr, 1htr, 1dc, 1ch) into each ch sp to end. Join with a ss to first dc. 8 petals. Break off B. Join in C.

4th round Using C, 2ch to count as first htr, *3ch, 1dc into tr of next petal, 4ch, 1dc into tr of next petal, 3ch, 1htr into 1ch sp before next petal, 3ch, 1htr into same ch sp, rep from * twice more, 3ch, 1dc in tr of next petal, 4ch, 1dc in tr of next petal, 3ch, 1htr into last 1ch sp

after last petal, 3ch. Join with a ss to 2nd of first 2ch.

5th round Using C, 1ch, *4ch, into 4ch sp work (3tr, 3ch, 3tr) to form corner, 4ch, 1dc into htr, 1dc into 3ch sp, 1dc into htr, rep from * twice more, 4ch, work corner, 4ch, 1dc into htr, 1dc into 3ch sp. Join with a ss to first ch. Break off C. Join in D.

6th round Using D, 1ch, *5ch, 1tr into each of next 3tr, 5ch, insert hook into 3rd ch from hook and work 1dc to form picot – called 5ch picot –, 2ch, 1tr into each of next 3tr, 5ch, ss into next dc, 4ch, insert hook into 3rd ch from hook and work 1dc to form picot – called 4ch picot –, 1ch, miss 1dc, ss into next dc, rep from * twice more, 5ch, 1tr into each of next 3tr, 5ch picot, 2ch, 1tr into each of next 3tr, 5ch, ss into next dc, 4ch picot, 1ch. Join with a ss to first ch. Fasten off.

Second motif
Using colours as required, work as given for 1st motif until 5th round has been completed.

6th round (joining round) Using any colour, 1ch, *5ch, 1tr into each of next 3tr, 2ch, with RS of 1st motif facing RS of 2nd motif work 1dc into 5ch picot at corner of 1st motif, 2ch, 1tr into each of next 3tr of 2nd motif, ss into first of 5ch after last tr on 1st motif, 4ch, ss into next dc of 2nd motif, 1ch, 1dc into 4ch picot of 1st motif, 1ch, miss 1dc on 2nd motif, ss into next dc on 2nd motif, 4ch, ss into last ch before next 3tr on 1st motif, 1tr into each of next 3tr on 2nd motif, 2ch, 1dc into 5ch picot at corner of 1st motif, 2ch, complete round as given for 1st motif. Work 16 more motifs in same way, using colours as required and joining each motif where edges touch, as shown in diagram.

To make up
Darn in all ends. Press on WS under a dry cloth with a cool iron.

Top edges Using No.5.00 (ISR) hook, A and with RS of work facing, rejoin yarn to corner picot at end of motif, 3ch to count as first tr, work 14 more tr evenly across first motif, work (15tr across next motif) twice. Turn. 45tr. Work 2 more rows tr. Fasten off. Work along other end in same way.
With RS facing fold motifs in half and join side seams as shown in diagram. Seam lining in same way. Turn bag RS out and insert loose lining. Fold top edge over handle to WS and sl st down. Work other handle in same way. Sl st top of lining to WS of top edge, easing in fullness. Sew lining to side edges of opening.

SQUARE AND WHEEL MOTIFS

The simple stitches you have learnt can be used for all sorts of motifs, including these two completely different lacy ones. The motifs can be worked in fine or thick yarns, depending on purpose or personal choice.

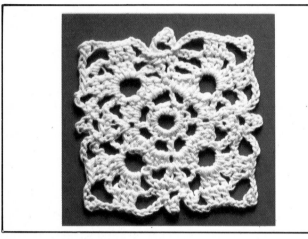

Square lace motif

Make 6ch. Join with ss to first ch to form circle.

1st round 2ch to count as first dc, work 15dc into circle. Join with ss to second of first 2ch.

2nd round 4ch to count as first htr and 2ch, *miss 1dc, 1htr into next dc, 2ch, rep from * 6 times more. Join with ss to second of first 4ch.

3rd round Work (1dc, 1htr, 1tr, 1htr, 1dc, 1ch) into each ch sp to end. Join with ss to first dc. 8 petals.

4th round 2ch to count as first htr, *3dc, 1dc into tr of next petal, 4ch, 1dc into tr of next petal, 3ch, 1htr into 1ch sp before next petal, 2ch, 1htr into same ch sp, rep from * twice more, 3ch, 1dc into tr of next petal, 4ch, 1dc into tr of next petal, 3ch, 1htr into last 1ch sp after last petal, 2ch. Join with ss to second of first 2ch.

5th round 1ch, *4ch, into 4ch sp work (3tr, 3ch, 3tr) to form corner, 4ch, 1dc into htr, 1dc into 2ch sp, 1dc into htr, rep from * twice more, 4ch, into 4ch sp work (3tr, 3ch, 3tr), 4ch, 1dc into htr, 1dc into 2ch sp. Join with ss to first ch.

6th round 1ch, *5ch, 1tr into each of next 3tr, 5ch, insert hook into third ch from hook to form a little loop (see diagram) and work 1dc to form picot – called 5ch picot – 2ch, 1tr into each of next 3tr, 5ch, ss into next dc, 4ch, insert hook into third ch from hook and work 1dc to form picot – called 4ch picot –

Forming a picot loop

1ch, miss 1dc, ss into next dc, rep from * twice more, 5ch, 1tr into each of next 3tr, 5ch picot, 2ch, 1tr into each of next 3tr, 5ch, ss into next dc, 4ch picot, 1ch. Join with ss to fir st ch. Fasten off.

Catherine wheel motif

Make 8ch. Join with ss to first ch to form circle.

1st round 1ch to count as first dc, work 15dc into circle. Join with ss to first ch. 16 sts. Do not break off yarn.

First spoke

1st row Make 14ch, work 1dc into third ch from hook, 1dc into next ch, work 10dc around, and not into, the ch, 1dc into each of last 3ch, ss into next dc along the circle, turn.

2nd row Work 1dc into each of first 3dc, (4ch, miss 1dc, 1dc into next dc) 5 times, 1dc into each of next 2dc, 1dc into second of first 2ch. Turn.

3rd row 1ch to count as first dc, 1dc into each of next 3dc, (4dc into 4ch loop, 1dc into next dc) 5 times, 1dc into each of last 2dc, ss into next dc along the circle, turn.

Second spoke

1st row Make 13ch, ss into centre st of third loop along first spoke, turn, work 1dc into each of next 3ch, work 10dc around the ch, 1dc into each of last 3ch, ss into next dc along circle, turn and complete as for first spoke but on next row end with 1dc into each of last 3dc instead of last 2dc and turning ch.

Work 6 more spokes in the same way and when working the last one, join the centre of the 3rd loop to the tip of the first spoke. Fasten off. 8 spokes.

Last round Rejoin yarn with ss to top of any spoke, 1ch to count as first dc, work 1dc into each st round outside edge of motif. Join with ss to first ch. Fasten off.

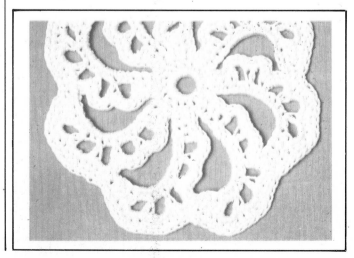

Cafe curtain

Size

Curtain 140cm (*55in*) wide by 140cm (*55in*) long, excluding tabs, each motif measures 13cm (*5in*) diameter

Materials

11 × 84m (*77yd*) balls of 4 ply cotton in main shade, A, 10 balls of contrast colour, B, 9 balls of contrast colour, C and 7 balls each of contrast colours, D and E. 1 ball makes 2 motifs
One No. 3.00 (ISR) crochet hook
Length of wooden curtain rail

Curtain

Make 22 catherine wheel motifs in A, 20 in B, 18 in C, 14 in D and 13 in E.

To make up

Join motifs tog as shown in diagram on opposite page.

Tabs Using No. 3.00 (ISR) hook, appropriate colour and with RS of first top motif facing, rejoin yarn with ss to fifth dc along edge, 3ch to count as first tr, work 1tr into each of next 5dc, turn. 6 sts. Cont working rows of tr across these 6 sts until tab is long enough to go over top of curtain rail and down to top of motif. Fasten off. Work 10 more tabs in same way. St tabs in place to back of each motif.

Place mat and coaster

Size
For place mat 28cm (11¼in) wide by 23cm (9in) deep and coaster 11cm (4½in) square. Each motif measures 5.5cm (2¼in) square

Materials
40grm of No. 20 cotton (1 ball makes approximately 23 motifs)
One No. 1.50 (ISR) crochet hook.

Mat
Work as given for square lace motif, joining 5 motifs to form one row, 4 rows in all, total 20 motifs.

Coaster
Work as given for square lace motif, joining 2 motifs to form one row, 2 rows in all, total 4 motifs.

Below: Crochet place mat and coaster

To join square lace motifs
Work first 5 rounds as given for motif.
6th round (joining round) 1ch, *5ch, 1tr into each of next 3tr, 2ch, with RS of completed motif A facing RS of motif B which is to be joined work 1dc into 5ch picot at corner of motif A, 2ch, 1tr into each of next 3tr of motif B, ss into first of 5ch after last tr on motif A, 4ch, ss into next dc of motif B, 1ch, 1dc into 4ch picot of motif A, 1ch, miss 1dc on motif B, ss next dc on motif B, 4ch, ss into last ch into before next 3tr on motif A, 1tr into each of next 3tr on motif B, 2ch, 1dc into 4ch picot at corner of motif A, 2ch. One side has been joined. Complete round motif B as given for square lace motif A. Fasten off. Where the squares have to be joined on two sides continue in the same way.

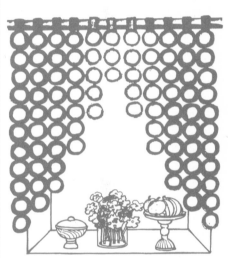

Above: Diagram to show how Catherine wheel motifs are joined for a cafe curtain

Above: Catherine wheel motifs used as edging for a circular tablecloth

USING COLOUR
PATCHWORK EFFECTS

This chapter explains how to work crochet, using various colours to form a patchwork effect, all in one process. Several samples are shown and explained in detail to help you follow the methods involved in this technique. As with patchwork crochet using separate shapes (see later) it is best to use the same weight of yarn throughout the work to make sure you keep an even tension and so give a good fabric. Multi-coloured fabrics can be worked in straight lines, or circles and other shapes in the same way as plain coloured crochet. The most popular stitch to give a good fabric is the double crochet.

Sample 1

Two colours of double knitting yarn, A and B, have been used to work this basic patchwork design which is formed from checked squares. The techniques covered in this sample are the method of joining in a new colour and the method of carrying the colour not in use in with the work. To help you work this first sample, we are giving both written instructions and a chart.
Using No.4.50 (ISR) hook and A, make a length of chain with multiples of 5+1 stitches.
Note Practise the method of joining in a new colour which is given in the 1st row as it is important that the new colour is joined into the stitch preceding the stitches to be worked in the new colour. Further

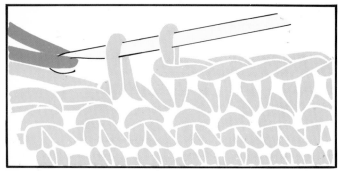

Joining in a new colour in the middle of a row

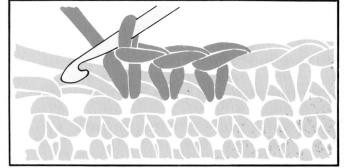

Working over the colour which is not in use

instructions for joining in new colours will not be given in detail, but this method should be used throughout. The colour not in use is held along the line of work and this is kept in place by the crochet stitch being worked over the yarn. This avoids ugly loops appearing on the work and also ensures that the work is completely reversible.

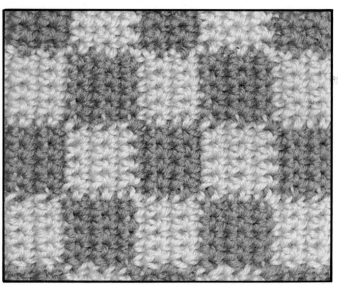

1st row Using colour A, into 3rd ch from hook work 1dc, 1dc into each of next 2ch, insert hook into next ch, yrh and draw through a loop, yrh with colour B and draw through both loops on hook, using colour B, work 1dc into each of next 5ch, using colour A, work 1dc into each of next 5ch, cont in this way working 5 sts alternately in A and B to end of row. Turn.
2nd row Using same colour as last 5dc of previous row and working over colour not in use as before, work 1ch to count as first dc, 1dc into each of next 4dc, change colour, 1dc into each of next 5dc, cont in this way to end of row, working last dc into turning ch. Turn.
3rd to 5th rows As 2nd.
6th to 10th rows As 2nd, working a square of colour A over colour B and a square of colour B over colour A. The 1st to 10th rows form the colour sequence for this sample. When you have completed this sample, you will see how the instructions compare with the squared diagram and you will be able to make up your own designs using this technique.

Sample 2

Here we have used the same techniques as explained in sample 1, but a much more varied effect has been achieved by using three colours and random shapes. As there is no definite pattern of shapes, oddments of colour can quite easily be used. A further technique is employed here, where the yarn not in use is left on the wrong side of the work ready for taking into the work again on the next row. This method is used when a coloured yarn is being used in one block only. Remember that should a colour of yarn which is already in use be required further along the row, then this yarn must be carried along the row until required. Using No.4.50 (ISR) hook and 3 colours of double knitting yarn, make 24ch. Work in double crochet and follow the chart to make our sample.

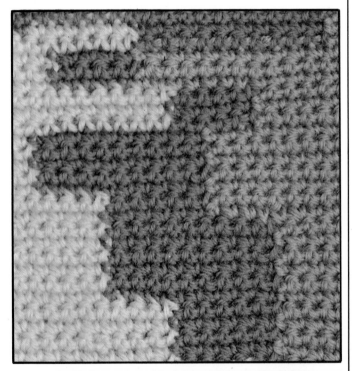

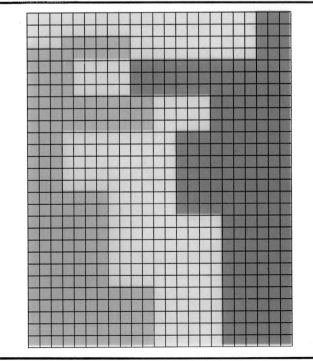

Sample 3

This is a lovely patchwork fabric made up of traditional church window shapes worked in many different colours. The effect of these colours and shapes is very fashionable when they are made into garments such as long skirts, waistcoats or tank tops. Household items such as cushion covers and rugs also look very attractive when they are worked in this way.

As so many colours are used it is a good idea to work a single church window shape to estimate how much yarn is required for each individual shape. Then, when you are deciding on your colours, wind each colour of yarn into balls of the correct length.

Using No.4.50 (ISR) hook and double knitting yarn, make a chain with multiples of 8+1 stitches and follow our diagram, changing colour for each shape. There is no need to work over the colour not in use. This should be left behind the work until the next row where it is required. When a shape in one colour is finished, leave the end of yarn hanging free and darn in all ends on the wrong side of the work when it is completed.

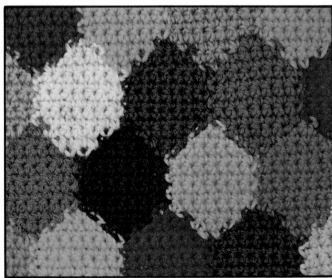

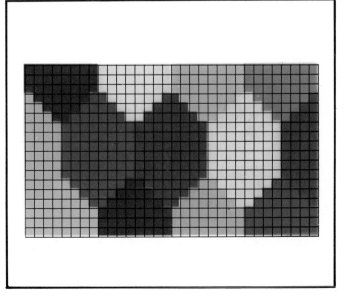

COLOUR DESIGNS

Here we continue our chapters on the use of different coloured yarns within a single piece of crochet work, by showing how lines of colour can be incorporated into a design. This sort of design would be ideal for border patterns on a plain piece of work such as a scarf, skirt or bedcover. In some of the samples shown here the lines of colour are raised from the background by applying a technique known as blistering and this is described in detail.

Sample 1
This is a double sided fabric, worked in two colours of double knitting yarn, A and B. Using No.4.50 (ISR) hook and A, make 21ch.

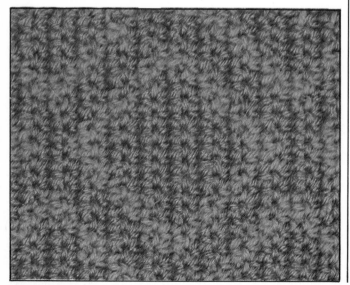

1st row Into 3rd ch from hook work 1dc, 1dc into next ch, join in B as explained in previous chapter, using B and working over A (see previous chapter), work 1dc into each of next 2ch, using A and working over B work 1dc into each of next 10ch, using B and working over A work 1dc into each of next 2ch, using A and working over B work 1dc into each of next 3ch. Turn. Continue in this way, working in pattern from the chart.

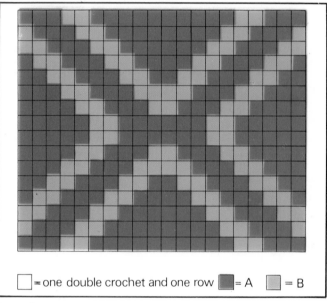

□ = one double crochet and one row ■ = A ■ = B

Sample 2
Here two colours of double knitting yarn, A and B, have been used to give a raised, or blistered, effect to the work. When working individual narrow lines of colour which follow through a design, it is not always necessary to carry the yarn not in use in with the work. Just leave this yarn behind the work ready to be worked into the crochet on the next row. There is a definite right and wrong side to the work when this technique is used. Using No.3.50 (ISR) hook and A, make 21ch.
1st row Into 3rd ch from hook work 1dc, 1dc into each of next 5ch, join in B as explained in previous chapter, leaving A hanging on WS of work, using B work 1dc into each of next 6ch joining in A on the last st, pull A taut to form a blister, using A work 1dc into each of next 7ch. Turn.
2nd row Using A work 1ch to count as first dc, miss first st, 1dc into each of next 6dc joining in B on the last st and placing A towards you whilst you work, 1dc into each of next 6dc using B and joining in A on the last st worked, leave B on WS of work (towards you) and pull A taut to form a blister, using A work 1dc into each of next 7dc. Turn.

3rd row Using A work 1ch to count as first dc, miss first st, 1dc into each of next 6dc joining in B on the last st, leave A on WS of work (away from you), work 1dc into each of next 6dc using B and joining in A on the last st, leave B on WS of work and pull A taut to form a blister, using A work 1dc into each of next 7dc. Turn.

The 2nd and 3rd rows are repeated throughout.

Sample 3

In this sample the two techniques of working over the yarn not in use or leaving it free at the back of the work are mixed. The background colour, A, is carried throughout, whilst the other colours in the design, B, C and D are left free at the back of the work when not in use. Using No. 3.50 (ISR) hook and A, make 17ch.

1st row Join in colour B see previous chapter, using B work 1dc into 3rd ch from hook, 1dc into each of next 2ch working over A, using A work 1dc into each of next 2ch, using C work 1dc into each of next

2ch, using A work 1dc into each of next 2ch, using D work 1dc into each of next 4ch, using A work 1dc into next ch. Turn.

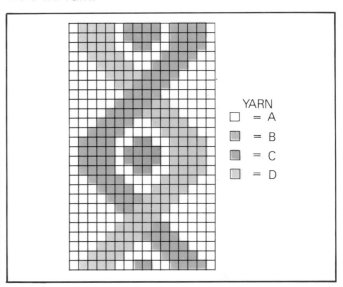

YARN
☐ = A
▨ = B
▨ = C
☐ = D

2nd row Using A work 1ch to count as first dc, miss first st, 1dc into next dc, using D work 1dc into each of next 4dc, using A work 1dc into each of next 4dc, using B work 1dc into each of next 4dc, using A work 1dc into each of next 2dc. Turn.

Continue working in this way from the chart, noting that yarn C forms a small area of colour so that the yarn may be cut after each motif is finished to avoid unnecessary yarns hanging behind the work.

Sample 4

Our belt has been worked in 3 colours of double knitting yarn, using a No.3.50 (ISR) hook. Follow the chart given for sample 3, omitting colour C and form a blistered or raised effect on the crossover lines by applying the technique used in sample 2 and keeping A taut whilst it is not in use. A large bead has been added as decoration in the centre of each diamond.

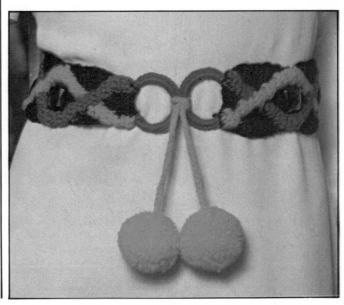

A hat of many colours

Size
To fit an average head

Tension
12htr and 9 rows to 5cm (*2in*) over patt worked on No.3.50 (ISR) crochet hook

Materials
1× one oz ball Lister Lavenda 4 ply in each of 5 colours, A, B, C, D and E
One No.3.50 (ISR) crochet hook

Note
When using two different coloured yarns in the same round, always work over the colour not in use and when changing colour, draw the new colour through all the loops on the hook of the last st in the old colour

Hat
Using No.3.50 (ISR) hook and A, make 6ch. Join with a ss into first ch to form circle.

1st round Using A, 2ch to count as first htr, 7htr into circle. Join with a ss into 2nd of 2ch. 8htr. Break off A.

2nd round Using B, 2ch to count as first htr, 1htr into st at base of ch, *2htr into next htr, rep from * to end. Join with a ss into 2nd of 2ch. 16htr.

3rd round Using 4 sts each of B and C all round, work 2ch to count as first htr, 2htr into next htr, *1htr into next htr, 2htr into next htr, rep from * to end. Join with a ss into 2nd of 2ch. 24htr.

Break off B and C.

4th round Using D, 2ch, 1htr into next htr, 2htr into next htr, *1htr into each of next 2htr, 2htr into next htr, rep from * to end. Join with a ss into 2nd of 2ch. 32htr.

5th round Using 5 sts each of D and E all round, work 2ch, 1htr into each of

next 2 htr, 2htr into next htr, *1htr into each of next 3 htr, 2htr into next htr, rep from * to end. Join with a ss into 2nd of 2ch. 40 htr. Break off E.

6th round Using D, 2ch, 1htr into each of next 3 htr, 2htr into next htr, *1htr into each of next 4 htr, 2htr into next htr, rep

each of next 7 htr, 2htr into next htr, rep from * to end. Join with a ss into 2nd of 2ch. 72htr. Break off A.

10th round Using E, 2ch, 1htr into each of next 7 htr, 2htr into next htr, *1htr into each of next 8 htr, 2htr into next htr, rep from * to end. Join with a ss into 2nd of 2ch. 80htr. Break off E.

11th round Using 4 sts each of B and D all round, 2ch, 1htr into each of next 8 htr, 2htr into next htr, *1htr into each of next 9 htr, 2htr into next htr, rep from * to end. Join with a ss into 2nd of 2ch. 88htr.

12th round Using 4 sts each of B and D and working into same colours in previous round, 2ch, 1htr into each htr to end. Join with a ss into 2nd of 2ch. Break off B and D.

13th round Using E, as 12th. Break off E.
14th round Using C, as 12th. Break off C.
15th round Using B, as 12th. Break off B.
16th round Using one st of A and 7 sts of D all round, as 12th.
17th round Using 3 sts of A and 5 sts of D all round, as 12th. Break off A and D.
18th round Using E, as 12th. Break off E.
19th round Using A, as 12th.
20th round Using 4 sts of A and 4 sts of C all round, as 12th.
21st round As 20th. Break off A and C.
22nd round Using B, as 12th. Break off B.
23rd round Using A, as 12th.
24th round Using C, as 12th.
25th round Using 3 sts of B and 5 sts of E all round, as 12th. Break off B and E.
26th round Using D, as 12th.
27th round As 26th.

Shape brim

28th round Using E, 2ch, 2htr into next htr, *1htr into next htr, 2htr into next htr, rep from * to end. Join with a ss into 2nd of 2ch. 132htr. Break off E.

29th round Using B, as 12th. Break off B.
30th round Using C, as 12th. Break off C.
31st round Using 8 sts of A and 4 sts of E all round, as 12th. Break off A and E.
32nd round Using D, 2ch, 1htr into each of next 4 htr, 2htr into next htr, *1htr into each of next 5 htr, 2htr into next htr, rep from * to end. Join with a ss into 2nd of 2ch. 154htr. Break off D.

33rd round Using A, as 12th.
34th round Using 4 sts of A and 3 sts of B all round, as 12th. Break off A and B.
35th round Using E, 2ch, 1htr into each of next 5 htr, 2htr into next htr, *1htr into each of next 6 htr, 2htr into next htr, rep from * to end. Join with a ss into 2nd of 2ch. 176htr. Break off E.

36th round Using D, as 12th. Break off D.
37th round Using C and working from left to right (i.e. in a backwards direction), work 1dc into each htr to end. Join with a ss into first dc. Fasten off.

from * to end. Join with a ss into 2nd of 2ch. 48htr. Break off D.

7th round Using C, 2ch, 1htr into each of next 4 htr, 2htr into next htr, *1htr into each of next 5 htr, 2htr into next htr, rep from * to end. Join with a ss into 2nd of 2ch. 56htr. Break off C.

8th round Using A, 2ch, 1htr into each of next 5 htr, 2htr into next htr, *1htr into each of next 6 htr, 2htr into next htr, rep from * to end. Join with a ss into 2nd of 2ch. 64htr.

9th round Using A, 2ch, 1htr into each of next 6 htr, 2htr into next htr, *1htr into

PATCHWORK CROCHET

Patchwork crochet

Traditionally we think of patchwork as a means of using oddments of fabric to obtain a quilt or garment. Today there is a great revival of interest in the art, and fabrics are carefully selected and co-ordinated to create colourful and exciting designs.

The same designs may be worked in crochet, again using oddments of yarn to use up scraps, or choosing a selection of colours to produce a desired effect. A pleasing choice of colours is a vital point in patchwork for this can make or mar a design. Closely related colours are usually a satisfactory choice, so that if you choose red, then you may use all the various shades of red from deep ruby to oranges and yellows. Our samples have been worked in blues and greens to illustrate the same idea.

Patchwork crochet has many purposes both for garments and in the home. Typical examples of household items are quilts, cushion covers, rugs, wall hangings and room dividers. The most suitable garments are ones which require little or no shaping, such as straight skirts, jerkins and belts.

In order to achieve a high standard of work, it is necessary to use the same weight of yarn throughout, although to add interest they may be of different textures. As the yarn should be of one weight, then the same size crochet hook may be used for each. Firm, even stitches, such as double crochet or half trebles, should be used for the crochet in order to make a precise shape.

The shapes described in this chapter are all geometrical and include the square, rectangle, diamond, triangle and hexagonal. They are all worked in a double knitting yarn using a No.4.00 (ISR) crochet hook.

To join the separate shapes you should place the right sides together and oversew with a firm stitch in the same yarn. The seam may be pressed on the wrong side under a damp cloth with a warm iron. Where there is more than one colour used in the same shape, such as samples 5 and 6, these are joined into the work as required.

Sample 1

To work the diamond shape Make 3ch.
1st row Into 3rd ch from hook work 1dc. Turn. 2 sts.
2nd row 1ch to count as first st, 1dc into st at base of ch, 1dc into turning ch. Turn. One st increased.
3rd row 1ch to count as first st, 1dc into st at base of ch, 1dc into next st, 1dc into turning ch. Turn. One st increased.
Cont in this way, inc one st at beg of every row, until there are 20 sts.
Next row 1ch to count as first st, miss next st, 1dc into next st, 1dc into each st to end, finishing with 1dc into turning ch. Turn. One st decreased.
Cont in this way, dec one st at beg of every row, until 2 sts rem. Fasten off.

Sample 2

To work the church window shape Work as given for sample 1, but when the required size or width is reached (20 sts, for example), work 14 rows without shaping. Then work the decrease shaping as before.

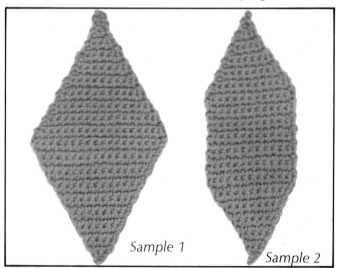

Sample 1

Sample 2

Sample 3

To work the triangle Make 3ch.
1st row Into 3rd ch from hook work 1htr. Turn. 2 sts.
2nd row 2ch to count as first htr, 1htr into st at base of ch, 2htr into 2nd of 2ch. Turn. 2 sts increased.
3rd row 2ch to count as first htr, 1htr into st at base of ch, 1htr into each of next 2 sts, 2htr into 2nd of 2ch. Turn. 2 sts increased.
Cont in this way, inc one st at each end of every row, until there are 24 sts or the triangle is the required size. Fasten off.

Sample 4

To work the hexagon Make 5ch. Join with a ss into first ch to form a circle.
1st round 4ch, *1tr into circle, 1ch, rep from * 10 times more. Join with a ss into 3rd of 4ch.
2nd round 3ch to count as first tr, 2tr into next 1ch sp, 1tr into next tr, 1ch, *1tr into next tr, 2tr into next 1ch sp, 1tr into next tr, 1ch, rep from * 4 times more. Join with a ss into 3rd of 3ch.
3rd round 3ch to count as first tr, 1tr into st at base of ch, 1tr into each of next 2tr, 2tr into next tr, 2ch, *2tr

into next tr, 1tr into each of next 2tr, 2tr into next tr, 2ch, rep from * 4 times more. Join with a ss into 3rd of 3ch. Fasten off.

This completes the sample illustrated, but a smaller or larger shape could be achieved by working in the same way, inc one st at each end of every block of tr and one ch between blocks on every round, until the shape is the desired size.

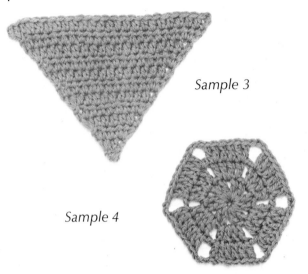

Sample 3

Sample 4

Sample 5

Four colours, A, B, C and D, are used for this sample which illustrates a square. See the effect of the colours when four squares are joined together. Using A, make 17ch.

1st row Into 3rd ch from hook work 1dc, 1dc into each ch to end. Turn. 16 sts.

2nd row 1ch to count as first dc, 1dc into each dc to end, finishing with 1dc into turning ch. Turn.

Rep last row twice more. Break off A. Join in B.

Note Care should be taken when joining in a new colour. It is better to work 2 turning chains instead of 1 and then pull up the old colour tightly. Work 4 rows in dc with each of B, C and D. Fasten off. Sew in the cut ends. Place squares to give the desired pattern and sew together.

Sample 6

Here four triangular shapes, as given in sample 3, have been worked with four colours in each and then joined together.

Work 2 triangles with 4 rows each in A, B, C and D, and then 2 more triangles using the colour sequence of D, C, B and A. Position with alternate colours meeting and then sew together. Neaten the cut ends by threading back into the work on the wrong side.

Sample 7

This sample is made up of brick shapes. There are 16 in all, 4 in each colour.

To work the brick shape Make 11ch.

1st row Into 3rd ch from hook work 1dc, 1dc into each ch to end. Turn. 10 sts.

2nd row 1ch to count as first dc, 1dc into each dc to end, finishing with 1dc into turning ch. Turn.

Rep last row 3 times more. Fasten off.

Work the required number of bricks in each colour and position carefully in rows of one colour before sewing into place. When finished, sew in all the cut ends on the wrong side of the work.

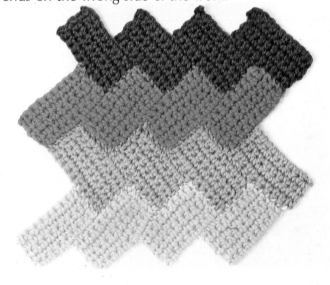

A patchwork jacket

Sizes

To fit 86.5[91.5:96.5:101.5]cm (34[36:38:40]in) bust/chest
Length to shoulder, 68.5[68.5:76:76]cm (27[27:30:30]in)
Sleeve seam, 46[46:51:51]cm (18[18:20:20]in)
The figures in brackets [ ] refer to the 91.5 (36), 96.5 (38) and 101.5cm (40in) sizes respectively

Tension

18 sts and 9 rows to 10cm (3.9in) over tr worked on No.3.50 (ISR) crochet hook

Materials

11[12:12:13] × 50grm balls of Mahony Killowen Double Knitting in main shade, A
2[2:2:2] balls each of contrast colours, B and C
1[1:1:2] balls of contrast colour, D
1[2:2:3] balls of contrast colour, E
One No.3.50 (ISR) crochet hook
66[66:71:71]cm (26[26:28:28]in) open ended zip fastener

Back

Using No.3.50 (ISR) hook and A, make 82 [88:94:96]ch.
1st row Into 4th ch from hook work 1tr, 1tr into each ch to end. Turn. 80[86:92:94]tr.
2nd row 3ch to count as first tr, miss first tr, 1tr into each tr to end. Turn.
Rep 2nd row 40[40:49:49] times more.
Shape raglan armholes
Next row Ss across first 6[6:7:7]tr, 1tr into each tr to last 6[6:7:7]tr, turn.
Next row 3ch to count as first tr, yrh, insert hook into next tr, yrh and draw through loop, yrh and draw through 2 loops on hook, yrh and insert hook into next tr, yrh and draw through loop, yrh and draw through 2 loops on hook, yrh and draw through 3 loops on hook – called dec 1 –, 1tr into each tr to last 3tr, dec 1, 1tr into last tr. Turn.
Rep last row 19[19:21:21] times more. Fasten off.

Sleeves

Using No.3.50 (ISR) hook and A, make 40 [40:49:49]ch. Work 1st row as given for back. 38[38:47:47]tr.
1st and 2nd sizes only
Work 2 rows tr.
4th row 3ch, 2tr into next tr – called inc 1 –, 1tr into each tr to last 2tr, inc 1, 1tr into last tr. Turn.
Work 2 rows tr without shaping. Cont inc in this way on next and every foll 3rd row until 34 rows have been worked from beg, then inc in same way on every foll 2nd row 5 times in all. 70[70]tr.

3rd and 4th sizes only

Work 4 rows tr. Inc as given for 1st and 2nd sizes on next and every foll 4th row until 21 rows have been worked from beg, then inc in same way on every foll 3rd row until there are 77[77]tr.
All sizes
Shape raglans
Next row Ss across first 6[6:7:7]tr, 3ch, 1tr into each tr to last 6[6:7:7]tr, turn.
Dec one st at each end of every row until 30[30:31:31]tr rem.
Next row 3ch, dec 1, 1tr into each of next 9tr, dec 1, 1tr into each of next 2[2:3:3]tr, dec 1, 1tr into each of next 9tr, dec 1, 1tr into last tr. Turn.
Next row 3ch, dec 1, 1tr into each of next 7tr, dec 1, 1tr into each of next 2[2:3:3]tr, dec 1, 1tr into each of next 7tr, dec 1, 1tr into last tr. Turn.
Cont dec in this way on next 4 rows. 6[6:7:7]tr. Fasten off.

Left and right fronts

Work motifs for fronts, noting that colours may be varied as required and should be twisted at back of work when changing colours.
1st motif
Using A, make 16[16:18:18] ch.
1st row Into 4th ch from hook work 1tr, 1tr into each ch to end. Turn. 14[14:16:16] tr.
2nd row 3ch to count as first tr, miss 1tr, 1tr into each tr to end. Turn.
Rep 2nd row 5[5:6:6] times more.
Fasten off and darn in ends. Work 1 more motif in same way using A, then 2 motifs each in B, C, D and E. 10 motifs, 5 for each front.
2nd motif
Using A, work first 2 rows as given for 1st motif. Break off A. Join in E. Complete as given for 1st motif. Work 1 more motif in same way, then 2 more using D and C and 2 more using E and B. 6 motifs, 3 for each front.
3rd motif
Using B, make 7[7:8:8] ch, join in D and make 9[9:10:10] ch.
1st row Using D, into 4th ch from hook work 1tr, 1tr into each of next 5[5:6:6] ch working last 2 loops of last tr with B – called 1trNc –, using B, work 1tr into each ch to end. Turn. 7[7:8:8] tr each in D and B.
2nd row Using B, 3ch to count as first tr, 1tr into each of next 6[6:7:7] tr, putting B to front of work and D to back under hook to work 1trNc with D on last tr, using D, work 1tr into each tr to end. Turn.
3rd row Using D, 3ch, work 1tr into each of next 6[6:7:7] tr, keeping yarn at back of work and working 1trNc with B on last

tr, using B, work 1tr into each tr to end. Turn.

Rep 2nd and 3rd rows twice more, then 2nd row 0[0:1:1] times more. Fasten off and darn in ends. Work 1 more motif in same way, then 2 motifs using A and D and 2 using C and E. 6 motifs, 3 for each front.

4th motif

Using B and C, work first 3 rows as given for 3rd motif.

4th row Using B, 3ch, 1tr into each tr to end. Turn.

5th row Using B, 3ch, 1tr into each of next 6[6:7:7] tr, keeping yarn at back of work join in C and work 1trNc on last tr, using C, 1tr into each tr to end. Turn.

6th row Using C, 3ch, 1tr into each of next 6[6:7:7] tr, putting C to front of work and B back under hook to work 1trNc with B on last tr, using B, 1tr into each tr to end. Turn.

7th row As 5th.

Rep 6th row 0[0:1:1] times more. Fasten off and darn in ends. Work 1 more motif.

5th motif

Using B, work first 3 rows as given for 1st motif, joining in E and working 1trNc on last tr. Break off B.

4th row Using E, 3ch, work 1tr into each of next 6[6:7:7] tr, join in C and work 1trNc on last tr, using C, 1tr into each tr to end. Turn.

5th row Using C, 3ch, work 1tr into each of next 6[6:7:7] tr, 1trNc with C on last tr using E, 1tr into each tr to end. Turn.

Rep 4th and 5th rows once more, then 4th row 0[0:1:1] times more. Fasten off and darn in ends. Work 1 more motif in same way, then 2 more using C, E and D and 2 more using A, B and E. 6 motifs, 3 for each front.

6th motif

Using E, make 7[7:8:8] ch, join in D and make 9[9:10:10] ch.

1st row Using D, into 4th ch from hook work 1tr, 1tr into each of next 4[4:5:5] ch, keeping yarn at back of work join in C and work 1trNc on last tr, using C, 1tr into each of next 2ch, keeping yarn at back of work join in E and work 1trNc on last tr, using E, 1tr into each of next 6[6:7:7] ch. Turn.

2nd row Using E, 3ch, 1tr into each of next 4[4:5:5] tr, putting E to front of work and C to back under hook and working 1trNc with C on last tr, using C, 1tr into each of next 4tr, putting C to front of work and D to back under hook and working 1trNc with D on last tr, using D, 1tr into each tr to end. Turn.

3rd row Changing colours as for 1st row, using D, 3ch, 1tr into each of next 3[3:4:4] tr, using C, 1tr into each of next 6tr, using E, 1tr into each tr to end. Turn.

4th row Changing colours as for 2nd row, using E, 3ch, 1tr into each of next 2[2:3:3] tr, using C, 1tr into each of next 8tr, using D, 1tr into each tr to end. Turn.

5th row Changing colours as for 1st row, using D, 3ch, 1tr into next tr, using C, 1tr into each of next 10tr, using E, 1tr into each tr to end. Turn.

6th row Changing colours as for 2nd row, using E, 3ch, 1tr into each of next 0[0:1:1] tr, using C, 1tr into each of next 12tr, using D, 1tr into each tr to end. Turn.

7th row Using C, 3ch, 1tr into each tr to end. Turn.

Rep 7th row 0[0:1:1] times more. Fasten off and darn in ends. Work 1 more motif in same way, then 2 using B, A and C, 2 using E, C and B, 2 using A, D and B, 2 using B, C and E and 2 using D, A and E. 12 motifs making 6 diamond shapes, 3 for each front.

Quarter raglan motif

Using D, make 10[10:12:12] ch. Work 1st row as given for 1st motif. 8[8:9:9] tr.

2nd row 3ch, dec 1, 1tr into each tr to end. Turn.

3rd row 3ch, 1tr into each tr to last 3tr, dec 1, 1tr into last tr. Turn.

Rep 2nd and 3rd rows twice more, then 2nd row 0[0:1:1] times more. Fasten off. Make another quarter motif in same way.

Three-quarter raglan motif

Using C, make 16[16:18:18] ch. Work 1st row as given for 1st motif. 14[14:16:16] tr.

2nd row 3ch, 1tr into next tr, dec 1, 1tr into each tr to end. Turn.

3rd row 3ch, 1tr into each tr to last 4tr, dec 1, 1tr into each of last 2 tr. Turn.

Rep 2nd and 3rd rows twice more, then 2nd row 0[0:1:1] times more. 8[8:9:9] tr. Fasten off.

Neck motif

Using E, make 16[16:18:18] ch.

1st row Into 4th ch from hook work 1tr, 1tr into each ch to last 4ch, dec 2 working over next 3ch as given for dec 1, 1tr into last ch. Turn.

2nd row 3ch, dec 2, 1tr into each tr to end. Turn.

3rd row 3ch, 1tr into each tr to last 4tr, dec 2, 1tr into last tr. Turn.

Rep 2nd and 3rd rows once more, then 2nd row once more. Fasten off.

To make up

Press each piece under a damp cloth with a warm iron. Sew motifs tog with cast off edge to cast on edge, with exception of 6th motif which must be sewn cast on edges tog to form diamond shape. Join 3 motifs, arranging as required or as shown in diagram, to form one row. Join 5 more rows in same way, then join these 6 rows tog to form one front to underarm. Join 2 motifs working from front edge for 7th row then join quarter raglan motif for armhole edge. Join one motif for front edge with three-quarter raglan motif for armhole edge for 8th row, then join neck motif to raglan edge of armhole, leaving 9tr at neck edge free for 9th row. Join other front in same way, reversing motifs.

Collar Using No.3.50 (ISR) hook, A and with RS of work facing, work 86[86:90:90] dc round neck edge. Work 1 row tr, dec one st at each side of sleeve, (4 dec). Cont dec in same way, work 1 row dc and 1 row tr. Work 2[2:3:3] rows dc without shaping. Fasten off.

Lower edge Using No.3.50 (ISR) hook, A and with RS of front facing, work 2[2:3:3] rows tr along lower edge for hem. Fasten off. Work other front in same way.

Front edges Using No.3.50 (ISR) hook, A and with RS of work facing, work 3 rows dc along each front edge. Fasten off. Join raglan, side and sleeve seams. Turn up hem at lower edge and sl st down. Turn up 2[2:3:3] rows tr at cuffs and sl st down. Sew in zip. Press seams.

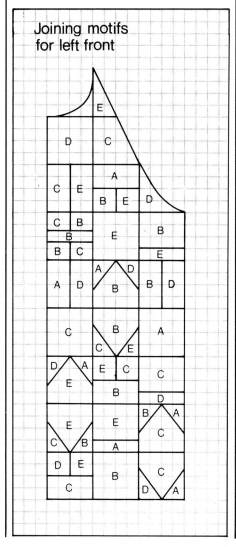

Joining motifs for left front

FREE SHAPING

This chapter illustrates a creative and individual application for crochet, the main feature of which is a breakaway from the accepted traditional methods of working in straight lines to and fro.

Here the method of making free and unusual lines and shapes, which are then worked around to form a flat fabric, is exploited. To achieve this type of work, increased and decreased stitches must be introduced at certain points on the work, so our samples are explained in detail to help you understand the technique and encourage you to try out your own ideas.

You will see that colour is very important here as the fabric is formed by using different colours of yarn for each new row, or section of a design so creating a patchwork effect.

Begin by making a square or rectangular shape which could be used as a cushion cover, or enlarged to make a rug. Later on fashion garments can be attempted or, more simply, a border design on a plain skirt.

Sample 1

The basic shapes here are two circles. By using the same method of work and varying the number of stitches between increases and decreases, you could use several circles in a row, three to form a triangle or four to form a square. The sample has been worked in five colours of double knitting yarn, A, B, C, D and E.

To work the basic circles (make 2) Using No.3.50 (ISR) hook and A, make 3ch. Join with a ss into first ch to form a circle.

1st round 1ch to count as first dc, 7dc into circle. Join with a ss into first ch.

2nd round 1ch, 1dc into st at base of ch, *2dc into next dc, rep from * to end. Join with a ss into first ch. 16dc.

3rd round 1ch, 1dc into st at base of ch, 1dc into next dc, *2dc into next dc, 1dc into next dc, rep from * to end. Join with a ss into first ch. 24dc.

4th round 1ch, 1dc into st at base of ch, 1dc into each of next 2dc, *2dc into next dc, 1dc into each of next 2dc, rep from * to end. Join with a ss into first ch. 32dc.

5th round 1ch, 1dc into st at base of ch, 1dc into each of next 3dc, *2dc into next dc, 1dc into each of next 3dc, rep from * to end. Join with a ss into first ch. 40dc. Break off A, but leave working st on a safety pin.

Join in B to either circle. **Replace working st on to hook, 1ch, 1dc into st at base of ch, 1dc into each of next 4dc, *2dc into next dc, 1dc into each of next 4dc, rep from * to end of round. Join with a ss into first ch.** Turn work.

1st row 1ch to count as first dc, miss first dc, 1dc into each of next 5dc. Turn work.

2nd–6th rows As 1st.

Join in 2nd circle Place circle to be joined behind the present work with RS tog and rep from ** to ** as given for 1st circle, working through double fabric for first 7 sts. Break off yarn, thread cut end through working st and pull up tightly.

Join in C With RS of work facing, join C to first increased dc of left hand circle (as shown in diagram) and work in an anti-clockwise direction around the circle, 1ch, 1dc into st at base of ch, 1dc into each of next 5 sts, (2dc into next dc, 1dc into each of next 5 sts) 5 times, cont along row ends of straight strip in B by working 2dc tog, 1dc into each of next 4 sts, work 2dc tog, then cont round right hand circle by working (1dc into each of next 5dc, 2dc into next dc) 6 times, 1dc into each of next 5dc and finally cont along 2nd side of straight strip in B by working 2dc tog, 1dc into each of next 4 sts, work 2dc tog, 1dc into each of next 5 sts. Join with a ss into first ch. Break off yarn, thread

cut end through working st and pull up tightly.

Join in D With RS of work facing, join in D by inserting hook into first ch of last round and cont in an anti-clockwise direction around entire shape by working 1ch, 1dc into st at base of ch, (1dc into each of next 6 sts, 2dc into next st) 5 times, 1dc into each of next 5 sts, work 2dc tog, 1dc into each of next 3 sts, work 2dc tog, 1dc into each of next 5 sts, (2dc into next st, 1dc into each of next 6 sts) 5 times, 2dc into next st, 1dc into each of next 5 sts, work 2dc tog, 1dc into each of next 3 sts, work 2dc tog, 1dc into each of next 5 sts. Join with a ss into first ch. Break off yarn, thread cut end through working st and pull up tightly.

Join in E With RS of work facing, join in E by inserting hook into first ch of last round and cont round shape by working 1ch, 1dc into st at base of ch, (1dc into each of next 7 sts, 2dc into next st) 5 times, 1dc into each of next 4 sts, work 3 sts tog using tr instead of dc, 1tr into each of next 2 sts, work 3tr tog, 1dc into each of next 4 sts, (2dc into next st, 1dc into each of next 7 sts) 5 times, 2dc into next st, 1dc into each of next 4 sts, work 3tr tog, 1tr into each of next 2 sts, work 3tr tog, 1dc into each of next 4 sts. Join with a ss into first ch. Break off yarn, thread through working st and pull up tightly.

Join in B With RS of work facing, join in B by inserting hook into first ch of last round and cont round shape by working 1ch, 1dc into st at base of ch, (1dc into each of next 8 sts, 2dc into next st) 5 times, 1dc into each of next 2 sts, work 3tr tog, 1tr into each of next 3 sts, work 3tr tog, 1dc into each of next 2 sts, (2dc into next st, 1dc into each of next 8 sts) 5 times, 2dc into next st, 1dc into each of next 2 sts, work 3tr tog, 1 tr into each of next 3 sts, work 3tr tog, 1dc into each of next 2 sts. Join with a ss into first ch. Break off yarn, thread through working st and pull up tightly.

Join in A Cont as before by working 1ch, 1dc into st at base of ch, (1dc into each of next 9 sts, 2dc into next st) 5 times, work 3tr tog, 1tr into each of next 4 sts, work 3tr tog, 2dc into next st, (1dc into each of next 9 sts, 2dc into next st) 5 times, work 3tr tog, 1tr into each of next 4 sts, work 3tr tog. Join with a ss into first ch.

Final round Using A, 1ch, 1dc into st at base of ch, (1dc into each of next 10 sts, 2dc into next st) 4 times, 1dc into each of next 29 sts, (2dc into next st, 1dc into each of next 10 sts) 4 times, 1dc into each of next 8 sts. Join with a ss into first ch. Fasten off.

Sample 2

Five colours of double knitting yarn, A, B, C, D and E have been used for this sample. Using No.3.50 (ISR) hook and A, make a chain with multiples of 6 + 1 stitches.

1st row Into 3rd ch from hook work 1dc, 1dc into each ch to end. Turn.

2nd row 1ch to count as first dc, miss first st, 1dc into each of next 5ch, *10ch, into 3rd ch from hook work 1dc, 1dc into each of next 7ch, 1dc into each of next 6dc, rep from * to end. Turn.

3rd row Join in B, 1ch, miss first st, 1dc into each of next 4dc, *work 2dc tog, 1dc into each of next 7dc, 3dc into tip of chain length, 1dc into each of next 7 sts, work 2dc tog, 1dc into each of next 4 sts, rep from * ending with 1dc into turning ch. Turn.

4th row Join in C, 1ch, miss first st, 1dc into each of next 3 sts, *work 2dc tog, 1dc into each of next 7 sts, (2dc into next st) twice, 1dc into each of next 7 sts, work 2dc tog, 1dc into each of next 3 sts, rep from * ending with 1dc into turning ch. Turn.

5th row Join in D, 1ch, miss first st, 1dc into each of next 2dc, *work 2dc tog, 1dc into each of next 7 sts, (2dc into next st) 3 times, 1dc into each of next 7 sts, work 2dc tog, 1dc into each of next 2 sts, rep from * ending with 1dc into turning ch. Turn.

6th row Join in E, 1ch, miss first st, 1dc into next dc, work 2dc tog, 1dc into each of next 7 sts, *(2dc into next st, 1dc into next st) twice, 2dc into next st, 1dc into each of next 7 sts, work 2dc tog, miss next st, work 2dc tog, insert hook into last dc but one just worked, yrh and draw up a loop through st on hook, (insert hook into next dc on right, yrh and draw through a loop, insert hook into next dc on left, yrh and draw through a loop, yrh and draw through all loops on hook) 7 times to join shapes tog, rep from * omitting joining on last rep and working in dc to end. Fasten off.

Counterpane in colour

Size

To fit average single bed, 91.5cm (*36in*) wide

Tension

Motifs 1, 2 and 3 measure 21.5cm (*8½in*) square

Materials

Wendy Double Knitting Nylonised
8 × 1oz balls Aquamarine, A
5 balls Turquoise, B
6 balls Clematis, C
8 balls Lincoln Green, D
9 balls Emerald, E
9 balls Black, F
6 balls Blue Velvet, G
5 balls Lichen Random, H
5 balls Purple Zodiac Random, I
One No. 5.50 (ISR) crochet hook

Counterpane

The counterpane is made of 8 square motifs using variations of 9 colours which are sewn tog and then borders and more motifs are worked on to the basic shape.

Square motif (1)

Using No. 5.00 (ISR) hook and A, work 4ch. Join with a ss into first ch to form a circle.
1st round 3ch, 11tr into circle. Join with a ss into 3rd of the 3ch.
2nd round Ss into first sp between tr, 3ch, 1tr into same sp, *2tr into next sp between tr, rep from * all round. Join with a ss into 3rd of the 3ch. Break off A and join in B.
3rd round Ss into first sp between tr, 3ch, 2tr into same sp, miss next sp, * 3tr into next sp, miss next sp, rep from * all round. Join with a ss into 3rd of the 3ch. Break off B and join in G.
4th round Ss into first sp between grs of 3tr, (3ch, 2tr, 1ch – to form corner sp, 3tr) into same sp, miss next 2 sp between tr, 1tr into each of next 4 sp, miss next 2 sp, *(3tr, 1ch, 3tr) into next sp, miss next 2 sp, 1tr into each of next 4 sp, miss next 2 sp, rep from * all round. Join with a ss into 3rd of the 3ch. Break off G and join in E.
5th round Ss into corner sp, (3ch, 2tr, 1ch, 3tr) into same sp, *miss next 2 sp between tr, 1tr into each of next 5 sp, miss next 2 sp, (3tr, 1ch, 3tr) into corner sp, rep from * all round. Join with a ss into 3rd of the 3ch. Break off E and join in A.
6th round Ss into corner sp, (3ch, 2tr, 1ch, 3tr) into same sp, *miss next 2 sp between tr, 1tr into each of next 6 sp, miss next 2 sp, (3tr, 1ch, 3tr) into corner sp, rep from * all round. Join with a ss

into 3rd of the 3ch.
Break off A and join in G.
7th round Ss into corner sp, (3ch, 2tr, 1ch, 3tr) into same sp, *(miss next 2 sp between tr, 3tr into next sp – thus forming 1sh) 3 times, (3tr, 1ch, 3tr) into corner sp, rep from * all round. Join with a ss into 3rd of the 3ch. Fasten off G and join in C.
8th round Ss into corner sp, (3ch, 2tr, 1ch, 3tr) into same sp, *(miss next sh, 3tr into sp between next 2 shs) 4 times, miss next sh, (3tr, 1ch, 3tr) into corner sp, rep from * all round. Join with a ss into 3rd of the 3ch. Break off C. Make another motif in the same way.

Square motif (2)

Make 3 motifs in the same way as above, but work in colour sequence as foll:
1st and 2nd rounds Work with H.
3rd round Work with A.
4th round Work with D.
5th round Work with E.
6th round Work with B.
7th round Work with H.
8th round Work with C.

Square motif (3)

Make 3 motifs using colour sequence as foll:
1st and 2nd rounds Work with B.
3rd round Work with I.
4th round Work with B.
5th round Work with F.
6th round Work with G.
7th round Work with D.
8th round Work with C.
Using C, join these 8 motifs tog as shown in diagram.
Next round Join E to corner sp marked (a) on diagram, (3ch, 2tr, 1ch, 3tr) into corner, *work a 4tr sh into each sp between shs to (b) on diagram, 2tr into (b), (4tr sh into each sp to next corner, (3tr, 1ch, 3tr) into corner) twice, rep from *all round motifs. Join with a ss into 3rd of the 3ch. Break off E and join in D.
Next round Ss into corner sp, (3ch, 2tr, 1ch, 3tr) into same sp, *4tr sh into each sp between shs to within one sp of point (b), 1tr into next sp, miss 2tr at (b), 1tr into next sp, (4tr sh into each sp to corner, (3tr, 1ch, 3tr) into corner) twice, rep from * all round. Join with a ss into 3rd of the 3ch. Break off D.

Semi-circular motif (4)

Using No. 5.50 (ISR) hook and A, work 4ch. Join with a ss into first ch to form a circle.
1st row 3ch, 6tr into circle. Turn.
2nd row Ss into first sp, 3ch, 1tr into same sp, 2tr into each sp to end. Turn. Break off A and join in B.

3rd row As 2nd row.
Break off B and join in E.
4th row Ss into first sp, 3ch, 1tr into same sp, miss next sp, *3tr sh into next sp, miss next sp, rep from * to last sp, 2tr into last sp. Turn. Break off E and join in H.
5th row 3ch, 3tr sh into each sp between shs, 1tr into 3rd of the 3ch. Turn.
6th row Ss into first sp, 3ch, 1tr into same sp, *4tr sh into next sp between shs, rep from * to last sp, 2tr into last sp. Turn. Break off H and join in E.
7th row 3ch, 4tr sh into first sp between shs, *5tr sh into next sp, rep from * to last sp, 4tr into last sp, 1tr into 3rd of the 3ch. Turn. Break off E.
Make 3 more motifs in the same way and join to the main section as shown in the diagram. Cont working a border round the main shape as foll:
1st round With RS of work facing join A to point (*) on diagram and work 4tr shs into each sp between shs to point (b), dec at (b) by working 1tr into sp at either side of previous dec, cont in shs to next corner, 4tr into corner, *3tr sh into 3rd tr of previous 5tr sh, 3tr sh into next sp between shs, rep from * all round semi-circular motif and cont round shape dec at each point (b), working (3tr, 1ch, 3tr) into each corner and working round motifs as shown above. Break off A and join in G.
2nd round As 1st round, but work 3tr shs into each sp between shs round motif 4. Break off G and join in F.
3rd round As 2nd round. Break off F and join in G.
4th round Work all round 1tr into each tr and 1tr into each sp, 1tr into each of 3 sp at point (b), (3tr, 1ch, 3tr) into each corner, missing 3tr between and after each corner sp. Break off G and join in F.
5th round Work all round 1tr into each tr, (3tr, 1ch, 3tr) into each corner, and at point (b) dec over 3tr by working 1tr into each of the 3tr and leaving the last 1p of each on hook, yrh and draw through all 4 lps on hook. Break off F and join in D.
6th round As 4th round, but dec over 5tr at each point (b). Break off D and join in F.
7th round As 5th round, but dec over 5tr at each point (b). Break off F and join in C.
8th round As 7th round, but work 2tr into every 10th tr round motif 4. Break off C and join in D.
9th round As 7th round. Break off D and join in F.
10th round As 7th round, but at each point (b) dec over 2tr, 1dtr into next tr, dec over next 2tr. Break off F and join in G.
11th round As 7th round, but dec over

210

2tr only at each point (b).
Break off G and join in H.

12th round As 7th round, but do not dec at point (b) and work 5tr shs into each corner sp. Break off H and join in B.

13th round As 12th round, but work 5tr into 3rd tr of previous 5tr sh at corners. Break off B and join in E.

14th round As 12th round.

Motif (5)

Work as given for semi-circular motif (4) until 2nd row has been completed. Break off A and join in B.

3rd row 3ch, miss first sp, 1tr into next sp, 2tr into each sp to last 2sp, 1tr into each of last 2sp. Turn. Break off B and join in E.

4th row 3ch, 1tr into first sp, *miss next sp, 3tr into next sp, miss next sp, 2tr into next sp, rep from * to end. Turn.

Break off E and join in H.

5th row 3ch, *2tr into next sp, 3tr into next sp, rep from * to end, 1tr into 3rd of the 3ch. Turn.

6th row 3ch, 1tr into first sp, *3tr into next sp, 2tr into next sp, rep from * to end. Turn. Break off H and join in E.

7th row 3ch, 3tr into each sp to end, 1tr into 3rd of the 3ch. Turn. Break off E and join in H.

8th row 3ch, 2tr into first sp, *3tr into next sp, rep from * to last sp, 2tr into last sp, 1tr into 3rd of the 3ch. Turn. Break off H and join in E.

9th row 4ch, 1dtr between 1st and 2nd tr (4dtr into next sp) twice, *4tr into next sp, rep from * to last 2 sp, 4dtr into each of next 2 sp, 1dtr between last 2tr, 1dtr into 4th of the 4ch. Turn.

10th row 4ch, 2dtr into first sp, 5dtr into

next sp, *5tr into next sp, rep from * to last 2 sp, 5dtr into next sp, 2dtr into last sp, 1dtr into 4th of the 4ch. Turn. Break off E and join in H.

11th row 4ch, 5dtr into first sp, *5tr into next sp, rep from * to last sp, 5dtr into last sp, 1dtr into 4th of the 4ch. Break off H.

Make one more motif in the same way and join to the main section as shown in the diagram. Cont with the border as foll:

15th round Join in A and work 1tr into each tr all round and (3tr, 1ch, 3tr) into 3rd tr of every 5tr sh. Break off A and join in D.

16th round *3tr sh into next sp, miss next 2 sp, rep from * all round, but work (3tr, 1ch, 3tr) into each corner. Break off D and join in A.

17th round Work 3tr shs into each sp and over motif (5), 4tr shs over the curves and (3tr, 1ch, 3tr) into each corner. Break off A and join in F.

18th round As 17th round. Break off F and join in C.

19th round As 17th round. Break off C and join in I.

20th round As 17th round. Break off I. Complete the counterpane by working the foll extensions:

1st row Join I to point marked (c) on diagram, 3ch and 3tr into same sp, 4tr sh into each sp between shs to point marked (d) on diagram. Turn. Break off I and join in B.

2nd row Ss into first sp between shs, 3ch and 3tr into same sp, 4tr sh into each sp to end. Turn. Break off B and join in E.

3rd row As 2nd row. Break off E and join in H.

4th row As 2nd row. Break off H and join in D.

5th row As 2nd row. Break off D and join in A.

6th row As 2nd row. Break off A. Work a similar extension at the opposite end of the cover, then work around the cover as foll:

Join E to any sp between shs, 3ch and 3tr into same sp, 4tr sh into each sp between shs all round, ss into 3rd of the 3ch. Break off E. Finish off all ends.

To make up

Tassels (make 6)

Cut 51cm (20in) lengths of every colour. Using 40 strands tog, tie them in the middle, fold in half and tie again 5cm (2in) from the top. Attach the tassels as shown in the diagram.

Fringe

Cut lengths of every colour as given for tassels. Using 8 strands draw centre of threads through each sp between shs round edge and knot.

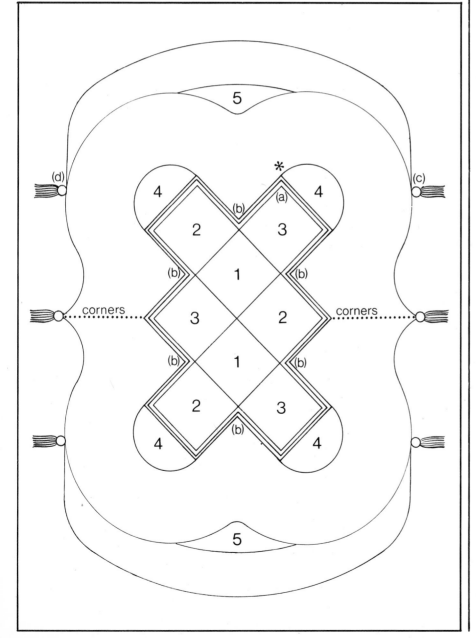

LACE CROCHET
FILET CROCHET

Filet crochet

Filet is the French name for 'net' and you will recognise this type of crochet by its simple lacy qualities. It is made up of two simple stitches, already learnt, the chain and treble. The trebles are worked in groups so forming a solid block and the space between each block is enclosed by a length of chain which corresponds in number to the group of trebles over which it is worked.

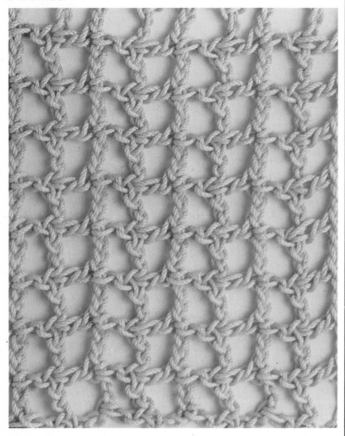

Filet net forms the basis of the work and this is composed very simply with single trebles and usually two chain separating them. However, when random spaces are filled in with trebles, a block is formed and from the basic net many different designs can be made.

An easy way of designing your own pattern is to use squared paper. Presume that each square across represents a stitch and each square up equals a row, then block in squares accordingly to create your own individual design.

Instructions are given for working the basic net and one of the many variations on this theme. Most yarns are suitable for filet crochet, although cotton or finer yarns are more popular as they add to the lightness and airiness of the work.

Basic filet crochet

Using No. 2.50 (ISR) hook and a cotton yarn, make 32ch.
1st row Into 8th ch from hook work ltr, *2ch, miss next 2ch, ltr into next ch, rep from * to end. Turn.
2nd row 5ch to count as first tr plus linking ch, miss first 2ch space, ltr into next tr, *2ch, miss next 2ch space, ltr into next tr, finishing with 1 tr into 3rd of the turning chain. Turn.
The last row is repeated throughout.

Filet crochet using blocks and spaces

Using No. 2.50 (ISR) hook and a cotton yarn, make 32ch.
1st row Work as given for 1st row of basic filet crochet.
2nd row 5ch to count as first tr plus linking ch, miss first 2ch space, ltr into next tr, *2ch, miss next 2ch space, (ltr into next tr, 2tr into next 2ch space) twice, ltr into next tr, rep from * once more, 2ch, miss next 2ch space, ltr into next tr, 2ch, ltr into 3rd of the turning chain. Turn.
3rd row 5ch, miss first 2ch space, ltr into next tr, *2ch, miss next 2ch space, ltr into each of next 7tr, rep from * once more, 2ch, miss next 2ch space, ltr into next tr, 2ch, 1tr into 3rd of the turning chain. Turn.

4th row 5ch, miss first space, ltr into next tr, 2ch, miss next space, ltr into next tr, (2ch, miss next 2tr, ltr into next tr) twice, 2tr into next space, (ltr into next tr, 2ch, miss next 2tr) twice, ltr into next tr, 2ch, miss next space, ltr into next tr, 2ch, ltr into 3rd of the turning chain. Turn.

5th row 5ch, miss first space, ltr into next tr, (2ch, miss next space, ltr into next tr) twice, 2ch, miss next space, ltr into each of next 4tr, (2ch, miss next space, ltr into next tr) 3 times, 2ch, 1tr into 3rd of the turning chain. Turn.

6th row 3ch, (2tr into next space, ltr into next tr) twice, (2ch, miss next space, ltr into next tr) 5 times, 2tr into next space, ltr into next tr, 2tr into last space, ltr into 3rd of the turning chain. Turn.

7th row 3ch, miss first tr, ltr into each of next 6tr, (2ch, miss next space, ltr into next tr) 5 times, ltr into each of next 5tr, ltr into 3rd of the turning chain. Fasten off.

If you have managed to work this sample successfully, then it's time to make up your own design using the method described above.

Very fine cotton used for this work produces a beautiful filet crochet lace. Worked into strips this can be used for a lace insertion or edging or make the strips a bit deeper and cover the cuffs of your favourite blouse. Follow the instructions below to make two simple lace edgings.

Lace edging 1

Make a chain the length that you require, making sure that you have a repeat of 3 stitches plus 2 extra.

1st row Into 4th ch from hook work ltr, ltr into every ch to end. Turn.

2nd row 5ch to count as first tr plus 2 linking ch, miss first 3tr, ltr into next tr, *2ch, miss 2 tr, ltr into next tr, rep from * finishing with 1 tr into 3rd of the turning chain. Turn.

3rd row 3ch, *2tr into next space, ltr into next tr, rep from * to end. Fasten off.

Lace edging 2

Make a chain the length that you require, making sure that you have a repeat of 6 stitches plus 5 extra.

1st row Into 8th ch from hook work ltr, ltr into each of next 3ch, * 2ch, miss next 2ch, 1tr into each of next 4ch, rep from * to end. Turn.

2nd row 5ch, miss first 3tr, *ltr into next tr, 2tr into next space, ltr into next tr, 2ch, miss 2tr, rep from * finishing with 1tr into next tr, 2tr into last sp and last tr into 3rd of the turning chain. Turn.

3rd row As 2nd. Fasten off.

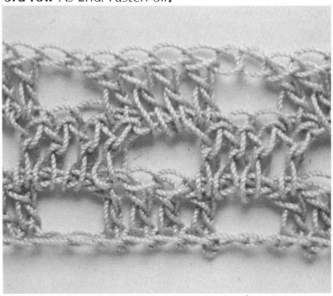

Using the same technique, and still working in very fine yarns, other items made this way are cushion covers, table cloths and other fine household items. Similar strips to those described above, if they are worked in thicker yarns make attractive braids and belts.

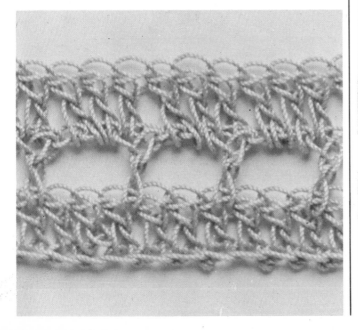

Belt with plastic strip threaded between trebles.

213

FILET LACE TRIMMINGS

This chapter continues our previous work on filet lace crochet which is comprised of blocks and spaces, with different and more advanced techniques. We shall particularly deal with the use of finer yarns for the more traditional types of work done in this form. A filet lace, or crochet lace as it is sometimes called, in its finest form is a popular trimming for underclothes, nightdresses and household linens. Today it is also fashionable for decorating roller blinds, Tiffany lamp shades and tablecloths – although probably for all of these you will need to use a slightly thicker yarn.

There is a fine cotton yarn available in a wide range of colours and thicknesses, varying from No.3 which is the thickest to No.100, the finest. The normal range of crochet hooks to use with fine cotton would vary in size from No.0.60 (ISR) hook to No.2.00 (ISR) hook.

Traditionally filet lace crochet is produced in white or ecru, but modern designs sometimes demand coloured yarns. It is particularly important if you are making underclothes or a nightdress to have the correct shade of lace. If this is unobtainable, dye your yarn with a water dye. The ball of cotton should first be rewound into a skein and then, for dyeing, follow the manufacturer's instructions.

When the lace trimming has been completed, it should be washed and pressed before it is applied to a garment. This will avoid any shrinkage at a later stage. Use neat hemming or chosen embroidery stitches to sew the lace on to the garment.

There are two methods of working the lace trimming – in narrow strips, beginning with the number of stitches required for the depth of the lace and working until the required length has been completed or working the number of stitches to give the required length of work and then working in rows to give the correct depth.

Our photograph shows a sample of filet lace crochet where blocks and spaces have been increased and decreased. You will also see a chart of this design. Earlier, we gave a simple way of charting a design, but now we shall teach you the professional way of charting.

In our chart here one space across represents either a block of trebles or a space and one space up represents a row. To help you follow the chart, the techniques of increasing and decreasing are explained in detail below and then there are instructions of how to work our sample.

To increase a block at the beginning of a row. Work 5ch. Into 4th ch from hook work 1tr, 1tr into next ch,

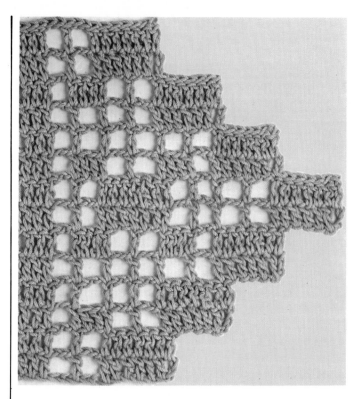

Use this chart to work the sample

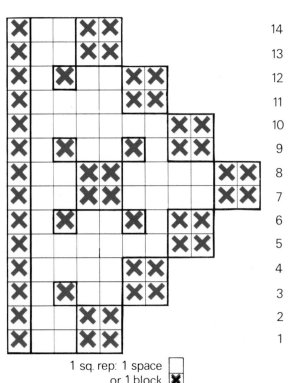

1 sq. rep: 1 space
or 1 block
& 1 row

1tr into next st (i.e. the last st of the previous row), continue across the row in pattern. To increase two blocks as in our chart, work 8ch. Into 4th ch from hook work 1tr, 1tr into each of next 4ch, 1tr into next st.

To increase a space at the beginning of a row Work 7ch which will represent a 2ch space at the end of the last row, 3ch to count as the first tr of the new row and another 2ch between the first tr and the next st, then work 1tr into last st of the previous row.

To decrease a block or space at the beginning of a row Miss the first st, ss loosely into each of the next 3 sts, then work 3ch to count as the first tr and continue in pattern.

To increase a block at the end of a row Provision has to be made for this increase by working 7ch at the beginning of the previous row, miss the first ch, ss into each of next 3ch, there are 3ch remaining which count as the first tr of the new row, then complete the row in pattern. At the end of the following row work 1tr into each of the 3ss, thus increasing one block.

To increase a space at the end of a row Work as given for increasing a block at the end of a row, but when the increasing is reached work 2ch, miss next 2 sts, 1tr into the last st.

To decrease a block or space at the end of a row Work to within the last block or space, then turn the work and proceed in pattern.

To work the sample
Make 18ch.

1st row Into 4th ch from hook work 1tr, 1tr into each of next 5 sts, (2ch, miss next 2ch, 1tr into next ch) twice, 1tr into each of next 3ch. Turn.

2nd row 3ch to count as first tr, 1tr into each of next 3tr, (2ch, 1tr into next tr) twice, 1tr into each of next 5tr, 1tr into 3rd of the 3ch. Turn.

3rd row Increase 2 blocks by working 8ch, 1tr into 4th ch from hook, 1tr into each of next 5 sts, (2ch, miss next 2 sts, 1tr into next st) twice, 1tr into each of next 3 sts, 2ch, miss next 2 sts, 1tr into each of next 3 sts, 1tr into 3rd of the 3ch. Turn.

Continue by working in pattern from the chart, increasing 2 blocks at the beginning of the 5th and 7th rows and decreasing 2 blocks at the beginning of the 9th, 11th and 13th rows. The 13 rows may be repeated to whatever length you require.

Here are the instructions and chart for a simple edging which would make an ideal tasselled trimming for a roller blind. You will notice that this sample is worked by using the required number of stitches for the width and working until the lace is the required length.

Trimming with tassels
Make 17ch.

1st row Into 8th ch from hook work 1tr, 1tr into each of next 3ch, (2ch, miss 2ch, 1tr into next ch) twice. Turn.

2nd row 5ch, 1tr into 2nd tr, 1tr into each of next 3 sts, 2ch, miss next 2 sts, 1tr into next st. Turn, thus decreasing one space.

3rd row 7ch thus increasing one space, 1tr into first tr, 1tr into each of next 3 sts, 2ch, miss next 2 sts, 1tr into next tr, 2ch, 1tr into 3rd of the 5ch. Turn.

The 2nd and 3rd rows are repeated throughout. Thread two tassels through each increased space.

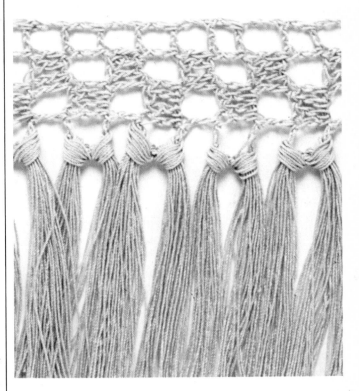

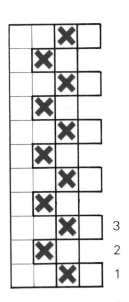

1 sq. rep: 1 space
or 1 block
& 1 row

DESIGNING AND WORKING CORNERS

The technique of designing and working corners in filet crochet may present problems, but here we shall explain these two processes in detail. If you follow our charts and instructions, you should no longer have any difficulty in producing a beautiful mitred corner suitable for use on a fitted divan cover or details on clothing such as square necklines.

In the last chapter we told you how to create your own designs in filet crochet by using squared paper, remembering that each square across represents either a block or a space and each square up represents a row. Our basic filet grid in the samples here is formed by working single trebles with two chain between each, but you can make the grid to your own design.

When designing a corner, first draw a diagram and then a line through the corner at an angle of 45 degrees from the outer edge of the design. On one side of the corner sketch in your pattern as you would like it to appear, stopping at the corner line, then mirror your design exactly over this line.

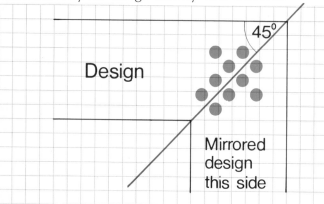

To work sample 1

In our photograph of a mitred corner two colours have been used to clarify the working process. You

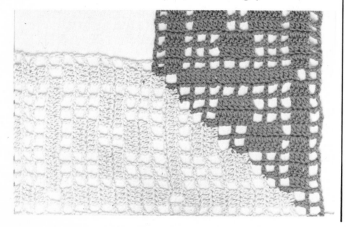

will also see a chart of the design which it will be necessary for you to follow in places. Make 41ch.

1st row Into 8th ch from hook work 1tr, 2ch, miss next 2ch, 1tr into each of next 25ch – thus forming 8 blocks –, (2ch, miss next 2ch, 1tr into next ch) twice. Turn.

2nd to 9th row Work in patt from the chart.

10th row Dec one square by missing first st, ss into each of next 3 sts, 5ch, miss 2tr, 1tr into each of next 25 sts, 2ch, miss 2tr, 1tr into next tr, 2ch, 1tr into 3rd of the 5ch. Turn.

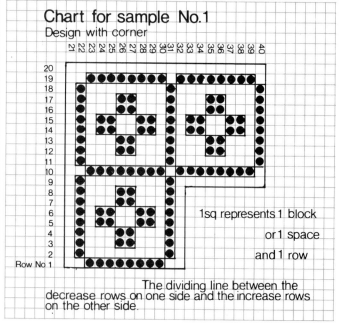

The dividing line between the decrease rows on one side and the increase rows on the other side.

11th row 5ch, miss 2ch, 1tr into each of next 4 sts, (2ch, miss 2tr, 1tr into next tr) 8 times, turn thus decreasing one square.

12th row Dec one square by missing first st, ss into each of next 3 sts, 5ch, miss 2ch, 1tr into next tr, 2ch, miss 2ch, 1tr into each of next 7 sts, (2ch, miss 2ch, 1tr into next tr) 3 times, 1tr into each of next 3tr, 2ch, 1tr into 3rd of the 5ch. Turn.

13th row 5ch, miss 2ch, 1tr into each of next 4tr, (2ch, miss 2ch, 1tr into next tr) 3 times, 1tr into each of next 6tr, 2ch, miss 2ch, 1tr into next tr, turn thus decreasing one square.

14th row Dec one square by missing first st, ss into each of next 3 sts, 5ch, miss 2tr, 1tr into next tr, 2ch, miss 2tr, 1tr into each of next 7sts, 2ch, miss 2ch, 1tr into each of next 4tr, 2ch, 1tr into 3rd of the 5ch. Turn.

15th row 5ch, miss 2ch, 1tr into each of next 4tr, 2ch, miss 2ch, 1tr into each of next 7tr, 2ch, miss 2ch, 1tr into next tr, turn thus decreasing one space.

16th row Dec one square by missing first st, ss into each of next 3 sts, 5ch, miss 2tr, 1tr into next tr, 2ch, miss 2tr, 1tr into next tr, 2ch, miss 2ch, 1tr into each of next 4tr, 2ch, 1tr into 3rd of the 5ch. Turn.

17th row 5ch, miss 2ch, 1tr into each of next 4tr, (2ch, miss 2ch, 1tr into next tr) twice, turn thus decreasing one space.

18th row Dec one square by missing first st, ss into each of next 3 sts, 5ch, miss 2ch, 1tr into each of next 4tr, 2ch, 1tr into 3rd of the 5ch. Turn.

19th row 5ch, miss 2ch, 1tr into next tr, 2ch, miss 2tr, 1tr into next tr, turn thus decreasing one space.

20th row Decrease one space by missing first st, ss into each of next 3 sts, 5ch, 1tr into 3rd of the 5ch of previous row. Turn the work and ss into each of the sts across the top of last space worked.

21st row 5ch, ss into corner of last space on left of the previous row. Do not turn.

22nd row 3ch, 1tr into each of next 2ch, (i.e. down side of space), ss into corner of last space on left of the previous row, turn, miss first st, ss into each of next 3 sts, 2ch, miss 2ch, 1tr into 3rd of the 5ch. Turn.

23rd row 5ch, miss 2ch, 1tr into each of next 4tr, 2ch, ss into corner of last space of the row on the left. Do not turn.

24th row 5ch, ss into corner of last space of the row on the left, turn, miss first st, ss into each of next 3 sts, 2ch, miss 2ch, 1tr into each of next 4tr, 2ch, 1tr into 3rd of the 5ch. Turn.

25th row 5ch, miss 2ch, 1tr into each of next 4tr, 2ch, miss 2ch, 1tr into each of next 6 sts, ss into corner of last space of the row on the left. Do not turn.

26th row 5ch, ss into corner of last space of the row on the left, turn, miss first st, ss into each of next 3 sts, 1tr into each of next 6tr, 2ch, miss 2ch, 1tr into each of next 4tr, 2ch, 1tr into 3rd of the 5ch. Turn.

27th row 5ch, miss 2ch, 1tr into each of next 4tr, 2ch, miss 2ch, 1tr into next tr, (2ch, miss 2tr, 1tr into next tr) twice, 1tr into each of next 5 sts, ss into corner of last space of the row on the left. Do not turn.

28th row 5ch, ss into corner of last space of the row on the left, turn, miss first st, ss into each of next 3 sts, 1tr into each of next 6tr, (2ch, miss 2ch, 1tr into next tr) 3 times, 1tr into each of next 3tr, 2ch, 1tr into 3rd of the 5ch. Turn.

29th row 5ch, miss 2ch, 1tr into each of next 4tr, (2ch, miss 2 sts, 1tr into next st) 6 times, 2ch, ss into corner of last space of the row on the left. Do not turn.

30th row 3ch, 1tr into each of next 2 sts, ss into corner of last space of the row on the left, turn, miss first st, ss into each of next 3 sts, 1tr into each of next 21 sts, 2ch, miss 2tr, 1tr into next tr, 2ch, 1tr into 3rd of the 5ch. Turn.

31st row 5ch, miss 2ch, 1tr into each of next 4 sts, (2ch, miss 2tr, 1tr into next tr) 8 times, 1tr into each of next 2 sts, ss into corner of last space of the row on the left. Do not turn.

32nd row 5ch, miss 2 sts (i.e. the side of last space in 10th row), 1tr into next st, turn, miss first st, ss into each of next 3 sts, 1tr into each of next 4tr, (2ch, miss 2ch, 1tr into next tr) 3 times, 1tr into each of next 6 sts, (2ch, miss 2ch, 1tr into next tr) 3 times, 1tr into each of next 3tr, 2ch, 1tr into 3rd of the 5ch. Turn.

33rd to 39th row Work in patt from the chart.

To work sample 2

Above we give details of how to work sample 1, but it is possible to work entirely from a chart. Practise working sample 2 from the chart. This illustrates the same technique, but it is worked in a very fine yarn and in one colour to give the true effect of the technique.

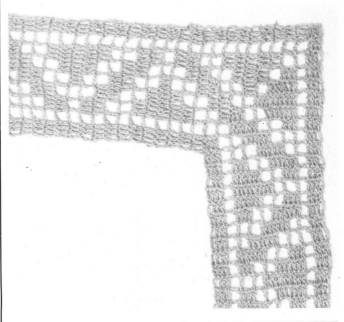

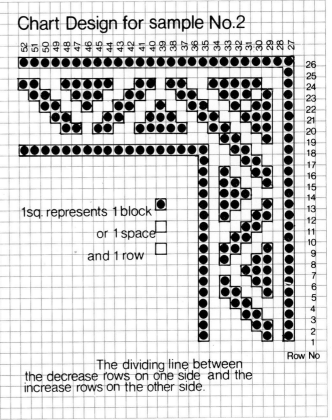

Chart Design for sample No.2

1sq. represents 1 block
or 1 space
and 1 row

The dividing line between the decrease rows on one side and the increase rows on the other side.

A butterfly top

Sizes
To fit 81.5[86.5:91.5]cm (32[34:36]in) bust
Side seam, 35.5[35.5:37]cm (14[14:14½]in)
The figures in brackets [] refer to the
86.5 (34) and 91.5cm (36in) sizes
respectively

Tension
8 sp and 12 rows to 10cm (3.9in) over
patt worked on No.3.00 (ISR) crochet
hook

Materials
3 × 20grm balls Wendy Minuit Lurex
One No.3.00 (ISR) crochet hook
3 press studs
2 glass beads for eyes

Back
Using No.3.00 (ISR) hook make 83[89:95]ch.
Base row Into 8th ch from hook work 1tr,
*2ch, miss 2ch, 1tr into next ch, rep from
* to end. Turn.
1st row 5tr to count as first tr and 2ch,
1tr into next tr, * 2ch, 1tr into next tr, rep
from * to end, working last tr into 3rd of
7ch. Turn. 26[28:30]sp. Rep last row
4[4:6] times more, noting that on
subsequent rows last tr will be worked
into 3rd of 5 turning ch.
Shape sides
1st row 3ch to count as first tr, 1tr into
first tr, patt to end, working 2tr into 3rd
of 5ch. Turn.
2nd row 3ch, 1tr into first tr, 1tr into
next tr, patt to end, working 2tr into
3rd of 3ch. Turn.
3rd row 3ch, 1tr into first tr, 1tr into each
of next 2tr, patt to last 2tr, 1tr into each
of next 2tr, 2tr into 3rd of 3ch. Turn.
4th row 5ch, miss 2tr, 1tr into next tr,
patt to last 3tr, 2ch, miss 2tr, 1tr into 3rd
of 3ch. Turn. 2 sp inc.
Rep last 4 rows twice more. 32[34:36] sp.
Cont without shaping until 31[31:33]
rows in all have been worked.
Next row 3ch, *2tr into next sp, 1tr into
next tr, rep from * to end. Fasten off.

Front
Work as given for back until 2[2:4] rows

have been completed. Commence
butterfly patt.
1st row Patt 7[8:9] sp, 1ch, 1tr into next
sp, 1tr into next tr, patt 10 sp, (1tr into
next sp, 1ch, 1tr into next tr, patt to end.
Turn.
2nd row Patt 7[8:9] sp, 1tr into next 1ch
sp, 1tr into each of next 2tr (1 block of
4tr has been worked), patt 4 sp, 1ch, 1tr
into next sp, 1tr into next tr, 1tr into next
sp, 1ch, 1tr into next tr, patt 4 sp, 1tr into
next tr, 1tr into next 1ch sp, 1tr into next
tr, patt to end. Turn.
3rd row Patt 6[7:8] sp, 2tr into next sp,
1tr into each of next 4tr, patt 4 sp, 1tr
into next 1ch sp, 1tr into each of next 3tr,
1tr into next 1ch sp, 1tr into next tr, patt
4sp, 1tr into each of next 3tr, 2tr into sp,
1tr into next tr, patt to end. Turn.
Cont working butterfly in this way from
chart, *at the same time* shaping sides as
given for back, until 28 rows of patt have
been completed.
Note The chart represents a filet crochet
grid of blocks, spaces, half blocks and
half spaces. Spaces are formed by
working single trebles with 2ch between
them and blocks are spaces which have
been filled in by working 2tr into the
appropriate 2ch sp. Here spaces have
been subdivided into half block/half
space by working 1tr and 1ch into a 2ch
sp.

Patt one more row in sp. Work last row
as given for back. Fasten off.

Straps (make 2).
Using No.3.00 (ISR) hook make 8ch.
1st row Into 4th ch from hook work 1tr,
1tr into each ch to end. Turn. 6tr.
2nd row 3ch to count as first tr, 1tr into
each tr to end. Turn.
Rep 2nd row until strap measures 35.5cm
(14in) from beg, or required length.
Fasten off.

To make up
Do not press. Join right side seam. Join
left side seam to within 7.5cm (3in) of
lower edge.
Edging Using No.3.00 (ISR) hook and
with WS of work facing, rejoin yarn to
first ch at lower edge, 3ch, *2tr into first
sp, 1tr into next tr, rep from * all round
lower edge. Turn.
Next row 3ch, *1tr into next tr, rep from
* to end.
Cont working in tr up side of opening
working 1tr into each tr and 2tr into each
sp, turn and work down other side in
same way. Fasten off.
Turn edging to WS on front edge of side
opening and sl st into position to form
overflap. Sew press studs along opening.
Sew straps in position. Sew on beads for
eyes.

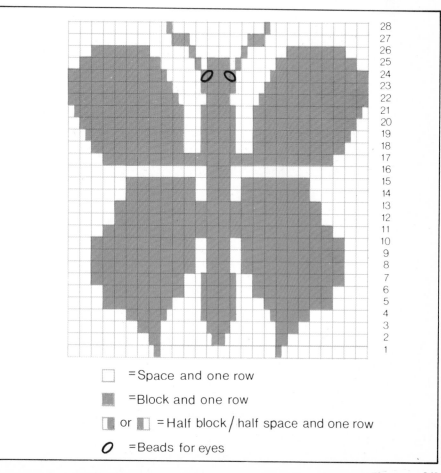

☐ =Space and one row

▦ =Block and one row

▨ or ▧ = Half block / half space and one row

O =Beads for eyes

Filet crochet smock

Sizes

To fit 81.5[86.5:91.5]cm (32[34:36]in) bust
Length to shoulder, 71[72.5:73.5]cm (28[28½:29]in)
Sleeve seam, 48.5cm (19in)
The figures in brackets [ ] refer to the 86.5 (34) and 91.5cm (36in) sizes respectively

Tension

24 sts and 12 rows to 10cm (3.9in) over tr worked on No.3.00 (ISR) crochet hook

Materials

11[12:12] × 50grm balls Patons Purple Heather 4 ply
One No.2.50 (ISR) crochet hook
One No.3.00 (ISR) crochet hook
11 small buttons

Back

Using No.2.50 (ISR) hook make 200[212:224]ch for lower edge.
1st row (WS) Into 3rd ch from hook work 1dc, 1dc into each ch to end. Turn. 199[211:223] sts.
Change to No.3.00 (ISR) hook. Commence patt.
2nd row 5ch to count as first tr and 2ch, miss first 3 sts, 1tr into next st, *2ch, miss 2 sts, 1tr into next st, rep from * to end. Turn.
3rd row 5ch, miss first tr, 1tr into next tr, *2ch, 1tr into next tr, rep from * ending with last tr into 3rd of 5ch. Turn.
The last row forms the main patt. Cont in patt until work measures 5cm (2in) from beg, ending with a WS row. Cont in patt, placing rose motifs as foll:
Next row 5ch, miss first tr, (1tr into next tr, 2ch) 1[2:3] times, work across next 85 sts as given for 1st row of rose motif from chart, (2ch, 1tr into next tr) 5[7:9] times, 2ch, work across next 85 sts as given for 1st row of rose motif from chart, (2ch, 1tr into next tr) 1[2:3] times, 2ch, 1tr into 3rd of 5ch. Turn.
Next row 5ch, miss first tr, (1tr into next tr, 2ch) 1[2:3] times, work across next 85 sts as given for 2nd row of rose motif from chart, (2ch, 1tr into next tr) 5[7:9] times, 2ch, work across next 85 sts as given for 2nd row of rose motif from chart, (2ch, 1tr into next tr) 1[2:3] times, 2ch, 1tr into 3rd of 5ch. Turn.
Cont working in this way until 30 rows of rose motif from chart have been completed. Cont in main patt as before until work measures 51cm (20in) from beg, ending with a RS row.

Shape yoke

Next row 3ch, (1tr into next 2ch sp, 1tr into each of next 2tr) 13[14:15] times, 1tr into next 2ch sp, 1tr into next tr, 1tr into next 2ch sp, 1tr into each of next 3tr, 1tr into each of next three 2ch sp, 1tr into each of next 3tr, 1tr into next 2ch sp, 1tr into each of next 3tr, 1tr into next 2ch sp, (1tr into next 2ch sp, 1tr into each of next 2tr) 13[14:15] times, 1tr into last ch sp, 1tr into 3rd of 5ch. Turn. 98[104:110] sts.
Next row 3ch, miss first st, 1tr into each st, ending with last tr into 3rd of 3ch. Turn.
Rep last row once more. **

Shape armholes

1st row Ss over first 3 sts and into next st, 3ch, (yrh, insert into next st, yrh and draw through a loop, yrh and draw through first 2 loops on hook) 3 times, yrh and draw through all 4 loops on hook – called dec 2 –, 1tr into each st to last 7 sts, dec 2, 1tr into next st, turn. 88[94:100] sts.
2nd row 3ch, miss first st, dec 2, 1tr into each st to last 4 sts, dec 2, 1tr into 3rd of 3ch. Turn.
3rd row 3ch, miss first st, (yrh, insert into next st, yrh and draw through a loop, yrh and draw through first 2 loops on hook) twice, yrh and draw through all 3 loops on hook – called dec 1 –, 1tr into each st to last 3 sts, dec 1, 1tr into 3rd of 3ch. Turn.
Rep last row 5[6:7] times more. 72[76:80] sts. Cont in tr without shaping until armholes measure 18[19:20.5]cm (7[7½:8]in) from beg, ending with a WS row.

Shape shoulders

Next row Ss over first 4[5:5] sts, 1dc into each of next 5 sts, 1htr into each of next 5 sts, 1tr into each st to last 14[15:15] sts, 1htr into each of next 5 sts, 1dc into each of next 5 sts. Fasten off.

Front

Work as given for back to **.

Shape armholes and divide for opening

1st row Ss over first 3 sts and into next st, 3ch, dec 2, 1tr into each of next 40[43:46] sts, turn. Cont on these 42[45:48] sts for first side as foll:
2nd row 3ch, miss first st, 1tr into each st to last 4 sts, dec 2, 1tr into 3rd of 3ch. Turn.
3rd row 3ch, miss first st, dec 1, 1tr into each st to end. Turn.
4th row 3ch, miss first st, 1tr into each st to last 3 sts, dec 1, 1tr into 3rd of 3ch. Turn.
Rep 3rd and 4th rows 2[2:3] times more. 34[37:38] sts.

2nd size only
Rep 3rd row once more. 36 sts.

All sizes
Cont in tr without shaping until armhole measures 11.5[12.5:14]cm (4½[5:5½]in) from beg, ending at armhole edge.

Shape neck

1st row 3ch, miss first st, 1tr into each st to last 9[10:11] sts, dec 2, 1tr into next st, turn.
2nd row 3ch, miss first st, dec 2, 1tr into each st to end. Turn.
3rd row 3ch, miss first st, 1tr into each st to last 4 sts, dec 2, 1tr into 3rd of 3ch. Turn.
Rep 2nd and 3rd rows once more. 19[20:21] sts. Cont without shaping until front matches back to shoulder, ending at armhole edge.

Shape shoulder

Next row Ss over first 4[5:5] sts, 1dc into each of next 5 sts, 1htr into each of next 5 sts, 1tr into each of next 5[5:6] sts. Fasten off.
With RS of work facing, return to beg of opening and leave centre 4 sts unworked, rejoin yarn to next st, 3ch, 1tr into each st to last 7 sts, dec 2, 1tr into next st, turn. Complete to match first side, reversing shapings.

Left sleeve

1st piece Using No.2.50 (ISR) hook make 23[25:27]ch.
1st row (WS) Into 3rd ch from hook work 1dc, 1dc into each ch to end. 22[24:26] sts.
2nd row 1ch to count as first dc, miss first st, 1dc into each st to end. Turn.
Rep last row until cuff measures 5cm (2in) from beg, ending with a WS row. Change to No.3.00 (ISR) hook.
Next row 5ch, miss first st, 1tr into next st, *2ch, 1tr into next st, rep from * to end. 64[70:76] sts.
Cont in main patt as given for back until 1st piece measures 10cm (4in) from beg, ending with a WS row. Fasten off.
2nd piece Using No.2.50 (ISR) hook make 14ch.
1st row (WS) Into 3rd ch from hook work 1dc, 1dc into each ch to end. 13 sts.
2nd row 1ch to count as first dc, miss first st, 1dc into each st to end. Turn.
Rep last row until cuff measures 5cm (2in), ending with a WS row. Change to No.3.00 (ISR) hook.
Next row 5ch, miss first st, 1tr into next st, *2ch, 1tr into next st. Turn. 37 sts.
Cont in main patt as given for back until 2nd piece matches 1st piece, ending with a WS row.
Next row Work in main patt across 37 sts of 2nd piece, 2ch, then with RS of work facing, patt across 64[70:76] sts of 1st piece. 103[109:115] sts. Turn.
** Cont in main patt until sleeve measures 54.5cm (18in) from beg measured at centre, ending with a RS row.

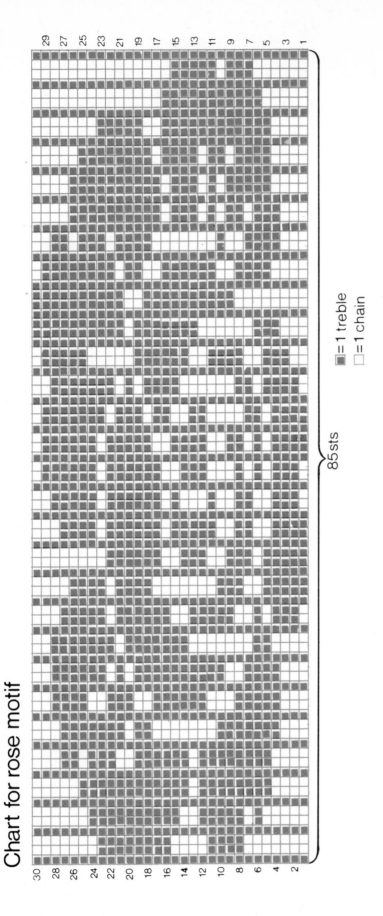

Chart for rose motif

= 1 treble
□ = 1 chain

85 sts

Shape top
1st row Ss over first 3 sts and into next st, 3ch, dec 1, 1tr into each st to last 6 sts, dec 1, 1tr into next st, turn.
2nd row 3ch, miss first st, dec 1, 1tr into each st to last 3 sts, dec 1, 1tr into 3rd of 3ch. Turn.
Rep last row 9[9:11] times more. 40[44:44] sts.
Next row 3ch, miss first st, dec 2, 1tr into each st to last 4 sts, dec 2, 1tr into 3rd of 3ch. Turn.
Rep last row 4[5:5] times more. 20 sts. Fasten off.

Right sleeve
1st piece Work as given for 2nd piece of left sleeve and fasten off.
2nd piece Work as given for 1st piece of left sleeve, but do not fasten off.
Next row Work in main patt across 64[70:76] sts of 2nd piece, 2ch, then with RS of work facing, patt across 37 sts of 1st piece. Turn. 103[109:115] sts. Complete as given for left sleeve from ** to end.

To make up
Press lightly under a damp cloth with a warm iron. Join shoulder seams. Set in sleeves. Join side and sleeve seams.
Neck edging Using No.2.50 (ISR) hook and with RS of work facing, rejoin yarn to top of right front neck and work 3 rows dc all round neck edge. Fasten off.
Left front border Using No.2.50 (ISR) hook and with RS of work facing, work 5 rows dc down left side of opening. Mark positions for 5 buttonholes on this border, first to come 1.5cm (½in) from base of opening and last 2 sts below top of neck with the others evenly spaced between.
Right front border Work as given for left front border, making buttonholes on 3rd row to correspond with markers by working 2ch and missing 2dc.
Catch down ends of borders to base of opening, right over left.
Sleeve opening border Using No.2.50 (ISR) hook and with RS of work facing, work 2 rows dc all round opening, working 3 buttonloops evenly spaced along cuff part of larger piece on 2nd row by making 3ch and missing 2dc.
Lower edging Using No.2.50 (ISR) hook and with RS of work facing, work 1dc into each of first 3 sts, *(ss, 5ch, ss, 5ch, ss, 5ch, ss) all into next st, 1dc into each of next 5 sts, *, rep from * to * 32[34:36] times more, 1dc into next st, rep from * to * 32[34:36] times more, (ss, 5ch, ss, 5ch, ss, 5ch, ss) all into next st, 1dc into each of last 3 sts. Join with a ss into first st. Fasten off. Press seams. Sew on buttons.

Next row 3ch, (1tr into next 2ch sp, 1tr into next tr) 16[17:18] times, 1tr into each of next two 2ch sp, (1tr into next tr, 1tr into next 2ch sp) 16[17:18] times, 1tr into 3rd of 5ch. Turn. 68[72:76] sts. Work 2 rows in tr.

OPEN LACE DESIGNS

Open lace designs

Open lace work is quick and easy to work in crochet as it is formed with large spaces between the stitches and so the pattern grows rapidly. Any type of yarn may be used and this will be determined by the nature of the work.

There are many uses for this type of crochet where an open effect is required. It can be used for entire garments but naturally these will need to be lined. More commonly strips of open lace work are used as insets especially on evening clothes where the laciness of the crochet looks most appropriate.

However these openwork designs do have everyday purposes as well. String bags, onion bags or simple cotton lace curtains for one of the windows in your home are examples of a few of the things that you can make once you have practised some of the samples of open lace work that are given below.

Solomon's knot stitch

Using No. 3.00 (ISR) crochet hook and a fine yarn make 35ch loosely.

1st row Extend loop on hook for 2cm ($\frac{3}{4}$ *in*), placing thumb of left hand on loop to keep it extended, yrh and draw through a loop, place hook from front to back under left hand vertical loop of stitch just worked, yrh and draw through a loop, yrh and draw through both loops on hook – called one Solomon st –, ss into 10th ch from last Solomon st, * 1ch, work 2 Solomon sts, ss into 5th ch from last Solomon st, rep from * to end. Turn.

2nd row 6ch, work 1 Solomon st, ss into st between first pair of Solomon sts on previous row, 1ch, * work 2 Solomon sts, ss into st between next pair of Solomon sts, rep from * ending with last ss into last of the turning ch of the previous row. Turn.

The last row is repeated throughout to create a very attractively lacy stitch with a 3-dimensional effect.

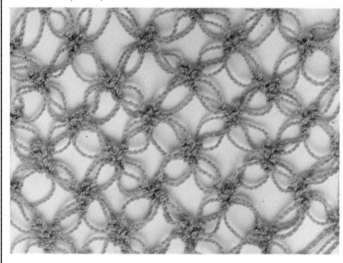

String stitch used as an insert on a bodice

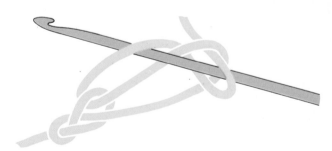

Working a Solomon's knot stitch.

Chain lace

Using No.3.00 (ISR) crochet hook and a fine yarn make 44ch.

1st row Into 12th ch from hook work 1dc, *8ch, miss next 3ch, 1dc into next ch, rep from * to end. Turn.

2nd row 8ch, 1dc into first 8ch loop, *8ch, 1dc into next loop, rep from * to end. Turn.

The last row is repeated throughout to form a very simple diamond shaped mesh.

It is an ideal stitch for an evening snood or a string bag like the one in our illustration.

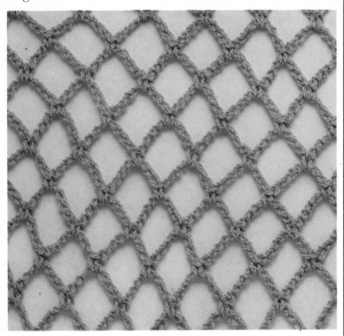

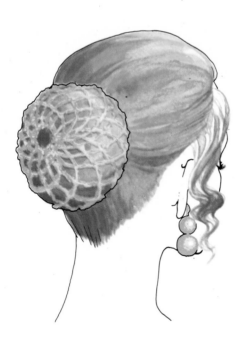

Chain lace used for a snood

To make a string bag

You will need one ball of parcel string, a brass curtain ring 3cm (1¼ inch) in diameter and a No.4.50 (ISR) crochet hook.

1st round Form a slip loop on the hook, 1dc into brass ring, *9ch, 1dc into ring, rep from * 21 times more, ss into first dc.

Next and all successive rounds Ss into first 4ch of next 9ch loop, 1dc into this loop, *9ch, 1dc into next loop, rep from * all round ending with 9ch, ss into first dc of the round. Turn.

When the bag is the required depth, fasten off and slot drawstrings through the spaces.

String stitch

Using No.2.50 (ISR) crochet hook and a fine yarn, make 43ch.

1st row Ss into 5th ch from hook, miss next ch, 1dc into next ch, *5ch, miss next 5ch, 1dc into next ch, 5ch, ss into dc last worked, 1dc into same ch as last dc, rep from * to end. Turn.

2nd row Ss to top of first 5ch loop, 6ch, ss into 5th ch from hook, 1dc into first loop, *5ch, 1dc into next 5ch loop, 5ch, ss into last dc worked, 1dc into same loop, rep from * to end. Turn.

The last row is repeated throughout to form the pattern.

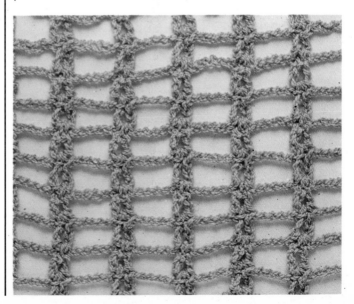

Mohair muffler

For a muffler about 30cm (12in) wide by 244cm (96in) long

Materials

150grm (5¼oz) of random coloured mohair yarn in a double knitting quality
One No. 4.50 (ISR) crochet hook

Muffler

Using the crochet hook make 20 Solomon's knots, drawing each loop up to a height of 2.5cm (1in).
Continue working in pattern until the work measures 244cm (96in) from the beginning. Fasten off.

Solomon's knot worked in mohair

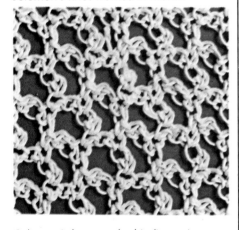

Solomon's knot worked in fine string

String shopping bag

Size

For a bag about 35cm (14in) wide by 40cm (16in) deep

Materials

2 balls of fine parcel string
One No. 3.50 (ISR) crochet hook

Bag

Using the crochet hook make 40 Solomon's knots, drawing each loop up to a height of 1.25cm (½in).
Continue in pattern until the work measures 81cm (32in) from the beginning.

Fasten off.
Make up the bag by folding it in half lengthwise. Join the side seams by over-sewing them, from the lower edge to within 15cm (6in) of the top edge.

Handle

Cut 12 lengths of string, each 91cm (36in) long for the handle.
Divide the string into 3 groups with 4 lengths in each and plait them together,

knotting each end.

Thread each plait through the last row at the top of the bag from the outer edge to the centre and tie the ends together to form a handle.

Complete the other handle in the same way.

Fringed shawl

Size

For a shawl measuring about 168cm (66in) across the top edge, excluding the fringe

Materials

100grm (3½oz) of 3 ply Botany Wool plus 25grm (1oz) extra for fringe
One No. 3.00 (ISR) crochet hook

Shawl

Using the crochet hook make 140 Solomon's knots, drawing each loop to a height of 1.25cm (½in), then shape the sides by working as follows:

Next row Miss knot on hook and next 4 knots, insert hook into centre of next knot and work 1dc, *make 2 knots, miss 1 knot along 1st row, 1dc into centre of next knot on 1st row, rep from * to end, working last dc into first ch.

Next row Make 3 knots, miss first knot, next unjoined knot and joined knot of last row, 1dc into centre of next unjoined knot of last row, *make 2 knots, miss next joined knot of last row, 1dc into centre of next unjoined knot of last row, rep from * to end.

Repeat the last row until 2 knots remain. Fasten off.

Cut lengths of yarn, each 40cm (16in) long.

Take 6 strands together at a time and knot into each space along side edges only.

Work 2 lines of fringing (see chapters on Trimmings and Braids later), each line 2.5cm (1in) below previous knots. Trim the fringe.

Solomon's knot worked in botany wool

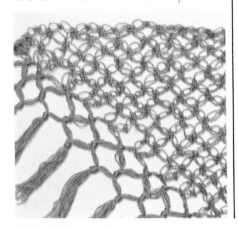

Solomon's knot stitch worked in 3-ply botany wool makes a gossamer shawl

FUR FABRICS AND LOOP STITCHES

Recently it has become very popular to represent fur fabrics with 'fun fur' fashions. In crochet this is equivalent to using loop stitch. Here we tell you how to work three basic loop stitches. The next section covers more advanced techniques.

Loop stitches give a very raised effect and form a solid, virtually windproof fabric which is ideal for cooler days. It is important not to underestimate the amount of yarn you will require for an item worked in loop stitches as this could be quite considerable.

Waistcoats, jackets and hats made entirely in loop stitch and bright paintbox colours are perfect for children's wear. Alternatively use the same stitches to give a 'fur' trimming effect on garments.

Clothes are not the only items you will come across in loop stitch. It is useful for making bathroom sets especially if a machine washable and quick drying yarn like Courtelle is used.

Loop stitch

This is loop stitch in its most usual form. It is worked into the fabric as you proceed in rows.

Using No.5.00 (ISR) crochet hook and a Double Knitting yarn, make 22ch.

1st row 1dc into 3rd ch from hook, work 1dc into every ch to end. Turn.

2nd row 1ch to count as first dc, miss first st of previous row, work a loop by inserting hook into next st, position yarn over 1st and 2nd fingers and extend yarn by lifting 2nd finger, draw through a loop as shown in diagram, then draw loop through

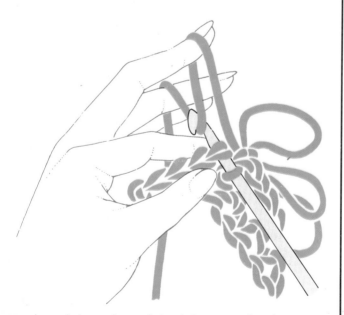

st, yrh and draw through both loops on hook, remove 2nd finger from loop, rep the action of making a

loop into every st to the end of the row, 1dc into the turning chain. Turn.

3rd row 1ch to count as first dc, miss first st of previous row, 1dc into every st to end, 1dc into the turning chain. Turn.

Repeat the 2nd and 3rd rows throughout to form the pattern.

Note You will see that the loops are on the back of the fabric as you are working. This is correct as you are making the loops from the wrong side of the work. The density of the loops can be altered by working them across the row on alternate stitches, and into the stitches between loops on following alternate rows.

Chain fur stitches

Again these chain loops are formed as part of the fabric. It has a close, curly fur effect that is reminiscent of many popular furs.

Using No.5.00 (ISR) crochet hook and a Double Knitting yarn, make 25ch.

1st row 1tr into 4th ch from hook, work 1tr into every ch to end. Turn.

2nd row 1ch to count as first dc, miss first st of previous row, *1dc into back loop only of next st, 10ch, rep from * to end of row, working last dc into the turning chain. Turn.

3rd row 3ch to count as first tr, missing the first st, work 1tr into every st of the last row worked in tr, inserting the hook into the loop missed in the previous row of dc, 1tr into the turning chain. Turn. Repeat the 2nd and 3rd rows throughout to form the pattern.

Cut fur stitch

Here the loops are added after the basic background —a mesh—has been worked.

Using No.5.00 (ISR) crochet hook and a Double Knitting yarn, make 25ch.

1st row 1dc into 3rd ch from hook, *1ch, miss next ch, 1dc into next ch, rep from * to end. Turn.
2nd row 1ch to count as first dc, 1dc into first 1ch **sp**, *1ch, 1dc into next 1ch sp, rep from * to last sp, 1ch, 1dc into the turning chain. Turn.
The 2nd row is repeated throughout.

To add the loops Cut lengths of yarn as required (approximately 13 centimetres (*5 inches*) long).
Take two pieces of yarn together each time and fold in half, with right side of work facing, insert the crochet hook horizontally through the first dc in the mesh, place the two loops of yarn over the hook and draw through the work, place the four cut ends of yarn over the hook and draw through the two loops on the hook. Pull up tightly to secure. Repeat this process into every dc throughout the mesh.
Note As with loop stitch you can vary the amount of cut loops and their position on the fabric. See how attractive these loops can look and the different designs you can create if you work them in various colours, or in shades of one colour like our sample.

▼ *Hat in loop stitch and chain fur stitch on jacket*

'Fun fur' pram cover

Colour chart for cover

1 Square = 1 Tr

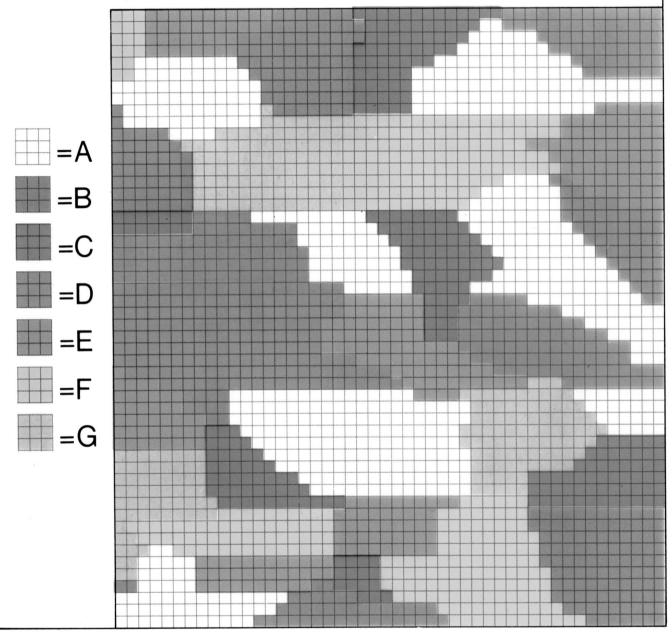

=A

=B

=C

=D

=E

=F

=G

Size
Crochet base measures 58.5cm × 34.5cm
(*23in × 13½in*)

Tension
13tr and 9 rows to 10cm (*3.9in*) worked on
No.4.00 (ISR) hook

Materials
10 × 20grm balls Wendy Courtellon

Double Knitting in main shade, A
3 balls each of contrast colours B, C, D,
E, F and G
One No.4.00 (ISR) crochet hook

Crochet base
Using No.4.00 (ISR) hook and A, make 50
ch.
1st row Into 4th ch from hook work 1tr,
1tr into each ch to end. Turn. 48tr.
2nd row 3ch to count as first tr, miss

first tr, 1tr into each tr, ending with 1tr
into 3rd of 3ch. Turn.
Rep last row 50 times more. Fasten off.

To make up
Cut rem balls of A and each ball of B, C,
D, E, F and G into 12.5cm (*5in*) lengths.
Following chart and using 2 strands of
yarn tog, knot round every tr in base.
Trim strands to desired length or leave
shaggy.

LOOPED BRAIDS AND EDGINGS

In this chapter we shall continue with more variations of the looped stitches you learnt in the last chapter. More advanced techniques are illustrated, including working with beads and we suggest how you might use these stitches.

Here the methods are used as a trim rather than an all over design because they are so decorative. To give the greatest contrast when using these trimmings on a crochet garment, the main stitches should be very basic such as double crochet or treble.

Accordion braid

This is formed by working many trebles into a small space on a background fabric of double treble to give a fluted effect.

Using No. 5.00 (ISR) crochet hook and a Double Knitting yarn, make 23ch.

1st row 1dtr into 5th ch from hook, work 1dtr into every ch to end. Turn.

2nd row 4ch to count as first dtr, miss first st in previous row, 1dtr into each st to end, 1dtr into the turning chain. Do not turn.

3rd row 3ch, work 6tr down side of first dtr, 1tr into st at base of this dtr, *work 7tr up side of next dtr in row, 1tr into st at top of this dtr, work 7tr down side of next dtr in row, 1tr into st at base of this dtr, rep from * to end of row. Fasten off.

Repeat the process on the first row of dtr that was worked.

This braid can be incorporated into a garment or applied to one that has been completed. It looks very effective round the outer edges of a long, simple evening coat as the bulkiness counteracts the length of the coat.

Accordion braid used to trim an evening coat

Triple loops worked over a bar

This is an unusual technique for making very thick loops. To be most effective it should be worked into the garment you are making as single rows or no more than three rows at the most. You could try spacing single rows at varying distances as in our illustration.

Work until the point in your garment where you wish to include triple loops, ending with a right side row.

Take a separate ball of yarn and wind it in a single strand over a piece of wood several times – a rule or a rug wool gauge used for cutting yarns for rug making and which has a groove down one side is ideal.

Next row Holding the wool-covered rule or gauge behind your work, begin at opposite end to ball of yarn, *insert hook into next st, then insert hook behind first 3 loops on rule, yrh and draw beneath the 3 loops of yarn and through the st of the previous row, yrh and draw through both loops on hook, rep from * to end of row, taking care to remove the yarn from the rule in consecutive order.
Remove the rule from the loops and cut the loop yarn at the end of the row. Work one row in double crochet before starting another triple loop row.

Vertical beaded loops

These are ideal for working a jabot around the front opening of an evening top.

Make sure that you buy beads that have the correct size hole for the yarn that you are using. Usually the beads will already be threaded on a coarse string when you purchase them, but you will need to transfer them on to the crochet yarn with which you will be working before you start work. To do this, make an overhand knot in one end of the bead thread, place the crochet yarn through this knot as in the diagram and carefully slide the beads from the thread on to the crochet yarn. Work to the position where a beaded row is required, ending with a right side row.

Next row Ss into the first st, *yrh and draw through a loop extending it for 15cm (6in), push up the required number of beads on the yarn and draw through the extended stitch, draw the enlarged st over the beaded loop and pull yarn tightly to secure (there is now no loop on the hook), insert hook into next st, yrh and draw through a st, ss into next st, *, rep from * to * until the required number of beaded loops have been worked. Use this same method to work beaded fringes, varying the number of beads used in a loop to give different depths.

ARAN CROCHET
BASIC STITCHES

Aran crochet

Aran is usually considered to be a knitting technique, but in this and following chapters we explain how you can achieve a similar effect working in crochet. It is a satisfying technique for those who prefer to crochet, giving quicker results and the same range of garments and items for the home can be made.

Traditional Aran work is usually seen in natural or off-white shades of yarn, but today many wool manufacturers make a special Aran yarn, which is very thick, in a variety of shades. The samples here explain how to work the basic patterns in crochet, which resemble the knitted versions quite closely.

Sample 1

Rib stitch This is the crochet version of the knitted rib. The fabric would be used from side to side across a garment, so that the foundation chain forms the side seam rather than the hem. If you are making a garment, this stitch is suitable for the welt. Using a smaller hook size than used for the rest of the garment, i.e. No.5.00 (ISR), make a length of chain to give the required depth of rib.

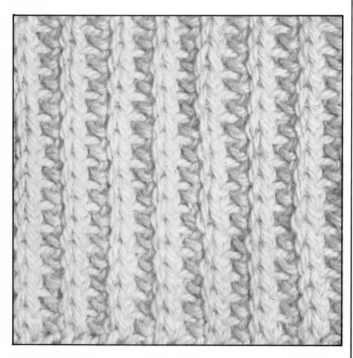

1st row Into 3rd ch from hook work 1dc, 1dc into each ch to end. Turn.

2nd row 1ch to count as first dc, miss first st, 1dc into each st to end, placing the hook into the horizontal loop under the normal ch loop of the dc, 1dc into turning ch. Turn.

Repeat the 2nd row throughout until the rib is the width of the garment.

To begin work on the main part of the garment, the ribbed fabric is turned so that the ridges run vertically. The loops formed by the row ends are then used as a basis for the first row of the main fabric. A larger hook, No.5.50 (ISR), is used for the main part and it may be

necessary to increase the number of stitches by working 2dc into some loops. In the following photograph the rib stitch is shown complete, followed by several rows of double crochet. This forms the basis of many Aran styles.

Sample 2

The following attractive stitches could be used as an all-over pattern or in a panel within an Aran design.

Even moss stitch Make a length of chain with multiples of 2 stitches.

1st row Miss first ch, ss into next ch, *1htr into next ch, ss into next ch, rep from * to end. Turn.

2nd row 1ch, miss first st, *1htr into next st, ss into next st, rep from * ending with last ss worked into turning ch. Turn.

The 2nd row is repeated throughout.

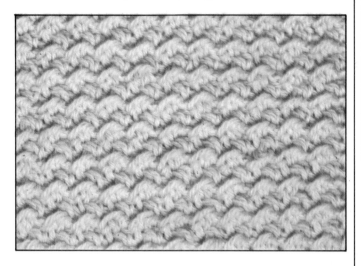

Uneven moss stitch Make a length of chain and work 1st and 2nd rows as given for even moss stitch.

3rd row 2ch to count as first htr, miss first st, ss into next st, *1htr into next st, ss into next st, rep from * to end, 1htr into turning ch. Turn.

4th row As 3rd.

5th row As 2nd.

6th row As 2nd.

The 3rd to 6th rows are repeated throughout.

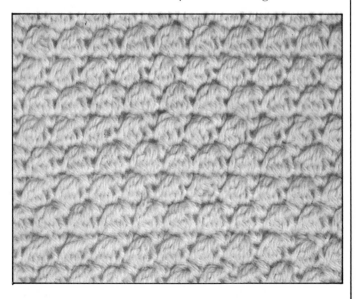

Sample 3

Even berry stitch Make a length of chain with multiples of 2 stitches.

1st row Into 3rd ch from hook work 1dc, 1dc into each ch to end. Turn.

2nd row 1ch to count as first ss, miss first st, *yrh and insert hook into next st, yrh and draw through a loop, yrh and draw through first loop on hook, yrh and insert hook into same st, yrh and draw through a loop, yrh

and draw through all 5 loops on hook, 1ch to secure st – called berry st –, ss into next st, rep from * ending with last ss worked into turning ch. Turn.

3rd row 1ch to count as first dc, miss first st, *ss into next berry st, 1dc into next ss, rep from * to end. Turn.

4th row 1ch to count as first ss, *1 berry st into next ss, ss into next dc, rep from * to end. Turn.

The 3rd and 4th rows are repeated throughout.

Uneven berry stitch Make a length of chain and work 1st to 3rd rows as given for even berry stitch.

4th row 1ch to count as first ss, 1 berry st into first dc, ss into next ss, *1 berry st into next dc, ss into next ss, rep from * to end. Turn.

5th row As 3rd.

The 2nd to 5th rows are repeated throughout.

RAISED DESIGNS

We have already shown you how to work the basic background effects necessary for Aran crochet, where the double crochet or treble stitches are very important. Here you will see how the background can be decorated with raised designs which are added after the main fabric has been completed. Practise our samples first on a piece of double crochet fabric before starting your own designs.

Sample 1

Raised lines may run horizontally, vertically or diagonally. For all samples of raised work begin at the lower edge and hold the crochet hook on top of the crochet (i.e. right side of work) with the incoming yarn held in the normal way, under the work. Using No.5.50 (ISR) hook, make a slip loop on the hook, insert hook into first hole on the foundation chain, yrh and draw through a loop drawing it through loop on hook, *insert hook into same hole as last st, yrh and draw through a loop (2 loops on hook), insert hook into next hole above last insertion, yrh and draw through a loop drawing it through both loops on hook – called one raised double crochet –, rep from * to end of line.

Other crochet stitches, such as slip stitch or treble, may be substituted instead of the raised double crochet, depending on the depth of stitch required.

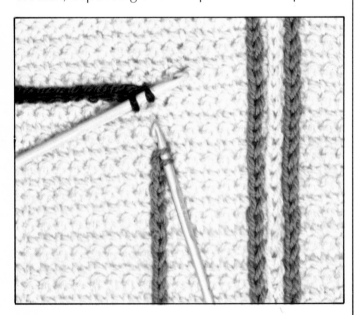

Sample 2

This sample depicts a variety of designs worked on a double crochet background. From left to right across the design there are 2 vertical rows of double crochet, then working from the diagram there is a row of twisted raised double crochet (work black line

first), 2 lines of twisted double crochet which form a diamond pattern, another line of twisted raised double crochet and finally, 2 more vertical lines of crochet.

These designs could be used as a pattern panel on a garment, or on a household article as with the cushion cover the instructions for which we give below.

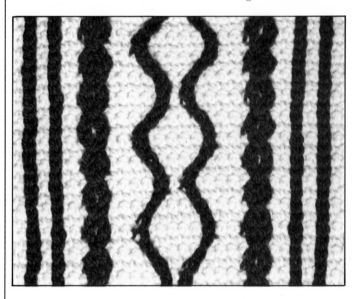

Aran Cushion cover
Size
56cm (22in) × 38cm (15in), excluding fringe

Tension
13 sts and 8 rows to 10cm (3.9in) over tr worked on No.4.00 (ISR) crochet hook

Materials
10 × 50grm balls Emu Aran
One No.4.00 (ISR) crochet hook
One No.5.50 (ISR) crochet hook
0.70 metres ($\frac{3}{4}$ yard) cotton lining material
Kapok for filling
1 × 50cm (20in) zip fastener

Cushion cover (make 2)
Using No.4.00 (ISR) hook make 72ch loosely.
1st row Into 4th ch from hook work 1tr, 1tr into each ch to end. Turn. 70tr.
2nd row 3ch to count as first tr, miss first tr, 1tr into each tr, ending with last tr into 3rd of 3ch. Turn.
Rep last row 28 times more. Fasten off.
Surface crochet This can be worked on either both sides or only one side as required. Using No.5.50 (ISR) hook and double yarn throughout, follow the chart and work in raised slip stitch following the direction

of the arrows throughout, noting that in row C the cable patt should first be worked by following the arrows, then in the opposite direction indicated by the dots.

To make up

With WS tog and using No.5.50 (ISR) hook and double yarn, join 2 short sides and 1 long side by working a row of dc through both thicknesses, working 1dc into each tr, 1dc into each row end and 3dc into each corner. On 4th side, work in dc along one side only leaving opening for zip. Sew in zip. Make up cushion pad to required size using lining material and fill with kapok. Insert into cushion cover.

Fringe Cut yarn into 30.5cm (*12in*) lengths and using 3 strands tog, knot through each dc along short edges.

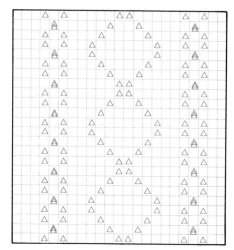

□ = one space between double crochet

△ = one raised double crochet

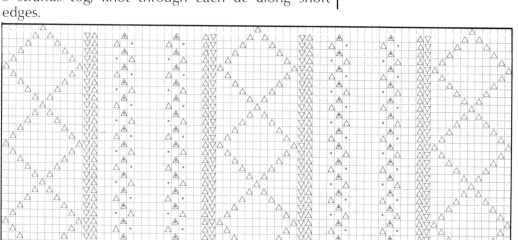

□ = one space between trebles

△ = one raised slip stitch

· = one raised slip stitch in opposite direction to arrows

BERRY STITCH MOTIFS

This chapter shows in detail how berry stitch, which was previously explained as an all-over design, can be worked into motifs on a double crochet background. The motifs are then outlined with raised double crochet to form a panel which could be incorporated into an Aran style garment.

Sample 1

This illustrates one method of grouping berry stitch. Using No.5.50 (ISR) hook and an Aran yarn, make a length of chain with multiples of 8+4 stitches.

1st row Into 3rd ch from hook work 1dc, 1dc into each ch to end. Turn.

2nd row 1ch to count as first dc, miss first st, 1dc into each st to end. Turn.

3rd row 1ch, miss first st, 1dc into each of next 3 sts, *ss into next st, yrh and insert into next st, yrh and draw through a loop, yrh and draw through first loop on hook, yrh and insert into same st, yrh and draw through a loop, yrh and draw through all loops on hook, 1ch to secure st – called berry st –, ss into next st, 1dc into each of next 5 sts, rep from * ending last rep with 1dc into each of next 4 sts. Turn.

4th row 1ch, miss first st, 1dc into each of next 3 sts, *1dc into next ss, ss into next berry st, 1dc into next ss, 1dc into each of next 5 sts, rep from * ending last rep with 1dc into each of next 4 sts. Turn.

5th row 1ch, miss first st, 1dc into each of next 2 sts, * ss into next dc, berry st into next dc, ss into next ss, berry st into next dc, ss into next dc, 1dc into each of next 3 sts, rep from * to end. Turn.

6th row 1ch, miss first st, 1dc into each of next 3 sts, *ss into next berry st, 1dc into next ss, ss into next berry st, 1dc into each of next 5 sts, rep from * ending last rep with 1dc into each of next 4 sts. Turn.

7th–8th rows As 3rd–4th rows.

9th row 1ch, miss first st, berry st into next dc, ss into next dc, *1dc into each of next 5 sts, ss into next dc, berry st into next dc, ss into next dc, rep from * to end. Turn.

10th row 1ch, miss first st, ss into next berry st, *1dc into each of next 7 sts, ss into next berry st, rep from * ending with 1dc into last st. Turn.

11th row 1ch, miss first st, *ss into next ss, berry st into next dc, ss into next dc, 1dc into each of next 3 sts, ss into next dc, berry st into next dc, rep from * to last 2 sts, ss into next ss, 1dc into last st. Turn.

12th row 1ch, miss first st, 1dc into next ss, ss into next berry st, *1dc into each of next 5 sts, ss into next berry st, 1dc into next ss, ss into next berry st, rep from * to last 3 sts, ss into next berry st, 1dc into next ss, 1dc into last st. Turn.

13th–14th rows As 9th–10th rows.

The 3rd to 14th rows are repeated to form the pattern.

Sample 2

This is a sample design where berry stitches in a diamond pattern have been included in a double crochet background and then the entire design has been emphasised with lines of raised double crochet. The technique of working raised double crochet was explained in detail previously and in our sample the lines are worked in varying colours to give them definition.

Using No.5.50 (ISR) hook and an Aran yarn, make 23ch.

1st row Into 3rd ch from hook work 1dc, 1dc into each ch to end. Turn.

Continue working in double crochet until one row before the position for starting berry stitch motif.

Next row Work across first 7 sts marking last st with a coloured thread, work across next 7 sts – this is the pattern area for the berry st motif, work across last 8 sts marking first st with a coloured thread. Turn.

1st patt row Work to marked position, 1dc into each of next 2 sts, ss into next st, berry st into next st, ss into next st, 1dc into each of next 2 sts, work to end. Turn.

Note From this point the instructions only refer to the centre 7 sts involved in the berry st design.

2nd patt row 1dc into each of next 3 sts, ss into next st, 1dc into each of next 3 sts.

3rd patt row 1dc into next st, (ss into next st, berry st into next st) twice, ss into next st, 1dc into next st.

4th patt row 1dc into each of next 2 sts, (ss into next st, 1dc into next st) twice, 1dc into next st.

5th patt row Ss into next st, (berry st into next st, ss into next st) 3 times.

6th patt row 1dc into next st, (ss into next st, 1dc into next st) 3 times.

7th–8th patt rows As 3rd–4th rows.

9th–10th rows As 1st–2nd rows.

Continue working in double crochet for the required depth, making more motifs if required. Complete the design by working the lines in raised double crochet from the chart.

Work in same way as sample 2, marking a centre panel to cover 7 sts. Repeat 1st–6th patt rows, 3rd–6th, 3rd–4th and then 1st and 2nd rows. Use the chart to work the lines of raised double crochet.

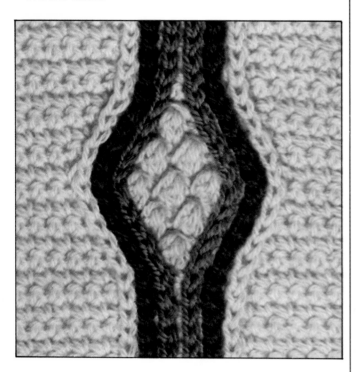

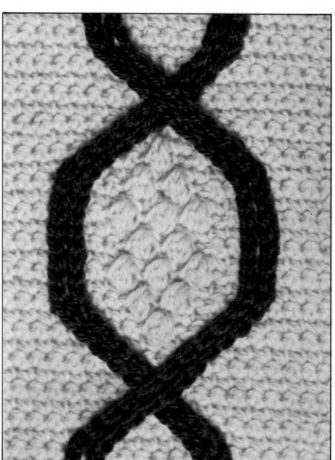

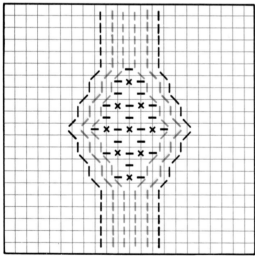

KEY

Each vertical line on each square = one double crochet
Each horizontal line on each square = one row
x = one berry stitch in place of a double crochet stitch
− = one slip stitch in place of a double crochet stitch
| = one raised double crochet worked vertically
/ = one raised double crochet worked diagonally

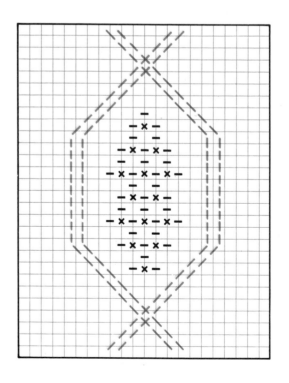

Sample 3

This is a variation on the previous sample with an enlarged berry stitch motif and double lines of raised double crochet which cross each other.

IRISH CROCHET
BASIC TECHNIQUES

Irish crochet

Irish crochet, also known as Honiton crochet, is a form of lace which originated as an imitation of the Guipure laces of Spain. The lace background and various motifs, such as the rose, leaf, shamrock plus other flowers and curves, are both major characteristics of this work.

This introductory chapter to the craft will cover some of the techniques for working the background and also a selection of some of the more simple motifs. The motifs may be applied directly on to the background or the lace mesh may be worked around the motif.

The samples shown here were worked in a No.5 cotton yarn with a No.2.00 (ISR) crochet hook. When you understand the basic techniques, try experimenting with some more unusual yarns and see what different effects may be achieved. All the net backgrounds seen here would make attractive evening shawls, especially if you work in one of the new mohair yarns.

Sample 1

To work the net background Make 50ch loosely.

1st row Into 10th ch from hook work 1dc, *6ch, miss 3ch, 1dc into next ch, rep from * to end of row. Turn.

2nd row 9ch, 1dc into first ch sp, *6ch, 1dc into next ch sp, rep from * to end of row. Turn.

The 2nd row is repeated throughout.

To work the rose motif Wrap the yarn 20 times round a pencil.

1st round Remove yarn carefully from the pencil work 18dc into the ring. Join with a ss into first dc.

2nd round 6ch, miss 2dc, 1htr into next dc, *4ch, miss 2dc, 1htr into next dc, rep from * 3 times more, 4ch. Join with a ss into 2nd of 6ch.

3rd round Into each 4ch sp work 1dc, 1htr, 3tr, 1htr and 1dc to form a petal. Join with a ss into first dc.

4th round Ss into back of nearest htr of 2nd round, *5ch, passing chain behind petal of previous round, ss into next htr of 2nd round, rep from * 5 times more.

5th round Into each 5ch sp work 1dc, 1htr, 5tr, 1 htr and 1dc. Join with a ss into first dc.

6th round Ss into back of ss of 4th round, *6ch, passing chain behind petal of previous round, ss into next ss of 4th round, rep from * 5 times more.

7th round Into each 6ch sp work 1dc, 1htr, 6tr, 1htr and 1dc. Join with a ss into first dc. Fasten off.

Sample 2

To work the net background Make 58ch loosely.

1st row Into 16th ch from hook work 1dc, 3ch, 1dc into same ch as last dc, *9ch, miss 5ch, 1dc into next ch, 3ch, 1dc into same ch as last dc, rep from * to end of row. Turn.

2nd row 13ch, 1dc into first ch sp, 3ch, 1dc into same sp, *9ch, 1dc into next ch sp, 3ch, 1dc into same sp

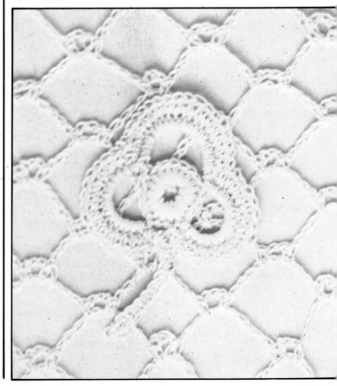

rep from * to end of row. Turn.

The 2nd row is repeated throughout.

To work the motif Wrap yarn 12 times round a pencil.

1st round Remove yarn carefully from the pencil, work 18dc into the ring. Join with a ss into first dc.

2nd round 8ch, miss 4dc, ss into next dc, 10ch, miss 4dc, ss into next dc, 8ch, miss 4dc, ss into next dc, work 12ch for stem, into 3rd ch from hook work 1dc, 1dc into each of next 9ch, turn.

3rd row Into first ch sp work 16dc, 20dc into next ch sp and 16dc into next ch sp. Turn.

4th row 3ch to count as first tr, miss first dc, 1tr into each dc to end of row. Fasten off.

Sample 3

To work the net background This background incorporates an attractive picot design. Make 47ch loosely.

1st row Work 4ch, ss into 4th ch from hook – called a picot –, 2ch, into 12th ch from picot work 1dc, *4ch, work a picot, 2ch, miss 4ch, 1dc into next ch, rep from * to end of row. Turn.

2nd row 6ch, work a picot, 2ch, 1dc into first ch sp, *4ch, work a picot, 2ch, 1dc into next ch sp, rep from * to end of row. Turn.

The 2nd row is repeated throughout.

To work the motif Wrap yarn 14 times round little finger of left hand.

1st round Remove yarn carefully from finger, work 38dc into the ring. Join with a ss into first dc.

2nd round *9ch, miss 6dc, ss into next dc, rep from * 4 times more, ss into each of next 3dc.

3rd round Into each 9ch sp work 12dc, work 14ch for stem, into 3rd ch from hook work 1dc, 1dc into each of next 11ch. Join with a ss into first dc.

4th round 3ch to count as first tr, miss first dc, 1tr into each dc on all 5 loops. Fasten off.

Sample 4

Here our sample has the same net background as sample 2, but it is worked in an ordinary parcel string and the raffia motif is made in the same way as the motif on sample 3. Use different coloured motifs to decorate a string hold-all.

Sample 5

Use the rose motif described in sample 1 to decorate a wedding veil. Our rose is worked in an extremely fine yarn and has beads sewn on to the motif over the background. The net here is a commercial one, but you could, with time and patience, make a valuable family heirloom if you worked your veil in a crochet net.

ADVANCED DESIGNS

To continue our series about Irish crochet we have ideas for a more complicated background net, also several different motifs.

The crochet lace background could be used for a scarf or evening shawl, made either into a stole shape or a large triangle trimmed with a fringe. Instead of using traditional cotton for Irish crochet try using mohair, lurex or a novelty cotton for an unusual effect. By working the motifs illustrated here you will learn the two techniques which are most common in this type of work. They both give a raised look to the work but by different means. One is working over several thicknesses of yarn and the other way is to insert the hook into the horizontal loop under the two loops where the hook is usually placed.

Shawl incorporating net background, rose and leaf motifs

The samples in this chapter were worked in a very fine cotton yarn, No.25, and a fine crochet hook, but the size of the hook will vary depending on the sort of yarn you use.

Sample 1
To work the net background Make 57ch loosely.

1st row Into 4th ch from hook work a ss – one picot formed –, 8ch, ss into 4th ch from hook, 2ch, 1dc into 8th ch from first picot worked, *6ch, ss into 4th ch from hook, 8ch, ss into 4th ch from hook, 2ch, miss 4ch, 1dc into next ch, rep from * to end. Turn.

2nd row 9ch, ss into 4th ch from hook, 8ch, ss into 4th ch from hook, 2ch, 1dc into first ch sp (i.e. between the 2 picots), *6ch, ss into 4th ch from hook, 8ch, ss into 4th ch from hook, 2ch, 1dc into next ch sp, rep from * to end. Turn.

The 2nd row is repeated throughout.

To work the rose motif Repeat the instructions given for the rose in the last chapter, do not fasten off but continue as follows:

Next round *7ch, passing chain behind petal of

previous round ss between the 2dc of next adjoining petals, rep from * 5 times more.

Next round Into each 7ch sp work 1dc, 1htr, 8tr, 1htr, 1dc. Join with a ss into first dc. Turn work.

Next round 1ch to count as first dc, miss first st, work 1dc into each st all round placing the hook into the horizontal loop behind the st in the previous row – this st gives a raised effect on the right side of the work. Fasten off.

To work the leaf motif All the double crochet stitches from a given point in the pattern are worked over four thicknesses of yarn to give a ridged effect. Cut four lengths of yarn, each 40.5cm (*16in*) long, and when the first dc to be worked in this way is indicated, place the yarn behind the work on a level with the stitch into which the hook is to be placed.

Make 16ch. Into 3rd ch from hook work 1dc, 1dc into each ch to last ch, 5dc into last ch to form tip of leaf, then work 1dc into each st on other side of chain. Work 3dc over the 4 thicknesses of yarn, still working over the yarn and continuing towards tip of leaf, work 1dc into each of next 12dc, working into back loop only of each st. Turn work, 1ch, miss first dc, working down one side of leaf and up the other side, work 1dc into each dc to within 4dc of tip of leaf. Turn work, *1ch, miss first st, 1dc into each dc of previous row to last 4dc of row and working 3dc into dc at base of leaf. Turn work. *. Repeat from * to * until the leaf is the required size.

Sample 2

Wrap yarn 14 times round a pencil.

1st round Remove yarn carefully from pencil, work 21dc into ring. Join with a ss into first dc.

2nd round 1ch to count as first dc, miss first st, 1dc into each dc all round. Join with a ss into first ch.

3rd round 1ch to count as first dc, miss first dc, 1dc into each of next 6 sts, (12ch, 1dc into each of next 7 sts) twice, 14ch. Join with a ss into first ch.

4th round 1ch to count as first dc, miss first dc, 1dc into each of next 4 sts, (22dc into next 12ch sp, 1dc into each of next 5 sts) twice, 24dc into next 14ch sp. Join with a ss into first ch.

5th round Ss into each of next 4 sts, *4ch, miss 2 sts, ss into next st, *, rep from * to * 6 times more, miss next 3 sts, ss into each of next 3 sts, rep from * to * 7 times, miss next 3 sts, ss into each of next 3 sts, rep from * to * 8 times. Join with a ss into first ss.

6th round 1ch to count as first dc, miss first st, 1dc into each of next 2 sts, (6dc into next 4ch sp) 7 times, ss into next st, work 18ch for stem, into 3rd ch from hook work 1dc, 1dc into each of next 15ch, ss into next st on main motif, (6dc into next 4ch sp) 7 times,

1dc into each of next 3 sts, (6dc into next 4ch sp) 8 times. Join with a ss into first ch. Fasten off.

Sample 3

Make 40ch.

1st row Into 3rd ch from hook work 1dc, 1dc into each ch to last ch, 5dc into last ch. Do not turn.

2nd row 1dc into each ch on opposite side of 1st row. Turn.

3rd row The petals are worked individually down each side of the stem beginning from the tip where the last dc was worked as follows: *12ch, ss into st at base of ch, 3ch, miss 2dc, ss into next dc, turn, work 25tr into 12ch sp, ss into first dc on row 1, turn, 1ch to count as first dc, miss first tr, 1dc into each tr round petal, ss into same ss as last ss – one petal has been completed –, rep from * to give the required number of petals noting that when the 25tr have been worked, the ss is placed in front of the previous petal by inserting the hook into the 3rd dc up from the base of the petal being worked. Fasten off.

To complete the other side, rejoin yarn at the tip and work the petals in the same way, but join the last of the 25tr behind the previous petal.

COMBINING MOTIFS AND BACKGROUNDS

During our previous chapters on Irish crochet instructions have been given for working the background and motifs separately. This chapter will deal with the alternative techniques of producing the background and motifs together.

Sample 1

This is a six-sided figure where the net background has been worked around the central motif. The shapes may eventually be joined together to form a whole fabric (the chapter on Square and Wheel Motifs gives the method) which would make an attractive bedcover or lampshade covering.

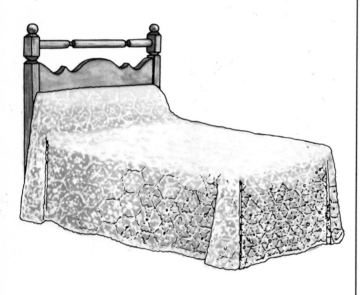

To work the sample Using a No.2.00 (ISR) crochet hook and a No.25 cotton yarn, make a rose motif as in preceding chapter.

Next round Ss into each of next 3 sts of first petal, *(5ch, miss 2 sts, ss into next st) twice, 5ch, miss 3 sts, ss into next st, rep from * 5 times more.

Next round Ss into each of next 2 sts, 6ch, *1dc into next 5ch sp, 5ch, rep from * 16 times more. Join with a ss into 2nd of 6ch.

Next round *Into next 5ch sp work 1dc, 1htr, 5tr, 1htr and 1dc, (5ch, 1dc into next 5ch sp) twice, 5ch, rep from * 5 times more. Join with a ss into first dc.

Next round Ss into each of next 5 sts, 6ch, (1dc into next 5ch sp, 5ch) 3 times, *1dc into centre tr of next petal gr, (5ch, 1dc into next 5ch sp) 3 times, 5ch, rep from * 4 times more. Join with a ss into 2nd of 6ch.

Next round Ss into each of next 2 sts, 6ch, *1dc into next 5ch sp, 5ch, rep from * 22 times more. Join with a ss into 2nd of 6ch.

Next round Ss into each of next 2 sts, 6ch, (1dc into next 5ch sp, 5ch) twice, into next 5ch sp work 1dc, 1htr, 5tr, 1htr and 1dc, *(5ch, 1dc into next 5ch sp) 3 times, 5ch, into next 5ch sp work 1dc, 1htr, 5tr, 1htr and 1dc, rep from * 4 times more, 5ch. Join with a ss into 2nd of 4ch.

Next round Ss into each of next 2 sts, 6ch, 1dc into next ch sp, 5ch, 1dc into next ch sp, 5ch, 1dc, into centre tr of next petal gr, *(5ch, 1dc into next ch sp) 4 times, 5ch, 1dc into centre tr of next petal gr, rep from * 4 times more, 5ch, 1dc into next ch sp, 5ch. Join with a ss into 2nd of 6ch.

Next round Ss into each of next 2 sts, 6ch, *1dc into next ch sp, 5ch, rep from * 28 times more. Join with a ss into 2nd of 6ch.

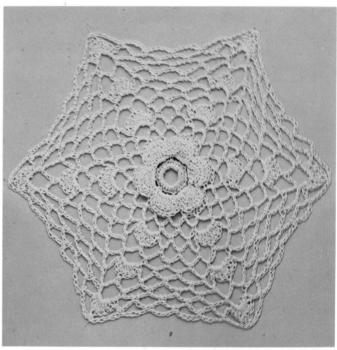

Next round Ss into each of next 2 sts, 6ch, 1dc into next ch sp, 5ch, into next ch sp work 1dc, 1htr, 5tr, 1htr, and 1dc, *(5ch, 1dc into next ch sp) 4 times, 5ch, into next ch sp work 1dc, 1htr, 5tr, 1htr and 1dc, rep from * 4 times more, (5ch, 1dc into next ch sp) twice, 5ch. Join with a ss into 2nd of 6ch.

Next round Ss into each of next 2 sts, 6ch, 1dc into next ch sp, 5ch, 1dc into centre tr of next petal gr, *(5ch, 1dc into next 5ch sp) 5 times, 5ch, 1dc into centre tr of next petal gr, rep from * 4 times more, (5ch, 1dc into next ch sp) 3 times, 5ch. Join with a ss into 2nd of 6ch. Fasten off.

Sample 2

The technique shown here is the method of working motifs and placing them on to paper so that a chain stitch may be worked to join the motifs together to form a fabric.

To work the circle Wrap yarn 20 times round a pencil.

1st round Remove yarn carefully from pencil, work 24dc into circle. Join with a ss into first dc.

2nd round 8ch, miss 2dc, *1tr into next dc, 5ch, miss 2dc, rep from * 6 times more. Join with a ss into 3rd of 8ch.

3rd round 3ch to count as first tr, 3tr into first ch sp, 4ch, ss into 4th ch from hook – called 1 picot –, 4tr into same ch sp, 1 picot, *(4tr, 1 picot) twice into next ch sp, rep from * 6 times more. Join with a ss into 3rd of 3ch. Fasten off.

To work the curve Cut ten lengths of yarn, each 18cm (7in) long. Work 60dc over yarn. Turn work and leave extra yarn to hang freely.

Next row 1ch, ss into 2nd dc, 3ch, miss 3dc, 1htr into next dc, (3ch, miss 3dc, 1tr into next dc) 5 times, (3ch, miss 2dc, 1tr into next dc) 8 times, (3ch, miss 2dc, 1htr into next dc) 3 times, 3ch, ss into last dc. Join with a ss into dc below 3rd tr worked at beg of row to give a circle plus a small length of work. Turn.

Next row Into first ch sp work 5dc, (4dc into next ch sp, 1 picot) 16 times, 4dc into next ch sp, double back the extra 10 lengths of yarn and work 4dc very tightly over the double length, 1dc into end loop, 1ch. Fasten off working yarn. Pull ten lengths of yarn tight to neaten, then cut away.

To join the motifs Make the desired number of motifs and tack on to a firm paper background. The green tacking stitches may be seen in the illustration and further tacks, rather than pins which tend to fall out, should be used as the filling-in progresses.

Our sample shows a circle and four curves, but any of the previous motifs which you have learnt could be incorporated in this method of working. Only half the filling-in has been completed so that the working method may be clearly seen.

A dress pattern of an evening bodice could be used as the paper backing and then the various motifs would be joined together to give the appearance of lace. It would then be necessary to make a lining for this lace.

Chain stitches are used for the filling-in which was started at the top right hand corner of the work. At random intervals a picot is worked by making four chain and slip stitching into the first of these. It is easiest to work in lines to and fro, so joining the motifs together and slip stitching back across some chain stitches where necessary or even breaking off the yarn and rejoining it at a new position on the work. When all the motifs are joined, the tacks may be removed and all the cut ends of yarn should be neatened on the wrong side of the work.

IRISH MOTIFS ON SQUARES

Our illustration shows a long evening skirt which is made up of simple crochet squares some of which are decorated with Irish crochet motifs. To make the skirt, which has no side seams or opening, work 80 squares with double knitting yarn and a No.5.00 (ISR) crochet hook as described later in this chapter. The squares are joined, using the same method as described in the chapter on Square and Wheel Motifs, into ten lines of eight squares each.

Use the crochet motifs, also described in this chapter and worked with the same yarn and crochet hook, to decorate various motifs and sew them on to the squares with a matching yarn using tiny stitches. Neaten the waist with a round of loosely worked quadruple trebles and then slot elastic, dyed to a matching shade if necessary, through the trebles. Two motifs may be placed at the centre front of the waistband to act as buckles.

To work the square motif Make 6ch. Join with a ss into first ch to form a circle.

1st round 3ch to count as first tr, work 19tr into the circle. Join with a ss into 3rd of 3ch.

2nd round 1ch to count as first dc, 1htr into next st, 1tr, 3ch, and 1tr into next st, 1htr into next st, 1dc into next st, *1dc into next st, 1htr into next st, 1tr, 3ch and 1tr into next st, 1htr into next st, 1dc into next st, rep from * twice more. Join with a ss into first ch.

3rd round 3ch to count as first tr, 1tr into each of next 2 sts, into corner 3ch sp work 2tr, 3ch and 2tr, *1tr into each of next 6 sts, into corner 3ch sp work 2tr, 3ch and 2tr, rep from * twice more, 1tr into each of next 3 sts. Join with a ss into 3rd of 3ch.

4th round 3ch to count as first tr, 1tr into each of next 4 sts, into corner 3ch sp work 2tr, 3ch and 2tr, *1tr into each of next 10 sts, into corner 3ch sp work 2tr, 3ch and 2tr, rep from * twice more, 1tr into each of next 5 sts. Join with a ss into 3rd of 3ch.

5th round 3ch to count as first tr, 1tr into each of next 6 sts, into corner 3ch sp work 2tr, 3ch and 2tr, *1tr into each of next 14 sts, into corner 3ch sp work 2tr, 3ch and 2tr, rep from * twice more, 1tr into each of next 7 sts. Join with a ss into 3rd of 3ch. Fasten off.

This gives a firm crochet square, as used in samples 1 and 2, where the corners are emphasised by a diagonal line of holes. Samples 3 and 4 have the same square as a basis, but are made more solid by replacing the 3ch at each corner with 1ch.

Sample 1

To work the wheel motif Wrap yarn 20 times round first finger of left hand.

1st round Remove yarn carefully from finger, work 20dc into circle. Join with a ss into first dc.

2nd round 12ch, into 3rd ch from hook work 1dc, work 11dc over complete length of chain instead of into each ch, miss next dc on circle, ss into next dc, *10ch, join with a ss into 6th dc up from circle of last 'petal', 1ch, work 12dc over the complete chain, miss next dc on circle, ss into next dc, rep from * 7 times

more, 10ch, join with a ss into 6th ch up from circle of last 'petal', 1ch, work 6dc over the complete chain, join with a ss into free end of first 'petal', work 6 more dc over complete chain. Join with a ss into circle. Fasten off.

Sample 2

This is known as the Clones knot and it is often seen in Irish lace. Here we use a very different yarn to the traditional as it is easier to work with, but you will need to practise before achieving a perfect knot.
To work the knots Make 10ch. Hold the length of chain firmly between thumb and first finger of left hand, *yrh, bring hook towards you, under the length of chain and draw through a loop, rep from * approx 18 times, noting that the yarn passing over the hook and length of chain should be loosely but evenly placed to give a good looped knot. When the required number of loops have been worked, yrh and draw through all the loops on the hook, ss into the ch just behind the looped knot. Continue by making as many lengths of chain and knots as required.
A stem may be added to complete the motif, by working 14ch after the last knot has been completed, into 3rd ch from hook work 1dc, work 14dc over complete length of chain, ss into last knot. Fasten off. Arrange the knots in position on the square and stitch in position.

Sample 3

This is a simple design achieved by making several small rings.
To work the rings Wrap yarn 12 times round first finger of left hand.
Next round Remove yarn carefully from finger, work 14dc into circle. Join with a ss into first dc. Fasten off. Make as many rings as required, then work a stem to complete the design.

To work a stem Make 14ch. Into 3rd ch from hook work 1dc, work 14dc over the complete length of chain. Fasten off.
Arrange the rings and stem on the square to give the desired effect and sew in place.

Sample 4

This is known as coiled work. Take 8 thicknesses of yarn, approx 57cm (*20in*) long, to form a filling core. We worked approx 25dc over the entire core, but you can experiment with any number you desire, then take the beginning of the work and twist up and behind the hook to form a circle, ss into 5th dc worked, continue by working another 25dc over the core and make it into a circle as before.
Continue in this way until the desired shape is achieved. Fasten off yarn and arrange in place on the square.

Glittering Irish crochet bolero

Sizes

To fit 81.5/91.5[94/101.5]cm (*32/36[37/40]in*) bust

Length to centre back, 40.5[43]cm (*16[17]in*)

Sleeve seam, 30.5cm (*12in*)

The figures in brackets [] refer to the 94/101.5cm (*37/40in*) size only

Tension

4½ shells and 16 rows to 10cm (*3.9in*) over patt worked on No.2.50 (ISR) crochet hook

Materials

10[11] × 20grm balls Wendy Minuit Lurex
One No.2.50 (ISR) crochet hook
One button

Note

It is easier to work with Minuit Lurex if the ball of yarn is first placed on a central spool. This can be done by rolling up a piece of card, about 12.5cm (*5in*) square, and securing the end with sticky tape

Jacket

Using No.2.50 (ISR) crochet hook make 90[99]ch and beg at neck edge.

Base row Into 3rd ch from hook work 1dc, 1dc into each ch to end. Turn. 89[98] dc.

1st inc row 1ch to count as first dc, 1dc into each of next 7dc, *2dc into next dc, 1dc into each of next 8dc, rep from * to end, working last dc into turning ch. Turn. 98[107]dc.

Next row 1ch, *1dc into next dc, rep from * to end. Turn.

2nd inc row (buttonhole row) 1ch, 1dc into each of next 2dc, 3ch, miss 3dc, 1dc into each of next 2dc, *2dc into next dc, 1dc into each of next 9[10]dc, rep from * to end. Turn. 107[116]dc.

Next row 1ch, 1dc into each dc to end, working 3dc into 3ch loop of previous row. Turn.

3rd inc row 1ch to count as first dc, 1dc into each of next 7dc, *2dc into next dc, 1dc into each of next 10[11]dc, rep from * to end. Turn. 116[125]dc.

Next row 1ch, 1dc into each dc to end. Turn.

Commence lace patt.

Base row 1ch to count as first dc, 1dc into each of next 6dc for right front border, *5ch, miss 2dc, 1dc into next dc, rep from * to last 7dc, turn and leave these 7dc for left front border. 34[37] 5ch loops.

1st row 1ch, *into next 5ch loop work (2dc, 3ch, ss into last dc to form picot, 3dc, 1 picot, 2dc) – called 1 shell –, ss into next dc, rep from * to end, working 1dc into last dc. Turn.

2nd row 7ch, 1dc into centre dc between first 2 picots, *5ch, 1dc into centre dc between 2 picots on next shell, rep from * to end, 3ch, 1dtr into last dc. Turn.

3rd row 1ch to count as first dc, into next 3ch loop work (1dc, 1 picot, 2dc), ss into next dc, *1 shell into next 5ch loop, ss into next dc, rep from * to end, ending with 2dc, 1 picot, 2dc into 7ch loop, 1dc into 4th of 7ch. Turn.

4th row 1ch to count as first dc, *5ch, 1dc into centre dc between 2 picots on next shell, rep from * to end, 3ch, 1dtr into last dc. Turn.

These 4 rows form patt, noting that on subsequent 1st patt rows the first shell will be worked into 3ch loop and last dc will be worked into 3rd of 5ch loop. Rep them once more, then first of them again.

Shape yoke

**1st inc row Patt 6[7] loops, (always counting ½ loops at ends of rows as 1 loop), (5ch, miss next picot and 2dc, 1dc into ss between shells, 5ch, 1dc between next 2 picots – called inc 1), patt 6[6] loops, inc 1, patt 7[8] loops, inc 1, patt 6[6] loops, inc 1, patt to end. 39[42] loops. Patt 3 rows without shaping.

2nd inc row Work as given for 1st inc row, working 11[12] loops in centre-back instead of 7[8] loops. 43[46] loops. Patt 3 rows without shaping.

3rd inc row Patt 3[4] loops, *inc 1, patt 5 loops, rep from * ending last rep with 3[5] loops. Patt 3 rows without shaping.

4th inc row Patt 3[5] loops, *inc 1, patt 5 loops, rep from * ending last rep with 3[5] loops. Patt 3 rows without shaping.

5th inc row Patt 2[3] loops, *inc 1, patt 5 loops, rep from * ending last rep with 1[3] loops. 68[71] loops. Patt 3 rows without shaping.

Divide for underarm

Next row Patt 12[13] loops, *work 15[18]ch, miss 11[12] shells, 1dc between next 2 picots, *, patt 19[20] loops, rep from * to * once more, patt to end. Turn.

Next row Patt 12[13] loops, *1dc into each of next 15[18]ch, *, patt 19[20] loops, rep from * to * once more, patt to end. Turn.

Next row Patt 12[13] loops, *5ch, miss first of 15[18]dc at underarm, 1dc into next dc, (5ch, miss 3dc, 1dc into next dc) 3[4] times, 5ch, 1dc between next 2 picots, *, patt 18[19] loops, rep from * to * once more, patt to end. Turn. 51[56] loops.

Keeping patt correct, cont without shaping until 13[15] picot rows in all have been worked from underarm. Fasten off.

Sleeves

Using No.2.50 (ISR) hook and with WS of work facing, rejoin yarn to centre dc at 15 underarm dc for 1st size and between 2 centre dc of 18dc for 2nd size.

Next row (5ch, miss 3dc, 1dc into next dc) once[twice], 5ch, 1dc into next dc, (5ch, 1dc between next 2 picots) 11[12] times, 5ch, 1dc into next dc before underarm, (5ch, miss 3dc, 1dc into next dc) twice. Turn. 16[18] loops.

Cont in patt until 14 picot rows in all have been worked from underarm, ending with a picot row.

Next row (inc) Patt 1 loop, inc 1 as given for yoke, patt 5[6] loops, inc 1, patt 6[7] loops, inc 1, patt to end. Turn. 19[21] loops.

Patt 7[9] more rows without shaping. Fasten off.

To make up

Do not press. Join sleeve seams.

Edging Using No.2.50 (ISR) hook and with WS of left front facing, rejoin yarn to 7dc at neck, 1ch, 1dc into each dc to end. Turn.

Next row 1ch, 1dc into each dc to end. Turn.

Rep this row until border, slightly stretched, fits down left front to lower edge. Fasten off.

Work other side in same way. Sl st borders into place.

With RS of work facing, rejoin yarn to right front at neck edge and work 1 row ss all round neck edge. Fasten off.

Sew on button to correspond with buttonhole.

Irish motif cushions

Sizes
Each cushion measures 40.5cm (16in) square

Tension
Brown and orange motif measures 7.5cm (3in) square worked on No.2.00 (ISR) crochet hook
Turquoise and lemon motif measures 11.5cm (4½in) between widest points worked on No.2.00 (ISR) crochet hook

Materials
Both cushions 1× 20grm ball Twilley's Lyscordet in each of two colours, A and B
One No.2.00 (ISR) crochet hook
0.45 metres (½yd) of 0.90 metre (36in) wide gingham material
40.5cm (16in) square cushion pad

Brown and orange motifs
1st motif
Using No.2.00 (ISR) hook and A, make 8ch. Join with a ss into first ch to form a circle.
1st round 4ch, leaving last loop of each on hook work 2dtr into circle, yrh and draw through all loops on hook – called 1st cluster –, *4ch, leaving last loop of each on hook work 3dtr into circle, yrh and draw through all loops on hook – called 1 cluster –, rep from * 6 times more, 4ch. Join with a ss to top of 1st cluster. Break off A.
2nd round Join B with a ss into any 4ch loop, work 1st cluster into this loop, (4ch and 1 cluster) twice into same loop, *3ch, 1dc into next 4ch loop, 3ch, 1 cluster into next 4ch loop, (4ch and 1 cluster) twice into same loop, rep from * twice more, 3ch, 1dc into next 4ch loop, 3ch. Join with a ss to top of first cluster. Break off B.
3rd round Join A with a ss to next 4ch loop, 1dc into same loop, *9ch, 1dc into next 4ch loop, (5ch, 1dc into next 3ch loop) twice, 5ch, 1dc into next 4ch loop,

rep from * 3 times, omitting last dc. Join with a ss into first dc.
4th round Using A work *7tr, 5ch and 7tr into 9ch loop, 1dc into next 5ch loop, 3dc, 3ch and 3dc into next 5ch loop, 1dc into next 5ch loop, rep from * 3 times more. Join with a ss into top of first tr. Fasten off.

2nd motif
Work as given for 1st motif until 3rd round has been completed.
4th round Work 7tr into first 9ch loop, 2ch, ss into corresponding 5ch loop on 1st motif, 2ch, 7tr into same 9ch loop on 2nd motif, 1dc into next 5ch loop, 3dc into next 5ch loop, 1ch, ss into corresponding 3ch loop on 1st motif, 1ch, 3dc into same 5ch loop on 2nd motif, 1dc

into next 5ch loop, 7tr into next 9ch loop, 2ch, ss into corresponding 5ch loop on 1st motif, 2ch, 7tr into same 9ch loop on 2nd motif, complete as given for 1st motif. Fasten off.
Make and join the 3rd and 4th motifs in the same way so that they form a square.
5th motif
Work as given for 1st motif, using B instead of A and A instead of B and joining to one free side of 1st motif on 4th round.
6th motif
Work as given for 5th motif and join on the 4th round to other free side of 1st motif, also joining to 5th motif at one corner.
7th and 8th motifs

round.

3rd round 5ch, *working across back work 1dc round stem of next tr in 1st round, 5ch, rep from * 4 times more. Join with a ss round last stem, taking in first 5ch.

4th round *Into next 5ch loop work 1dc, 1htr, 5tr, 1htr and 1dc, rep from * to end.

5th round *7ch, 1dc into back of dc between petals of previous round, rep from * all round, ending with 7ch, 1dc into back of next dc between petals, taking in the base of the 7ch.

6th round Into next 7ch loop work 1dc, 1htr, 7tr, 1htr and 1dc, rep from * all round. Join with a ss into first dc. Break off A.

7th round Join in B to dc between petals, 1dc into same place, *8ch, 1dc into 4th of 7tr of next petal, 8ch, 1dc between petals, rep from * all round. Join with a ss into first dc.

8th round Ss into first 4ch, 1dc into 8ch loop, *12ch, 1dc into next 8ch loop, 1dc into next 8ch loop, rep from * omitting dc at end of last rep. Join with a ss into first dc.

9th round *1dc into each of next 6ch, 3ch, 1dc into each of next 6ch, 1dc between 2dc of previous round, rep from * to end. Join with a ss into first dc. Fasten off.

2nd motif

Work as given for 1st motif until 8th round has been completed.

9th round 1dc into each of first 6ch, 1ch, ss into 3ch loop on 1st motif, 1ch, 1dc into each of next 6ch on 2nd motif, work as given for 1st motif, joining as before on the next 3ch loop, complete as given for 1st motif. Fasten off.

Make 7 more motifs, joining as before into 3 rows with 3 motifs in each.

Small motif

Using No.2.00 (ISR) hook and A, make 5ch. Join with a ss into first ch to form a circle.

1st round 3ch, 11tr into circle. Join with a ss into 3rd of 3ch.

2nd round 1dc into sp between 3ch and next tr, *8ch, miss next 2 sp between tr, 1dc into sp between next 2tr, rep from * to end. Join with a ss into same sp as first dc.

3rd round Ss into first 4ch, 1dc into 8ch loop, *6ch, 1dc into join of large motifs, 6ch, 1dc into next 8ch loop on small motif, rep from * 3 times more, working last dc into first dc.

Fasten off. Make 3 more small motifs and join to large motifs in the same way.

To make up

Complete as given for other cushion.

Work as given for 5th motif, but join to the two free sides of 3rd motif and to each other at one corner.

Small flowers

Using A only, work as given for 1st motif until 1st round has been completed.

2nd round Work 3dc, 3ch and 3dc into each 4ch loop to last loop, 3dc into last loop, 1ch, ss to free 5ch loop of motif of opposite colour, 1ch, 3dc into same 4ch loop. Join with a ss to first dc. Fasten off. Make 3 more motifs in A and 2 in B.

To make up

Cut a piece of gingham 86.5cm (*34in*) square, fold in half and seam along 3 edges, leaving 1.5cm (½*in*) turnings. Turn

to RS and insert a piece of card into the case to make pinning the motifs easier. Pin crochet in position on cover, then sew using a matching colour. Place pad in cover, turn in raw edges and oversew the seam.

Turquoise and lemon motifs
1st motif

Using No.2.00 (ISR) hook and A, make 8ch. Join with a ss into first ch to form a circle.

1st round 6ch to count as first tr and 3ch, 1tr into circle, *3ch, 1tr into circle, rep from * 3 times more, 3ch. Join with a ss into 3rd of 6ch.

2nd round *Into next 3ch loop work 1dc, 1htr, 3tr, 1htr and 1dc, rep from * all

COLOURED PATTERNS
ZIGZAG STRIPES

Zig-zag crochet designs

The technique of working this very attractive form of patterning is very different to those learnt in previous chapters. Crochet formed in this way with a double knitting yarn gives a very decorative, thick fabric which is suitable for jackets and jerkins. The same technique could be worked in Lurex for evening bags and belts, or in raffia yarns for more casual accessories. Instructions for working the technique and several variations on the design are given here.

Sample 1

Two colours of double knitting yarn, A and B, have been used for this sample. Using No.3.50 (ISR) hook and A, make a chain with multiples of 10 + 2 stitches.
1st row Into 3rd ch from hook work 1dc, 1dc into each ch to end. Turn.
2nd row 1ch to count as first dc, miss first st, 1dc into each st, ending with last dc into turning ch. Turn.
3rd–6th rows As 2nd. Do not break off A.
7th row Using B, 1ch to count as first dc, *1dc into next st missing 1 row, noting that each time the hook is inserted into a stitch missing a row, the yarn forming the loop on the hook must be extended to meet the

previous st of the working row, 1dc into next st missing 2 rows, 1dc into next st missing 3 rows, 1dc into next st missing 4 rows, 1dc into next st missing 5 rows, 1dc into next st missing 4 rows, 1dc into next st missing 3 rows, 1dc into next st missing 2 rows, 1dc into next st missing 1 row, 1dc into next st, rep from * to end. Turn.
8th–12th rows Using B, as 2nd.
13th row 1ch (this does not count as first st), 1dc into first st missing 5 rows, *1dc into next st missing 4 rows, 1dc into next st missing 3 rows, 1dc into next st missing 2 rows, 1dc into next st missing 1 row, 1dc into next st, 1dc into next st missing 1 row, 1dc into next st missing 2 rows, 1dc into next st missing 3 rows, 1dc into next st missing 4 rows, 1dc into next st missing 5 rows, rep from * to end. Turn.

14th–18th rows Using A, as 2nd.
The 7th–18th rows inclusive are repeated throughout.
Note It is a good idea at the beginning of a row when changing colour to wind the working colour around the yarn not in use in order to make a neat edge to the work.

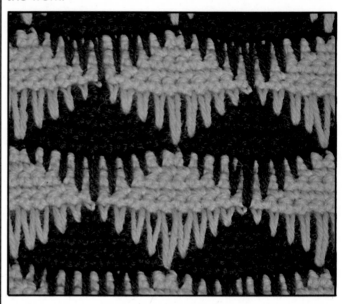

Sample 2

Here we have used three colours of a double knitting yarn, A, B and C. Using No.3.50 (ISR) hook and A, make a chain with multiples of 14 + 4 stitches.
1st–6th rows As 1st–6th rows of sample 1. Do not break off A.

7th row Using B, 1ch to count as first dc, 1dc into each of next 2 sts,*1dc into next st missing 1 row, 1dc into next st missing 2 rows, 1dc into next st missing 3 rows, 1dc into next st missing 4 rows, 1dc into each of next 3 sts missing 5 rows, 1dc into next st missing 4 rows, 1dc into next st missing 3 rows, 1dc into next st missing 2 rows, 1dc into next st missing 1 row, 1dc into each of next 3 sts, rep from * to end. Turn.

8th–12th rows Using B, as 2nd row of sample 1. Do not break off B.

13th–18th rows Using C, as 7th–12th rows. Do not break off C.

19th–24th rows Using A, as 7th–12th rows. The 7th–24th rows are repeated throughout.

Sample 3

The four colours of double knitting yarn used here are denoted as A, B, C and D. Using No.4.50 (ISR) hook and A, make a chain with multiples of 6+1 stitches.

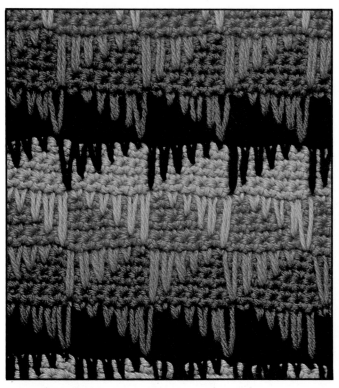

1st–6th rows As 1st–6th rows of sample 1. Do not break off A.

7th row 1ch to count as first dc, *1dc into next st missing 1 row, 1dc into next st missing 2 rows, 1dc into next st missing 3 rows, 1dc into next st missing 4 rows, 1dc into next st missing 5 rows, 1dc into next st, rep from * to end, omitting 1dc at end of last rep. Turn.

8th–12th rows Using B, as 2nd row of sample 1. Do not break off B.

13th row Using C, 1ch (this does not count as first st), *1dc into first st missing 5 rows, 1dc into next st missing 4 rows, 1dc into next st missing 3 rows, 1dc into next st missing 2 rows, 1dc into next st missing 1 row, 1dc into next st, rep from * to end. Turn.

14th–18th rows Using C, as 2nd row of sample 1. Do not break off C.

19th–24th rows Using D, as 7th–12th rows. Do not break off D.

25th–30th rows Using A, as 13th–18th rows.

The 7th–30th rows inclusive form the pattern and colour sequence for this design.

Sample 4

Shiny and matt raffia in four colours, A, B, C and D have been used for this unusual sample. Using No.3.50 (ISR) hook and A, make a chain with multiples of 6+2 stitches.

1st–4th rows As 1st–4th rows of sample 1. Do not break off A.

5th row Using B, 1ch (this does not count as first st), 1dc into first st, *1dc into next st missing 1 row, 1dc into next st missing 2 rows, 1dc into next st missing 3 rows, 1dc into next st missing 2 rows, 1dc into next st missing 1 row, 1dc into next st, rep from * to end. Turn.

6th–8th rows Using B, as 2nd row of sample 1. Do not break off B.

9th row Using C, 1ch (this does not count as first st), 1dc into first st missing 3 rows, *1dc into next st missing 2 rows, 1dc into next st missing 1 row, 1dc into next st, 1dc into next st missing 1 row, 1dc into next st missing 2 rows, 1dc into next st missing 3 rows, rep from * to end. Turn.

10th–12th rows Using C, as 2nd row of sample 1. Do not break off C.

13th–16th rows Using D, as 5th–8th rows. Do not break off D.

17th–20th rows Using A, as 9th–12th rows.

The 5th–20th rows inclusive are repeated throughout.

CHEVRON DESIGNS AND BRAIDS

More zig-zag designs in crochet

A different kind of zig-zag design which is very simple to work is illustrated in this chapter. Both wavy lines and pronounced zig-zags are formed by this method, either to give an all-over patterned fabric or a strip of crochet braid.

If double knitting yarn is used, this crochet work makes beautiful bed covers, rugs and cushion covers or could be used as a pattern on a fashion garment such as a jacket where a scalloped edge is required as a design feature. More unusual yarns, string and raffia in particular, could be used to make bags, belts and shoe uppers.

Our samples show different stitches for you to experiment with before starting an article of your choice.

Sample 1

Using No.4.50 (ISR) hook and double knitting yarn in various colours, make a length of chain with multiples of 17 + 4 stitches.

1st row Into 4th ch from hook work 3tr, **1tr into each of next 5ch, *yrh and insert hook into next ch, yrh and draw through a loop, yrh and draw through first 2 loops on hook, yrh and insert hook into next ch, yrh and draw through a loop, yrh and draw through first 2 loops on hook, yrh and draw through all 3 loops on hook – called dec 1tr –, *, rep from * to * twice more, 1tr into each of next 5ch, 4tr into next ch, rep from ** to end. Turn.

2nd row 3ch to count as first tr, miss first 2 sts, 3tr into next st, *1tr into each of next 5 sts, dec 3tr over next 6 sts, 1tr into each of next 5 sts, 4tr into next st, rep from * ending last rep with 4tr into 3rd of 3ch. Turn.

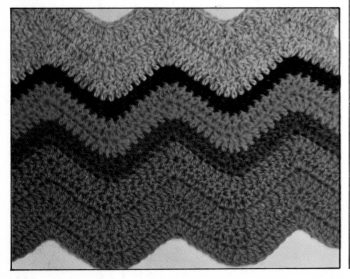

Repeat 2nd row throughout, alternating the colours as required. You will see that the pattern gives a flowing, wavy line.

Sample 2

This design, which gives a very ribbed zig-zag pattern, has been worked throughout in four rows each of two colours of double knitting yarn, A and B. Using No.4.50 (ISR) hook and A, make a length of chain with multiples of 16 + 4 stitches.

1st row Insert hook into 3rd ch from hook, yrh and draw through a loop, insert hook into next ch, yrh and draw through a loop, yrh and draw through all 3 loops on hook, **1dc into each of next 6ch, 3dc

into next ch, 1dc into each of next 6ch, *insert hook into next ch, yrh and draw through a loop, *, rep from * to * twice more, yrh and draw through all 4 loops on hook – called dec 2dc –, rep from * to end. Turn.

Note From this point, insert hook into back loop only of each st throughout.

2nd row 2ch, insert hook into st at base of ch, yrh and draw through a loop, insert hook into next st, yrh and draw through a loop, yrh and draw through all loops on hook, *1dc into each of next 6 sts, 3dc into next dc, 1dc into each of next 6 sts, dec 2dc over next 3 sts, rep from * ending last rep by working into 2nd of 2ch. Turn. The 2nd row is repeated throughout the design.

Sample 3

Two colours of a double knitting yarn, A and B, have been used for this sample. Using No.4.50 (ISR) hook and A, make a length of chain with multiples of 13 + 6 stitches.

1st row Yrh and insert into 4th ch from hook, yrh and draw through a loop, yrh and draw through first 2 loops on hook, *yrh and insert into next ch, yrh and draw through a loop, yrh and draw through first 2 loops on hook, *, rep from * to *, yrh and draw through 4 loops on hook, **1tr into each of next 4ch, 4tr into next ch, 1tr into each of next 4ch, rep from * to * 4 times, yrh and draw through all 5 loops on hook – called dec 3tr –, rep from ** to end, 2ch. Fasten off A. Do not turn.

2nd row Join B to 3rd of 3ch at beg of previous row, 1ch to count as first dc, 1dc into front loop of each st to end. Fasten off B. Do not turn.

3rd row Join A to first ch at beg of previous row, 3ch, working into back loop only of each st in previous alternate row, *yrh and insert into next st, yrh and draw through a loop, yrh and draw through first 2 loops on hook, *, rep from * to * twice more, yrh and draw through all loops on hook, **1tr into each of next 4 sts, 4tr into next st, 1tr into each of next 4 sts, dec 3tr over next 4 sts, rep from ** to end, 2ch. Fasten off A. Do not turn.

The 2nd and 3rd rows complete the design and should be repeated throughout.

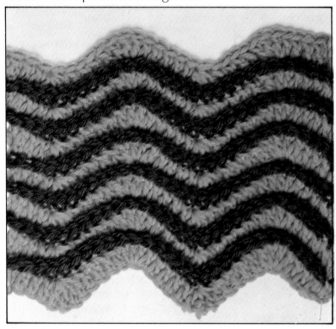

Sample 4

Sometimes zig-zag designs require at least one straight edge, as on a belt. Here our sample illustrates this method of work with two zig-zag lines between the straight edges. Two colours of a double knitting yarn, A and B, have been used so that it is easy to distinguish between the straight lines and zig-zag.
Using No.4.50 (ISR) hook and A, make a length of chain with multiples of 13 + 4 stitches. The 4 extra

chains are not turning chains but are for the 4 slip stitches at each end of the pattern repeat.

1st row Miss first ch, ss into each of next 3ch, *1dc into next ch, 1htr into next ch, 1tr into next ch, 1dtr into next ch, 1tr tr into next ch, 1dtr into next ch, 1tr into next ch, 1htr into next ch, 1dc into next ch, ss into each of next 4ch, rep from * to end. Turn. Break off A.

2nd row Join B to first st, 3ch, *yrh and insert into next st, yrh and draw through a loop, yrh and draw through first 2 loops on hook, *, rep from * to * twice more, yrh and draw through all loops on hook, **1tr into each of next 4 sts, 4tr into next st, 1tr into each of next 4 sts, rep from * to * 4 times, yrh and draw through all loops on hook, rep from ** to end. Turn.

3rd row As 2nd, working 4tr group between 2nd and 3rd tr of 4tr group of previous row. Fasten off B.

4th row This shows how to end a zig-zag design with a straight edge. Join A to last st worked in previous row, 4ch to count as first tr tr, *1dtr into next st, 1tr into next st, 1htr into next st, 1dc into next st, ss into each of next 4 sts, 1dc into next st, 1htr into next st, 1tr into next st, 1dtr into next st, 1tr tr into next st, rep from * to end. Fasten off.

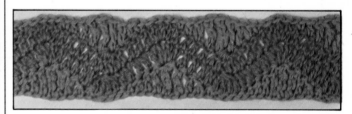

Sample 5

Here is one of the many interesting effects that can be achieved using the techniques here. Make two lengths of crochet by working the first two rows as given for sample 2, using only 4dc between each increase and decrease. Then twist the lengths around each other to give this plaited effect which could be used as a braid or a belt.

Crochet dress with chevron skirt

Sizes

To fit 81.5[86.5:91.5:96.5:101.5]cm
(32[34:36:38:40]in) bust
Length to shoulder, 95[96.5:98:99:100.5]
cm (37½[38:38½:39:39½]in)
Long sleeve seam, 40.5[42:42:43:43]cm
(16[16½:16½:17:17]in)
Short sleeve seam, 10cm (4in)
The figures in brackets [ ] refer to the
86.5 (34), 91.5 (36), 96.5 (38) and 101.5cm
(40in) sizes respectively

Tension

20 sts and 24 rows to 10cm (3.9in) over
dc worked on No.3.50 (ISR) crochet hook

Materials

Dress with long sleeves 18[19:20:21:22]
× 1oz balls Lee Target Motoravia 4 ply
or 17[18:19:20:21] × 20grm balls Lee
Target Duo 4 ply Crepe Tricel Nylon in
main shade, A
6[6:6:7:7] × 1oz balls or 6[7:8:9:9] ×
20grm balls of contrast colour, B
Dress with short sleeves 16[17:18:19:20]
× 1oz balls Lee Target Motoravia 4 ply or
15[16:17:18:19] × 20grm balls Lee Target
Duo 4 ply Crepe Tricel Nylon in main
shade, A
4[4:5:5:6] × 1oz balls or 5[6:6:7:8] ×
20grm balls of contrast colour, B
One No.3.00 (ISR) crochet hook
One No.3.50 (ISR) crochet hook
One No.4.00 (ISR) crochet hook
1 × 55cm (22in) zip fastener

Dress

(worked in one piece to underarm)
Using No.4.00 (ISR) hook and A, make
244[260:276:292:308] ch for entire lower
edge.
1st row (RS) Into 4th ch from hook work
1tr, *1tr into each of next 6ch, miss 3ch,
1tr into each of next 6ch, 3tr into next
ch, rep from * ending last rep with 2 tr
into last ch instead of 3. Turn.
2nd row 3ch to count as first tr, 1tr into
st at base of ch, *1tr into each of next
6tr, miss 2tr, 1tr into each of next 6tr,
3tr into next tr, rep from * ending last
rep with 2tr into 3rd of 3ch instead
of 3. Turn.
The 2nd row forms the patt. Cont in

patt until work measures 15cm (6in)
from beg.
Next row 3ch, miss first tr, 1tr into each
of next 6tr, *miss 2tr, 1tr into each of
next 13tr, rep from * to last 9tr, miss
2tr, 1tr into each of next 6tr, 1tr into 3rd
of 3ch. Turn.
Next row 3ch, 1tr into st at base of ch,
*1tr into each of next 5tr, miss 2tr, 1tr
into each of next 5tr, 3tr into next tr,
rep from * ending last rep with 2tr into
3rd of 3ch. Turn.
The last row forms the patt. Cont in
patt until work measures 30.5cm (12in)
from beg.
Next row 3ch, miss first tr, 1tr into each
of next 5tr, *miss 2tr, 1tr into each of
next 11tr, rep from * to last 8tr, miss 2tr
1tr into each of next 5tr, 1tr into 3rd
of 3ch. Turn.
Next row 3ch, 1tr into st at base of ch,
*1tr into each of next 4tr, miss 2tr, 1tr
into each of next 4tr, 3tr into next tr,
rep from * ending last rep with 2tr into
3rd of 3ch. Turn.
Cont in patt as now set until work
measures 45.5cm (18in) from beg.
Next row 3ch, miss first tr, 1tr into each
of next 4tr, *miss 2tr, 1tr into each of
next 9tr, rep from * to last 7tr, miss 2tr,
1tr into each of last 4tr, 1tr into 3rd of
3ch. Turn.
Next row 3ch, 1tr into st at base of ch,
*1tr into each of next 3tr, miss 2tr,
1tr into each of next 3tr, 3tr into next
tr, rep from * ending last rep with 2tr
into 3rd of 3ch. Turn.
Cont in patt as now set until work
measures 53.5cm (21in) from beg, ending
with a WS row. Change to No.3.50 (ISR)
hook.

Shape waist

1st row 1ch to count as first dc, miss
first st, *1dc into next tr, 1htr into next tr,
1tr into next tr, 1dtr into each of next
2tr, 1tr into next tr, 1htr into next tr,
1dc into next tr, miss next tr, rep from *
to end working 1dc into 3rd of 3ch.
Turn. 122[130:138:146:154] sts.
2nd row (eyelet hole row) 3ch to count
as first tr, miss first st, 1tr into next st,
*1ch, miss next st, 1tr into each of next
3 sts, rep from * to end. Turn.
3rd row 1ch to count as first dc, miss

first st, work 1dc into each tr and ch
sp to end. Turn.
4th row 1ch to count as first dc, miss
first st, 1dc into each dc to end. Turn.
Join in B. Using B, rep 4th row twice.
Using A, rep 4th row twice. The last 4
rows form the stripe patt for the bodice
which is repeated throughout.

Shape bodice

Next row 1ch, miss first st, 1dc into each
of next 28[30:32:34:36]dc, 2dc into each
of next 2dc, 1dc into each of next 60[64:68:
72:76]dc, 2dc into each of next 2dc, 1dc
into each of next 29[31:33:35:37]dc.
Turn.

Next row Work in dc.

Next row 1ch, miss first st, 1dc into each
of next 29[31:33:35:37] sts, 2dc into each
of next 2dc, 1dc into each of next 62[66:70:
74:78]dc, 2dc into each of next 2dc, 1dc
into each of next 30[32:34:36:38]dc.
Turn.
Cont inc 4dc in this way on foll alt rows
until there are 138[146:158:166:178] sts,
then on every foll 4th row until there
are 166[174:186:194:206] sts. Cont without
shaping until work measures 78.5cm
(31in) from beg, ending with a WS row.

Divide for back and front armholes

Next row 1ch, miss first st, 1dc into each
of next 38[40:43:45:48]dc, turn.
Cont on these 39[41:44:46:49] sts for left
back.
Next row 1ch, miss first 2 sts, 1dc into
each dc to end. Turn.
Next row 1ch, miss first st, 1dc into each
dc to last 2dc, miss next dc, 1dc into
last st. Turn.
Rep last 2 rows 3[3:4:4:5] times more.
31[33:34:36:37] sts. Cont without shaping
until armhole measures 16.5[18:19:20.5:
21.5]cm (6½[7:7½:8:8½]in) from beg,
ending at back edge.
Shape shoulder
Next row Patt to last 8 sts, turn.
Next row Ss into each of next 8[10:11:
13:14] sts, patt to end. Fasten off.
With RS of work facing, return to main
part, miss 5 sts for underarm, rejoin yarn
to next st and work 1ch, 1dc into each
of next 77[81:87:91:97]dc, turn. Cont on
these 78[82:88:92:98] sts for front.
Next row 1ch, miss first 2 sts, 1dc into
each dc to last 2dc, miss next dc, 1dc

into last st. Turn.

Rep last row 7[7:9:9:11] times more. 62[66:68:72:74] sts. Cont without shaping until work measures 14 rows less than back to shoulder shaping.

Shape neck
Next row Patt across 23[25:26:28:29] sts. Turn.

Next row 1ch, miss first 2 sts, patt to end. Turn.

Next row Patt to last 2 sts, miss next dc, 1dc into last st. Turn.

Rep last 2 rows twice more, then first of them again. 16[18:19:21:22] sts. Cont without shaping until work measures same as back to shoulder, ending at armhole edge.

Shape shoulder
Next row Ss into each of next 8 sts, patt to end. Fasten off.

With RS of work facing return to rem sts at front, miss centre 16 sts for front neck, rejoin yarn to next st, 1ch, patt to end. Turn. Complete to match first side of neck, reversing shapings.

With RS of work facing return to main part, miss 5 sts for underarm, rejoin yarn to next st, 1ch, patt to end for right back. Complete to match left back, reversing shapings.

Long sleeves
Using No.3.00 (ISR) hook and A, make 39 [41:43:45:47]ch.

1st row Into 3rd ch from hook work 1dc, 1dc into each ch to end. Turn. 38[40:42:44:46] sts.

2nd row 1ch to count as first dc, miss first st, 1dc into each dc to end, finishing with last dc into turning ch. Turn.

Join in B. Using B, rep 2nd row twice. Using A, rep 2nd row twice more. These 4 rows form the stripe patt which is repeated throughout. Cont in patt until work measures 5cm (2in) from beg. Change to No.3.50 (ISR) hook. Cont in patt, inc one dc at each end of next and every foll 6th row until there are 60[64:68:72:76] sts. Cont without shaping until work measures 40.5[42:42:43:43]cm (16[16½:16½:17:17]in) from beg.

Shape top
1st row Ss into each of next 4 sts, 1ch, patt to last 3 sts, turn.

2nd row Patt to end. Turn.

3rd row 1ch, miss 2 sts, 1dc into each st to last 2 sts, miss next dc, 1dc into last st. Turn.

Rep 2nd and 3rd rows until 36[36:40:40: 44] sts rem, then rep 3rd row until 14 sts rem. Fasten off.

Short sleeves
Using No.3.50 (ISR) hook and A, make 53[57:61:65:69]ch.

1st row Into 3rd ch from hook work 1dc, 1dc into each ch to end. Turn. 52[56:60: 64:68] sts.

2nd row As 2nd row of long sleeves. Join in B and working in stripe sequence as given for bodice, inc one dc at each end of next and every foll 6th row until there are 60[64:68:72:76] sts. Cont without shaping until work measures 10cm (4in) from beg.

Shape top
Work as given for long sleeves.

To make up
Press each piece according to manufacturer's instructions. Join shoulder and sleeve seams. Set in sleeves.

Neck edging Using No.3.00 (ISR) hook and A, work 5 rows dc evenly round neck edge.

Sew in zip, joining rem back seam. Using 6 strands of A tog, make a twisted cord approx 152.5cm (60in) long and thread through eyelet holes at waist. Press seams.

CHECK PATTERNS

Check patterns in crochet

Effective check crochet patterns in one or more colours may be worked which, because of the method used, form a thick fabric suitable for warm outer garments such as coats, jackets and skirts. The stitches used to form the checks pass over previous rows so forming a double fabric in some designs. Some of the designs may be reversible and this should be taken into account when deciding on the kind of garment which you are going to make.

Double knitting yarn and a No.4.50 (ISR) crochet hook are recommended for the samples which you see illustrated. Samples 2 and 3 are worked from one side, therefore the crochet could be worked in continuous rounds without turning the work or breaking the yarn at the end of each row. This technique would be ideal for making a skirt as it would avoid any side seams.

Sample 1

Make 26ch.

1st row Into 4th ch from hook work 1tr, 1tr into each ch to end. Turn. 24tr.

2nd row 3ch to count as first tr, miss first tr, (1tr into next tr inserting the hook from the front of the work horizontally from right to left under the vertical bar of the tr in the previous row so that the hook is on the front of the work) 3 times, (1tr into next tr inserting the hook from the back of the work from right to left over the vertical bar of the tr in the previous row so that

the hook is on the back of the work) 4 times, cont in this way working 4tr to the front and 4tr to the back of the work to the end of the row, working last tr into 3rd of the 3ch. Turn.

3rd row As 2nd.

4th row 3ch to count as first tr, miss first tr, work 1tr to the back of each of the next 3tr, work 1tr to the front of each of the next 4tr, cont in this way so reversing the check effect to the end of the row, working the last tr into 3rd of the 3ch. Turn.

5th row As 4th.

Rows 2 to 5 form the pattern and are repeated throughout.

Sample 2

This is worked in 2 colours, A and B. With A, make 26ch.

1st row Into 3rd ch from hook work 1dc, 1 dc into each ch to end. 25dc. Fasten off yarn. Do not turn.

Note Unless otherwise stated, work into the back loop only of each st to end of design.

2nd row Join B to beg of previous row, 1ch to count as first dc, miss first st, 1dc into each st to end. Fasten off yarn. Do not turn work.

3rd and 4th rows As 2nd.

5th row Join A to beg of previous row. 1ch to count as first dc, miss first st, insert hook under horizontal front loop of next st, yrh and draw through a loop, (insert hook under horizontal front loop of st immediately below st just worked into, yrh and draw

through a loop) 3 times, (yrh and draw through first 2 loops on hook) 4 times – 1 connected quad tr has been worked –, *1dc into each of next 3 sts, 1 connected quad tr into next st, rep from * to last 2 sts, 1dc into each of next 2 sts. Fasten off yarn. Do not turn work.

6th to 8th rows As 2nd.

9th row Join A to beg of previous row, 1ch to count as first dc, miss first st, 1dc into each of next 3 sts, *1 connected quad tr into next st, 1dc into each of next 3 sts, rep from * to last st, 1dc into last st. Fasten off yarn. Do not turn.

Rows 2 to 9 form the pattern and are repeated throughout.

Sample 3

Three colours are used for this sample, A, B and C. Unless otherwise stated, insert the hook into the back loop only of each st. With A, make 26ch.

1st row Into 3rd ch from hook work 1dc, 1dc into each ch to end. 25dc. Fasten off yarn. Do not turn.

2nd row Join A to beg of previous row. 1ch to count as first dc, miss first st, 1dc into each st to end. Fasten off yarn. Do not turn.

3rd row As 2nd.

4th row Join B to beg of previous row. 1ch to count as first dc, miss first st, 1dc into next st, yrh 3 times, insert hook under horizontal front loop of next st in 4th row below, yrh and draw through a loop, (yrh and draw through first 2 loops on hook) 4 times – 1 surface tr tr has been worked –, 1 surface tr tr into each of next 2 sts, *1dc into each of next 3 sts, 1 surface tr tr into each of next 3 sts, rep from * to last 2 sts, 1dc into each of next 2 sts. Fasten off yarn. Do not turn.

5th and 6th rows With B, as 2nd.

7th row Join C to beg of previous row. 1ch to count as first dc, miss first st, 1dc into each of next 4 sts, *1 surface tr tr into each of next 3 sts, 1dc into each of next 3 sts, rep from * to last 2 sts, 1dc into each of last 2 sts.

Fasten off yarn. Do not turn.

8th and 9th rows With C, as 2nd.

10th to 12th rows With A, as 4th to 6th rows.

13th to 15th rows With B, as 7th to 9th rows.

16th to 18th rows With C, as 4th to 6th rows.

Rows 1 to 18 form the pattern and colour sequence for this sample.

Sample 4

Two colours, A and B, are used for this sample. With A, make 22ch.

1st row Into 3rd ch from hook work 1dc, 1dc into each ch to end. Turn. 21dc.

2nd row 1ch to count as first dc, miss first dc, 1dc into front loop only of each st to end. Turn. Fasten off yarn.

3rd row Join in B. 2ch to count as first htr, miss first st, 1htr into each st to end placing hook under both loops. Fasten off yarn. Do not turn.

4th row Join A to beg of previous row. 1ch to count as first dc, (1dtr into front loop only of next st in 3rd row below) twice, 1dc into back loop only of next 3 sts, *1dtr into each of next 3 sts placing the hook as before, 1dc into back loop only of next 3 sts, rep from * to last 3 sts, 1dtr into each of next 2 sts, 1dc into last st. Fasten off yarn. Do not turn work.

5th row As 3rd.

6th row Join A to beg of previous row. 1ch to count as first dc, 1dc into back loop only of next 2 sts, *(1dtr into front loop only of next st in 3rd row below) 3 times, 1dc into back loop only of next 3 sts, rep from * to end. Fasten off. Do not turn.

7th row As 3rd.

Rows 4 to 7 form the pattern.

CROCHET WITH LEATHER AND SUEDE

In this chapter we have used circular leather motifs and crochet stitches together to give some interesting results. This type of work lends itself especially to the making of belts, bags, jerkins and waistcoats. A firm, good quality leather, suede or grain skin should be chosen to withstand the pull of the crochet work. Most local handicraft shops will sell off-cut leather pieces suitable for this purpose. First mark the shape on the wrong side of the skin by drawing round a circular object with a pencil. Cut out the circles with a sharp pair of scissors to avoid making a rough edge. You will need a special tool, called a leather punch, to make the holes which must be evenly spaced around the circle, but not too near the edge. Also make sure that the holes are the correct size to take the yarn and crochet hook which you are using.

We have used various sized circles decorated with a double knitting yarn, string and a lurex yarn, and a No.2.00 (ISR) crochet hook. There are a number of methods for working crochet round leather circles which are demonstrated here, together with instructions for joining the circles.

Sample 1
This illustrates a 4cm (1½in) leather circle with the holes cut out ready for work to commence.

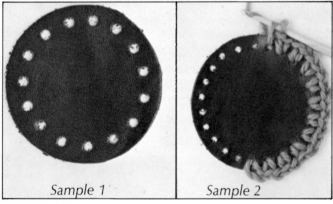

Sample 1   *Sample 2*

Sample 2
This is a 5.5cm (2¼in) circle with the surrounding crochet in progress.

To work the crochet Hold the leather circle so that the right side is facing you and place the working yarn behind the circle, insert hook through any hole, yrh and draw through hole, yrh and draw through loop on hook, 2ch, *insert hook into next hole, yrh and draw yarn through hole, yrh and draw. yarn through both loops on hook – 1dc has been worked into the hole –, 1ch, rep from * until the circle is complete. Join with a ss into first ch to neaten. Fasten off.

Sample 3
The double crochet edging round this circle is now complete.

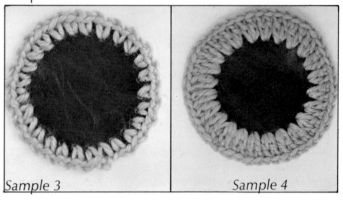

Sample 3   *Sample 4*

Sample 4
Using the same technique as described in sample 2, work 3ch at the beginning of the edging and work 1tr into the same hole, *2tr into next hole, rep from * to the end of the circle. Join with a ss into 3rd of 3ch. Fasten off.

Sample 5
Here is a grouping of circles ranging in sizes from 2.5cm (1in) to 5.5cm (2¼in). The surrounding stitches vary in depth to give a 'clam' appearance.

Begin by working 2ch into the first hole, 1dc into each of next 2 holes with 1ch between them, then continue by working 2 sts into each hole and increase the stitch depth by working into the same number of holes in each of htr, tr and dtr, then decrease the st size in the same way. The number of sts in each group will have to be varied according to the size of the circle and number of holes.

Samples 6, 7, 8 and 9 show a more experimental way to edge the leather. These would make ideal edgings for a plain leather jerkin.

Sample 6

1st round Beg with 2ch and 1dc into first hole, 2dc into each hole all round. Join with a ss into 2nd of 2ch.

2nd round 2ch, (yrh and insert into st at base of ch, yrh and draw through a loop extending it for 1cm ($\frac{3}{8}$in), twice, yrh and draw through all 5 loops on hook, 1ch, miss next st, *yrh and insert into next st, yrh and draw through a loop extending it for 1cm ($\frac{3}{8}$in), (yrh and insert into same st as last, yrh and draw through an extended loop) twice, yrh and draw through all 7 loops on hook, 1ch, miss next st, rep from * to end of circle. Join with a ss into 2nd of 2ch.

3rd round 1ch to count as first dc, *2dc into next sp between bobbles, 1dc into top of next bobble, rep from * to end, 2dc into next sp. Join with a ss into first ch. Fasten off.

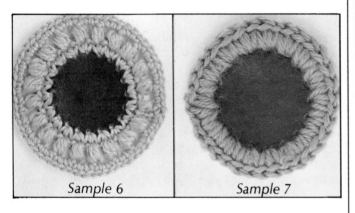

Sample 6   *Sample 7*

Sample 7

Cut 8 thicknesses of yarn to fit all round the outer edge of the circle.

Next round Working over 8 thicknesses of yarn to produce a rounded effect, commence with 2ch and 1dc into first hole, 2dc into each hole to end of round. Join with a ss into 2nd of 2ch. Fasten off.

Sample 8

Two colours, A and B, were used for this sample.

1st round Using A, beg with 3ch and 1tr into first hole, 2tr into each hole to end of round. Join with a ss into 3rd of 3ch.

2nd round Join in B. Work 1dc into each st, working from left to right (i.e. working backwards round circle) instead of right to left. Fasten off.

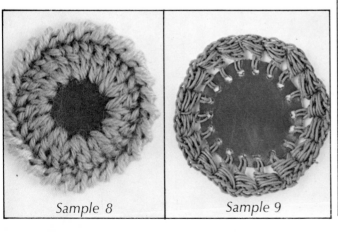

Sample 8   *Sample 9*

Sample 9

Green parcel string was used for this sample.

1st round Beg with 4ch into first hole, (yrh and take hook in front of chain, round to the back and yrh) 3 times, yrh and draw through all 7 loops on hook, 1ch, *1tr into next hole, (yrh and take hook in front of tr, round to the back and yrh) 3 times, yrh and draw through all 7 loops on hook, 1ch, rep from *.to end of round. Join with a ss into 3rd of 4ch. Fasten off.

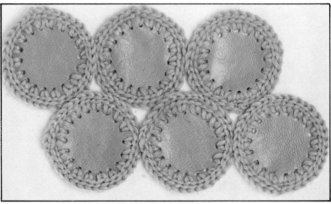

Sample 10

1st round Beg with 2ch, then work 1dc and 1ch into each hole to end of round. Join with a ss into 2nd of 2ch.

2nd round Ss into back loop only of each st to end of round.

To join the circles At the point where two circles are to be joined on the 2nd round, insert the hook into the next st of the circle on which you are working and then into any stitch of the circle to be joined, yrh and draw though all loops on hook. In our sample three stitches were used at each joining point. Our circles were all the same size, but if there are a variety of sizes then they may be joined in the same way.

Sample 11

This gold belt illustrates the method of edging used in sample 7. Twelve circles, each 5cm (2in) in diameter were used to fit a 68.5cm (27in) waist. Work round half the circle in crochet before joining on to the next circle, and when the complete length has been worked, the return crochet is worked on the second half of each circle.

Brass rings are used as a fastening with a cord worked in double chain threaded through to link them.

LEATHER OR PVC PROJECTS

The technique of working crochet around leather circles was dealt with in the last chapter, and now we shall show you more ideas for using this technique with a variety of shapes and materials.

PVC is an interesting fabric to work with as it has a very glossy surface which is a good contrast to most crochet yarns. Also it has the additional advantage that it can be cut without the edges fraying in the same way as leather. There are two types of PVC which are available, one with and one without a light backing fabric, and both are suitable to use.

To make the satchel
You will need four pieces of PVC, two measuring 20.5cm (*8 inches*) by 26.5cm (*10½ inches*) for the outer piece and lining and another two measuring 40.5cm (*16 inches*) by 26.5cm (*10½ inches*). The larger piece is for the back and folds over to form the flap, and should have all the corners rounded. Only the corners of the lower edge of the smaller piece (front) need to be rounded.

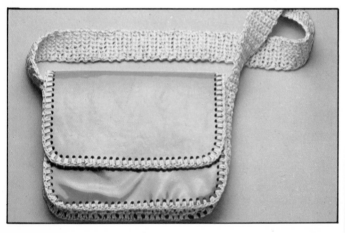

A middle layer of thick bonded interfacing is stuck with an adhesive suitable for fabric between the outer PVC and the lining. The three layers are then treated as one. Holes are punched evenly all round the PVC pieces at least 0.5cm (¼ *inch*) in from the edge.

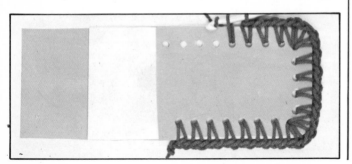

The back and front are linked with a crochet gusset which extends to form the handle.

To work the gusset Using No.4.00 (ISR) crochet hook and a very strong knitting yarn or string (we used a fine ribbon similar to Russia braid), make 9ch.

Next row Into 3rd ch from hook work 1dc, 1dc into each ch to end. Turn.

Next row 1ch to count as first dc, 1dc into each st to end. Turn.

Rep last row until work measures 145cm (*57 inches*) from beg. Fasten off. Join 2 short ends to form a circle.

To work the edging and join the sections together
Begin with a slip loop on the hook and hold the bag section with RS towards you, insert hook from front to back into first hole at right hand side of flap, yrh and draw through a loop, yrh and draw through both loops on hook – 1dc has been worked into the hole –, *1ch, work 1dc into next hole, rep from * to halfway down first long side (i.e. where back begins), then join bag on to gusset by placing hook through next hole as before and also through edge of gusset and complete the st in the normal way, cont in this way until all the back and flap section has been worked. Work round the front section and join to the gusset in the same way.

To make the leather belt
The same techniques have been incorporated into the making of a belt. According to the size required, you will need approximately ten rectangles of leather each 4.5cm (*1¾ inches*) by 6.5cm (*2½ inches*). In addition a strong bonded interfacing is again stuck to the wrong side of each shape.

To work the crochet Using a No.3.50 (ISR) hook, a lurex yarn and with the RS of the shape facing you, insert the hook from front to back into a hole, yrh and draw through hole, yrh and draw through a loop – 1ch has been worked –, *insert hook into next hole, yrh and draw through hole, yrh and draw through first loop on hook, yrh and draw through both loops on hook, rep from * all round shape, working 3 sts into each corner hole. Fasten off and neaten ends.

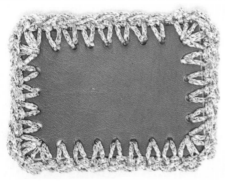

To join the shapes Place two shapes with right sides together so that the chain of each stitch is uppermost on the right side to give a pronounced ridge effect and sew together.

To fasten the belt Two large eyelets, available at most chain stores, have been placed at either side of the centre front opening. A double chain tie has been made to lace through the eyelets, but this must be made long enough to allow the belt to open sufficiently to allow the wearer to slip the belt over her hips. Four loops of beads have been added to each end of the tie to decorate them.

To make the slippers

Another use for this form of patchwork is the attractive slippers which are so easy to make and fit a size 5–6 foot. The pattern for the upper is divided into five shapes and each piece is cut out in suede and in a heavy bonded interfacing, which is then stuck to the suede. Holes are then punched all round each shape.

To work the crochet Using No.3.50 (ISR) crochet hook, a chenille yarn (or any other type of heavy yarn) and with the RS of the shape facing you, insert hook into hole from front to back, yrh and draw through hole, yrh and insert into same hole, yrh and draw through a loop, yrh and draw through all 4 loops on hook, cont in this way all round shape, working 3 sts into each corner hole.

To join the shapes together When the 5 shapes are complete, sew them firmly together on the wrong side. A lining fabric can also be hemmed into place at this stage, if you wish.

The insole is cut out in a plastic fabric and has a bonded interfacing backing stuck to it. Holes are punched all round the sole. The stitches described for the suede shapes are worked into the holes, noting that 1ch should be worked between the stitches at the heels and toes, also that the upper should be joined to the insole between the marked positions by inserting the hook into the upper and then into the insole, completing the stitch in the normal way. At this point the completed work is then stuck to a main rubber sole with a suitable adhesive. These instructions are repeated for the second sandal, making sure that the pattern pieces are reversed.

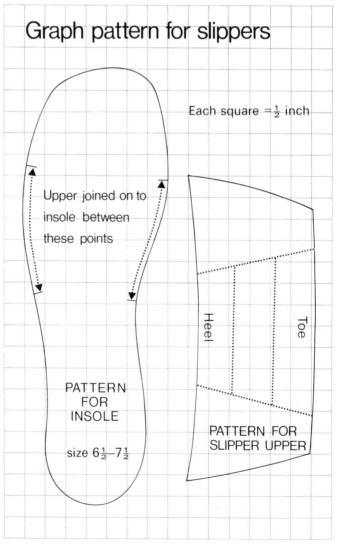

Graph pattern for slippers

Each square = ½ inch

Upper joined on to insole between these points

Heel

Toe

PATTERN FOR INSOLE

size 6½–7½

PATTERN FOR SLIPPER UPPER

COVERED RINGS
BASIC TECHNIQUES

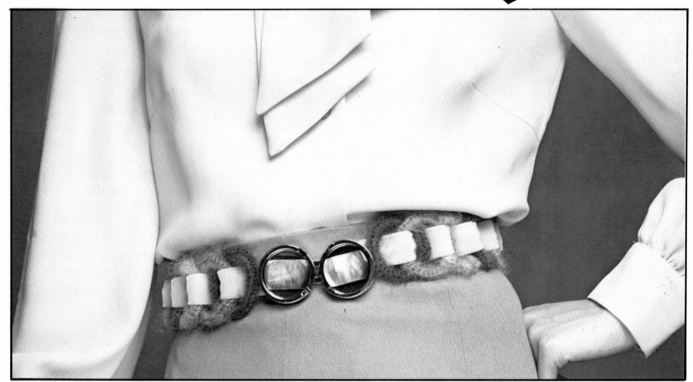

Crochet covered rings can be used in a variety of ways such as for belt fastenings and window hangings. There are several different methods of covering rings, some of which have already been illustrated, such as covering with a looped or button-hole stitch or with crochet stitches.

This chapter develops the technique further and shows what can be done by using several rings on a belt. All types of curtain rings, obtainable from the haberdashery counters of large stores, are suitable. The type of yarn is dependent upon the item being made, but most yarns can be used. The crochet hook should be one size smaller than usual in order to obtain a close stitch, which will cover the ring completely.

To make the belt

For a belt which is approximately 71cm (28in) long, you will need 23 rings with a 4cm (1½in) diameter, five different shades of mohair yarn, a length of 2.5cm (1in) wide velvet ribbon, a clasp and a No.3.00 (ISR) crochet hook.

Before starting work on covering the ring note that the cut end of yarn at the beginning can be laid along the ring and worked over in order to neaten it. Remember to keep the stitches close together, so that the ring is completely covered. Hold the yarn in

the left hand in the usual way and place the ring over the yarn and hold between the thumb and first finger of the left hand, insert the hook from front to back into the centre of the ring, yrh and draw through a loop, place the hook over the top of the ring, yrh and draw yarn through loop on hook, *insert hook from front to back into the centre of the ring, yrh and draw through a loop, place hook over top of the ring, yrh and draw through both loops on hook, rep from * until the ring is completely covered. Join with a ss into first st. Break off the yarn and darn in the cut end.

Slot ribbon through the rings as shown in the diagram to form a continuous belt and attach the clasp to either end.

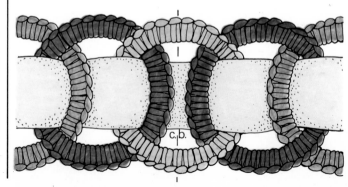

Alternative methods of working and joining rings suitable for belts

(a) Here the method of work is the same as that used for the belt rings, except that the rings are covered and joined continously in one operation. Using No.3.00 (ISR) hook, a double knitting yarn and 3.5cm (1¼in) diameter rings, you should work 14 stitches as previously explained to cover half the ring, then work the same number of stitches in a semi-circle around the next ring and so on until the required number of rings are joined and half covered in crochet. Work completely round the last ring and continue back along the other side of the rings.

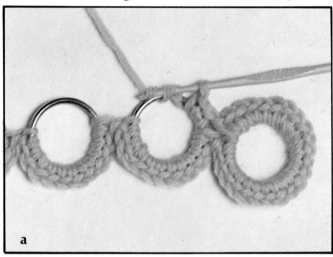

a

(b) Using No.3.00 (ISR) crochet hook, a cotton yarn and 3.5cm (1¼in) rings, work in the same way as given

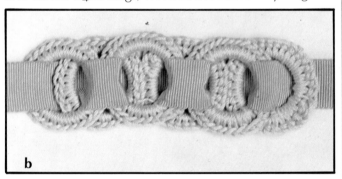

b

for the belt and cover each ring individually. Thread petersham ribbon through the rings as shown in the diagram.

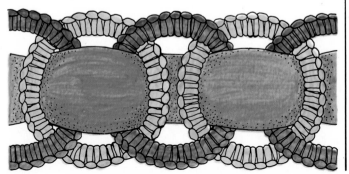

Alternative methods of covering individual rings

Each ring here is 5cm (2in) in diameter and a No.3.00 (ISR) hook is used for all the work.

(a) Here 34 stitches worked in raffia yarn are needed to cover the ring. The raffia gives a distinct chain edging to the circumference.

(b) Chenille yarn gives a softer appearance to this ring. You will need to work 46 stitches to cover the ring completely. The reverse side of the work is illustrated as this gives a more looped stitch.

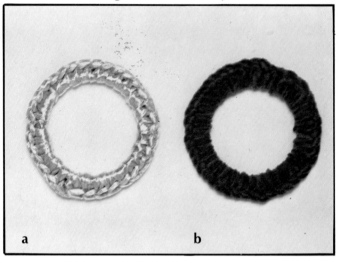

a   b

(c) Two rounds in two different yarns are worked over this ring. Using a double knitting yarn work 50 stitches into the ring as given for the belt. Lurex yarn is used for the 2nd round where double crochet is worked into each stitch in the 1st round, working from left to right instead of from right to left.

(d) Work in the same way as the previous sample until the 1st round has been completed. For the 2nd round, instead of working into all the stitches of the previous round, the hook is inserted into the centre of the ring at various intervals. In this sample, using Lurex yarn, work, *1dc into each of next 3 sts, 1dc inserting hook into centre of ring, 1dc into each of next 3 sts, 3dc inserting hook into centre of ring, repeat from * to end of round. Join with a ss into first st. Fasten off.

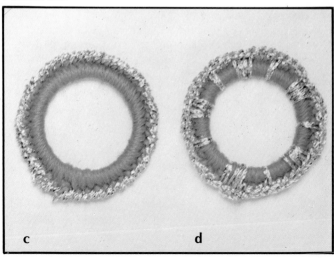

c   d

LARGE CIRCULAR MOTIFS

In this chapter, by telling you how to work our attractive window hanging, we shall increase your knowledge of working circular motifs and combine it with two new techniques which you will learn from these instructions. These are: the method of covering a large ring and making loops so that crochet work may be attached to the ring; and the method of making small circles by wrapping yarn round the fingers to form the basis of the ring.

Window hangings are a popular continental form of decoration. Usually white yarn is used for this form of work as many of the designs are based on snowflake patterns. Once you know the new methods of working described in this chapter, use them with the various techniques and stitches which we have dealt with in previous chapters and you will be able to design your own circular motifs.

To cover the ring

The most suitable ring to use is a plastic covered lamp shade ring. Ours is 30.5cm (12in) in diameter and the plastic will prevent rust marks from appearing and spoiling the white yarn.

Work **eleven** pairs of reversed half hitch knots, making a picot between each group of **eleven** knots by leaving 1.5cm ($\frac{1}{2}$in) of yarn free before working the next knot. Continue in this way until 24 picots have been made, join to first knot and fasten off. The covered ring will next be needed in the final round of the crochet work.

To work the window hanging

Using No.2.00 (ISR) hook and a cotton yarn, wrap yarn 20 times round first two fingers of your left hand, insert hook under all the strands of yarn, yrh and draw through a loop which is your working st.

1st round 1ch to count as first dc, work 47dc into the circle of yarn. Join with a ss into first ch.

2nd round 3ch, 1tr into same place as ss, *11ch, miss 5dc, leaving the last loop of each on hook, work 2tr into next dc, yrh and draw through all 3 loops on hook, rep from * 6 times more, 11ch. Join with a ss into 3rd of the 3ch.

3rd round *13dc into next 11ch sp, ss into top of pair of tr in previous round, rep from * 7 times more.

4th round **Ss into each of next 5dc, 5ch, miss 3dc, yrh 4 times and insert hook into next dc, yrh and draw through a loop, (yrh and draw through first 2 loops on hook) 5 times – called a quad tr–, *8ch, work a ring as foll: wrap yarn 10 times round second finger of left hand, insert hook under all the strands of yarn, yrh and draw a loop through the working st on the hook, remove yarn from finger, work 23dc into the circle, join with a ss into first st, (10ch, miss next 5dc on ring, ss into next dc) twice, 8ch, ss into top of pair of quad tr at base of previous 8ch, *, 17ch, 1 quad tr into 5th dc of next sp, miss 3dc, 1 quad tr into next dc, rep from * to *, work 5ss down side of next quad tr, ss into each of next 5dc of sp, 21ch, into 3rd ch from hook work 1dc,

1dc into each ch just worked, **, rep from ** to ** 3 times more. Join with a ss into first ss of round. Fasten off.

5th round *Rejoin yarn into the top of the length of ch just worked, 6ch, 6dc into first 10ch sp above next ring, 6dc into next 10ch sp above same ring, 5ch, leaving the last loop of each on hook work 3tr into next 17ch sp, yrh and draw through all 4 loops on hook, 5ch, (6dc into next 10ch sp above ring) twice, 6ch, ss into top of next length of 20ch, rep from * 3 times more.

6th round *1ch, 6dc into next 6ch sp, ss into each of next 12dc, (6dc into next 5ch sp) twice, ss into each of next 12dc, 7dc into next 6ch sp, rep from * 3 times more working 7dc at beg of each rep instead of 1ch, 6dc. Join with a ss into first ch.

7th round 3ch to count as first tr, 1tr into same place, *5ch, miss next 4 sts, leaving the last loop of each on hook work 2tr into next st, yrh and draw through all 3 loops on hook, rep from * all round, ending with 5ch. Join with a ss into 3rd of the 3ch.

8th round This is the round where the crochet motif is joined into the circle. Work 1ch, 5dc into first 5ch sp, 6dc into each sp to end of round, *at the same time* after every 10th dc, remove hook from working loop, insert it into picot on ring from front to back, reinsert hook into working loop and draw through picot. Join with a ss into first ch.

A window hanging

Our last chapter dealt with the basic techniques involved in working large circular motifs which are popularly used as window hangings. The intricate design shown here involves three more complicated techniques in crochet. These are the method of covering a narrow tube, enclosing spheres with crochet and a different method of covering and joining the centre motif into the ring.

Follow our step by step instructions for making the window hanging and learn these new methods. You will also find them useful for other forms of crochet work as the spheres could be used as a decorative fringe on a lampshade.

Once again a plastic covered lampshade ring, 30.5cm (12in) in diameter, was used for the large circle. Also used were a fine cotton yarn and a No.2.00 (ISR) crochet hook.

To cover the tube

Make a slip loop on the hook. * Holding the tube between thumb and first finger of left hand and having the yarn behind the tube, insert hook inside tube from top to lower edge, yrh and draw through tube taking hook behind tube, yrh and draw through both loops on hook, rep from * 47 times more. Join with a ss into first st. Fasten off.

Move the chain ridge formed by the previous row to give a zig-zag pattern with 3 points at each edge of the tube.

To work the centre motif

1st round Join yarn into one of the zig-zag points, *6ch, ss into next point at same edge, rep from * twice more.

2nd round 12dc into first 6ch sp, 12ch into each of next 2 sp.

3rd round *6ch, miss 5 sts, ss into next st, rep from * 5 times more.

4th round Work 1dc into each dc worked on 2nd round. 36dc. Join with a ss into first dc.

5th round *4ch, ss into next 6ch sp, 4ch, ss into 6th dc of previous round (i.e. behind the joining point of two 6ch sp), rep from * 5 times more.

6th round Work 5dc into each 4ch sp all round. Join

with a ss into first dc.

7th round 9ch, miss 4dc, ss into next dc, ss into next to last ch just worked, *7ch, miss 4dc, ss into next dc, ss into next to last ch just worked, rep from * 9 times more, 5ch. Join with a ss into 2nd of first 9ch.

8th round Work 7dc into each 5ch sp all round. Join with a ss into first dc.

9th round 3ch to count as first tr, 2tr into st at base of ch, *7ch, miss 6dc, 2dtr into next dc, 7ch, miss 6dc, 3tr into next dc, rep from * 4 times more, 7ch, miss 6dc, 2dtr into next dc, 7ch, miss 6dc. Join with a ss into 3rd of first 3ch.

10th round 1ch to count as first dc, 1dc into each of next 6 sts, 10ch, miss 8 sts, *1dc into each of next 11 sts, 10ch, miss 8 sts, rep from * 4 times more, 1dc into each of next 4 sts. Join with a ss into first ch. Fasten off.

Rejoin yarn into one of the zig-zag points at the other end of the tube and repeat 1st to 10th rounds, so giving a 3-dimensional effect to the work.

To cover the small spheres

These are made from a crochet casing filled with cotton wool which forms a firm ball shape approximately 4cm (1½ in) in diameter. You will need six balls for our window hanging.

Using the same yarn and crochet hook, leave a length of yarn 35cm (14in) long and then make 3ch. Join with a ss into the first ch to form a circle.

1st round 1ch to count as first dc, work 9dc into circle. Join with a ss into first ch.

2nd round 1ch to count as first dc, 2dc into next dc, *1dc into next dc, 2dc into next dc, rep from * to end. Join with a ss into first ch. 15dc.

3rd round 2ch to count as first cluster st, *yrh and insert into next dc, (yrh and draw through a loop extending it for 1cm (⅜in)) 4 times, yrh and draw through all loops on hook – called 1 cluster st, 1ch to secure the st, rep from * into each dc all round. Join with a ss into 2nd of the 2ch.

4th round 2ch to count as first cluster st, work 1 cluster st and 1ch into each cluster st all round. Join with a ss into 2nd of the 2ch.

Taking care that the right side of the work is on the outside, insert the cotton wool into the ball at this point.

5th round *1ch, (yrh and insert into next cluster st, yrh and draw through a loop) twice, yrh and draw through all 5 loops on hook – thus dec 1dc, rep from * all round. Join with a ss into first ch.

6th round 1ch to count as first dc, 1dc into each st of previous round. Join with a ss into first ch.

Thread yarn carefully through each st of last round and draw through the last st on the hook. Leave a length of yarn 35.5cm (14in) long for attaching sphere on to work.

To cover the ring and join in the centre motif

To work the covering of our lampshade ring, we used a No.3.00 (ISR) crochet hook and a slightly thicker cotton. First place a slip loop on to the crochet hook, keeping the yarn behind the ring, insert the hook into the ring from top to lower edge, yrh and draw through both loops on hook. Repeat this stitch until the ring is completely covered. You will need 258 stitches if you are using the same size ring as we are. Fasten off.

Next round Rejoin yarn into any st and draw through yarn thus making a st, work 1dc into each st all round. Join with a ss into first st.

Next round *36ch, miss 42dc, ss into next dc, rep from * 5 times more.

Next round Ss into each of next 2ch, 3ch, 1tr into st at base of 3ch, (2ch, miss next 2ch, leaving the last loop of each on hook work 2tr into next ch, yrh and draw through all 3 loops on hook – called a joint tr) 5 times, 1ch, remove hook from working loop and insert it from back to front into any of the 10ch sp of 10th round of either section of centre motif, * pick up working loop and work 1ch, miss 2ch, (a joint tr into next ch, 2ch, miss 2ch) 5 times, a joint tr into next ch, miss 2ch, a joint tr into next ch, (2ch, miss 2ch, a joint tr into next ch) 5 times, remove hook from working loop and insert it into next 10ch sp of *same* section as before, *, rep from * to * 4 times more, pick up working loop and work 1ch, miss 2ch, (a joint tr into next ch, 2ch, miss 2ch) 5 times, a joint tr into next ch. Join with a ss into 3rd of the 3ch.

To join the spheres

Using the 10ch sp of the other section of the centre motif, attach one end of the sphere firmly to the centre of the space. At the other end of the sphere, crochet 4ch and attach to the point where two joint treble meet at the point of a star on the ring.

CROCHET ON MESH
CROCHET ON NET

Crochet on net

This is an unusual and unexpected use for crochet – working on to net to give a design, which can eventually be built up to give the appearance of lace. However, the samples in this chapter demonstrate the basic techniques and are worked in straight lines, but they need to be practised before attempting anything more complicated.

Several types of net are available, usually made from nylon, silk or rayon. Although coloured nets are easy to obtain, white is the most popular colour, especially as it can be very wide which is ideal for wedding veils. For beginners the usual commercial net is rather fine to work with at first, so for our samples we have used one with a larger hole. Work with a No.2.00 (ISR) hook and a double knitting yarn when practising. If the larger holed net for practising is difficult to obtain, we suggest using the plastic net covering for oranges and other fruits which is often found in supermarkets.

You may find it easier to work the crochet if the net is first placed into an embroidery ring. In this way the net is held taut in the ring, and this will make the insertion of the hook much easier.

Sample 1

The chain on net is the first basic stitch, and all the other designs are variations on this, therefore it is important to master this technique first. Place the net firmly in the ring. Begin working from the outer edge of the ring and plan to work in an upward direction. This is the easiest way to start, but when you are more familiar with this technique you will be able to work in all directions. Holding yarn under net on ring and hook over net on ring, insert hook into one hole, yrh and draw through a loop, *insert hook into next hole above as shown in the diagram, yrh and draw through

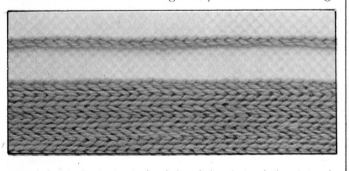

a loop, drawing it through loop already on hook – one chain st has been worked over one hole in the net –, rep from * for the required length.

Note It is important to keep your chain stitches fairly loose, otherwise the net will pucker and not lie flat.

Sample 2

Chain stitch is used again, but the hook is placed into alternate holes.

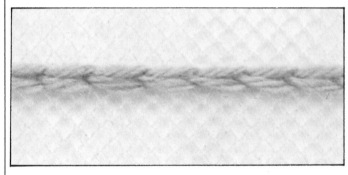

Sample 3

This is worked in the same way as sample 2, but in 8 rows of 4 colours to give a striped block. The chain is worked backwards and forwards, turning the ring for each new row and only cutting the yarn when changing colours.

Sample 4

Straight lines have been used again here, but a zig-zag effect has been achieved by, *working 8 sts into alternate diagonal holes in a left to right direction, then another 8 sts into alternate diagonal holes in a right to left direction, rep from * for the required length. Two rows have been worked in a variety of colours, leaving a space of two rows of holes between each new colour.

Sample 5

Here a variety of stitches have been worked using the same technique. First place the net in the ring as given for sample 1.

(a) Insert hook into one hole on the edge of the ring,

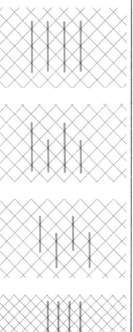

and again work upwards, yrh and draw through a loop extending it to reach 3rd hole on right, insert into this hole, yrh and draw through a loop drawing it through loop on hook, *insert hook into adjacent hole above last st on left, yrh and draw through a loop extending it as before, insert hook into 3rd hole on the right, yrh and draw through all loops on hook, rep from * to end of line.

(b) Following the diagram work in a similar way to previous sample, extending the stitches alternately two and three spaces to the right.

(c) You will see from the diagram that this sample has been worked over 3 sts in a zig-zag direction.

(d) Two rows of sts as given for sample (a) have been worked side by side (i.e. work one row as explained for sample (a), then turn the ring so that the completed row is on the right and work a second row like the first so that the chain sts are worked in adjacent rows).

Sample 6

These stitches are all a zig-zag variation of chain stitch.

(a) Place net in ring as given for sample 1. Working upwards as before, insert hook into hole at left edge, yrh and draw through a loop, miss one hole on the right, insert hook into next hole on the right, yrh and draw through a loop drawing it through loop on hook, *insert hook into next hole above last st on the left, yrh and draw through a loop drawing it through loop on hook, miss one hole on the right, insert hook into next hole above last st on the right, yrh and draw through a loop drawing it through loop on hook, rep from * to end of line.

(b) This is worked in the same way as sample (a), but slightly more spaced (i.e. there is one hole missed between each st worked on the left and the right).

(c) Here is another variation where the hook is inserted to give a diamond effect.

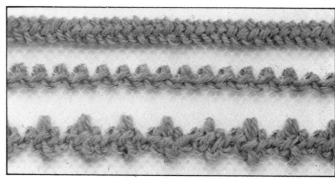

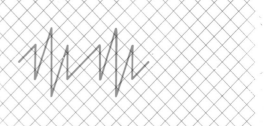

CROCHET ON RUG CANVAS

Crochet on rug canvas

Stitches on all varieties of canvas are usually worked with a needle, but many interesting effects will be illustrated in this chapter using crochet techniques.

In the last chapter, we demonstrated how crochet is worked on to net where the holes do not come immediately above each other, but to either side on each new row. With canvas, however, the holes are immediately next to and above each other and so designs can easily be worked out on ordinary squared graph paper.

Both double and single weave canvas can be used for this technique and very delicate work can be achieved by using a finer canvas which has more holes to the square inch. Choose a hook which will easily enter the holes in the canvas and a yarn which will completely cover the weave when the stitches are worked. Too fine a yarn used with a thick canvas will result in unsightly gaps.

No frame is necessary if you are using a stiff canvas. If a large amount of work is required and a finer canvas is being used, a slate or traditional embroidery frame is recommended, which can be obtained from any good crafts supplier or shop. For our samples we have used an ordinary rug canvas, a chunky knitting yarn and a No.3.50 (ISR) crochet hook. This combination of materials is suitable for making shoulder bags, holdalls and stool or chair seats.

Sample 1

At the top of the sample a straight line of chain stitch has been worked in every adjacent hole. This was worked upwards from the lower edge of the canvas and then turned to give a horizontal line of stitches. Two lines have been completed and the third is in the process of being worked.

To work the stitches Holding the yarn under the canvas in the normal way and the hook above the right side of the canvas, insert hook into one hole on the line of canvas to be worked, yrh and draw loop through hole, *insert hook into next hole upwards, yrh and draw through a loop drawing it through loop on hook, rep from * for the required length of chain.

To the left of the photograph the same chain stitches have been worked vertically. The canvas can be turned at the end of every row in order to keep working in an upwards direction.

The remaining sample shows chain stitches worked into a zig zag design. Again work up the canvas and follow the chart which shows where to insert the hook.

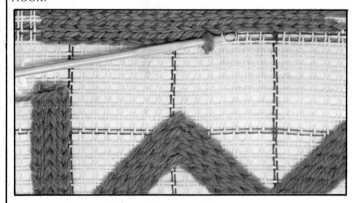

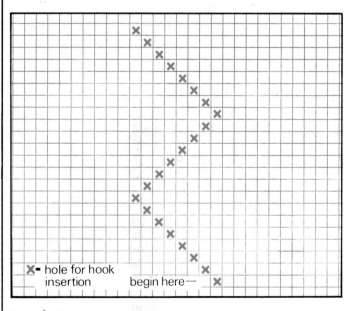

X = hole for hook insertion   begin here—

Sample 2

This is a square design worked in chain stitch which can be enlarged to form one pattern, or a number of smaller squares can be used together as motifs.

Each new round of our sample has been worked in a different colour and yarn, including raffene. Follow the diagram for the order of working, beginning with the 1st round which is worked over four holes at the centre.

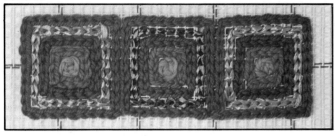

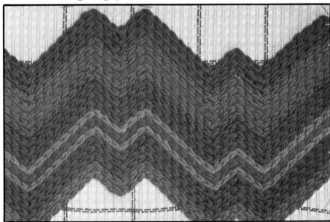

○ = 1st round

□ = 2nd ·

△ = 3rd ·

◇ = 4th ·

▽ = 5th ·

Sample 3

This is an imitation of Florentine embroidery, the zig zag stitchery which is often seen on canvas. Careful colour selection is necessary and the work can be made much more effective by varying the number of rows worked in each colour. The chart illustrates our design, but it is quite easy to adapt your own ideas into zig zag patterns.

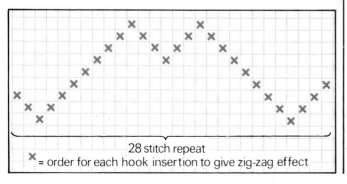

28 stitch repeat
× = order for each hook insertion to give zig-zag effect

Sample 4

This illustrates three stitches which could be used on rug canvas in place of chain stitch. Follow the instructions given to learn how to work these stitches.

a) Holding the yarn and hook as given for sample 1 and working in an upwards direction, insert hook into one hole on the line of work, yrh and draw through a loop, insert hook into next hole up, yrh and draw through a loop drawing it through loop on hook, *insert hook into next hole up on 2nd row to the left, yrh and draw through a loop extending it to meet the next hole above last st worked on the right, insert hook into that hole, yrh and draw through a loop drawing it through both loops on hook, rep from.* for the required length.

b) Holding the yarn and hook as given for sample 1 and working in an upwards direction, insert hook into one hole on the line of work, yrh and draw through a loop, insert hook into next hole up, yrh and draw through a loop drawing it through loop on hook, insert hook into next hole up on 2nd row to the left, *yrh and draw through a loop extending it to meet the next hole above last st worked on the right, insert hook into that hole, yrh and draw through a loop drawing it through both loops on hook, *, – one long st has been worked –, insert hook into next hole up on the next row to the left and rep from * to * so forming a short st, cont working a long and a short st alternately to end of the line. Turn work and repeat a second line of crochet opposite the first, working a long st next to a short st and a short st next to a long st.

c) Holding the yarn and hook as given for sample 1 and working in an upwards direction, insert hook into one hole on line of work, *insert hook into next hole up to the left, yrh and draw through a loop drawing it through loop on hook, insert hook into next hole to the right, yrh and draw through a loop drawing it through loop on hook, rep from * for the required length.

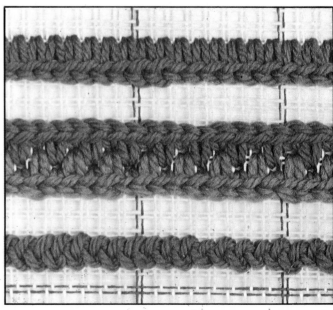

EMBROIDERY ON CROCHET

Crochet plus stitchery

A background of simple crochet lends itself attractively to decorative stitchery and many of the traditional embroidery stitches can be worked on to crochet fabrics.

To work the crochet background This is a basic mesh which is quick and simple to work. You can vary the size of the mesh by working a smaller or larger crochet stitch with more or less chain stitches between as required. Any yarn may be used, but for these samples we have used a No. 3.50 (ISR) crochet hook and a double knitting yarn. Make a length of chain with multiples of 4 plus 11 stitches.

1st row Into 11th ch from hook work 1dtr, *3ch, miss next 3ch, 1dtr into next ch, rep from * to end. Turn.

2nd row 7ch to count as first dtr and 3ch, miss first dtr, 1dtr into next dtr, *3ch, 1dtr into next dtr, rep from * ending with last dtr into 4th of turning ch. Turn.

Rep the 2nd row for the required depth of work. Throughout these samples we have used an embroidery stitch which is a form of darning. Again any yarn can be used, but choose it carefully and work a trial piece before commencing work as stitches can look entirely different depending on the yarn used. Many varied and attractive designs can be made using this basic stitch technique including table linen, bedcovers and curtains. A more delicate effect can be made by using a finer cotton yarn and a smaller sized crochet hook.

Sample 1

Here is a design which is suitable for an all-over pattern. Certain squares in the background have been filled in with the darning or weaving stitch as shown in the diagram. The chart shows which squares are to be filled in.

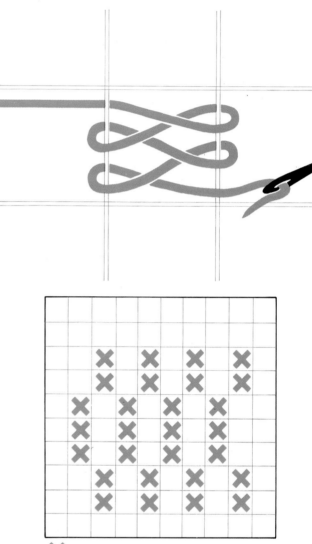

✖ = sq. to be filled in with 'darning' stitch

Sample 2

This basic background has a shaped edge so that the finished piece of work could be used as a window pelmet or an edging on a roller blind.

To work the background Work 3 rows as given for the basic background.

4th row Ss over first 4 sts so dec one square, 7ch, patt to end. Turn.

5th row Patt to last square, turn so dec one square.

6th row 8ch to count as first dtr of this row and space at end of next row, ss into each of first 4ch, 3ch, patt to end. Turn.

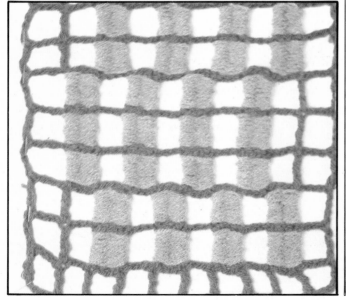

7th row Patt to end, working last dtr into final ss of previous row so inc one square. Turn.

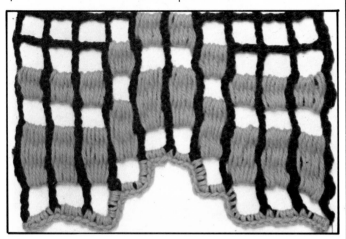

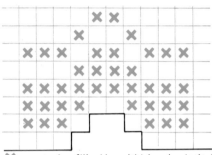

✕ = sq. to be filled in with 'darning' stitch

8th row 10ch so inc one square, 1dtr into first dtr, patt to end. Turn.

9th-10th row Patt to end. Turn.

These 10 rows form the basic shape which can be repeated for the required length.

Darn the appropriate squares as shown in the chart and then, using the same yarn as for the darning, complete the shaped edge by working 3dc into each square and 1dc into each dtr or corner of a square.

Sample 3

Circular motifs have been added to the basic background. Using two strands of a 4 ply yarn together,

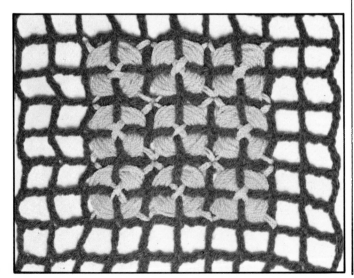

thread the motifs over four squares as shown in the diagrams. The photograph shows the motifs worked over adjacent groups of four squares.

Sample 4

Here a single flower motif has been worked on to a basic background using a chunky yarn. After working the four basic lines as shown in the diagram twice, the thread is woven round the centre by passing the needle (under the blue line, over the green, under the red and over the brown) six times in all. All the cut ends of yarn should then be neatened on the wrong side of the work.

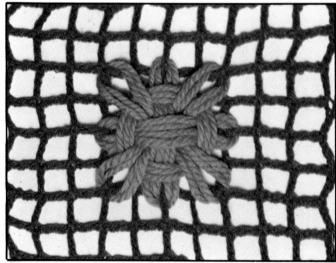

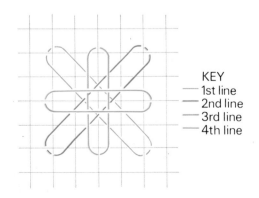

KEY
— 1st line
— 2nd line
— 3rd line
— 4th line

MORE EMBROIDERY DESIGNS

This is a continuation of our chapter about weaving designs on to a crochet mesh background. We also give instructions for working an unusual and decorative shawl, which is simple to make and employs the techniques shown in recent chapters. Practise the samples shown here before starting work on the shawl.

Sample 1

To work the background Using No.3.00 (ISR) crochet hook and a 4 ply yarn, make a length of chain with multiples of 4 + 11 stitches.

1st row Into 11th ch from hook work 1dtr, *3ch, miss 3ch, 1dtr into next ch, rep from * to end. Turn.

2nd row 7ch to count as first dtr and 3ch, miss first sp, 1dtr into next dtr, *3ch, 1dtr into next dtr, rep from * ending with last dtr into 4th of turning ch. Turn.

The 2nd row is repeated throughout.

Sample 2

Work the mesh as given for sample 1, weave the flower with a double thickness of contrasting yarn following the diagram for sample 4 on previous page.

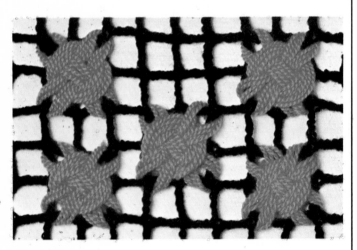

To work the flower Using double thickness of a contrasting yarn and a large blunt-eyed bodkin, follow the diagram and work the yarn through the crochet mesh.

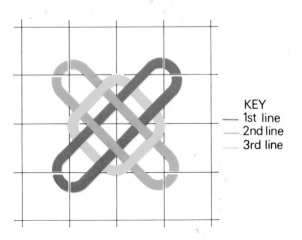

KEY
- 1st line
- 2nd line
- 3rd line

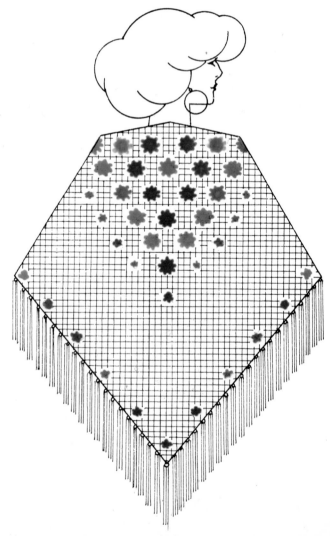

Crochet shawl

Size
Triangle measures approx 114.5cm (*45in*) across top and 76cm (*30in*) from centre of top edge to point

Tension
5ch sp and 6 rows to 7.5cm (*3in*) over patt worked on No.3.00 (ISR) crochet hook

Materials
12 × 25grm balls Twilley's Cortina
Oddments of six contrasting colours
One No.3.00 (ISR) crochet hook

Shawl
Using No.3.00 (ISR) hook and A, make 327ch loosely.
1st row Into 11th ch from hook work 1dtr, *3ch, miss 3ch, 1dtr into next ch, rep from * to end. Turn. Eighty 3ch sp.
2nd row 7ch to count as first dtr and 3ch, miss first sp, 1dtr into next dtr, *3ch, 1dtr into next dtr, rep from * ending with last dtr into 4th of turning ch. Turn.
3rd and 4th rows As 2nd.
5th row (dec row) 7ch to count as first dtr and 3ch, miss first sp, (1dtr into next dtr) twice – i.e. miss the 3ch between dtr, so dec one sp –, *3ch, 1dtr into next dtr, rep from * to last 2 sp, 1dtr into next dtr, 3ch, 1dtr into 4th of turning ch. Turn. 2 sp decreased.
6th and 7th rows As 2nd.
8th row As 5th.
Cont in this way, dec 2 sp on every foll alt row, until 46 sp rem, then on every row until 2 sp rem. Fasten off.

To make up
Using the contrasting colours apply motifs as shown in the diagram. Care should be taken to keep all the cut ends neatly finished on the wrong side of the work.
Fringe Cut 10 strands of yarn each 33cm (*13in*) long, fold in half and using crochet hook pull folded end through first space at side of shawl, pull cut ends through loop thus made and pull tight to form a knot. Rep these knots into each space along 2 sides of the triangle. Trim fringe to an equal length.

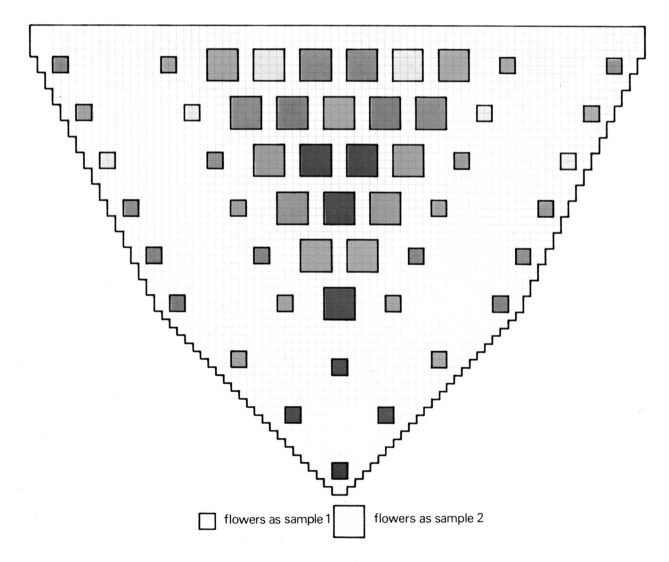

☐ flowers as sample 1   ☐ flowers as sample 2

BEADED DESIGNS

Beaded designs may easily be incorporated into the crochet work during the process of making an article. There are numerous types of beads, normally made of glass, china or wood, which are available from most large multiple stores.

The size of beads varies dramatically, but any type can be used for this kind of work providing that the hole in the bead is large enough to take the yarn which is being used. To thread the beads on to the yarn, see the second chapter on Loopy Stitches. Each bead is positioned so that it forms part of a design and care must be taken to see that the beads are placed on the right side of the work.

It should be remembered that the beads are quite heavy if they are used in large quantities. Therefore small articles are really the most suitable, or isolated areas to form a border pattern. These articles would need to be lined to strengthen the work and to take the weight of the beads.

Beads are particularly popular for evening wear. Very attractive patterns using beads may be designed and applied to evening waistcoats and bags, or as a border design around the hem of a long evening coat or skirt. There are two distinct methods of applying the beads. One way is to thread the beads on to the yarn which you will be using, before you start working. The bead is then pushed up and positioned as it is required and the following stitch is then worked in the usual way. This technique is illustrated in samples 1 and 2. Another method, used in sample 3, is to thread the beads on to a separate ball of yarn. When a bead row is being worked, the yarn on either side of the bead is caught into place during the working of the crochet, by looping the working yarn round the yarn holding the beads. Our samples show some simple designs which follow the methods described above. If you practise these samples from our instructions you will soon become familiar with the art of beaded crochet.

Sample 1

Using a fine yarn and No.2.50 (ISR) crochet hook, make 40ch.

1st row Into 3rd ch from hook work 1dc, 1dc into each ch to end. Turn.

2nd–7th rows 1ch to count as first dc, 1dc into each dc to end. Turn.

8th row 1ch to count as first dc, 1dc into each of next 6 sts, *push up one bead, placing it at back of the work which will be the right side, 1dc into next st – called 1 Bdc –, 1dc into each of next 7 sts, rep from * 3 times more. Turn.

9th row 1ch to count as first dc, 1dc into each of next 6 sts, *noting that beads are placed at the front of the work, 1Bdc into each of next 2 sts, 1dc into each of next 6 sts, rep from * 3 times more. Turn.

10th row 1ch to count as first dc, 1dc into each of next 5 sts, *1Bdc into each of next 3 sts, 1dc into each of next 5 sts, rep from * 3 times more, ending last rep 1dc into each of next 6 sts. Turn.

11th row 1ch to count as first dc, 1dc into each of next 5 sts, *1Bdc into each of next 4 sts, 1dc into each of next 4 sts, rep from * 3 times more, ending last rep 1dc into each of next 5 sts. Turn.

12th row 1ch to count as first dc, 1dc into each of next 4 sts, *1Bdc into each of next 5 sts, 1dc into each of next 3 sts, rep from * twice more, 1Bdc into each of next 5 sts, 1dc into each of next 5 sts. Turn.

13th row As 11th.

14th row As 10th.

15th row As 9th.

16th row 1ch to count as first dc, 1dc into each of next 2 sts, *1Bdc into next st, 1dc into each of next 3 sts, rep from * 8 times more. Turn.

17th row 1ch to count as first dc, 1dc into each of next 2 sts, *1Bdc into each of next 2 sts, 1dc into each of next 6 sts, rep from * 3 times more, 1Bdc into each of next 2 sts, 1dc into each of next 2 sts. Turn.

18th row 1ch to count as first dc, 1dc into next st, *1Bdc into each of next 3 sts, 1dc into each of next 5 sts, rep from * 3 times more, 1Bdc into each of next 3 sts, 1dc into each of next 2 sts. Turn.

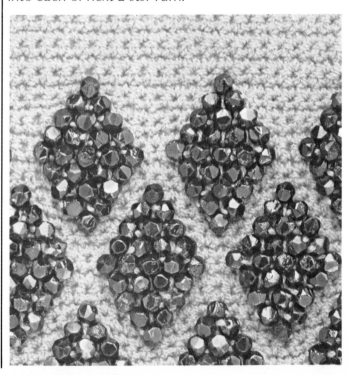

19th row 1ch to count as first dc, 1dc into next st, *1Bdc into each of next 4 sts, 1dc into each of next 4dc, rep from * 3 times more, 1Bdc into each of next 4 sts, 1dc into last st. Turn.

20th row 1ch to count as first dc, *1Bdc into each of next 5 sts, 1dc into each of next 3 sts, rep from * 3 times more, 1Bdc into each of next 5 sts, 1dc into last st. Turn.

21st–24th rows As 19th–16th rows in that order. The 9th row is then repeated to complete the pattern and start the next diamond shape.

Sample 2

Using a cotton yarn and No.2.50 (ISR) crochet hook, make 40ch.

1st row Into 3rd ch from hook work 1htr, 1htr into each ch to end. Turn.

2nd row 2ch to count as first htr, 1htr into each of next 6 sts, *push up one bead, placing it at back of work which will be the right side, 1htr in the next st – called 1Bhtr –, 1htr into each of next 7 sts, rep from * 3 times more. Turn.

3rd row 2ch to count as first htr, *1htr into each of next 5 sts, 1Bhtr into next st, 1htr into next st, 1Bhtr into next st, rep from * 3 times more, 1htr into each of next 6 sts. Turn.

4th row 2ch to count as first htr, 1htr into each of next 4 sts, *1Bhtr into next st, 1htr into each of next 3 sts, rep from * 7 times more, 1Bhtr into next st, 1htr into each of next 2 sts. Turn.

5th row 2ch to count as first htr, 1htr into each of next 3 sts, *1Bhtr into next st, 1htr into each of next 5 sts, 1Bhtr into next st, 1htr into next st, rep from * 3 times more, 1htr into each of next 3 sts. Turn.

6th row 2ch to count as first htr, 1htr into each of next 2 sts, *1Bhtr into next st, 1htr into each of next 7 sts,

rep from * 3 times more, 1 Bhtr into next st, 1htr into each of next 3 sts. Turn.

7th–10th rows As 5th–2nd rows in that order. The 2nd to 10th rows form the pattern.

Sample 3

Wooden beads, approximately 2cm ($\frac{3}{4}$in) long were used for this sample. Thread them on to a separate ball of yarn.

Using a cotton yarn and No.3.00 (ISR) crochet hook, make 33ch.

1st row Into 3rd ch from hook work 1dc, 1dc into each ch to end. Turn.

2nd–8th rows 1ch to count as first dc, 1dc into each dc to end. Turn.

9th row 1ch to count as first dc, 1dc into next st, *hold the yarn with the beads behind the work, place the working yarn round the yarn holding the beads, work 1dc into next st, work 1dc into each of next 3 sts using the main yarn, push up one bead into position behind the work, *, rep from * to * 9 times more, ending last rep with 1dc into each of next 2 sts. Turn. Cut off yarn holding beads.

10th row Work in dc.

11th row 1ch to count as first dc, 1dc into each of next 3 sts, rep from * to * of 9th row to complete the row. The 9th and 11th rows show the sequence of working the beads so that they lie in alternate spaces. You may make your own designs by using this sequence but remember that the beads are always placed from the opposite side of the work, so that you will have to cut the yarn after each bead row.

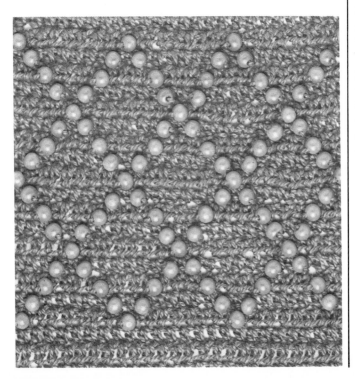

NEEDLE WEAVING
BASIC DESIGNS

Crochet with needle weaving

This chapter gives instructions for working a crochet background into which various materials may be woven to give a solid fabric. The background is formed by working in trebles with one chain separating them, and on subsequent rows the trebles are worked into those in the previous row to give a straight vertical line. The chains of each space or the trebles worked between the spaces form bars either over or under which the weaving threads may pass, according to the design.

A crochet hook or bodkin is used to pass the threads vertically, horizontally or diagonally across the fabric, breaking off the yarn after each row. It is interesting to experiment with different yarns and ribbons for weaving. We have used four thicknesses of the same yarn, rug wool, various ribbons and strips of plastic. Strips of fur could be used to give a more expensive-looking fabric.

The weaving threads help to keep the crochet in position, and as the fabric formed is thick and warm, it is especially suitable for outer garments such as jackets, coats, scarves and skirts. The fabric made by this technique is also ideal for cushions and rugs.

Follow the instructions for our samples before experimenting with your own designs and yarns.

Sample 1

This is the basic open background for needle weaving. Using No.4.00 (ISR) hook and a double knitting yarn, make 30ch.

1st row Into 6th ch from hook work 1tr, *1ch, miss next ch, 1tr into next ch, rep from * to end. Turn.

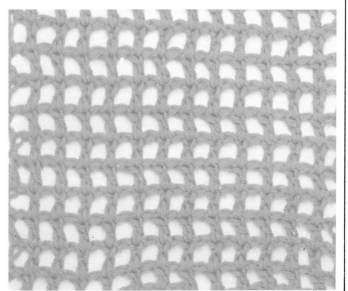

Note A firmer fabric is produced by placing the hook under three loops of each tr, instead of the normal one or two loops.

2nd row 4ch to count as first tr and 1ch, miss first ch sp, 1tr into next tr, *1ch, miss next ch sp, 1tr into next tr, rep from * to end, working last tr into 4th of 5ch. Turn.

The 2nd row is repeated throughout, noting that each subsequent row will end with last tr worked into 3rd of 4ch.

One attractive item to make entirely in this stitch is a bag. It is quick and easy to work in one piece which is folded in half and seamed at the sides. A line of crochet chain gathers the top edges and at the same time joins them to wooden handles.

Sample 2

Work a basic background as given for sample 1. Ribbon, 0.5cm ($\frac{1}{4}$in) wide, is then woven vertically through the spaces.

1st weaving row Take the ribbon under the ch of the foundation row and through into the first space, *miss the next space up and insert ribbon from front to back into the next space up, take ribbon from back to front into the next space up, *, rep from * to * to end of fabric.

2nd weaving row Insert ribbon from front to back into first space of next row, then take ribbon from back to front into second space, rep from * to * of 1st weaving row to end of fabric.

3rd weaving row Insert ribbon from front to back into second space of next row, then take ribbon from back to front into third space, rep from * to * of 1st weaving row to end of fabric.

The 3 weaving rows are repeated vertically across the fabric.

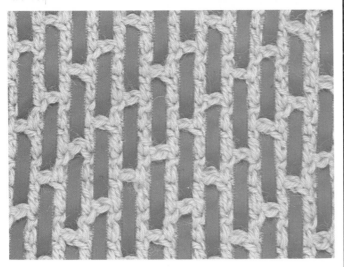

Sample 3

Green parcel string has been used for the background of this sample. Using No.5.00 (ISR) hook make 31ch.

1st row Into 7th ch from hook work 1dtr, *1ch, miss next ch, 1dtr into next ch, rep from * to end. Turn.

2nd row 5ch, miss next sp, 1dtr into next dtr, *1ch, 1dtr into next dtr, ending with last dtr into 5th of 6ch. Turn.

The 2nd row is repeated throughout, noting that each subsequent row will end with last tr worked into 4th of 5ch.

2cm ($\frac{3}{4}$ in) wide petersham ribbon is woven horizontally through each space in the first row, and then through alternate spaces in the next row.

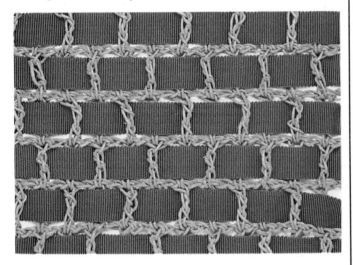

Sample 4

Work a basic background as given for sample 1.

There are two types of weaving involved in this design. Firstly thick rug wool is placed vertically round each treble stitch working up the fabric. Instead of working in and out of the crochet fabric, the rug wool is placed under each treble from left to right working upwards on the first row and following

alternate rows. On the remaining rows the rug wool is threaded in the same way but it is passed from right to left.

Strips of plastic 0.5cm ($\frac{1}{4}$ in) wide, matching the background colour, and ribbon 0.5cm ($\frac{1}{4}$ in) wide, matching the rug wool are then woven alternately between each row of trebles. The plastic is threaded so that on the right side the strip passes completely over one space, whilst the ribbon goes into alternate spaces.

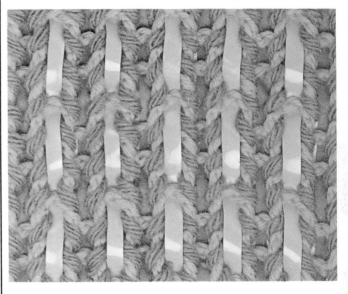

Sample 5

Work a basic background as given for sample 1.

The weaving is worked in two different colours, A and B, of double knitting yarn, using four thicknesses together each time. With A work into horizontal alternate spaces in the first row. Continue with A into each horizontal row throughout the fabric, alternating the spaces worked into with those in the previous row.

Colour B is woven vertically into each row in the same way as A, going in and out of the strands of A as well as the bars of the background fabric.

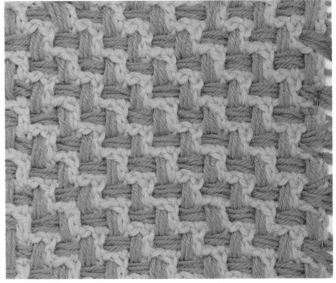

EXPERIMENTAL TECHNIQUES

The basic methods of needle weaving were dealt with in the last chapter, and now we shall illustrate some more experimental uses of this technique with different yarns and other ways of employing the weaving material.

Two of the samples are check fabrics worked into the basic background and these are thick and warm because of the method of working. Other samples are worked in alternative crochet stitches to form a background. Most of these samples of needle weaving are suitable for an all-over fabric, but some (such as sample 4) may be adapted to make an attractive border for a jacket or long skirt.

Sample 1
To work the background This is worked in two colours of double knitting yarn, A and B. Using No.4.50 (ISR) hook and A, make 30ch.
1st row Into 6th ch from hook work 1tr, *1ch, miss 1ch, 1tr into next ch, rep from * to end. Turn.
2nd row 4ch to count as first tr and 1ch, miss 1 ch sp, 1tr into next tr, *1ch, miss 1 ch sp, 1tr into next tr, rep from * finishing with last tr into 5th of 6ch. Turn.
Join in B and rep 2nd row twice more, noting that on subsequent rows the last tr is worked into 3rd of 4ch. Continue in this way, working 2 rows in each colour, for the required length.
To work the weaving Using 4 thicknesses of A together, weave in and out of each vertical space in the first row. Then using A again, work into each space in the next row alternating where the yarn passes over or under a bar. Alternating A and B, repeat this process in two row stripes throughout the fabric.

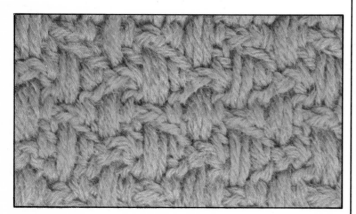

Sample 2
To work the background This is worked in three colours of double knitting yarn, A, B and C. Using No.4.50 (ISR) hook make a background as given for sample 1, but work one row in A, two rows in B and

three rows in C. Note also that colours A and C will have to be cut at the end of the line so that the yarn will be in the correct position for the repeat of colour sequence.
To work the weaving This is worked in the same way as sample 1, but work one vertical line in A, two lines in B and three lines in C.

Sample 3
Two colours of double knitting yarn are used for this sample, colour A for the background and B for the needle weaving.
To work the background Using No.4.50 (ISR) hook and A, make 27ch.
1st row Into 5th ch from hook work 4tr leaving last loop of each on hook, yrh and draw through all loops on hook, 1ch, miss 1ch, 1dc into next ch, *1ch, miss 1ch, into next ch work 4tr leaving last loop of each on hook, yrh and draw through all loops on hook, 1ch, miss 1ch, 1dc into next ch, rep from * to end. Turn.

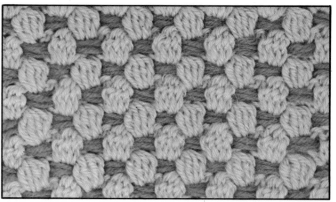

2nd row 3ch, into first dc work 3tr leaving last loop of each on hook, yrh and draw through all loops on hook, 1ch, *1dc into top of next 4tr gr, 1ch, into next dc work 4tr leaving last loop of each on hook, yrh and draw through all loops on hook, 1ch, rep from *

finishing with last 4tr gr into turning ch. Turn.

3rd row 2ch, * into next dc work 4tr leaving last loop of each on hook, yrh and draw through all loops on hook, 1ch, ldc into top of next 4tr gr, 1ch, rep from * to end omitting 1ch at end of last rep. Turn.

The 2nd and 3rd rows are repeated throughout.

To work the weaving Four thicknesses of colour B are placed horizontally across every row by weaving them under each four treble group and over each double crochet.

Sample 4

The crochet background illustrates an attractive stitch made up of blocks and spaces.

To work the background Using No.4.50 (ISR) hook and a double knitting yarn, make 29ch.

1st row Into 5th ch from hook work 2dtr, miss 2ch, ldc into next ch, *3ch, miss 3ch, 3dtr into next ch, miss 2ch, ldc into next ch, rep from * to end. Turn.

2nd row 4ch, 2dtr into first dc, ldc into next 3ch sp, *3ch, 3dtr into next dc, ldc into next 3ch sp, rep from * finishing with last dc into turning ch. Turn.

The 2nd row is repeated throughout.

To work the weaving Following the diagram, thread the ribbon and four thicknesses of yarn in alternate strips over the vertical bars formed by three chain in the background.

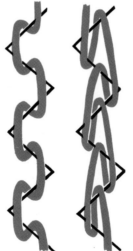

Sample 5

To work the background Using No.4.50 (ISR) hook and a mohair yarn, make 29ch.

1st row Into 7th ch from hook work 1dc, 2ch, miss next ch, 1tr into next ch, *2ch, miss next ch, 1dc into next ch, 2ch, miss next ch, 1tr into next ch, rep from* to end. Turn.

2nd row 3ch to count as first dc and 2ch, *1tr into next dc, 2ch, 1dc into next tr, 2ch, rep from * to end, working last dc into 3rd of turning ch. Turn.

3rd row 5ch to count as first tr and 2ch, 1dc into first tr, 2ch, 1tr into next dc, 2ch, rep from * to end, working last tr into 2nd of 3ch. Turn.

The 2nd and 3rd rows are repeated throughout.

To work the weaving Diagonal lines of alternate strips of velvet ribbon and four thicknesses of a contrasting shade of mohair are worked over the diagonal chain bars and under the treble stitches in each row.

This fabric is very light, warm and luxurious and would be very suitable for a long evening skirt, straight evening stole or travelling rug.

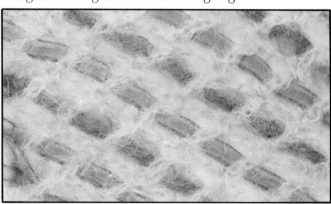

Sample 6

This beautiful evening belt is made very simply by following the needle weaving techniques. Using No.3.50 (ISR) hook and a lurex yarn, make a length of chain long enough to fit round your waist or hips minus combined diameters of the two rings used for fastening. Into the chain work 6 rows as given for the basic background in the previous chapter.

Two colours of Russia braid are threaded through the background to give a raised effect. Secure the ends of the belt over the fastening rings (ours are large brass rings, 5cm (*2in*) in diameter) and crochet a length of cord to bind the rings together.

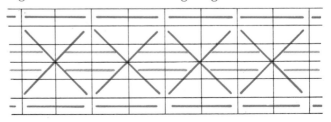

A woven crochet rug

Base row Into 6th ch from hook work 1tr, *1ch, miss 1ch, 1tr into next ch, rep from * to end. Turn. 95 sp.

1st row 3ch to count as first tr, *1tr into next tr, 1ch, rep from * to last sp, miss 1ch, 1tr into 4th of first 5ch. Turn. The last row forms patt. Rep last row 3 times more. Break off A. Cont in patt, working striped sequence of 5 rows B, 5 rows C and 5 rows A throughout. Rep striped sequence 6 times more. Fasten off.

To make up

Sew in ends. Press lightly under a dry cloth with a cool iron.

Weaving Cut 70 lengths of A, 60 lengths of B and 60 lengths of C, all 223.5cm (*88in*) long. Take 2 strands of A and, taking care not to twist strands, weave vertically over and under 1ch bars separating tr, beg with 1st row of sps and leaving 15cm (*6in*) hanging free. A firmer edge will be obtained if needle is passed through first ch on lower edge rather than into sp and also through final ch in top edge. Do not pull yarn too tightly, but weave at a tension that will leave 15cm (*6in*) hanging free at top edge. Work a further 4 rows in A weaving over alt bars to preceding row. Cont in

same way in striped sequence as given for rug.

Fringe Cut two 33cm (*13in*) lengths of colour required for each sp along both edges of rug. Fold strands to form a loop. Insert hook into first sp at lower edge, draw loop through, draw woven ends through loop then draw fringe ends through loop and draw up tightly. Rep along lower edge and upper edge, taking care to keep same side of rug uppermost while knotting fringe. Trim fringe.

Size

The finished dimensions of the travelling rug should measure 152.5cm x 132cm (60in x 52in), excluding fringe.

Tension

10tr and 10 sp and 10 rows to 14cm ($5\frac{1}{2}$*in*) over patt worked on No.6.00 (ISR) crochet hook

Materials

15 × 50grm balls Sirdar Wash'n'Wear Chunky Bri-Nylon Courtelle in main shade, A

13 balls each of contrast colours B and C

One No.6.00 (ISR) crochet hook

Large tapestry needle or bodkin

Note

To obtain an even background insert hook under 3 top strands of tr of previous row working into body of st

Rug

Using No.6.00 (ISR) hook and A, make 194ch.

CROCHET TRIMMINGS
INSERTIONS

Crochet as an insertion

An insertion is usually thought of as a decorative open work strip which joins two pieces of fabric together, so adding a pretty, patterned panel to a dress or down the side seams of trousers. In this chapter we deal with making straight insertions which are applied directly on to straight pieces of fabric, so working the crochet and joining the pieces together in one easy stage. Dress patterns with simple seams could easily employ this method, but remember that the crochet has a certain depth and therefore the appropriate amount should first be cut away from your pattern (i.e. half the width of the total insertion could be removed from both pattern pieces being joined). Before beginning work on a sample, turn under 5cm (*2 inches*) seam allowance or for a garment, press back the seam on the fitting line, then follow our instructions to learn the techniques and some interesting designs.

Sample 1

This sample shows the seam pressed back and ready for work to begin. As a crochet hook can not be inserted directly into the majority of dress fabrics, an even back stitch has been worked along the fitting line (this has been emphasised in our sample by the use of green wool). The size of the sewing stitch should be large enough to allow the crochet hook to pass through it.

Sample 2

Here the first line of crochet is being worked. Make a slip loop on the hook, then working from right to left with the right side of the work facing, remove hook from loop and insert into first st on fabric, replace the loop on the hook and draw through the st on the fabric, 2ch, *insert hook into next sewing stitch, yrh and draw through a loop, yrh and draw through both loops (i.e. 1dc has been worked), 1ch, rep from * to end of work. Fasten off.

Note Our sample illustrates 1dc followed by 1ch, but if the back stitches are smaller there is no need for 1ch between stitches.

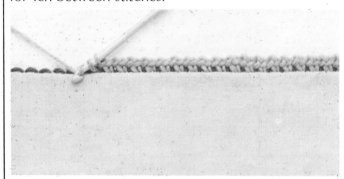

Sample 3

This is the completed insertion. First work along the edges of fabrics, A and B, as described in sample 2. With RS of work facing and working from right to left, insert hook into first ch of fabric A, work 5ch, slip hook out of st and insert into first ch of fabric B again with RS facing, *replace st on the hook and draw through the st on B, yrh 3 times, insert hook into next ch of fabric A, yrh and draw through a loop, (yrh and draw through first 2 loops on hook), 4 times – 1tr tr has been worked –, remove hook from st and insert into next ch on fabric B, rep from * to end. Fasten off yarn by replacing st and draw through the ch sp on fabric B, yrh and draw through, cutting end.

Note When joining two pieces of fabric together in this way, it is important that the two rows of back stitches are exactly the same in size and number.

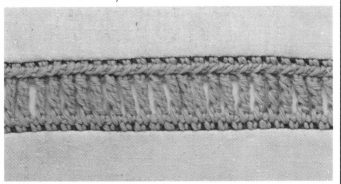

Sample 4

This sample has been made in the same way as sample 3, but a further development has been incorporated. A cord has been worked through pairs of tr tr – denoted as A and B. To do this, follow our diagram and place first tr tr – A over second tr tr – B and then take the cord under B and over A. Repeat over each pair of tr tr. Here the insert has been used vertically as it would be in a trouser seam.

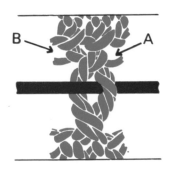

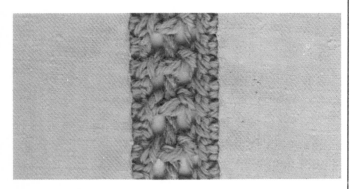

Sample 5

Work a row of dc along two pieces of fabric, A and B, as given for sample 2. To work the crochet joining the two pieces together, with RS of work facing and working from right to left, join yarn to first st on fabric A, work 9ch, slip hook out of st and insert hook into first st on fabric B again with RS of work facing, *replace the st on the hook and draw through the st on fabric B, yrh 8 times, insert hook into next st on fabric A, yrh and draw through a loop, (yrh and draw through first 2 loops on hook) 9 times – called 1tr8 –, remove st from hook and insert into next ch on

fabric B, rep from * to end. Fasten off yarn by replacing st on hook, then draw through the st on fabric B, yrh and draw through yarn, cutting off end. The diagram shows the method of threading cord through the stitches.

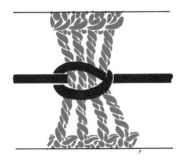

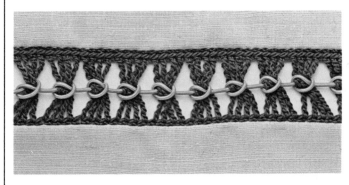

Sample 6

Work as given for sample 5, working 10ch at the beginning and working a 1tr9 by placing yrh 9 times and (yrh and draw through first 2 loops on hook) 10 times.

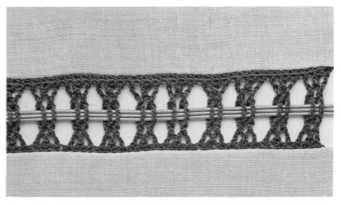

The diagram shows the method of working three rows of cord through the stitches.

EDGINGS

One of the neatest and most attractive ways of finishing off the outer edges of a garment, whether it is knitted or worked in crochet, is by using a crochet edging.

The edging may be worked in rounds or rows. It normally consists of only one row or round of crochet, but it may be necessary to work a foundation row or round of double crochet to give a firmer edge. These edgings are worked into the stitches round the outer edges of a garment or piece of crochet work after the main part has been completed and stitched together. Edgings can be either subtle or a feature of the design depending on the nature of the main work. A decorative edging can liven up a plain jacket, whilst a very simple edging may be all that is needed to neaten a heavily patterned piece of work. Choose a yarn that is applicable to the type of work you are doing. You will probably want to use the same yarn as you used for the rest of the garment, maybe in a different colour to add contrast. Should you want to make more of a feature of the edging however and use an entirely different yarn, remember the quality of the rest of the work, e.g. do not pick a thick, heavy yarn for delicate baby clothes.

There are an infinite number of edgings and below we give instructions for a number of the most unusual including basic picots, shells and clusters. One of these would be suitable for practically everything you can crochet from heavy outer garments to baby clothes and fine household linens.

Edging 1 Into first st work 1dc, *3ch, miss next st, 1dc into next st, rep from * to the end.

Edging 2 This is called crab stitch. It is simply double crochet into every stitch, but working from left to right instead of the normal right to left.

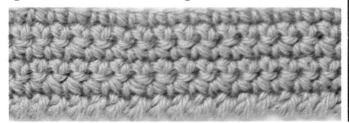

Edging 3 This is the most usual way of working a picot. Work 1dc into each of first 3 sts, *4ch, remove hook from st and insert it into first ch worked from front to back, pick up the st that was left and draw through the loop on the hook – 1 picot has been formed –, 1dc into each of next 3 sts, rep from * to end.

Edging 4 Here is a more decorative picot edging. Work 1dc into each of first 3 sts, *4ch, 1dc into 3rd ch from hook, 1ch, miss next st, 1dc into each of next 3 sts, rep from * to end.

Edging 5 The picots worked here form a very dense edge. Ss into first st, *4ch and work a picot into 4th ch from hook as described in edging 3, ss into next st, rep from * to end.

Edging 6 This is an easy way of making a looped edging. *Work 1dc into first st, extend loop on hook and transfer it to a No.1 knitting needle, keeping the needle at the back of the work, reinsert hook into last dc worked, yrh and draw through a loop, 1dc into next st, rep from * to end.

Edging 7 Ss into each of first 2 sts, *1dc into next st, 3ch, ss into same st where last dc was worked, ss into each of next 2 sts, rep from * to end.

Edging 8 The group of stitches in this edging form a decorative scallop shape. Work 3ch, into st at base of ch work (1htr, 1ch, 1tr, 1ch and 1dtr), *miss next 2 sts, ss into next st, (1htr, 1ch, 1tr, 1ch and 1dtr) into same st as ss, rep from * to end.

Edging 9 More loops, but this time formed by chain stitches. Work 1dc into first st, *3ch, ss into same st where last dc was worked, miss next st, 1dc into next st, rep from * to end.

Edging 10 The stitches in each group form a shell. Join in yarn and into 3rd st from hook work (2tr, 1ch, 1dtr, 1ch, 2tr), *miss next 2 sts, ss into next st, miss next 2 sts, (2tr, 1ch, 1dtr, 1ch, 2tr) into next st, rep from * to end.

Edging 11 This edging gives an unusual geometric outline. *Work 7ch, into 3rd ch from hook work 1dc, 1htr into next ch, 1tr into next ch, 1dtr into next ch, 1tr tr into next ch, miss next 3 sts, ss into next st, rep from * to end.

Edging 12 Here a cluster of stitches gives an interesting variation. Work 2ch, miss first st, 1htr into next st, *(yrh and insert into the ch sp at right of htr just worked from front to back, yrh and draw through a loop) 3 times, yrh and draw through all 7 loops on hook, 1ch, miss next st, 1htr into next st, rep from * to end.

SIMPLE BRAIDS AND CORDS

Decoration plays an important part in fashion today, both for the fashions we wear and for those in the home. One type of decoration is to apply braids and cords to form an additional design. Here we shall tell you how to work a number of braids which are suitable for all types of garment.

A braid is usually considered to be a narrow piece of work made in a chosen yarn to complement the main garment which is then applied as a binding to cover or neaten a raw edge of fabric, or as a fashion detail. The colour, texture and width of the braid must be chosen carefully in conjunction with the fabric with which it is to be used and the trimming design must be worked out in relation to the whole garment so that it does not end up looking as though it has been added as an afterthought.

The cords illustrated in this chapter may be used for any form of tie lacing or decoration. Several strips of cord can be applied side by side to give a wider trim.

Sample 1

This is a simple cord made with a No.4.00 (ISR) hook and a double knitting yarn. Work a length of chain, and then slip stitch back along the length by placing the hook into the loop on the reverse side of each chain.

Sample 2

Make a length of chain in the same way as sample 1 and then slip stitch back along the length by placing the hook into the single top loop on the front of each chain. The reverse side has been illustrated and this has an attractive knotted effect.

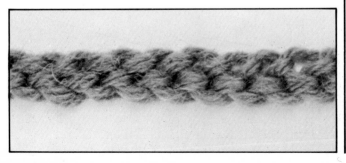

Sample 3

Using No.4.00 (ISR) hook and a double knitting yarn, make a length of chain very loosely. When the chain is the required length, thread four thicknesses of a chenille yarn through the chain stitches.

Sample 4

In this sample four thicknesses of chenille yarn are threaded into the cord as you are working it. Using No.4.00 (ISR) hook and a double knitting yarn, make a length of chain, but at the same time pass the chenille to and fro over the incoming yarn behind the hook between every two stitches worked. The reverse side of the chain has been illustrated.

Sample 5

This attractive beaded cord has been worked in a similar way to sample 4. Thread the small wooden beads on to a separate length of yarn. Using a No.4.00 (ISR) hook and a double knitting yarn, make a length of chain and at the same time pass a doubled length of beaded yarn to and fro between every four chain stitches. In the illustrated sample the beads have been positioned in fives followed by threes on either side of the chain.

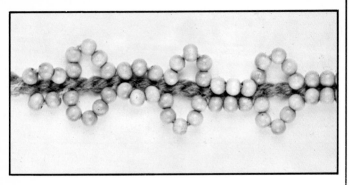

Sample 6

This sample has been worked with a modern interpretation of a lucet which is an old-fashioned tool for making a chain type cord. It is usually in the shape of a lyre and is also known as a chain fork. However, two crochet hooks placed together as in our diagram can be used to make this cord.

Rug wool has been used for this particular cord and you will also need two No.7.00 (ISR) hooks plus a No.2.50 (ISR) hook to work the chain. Place a slip loop on the left hand hook and then hold the two hooks together. Wrap the yarn behind the right hook and in front of the left hook. Hold the yarn behind the hooks and using the smaller hook slip the loop on the left hook over the yarn. *Place yarn behind the right hook in front of both loops, holding it behind the hooks, then slip the under loop over the top loop on both hooks. *. Repeat from * to * for the required length.

Sample 7

Here the same method as sample 6 is illustrated using two No.5.00 (ISR) hooks in place of the lucet, a double

knitting yarn and a No.2.50 (ISR) hook for working the chain.

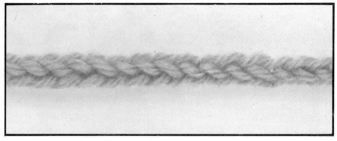

Sample 8

Using two No.6.00 (ISR) hooks in place of the lucet, two thicknesses of double knitting yarn together and a No.2.50 (ISR) hook, place a slip loop on the left hook and then *wrap the yarn round the right hook from behind and then round the left hook from behind as in the diagram. Slip the under loop over the top loop on both hooks. *. Repeat from * to * for the required length. This forms a much firmer cord suitable for a tie belt.

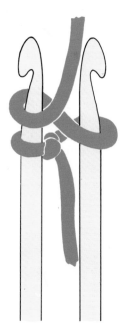

Sample 9

After the completion of a braid made with a lucet, a narrow ribbon has been threaded in and out of the chain, and then it has been drawn up to give a zigzag effect.

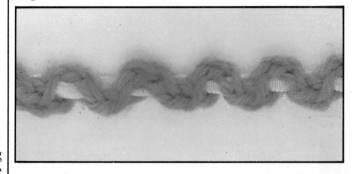

290

INTRICATE BRAIDS

Here are some braids and trimmings more intricate than the simple cords suitable for lacing or ties which were described in the last chapter. The samples in this chapter are worked in a different way and produce slightly wider trimmings which are suitable for clothes, or lampshade braids and roller blind hems. Again, remember that the choice of yarn for working the trimming is very important and should compliment the fabric on which it will be used.

Sample 1

A very attractive braid is formed by a new technique where the work is turned after each individual stitch has been worked. Using a No.4.50 (ISR) hook and a double knitting yarn, make a slip loop on the hook. Yrh and draw through loop, insert hook into first loop made, yrh and draw through loop, yrh and draw through both loops on hook. Turn work. Insert hook from right to left into the small loop on the left hand side, yrh and draw through a loop, yrh and draw through both loops on hook. Turn work. *Insert hook from right to left into the two loops on the left hand side, yrh and draw through a loop, yrh and draw through both loops on hook. Turn work. *. Repeat from * to * for required length of braid.

Sample 2

Both sides of this unusual braid are illustrated here as each has a completely different appearance. Using two thicknesses of a double knitting yarn and

a No.5.00 (ISR) hook, make a slip loop on the hook. Yrh and draw through loop, insert hook into first loop made, yrh and draw through loop, yrh and draw through both loops on hook. Turn work. Insert hook from right to left into the small loop on the left hand side, yrh and draw through a loop, yrh and draw through both loops on hook. Turn work. *Insert hook from right to left into the two loops on the left hand side as given for sample 1, yrh and draw through a loop, yrh and draw through both loops on hook. *. Turn work from right to left. Repeat from * to *. Turn work from left to right. Continue in this way, turning work alternately from right to left and then from left to right for the required length of the cord. One way of using this braid is for trimming a pocket as in our photograph.

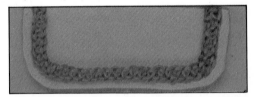

Sample 3

This is worked in the same way as sample 1, but in trebles instead of double crochet. A double length of mohair yarn has then been threaded through the vertical loops on the surface.

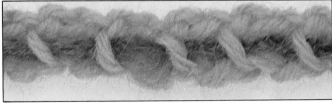

Sample 4

Using a very thick embroidery yarn and a No.5.00 (ISR) hook, work in the same way as sample 1 in half trebles instead of double crochet.

Sample 5

Here is a very pretty shell design which is very easy to make. Using a No.4.50 (ISR) hook and a double knitting yarn, make 8ch. Join with a ss into first ch to form a circle. 3ch to count as first tr, work 7tr into circle, 6ch, work 1dc into circle. Turn work. *3ch to count as first tr, work 7tr into 6ch sp, 6ch, 1dc into 6ch sp. Turn work. *. Repeat from * to * for the required length.

Sample 6

Using two thicknesses of a double knitting yarn and a No.5.00 (ISR) hook, make 4ch. Into 4th ch from hook work 1tr tr and 1dc. Turn work. *3ch, into dc work 1tr tr and 1dc. Turn work. *. Repeat from * to * for the required length. This produces a thick, chunky accordion type braid.

Sample 7

Raffene has been used for this braid to give a shiny and crunchy texture. Using a No.5.00 (ISR) hook work in the same way as sample 1, but instead of double crochet make a 7 loop treble by placing (yrh, insert hook into stitch, yrh and draw through a loop) 3 times, yrh and draw through all 7 loops.

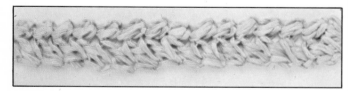

Sample 8

Bobble stitches give an interesting chunky look to this braid. Using No.5.00 (ISR) hook and two thicknesses of a double knitting yarn, make 2ch. (Yrh and insert into first ch worked, yrh and draw through a loop) 3 times, yrh and draw through all loops on hook, 3ch, 1dc into first ch worked. Turn work. *(Yrh and insert into 3ch sp, yrh and draw through a loop) 3 times, yrh and draw through all loops on hook, 3ch, 1dc into 3ch sp. Turn work. *. Continue in this way for the required length.

You will see that the bobbles lie in an alternating pattern with the outer edges forming gently scalloped lines on either side of the braid.

Sample 9

An interesting frieze has been created by working crochet stitches within a border. Using No.4.50 (ISR) hook and a double knitting yarn, make a chain the required length with multiples of 4 stitches.

1st row Into 3rd ch from hook work 1dc, 1dc into each ch to end. Turn.

2nd row 4ch, miss first 2dc, *leaving last loop of each on hook work 2dtr into next dc, yrh and draw through all 3 loops – called a joint dtr –, 3ch, work a joint dtr into same dc as before, miss next 3dc, rep from * finishing with 1dtr into last dc. Turn.

3rd row Work 1dc into each st to end of row. Fasten off.

Sample 10

Two colours of a double knitting yarn, A and B, create an unusual effect in this braid. Using a No.4.50 (ISR) hook and A, make 5ch.

1st row Into 2nd ch from hook work 1dc, 1htr into next ch, 1tr into next ch, leaving the last loop of each on hook work 3dtr into next ch, yrh and draw through all loops on hook. Turn.

2nd row Join in B. *Work 1dc into first st, 1htr into next st, 1tr into next st, leaving the last loop of each on hook work 3dtr into next st, yrh and draw through all loops on hook. Turn. *.

3rd row Join in A. Rep from * to * of 2nd row.

Repeat 2nd and 3rd rows for the required length.

Note Work over the colour not in use to keep the loose ends of yarn behind the work.

BRAIDS USING RIBBON

Braids using ribbons

Most of the braids illustrated can be used for either a trimming added to a garment, or a chosen sample could be incorporated as part of the design of a garment and worked in with the normal crochet stitches. They could be used as trimmings round the hemline of a plain skirt, trousers or jerkins. If the braid is placed on the waistline of a garment, then the ribbon can act as a means of drawing in the waist.

Sample 1

This demonstrates the basic technique used in this chapter and the samples following show developments of this method of work.

Using No.4.00 (ISR) hook and a cotton yarn, make a length of chain with multiples of 2 stitches.

1st row Into 3rd ch from hook work 1htr, 1htr into each ch to end. Turn.

2nd row 4ch to count as first tr and ch sp, miss first 2 sts, 1tr into next st, *1ch, miss next st, 1tr into next st, rep from * to end. Turn.

3rd row 2ch to count as first htr, 1htr into each ch sp and tr, ending with 1htr into 4ch sp, 1htr into 3rd of 4ch. Fasten off.

The ribbon has been threaded through alternate trebles in the 2nd row.

Sample 2

Using No.3.00 (ISR) hook and a cotton yarn, make a chain with multiples of 4+2 stitches.

1st row Into 3rd ch from hook work 1dc, 1dc into each ch to end. Turn.

2nd row 4ch to count as first dtr, 2dtr leaving last loop of each on hook into st at base of ch, yrh and draw through all loops on hook, *3ch, miss next 3 sts, 3dtr leaving last loop of each on hook into next st, yrh and draw through all loops on hook, rep from * to end. Turn.

3rd row 1ch to count as first dc, 1dc into each st to end. Fasten off.

Velvet ribbon has been threaded in and out of alternate double treble groups.

Sample 3

Using No.3.00 (ISR) hook and a cotton yarn, make a length of chain with multiples of 6+3 stitches.

1st row Into 3rd ch from hook work 1dc, 1dc into each ch to end. Turn.

2nd row 1ch to count as first dc, 1dc into each st to end. Turn.

3rd row As 2nd.

4th row 1ch to count as first dc, 1dc into each st working into same sts as for 3rd row – this gives a very firm ridge. Turn.

5th row 6ch to count as first st and ch sp, miss first 2 sts, *yrh 5 times, insert hook into next st, yrh and draw through a loop, (yrh and draw through first 2 loops on hook) 6 times – called 1tr5 –, (1ch, miss next st, 1tr5 into next st) twice, 1ch, yrh twice, take hook in front of last 3 vertical bars worked to the back, yrh and draw through a loop, yrh and draw through one loop, yrh twice, miss next st, insert hook into next st, yrh and draw through a loop, (yrh and draw through first 2 loops on hook) 6 times, rep from * to end, beg each new rep with first 1tr5 into same st as last 1tr5. Turn.

6th row 1ch to count as first dc, 1dc into each st to end. Turn.

7th row 1ch to count as first dc, 1dc into each st working into same sts as for 6th row. Turn.

8th and 9th rows As 2nd. Fasten off.

Ribbon has been threaded through alternate groups of crossed stitches.

Sample 4

Using No.3.00 (ISR) hook and a cotton yarn, make a length of chain with multiples of 6+2 stitches.

1st to 3rd rows As 1st to 3rd rows of sample 3.

4th row 9ch, miss first 6 sts, ss into next st, *9ch, miss next 5 sts, ss into next st, rep from * to end. Turn.

5th row 1ch to count as first dc, 10dc into first 9ch sp, 11dc into each 9ch sp to end. Turn. Fasten off.

6th row Join yarn into 3rd st of first sp between half circles, *9ch, ss into 3rd ch of next sp passing ch length in front of work, rep from * taking the ch length behind and in front of work alternately. Turn.

7th row As 5th.

8th row Make a slip loop on the hook, 2ch, ss into 6th dc of first half circle, *2ch, ss into 6th dc of next half circle, rep from * to end, 2ch. Turn.

9th row 1ch to count as first dc, 1dc into each st to end. Turn.

10th and 11th rows As 9th.

This braid is reversible and petersham ribbon has been threaded through as illustrated.

Sample 5

Using No.3.50 (ISR) hook and a double knitting yarn, make 2ch. (Yrh and insert into first ch worked, yrh and draw through a loop) 3 times, yrh and draw through all loops on hook, 3ch, 1dc into first ch worked. Turn. *(Yrh and insert into ch sp, yrh and draw through a loop) 3 times, yrh and draw through all loops on hook, 3ch, 1dc into same ch sp. Turn. * Rep from * to * for required length.

Double chain has been threaded in and out of the chain spaces.

Sample 6

Using No.3.50 (ISR) hook and a double knitting yarn, make a length of chain with multiples of 4+3 stitches.

1st row Into 5th ch from hook work 1dc, *1ch, miss next ch, 1dc into next ch, rep from * to end. Turn.

2nd row *5ch, 3dtr into 4th ch from hook, miss next ch sp, 1dc into next ch sp, rep from * to end. Break off yarn.

3rd row Rejoin yarn to other side of foundation ch and rep 2nd row, working the dc into the sp missed on that row.

A narrow velvet ribbon has been threaded in a spiral over the centre core, working in and out of the spaces below the double trebles.

Sample 7

This sample is worked with a No.3.50 (ISR) hook and a double knitting yarn.

1st line *6ch, (yrh and insert into first ch, yrh and draw through a loop) 3 times, yrh and draw through all loops on hook, rep from * for required length.

2nd line *3ch, sl working loop off hook and insert into next 6ch sp of first line, pick up working loop and draw through to front of work, 3ch, (yrh and insert into first ch worked, yrh and draw through a loop) 3 times, yrh and draw through all loops on hook, rep from * joining each 6ch length to the next 6ch sp of the 1st line. Fasten off. Narrow velvet ribbon has been threaded in and out between the 6 chain spaces.

Hatband with leather trim

Size
2.5cm (1in) wide by 58.5cm (23in) long

Tension
12 sts to 10cm (3.9in) and 1 row to 2.5cm (1in) over tr worked on No.4.00 (ISR) crochet hook

Materials
Approximately 8.25 metres (9yds) of garden twine
Approximately 3.65 metres (4yds) of leather thonging for trimming
One No.4.00 (ISR) crochet hook

Hatband
Using No.4.00 (ISR) hook and twine, make 72ch.
1st row Into 6th ch from hook work 1tr, *1ch, miss 1ch, 1tr into next ch, rep from * to end.
Fasten off.

To make up
Press under a damp cloth with a warm iron. Darn in ends.
Leather thonging Cut leather thonging into 3 lengths. Thread through holes in hatband, leaving ends to tie at centre back.

EDGINGS FOR LINEN

Crochet trimmings for household linens
The theme of this chapter is household linens. The samples illustrated are worked in white as traditionally these 'laces' would have been used on white linen sheets and pillowcases. As the trend today is for coloured and patterned bed linen, the trimmings could still make attractive decorations on a number of plainer items such as a tailored bedcover or edging on a sheet.

You must first decide where the trim is to be placed, either on the edge of the work or within the main fabric. This will determine whether you have a trim with a definite straight edge (the other edge being curved, scalloped, pointed or fringed) which is required for sewing on to the very edge of an article or a double sided trim (the two edges are exactly the same) which is suitable for the main fabric and is usually placed well within a border or the hem.

All the designs illustrated may be used as an edging, or can be made into a double sided trim by repeating the design on the opposite side of the foundation chain, as in sample 7. Remember to wash and press all trimmings before adding to the linen to prevent any shrinkage during laundering.

Sample 1
Using No.3.50 (ISR) hook and a cotton yarn, make a length of chain with multiples of 4+3 stitches.
1st row Into 3rd ch from hook work 1htr, 1htr into each ch to end. Turn.
2nd row 2ch to count as first htr, 1htr into next htr, *6ch, into 4th ch from hook work 1tr, 1tr into each of next 2ch, miss 2htr, 1htr into each of next 2htr, rep from * ending with last htr into top of turning ch. Fasten off.

Sample 2
Using No.3.50 (ISR) hook and a cotton yarn, make a length of chain with multiples of 6+8 stitches.

1st row Into 8th ch from hook work 1tr, *2ch, miss next 2ch, 1tr into next ch, rep from * to end. Turn.
2nd row *3ch, 3dtr into next ch sp, 3ch, 3dc into next ch sp, rep from * to last ch sp, 3ch, 3dtr into last ch sp, 3ch, ss into ch sp. Fasten off.

Sample 3
Using No.3.50 (ISR) hook and a cotton yarn, make a length of chain with multiples of 6+4 stitches.
1st row Into 6th ch from hook work 1tr, *1ch, miss next ch, 1tr into next ch, rep from * to end. Turn.
2nd row Ss into first ch sp and into next tr, *5ch, miss next ch sp, (ss into each of next tr and ch sp) twice, ss into next tr, rep from * finishing with 3ss instead of 5 at end of last rep. Turn.
3rd row *Into next 5ch sp work 5tr, 5ch, ss into 4th ch from hook, 1ch and 5tr, ss into 3rd of next 5ss, rep from * to end. Fasten off.

Sample 4
Using No.3.50 (ISR) hook and a cotton yarn, make a length of chain with multiples of 5+1 stitches.
1st row Into 3rd ch from hook work 1dc, 1dc into each ch to end. Turn.
2nd row 1ch to count as first dc, miss first st, 1dc into each st to end. Turn.
3rd row As 2nd.
4th row 4ch to count as first dtr, 1dtr into first st, *miss next 3 sts, leaving last loop of each on hook work 2dtr into next st, yrh and draw through all 3 loops on hook – called a joint dtr –, 3 ch, a joint dtr into next st, rep from * to last 4 sts, miss next 3 sts, a joint dtr into last st. Turn.
5th row 4 ch to count as first dtr, 1dtr into first st, *3ch, a joint dtr into top of next joint dtr in previous row, miss next 3 sts, a joint dtr into top of next joint dtr in previous row, rep from * to last 2dtr, 3 ch, a joint dtr into last 2dtr. Turn.
6th-8th rows 1ch to count as first dc, 1dc into each st to end. Turn.
9th row 6ch, miss first 4 sts, ss into each of next 2 sts, *6ch, miss next 3 sts, ss into each of next 2 sts, rep from * finishing with a ss into last st. Turn.

10th row Into each 6ch sp work 3dc, 3ch, 1tr, 3ch and 3dc. Fasten off.

Sample 5

Using No.3.50 (ISR) hook and a cotton yarn, make 13ch.

1st row Into 4th ch from hook work 1tr, 1tr into each of next 3ch, 2ch, miss next 2ch, 1tr into each of next 4ch, 2ch, 1tr into last ch. Turn.

2nd row 3ch, miss ch sp, 1tr into each of next 4tr, 2ch, 1tr into each of next 4tr. Turn.

3rd row 3ch to count as first tr, 1tr into each of next 3tr, 2tr into next 2ch sp, 1tr into each of next 4tr, 5tr into next ch sp at beg of 2nd row, 5tr into next ch sp at end of 1st row. Do not turn.

4th row 1 ch to count as first dc, work 1dc into front loop only of each st to end of row working from left to right instead of right to left. Do not turn.

5th row 3ch to count as first tr, 1tr into each of next 3 sts placing hook into back loop only of each st, 2ch, miss next 2 sts, 1tr into back loop only of next 4 sts, 2ch, 1tr into next st. Turn.

Repeat 2nd to 5th rows inclusive for required length.

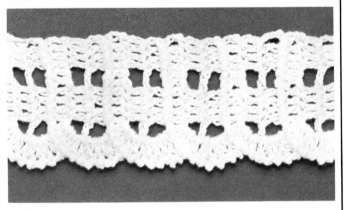

Sample 6

Using No.3.50 (ISR) hook and a cotton yarn, make a length of chain with multiples of 10+9 stitches.

1st row Into 5th ch from hook work 1tr, *1ch, miss next ch, 1tr into next ch, rep from * to end. Turn.

2nd row 3ch to count as first tr, 1tr into first ch sp, 3ch, miss next ch sp, *2tr into next ch sp, 3ch, miss next ch sp, rep from * ending with 1tr into last ch sp, 1tr into 4th of 5ch. Turn.

3rd row 4ch, 1tr into first ch sp, *1ch, 1tr into next ch sp, 1ch, 1tr into same ch sp, rep from * to last ch sp, 1ch, 1tr into last ch sp, 1ch, 1tr into 3rd of 3ch. Turn.

4th row 1ch to count as first dc, 2dc into first ch sp, 8ch, *3dc into each of next 3 ch sp, 8ch, rep from * to last ch sp, 2dc into last ch sp, 1dc into 3rd of 4ch. Turn.

5th row Ss into each dc worked and into each 8ch loop work 2dc, 2htr, 9tr, 2htr and 2dc. Fasten off.

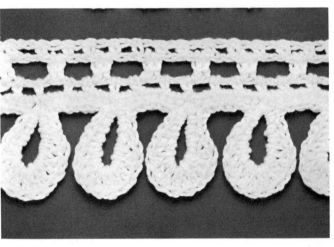

Sample 7

Using No.3.50 (ISR) hook and a cotton yarn, make a length of chain with multiples of 8 stitches.

1st row Into 6th ch from hook work 1tr, *1ch, miss next ch, 1tr into next ch, rep from * to end. Turn.

2nd row 4ch, 1tr into first sp, 1ch, 1tr into next sp, *6ch, miss next sp, 1tr into next sp, 1ch, 1tr into next sp, 1ch, 1tr into next sp, rep from * to end. Turn.

3rd row Ss into each of next sp, tr and foll sp, * into 6ch sp work 2dc, 2htr, 5tr, 2htr and 2dc, ss into each of next 3 sts, rep from * to end. Turn.

4th row *3ch, 1tr into first tr of 5tr gr, 3ch, 1dtr into centre tr of gr, 3ch, 1dtr into same tr, 3ch, 1tr into last tr of gr, 3ch, 1tr into centre ss, rep from * to end. Turn.

5th row *3dc into each of next 2 sp, into next sp work 3dc, 4ch, ss into first ch worked so forming a picot and 3dc, 3dc into each of next 2 sp, rep from * to end. Fasten off. This forms an edging with one straight edge, but the crochet design may be worked on the other side of the foundation chain to give a double sided trim as in our illustration.

EDGINGS FOR SOFT FURNISHINGS

Trimmings for soft furnishings

In the last chapter we showed samples of edgings and double sided braids suitable for household articles. Here we extend the theme to include more decorative and deeper trimmings such as deep shaped edgings and crochet braids with long tassels and pompons. This work is ideal for lampshades, both hanging from the ceiling and table lamps, roller blinds, curtains and pelmets.

Our samples have been worked in cotton yarns, but of course other colours and types of yarn are quite suitable for most of the designs. One word of warning – if you are making tassels the yarn must not fray when cut so leave the tassel in uncut loops to avoid this happening with yarn which unravels.

Sample 1

Using No.3.50 (ISR) hook and a cotton yarn, make a length of chain with multiples of 2 stitches.

1st row Into 3rd ch from hook work 1dc, 1dc into each ch to end. Turn.

2nd row 1ch to count as first dc, miss 1dc, 1dc into each dc to end. Turn.

3rd row 4ch to count as first tr and sp, miss first 2dc, 1tr into next dc, *1ch, miss next dc, 1tr into next dc, rep from * to end. Turn.

4th row 3ch to count as first tr, *(yrh and insert into next ch sp, yrh and draw through a loop) 4 times, yrh and draw through all loops on hook, 1ch, rep from * omitting 1ch at end of last rep and ending with 1tr into 3rd of 4ch. Turn.

5th row 4ch to count as first tr and sp, *miss next bobble, 1tr into next ch, 1ch, rep from * omitting 1ch at end of last rep and ending with last tr into 3rd of 3ch. Fasten off.

Fringe Cut 5 lengths of yarn each 12.5cm (*5in*) long and fold in half lengthwise. Insert folded end through ch sp in the 5th row, then pull the cut ends through the loop. Pull up tightly. Repeat into each ch sp along the row. Trim ends to an equal length.

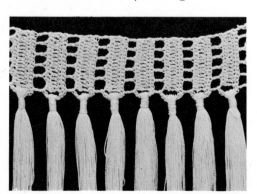

Sample 2

Using No.3.50 (ISR) hook and a cotton yarn, make a length of chain with multiples of 4+1 stitches.

1st–2nd rows As 1st–2nd rows of sample 1.

3rd row (crossed triple trebles) Ss into each of first 4 sts, 5ch to count as first tr tr, yrh 3 times, insert hook behind ch length into next st at right of ch just worked, yrh and draw through a loop, (yrh and draw through first 2 loops on hook) 4 times – called 1tr tr –, work 1tr tr into each of next 2 sts to the right of last tr tr, *miss 3 sts to left of first tr tr, 1tr tr into next st, 1tr tr into each of next 3 sts to the right of last tr tr always placing hook behind the last st worked, rep from * to end. Turn.

4th row 1ch to count as first dc, 1dc into each st to end. Turn.

5th row As 4th.

6th row 6ch, miss first 2 sts, ss into next st, *3ch, miss next st, ss into next st, 6ch, miss next st, ss into next st, rep from * to end. Fasten off.

Fringe Work as given for sample 1, and thread through each 6ch loop in 6th row.

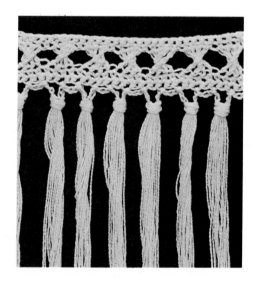

Sample 3

Using No.3.50 (ISR) hook and a cotton yarn, make 20ch.

1st row Into 8th ch from hook work 1tr, *2ch, miss 2ch, 1tr into next ch, rep from * to end. Turn.

2nd row 1ch to count as first dc, miss first st, 1dc into each st to last ch sp, 2dc into ch sp, 1dc into 5th of 7ch. Turn.

3rd row 3ch to count as first tr, miss first st, 1tr into each st to end of row. Turn.

4th row As 2nd row working last dc into 3rd of 3ch, but do not turn, 5ch, ss into base of first dc in 2nd row, 7ch, ss into top of last dc worked. Turn.

5th row 5ch, miss first 3 sts, 1tr into next st, *2ch, miss next 2 sts, 1 tr into next st, rep from * to end. Fasten off. The 2nd to 5th rows inclusive form the pattern and are repeated for the required length.

Fringe Cut yarn into 30.5cm (*12in*) lengths and using 34 of these lengths together, place over a length of double chain. Tie very securely in place below the chain. Repeat into each length of double chain along the row, and then trim the ends.

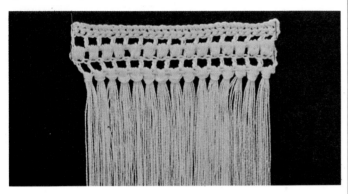

Sample 4

Using No.4.00 (ISR) hook and a thick cotton yarn, make a chain the required length with multiples of 4+3 stitches.

1st row Into 3rd ch from hook work 1dc, 1dc into each ch to end. Turn.

2nd row (crossed trebles) Ss into each of first 2 sts, 3ch to count as first tr, placing the hook behind the length of chain work 1tr into next st to the right of the chain, *miss next st to left of first tr, 1tr into next st, placing the hook in front of the last tr worked 1tr into next st to the right, miss next st, 1tr into next st, placing the hook behind the last tr worked 1tr into next st to the right, rep from * to end. Turn.

3rd row 1ch to count as first dc, 1dc into each st to end. Turn.

4th row 6ch, miss first 4 sts, 1dc into next st, *5ch, miss 3 sts, 1dc into next st, rep from * to end. Fasten off.

Pompons Cut two circular pieces of card both 5cm (*2in*) in diameter and each having a central hole, 2.5cm (*1in*) in diameter. Use the circles to make a pompon in the usual manner.

Work a length of chain for attaching on to the 5ch loops in the 4th rows.

Sample 5

This is a variation on the traditional filet crochet known as filet guipure. The techniques of working filet crochet are described in detail in the chapters on Filet Crochet given earlier. Here we give a chart which comprises blocks and spaces for you to follow. As usual the spaces are formed by one treble at either side of two chain, and blocks are spaces filled in with two trebles. Also in this design a double space has been worked in an unusual way by making three chain, then working one double crochet where the normal treble would be, three more chain and working the next tr in its usual position. On the following row five chain will be worked above this particular group. This variation is denoted in the chart by the symbols in the following diagram.

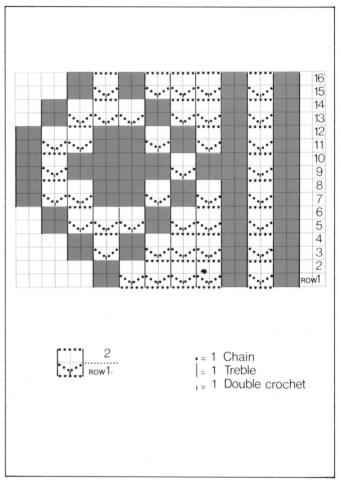

• = 1 Chain
| = 1 Treble
ı = 1 Double crochet

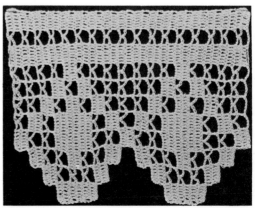

FRINGES

Continuing our chapters on trimmings and braids, we now give you instructions for making some more using fringes as the focal point. These are formed during the working of the crochet by an unusual technique of twisting the yarn to form the fringe. It is a method which requires some practise in order to achieve a good standard of work. Depending on the yarn chosen, the fringes are suitable for both household and dress trimmings.

Sample 1

Using No.4.00 (ISR) hook and a rayon yarn, make a chain the required length.

1st row Into 3rd ch from hook work 1htr, 1htr into each ch to end. Turn.

2nd row (loop row) 1ch to count as first st, miss first st, *insert hook into next st, yrh and draw through a loop, yrh and draw through both loops on hook extending loop on hook for 15cm (6in), hold work over st with thumb and first finger of left hand and with the hook in the extended loop, twist in a clockwise direction approx 24 times, halve the twisted yarn placing the hook into the last st worked, the extended

st will twist firmly in an anti-clockwise direction, yrh and draw through both loops on hook, rep from * to end of row. Fasten off. This completes the fringe.

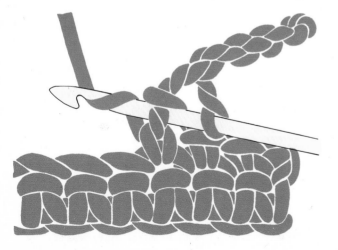

Note The depth of the fringe will depend on the length of the extended stitch and the number of times that it is twisted. You must practise this stitch to obtain perfect results.

Sample 2

Using No.4.00 (ISR) hook and a rayon yarn, make a chain the required length.

1st row Into 4th ch from hook work 1tr, 1tr into each ch to end. Turn.

2nd row Work loop row as given for sample 1. Fasten off.

Velvet ribbon, 1.5cm (½in) wide, is threaded between alternate trebles in the 1st row.

Sample 3

Using No.4.00 (ISR) hook and a double knitting yarn, make a chain the required length.

1st row Work a length of braid as given for sample 1 on page 291. Fasten off.

Join in a different colour of rayon yarn and work the loop row as foll:

2nd row Insert the hook into the loop at the top right hand edge of the braid and work a twisted loop as given for sample 1 extending the loop for 12.5cm (5in), insert the hook into the next loop but at the lower edge of the braid and make a twisted loop so forming a stitch over the braid, continue in this way working twisted loops into alternate stitches at top and lower edges for the complete length of the braid. Fasten off.

Sample 4

Using a No.4.00 (ISR) hook and a double knitting yarn, make a length of chain with multiples of 4 + 2 stitches.

1st row Into 3rd ch from hook work 1dc, 1dc into each st to end. Turn.

2nd row 1ch to count as first dc, miss first st, 1dc into next st, *1tr tr into next st, 1dc into each of next 3 sts, rep from * to last 3 sts, 1tr tr into next st, 1dc into each of next 2 sts. Turn.

3rd row 1ch to count as first dc, miss first st, 1dc into each st to end. Turn. Fasten off.

Join in a different colour of rayon yarn and work the loop row as foll:

4th row Work as given for loop row of sample 1, placing hook first into (a) next st of last row, then (b) into next st of row below, then (c) into next st of row below that, rep in the order of (b), (a), (b), (c), (b) and (a) for the required length. Fasten off.

Sample 5

Using No.4.00 (ISR) hook and a rayon yarn, make a chain the required length.

1st row Into 4th ch from hook work 1tr, 1tr into each ch to end. Turn.

2nd row 1ch to count as first dc, miss first st, work 1dc into each st to end placing hook from back to front into sp between normal chain st and horizontal loop below it – this gives a raised chain effect on the right side of the work. Turn.

3rd row (loop row) This is slightly different from the loop row of sample 1. Work 4ch to count as first tr

and sp, miss first 2 sts, *yrh and insert into next st, yrh and draw through a loop, (yrh and draw through first 2 loops on hook) twice, extend loop on hook twisting it as before, insert hook into last st worked, yrh and draw through both loops on hook, 1ch, miss next st, rep from * ending with last tr into turning chain. Fasten off. Velvet ribbon has been threaded between alternate trebles of the loop row.

Sample 6

Using No.3.00 (ISR) hook and a cotton yarn, make a chain the required length.

1st row Into 4th ch from hook work 1tr, 1tr into each ch to end. Turn.

2nd row 1ch to count as first dc, 1dc into each st to end. Turn.

3rd row 1ch to count as first dc, 1dc into back loop only of each st to end. Turn.

4th row 2ch to count as first tr, 1tr into each single loop rem from last row – now to the back of the work – to end of row. Turn.

5th row (loop row) Work as given for loop row of sample 1. Fasten off.

6th row (loop row) Rejoin yarn to sts of row 3 on front of braid and work as given for loop row of sample 1. Velvet ribbon has been threaded between alternate trebles in the 1st row.

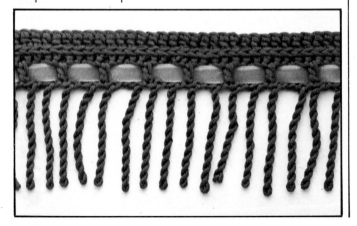

DECORATIVE FRINGES

Decorative fringes

Exciting fringes may be worked in many ways and in this chapter we cover a variety of very decorative ones which would be suitable for fashion garments. The fringes illustrated could be used on jerkins, long scarves, stoles and dresses. Master the techniques described here and when you feel competent, try experimenting with different yarns, beads and threads.

Sample 1

This has been worked in two yarns, a gold ribbon – A, and a tubular rayon – B. Using No.4.00 (ISR) hook and B, make 6ch.

1st row Place yarn A between the incoming yarn B and the hook, placing the cut end to the right hand side of the work, 1ch with B, *take yarn A from left to right placing it between incoming yarn B and the hook leaving a 7.5cm (3in) folded loop, 1ch with B, take yarn A now on the right and place between the incoming yarn B and the hook leaving no loop, 1ch with B, rep from * for the required length of fringe, work 12ch with B. Break off A and reverse work.

2nd row Fold the 12ch length just worked in half and hold in the left hand with the loops to the right, the incoming yarn should be under or behind the work and the hook on top or towards you, *place hook over single thickness of next loop, yrh and draw through st on hook, place hook over next single thickness of same loop, yrh and draw through st on hook, rep from * to end of loops, work 12ch and reverse work.

3rd row Fold the 12ch length just worked in half and hold in the right hand with the loops to the left, rep as given from * of 2nd row to end.

The 2nd and 3rd rows are repeated to give the required proportion of heading to the looped fringe.

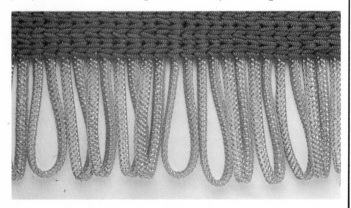

Sample 2

Two types of yarn have been used for this sample,

A for the working yarn and 4 thicknesses of B together for the fringe. Using No.3.50 (ISR) hook and A, make 6ch.

1st row Place yarn B (all 4 thicknesses) between the incoming yarn A and the hook, placing the cut ends to the right hand side of the work, 1ch with A, * take yarn B from left to right placing it between incoming yarn A and the hook leaving a 7.5cm (3in) folded loop, 1ch with A, take yarn B now on the right and place between the incoming yarn A and the hook leaving no loop, 1ch with A, rep from * for the required length of fringe, work 12ch with A. Break off B and reverse work.

2nd row Fold the 12ch length just worked in half and hold in the left hand with the loops to the right, the incoming yarn should be under or behind the work and the hook on top or towards you, *place hook over 4 thicknesses of next loop, yrh and draw through st on hook, place hook over next 4 thicknesses of same loop, yrh and draw through st on hook, rep from * to end of loops, work 12ch and reverse work.

3rd row Fold the 12ch length just worked in half and hold in the right hand with the loops to the left, rep as given from * of 2nd row to end.

The 2nd and 3rd rows are repeated to give the required proportion of heading to the fringe. The loops can either be cut as in our sample or left uncut .

Sample 3

Here is an attractive method of making a beaded fringe. A lurex yarn has been used for the crochet, whilst the beads have been threaded on to a separate length of yarn. The number of beads will of course depend on the amount of fringing required. Using No.3.50 (ISR) hook and lurex yarn, make 6ch.

1st row With cut end to the right, place yarn with beads between incoming yarn and the hook, 1ch with lurex yarn, *place yarn with beads from left to right, placing 21 beads on a loop plus 2.5cm (1in) of free yarn, between incoming yarn and hook, 2ch with lurex yarn, place yarn with beads from right to left, leaving no loop between incoming yarn and hook, work 1ch with lurex yarn, rep from * to give required length of fringe, work 12ch with lurex yarn. Break off yarn with beads and reverse work.

2nd row Hold the work with the chain heading to the left and beaded loops to the right, work 1ch over next length of yarn with beads having one bead on the left, *1ch, 1ch over next length of yarn with beads having one bead on the left, rep from * to end of fringe, work 12ch. Reverse work.

3rd row Hold the work with the chain heading to the right and beaded loops to the left, work as given for 2nd row. Fasten off.

Note The yarn with beads will require tightening in order to give an all beaded loop with no yarn showing between the beads.

Sample 4
Using No.4.00 (ISR) hook and a double knitting yarn, make 6ch.

1st row Into 3rd ch from hook work 1dc, 1dc into each ch to end. Turn. 4 sts.

2nd row 1ch to count as first dc, miss first st, 1dc into each of next 3 sts. Turn.

3rd row As 2nd.

4th row As 2nd, but do not turn, work 24ch. Turn.

5th row Into 4th ch from hook work 3tr, 4tr into each of the next 20ch, 1tr into each of next 4 sts. Turn.

The 2nd to 5th rows inclusive are repeated for the length of trimming required.

Sample 5
To work the braid Using No.4.00 (ISR) hook and a double knitting yarn, make a chain with multiples of 4+2 stitches.

1st row Into 3rd ch from hook work 1dc, 1dc into each ch to end. Turn.

2nd row 1ch to count as first dc, miss first st, 1dc into each st to end. Turn.

3rd row 4ch to count as first tr and sp, miss first 2 sts, *(yrh and insert into next st, yrh and draw through a loop, yrh and draw through first 2 loops on hook) 9 times always inserting hook into same st, yrh and draw through all 10 loops on hook, work 1ch very tightly to hold bobble, 1ch, miss next st, 1tr into next st, 1ch, miss next st, rep from * ending with 1tr into last st. Turn.

4th row 1ch to count as first dc, *1dc into next ch sp, 1dc into top of next bobble, 1dc into next ch sp, 1dc into next tr, rep from * to end. Turn.

5th row As 2nd. Fasten off.

To work the crochet balls Using same yarn and hook, place the cut end of yarn in the palm of left hand and wrap yarn once round first finger, insert hook into loop round finger from underneath, yrh and draw through a loop, slip loop off finger and hold between finger and thumb of left hand, *insert hook into ring, yrh and draw through a loop, yrh and draw through both loops on hook, rep from * 7 times more. Tighten ring by pulling cut end of yarn. Mark beg of each round with a coloured thread.

Next round Work 2dc into each of 8 sts. Do not join.

Next 2 rounds Work 1dc into each of 16 sts. Do not join. Place cotton wool stuffing into ball.

Next round (Work 2dc tog) 8 times. Do not join.

Next round Work 1dc into each of 8 sts. Draw sts tog by threading working st through each free st to make a neat end, do not break off yarn, 9ch, ss to braid below bobble, ss back along chain to ball, 9ch, miss next bobble on braid, ss to braid below next bobble, ss back along chain and fasten to ball. Continue in this way, first fastening each new ball below the bobble omitted in the previous joining and so forming a cross-over design.

FRILLS

Crochet frills are easy to work and make effective trimmings for a variety of garments. When working a frill, choose a yarn which is appropriate to the purpose and fabric of the main garment such as a lurex yarn for evening wear or a fine cotton yarn for lingerie. Our samples in the photographs are worked with a No.4.50 (ISR) crochet hook and a double knitting yarn.

We also explain two methods of making frills. One way is to work more than one stitch into each stitch of the previous row and this is illustrated in samples 1, 2, 4 and 5. Sample 3 demonstrates the method of gathering crochet to form a frill. It is simple to work and would look very attractive in a white or ecru yarn. If you prefer, you could starch the crochet frill before applying it to the garment.

Sample 1

Make 31ch. This can be made longer by adding multiples of 4 stitches.

1st row Into 3rd ch from hook work 1dc, 1dc into each ch to end. Turn.

2nd row 5ch, miss first 4dc, ss into next dc, *(5ch, miss 3dc, ss into next dc), rep from * 5 times more. Turn. Seven 5ch sp.

3rd row 1ch to count as first dc, 7dc into first 5ch sp, 8dc into each 5ch sp to end.

Rep 2nd and 3rd rows along the opposite side of the foundation chain. Turn.

4th row 4ch to count as first tr and ch, *1tr, 1ch into next dc, rep from * round both sides of foundation chain. Turn.

5th row Using a contrast colour, join yarn into first 1ch sp, ss into same sp, *3ch, ss into next ch sp, rep from * to end. Fasten off.

Use this frill to decorate the centre front of a long evening gown.

Sample 2

This frill is ideal for a decorative cuff. To work the fabric shown in our sample, make 26ch.

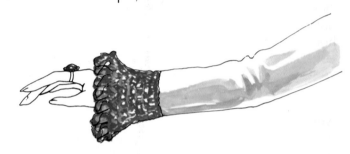

1st row Leaving the last loop of each on hook, work 1tr into each of 4th and 5th ch from hook, yrh and draw through all 3 loops on hook, 1 ch, * leaving the last loop of each on hook, work 1tr into each of next 2ch, yrh and draw through all 3 loops on hook, 1ch, rep from * to last ch, 1tr into last ch. Turn.

2nd row 3ch to count as first tr, *leaving the last loop of each on hook, work 2tr into next 1ch sp, yrh and draw through all 3 loops on hook, 1ch, rep from * ending with 1tr into 3rd of the turning ch. Turn.

The 2nd row is repeated throughout.

To work the frill

1st row 5ch, ss into top of first pair of tr, *5ch, ss into top of next pair of tr, rep from * to end. Turn.

2nd row 3ch to count as first tr, 2tr into first sp, 3ch, 3tr into same sp, *2ch, ss into next sp, 2ch, (3tr, 3ch, 3tr) into next sp, rep from * to end. Turn.

3rd row 1ch to count as first dc, 1dc into each st to end, working 5dc into each 3ch sp. Turn.
4th row 3ch to count as first tr, 1tr into each of next 4 sts, *2tr into each of next 3 sts, 1tr into each of next 13 sts, rep from * ending last rep with 1tr into each of next 3 sts, 1tr into the turning ch. Fasten off.

Sample 3
This sample would also be very effective as a cuff trimming. Using the first colour, make a foundation chain to fit the required measurement, say 30 chain.
1st row Work 1tr by placing the hook under the complete ch so that the st will move freely over the chain when complete, *3ch, work 1tr in the same way, rep from * 8 times more. Turn.
2nd row *3ch, ss into next ch sp, rep from * to end. Turn.
3rd row *5ch, ss into next ch sp, rep from * to end. Turn.
4th row *7ch, ss into next ch sp, rep from * to end. Turn.
5th row *9ch, ss into next ch sp, rep from * to end. Turn.

6th row *11ch, ss into next ch sp, rep from * to end. Turn.
7th row Into each 11ch sp work 12dc. Fasten off.
Next row Using second colour, join yarn into right hand sp at base of first tr worked on the foundation ch, 6ch to count as first tr and 3ch, 1tr into next sp between tr working over foundation ch as before, *3ch, 1tr into next sp between tr, rep from * to end. Turn.
Next 4 rows Rep 2nd to 5th rows as given for first colour.
Next row Into each 9ch sp work 11dc. Fasten off.
Note When using the second colour, if the same side of the dc row is to appear on both frills then the yarn should be cut and rejoined between the 5th and 6th rows in order to work from the correct side. The trebles are arranged along the foundation chain to give the required amount of frilling.

Sample 4
Worked in a fine yarn, this frill will look very good on nightwear or in a thicker yarn, it could be added to a circular hat such as a beret. The basic fabric in our samples is composed of trebles. When working your own sample make sure that you have a repeat of 5 stitches plus one extra. Work until the position for the frill is reached then continue as follows:
Next row *5ch, miss next 4 sts, ss into next st, rep from * to end. Turn.
Next row Into each ch sp work 1dc, 1htr, 1tr, 3ch, 1tr, 1htr, 1dc. Turn.
Continue in trebles until the position for the next frill is reached.

Sample 5
This is a narrow frill which could be used for all kinds of trimming. Make a foundation chain the required length of the frill.
1st row Into 3rd ch from hook work 1dc, 1dc into each ch to end. Turn.
2nd row *5ch, miss next st, ss into next st, rep from * to end. Turn.
3rd row Into each ch sp work 1dc, (3ch, 1dc) 5 times. Fasten off.

FINISHING TOUCHES
BUTTONS

Sample 1   Sample 2   Sample 3

Covered buttons

So often it is difficult to purchase the right button for a garment that you are making. Either the size is wrong or you are unable to match the colour, or maybe you would like an unusual button at a reasonable price as a feature on a plain garment. Crochet covered buttons can be very decorative and add greatly to any simple outfit.

The wooden or metal forms for covering are available from most haberdashery counters in a variety of shapes and sizes. The method of work is simple, but try a sample piece of crochet using your chosen yarn and hook size first. This sample must look correct on the garment for which the buttons are being made and the crochet fabric must be firm enough to entirely cover the form beneath it, so for this reason a smaller hook size than usual is recommended in order to achieve a close stitch.

Sample 1

5.50 metres (*6 yards*) of Russia braid is required to cover this large round button which is 4.5cm (*1¾in*) in diameter.

1st round Make a circle with the braid in the left hand, using No.3.00 (ISR) hook, work 8dc into this circle, draw the short end tight to close circle. Join with a ss into first dc.

2nd round 1ch to count as first dc, 1dc into st at base of ch, *2dc into next dc, rep from * to end. Join with a ss into first dc.

3rd round 1ch, 1dc into st at base of ch, 1dc into next dc, *2dc into next dc, 1dc into next dc, rep from * to end. Join with a ss into first dc.

4th round 1ch, 1dc into each dc to end. Join with a ss into first dc.

5th round As 4th.

In this case the back of the crochet work is the most effective and this has been placed on to the button shape as the right side. Lace the edge of the crochet circle on to the wrong side of the shape and secure very firmly in several places all round the edge. Place the metal covering disc over the back or neatly hem a circle of lining fabric to cover the edges. All button shapes should be neatened in this way.

Sample 2

This is a more unusual method of working the crochet covering for a 4.5cm (*1¾in*) button. Five shades of yarn and a No.3.50 (ISR) crochet hook are used. Using A make 7ch.

1st row Into 3rd ch from hook work 1dc, 1dc into each ch to end. Turn.

2nd row 1ch to count as first dc, 1dc into st at base of ch, 2dc into each st, ending with 2dc into turning ch. Turn. 12dc.

3rd row 1ch, 1dc into st at base of ch, 1dc into next st, *2dc into next st, 1dc into next st, rep from * ending with 1dc into turning ch. Turn. 18dc.

4th row 1ch, 1dc into st at base of ch, 1dc into each of next 2 sts, *2dc into next st, 1dc into each of next 2 sts, rep from * ending with last dc into turning ch. Turn. Break off A.

5th row Using B, 1ch, miss first st, 1dc into each of next 8 sts, using C, 1dc into same st as last dc, 1dc into each of next 4 sts, using D, 1dc into same st as last dc, 1dc into each of next 4 sts, using E, 1dc into same st as last dc, 1dc into each of next 7 sts. Turn.

Note When joining in new colours, follow the instructions given earlier.

6th row As 5th, dec one st at each end of row and omitting increased sts between colours.

7th row As 5th, dec one st at each end of row and inc

between colours as before.

Dec one st at each end of every row and omitting increased sts, cont in this colour sequence until there are no sts left. Fasten off.

Sample 3

Eight colours of cotton and a No.3.00 (ISR) hook have been used here to give a subtly shaded look to another 4.5cm ($1\frac{3}{4}$in) diameter button. Using a new colour for each round, follow the instructions given for 1st–3rd rounds of sample 1. Continue in rounds of dc, working 1 more dc between the increased stitches on each round.

Sample 4

This tiny, 1.5cm ($\frac{1}{2}$in) diameter, button has been delicately covered in a very fine Lurex embroidery thread. Using No.0.60 (ISR) hook, work as given for sample 3.

Sample 5

Using a Lurex yarn and No.3.00 (ISR) hook, work as given for sample 3.

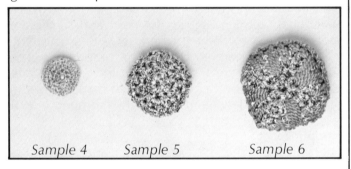

Sample 4   *Sample 5*   *Sample 6*

Sample 6

Lurex and cotton yarns are combined in this design to cover a 2.5cm (1in) diameter button. Using No.3.00 (ISR) hook and the Lurex yarn, work as given for 1st–3rd rounds of sample 1. Break off yarn.

4th round Using cotton yarn, 2ch, *1dc into next st, 1dc into next st inserting hook into 2nd round, 2dc into next st in 1st round, 1dc into next st in 2nd round,

1dc into next st, 1ch, rep from * omitting 1ch at end of last rep. Join with a ss into first ch.

5th round 1ch to count as first dc, 1dc into each st to end. Join with a ss into first ch. Fasten off.

Sample 7

Seven colours of a cotton yarn have been used to cover this square button in varying widths of diagonal stripes. You can vary the colours in any way you want. Using No.3.00 (ISR) hook make 3ch.

1st row Into 3rd ch from hook work 1dc. Turn.

2nd row 1ch to count as first dc, 1dc into st at base of ch, 2dc into next st. Turn.

3rd row 1ch, 1dc into st at base of ch, 1dc into each st to turning ch, 2dc into turning ch. Turn.

Cont inc one st at each end of every row in this way until the crochet is the correct diagonal width for the button shape required. Dec one st at each end of every row until there are no sts left. Fasten off.

Sample 8

This button cover consists of 2 triangular shapes joined together, then decorated with chain stitch. Three colours of cotton yarn, A, B and C and a No.3.00 (ISR) crochet hook are required. Using A, make 15ch.

1st row Into 3rd ch from hook work 1dc, 1dc into each of next 5 sts, join in B as explained in Patchwork Effects, 1dc into each of next 7 sts. Turn.

2nd row Using B, 1ch to count as first dc, 1dc into each of next 6 sts, using A, 1dc into each of next 7 sts. Turn. Working in colours as above, dec one st at each end of every row until there are no sts left. Make another triangle in the same way, then crochet the shapes together and, using C, work a chain st over the colour join.

Sample 9

Work in the same way as sample 8, using 3 colours for each triangle and begin by working 7dc in A, 3dc in B and 4dc in C. When 2 triangles have been completed, place the alternate colour sequence side by side and crochet together.

Sample 7   *Sample 8*   *Sample 9*

FASTENINGS

Crochet fastenings

This chapter illustrates some useful and decorative fastenings all worked by using various crochet techniques. These fastenings are useful when working with fabrics where it is difficult to work the traditional types of fastening such as fabric or machined buttonholes.

The crochet stitches which have been used are all simple and have been explained in previous chapters. It is important to bear in mind the function of the garment and just how decorative you want the fastening to be when you are deciding on the yarn to use.

Sample 1

This toggle fastening is most suitable for a casual garment. Using string make two lengths of cord, one 17.5cm (7in) and the other 30.5cm (12in) long, as

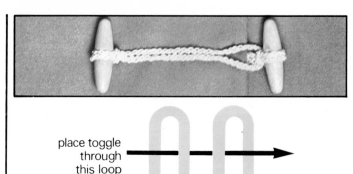

place toggle through this loop

described in sample 10 of chapter 34. The longer piece of cord is fastened into a circle and looped over a traditional wooden toggle. The cord and toggle are then sewn on to the right hand side of a garment, leaving a loop extension over the outer edge. The shorter piece of cord is not joined into a circle, but is looped over another toggle which is then sewn in position on the left hand side of the garment.

Sample 2

The finished effect of these loops and buttons is more decorative, but this will depend on the buttons and yarn which you choose to use. To make the loops in our sample you will need a Lurex yarn, a medium thickness of string and a No.3.00 (ISR) crochet hook. Hold the string in the left hand with the cut end to the right and the incoming string to the left. Holding the yarn in the usual way, place the hook under the string and catch yarn to form a loop on the hook, place hook over string, yrh and draw yarn through loop on hook, *place cut end of string in the right hand and continuing to hold incoming

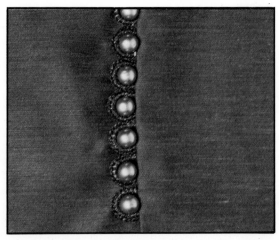

yarn in the left hand, place hook under string, yrh, place hook over string, yrh and draw through both loops on hook, rep from * for the required length. (Our sample took approx 6.5cm (2½in) of string for each loop.) Position the loops one below another so that the chain extends over the outer edge, on the right side of the fabric, making all loops an even size. Tack firmly in place as shown in the diagram. With right sides of the fabric together, tack the facing over the cording and machine firmly along the stitching line. Line up the extended loop with the left hand side of the garment and attach buttons.

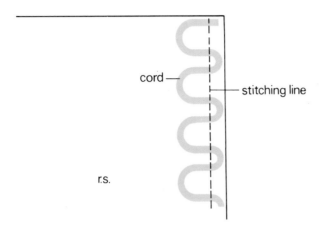

Sample 3
This single frog fastening is more decorative still and would probably be used on its own on an evening cape. Using No.3.00 (ISR) hook and Lurex yarn, work

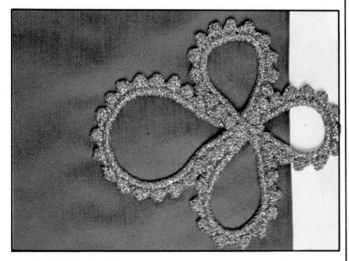

over piping cord, 38.5cm (15in) to 50.5cm (20in) long as explained in sample 2. Then work the second line by turning the work so that you crochet back along the first line, *(yrh, insert hook into next st, yrh and draw through a loop) 3 times into same st, yrh and draw through all loops on hook, ss into each of next 2 sts, rep from * to end of cord.
Form the cord into the required shape for four loops on the right hand side of the garment with one loop extending over the outer edge and sew neatly, but firmly, in place. Line up the extended loop with the left hand side of the garment and attach button.

Sample 4
For the cord you will require two lengths of No.4 piping cord, one approx 50.5cm (20in) long and the other approx 40cm (17in) long, a No.3.50 (ISR) crochet hook and a chenille yarn. Make 4ch. Join with a ss into first ch to form a circle. Thread No. 6 piping cord through the circle. Tie in an overhand knot about 15cm (6in) from the end of the cord and place the knot behind the circle so that the free cord is coming towards you.
To work the crochet Insert the hook into the back or lower single loop of the first ch, yrh and draw through the loop and st on the hook – one ss has been worked – * insert the hook into the back or lower single loop of the next st and work one ss, rep from * working round and round the cord until the required length has been covered. Position the longer piece of cord on the

right hand side of the garment, forming the desired size of loops with one loop extending over the outer edge. Sew in place. Line up the extended loop with the left hand side of the garment and position the shorter length of cord to give three loops equal in size to those at the opposite side. A covered button has been sewn on to the join of the loops on both the right and left hand side.
To cover the button shape You will need a 2.5cm (1in) ball button, some chenille yarn and a No.3.50 (ISR) crochet hook. Form a circle with the yarn in the left hand, work 8dc into this circle, draw the cut end of yarn tightly to close the circle and ss into the first dc worked.
2nd round 1ch to count as first dc, 1dc into st at base of ch, *2dc into next st, rep from * to end. Join with a ss into first ch.
3rd round 1ch, 1dc into st at base of ch, 1dc into next st, *2dc into next st, 1dc into next st, rep from * to end. Join with a ss into first ch.
4th round 1ch, 1dc into each st to end. Join with a ss into first ch.
5th round As 4th.
6th round 1ch, work 2dc tog over next 2 sts, *1dc into next st, work 2dc tog over next 2 sts, rep from * to end. Join with a ss into first ch.
7th round 1ch, *work 2dc tog over next 2 sts, rep from * to last st, 1dc into last st. Join with a ss into first ch. Fasten off.

FLOWERS

Fluted crochet

Artificial flowers are very much a part of the fashion scene. They are used on day and evening dresses, hats and other accessories. Most commercial flowers are made up in fabric, but here we illustrate how you can make your own by using the technique of fluted crochet.

The type of yarn you choose for making your flower will depend on the sort of outfit you will be wearing it with, perhaps a crisp cotton to trim a hatband or a glitter yarn for an evening outfit. A selection of centres are shown for different flowers.

5th round Ss into each of first 3ch of next loop, ss into centre of same loop, 7ch, *ss into centre of next ch loop, 7ch, rep from * to end. Join with a ss into ss at centre of first loop. Fasten off.
2nd circle Using No.4.00 (ISR) hook and a 4 ply yarn, make 5ch. Join with a ss into first ch to form a circle.
1st round 1ch to count as first dc, 20dc into circle. Complete as given for 1st circle.
To make up Place the larger, more fluted circle over the first circle and stitch the centres together. In our sample wooden beads in groups of three, five and seven on a loop have been used as additional decoration.

1st flower

This flower consists of two circles.
1st circle Using No.4.00 (ISR) hook and a 4 ply yarn, make 5ch. Join with a ss into first ch to form a circle.
1st round 1ch to count as first dc, 15dc into circle. Join with a ss into first ch.
2nd round *4ch, ss into next dc, rep from * to end. 16 ch loops.
3rd round Ss into each of first 2ch of next loop, ss into centre of same loop, 5ch, *ss into centre of next ch loop, 5ch, rep from * to end. Join with a ss into ss at centre of first loop.
4th round Ss into each of first 3ch of next loop, ss into centre of same loop, 6ch, *ss into centre of next ch loop, 6ch, rep from * to end. Join with a ss into ss at centre of first loop.

2nd flower

Using No.4.00 (ISR) hook and a 4 ply yarn, make 6ch. Join with a ss into first ch to form a circle.
1st round 1ch to count as first dc, 20dc into circle. Join with a ss into first ch.
2nd round 3ch to count as first tr, 1tr into st at base of ch, *2tr into next dc, rep from * to end. Join with a ss into 3rd of 3ch. 42 sts.
3rd round 3ch to count as first tr, 1tr into st at base of ch, *2tr into next tr, rep from * to end. Join with a ss into 3rd of 3ch. 84 sts.
4th round As 3rd. 168 sts.
5th round 1ch to count as first dc, 1dc into each of next 9 sts, insert hook from front to back into next st, miss next 9 sts, insert hook from front to back into next st, yrh and draw through first 2 loops on hook, yrh and draw through both loops on hook, *1dc into each of next 10 sts, insert hook from front to back

into next st, miss next 9 sts, insert hook from back to front into next st, yrh and draw through first 2 loops on hook, yrh and draw through both loops on hook, rep from * to end. Fasten off.

To make up Make the tufted centre by cutting 40 lengths of yarn, each 7.5cm (*3in*) long and firmly bind together around the centre with another piece of yarn. Fold the lengths in half and insert the bound section into the centre of the flower.

3rd flower

Using No.3.00 (ISR) hook and a Lurex yarn, make 6ch. Join with a ss into first ch.

1st round 1ch to count as first dc, 17dc into circle.

2nd round 5ch, miss next 2dc, *1dc into next dc, 4ch, miss next 2dc, rep from * to end. Join with a ss into 2nd of first 5ch. 6ch loops.

3rd round *Into next 4ch loop work 1dc, 1htr, 5tr, 1htr and 1dc, rep from * to end. Join with a ss into first dc.

4th round *5ch, pass this ch length behind next gr of sts and work 1dc into next dc of 2nd round inserting the hook from behind, rep from * to end.

5th round *Into next 5ch loop work 1dc, 1htr, 10tr, 1htr and 1dc, rep from * to end. Join with a ss into first dc.

6th round *7ch, pass this ch length behind next gr of sts and work 1dc into next dc of 4th round inserting the hook from behind, rep from * to end.

7th round *Into next 7ch loop work 1dc, 1htr, 15tr, 1htr and 1dc, rep from * to end. Join with a ss into first dc.

8th round *8ch, pass this ch length behind next gr of sts and work 1dc into next dc of 6th round inserting the hook from behind, rep from * to end.

9th round *Into next 8ch loop work 1dc, 1htr, 5tr, 10dtr, 5tr, 1htr and 1dc, rep from * to end. Join with a ss into first dc. Fasten off.

A large pearl bead makes an attractive centre to this silver flower.

4th flower

Here is an unusual method of working a chrysanthemum. Using No.3.00 (ISR) hook and a cotton yarn, make 21ch. Miss first ch, ss into each ch to end, turn. *Miss first st, ss into each of next 2 sts inserting hook into back loop only of each st, work 17ch, miss first ch, ss into loop at back of each ch to end, turn, *, rep from * to * until approximately 60 to 70 petals have been completed. Fasten off.

To make up Beginning at one end of the work, twist the base of the petals round and round, securing with sewing stitches, until all the crochet is in place.

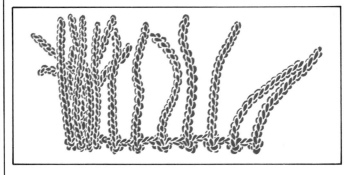

TUNISIAN CROCHET
BASIC STEPS

Tunisian crochet

This is a form of crochet which is similar to both crochet and knitting, and it is also known as Tricot work. The first similarity is in the special tool used for this craft which is a single hooked needle, or Tunisian crochet hook. These hooks are extra long to accommodate the large number of stitches in use and come in an international size range (ISR) with the smallest starting at 2.50 with the numbers 3.00, 3.50, 4.00, 4.50, 5.00, 5.50, 6.00 and 7.00 becoming gradually larger. The fabric produced is very strong and firm and, depending on the stitch used, the finished appearance can resemble crochet or look deceptively like knitting. It is ideal for making furnishing fabrics, for which there are special hooks in three sections that screw together to make an even longer one. Also Tunisian crochet is suitable for heavier outer garments where the intricacies of fine detail would be superfluous.

Several basic points make this form of crochet different to ordinary crochet and they should be referred to throughout all Tunisian crochet instructions.

a) When making an initial length of chain stitches to begin work, you will not require any extra chains for turning, i.e. a chain length of 20 will give you exactly 20 working stitches.

b) The work is not turned at the end of each row so that the right side of the work faces you throughout.

c) Tunisian crochet is worked in pairs of rows, i.e. the first row is worked from right to left and then it requires another row worked from left to right to complete it.

d) Apart from a very small number of exceptions, no turning chains are required at the beginning of each new row.

To work the basic stitch – Tricot stitch Using No.4.50 (ISR) Tunisian crochet hook and a double knitting yarn, make a length of chain.

1st row Working from right to left, miss first ch, insert hook into 2nd ch from hook, yrh and draw through a loop, *insert hook into next ch, yrh and draw through a loop, rep from * to end of ch length so keeping all loops on hook.

2nd row Working from left to right, yrh and draw through first 2 loops on hook, *yrh and draw through next 2 loops on hook, rep from * to end so leaving one loop on hook.

3rd row Working from right to left, miss first vertical loop on the front of the fabric, insert hook from right to left into next vertical loop, yrh and draw through a loop, rep from * to end so keeping all loops on hook.

4th row As 2nd.

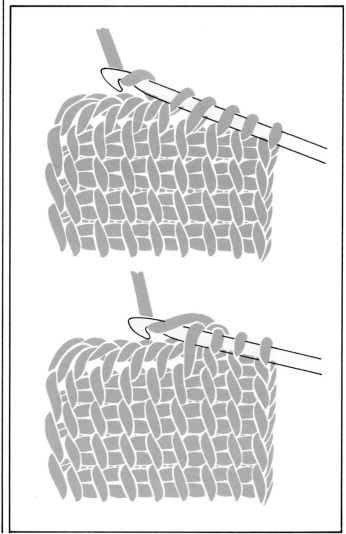

The 3rd and 4th rows are repeated throughout.

Note Care should be taken to check the number of stitches at the end of each row as it is very easy to miss the last stitch when working the 3rd row.

Shaping a Tunisian crochet fabric

When it is necessary to increase or decrease, this is usually done on the first of the pair of rows which you must work.

To increase on the sides of your work The increased stitch is worked by inserting the hook into the single horizontal loop between two vertical loops. To increase one stitch at the beginning of a row, this is usually done between the first and second vertical loops and between the last and last but one vertical loops to increase one stitch at the end of a row.

To increase in the middle of a row One stitch is simply increased in the middle of a row by inserting the hook into the single horizontal loop between vertical loops at the position where the increased stitch is required.

To increase more than one stitch at the beginning or end of a row Remembering that increases are made on the first row of the required pair, to increase several stitches at the beginning of a row, work the extra chain stitches required and go back along these extra chains picking up the working stitches. To increase several stitches at the end of a row complete the row then take a spare length of matching yarn and join this into the last stitch. Work the extra chain stitches required with the spare yarn, then continue working into this extra chain length with the main yarn.

To decrease on the sides of your work One stitch is decreased just inside the beginning of a row by inserting the hook into the 2nd and 3rd vertical loops and working the stitch in the usual way. At the end of a row the last two stitches before the end stitch are worked together in the same way.

To decrease in the middle of a row At the required position, decrease one stitch as given above.

To decrease more than one stitch at the beginning or end of a row At the beginning of a row slip stitch over the required number of decreased stitches and at the end of a row work until the required number of stitches to be decreased are left, then work the second of the pair of rows required.

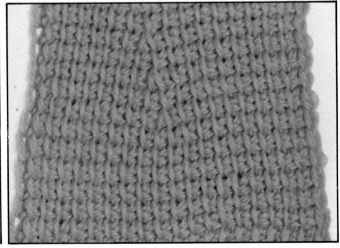

FABRIC STITCHES

An introduction to Tunisian crochet was made in our last chapter. The stitches may be worked in a variety of ways to give very different patterned effects and textures. These are achieved by different positions of the hook insertion on the first row of the pair necessary for Tunisian crochet. For all our samples, it is only the first row which varies and the second is the same throughout.

3rd row *Insert hook into space between vertical loops from front to back, yrh and draw through a loop, rep from * to end.
4th row As 2nd.

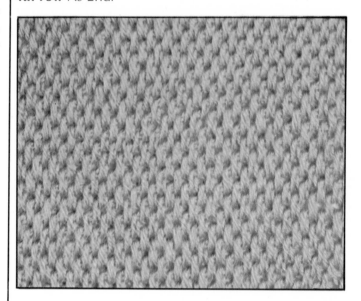

5th row Miss space between first two vertical loops, *insert hook into space between next two vertical loops from front to back, yrh and draw through a loop, rep from * to end, inserting hook into last vertical loop.
6th row As 2nd.
The 3rd-6th rows are repeated throughout.

Sample 2
Using No.4.50 (ISR) Tunisian crochet hook and double knitting yarn, make a length of chain.

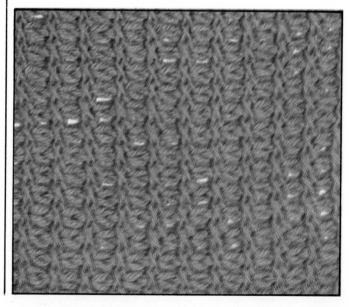

Sample 1
Using No.4.50 (ISR) Tunisian crochet hook and double knitting yarn, make a length of chain.
1st row Insert hook into second ch from hook, yrh and draw through a loop, *insert hook into next ch, yrh and draw through a loop, rep from * to end.
2nd row Yrh and draw through first 2 loops on hook, *yrh and draw through next 2 loops on hook, rep from * to end so leaving one loop on hook.

1st-2nd rows As 1st-2nd rows of sample 1.
3rd row Miss first vertical loop, *miss next vertical loop, insert hook from right to left through next vertical loop, yrh and draw through a loop, insert hook from right to left through the missed vertical loop, yrh and draw through a loop, rep from * to end, inserting hook into last vertical loop.
4th row As 2nd.
The 3rd and 4th rows are repeated throughout.

Sample 3
Using No.4.50 (ISR) Tunisian crochet hook and double knitting yarn, make a length of chain with multiples of 3 + 2 stitches.
1st-2nd rows As 1st-2nd rows of sample 1.

3rd row Miss first vertical loop, *yarn over hook from front to back, (insert hook into next vertical loop, yrh and draw through a loop) 3 times, pass 4th loop from hook from right to left over last 3 loops on the hook, rep from * to end, insert hook into last vertical loop, yrh and draw through a loop.
4th row As 2nd.
The 3rd and 4th rows are repeated throughout.

Sample 4
Using No.4.50 (ISR) Tunisian crochet hook and double knitting yarn, make a length of chain.
1st-2nd rows As 1st-2nd rows of sample 1.

3rd row Miss first vertical loop, *insert hook directly through centre of next vertical loop from front to back

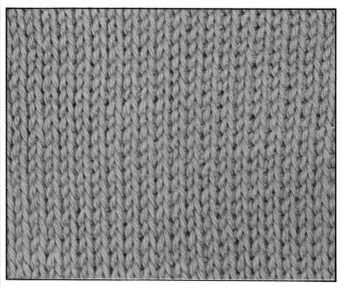

of work, yrh and draw through a loop, rep from * to end.
4th row As 2nd.
The 3rd and 4th rows are repeated throughout.

Sample 5
Using No.4.50 (ISR) Tunisian crochet hook and double knitting yarn, make a length of chain with multiples of 3 + 2 stitches.
1st-2nd rows As 1st-2nd rows of sample 1.

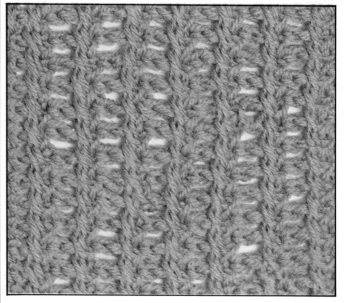

3rd row Miss first vertical loop, *insert hook under next three vertical loops, yrh and draw through a loop, insert hook under middle loop only of this group of three, yrh and draw through a loop, insert hook under first loop only of this group of three, yrh and draw through a loop, rep from * to end, insert hook into last vertical loop, yrh and draw through a loop.
4th row As 2nd.
The 3rd and 4th rows are repeated throughout.

DECORATIVE STITCHES

There are so many different patterns to be achieved when working Tunisian crochet that we are giving the instructions of several more for you to practise.

The tension of your work can be gauged in the same way as for plain crochet and this will need careful checking if you are making a garment. Any tendency for the fabric to curl and twist can be overcome by working the stitches fairly loosely. Always pull the yarn round the hook adequately through the stitch and, when working back along a row from left to right, never pull the first stitch through so tightly that the height of the row is flattened.

Sample 1

This is a variation of the basic Tricot stitch. Using No.4.50 (ISR) Tunisian crochet hook and double knitting yarn, make a length of chain with multiples of 2 stitches.

1st row Insert hook into second ch from hook, yrh and draw through a loop, *insert hook into next ch, yrh and draw through a loop, rep from * to end.

2nd row Yrh and draw through first 2 loops on hook, *yrh and draw through next 2 loops on hook, rep from * to end so leaving one loop on hook.

3rd row Miss first vertical loop, *insert hook from right to left through next 2 vertical loops on RS of work, yrh and draw through a loop, insert hook from right to left into first of these loops, yrh and draw through a loop, rep from * to end, insert hook into last vertical loop, yrh and draw through a loop.

4th row As 2nd.

5th row Miss first vertical loop, insert hook into next vertical loop, yrh and draw through a loop, *insert hook from right to left through next 2 vertical loops on RS of work, yrh and draw through a loop, insert hook from right to left into first of these loops, yrh and draw through a loop, rep from * to end.

6th row As 2nd.

The 3rd to 6th rows are repeated throughout.

Sample 2

Here crossed stitches within the pattern give a vertical ribbed effect. Using No.4.50 (ISR) Tunisian crochet hook and double knitting yarn, make a chain with multiples of 2 stitches.

1st-2nd rows As 1st–2nd rows of sample 1.

3rd row 1ch, miss first 2 vertical loops, insert hook from right to left through next vertical loop on RS of work, yrh and draw through a loop, insert hook into missed vertical loop to the right of the one just worked into, yrh and draw through a loop, cont in this way, working in groups of 2 and crossing the threads, ending by inserting hook into last vertical loop, yrh and draw through a loop.

4th row As 2nd.

The 3rd and 4th rows are repeated throughout.

Note If you are using this pattern for a shaped garment where you are increasing and decreasing, take care to see that the crossed stitches come immediately above those in the previous row so that the ribbed effect will not be broken.

Sample 3

Here bobbles are made on a basic Tricot background by working extra lengths· of 4ch before continuing with the next stitch. Using No.4.50 (ISR) Tunisian crochet hook and double knitting yarn, make a length of chain with multiples of 6+1 stitches.

1st –2nd rows As 1st–2nd rows of sample 1.

3rd row 1ch, miss first vertical loop on front of fabric, 1 vertical stitch into next vertical loop, *insert hook into next vertical loop on front of fabric, yrh and draw through a loop, 4ch, insert hook into horizontal loop at base of ch on WS of work, yrh and draw through 2 loops on hook – called B1 –, work 1 vertical stitch into each of next 2 vertical loops, rep from * to last 2 loops, B1 into next vertical loop, 1 vertical stitch into last vertical loop.

4th–6th rows Work in basic Tunisian crochet.

7th row 1ch, miss first vertical loop, *B1 into next vertical loop, 1 vertical stitch into each of next 2 vertical loops, rep from * to end of row.

8th row As 2nd.

The 3rd–8th rows are repeated throughout.

Sample 4

An eyelet stitch gives this sample a simple openwork pattern. Using No.4.50 (ISR) Tunisian crochet hook and double knitting yarn, make a chain with multiples of 2+1 stitches.

1st row Yrh twice, insert hook into 3rd ch from hook, yrh and draw through a loop, yrh and draw through first 2 loops on hook, *miss next ch, yrh twice, insert hook into next ch, yrh and draw through a loop, yrh and draw through first 2 loops on hook, rep from * to end.

2nd row As 2nd row of sample 1.

3rd row 2ch, *yrh twice, insert hook into both next vertical loop and slightly sloping vertical loop to right of it made in previous row, yrh and draw through a loop, yrh and draw through first 2 loops on hook rep from * to end.

4th row As 2nd.

The 3rd and 4th rows are repeated throughout.

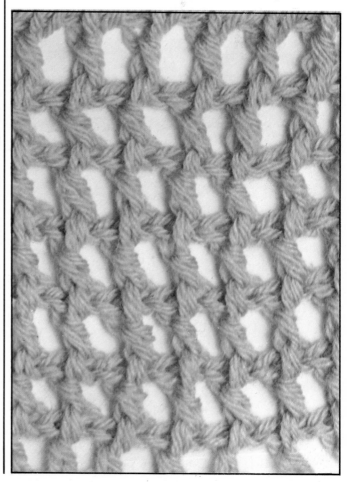

ADVANCED TUNISIAN STITCHES

More advanced designs for Tunisian crochet

Five more interesting Tunisian crochet stitches are illustrated in this chapter, including two which show the technique of using different colours within the work. As all the samples are worked in a chunky knitting yarn they would be ideal for cushions, rugs and blankets. Reference should be made to the first of these chapters on Tunisian crochet, and checks should be made during the working of these samples to keep the number of stitches correct.

Sample 1

Using No.5.00 (ISR) Tunisian crochet hook and chunky yarn, make a length of chain with multiples of 2 stitches.

1st row Insert hook into 2nd ch from hook, yrh and draw through a loop, *insert hook into next ch, yrh and draw through a loop, rep from * to end.

2nd row *Yrh and draw through two loops, rep from * to end. One loop rem on hook.

3rd row Miss first vertical loop, *yrh from front to back, insert hook under next 2 vertical loops, yrh and draw through a loop, rep from * to last vertical loop, insert hook into last vertical loop, yrh and draw through a loop.

4th row As 2nd.

The 3rd and 4th rows are repeated throughout.

Sample 2

Using No.5.00 (ISR) Tunisian crochet hook and chunky yarn, make a length of chain with multiples of 2 stitches.

1st-2nd rows As 1st-2nd rows of sample 1.

3rd row Miss first vertical loop, *insert hook into hole under chain st to right of next vertical loop, yrh and draw through a loop, insert hook under vertical loop to left of last loop made, yrh and draw through a loop, drawing it through one loop on hook, rep from * to last vertical loop, insert hook into last vertical loop, yrh and draw through a loop.

4th row As 2nd

The 3rd and 4th rows are repeated throughout.

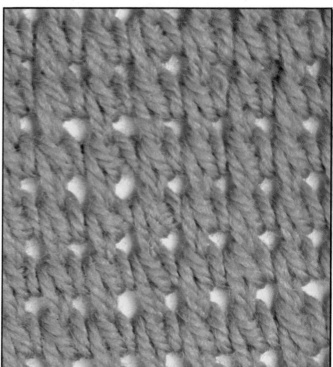

Sample 3

Using No.5.00 (ISR) Tunisian crochet hook and chunky yarn, make a length of chain with multiples of 2+1 stitches.

1st row (Yrh and insert into 3rd ch from hook, yrh and draw through a loop) twice, yrh and draw through 2 loops on hook, yrh and draw through 3 loops on hook, *miss next ch, (yrh and insert into next ch, yrh and draw through a loop) twice, yrh and draw through 2 loops on hook, yrh and draw through 3 loops on hook, rep from * to end.

2nd row Yrh and draw through one loop, *1ch, yrh and draw through 2 loops, rep from * to end. One loop rem on hook.

3rd row 2ch, *yrh from front to back, insert hook from front to back into space on right of next st, yrh and draw through a loop, yrh from front to back and insert into space on left of same st, yrh and draw through a loop, yrh and draw through 2 loops on hook, yrh and draw through 3 loops on hook, rep from * ending with last st worked completely into last space.
4th row As 2nd.
The 3rd and 4th rows are repeated throughout.

Sample 4
For this sample you will need two colours of chunky yarn, coded as A and B. Using No.5.00 (ISR) Tunisian crochet hook and A, make a length of chain.
1st-2nd rows As 1st-2nd rows of sample 1.
3rd-6th rows Work 4 rows basic Tunisian crochet. Do not break off yarn. Join in B.
7th row Using B, 2ch, *yrh, insert hook from front to back through work under next horizontal st, yrh and draw through a loop extending it to length of 2ch, rep from * ending with last st worked into last horizontal space.

8th row Yrh and draw through 2 loops on hook, *yrh and draw through 3 loops on hook, rep from * to end.
9th row Draw A through loop on hook, *yrh and insert into horizontal loop at back of long st, rep from * to end.
10th-12th rows Work 3 rows basic Tunisian crochet. Repeat 7th-12th rows throughout.

Sample 5
Here we have used two colours of double knitting yarn coded as A and B. Using No.4.00 (ISR) Tunisian crochet hook and A, make a length of chain with multiples of 4+7 stitches.
1st-6th rows As 1st-6th rows of sample 4.
7th row Miss first vertical loop, insert hook into next vertical loop, yrh and draw through a loop – called one basic tricot st –, one basic tricot st into next

loop, *using B, (yrh and insert into 3rd vertical loop down from next st, yrh and draw through a loop extending it to meet working st) 4 times, yrh and draw through all loops in B on hook, insert hook into next vertical loop behind bobble, yrh and draw through a loop drawing it through one loop in B on hook – one bobble has been worked –, using A, work one basic tricot st into each of next 3 loops, rep from * to end.
8th-14th rows Using A, work 7 rows basic Tunisian crochet.
15th row Miss first vertical loop, *using B, work one bobble into 3rd vertical loop down from next st, using A, work one basic tricot st into each of next 3 loops, rep from * to last 2 loops, one bobble into next loop, one basic tricot st into last loop.
16th row Work in basic Tunisian crochet.
Continue in this way, working 7 rows of basic Tunisian crochet between each bobble row, for the required depth of pattern.

Clutch bag with woven threads

Size
Width, 35.5cm (14in)
Depth, 23cm (9in)

Tension
14sts and 14 rows to 10cm (3.9in) over basic tricot stitch worked on No. 6.00 (ISR) long blanket Tunisian crochet hook

Materials
2 hanks of Twilley's Health Vest Cotton No. 1
Oddments of contrasting colours for decoration
One No. 6.00 (ISR) long blanket Tunisian crochet hook
Lining material
Heavy-weight interlining
Velcro for fastening

Bag main part
Using No. 6.00 (ISR) long blanket Tunisian crochet hook make 50ch. Work in basic tricot stitch until crochet measures approx 66 cm (26in) from beg. Fasten off.

Gusset (make 2)
Using No. 6.00 (ISR) long blanket Tunisian crochet hook make 14ch. Work 8 pairs of rows. Dec one st at each end of next and every foll 4th pair of rows until 6 working sts rem. Work 4 more pairs of rows. Fasten off.

To make up
Cut out a piece of interlining the same size as the main part of the bag. Sew the crochet neatly on to the interlining to hold its shape and steam press. The gussets are not interlined. Cut out lining material to fit the main part and gussets, allowing 1.5cm ($\frac{1}{2}$in) turnings on all sides. Using the same yarn, a tapestry needle and oversewing stitches, sew in the gussets to the main part as shown in the diagram. Make up the lining as given for the bag, sewing in the gussets. Hem lining on to the crochet. Sew the two pieces of velcro fastening in position, one to the underside of the flap and one

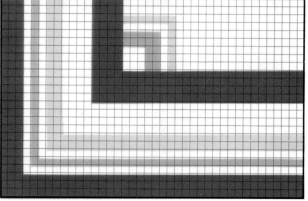

on the corresponding bag section. Follow the diagram and work the required crochet design on the bag flap.

Working the design
You will notice that horizontal and vertical lines of loops are produced on the right side of the crochet fabric. A contrasting coloured or textured yarn is then woven over and under these loops or stitches in straight lines. To achieve a good line, it is necessary to use several thicknesses of the yarn for decoration and a long Tunisian crochet hook in a size smaller than the hook used for the background to pull the threads through the work.

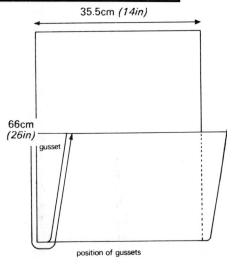

35.5cm (14in)

66cm (26in)

gusset

position of gussets

AN INTRODUCTION TO EMBROIDERY

Although I am more generally associated with knitting and crochet and cannot claim to be a specialist in any other field, I have always strongly believed that one must have an overall interest in all crafts, in order to explore the full possibilities of any particular field. The structure and embellishment of different types of fabric may point the way to a new approach in almost any craft, and embroidery, in particular, has many applications in both knitting and crochet. A knowledge of something like herringbone stitch – called casing stitch in knitting terms – is essential for some stages in making up garments, and simple embroidery stitches look most effective when worked on a knitted background.

Before primitive man had even learned to cure skins or weave and knot fabrics, he had already begun the search for some way to distinguish himself from the animal kingdom and proclaim his creative ability. Body painting was, and still is in some remote parts, a form of art which satisfied this need. Once the human race began to clothe itself, this creative urge was so strong that it was not sufficient to make a warm and protective covering, and ways of displaying wealth and individuality had to be devised as a form of decoration.

The art of embroidering with a needle had already reached a high standard in Old Testament days and has since formed a part of the cultural development of almost every nation in the world. Embroidery has evolved into many different forms and the overall names of some of these categories have a ring of grandeur about them. Groups of stitches which comprise Hardanger, Hedebo and Assisi techniques all evoke memories of past glory and history.

Some stitches, such as cross stitch and chain stitch, are so simple that a child can easily master them. Others are so complex that even a small example could eventually become a prized heirloom. The Victorians had a passion for exquisite embroidery and their method of perfecting as many stitches as possible could well be adopted today. A child would be encouraged to begin a sampler of stitches, which would be continued throughout adult life to form a unique and lasting record of achievement. Another popular form of sampler for a child to undertake would be worked entirely in cross stitch, to build up a series of pictures and quotations, mostly biblical, and proudly completed with a signature and date.

Although I have experimented with embroidery in the past, I must class myself as a beginner. Many of the simple stitches, such as lazy-daisy, cross stitches, French knots, smocking and back stitch, all play a part in the formation of knitted and crochet designs, so I am familiar with these. I have also enjoyed simple canvas work and have even tried my hand at drawn thread work. Despite an interest in more advanced techniques, such as quilting and cut work, I have been prevented from exploring these more fully because I have never been able to find a reference book which did not assume that I was already familiar with these methods.

In introducing this book, I have greatly enriched my own knowledge of this craft and I intend to try and develop my meagre skills. I find the clear and concise instructions, and simple illustrations of the working methods, very easy to follow and the text is presented in a logical way, which means you can begin with something quite simple but effective, before progressing to more difficult examples. With the aid of this book, I hope that you and I together can extend our knowledge, and explore the possibilities which this craft has to offer.

Pam Dawson

BASIC SKILLS
EQUIPMENT

The basic tools of the embroideress are simple: a pair of good embroidery scissors with fine points; a pair of paper-cutting scissors or blunt, older scissors for making a design of cut paper shapes – embroidery scissors should never be used to cut paper; a thimble; assorted needles, i.e. crewels, betweens, sharps, tapestry, a large chenille needle or a thick needle such as is used in the making-up of heavy wool garments and called a 'stiletto', used to take heavy threads through to the back of your work by means of a sling for certain embroidery methods. However, the correct needle choice for each method of work is given in the relevant chapter. Other essentials are beeswax for waxing thread, necessary for some methods of embroidery; a piece of tailor's chalk or a white dressmaking pencil for use on darker materials; tacking cotton; pins, embroidery threads; and a frame to hold the fabric firm as you work.

Embroidery fabrics

There are many fabrics for embroidery, providing a constant source of inspiration for both beginner and expert.

Linen is a favourite choice and is woven in many weights and colours and in both even-weave and coarser textures. Suitable cotton materials include dress fabrics, poplin, organdie, gingham, cotton satin and glazed cotton. Woollen fabrics are suitable for many stitches, particularly even-weave wool, flannel and wool tweeds, both in light and heavy weights. There is also silk in all its varying weights. and textures, from thin Chinese silk to wild silk and the heavier silk tweeds. Many man-made furnishing fabrics make excellent backgrounds for stitchery and make the choice for the embroideress even wider. A comprehensive chart to guide you in your choice of fabrics, threads and needles is included later.

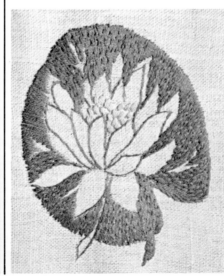

Embroidery frames

For a really professional finish in embroidery, a frame is essential. This holds the fabric taut while you are working and helps you to form the stitches evenly and accurately as you go along.

Before starting work, oversew the edges of the fabric. This will prevent the edges fraying once the fabric has been placed in the frame.

Types of embroidery frame

There are two main types of embroidery frame, the round, or tambour, frame which is used for small pieces of work with surface or counted embroidery, and the traditional slate frame which is used for large pieces of embroidery.

Round frames

These are available in different sizes from 7.5cm–30.5cm (3 inch–12 inch) diameter and are usually made from wood, although it is sometimes possible to buy them in aluminium which holds the fabric more securely.

The frame consists of two circular hoops, one over which the fabric is stretched and another hoop, slightly larger, which fits over the first one and holds the fabric in place. This second hoop has a screw which can be adjusted to tighten or slacken the fabric as required.

To prevent the fabric from slipping through the frame when you are mounting it, it is advisable to bind the inner hoop with tape or strips of cotton fabric first. To mount the fabric, stretch the section of embroidery to be worked over the inner hoop, keeping the grain of the fabric square, press down the outer hoop and tighten the screw.

Traditional frames

Embroidery worked in this kind of frame rarely needs pressing before mounting and this is a great advantage when various methods and stitchery have been combined which might react differently to heat and damp.

The frames are available in different sizes from about 46cm–76.5cm (18 inches–30 inches), although it is possible to obtain larger ones still, often combined with a floor stand.

The frame consists of two rollers which form the top and bottom of the rectangle and two flat strips which form the side slats of the frame. The side pieces have a series of holes down their length which enables them to be fitted into the rollers – with wooden pegs or screws – at any point to make a frame of the right size for your embroidery. Each roller has a strip of tape or webbing nailed along the edge

to which the fabric is firmly sewn.

For embroidery which will not be damaged by rolling, such as petit point and some forms of canvas work, it is possible to buy frames with rotating rollers so the work can be rolled up as it progresses.

A less expensive substitute for the rectangular frame is a canvas painting stretcher, obtainable from art suppliers in various sizes. The embroidery fabric is attached to it with drawing pins, but care must be taken to ensure that enough pins are used and that the fabric is firmly pinned under tension so that it is completely taut.

Preparing a traditional frame

Preparing a traditional frame for embroidery is known as dressing the frame.

1 Assemble the frame by inserting the side pieces into the rollers at the required height and secure in place.

2 Mark the centres of the tape or webbing on both rollers with coloured thread.

3 Make a 1.3cm ($\frac{1}{2}$ inch) turning along the top and bottom edges of the fabric and hem them if the fabric is likely to fray. Mark the centre points of the edges.

4 Turn under the side edges of the fabric for 1.3cm ($\frac{1}{2}$ inch), enclosing a length of cord or string to give strength for attaching it to the side slats. Machine stitch in place.

5 Match the centre of the top edge of the fabric to the centre of the roller and pin it in position, working from the centre out to each side. Then overcast it, using strong thread.

6 Repeat on the bottom roller so that the fabric is quite taut between the two rollers.

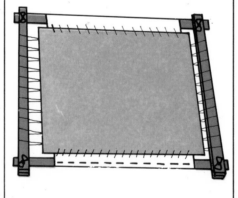

7 To secure the fabric to the side pieces, use very strong thread or fine string and a heavy needle and lace them together using a diagonal movement, placing the stitches about 2.5cm (1 inch) apart. Leave a good length of string at the ends, pull taut, then tie through the last hole at the

top and bottom of the slat.

Attaching fine fabrics

If you are mounting a very fine fabric, such as jap silk or organdie, which is likely to tear if laced, a different method of attaching the edges to the side slats should be used.

1 Using long pieces of 2cm ($\frac{3}{4}$ inch) wide tape, start at the top and pin the tape to the side edge of the fabric, placing the pin about 1.3cm ($\frac{1}{2}$ inch) from the edge.

2 Fold the tape back over the pin (to prevent it from pricking you while you work) and take it over and around the side slat. Pin it to the fabric about 2.5cm (1 inch) further down, then take it over the side slat again. Continue in this way to the bottom of the fabric and then complete the opposite side.

Backing the fabric

If you are using a variety of threads in different weights or beads for the embroidery which might be too heavy for the fabric alone, it is advisable to back the fabric to add strength. The backing can be washed linen, cotton or sheeting – unbleached calico is normally too firmly woven for this purpose.

The embroidery is worked through the double thickness and when it is finished the surplus backing fabric is cut off and trimmed back to the line of embroidery. The method of dressing a frame when using a backing is slightly different.

1 Tack a line down the centre of the backing and of the embroidery fabric. Working on a flat surface, place the fabric on to the backing, matching the centre lines. Pin in position, working out from the centre and with the pins pointing inwards to avoid puckering. Take care not to stretch either layer. Firmly tack the layers together all round the outer edge.

2 Turn under the side edges of the backing for 1.3cm ($\frac{1}{2}$ inch), enclosing a length of cord or string to give strength for attaching it to the side slats. Machine stitch in place.

3 Attach the top and bottom edges to the rollers and lace the sides to the slats as for unbacked fabrics.

Backing small pieces of embroidery

If the embroidery fabric is much smaller than the backing fabric, pin it in position on to the backing using fine pins or needles to avoid leaving marks. Overcast it by taking the needle from the embroidery fabric, and down into the backing fabric 1cm ($\frac{3}{8}$ inch) above the edge of the embroidery fabric. This pulls the fabric completely taut on the backing.

DESIGN TRANSFERS

There are three main methods of transferring embroidery designs to fabric and usually the type of design and fabric decides which method is most suitable. Whichever method you do choose, however, it is normally best to transfer the design before the fabric has been mounted into a frame because it will be difficult to keep the fabric completely flat owing to the bulk of the frame.

For all methods, start by making a tracing of your design – whether it is freely drawn, copied from an illustration or composed of cut paper shapes – using tracing or greaseproof paper and a non-smudge pencil.

Tacking
Use this method for transferring a design on to a fabric with a pile e.g. velvet.

1 Pin the tracing in place on the fabric. Using a contrasting thread and small stitches, tack along the lines of the design.

2 Remove the paper by tearing it away.

Dressmaking carbon
Use this method on fabrics with very fine and even weave, without irregular slub threads. Do not use it if the design contains any fine detail, as the prick and pounce method is the only reliable one. The carbon paper is available in light colours for use on dark fabrics and vice versa. Simply place the carbon paper under your tracing in the correct position on the fabric and trace over the design with a sharp pencil.

Prick and pounce method
This method is the only reliable one for transferring designs with fine detail or where you are using fabric with irregular slub threads.

Basically, prick holes are made through the tracing paper along the lines of the design and the design is transferred to the fabric underneath by rubbing a mixture of 'pounce' over the paper. When the paper is removed, the design shows up on the fabric as a series of fine dots where the pounce penetrated the prick holes.

'Pounce' was originally a powder made from ground cuttlefish bone used as a wig powder in the 18th century, but nowadays it is made from powdered chalk for dark fabrics and powdered charcoal for light fabrics. A mixture of powdered chalk and charcoal is the most useful and can be obtained from wholesale drapery suppliers; alternatively you can use talcum powder.

To apply the pounce, you need a felt pad which can be made by rolling up several thicknesses of felt and securing the roll with oversewing.

1 Place the tracing paper on to a folded towel or ironing blanket to give a good base for pricking the design.

2 Use a fine needle for smooth fine fabrics or designs with a lot of detail and a larger needle for heavier fabrics. Insert the eye of the needle into a cork to make it easier to handle.

3 Go over the lines of the design, pricking it with holes 0.15cm ($\frac{1}{16}$ *inch*) apart on fine fabrics and 0.3cm ($\frac{1}{8}$ *inch*) apart on heavier ones.

4 Pin the tracing in position on the embroidery fabric. It is advisable to weight the edges of the tracing with something heavy to prevent it moving.

5 Using the felt pad, rub the pounce all over the paper. Lift off the paper carefully.

6 Paint in the lines of the design, using a fine brush and white poster paint mixed with a little blue or yellow to make the design clearer on a white or very light fabric. Water colour paint can be used instead of poster paint but it does not give as good an outline and is best for fine transparent fabrics. As you work the embroidery the paint can be flicked off with the point of a needle.

Transferring designs on to sheer fabrics
1 Trace the design on to paper using a hard pencil or waterproof ink. Check whether this shows through the fabric, and if necessary go over the design with white poster paint or a light crayon.

2 Place the fabric over the tracing and weight down to prevent it moving. Paint over the lines of the design, using a fine brush and poster or water colour paint as in the prick and pounce method.

Transferring designs to canvas
For simple designs use the tacking method, or for more complicated designs place the canvas over the tracing and trace the

Transferring designs using the prick and pounce method.

Making the prick holes through the tracing paper.

Using the felt pad, rub the pounce all over the paper.

Finally, paint in the lines of the design.

outline with waterproof ink.

Enlarging and reducing designs

Whether you are using your own design or a pattern or illustration you have copied, you will often need to enlarge or reduce it to fit the size you need. This is easy to do if you divide the design into little squares and divide the area where you want it enlarged into the same number of squares: you will find you can easily copy each square individually and so build up the whole design. You can reduce a design in just the same way, but copying on to smaller squares.

To avoid marking the original design, and to save the bother of drawing out lots of little squares, transfer the design on to graph paper. To do this, you can either trace it direct, if the graph paper is thin enough, or use tracing paper.

Trace the design on to tracing paper.

1 Lay this over graph paper. If you can see the squares clearly through the tracing paper, stick it down with clear tape, taking care that the tracing paper lies flat. This way, you can re-use the graph paper.

2 If, however, you cannot see the squares clearly through the tracing, transfer the design to the graph paper either with carbon paper (dressmakers' carbon is fine) or by shading the back of the tracing paper with a soft pencil and drawing firmly over the design with a ballpoint.

3 Draw a rectangle to enclose the design. This will be divided into a certain number of squares by the graph paper. If you are using plain paper you must, at this stage, divide the rectangle up by marking off each side and joining up the marks to make a lot of small squares. It is helpful to number these for reference.

4 Draw, preferably on tracing paper as before, a second rectangle, to the size you want the finished design to be and in the same proportions as the first one. Do this by tracing two adjacent sides of the first rectangle and the diagonal from where they meet. Extend them as much as you need and then draw in the other sides of the second rectangle. Divide this into the same number of squares as the smaller one. A backing sheet of graph paper will make this process easier.

5 Carefully copy the design square by square. If you have to copy a flowing, curved line across several squares, mark the points at which it crosses the squares and then join them up in one flowing movement.

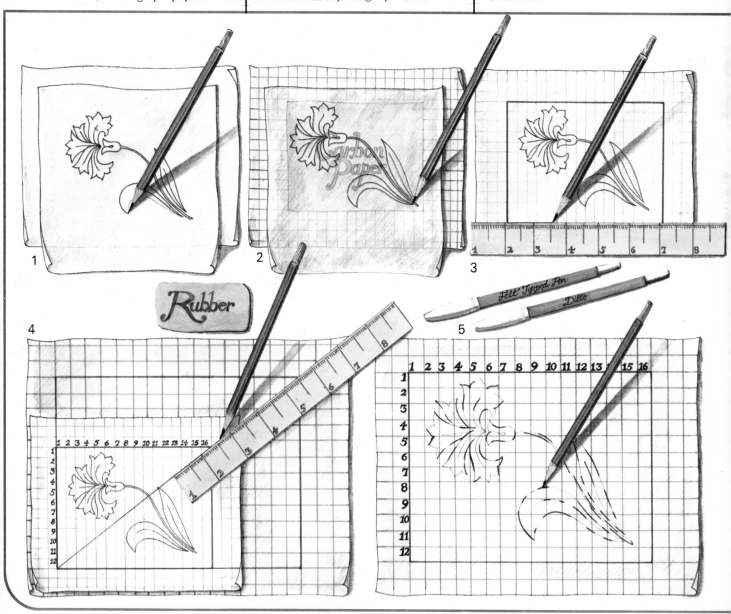

1 *Draw the design carefully onto the tracing paper.*

2 *Lay the tracing paper over the graph paper.*

3 *Draw a rectangle to enclose the design and number the squares in it.*

4 *Draw the second rectangle by tracing two sides and a diagonal from the first.*

Extend as needed.

5 *Transfer the design square by square till it is complete. Try to use one flowing movement for joining curves.*

SIMPLE STITCHES
Line and straight stitches

A knowledge of basic stitchery is the prime factor in the many methods which combine to make embroidery a creative and stimulating hobby, and it is essential if you intend to create your own individual embroideries.

Probably the simplest stitches with which to start are line or straight stitches. These are illustrated below and can be used for any of the designs illustrated using the trace patterns illustrated overleaf. A basic guide to these elementary stitches can be found in the Guide to Basic Stitches (Page 41).

Basic stitches

Running stitch

Make the stitches on the right side the same length as those on the wrong side.

Laced running stitch

This can be effective using either the same or contrasting yarn. Use a tapestry needle and thread it in and out of the running stitches without catching in the cloth. This lacing can be used with other stitches.

Back stitch

Bring the needle through to the right side of the fabric and make a small stitch backwards. Bring the needle through again a little in front of the first stitch and

make another stitch backwards to make a continuous line.

Stem stitch

Make a sloping stitch along the line of the design, and then take the needle back and bring it through again about halfway along the previous stitch.

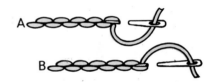

Cable stitch

Work lower stitch A on line of design, as shown; then work upper stitch B in same way with yarn above needle.

Ideas for using the motifs – brightening up a pretty nightdress.

A simple dress in a plain colour is made demurely pretty with a few motifs.

The use of an ice-cream cone motif gives this blouse a distinctive look.

Motifs to use on their own or in groups.
Trace the motifs off the page, transfer
them to the fabric, then embroider them
in pretty colours, using any of the
straight stitches illustrated.

Satin stitches

Although satin stitch is essentially a simple over-and-over stitch, skill is required to produce the beautiful satiny effect that its name implies. It is a surprisingly versatile stitch and, as it imposes no pattern of its own, is invaluable in pictures when stitches of varying lengths and shades produce illusions of distance and depth. There are several variations, one of which is padded and gives the effect of an extra dimension (see the Essential Stitches, later).

Satin stitch flower motif
This simple flower motif is a good example of the stitch when worked with long and short and split stitch. The motif below can be worked in stranded cottons on a table napkin, dress or blouse.

You will need
Stranded cotton (used with three strands in the needle) in six or seven colours. You should allow about one skein of yarn in each colour but the exact amount you use will depend on the fabric used.

The design
1 Work the motif into the corner of the napkin, placing it about 2.5cm (1 inch) from the sides.
2 The flowers of the design are worked in long and short stitch, the four upper leaves in satin stitch and the lowest leaf in split stitch. French knots (page 20) decorate the flower centres.
3 The dotted line on the trace pattern (below) indicates the meeting point for stitches and suggests the position of the leaf vein. Transfer the design by the tissue paper method.
Begin by working the leaves, stitching from the inner line towards the outer edge. Work flower colour 4 first, then colour 6, taking the stitches just into the edge of the leaves. Finally, work flower colour 5. Work each half of each leaf in turn. Make dots with a couple of small satin stitches or French knots at the centres.

▲ *A beautiful example of satin stitch worked in silk for picture making.*

▼ *The motif worked in cotton on a linen napkin.*

A delightful embroidery design 'Panier de Fleurs' is featured on this cushion. It is worked in wool on canvas and satin stitch is used throughout. Designed by Jean-Yves Rocher for the D.M.C. 'New Tapestry Collection'.

Guatemalan motifs

Reversible satin stitch worked in bright colours in geometric designs is a popular feature of Guatemalan peasant embroidery as shown in the poncho and bag in the photograph. A similar motif can also look effective on the flap of a clutch bag and, because it is reversible, the motif will look equally good when the bag is closed or open.

Making a clutch bag

Make the clutch bag from a rectangle of loosely woven fabric, such as coarse linen. The minimum size of fabric for the motif is 45cm (*18 inches*) × 23cm (*9 inches*).

Working the motif

Draw the motif (right) to scale and trace it on to tissue paper. Place the tracing in position on the top third of the rectangle. Tack over the lines indicating the colour areas and then pull away the paper. Start stitching each area, working from the middle outwards.

Making up

Fold up the bottom third of the rectangle with wrong sides together to form the pocket and pin the sides. Trim the edge of the flap to within 1.5cm (½ *inch*) of the stitching. Cover the turnings and raw edge of the flap with a continuous length of bias binding machine stitched on both sides.

Top: Graph pattern for Guatemalan motif. Work it in bright colours for a bag.

Right: The poncho and bag embroidered with Guatemalan motifs.

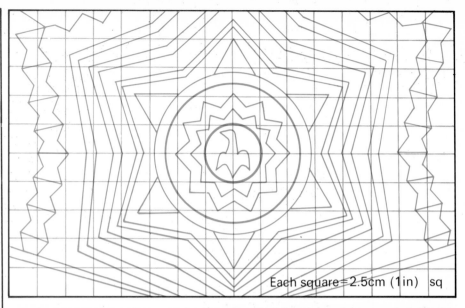

Each square = 2.5cm (1in) sq

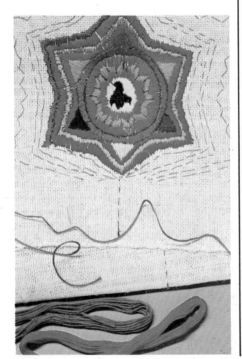

Chain stitches: continuous

Chain stitch has no single origin but can be traced to all parts of the world where ancient fabrics have been found. Chain stitch was found on basket-work from pre-dynastic Egypt (c.350 BC), on the earliest surviving Egyptian textiles, in graves in the Crimea dating from the 4th century BC and on some old textiles in China and Japan worked during the 7th and 8th centuries AD and still extant.

The Chinese worked chain stitch using silk thread on silk in a single line technique, widening or tightening the loop with a thread of uniform thickness to produce an effect of variable depths of colour and shadow. Some of the finest examples worked with chain stitch alone, using silk thread on satin, are 18th– and 19th–century Indian garments from Kutch.

In mediaeval western Europe the grandest embroidery used more elaborate stitches and chain stitch only appeared on more humble objects. In 18th-century England chain stitch was revived and widely used, often under Chinese influence, to decorate silk coats and satin bedspreads. It appears independently in peasant work throughout the world.

Using chain stitch

Chain stitch worked in lines and curves is very versatile. The stitch can be worked large or small to give a fine or a bold outline. For a regular appearance the proportions should remain the same; as a rough guide the width should be two-thirds of the length of the stitch.

Chain stitch adapts well to tight curves and can be worked round and round to partially fill in areas.

Chain stitch

When worked, this stitch makes a chain of loops on the right side of the fabric and a line of back stitches at the back. Bring the needle through on the line of the design, loop the yarn under the point of the needle and draw the needle through. Insert the needle close to where the yarn came out. Bring the needle through a little further along the line of the design, loop the yarn under the point of the needle and draw through (see below). Continue in this way until the required length has been worked.

Suitable yarns

Small stitches worked in a thick yarn give a solid line, while larger stitches in fine yarn give an open stitch. Use these characteristics to their fullest advantage.

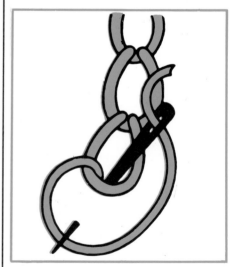

▲ *Working a line of chain stitch.*

Using chain stitch to brighten up the back of a plain jacket.

These designs are shown about one-third of their actual size, but they may be enlarged to the size you require.

This pretty butterfly picture would be ideal for a girl's bedspread or embroided on to a dress or apron pocket.

An appropriate design for a beach bag or beach cover-up – a colourful landscape scene with rolling waves.

Brighten up plain table mats with this simple motif. All these designs are worked in Soft Embroidery Cotton.

Any of the finer yarns previously mentioned are suitable for chain stitch but for quickly worked chain stitch use a thick embroidery yarn (such as one of those shown below) on a large weave backing.

2 ply Crewel wool: a twisted, matt wool. Use one or, more usually, several strands.

Tapestry wool: a twisted, matt, separable wool.

Twilley's Lyscordet: a twisted knitting cotton.

Mercer Crochet Cotton: a fine knitting cotton.

Sudan Wool: a twisted, matt, separable wool.

Paton's Turkey Rug Wool: a twisted, matt wool for using on rug canvas.

To work the designs

Choose your fabric – perhaps a T-shirt, cotton jacket or whatever you wish to embroider on. Enlarge the design to the required size. Transfer the design to the material in one of the ways already suggested. If you are using thick yarn you will need a chenille needle.

Follow the lines of the design with closely worked chain stitch until you have covered them.

Flower bed cushion

Fabric required

Single thread even weave linen, 26 threads per 2.5cm (*1 inch*), 36.5cm × 36.5cm (*14 inches × 14 inches*).

You will also need

☐ Soft Embroidery Cotton, 3 skeins purple, 4 skeins red, 4 skeins mauve, 5 skeins lilac, 6 skeins light green, 6 skeins dark green, 6 skeins orange.

☐ Fabric for back of cushion 36.5cm × 36.5cm (*14 inches × 14 inches*).

☐ Square cushion pad 35cm × 35cm (*14 inches × 14 inches*).

The design

1 Transfer the pattern on facing page centrally to the linen.

2 Lightly mark a square 2cm ($\frac{3}{4}$ *inch*) in from outer edges with a transfer pencil.

3 Work the design in fairly small chain stitch, working over 2 or 3 threads to make stitches uniform in length.

4 Work around the edge of the square in chain stitch and work two more squares of chain just inside the first.

5 Make up into a cushion stitching 1.25cm ($\frac{1}{2}$ *inch*) seams.

This flower bed design is set off well by a natural-coloured background.

Detached chain stitch

Although chain stitches can be used continuously this stitch can also be used individually and arranged to form flower or leaf shapes. This is known as daisy or detached chain stitch. The stitches may be worked in any size you require, but remember, if the stitches are very long they will catch easily and so are not suitable for working on articles that are used every day.

Cotton mesh

This is an embroidery fabric woven in blocks of cotton strands separated by holes through which the needle is drawn. The number of holes per centimetre (inch) vary: 6 holes per 2.5cm (6 holes per inch) have been used here and embroidery on this scale grows quickly. Penelope Binca and Panama cotton mesh are examples of this type of embroidery fabric. Cotton mesh is also available in small sizes for finer work. This fabric may be used for making cushions, table linen, chairbacks or stool tops.

After care

Wash in warm water and pure soap. Squeeze the fabric gently in the soapy water. Rinse thoroughly in warm water and squeeze gently by hand to remove excess water. Leave the fabric on a towel, lying flat, until it is half-dry. Press on the wrong side, using a moderately hot iron, working from the centre outwards until the fabric is completely dry. Alternatively the fabric may be dry cleaned.

Basic stitches

Detached chain stitch

Make a chain stitch and instead of re- inserting the needle inside the loop, make a tiny stitch over the loop to hold it in place (A). Leave a space and bring the needle out again to begin the next stitch. Work daisy stitches in the same way as for detached chain but position the stitches to form a flower shape (B).

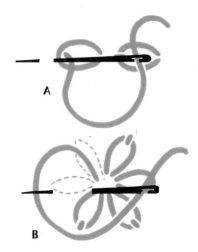

Daisy stitch cushion

The flowers are meant to be worked in a random fashion, so embroider the largest flowers first, spacing them out, and then fill the spaces in between with the smaller flowers. In the remaining spaces work the tiny four-petalled flowers and either bunches of, or single, leaves.

Fabric required

35cm (14 inch) square of cotton mesh, 6 holes per 2.5cm (1 inch)

You will also need

☐ 11 skeins of embroidery wool in 11 different colours
☐ Tapestry needle No. 18
☐ Material for back of cushion-cover, 35cm (14 inches) square
☐ Cushion pad, 32cm (13 inches) square

Working the design

1 Work the required number of flowers over the fabric leaving a 2.5cm (1 inch) border unworked. To give the edge of the cushion definition, work a border of leaves 2.5cm (1 inch) in from the edge. Vary the height of the leaves so that they frame the flowers.

Note While working with the wool it is important to twist it to the right to keep the ply tightly twisted. This gives a clean line to shapes. Work the larger flowers one at a time.

2 Leave the ends on the wrong side and sew them in neatly at the back of the work.

This colourful cushion displays a random pattern of flowers in detached chain stitch. Fabric: Penelope Binca.

3 The detached chain stitches are held in place in two ways; either by bringing the yarn over the loop through the same hole (see below) or by bringing the yarn over the

Compact detached chain stitch.

loop, over one block and through the next hole to form a stem (below).

Detached chain stitch with a stem.

To make up

1 Fold the edges of the fabric to the wrong side so that the border of leaves is right on the edge, and pin. Fold the back of the cover to the same size and shape and pin the edges to secure them. Pin the back and front together, wrong sides facing as below. Slip stitch around three edges,

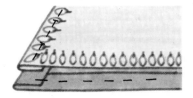

Pin with wrong sides together.

insert cushion pad and slip stitch along the fourth side. The cushion is now complete.

2 The motifs show the variety of shapes that can be worked over a similar number of squares. Each square represents the number of blocks worked over – ie, if the 'petal' covers three squares there are two holes missed between inserting and drawing out the needle. Work out the position of the motifs to form a pleasing design on the fabric.

Bright and pale colours show up well against either dark brown or cream backgrounds. The motifs may be arranged to make a pattern the same as, or similar to, the one opposite. The motifs given are only a few of the many you can work.

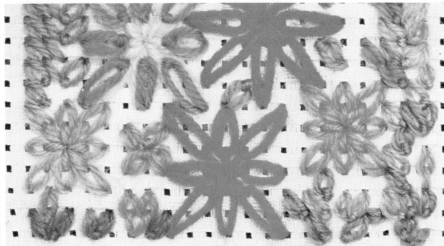

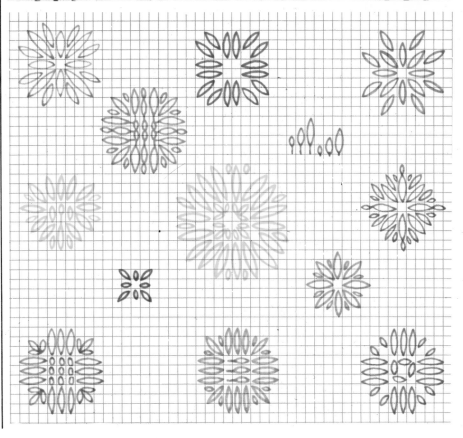

Chain stitch as a filling stitch

When using chain stitch as a filling stitch it is easiest to start off with shapes which are fairly round. With these shapes it is easier to work round and round and keep the lines of stitches close together. Once you have completed a few such shapes you will be able to tackle irregular ones.

When working a design which is filled in with closely packed stitches, choose a medium-weight dress or furnishing fabric which is comparable to the weight of the stitching. Also, to obtain the most successful results, choose a colour and texture which is suited to the design.

When filling in a shape, work the stitches around the outline of the shape, then, as you return to the starting point, bring the needle point just inside the first round of stitches so that the start of the second round is hardly visible when the work is completed (see below). Keep working round and round, completely covering the background, until the centre is reached, then bring the needle over the last loop and draw the yarn through to the back. Fasten off.

Filled chain stitch can be made to look almost three-dimensional if you start along the outline with larger chain stitches and gradually make them smaller and smaller as you progress towards the centre.

However, if you want the surface of the fabric to be completely covered with embroidery, it will be necessary to fill in the centre of the outer chain stitches with detached chain stitches.

Yarn

To use chain stitch as a filling stitch it is important to select a yarn of proportionate thickness to the weight of the fabric, which is why 6-stranded cotton is often the most appropriate. Before you start the embroidery, work a few stitches to find out how many strands you need to achieve a stitch size which is completely filled in with the yarn.

Pressing and stretching

When stitches are worked very close together the fabric sometimes becomes puckered because the tension of the stitching is too tight. Always try to maintain the same even tension.

All embroidery should be pressed on the wrong side with a warm iron to give it a finished appearance, but if the fabric is distorted it must be pressed and stretched to make it smooth.

To press the embroidery

Pad a large surface with a blanket and ironing cloth or use a well-padded ironing board. Place the fabric on the ironing cloth, wrong side uppermost, and press with a damp cloth.

To stretch the fabric

Pad a board with clean, damp blotting paper or, if blotting paper is not available, lay the fabric over several thicknesses of damp, white cotton fabric. Place the fabric on the blotting paper, right side uppermost. Fix one edge of the fabric to the board with drawing pins, aligning the horizontal strands with the edge of the board. Repeat on the opposite edge and at the sides, aligning the vertical strands with the edge of the board.

If the sides of the board are not at right angles, use graph paper or lined blotting paper to obtain accurate stretching. If using graph paper place it under the blotting paper.

To work the iris design

The contrast between the nubbly, dull linen background and the lustrous stranded cotton makes the textural effect more exciting. Note, too, how the narrow spacing between the random, horizontal lines integrates the background cloth with the embroidery; without these lines the embroidery would appear superimposed.

Size

The design enlarged to 17cm × 21.5cm ($6\frac{3}{4}$ inches × $8\frac{1}{8}$ inches).

Fabric required

A piece of natural coloured linen-look fabric, 25.5cm × 27cm (10 inches × $10\frac{1}{2}$ inches).

You will also need

☐ Stranded cotton; for flowers, 2 skeins of peacock blue and 2 skeins of natural; for leaves, 1 skein dark grey, 1 skein chestnut; for horizontal background lines, 1 skein beige; for buds, 1 skein cinnamon.
☐ 1 crewel needle.

The stitches are all worked with two strands of the stranded cotton. While working it is important to remove any kinks from the strands so that they lie side by side to give a smooth appearance.

The design as a picture

Fray the top and bottom edges of the fabric and oversew very neatly to prevent further fraying. The sides may be either frayed and oversewn or turned under and hemmed. Mount the fabric on a coloured cardboard background, leaving about 2.5cm (1 inch) border all round and set in a picture frame.

The design as a cushion

Centre the design on a piece of cloth about 32cm × 40cm (13 inches × 16 inches) and make up into a cushion 30cm × 38cm (12 inches × 15 inches).

The design on a dress

Work the design directly on to the front of a plain woollen dress.

This beautiful piece of embroidery is made up entirely of very small chain stitches, some worked round and round to make up the iris flowers and buds, others in lines to represent the leaves and the background. Yarn: Anchor Stranded Cotton. Designed by Shifrah Fram.

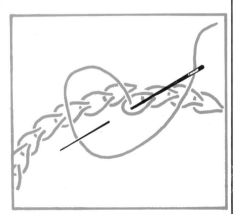

Bring the needle through just inside the first line of embroidery.

French knots and other stitches

For picture making choose a theme with bold and simple shapes. Break down the composition into stitch areas, fitting an appropriate stitch to the type of texture which will best express each part. As you gain experience, more detailed subjects may be attempted with the texture provided by a greater variety of stitches, and you will probably be able to add some invented by yourself.

Background

To start with, choose a finely woven, natural-coloured fabric. When you have become more confident you can use backgrounds which will play a part in the composition of the design with textures of the fabric as well as the stitching becoming an integral part of the picture.

Borders

If you wish to embroider a frame around a picture, choose one that is in keeping with the subject – a rose-festooned one as shown here – or a geometric border for a more modern picture. Of course, many pictures look their best when set in a plain picture frame.

Yarn quantities

For a small picture, such as the one shown, one skein of each colour is usually more than enough. However, if one colour predominates or if the stitches are very closely or thickly worked, two skeins may be needed.

Apple blossom picture

The apple blossom on the tree in the picture is superbly suggested by the use of French knots. These are also used on the girl's dress and hair band and this holds the picture together. Bold straight stitches which lie flat are used for the trellis in front of the bushes. These add a little perspective and contrast in texture.

The colours used are light to medium tones and give the whole picture a pretty, country air.

Trace the design on to tissue paper, being careful not to tear it. Lay the tissue paper over the fabric. Using sewing or tacking cotton and a fine needle, sew through the tissue paper and fabric with back or small running stitches round the outline or indicate the position of the areas to be embroidered. Tear the tissue paper away.

The stitches not hidden by the embroidery are removed when the embroidery is complete.

Fabric required

Piece of fabric 38cm (15 inches) × 30cm (12 inches)

You will also need

- [ ] 1 skein each of stranded cotton in the following colours: brown, pale pink, rose pink, light green, mid green, sage green, golden brown, white
- [ ] 1 ball pearl cotton No. 5 in two shades of brown and pale blue
- [ ] Small amount of gold lurex yarn for trellis

The design

1 Enlarge the picture to measure 33cm (13 inches) × 25cm (10 inches) – see Enlarging designs, earlier.

2 Using pearl cotton, work as follows: The girl's dress, chain stitch and stem stitch. Bark of tree and branches, stem stitch.

3 Using all strands of 6-stranded cotton, work as follows:
apple blossom, flowers under tree, girl's hairband and part of girl's dress: closely worked, loose French knots. Place some knots over the branches of the tree.
Grass and flower leaves, random straight stitches.
Background bush, feather stitch.
Foreground bush, herringbone stitch outlined with stem stitch.
Girl's hair and feet, stem stitch.
Girl's hairband, French knots.
Girl's arms, backstitch.

The trellis

Use all strands of cotton and work a lattice, couching it with the gold lurex yarn. In front of the trellis work the flowers in French knots and leaves in detached chain stitch.

The border

The border consists of herringbone in stranded cotton with stem stitch in pearl cotton on either side.
Work the rosettes in stem stitch from the outside towards the centre, and add one or two French knots at the centre. Work leaves in detached chain stitch.
To press the picture, lay it right side downwards on a well-padded ironing board, cover with a damp cloth and press it lightly. When dry mount the picture.

Basic stitches

French knots (Figure 1)

Bring the thread out at the required position, hold the thread down with the left thumb and encircle it twice with the needle as in A. Still holding the thread firmly, twist the needle back to the starting point and insert it as close as possible to where the thread first emerged. Pull the thread through to the wrong side and secure if you are working a single knot or pass to the next.

Couched lattice (Figure 2)

Lay threads along the lines of the design and, with another thread, secure the intersections down by taking a small stitch into the fabric.

Feather stitch (Figure 3)

Work in a vertical line. Bring the needle through to the right of the centre line of the design and take a small vertical stitch to the right as shown, catching the thread under the point of the needle. Continue making a series of stitches to the left and right of the design line, catching the thread under the needle.

Herringbone stitch (Figure 4)

Work from left to right. Bring the needle through above the centre line of the design and insert it below this line to the right, taking a small stitch to the left, keeping the thread above the needle. Then insert the needle on the upper line a little to the right, taking a small stitch to the left with the thread below the needle. Continue working these two movements alternately.

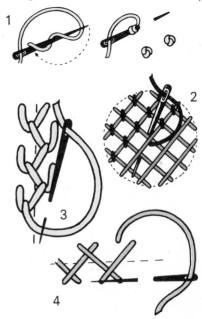

Texture is created in this pretty picture by the use of French knots for blossom and couching for the trellis.

Cross stitch

Cross stitch is one of the simplest and most ancient of all embroidery stitches. It dates back to the Coptic period and has been a form of peasant art for many centuries, appearing in one form or another throughout the world.

The best examples of this work come from the Slavonic countries of Eastern Europe where it has been used to adorn national dress.

Cross stitch can be exciting and absorbing to work and in Victorian times in Britain it was a popular pastime to make cross stitch pictures, often mis-named 'samplers' (true samplers should consist of several stitches).

Many of these pictures were made by small girls and consisted of the alphabet, a text, their age and the date of working, all in minute cross stitch.

How to use cross stitch

Cross stitch can be used for exciting designs on clothes, such as smocks, blouses, and dresses; for accessories, to decorate bags, belts and slippers; and for the home for rugs, table linen, cushions and curtains.

Whether it is worked in an all-over design or simply in a border pattern depends on the size of the item and the background fabric.

The design

Because of the geometrical nature of the stitch, it looks its best when the design is formal and has a repeating pattern, such as shown on the border in the photograph. The shape of the spaces between the areas is as important as those areas filled with the stitch. Often main areas are left unworked and the spaces suggest detail – a technique known as voiding – which is the main characteristic of another form of cross stitch, Assisi work (see Assisi work, later).

The colours

Cross stitch is usually worked in colours – often very bright – which contrast with the background fabric, and the interplay of the colours you choose is all-important. It is often more effective to use several tones of one colour rather than introducing completely different colours.

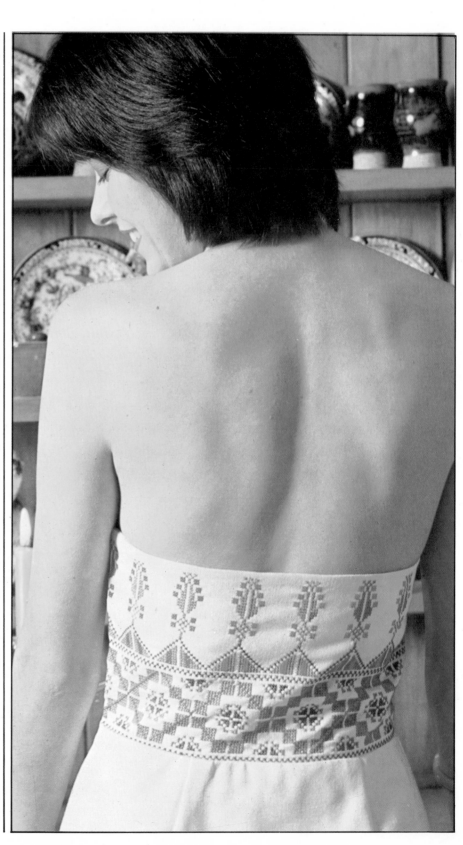

Planning your design

Although it is possible to buy transfers of cross stitch patterns to print on to fabric, it is much more satisfying to use an even-weave fabric and make up your own designs.

To plan your design, draw it first on to graph paper, using different coloured pencils or symbols to represent each colour, with one square representing one stitch or unit. When working from the graph each square or unit may be considered as consisting of one or more threads, which remains standard throughout the work.

A unit of three threads usually makes a good average size cross, each stitch being made by counting three threads along the fabric and then three threads up.

By reducing or increasing the number of threads in the units − or by using fabric with fewer or more threads to the centimetre (inch) − a design may be made smaller or larger accordingly.

An essential point in working cross stitch is that the counting of both stitches and threads must be accurate, and if you are using a transfer it is important to ensure that the lines of the crosses lie on the weave of the fabric.

The fabric

Even-weave fabrics with threads which are easy to count are obviously the best to use for cross stitch and as well as the traditional embroidery linens you can also use hessian, hopsack, 'Hardanger' cotton, Binca and many synthetic furnishing fabrics. Checked fabrics can also be used even if the weave is uneven as the size of the crosses can be determined by the size of the checks.

The threads

Any threads − cotton, silk, linen and wool − can be used provided that they are suitable in weight to the background fabric. A coarse fabric needs a thread of heavier weight while a fine fabric needs lighter threads. Variety can be introduced by using threads of different textures.

The stitches

Cross stitch is formed by two oblique stitches, crossing in the centre. There are two basic methods in which it can be worked, either by making one complete stitch at a time or by making a line of single oblique stitches in one direction, then completing the stitch on the return journey.

It is important that the upper half of the stitch should lie in the same direction if an even and regular effect is to be achieved. Traditionally the upper stitch should slope from bottom left to top right.

Combining cross stitch

While there are numerous variations of cross stitch which are used in other methods of embroidery, the stitch which is most often allied to regular cross stitch is Holbein or double running. This is a small line stitch which is used to break up a mass of cross stitch pattern and lighten it. It produces a light filigree effect and is always worked in two journeys.

The first journey is worked along the required outline in running stitches which are of equal length to the spaces left between them. The work is turned for the return journey when the spaces left between the first stitches are filled in, thus making a solid line. To keep the second line of stitches straight and even, bring the needle out of the fabric immediately below the stitch that was made on the first journey, but still using the same hole of the fabric.

Working the design

The design shown in the photographs here is made up of two simple repeat motifs and it can easily be adjusted to make borders for other garments or to decorate soft furnishings for the home (see diagram below).

The top motif is 5cm (2 inches) wide × 8.5cm ($3\frac{1}{4}$ inches) high. The border motif is 7cm ($2\frac{3}{4}$ inches) wide × 8cm ($3\frac{1}{8}$ inches) high.

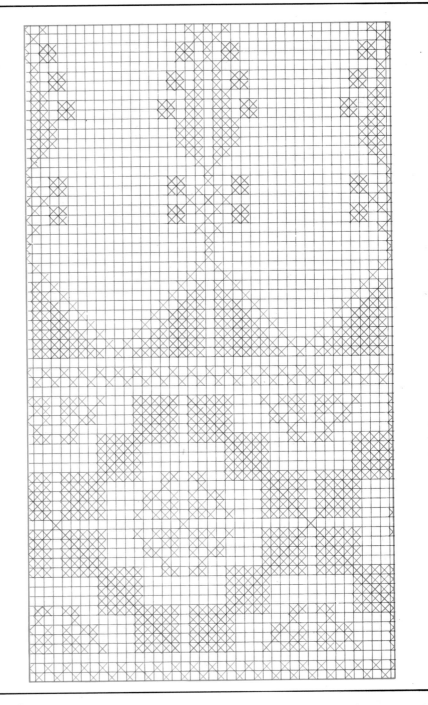

Cross stitch motif

The photograph opposite shows a charming example of the kind of pictorial 'sampler' worked by Victorian children. Notice how the spaces between stitches are used to suggest features. If you do not wish to make a complete item from even-weave fabric, you could work the embroidery only on it, cut round leaving a margin of about 5cm (½ inch) and apply it as a patch on to the finished item.

Fabric required

The motifs, shown worked individually, were done in stranded cotton on linen fabric. Alternatively, you could work in wool to brighten up a favourite cardigan or sweater.

You will also need

☐ Remnants of stranded cotton or knitting wool in various colours. Try to match the weight of the yarn to the background using six strands of cotton or a double-knitting wool on a heavy background.

The design

1 Working over two or three threads of the fabric, work the stitches in the appropriate shades as shown in the charts. Darn all ends neatly through the backs of the stitches on the wrong side.

2 The size of the motif will of course vary according to the weave of the background.

3 On a fabric with 19 threads per 2.5cm (1 inch) for example, the cow motif would be about 11cm (4½ inches) by 5cm (2 inches) when each stitch is worked over two threads.

On a knitted background, work over a unit of one or two knitted stitches counted vertically and horizontally.

Basic cross stitch

To work cross stitch in two journeys, bring the needle through on the lower right line of the cross and insert at the top left line of the cross. Take a straight stitch along the wrong side of the fabric and bring the needle through on the lower right line

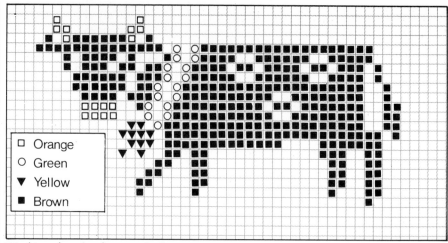

Key	
☐	Orange
○	Green
▼	Yellow
■	Brown

Working chart for the cow. Each square represents one cross stitch.

The cow worked on linen with 19 threads per 2.5cm (1 inch); each stitch = two threads.

of the next stitch. Continue to the end of the row in this way (Figure 1a). To complete the stitch, work left to right in a similar way (Figure 1b).

Outlines and single stitches

To work cross stitch individually, start as for the two-stage stitch but complete the cross each time before beginning the next stitch. Pass the thread on the wrong side of the fabric to the lower right line of the position of the next and subsequent stitches.

Double running stitch

Working from right to left, work a row of running stitch, making the stitches and spaces the same length as the crosses. To complete the stitch, work from right to left, filling in the spaces left in the first row.

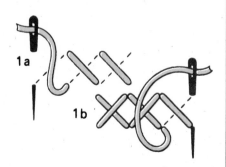

Two-stage stitch

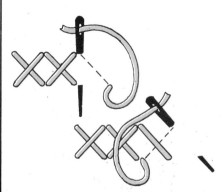

Individually worked stitches

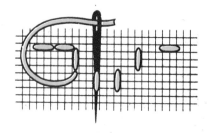

Completing double running stitch

Work this charming cross stitch picture for a nursery or use the motifs individually.

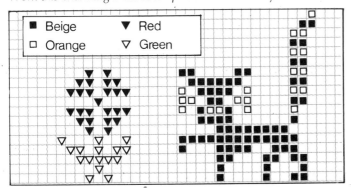

Working chart for the flower and cat

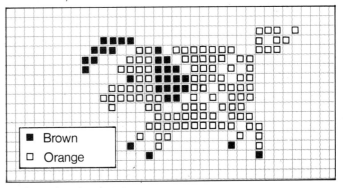

Working chart for the pig

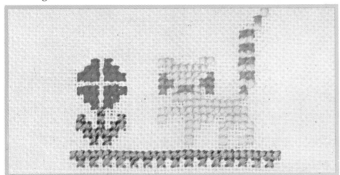

The cat worked on linen as above

The pig worked on linen as above

Cross stitch alphabet

Cross stitch has long been a favourite for embroidered lettering and monograms because it is quick and easy to work. No preliminary outline or transfer is needed when an evenweave fabric is used for the background because the fabric threads can be counted to form each letter. Although cross stitch designs based on counting threads are necessarily geometric in formation, they still leave plenty of opportunity for embellishment, as shown by the alphabet in the photograph. These letters have been worked in a modern version of the popular Victorian sampler, but you can easily extract the appropriate letters from the chart and use them individually to give a personal finish to your table linen or sheets, or you could combine them to form a monogram to decorate the pocket of a dress or the flap of a bag.

Working the alphabet

1 The alphabet in the photograph is worked on an even-weave cotton with 7 threads to 1cm (*18 threads to 1 inch*) in stranded embroidery cotton, using three strands throughout.

2 Each stitch is worked over one thread of the fabric and the letters are about 3cm ($1\frac{1}{4}$ *inches*) high.

Enlarging the letters

If you simply want to double the size of the letters – and this means increasing their width too – you can work the stitches over two threads of the fabric.

Alternatively, work four stitches for every one stitch indicated on the chart. If you do not want the increase to be so great, you can work the stitches over two threads but on a finer fabric.

Reducing the letters

The only method of reducing the size of the letters is to use a fine fabric.

Monograms

Composite intertwined initials are fun to plan and work. The initials may be arranged so that the base lines are level or you could place them diagonally (see below).

Sketch out your monogram on graph paper before you start work so that you can see how the initials link and where they will have stitches in common.

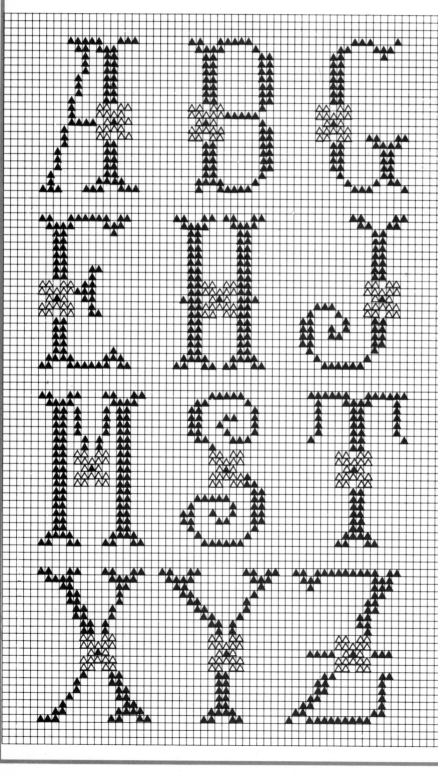

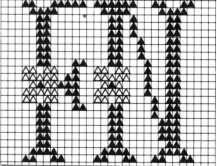

Above Using two of the letters as a monogram.

Left Trace patterns for some of the more complex letters.

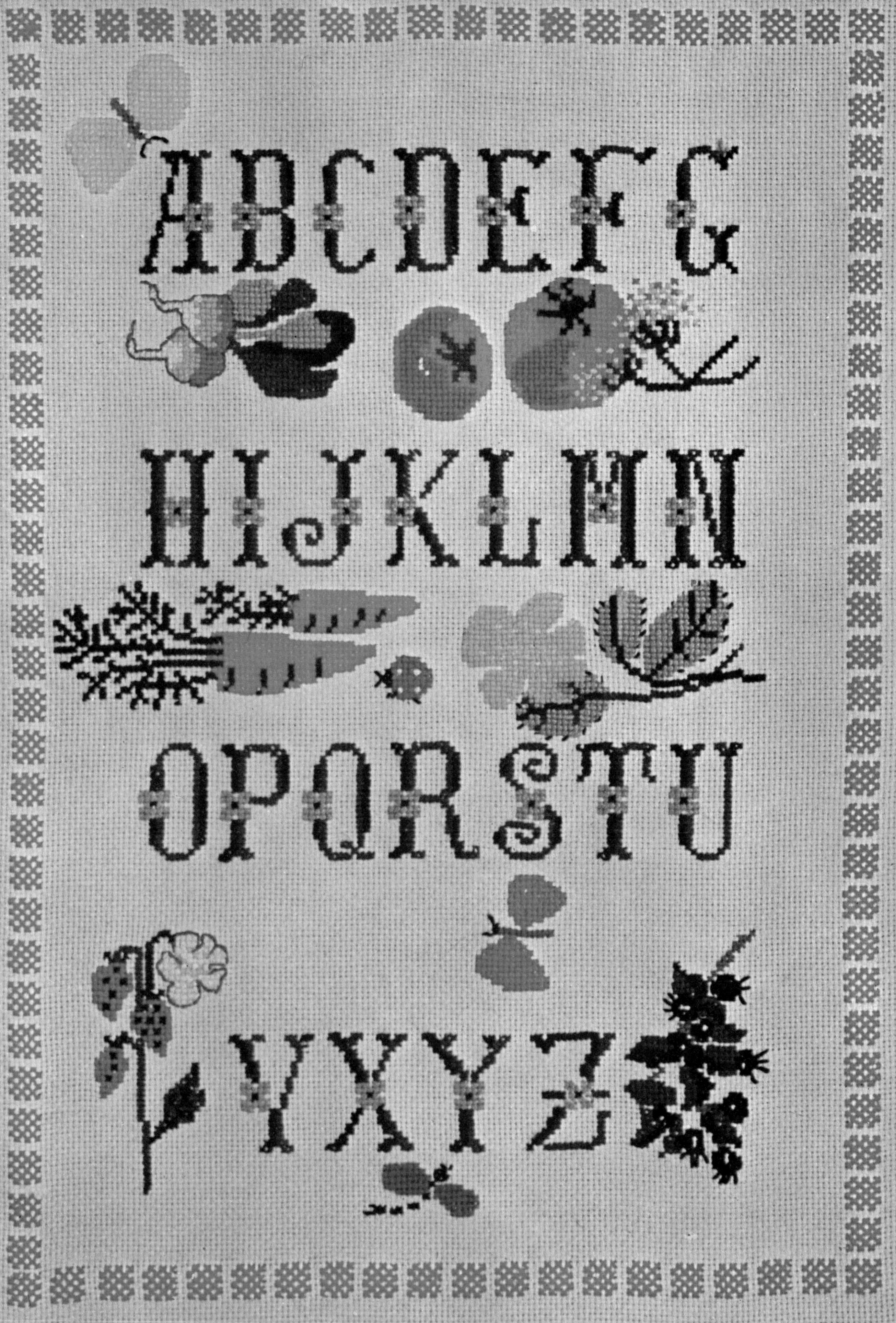
ABCDEFG
HIJKLMN
OPQRSTU

FIRST PROJECTS
Simple peasant design

This beautiful embroidery design is worked with the simplest of stitches. The beginner will be able to work the design after following the previous few chapters – and the experienced embroiderer will have no difficulty at all. The design is suitable for a garment with yoke and sleeves.

To work the embroidery
Materials required

☐ Clark's Anchor Stranded Cotton: 3 skeins each of 047 turkey red, 052 rose pink, 0100 violet, 0130 cobalt blue, 0218 forest green, 0264 moss green, 0304 amber gold

☐ 1 each crewel needle Nos.5 and 7

Placing the motifs

The trace pattern gives half the design used on the yoke with the broken lines indicating the fold. The section within the dotted outline gives half the design used on the sleeve.

Mark centre-front of blouse yoke with a line of tacking stitches.

Placing fold line to centre-front trace motif on to right hand side of yoke.

Reverse and trace on to the left hand side.

Trace section given within dotted outline on to sleeves, approximately 12.7cm (5 inches) from cuff. Repeat in reverse to complete the design as shown.

Method of working

Following diagram 1 and number key, work the embroidery. Use 6 strands of cotton and No.7 needle for the French knots and 3 strands with No.5 needle for the remainder.

Most of the design is worked in simple satin stitch, stem stitch and French knots, with the centres of flowers in spider's web filling stitch. Work this as shown below. Work nine straight stitches on each side of the fly stitch tail, into the centre of the circle. This divides the circle into nine equal sections and the spokes form the foundation of the web. Weave over and under the spokes until the circle is filled.

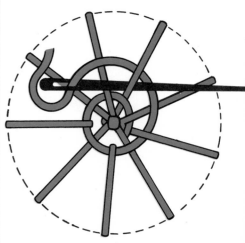

Spider's web filling stitch

KEY TO DIAGRAM

1 — 047
2 — 052
3 — 0100
4 — 0130 } Satin Stitch
5 — 0218
6 — 0264
7 — 0304

8 — 0100
9 — 0218 } Stem Stitch
10 — 0264
11 — 0304

12 — 0304 Spider's Web Filling Stitch

13 — 0304 French knots

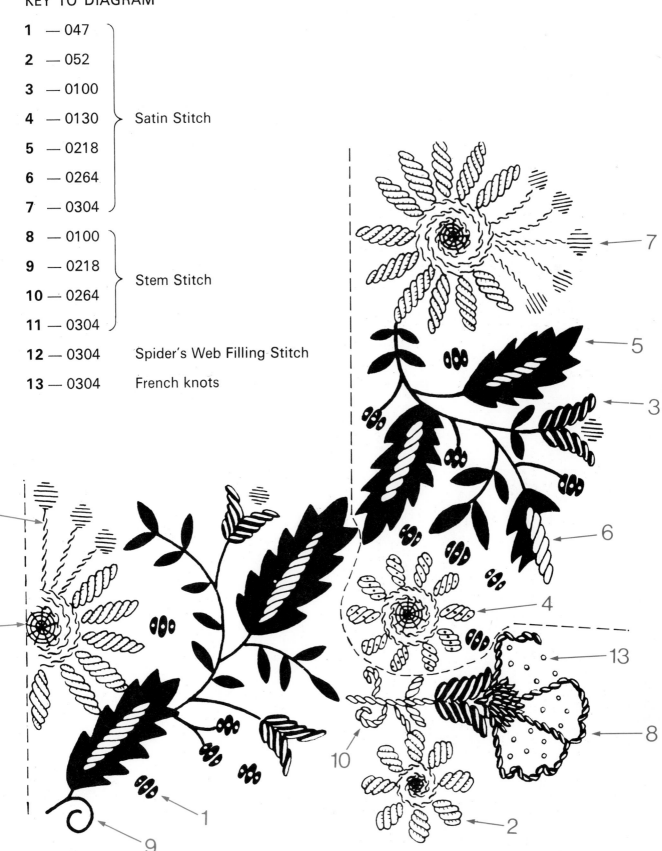

351

A magnificent dragon

In China the dragon is regarded as the lord of all animals, a rain bringer and symbol of the highest intelligence. This magnificent dragon, embroidered on the back of an emerald green kimono, is chasing a flaming pearl, another popular Chinese symbol which represents the spring moon, herald of the fertile rainy season. A bat, symbol of happiness, is worked on the pocket.

Fabric required
Length of emerald green fabric

You will also need
☐ Anchor Stranded Cotton in the following colours and quantities: 2 skeins each 0187 jade and 0307 amber gold; 1 skein each 0132 cobalt blue; 0185 and 0189 jade; 0242 and 0245 grass green; 0297 buttercup; 0300 gorse yellow; 0305 and 0309 amber gold; 0335 flame
☐ Alternative thread: Anchor Pearl Cotton No. 8 (10grm ball), 1 ball each: 0132 cobalt blue; 0185, 0187 and 0189 jade; 0243 and 0245 grass green; 0297 buttercup; 0300 gorse yellow; 0306, 0307 and 0309 amber gold; 0335 flame
☐ McCalls kimono pattern No. 3738
☐ Milward 'Gold Seal' crewel needle No. 8

The design
1 Lay out the pattern pieces on the fabric as directed in the pattern. Do not cut out the back and pocket pieces, but mark the cutting line on the fabric with either small tacking stitches or with a tracing wheel and dressmakers' carbon paper. This is because the embroidery may pull and distort the fabric slightly.
2 Enlarge the design on to graph paper and transfer on to the fabric. To do this either use an embroidery transfer pencil or trace the design on to tissue paper and sew it to the fabric with small tacking stitches along the lines of the design, tearing the paper away afterwards.
3 Position the dragon on the back of the kimono 7.5cm (3 inches) from the neck edge. The bat and pearl should be placed centrally on the pocket.

To work the embroidery
4 Use two strands of Stranded Cotton in the needle throughout. Follow the diagram and stitch key to work the embroidery. All parts similar to the numbered parts are worked in the same colour and stitch.
5 To complete the dragon work a French knot in the centre of each eye on top of the satin stitch.

To make up the kimono
6 Press the embroidery on the wrong side under a damp cloth.
7 Lay the pattern pieces on the embroidered back and pocket pieces. Check that the outlines of the pattern on the fabric have not been distorted by the embroidery. Adjust if necessary. Make up the kimono as directed by the pattern.

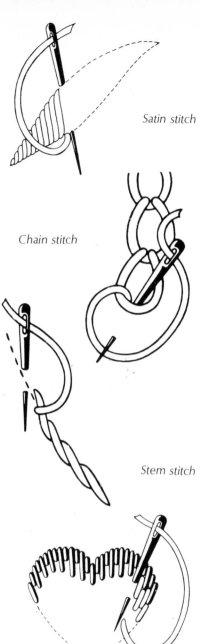

Satin stitch

Chain stitch

Stem stitch

Long and short stitch

A

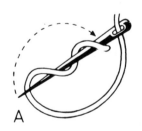

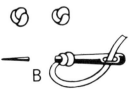

B

French knot

Graph pattern for dragon design

each square = 2.5 cm (1 in) sq

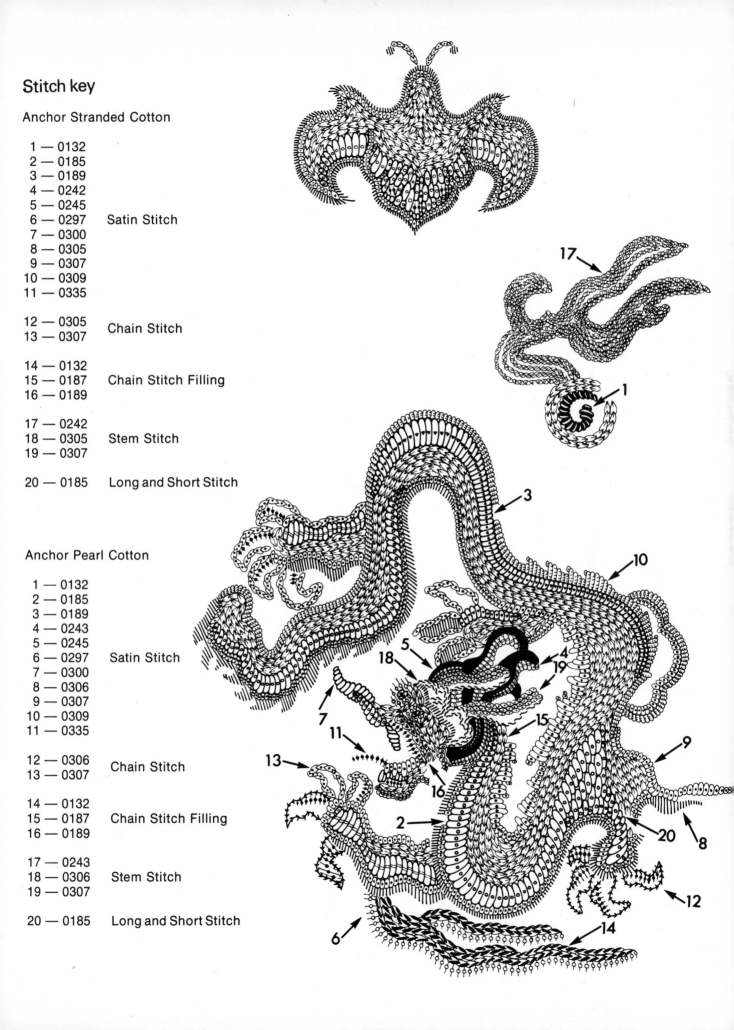

Stitch key

Anchor Stranded Cotton

1 — 0132		
2 — 0185		
3 — 0189		
4 — 0242		
5 — 0245		
6 — 0297	Satin Stitch	
7 — 0300		
8 — 0305		
9 — 0307		
10 — 0309		
11 — 0335		
12 — 0305	Chain Stitch	
13 — 0307		
14 — 0132		
15 — 0187	Chain Stitch Filling	
16 — 0189		
17 — 0242		
18 — 0305	Stem Stitch	
19 — 0307		
20 — 0185	Long and Short Stitch	

Anchor Pearl Cotton

1 — 0132		
2 — 0185		
3 — 0189		
4 — 0243		
5 — 0245		
6 — 0297	Satin Stitch	
7 — 0300		
8 — 0306		
9 — 0307		
10 — 0309		
11 — 0335		
12 — 0306	Chain Stitch	
13 — 0307		
14 — 0132		
15 — 0187	Chain Stitch Filling	
16 — 0189		
17 — 0243		
18 — 0306	Stem Stitch	
19 — 0307		
20 — 0185	Long and Short Stitch	

Circles and spirals

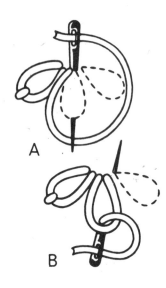

Detached chain stitch

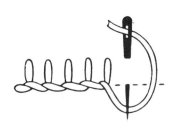

Buttonhole stitch

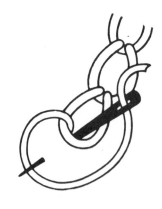

Chain stitch

The colourful design on this cushion is based on a theme of circles. A vibrant range of colours and a few simple stitches combined to give this effect. A more striking finish could be achieved by matching one embroidered cushion with others in plain fabrics, chosen to pick up the embroidery thread colours.

Fabric required
2 × 43cm (*17 inch*) squares of furnishing cotton

You will also need
- ☐ 1 × 40.5cm (*16 inches*) square cushion pad
- ☐ Crewel needles, No. 6 and No. 7
- ☐ Contrast bias binding
- ☐ Coats Anchor Stranded Cotton in the following colours and quantities: 1 skein each 0125 indigo; 061 magenta; 097 violet; 0889 bark; 0122 delphinium; 0853 tawny beige; 0893 muted pink; 0117 periwinkle; 0164 kingfisher

The design
Work the chain stitch flowers with three strands of cotton. Stitch in a spiral from the outer edge to the centre. The violet flowers are worked in a long detached chain stitch angled towards the centre point. Work a smaller second stitch within each petal. The florets in the delphinium are made with closely stitched buttonhole wheels. Use four strands in the needle.

To make up the cushion
Press the embroidery face down over a thick pad. Decorate the edges with a bias binding piping. Match it to one of the colours in the embroidery. Pin the two cushion pieces, right sides together, with the folded bias binding sandwiched between the two layers. The fold of the binding faces into the centre. Stitch three sides together through all layers. On the fourth side, the binding is stitched to the seam line of the embroidered square. Turn to the right side and press. Insert the cushion pad and close with oversewing, with a zip, or with press studs.

Trace pattern for cushion

Colour key

1 0125 indigo
2 061 magenta
3 097 violet
4 0889 bark
5 0122 delphinium
6 0853 tawny beige
7 0893 muted pink
8 0117 periwinkle
9 0164 kingfisher

Continue outer leaf pattern
to match opposite side

Working a family tree

One of the best ways of using stitches recently learned and to put them into practice is to make up a sampler. This family tree uses four simple stitches illustrated in the previous pages and will make a beautiful and personal addition to your home.

This adaptable embroidered version of a family tree was worked by Mrs Mary Pilcher for her grandson Robin (at the top of the tree), who is the fifth generation of Pilchers shown.

This family tree was worked as a present for Robin's second birthday, but a family tree for your own family would make an equally appropriate wedding or christening gift. The number of branches and sprigs will, of course, vary with the size of the family represented and also with the degree of lineage shown.

Choose your own fabric and colours, remembering that the more personal the choice, the more your embroidered family tree will mean to you and to those who will, in time, inherit it.

Be sure to date your tree too, as Mrs Pilcher has done, because one day some member of a future generation will regard it with pride as a family heirloom.

To make the family tree
Size
25.5cm (10 inches) by 40cm (15¾ inches) dimensions of mounting board as frame: 33cm (13 inches) by 47.5cm (18¾ inches)

Fabric required
☐ 46cm (½ yard) ivory linen
☐ 46cm (½ yard) textured linen or similar fabric in contrasting colour.

You will also need
☐ Anchor Stranded Cotton in the following colours: 0258 medium moss green, 0269 dark moss green, 0280 medium muscat green, 0281 dark muscat green, 0308 amber gold, 0358 medium peat brown, 0359 dark peat brown, 0326 dark orange, 0332 flame
☐ Shelf paper or similar and grease-proof or tracing paper, each sheet measuring approximately 25.5cm (10 inches) by 35.5cm (14 inches)
☐ Two pieces heavy card for mounting, measuring 25.5cm (10 inches) by 40cm (15¾ inches) and 33cm (13 inches) by 47.5cm (18¾ inches)
☐ 1.83m (2 yards) ricrac trim
☐ Rubber adhesive
☐ 2.3m (2½ yards) gum strip.

The design
Planning the design
1 Use the design given as a basic pattern for your own family tree, altering it as required.

Each square 2·5cm (1in) sq

The design for the family tree shown here reduced by half. Alter the design to accommodate a larger or smaller family.

Work out these alterations on a sheet of shelf paper, doing this preliminary work in pencil so that changes can be easily made.

2 Fold the sheet of shelf paper in half length-ways, making a sharp crease. Open it out and use the centre, vertical fold as a guide line for the tree trunk. Draw in the tree trunk with a pencil. Make a list of the baby's relations or member of the family to be included, and decide how many branches the tree will need. If working the tree for a baby, the names of his parents and grandparents will be embroidered down the main trunk of the tree and great aunts, uncles and cousins on the side branches. Additional side branches can be worked in if necessary and a strategically placed flower or leaf will balance the design if it becomes asymmetrical. After adjusting the design of the tree, outline it in ink. Underline the names to be worked in ink, but omit the names on this pattern.

Transferring the design

1 Fold the greaseproof or tracing paper vertically as above, open it out and place over the design, matching the centre folds. Trace all the lines you will need for the embroidery.

2 Fold the background material in half length-ways, making certain the fold is along the straight grain of the fabric. Put a few pins along the centre fold as a guide-line. Place the tracing of the design over the material, matching the folds; then pin and tack them together.

3 With small tacking stitches tack along all the lines for embroidery, being careful to start and finish securely so that the tacking threads won't pull out. Tear away the paper, leaving the tacked design on the background fabric. The tacking stitches are removed as the embroidery progresses: snip the thread and pull out a short length at a time.

Working the embroidery

Follow the working chart and key for stitches and colours to be used in the design. The key also indicates the number of strands to be used in each area.

Mounting the embroidery

1 Use two pieces of heavy card to mount the embroidered panel and 'frame' it. The smaller piece measures 25.5cm (*10 inches*) by 40cm (*15¾ inches*) and the larger, 33cm (*13 inches*) by 47.5cm (*18¾ inches*).

2 Place the smaller piece of card on a table so that one side projects over the edge by a few inches. Lay the embroidery over it, right side up, centring the work as carefully as possible. Starting at the centre of one side, feel the edge of the card through

KEY TO DESIGN FOR FAMILY TREE				
Grass	outer row	chain stitch	2 strands	0268 med. moss green
	middle row	stem stitch	1 strand	0281 dk. muscat green
	inner rows (two)	stem stitch	1 strand	0280 med. muscat green
Tree trunk	outer row	stem stitch	3 strands	0359 dk. peat brown
	inner row	stem stitch	2 strands	0358 med. peat brown
	inner row	stem stitch	1 strand	0308 amber gold
Roots		stem stitch	3 strands	0359 dk. peat brown
		stem stitch	2 strands	0358 med. peat brown
		stem stitch	2 strands	0281 dk. muscat green
Flowers		detached chain stitch	2 strands	0332 flame
			2 strands	0326 dk. orange
Sun	centre	stem stitch	1 strand	0308 amber gold
		stem stitch	1 strand	0332 flame
		stem stitch	1 strand	0326 dk. orange
	rays	open Cretan stitch	1 strand	0326 dk. orange
Leaves	outer row	stem stitch	3 strands	0269 dk. moss green
	centre	open Cretan stitch	3 strands	0268 med. moss green
		open Cretan stitch	3 strands	0280 med. muscat green
		open Cretan stitch	3 strands	0281 dk. muscat green
Lettering		stem stitch	1 strand	0359 dk. peat brown
Underlining		stem stitch	1 strand	0326 dk. orange
Butterflies		stem stitch	3 strands	0308 amber gold
		French knots	3 strands	0308 amber gold

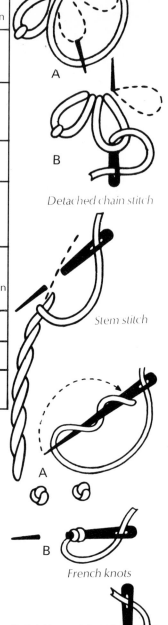

Detached chain stitch

Stem stitch

French knots

Open Cretan stitch

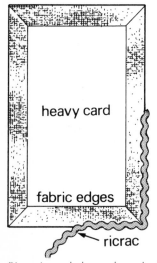

Ricrac is stuck down along the back edge of the panel to add a decorative trim.

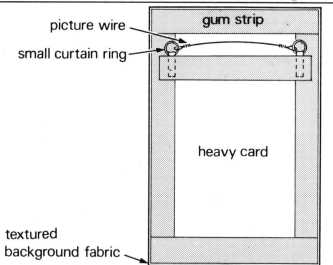

picture wire — gum strip
small curtain ring —
heavy card
textured background fabric —

Finish off the back of the completed panel with gum strip and curtain rings for hanging

the material with your left thumb and pin at 2.5cm (1 inch) intervals. Stick the pins straight through the edge of the card, perpendicular to it. Turn the card round and pin along the opposite edge, pulling as tight as possible. Check to see that the embroidery is centred on the card and that the grain of the fabric is straight in both directions; take the pins out and adjust accordingly. Then pin the third side and the fourth, so that the fabric is very tight but the embroidery not distorted.

3 When you are quite certain that the embroidery is positioned correctly, turn the card over and stick down the edges with rubber adhesive. Leave the pins in place until the adhesive is dry; then remove them and trim the corners.

4 Cover the larger piece of card with the textured background fabric in the same way. Spread a small amount of rubber adhesive in the centre of the material to join the two panels.

5 If ricrac trim is to be used, stick it down along the back edge of the smaller panel before joining the two panels. Start sticking down the ricrac half way down one side of the panel, adjusting as necessary from the front. Make certain that a loop appears at each corner, stretching or easing the ricrac to make this possible.

If you prefer not to frame the finished panel, cover the raw edges of the material on the back with gum strip. Slip a short length of tape through each of two small curtain rings and fix in place with gum strip. A length of picture wire can be extended between the two rings, and the panel hung by this wire.

THE ESSENTIAL STITCHES

Stitches can be divided into six main groups, according to their general method of construction, and as you become more expert you will see how they can be adapted to add interest and individuality. In cases where you pass the needle under the stitches without penetrating the fabric it is easier to do so if you reverse the needle and lead with the head.

Line stitches
Stem stitch

This stitch is used principally as a line or outline stitch. Work from left to right taking small slanting stitches along the line of the design. The thread should always emerge on the left-hand side of the previous stitch.

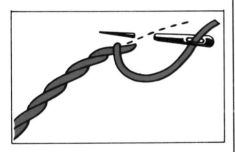

Back stitch

Work from right to left. Bring the thread through the stitch line, take a small stitch back into fabric and bring out the needle the same distance in front of the first stitch. To repeat, insert the needle into the fabric at the point of the first stitch.

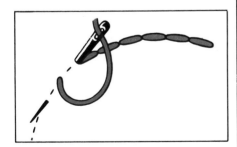

Split stitch

This can be used as a line stitch and a filling stitch when worked closely together. Work from left to right. Bring the thread through the stitch line and make a small stitch with the needle pointing backwards.

Bring the needle up piercing the working thread and splitting it.

Running stitch

Work from right to left. Insert the needle into the fabric making stitches of equal length above and below the fabric so that on both sides the stitches and spaces are of equal length.

Pekinese stitch

Work a row of back stitch, then interlace it with a different, preferably heavier thread, for contrast. The bottom part of the interlacing should lie flat, leaving a looped edge on the upper side of the back stitch.

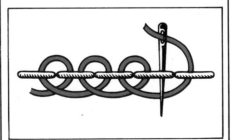

Flat or filling stitches
Satin stitch

This is a close straight stitch which is usually used as a filling stitch. The stitches

should lie flat and even on the right side of the work.

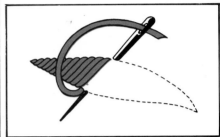

Herringbone stitch

Work from bottom left to upper right. Bring the needle out on the lower line at left and insert at top right, making a small stitch to the left and keeping the thread below the needle. Repeat, making a small stitch at bottom and top as you progress. The stitch can be laced in a variety of ways with ribbon or thread and can be as narrow or as wide as required.

Encroaching satin stitch

This is another useful way of shading. Work the tops of the stitches in the second and subsequent rows in between the bases of the stitches in the row above.

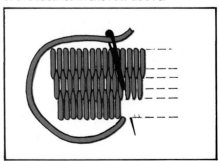

Padded satin stitch

For small surfaces in a design and to give additional texture, some parts may be padded with rows of small running stitch before the satin stitch is worked. To make a neat contour you can outline the edge first with split stitch and then work satin stitch over the whole shape.

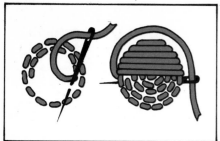

Raised satin stitch

This is effective for small parts of pictures where you want a three-dimensional effect, Start in the same way as for padded satin stitch across the shape. Then work a second layer at right angles to the first one.

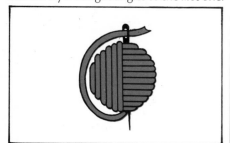

Chevron stitch

Work from bottom left to top right and from top right to bottom left alternately making small back stitches. Bring out the needle halfway along each back stitch, keeping the thread alternately above and below the needle as the stitch progresses.

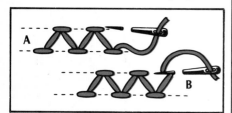

Fishbone stitch

This is a useful filling stitch which should be kept even and compact. Note the small straight stitch at the beginning which is not repeated. Bring the thread through at A and make a small straight stitch along the centre line of the shape. Bring the thread through again at B and make a sloping stitch across the centre line at the base of the first stitch. Bring the thread through at C and make a similar sloping

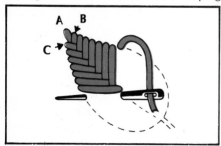

stitch to overlap the previous stitch. Continue working alternately on each side until the shape is filled.

Looped stitches

This group of stitches shows only some of the many which are formed by looping thread round a needle.

Buttonhole stitch

Work from left to right, starting on the bottom line. Insert the needle into the fabric above the line at required distance, take a straight downward stitch, and bring out the needle with the thread under it. Pull up the stitch to form a loop and repeat the process. Once the basic method of working the stitch is mastered, the variations such as closed, up and down and knotted buttonhole stitch are not difficult.

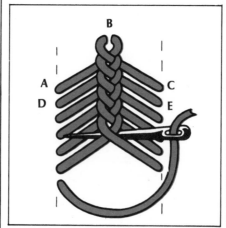

Vandyke stitch

This stitch closely worked will form a thick plaited line but it can also be used as a filling stitch. It must be worked very evenly to form a good plait. Bring the thread through at A. Take a small horizontal stitch at B and insert the needle at C. Bring the thread through at D. Without piercing the fabric, pass the needle under the crossed threads at B and insert at E. Do not pull the stitches too tightly or the regularity of the centre plait will be lost.

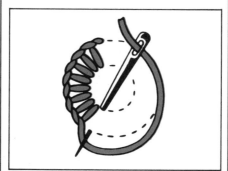

Cretan stitch

A most useful and versatile stitch with a number of uses when worked closely or

openly and irregularly. Work from left to right. Bring the needle through on the left-hand side, take a small stitch on lower line with the needle pointing upwards and the thread behind it. Take a stitch on the upper line with the thread under the needle. Repeat movements.

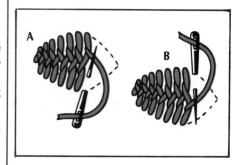

Loop stitch

This is similar to Vandyke stitch but its effect is not so heavy and the two should not be confused. Work from right to left. Start at centre of the stitching line, take the thread through at A and insert at B, bring through at C immediately below B. Keep the thread to the left and under the needle, pass the needle under the first stitch without entering the fabric.

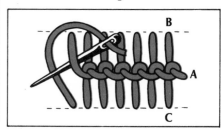

Feather stitch

This stitch is seen at its best in the traditional forms of Dorset feather stitchery but is not so often used today. The stitch gives a feathery effect but must be worked very evenly to prevent it becoming straggly. Bring out the needle at top centre, hold the thread down with the left thumb, insert the needle a little to the right on the same level and take a small stitch down to the centre, keeping the thread under the needle point. Insert the needle a little to the left on the same level and take a stitch to centre, keeping the thread under the needle. Work these two movements alternately.

Fly stitch

This can be worked closely as a line and either regularly or sparsely as a filling. Work from the left when using it horizontally and from the top when working on a vertical line. Bring the thread through at top left, hold it down with the left thumb, insert the needle to the right on the same level and take a small stitch down to the centre with the thread below the needle. Pull through and insert the needle below the centre stitch to hold the loop and bring it through in position to begin the next stitch.

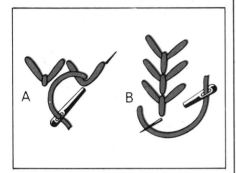

Chained stitches

There are at least nine varieties of chain stitch and the simpler versions, such as ordinary chain, twisted chain and open chain, can be whipped, overcast or threaded.

Chain stitch

This is usually worked from top to bottom vertically and from right to left horizontally. Start by bringing the thread through at the top and inserting the needle again at the same place, forming a loop. (If you are working in the hand, you may find it easier to hold the loop down with your left thumb.) Take a small stitch forward, bringing the needle up through the loop, keeping the thread under the needle. Repeat the stitch, varying its length as required.

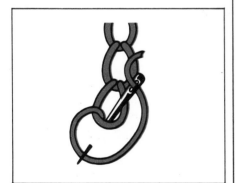

Twisted chain stitch

This is a most useful stitch which should be worked closely and evenly to produce a firm twisted line. Work as for ordinary

chain stitch but insert the needle just outside the last loop and at a slight angle to the stitching line with the thread below the point of the needle, as shown.

Open chain stitch

This must be worked evenly to prevent it from becoming very loose and untidy. Bring the needle through at A, hold down the thread and insert the needle at B, the required width of the stitch. Bring the needle through at C, the required depth of the stitch, leaving the loop thus formed slightly loose. Insert the needle at D and, with the thread under the needle, bring it through for the next stitch. Secure the last loop with a small stitch at each side.

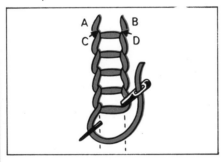

Heavy chain stitch

This makes a very firm close line. Start at the top and work down. Bring out the thread at point A and make a small vertical stitch. Bring the thread through at B and pass the needle under the vertical stitch without penetrating the fabric (use the head of the needle, rather than the point, as this is easier). Insert the needle again at B and bring it out at C. Pass the needle under the vertical stitch and insert again at C. Continue forming stitches in this way, passing the needle under the two preceding loops.

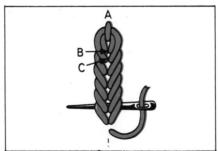

Rosette chain

For this stitch to be effective with either thick or thin threads it must be worked evenly and closely, with no loose top edge. Work from right to left and bring the thread through at the right end of the upper line, pass it to the left and hold down with the left thumb. Insert the needle into the upper line a short distance from where it first emerged and bring it out on the lower line with the thread under the needle point. Draw the needle through the loop and, using the head of the needle, pass it under the top edge of the stitch.

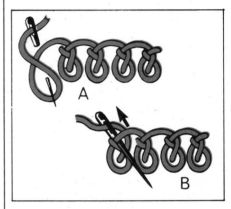

Wheatear

This is a simple stitch which combines straight stitches and a chain stitch. Work two straight stitches at A and B. Bring the thread through below these at C and pass the thread under the two straight stitches without penetrating the fabric. Insert the needle again at C, bring it through at D and repeat.

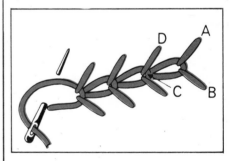

Knotted stitches

Some of the stitches in this group, such as French knots and bullion, are intended to be worked as single stitches while others are more suitable for use as line stitches.

French knots

Bring out the needle at the required position, hold the thread down with the left thumb and encircle the thread with the needle two or three times (depending on the thickness of the thread and the size of knot required). Still holding the thread firmly, return the needle to the starting point and insert *very close* to where the thread emerged. Pull the thread through to the wrong side of the fabric and secure if working a single stitch or pass on to the position of the next stitch if you are working a group. It is a common error to insert the needle too far from the point where the stitch was started, making a loose, untidy knot.

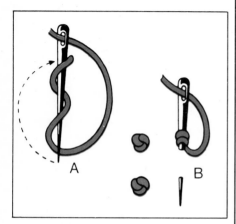

Bullion stitch

The second part of this stitch is taken back over the first part so it is this first part which dictates the finished length of the stitch. Pick up a back stitch of the required length, bringing the needle point out where it first emerged from the fabric. Coil the thread round the needle point as many times as required to equal the space of the back stitch, hold the coiled thread down with your left thumb and pull the needle through. Still holding the coil, return the needle to where it was first inserted (see arrow) and pull through until the stitch lies flat.

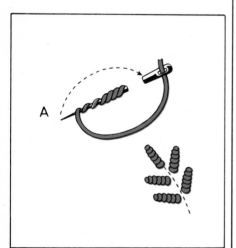

Coral stitch or knot

This is best worked as a firm line as it becomes weak and straggling if the knots are too far apart. Work from right to left or from top to bottom. Bring the thread out at the starting point and lay it along the line to be worked, holding it down with the left thumb. Take a small stitch under

the line where the knot is to be spaced (the thread lies on top of the needle as it enters the fabric) and pull through, taking the needle over the lower loop to form the knot.

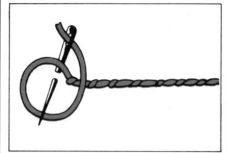

Double knot

This is a slightly more complicated knot stitch. The knots should be spaced evenly and closely to obtain a beaded effect. Bring the thread through at A and take a small stitch across the line to be worked at B. Pass the needle downwards under the stitch just made without penetrating the fabric as at C. With the thread under the needle, pass it under the first stitch again as at D. Pull the thread through to form a knot.

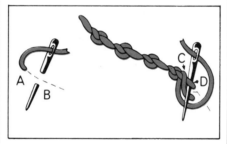

Knotted cable chain

Work from right to left. Bring the thread through at A and place it along the line to be worked. With the thread under the needle, take a stitch at B (which is a coral knot). Pass the needle under the stitch between A and B without penetrating the fabric, as shown at C. With the thread under the needle, take a slanting stitch across the line of stitching at D, close to the coral knot. Pull the thread through to form a chain stitch.

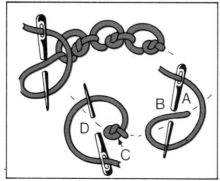

Composite stitches

These form a group which are usually worked on a foundation of satin stitch bars and they can be used as filling or line stitches. The satin stitch bars can be lengthened or shortened as required.

Portuguese border stitch

Work the required number of horizontal straight stitches (satin stitch bars). Working from the bottom upwards, bring the thread through at the centre and below the first bar (point A). Keeping the thread to the left of the needle take the thread over and under the first two bars, over the first two bars again and then under the second bar only without penetrating the fabric. With the thread now at B, work the second pair of stitches in a similar way and continue upwards to the top of the row. Return to point A and work the second row of stitches up the foundation bars, keeping the thread to the right of the needle. Do not pull the surface stitches too tightly.

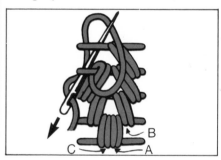

Raised chain band

If worked as a heavy line stitch it is advisable to use a finer thread for the foundation bar, but this should be of suitable weight to carry the chain stitch which can be in a heavier thread (for example Anchor Stranded for the bars and Anchor Soft for the chain stitches). Work the required number of satin stitch bars. Starting at the top and working down, bring the needle through at A in the centre of the first bar. Pass the needle up to the left and down to the right under the foundation bar, as shown, then through the chain loop thus formed. Repeat for the following stitches.

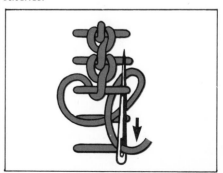

Raised stem band

This is worked in a similar way as for raised chain band but substituting stem stitch for chain stitch. The stem stitch can be worked from top to bottom but the effect is more even if worked from the bottom up.

Woven band

This stitch is worked on evenly spaced foundation bars from the top down. You will require two needles with contrasting thread and you will obtain a better effect if one is shiny and the other dull in the same colour, rather than with two contrasting colours. Bring both threads through at the top of the foundation bars with the lighter or silky thread to the left. Pass the light thread under the first bar and leave it lying. Take the darker or dull thread over the first bar, under the second bar and under the light thread. Leave the dark thread lying and pass the light thread over the second bar, under the third bar and under the dark thread. Continue in this way to the end of the band. Begin each following row at the top. By altering the sequence of the contrasting thread, various patterns can be achieved.

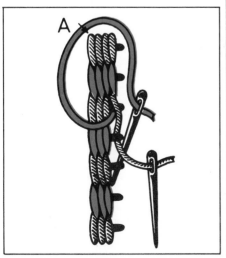

Interlaced band

This stitch is composed of two rows of back stitch with an interlacing band. The distance between the back stitch rows depends on the thickness of the interlacing thread, and should be greater when using a thick thread. For the back stitch, the centre of the stitches in the bottom row should be directly in line with the end of the stitches in the top row so that the interlacing can be worked evenly. Bring the lacing thread through at A and interlace through every stitch as shown.

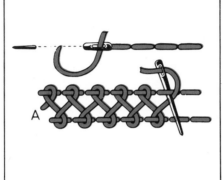

Spider's web

This is a useful and decorative stitch of which there are two varieties.

Back-stitched spider's web Work an even number of equal or unequal length stitches radiating from a centre point – six or eight stitches is the usual number. Bring the needle through the centre. Working from right to left as you progress round the spokes of the web, work a back stitch over each spoke. Pass the needle under the next thread before working the back stitch over it. To finish off, take the thread down into the fabric immediately under a spoke and fasten off underneath. The spokes of the web can be completely filled in but a better effect is made by leaving some unworked with the spokes showing.

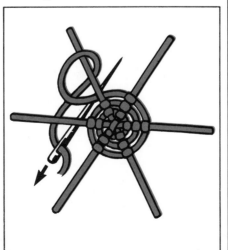

Woven spider's web or woven wheel

Work an uneven number of stitches radiating from a centre point. Bring the needle up in the centre and weave the thread over and under the spokes. This can be worked from left to right or vice versa. Finish off as for the back-stitched web.

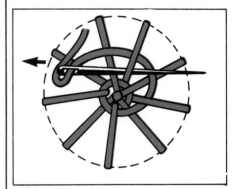

Couching

Couching a line means to lay a line of thread (heavy, light, thick or thin) on the fabric on the line of the design and stitch it down at regular intervals with another thread which may be contrasting. The stitching must be evenly spaced.

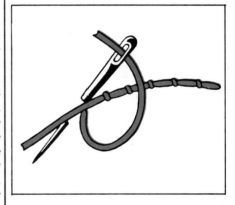

Sheaf stitch

This is a useful stitch which can be used as a filling or as an isolated stitch. It can be worked at spaced intervals or closely grouped. It consists of three vertical satin stitches which are overcast with two horizontal satin stitches, worked with the head of the needle without penetrating the fabric.

ADVANCED STITCHERY
ASSISI WORK

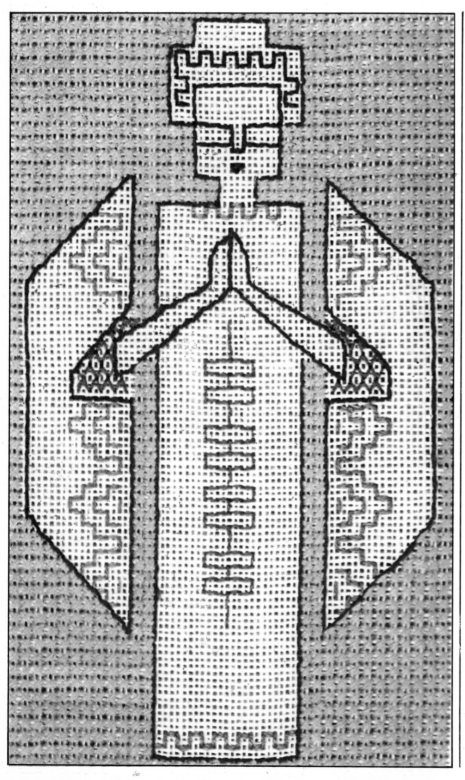

Assisi work is basically a form of cross stitch embroidery although the principle of the work is reversed and the stitches form the background of the design while the basic shapes are left unworked. (This technique is known as 'voiding'.)

As its name suggests, Assisi work originated in Italy. For centuries it has been used to decorate ecclesiastical linen and vestments as well as peasant clothing and household linen. Today it can be used to decorate cushions, place mats and tray cloths or it can form an unusual embroidery on a child's dress or on an accessory such as a bag or belt.

The designs

Traditionally the designs for Assisi work were formal and generally naturalistic; representing animals, birds or flowers in a stylised manner.

Contemporary Assisi work can be inspired by designs from many sources; mosaics, carvings, wrought iron work, screen walling, architectural details, geometric patterns and lettering.

Abstract shapes or stylised reversed initials can also look effective in a border or on the pocket of a dress.

Making your own design

The simplest way is to draw the design on to a graph starting by outlining the motif in straight lines following the lines on the graph and then filling in the background so that you can get an idea of the effect.

As with cross stitch, (see earlier) each square on the graph should represent a unit or stitch. The basic stitch is then worked over three or four threads of an even weave fabric to form a regular and stylised pattern.

The colours

The traditional colours for the embroidery fabric in Assisi work were either white or natural linen with the stitches worked in two colours – usually browns, blues or dark reds, outlined either in a darker tone of the same colour or in black.

A contemporary colour scheme could be dark blue or navy threads worked on a

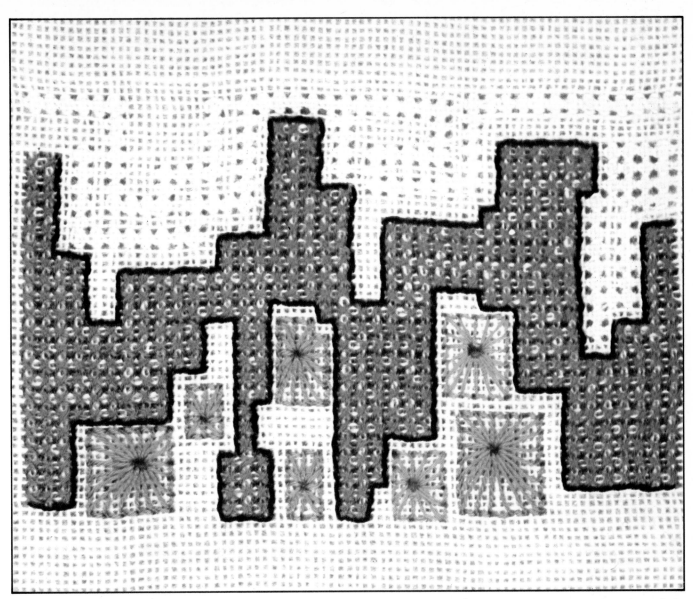

paler blue fabric or orange on yellow, but it is best not to mix colours for the stitchery.

Fabrics
Because all the stitches are worked over a specific number of threads, an even-weave fabric is essential, whether linen, cotton, wool or a synthetic furnishing fabric.

Threads
Pearl cotton, coton à broder and linen threads of a suitable weight for the fabric can all be used for Assisi work.

Needles
Use tapestry needles of a suitable size for the fabric and thread.

Method
There are only two stitches used for this type of embroidery – cross stitch for the background and Holbein (or double run-ning) for the outlining of the motif. The

design illustrated above also used Algerian eye stitch as a filling to give variety to the design.

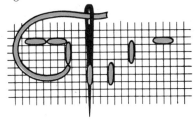

Start by working the Holbein stitch round the outline, counting the threads carefully. Make the stitches about three threads long, with equal spaces. Work round any offshoots of the design, carrying the thread out to the end of the line and back again to the main outline.

On the completion of the first journey the design may look rather disjointed and muddled, but on the second journey the stitch gaps are filled in and the design begins to take form. When all the out-lining is complete the background can be

filled in with cross stitch. Either of the two methods of cross stitch given earlier can be used. For large embroidered areas you may find it quicker to work it in two stages. Make sure that the upper stitch in each cross lies in the same direction and that you take the stitches right up to the outline or the character of the work could be lost.

Adding a border
When the background is complete the embroidery should have a very solid appearance and quite often needs a small border to soften it slightly. This can be a small geometric repeating pattern in Hol-bein worked either side of the design.

Finishing the edges
Final hems should be narrow and un-obtrusive in order not to detract from the work. On table linen a hemstitched hem is usually sufficient, while on a dress, pocket or belt the work can be finished with an invisible hem.

Assisi work tablecloth

The design in Assisi work is achieved by working over counted threads on an even-weave fabric, with a yarn which should be of a similar thickness to the warp and weft threads of the fabric. The finer the weave, the more attractive the design will be.

The actual motifs are formed by outlining them first in Holbein (double running) stitch and then filling in the background area with cross stitch. The fabric is thus left showing through the shape of the motifs. As the embroidery is worked over counted threads, the design has a stylised geometric look, and curves can only be indicated by stepped stitches or by diagonal stitches.

If you wish to make up or adapt your own design, it is best to work it out on graph paper first (10 squares to 2.5cm (1 inch) is suitable). Each square on the graph paper should represent one stitch and then, according to the fabric used, you can decide how many threads to work each stitch over. Most designs are repetitive and can be varied to suit the size required. Figures 1 and 2 show two simple treatments of a flower form and figure 3 shows a bird form.

Assisi work table cloth
Size
1.12m (44 inches) square

Fabric required
1.2m (1⅓ yards) × 140cm (54 inches) wide cream evenweave fabric, 30 threads to 2.5cm (1 inch)

You will also need
☐ Anchor Pearl Cotton No. 8 in the following colours and quantities: 3 balls 0132 blue; 1 ball 0403 black
☐ Milward 'Gold Seal' tapestry needle No. 24
☐ Embroidery ring frame

The design
1 Trim the fabric to an exact square with 117cm (46 inch) sides, cutting along the grain lines. Find the centre by folding the fabric in half both horizontally and vertically and tacking along the creases with a contrast thread, following the grain. The point of intersection marks the centre of the cloth.

2 Turn under 0.6cm (¼ inch) all round the edges and tack to prevent the fabric from fraying while you are working.

3 The chart gives just over half of one side of the square design in the centre of the cloth. Each square represents one stitch worked over three threads of evenweave fabric. The centre is indicated by the white arrow which should coincide with one of the lines of tacking stitches. Commence the Holbein stitch outline at the small black arrow, 213 threads down from the crossed tacking stitches, and follow the pattern as shown on the chart.

4 The design is repeated as a mirror image on the other half of the first side. Work the remaining three sides to correspond.

Working the outline
Work all the embroidery in a ring frame. Embroider the entire outline of the bird and flower design first in Holbein stitch, using black Pearl Cotton. Holbein stitch is worked in two stages. The first row is formed by working running stitch over and under three threads of fabric, following the shape of the design. When this is completed, work back in the opposite direction, filling in the spaces left in the first row. The diagonal stitches are formed by counting three across and three down (or up as required) and inserting the needle at this point. Work the lines of the pattern inside the motifs, for example the bird's eye, at the same time as working the outline.

Working the background
When the black outline is completed, fill in the background with horizontal lines of cross stitch, using blue Pearl Cotton. It is important to work all the stitches with the top stitch facing the same way.

1 Continue each row as far as it will go and fill in any separate areas later. As the back of the cloth should look as perfect as the front, the thread should not be carried over any of the unworked motifs.

2 Where the outline takes a diagonal direction, it may be necessary to use half a cross stitch only in filling in the background. Finally, work the inner and outer borders in Holbein and cross stitch as indicated on the chart, using blue Pearl Cotton.

Finishing off
Press the embroidery on the wrong side. Turn under a 2cm (¾ inch) hem all round, mitring the corners as shown in the diagram, and slip stitch in place. A more decorative hem can be worked if desired by withdrawing one or two threads around the edges of the cloth and finishing off with hem stitch. Finally, repeat the Holbein and cross stitch border about 7.5cm (3 inches) from the edge of the cloth.

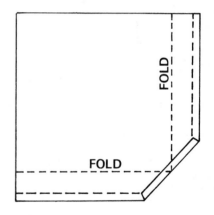

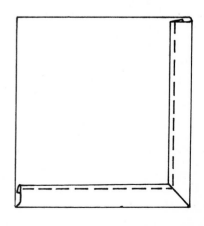

Stitch chart for
Assisi work cloth

Figs 1, 2 Two simple treatments of a flower motif.

Fig 3 A basic bird motif is reversed and a simple
outline added to create an effective design.

centre
of design

The Holbein stitch outline is worked in black Pearl
Cotton and the cross stitch background and the
borders in blue Pearl Cotton ►

A

B

Cross stitch

Holbein or double running stitch   Each square represents one stitch worked over three threads of fabric

BLACKWORK

Blackwork is a monochrome method of embroidery, and relies for effect on the contrasting tone values produced by varying the density of the pattern fillings and the weight of yarn used.

Blackwork became fashionable in England during the reign of Henry VIII when it was used mainly for the decoration of garments. Later it was also used to decorate household articles and soft furnishings.

Although its name derived from the method of working a geometric pattern in black silk or cotton threads on a white or cream background, any combination which gives a good contrast between dark thread and lighter fabric can be used. In the Tudor period it was frequently worked with a dark red silk on a cream fabric.

The fabric

Blackwork is a counted thread method of embroidery, so choose a fabric which is evenly woven and where the threads can be easily counted.

You could also use a heavy slubbed even-weave linen or cotton which will give a slightly uneven but attractive variation to the stitchery.

The threads and needles

You will need a selection of threads of all weights to provide the depth of tone and contrast in the stitchery. Machine Embroidery cotton No. 30, pure sewing silk, stranded cotton, pearl cotton Nos. 5 and 8, coton à broder and Anchor soft (on a heavier fabric) are all suitable and some of the various types of lurex and metal threads can also be incorporated. You will need tapestry needles in a variety of sizes to suit the fabric and threads.

The stitches

The stitches are simple and mostly variations of backstitch. Holbein or double running stitch can also be used for building up a border pattern incorporating blackwork filling stitches.

The patterns

The basis of all blackwork patterns is a simple geometric shape which can be adapted to the depth of tone required either by using a heavier or lighter thread or by adding and subtracting additional straight stitches. The spacing of the pattern will also enable a lighter or darker tone to be achieved.

The traditional method of working blackwork was to use the patterns as fillings for shapes of flowers, birds or animals, with the shape outlined with a heavier thread. Nowadays these heavy outlines are usually omitted.

If you are experimenting with blackwork, start by using one basic pattern, working it first over four threads of fabric and then altering the tone or size of the pattern by adding or subtracting part of it. Alternatively, work the pattern over a different number of threads.

The pattern shown below can be made to appear darker, for example, by working a small cross stitch in the centre of each shape. It would appear lighter in tone if each alternate small cross was omitted.

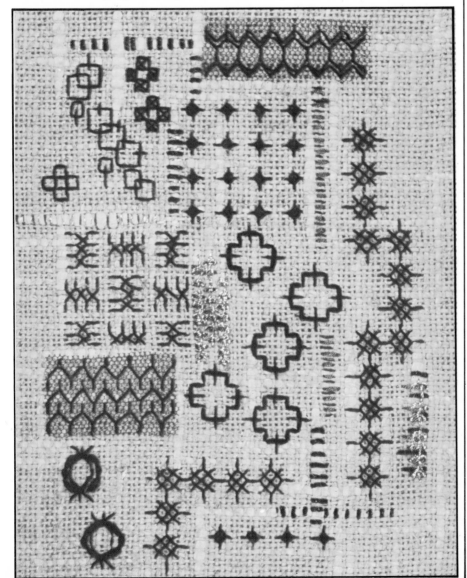

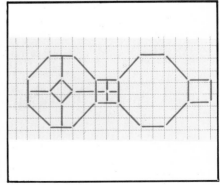

Embroidered chessboard

The chessboard (illustrated overleaf) is in fact a blackwork sampler, showing a variety of filling patterns. By working the patterns in alternate squares with blank squares in between, the sampler becomes an attractive chessboard as well as a permanent reference for the various patterns. The sampler was stretched over plywood, covered in glass to keep it clean and give a good playing surface for chess, and then framed. The materials given below are for a chess-board 40cm (*16 inches*) square, excluding the border, with 5cm (*2 inch*) individual squares.

Fabric required

Evenweave embroidery fabric, 60cm (24

Right A simple design in blackwork ideal to form a border.
Below A complex arrangement of blackwork stitches used to create an abstract design for a wallhanging or picture.

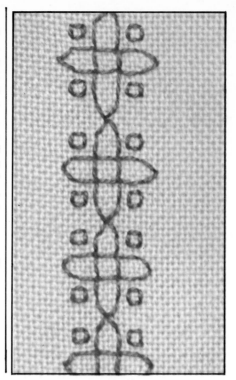

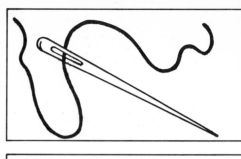

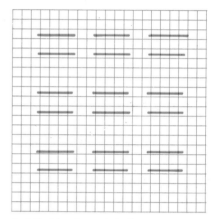

1a *Working in straight lines.*

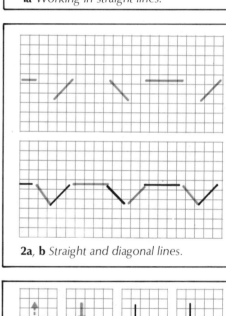

2a, b *Straight and diagonal lines.*

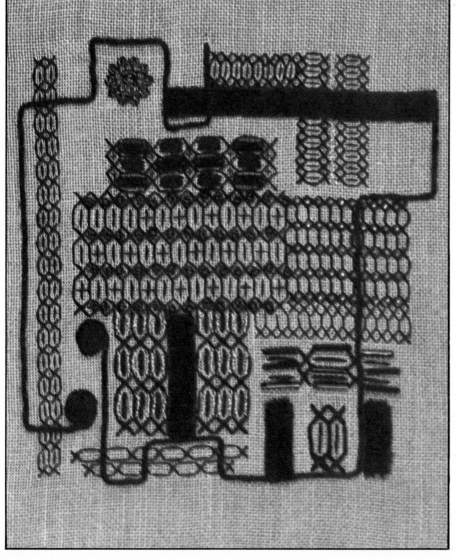

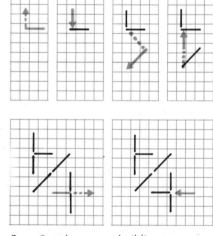

3a–o *Step by step to building up individual units by working in circular movements. This pattern could have been*

Creating blackwork patterns

All you need to create your blackwork patterns are graph paper, a ruler and a sharp pointed pencil. Work on the basis of one line on the graph equalling one thread of fabric and draw the patterns using basic geometric shapes from which you can develop intricate and interesting patterns. In order to stitch continuously round the design, so that you do not waste thread, you can work straight lines to form a plain grid or straight lines including diagonals or you can move in continuous circles for complicated patterns.

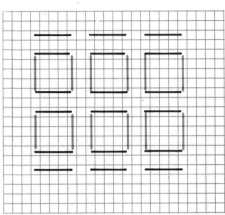

1b Completing the basic grid.

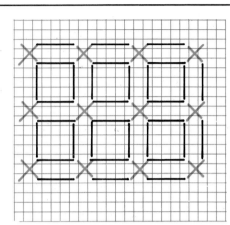

1c Filling in with cross stitch

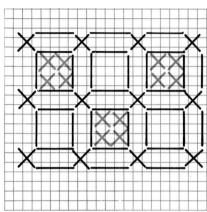

1d The complete pattern.

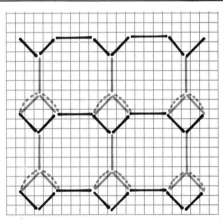

2c Completing the basic grid.

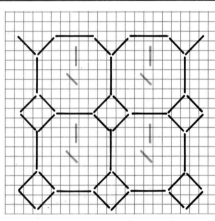

2d Starting the inner grid.

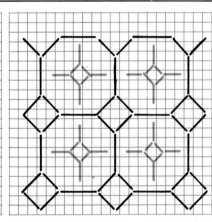

2e The complete pattern.

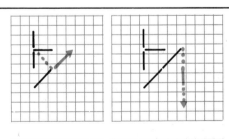

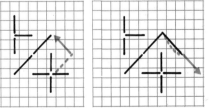

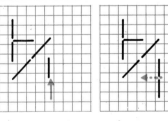

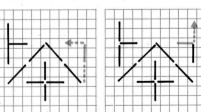

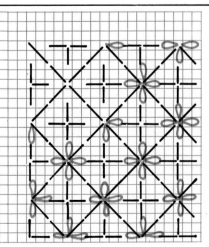

worked in lines to form the grid although it would need long stitches on the wrong side, but by stitching complicated patterns in circular movements you can work more quickly, and use less thread.

The plain grid (top left) with the pattern completed by rosettes of detached chain stitch.

373

inches) square, with 18 threads per 2.5cm (*1 inch*)

You will also need

☐ Threads, pearl cotton, one 10grm ball No. 5 and two 10 grm balls No. 8 in black, seven reels twisted silk.
☐ Tapestry needles, No. 26 for silk thread and No. 22 for pearl cotton.
☐ Plywood 50cm (*20 inches*) square (this can be larger if you want a wide frame)
☐ Staples and staple gun
☐ Glass and framing materials

The design

1 Check that the fabric is cut on the straight grain or straighten if necessary.
Find the centre of each side of the fabric by folding it in half and marking the fold at each end with a few tacking stitches. Open out the fabric, refold the other way and mark the fold again.
2 Starting at the centre, and 10cm (*4 inches*) in from the edge on one side, start by outlining the shape of the board in back stitch, using the No. 5 pearl cotton and working each stitch over three threads of the fabric. At 5cm (*2 inch*) intervals all the way round on the back-stitch border, work a single stitch of the same size at right angles and facing inwards to indicate the grid for the squares (if you do this there will be no need to recount the threads). Complete the grid by joining up the single stitches in lines across the board.
3 Work the patterns of your choice using different threads to give variety. Work the border to the size you require.

Making up

4 Press the embroidery on the wrong side. Stretch over the plywood and secure on the wrong side with staples. Cover with glass and frame.

This town scene, designed by Pauline Liu, is a clever example of how blackwork gives contrasting tone values by varying the density of the stitchery.

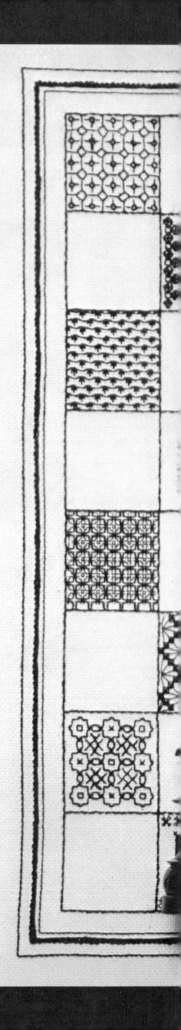

One way of keeping a permanent record of blackwork patterns is to work a sampler, such as this one designed as a chessboard by Pamela Tubby.

DRAWN AND PULLED THREAD WORK
Drawn thread work

Drawn thread work is a method of embroidery which creates a lacy fabric from a plain, closely woven one. It is primarily used for decorative borders for table linen where threads parallel to the edge of the fabric are withdrawn and the remaining threads in the border (those at right angles to the edge) are grouped together by simple stitchery.

The fabric

When choosing a fabric for drawn thread work the most important considerations are that it should be even-weave (with an equal number of warp and weft threads) and the threads should be easily counted and withdrawn.

Linen is the traditional choice for drawn thread work (not least because of its durability for table linen), and it is available in an even-weave with a thread count which varies from very fine to the coarser heavier variety.

There are many other suitable even-weave fabrics, including some synthetics, which do not need ironing and are very practical for place mats, tray cloths, table cloths, etc. To decide whether a fabric is even-weave, cut a hole 2.5cm (1 inch) square in a piece of card, hold it over the fabric and count the threads enclosed in the 'window' – there should be the same number in both directions.

The threads

Threads for this type of embroidery need to be strong and hard wearing. It is usually best to choose a matching thread which is slightly heavier than the threads of the fabric for the decorative stitching and a finer one for hem stitching and button-holing. On a medium-weight linen, for example, a Sylko perlé thread No.12 is suitable for hem-stitching and button-holing, with a No.8 thread for the additional stitchery. However, it is worth trying out the thread on a spare piece of fabric as it might be suitable and effective to use one thread throughout.

The needles

Tapestry needles of appropriate size should always be used because their blunt points separate the threads of the fabric which a regular sewing needle would split.

The stitches

The simplest form of drawn thread work is hem-stitching, in which the outer edge of the border is level with the inner edge of the hem so that the stitching can be worked alternately to secure the hem

Cafe curtains, given a neat but delicate border by the use of drawn thread work.

and group the threads in the border. There are numerous ways in which the threads of the border can be stitched, twisted or knotted together decoratively. Some of the most commonly used stitches are ladder stitch, coral knot, double knot and herringbone stitch.

Hem-stitched borders

Before starting a major project, it is advisable to work a simple hem-stitched border for a tray cloth, place mat or napkin.

1 Decide on the finished depth of the hem and measure in double this amount plus the depth of the first turning.

2 Using the point of a tapestry needle, pull out the thread immediately above the total depth of the hem and withdraw it across the width of the fabric.

3 Continue to pull out threads of fabric until the border is the required depth.

4 Turn up the hem to the edge of the border and tack in place.

5 To work the hem-stitching, first knot the end of the thread and run it along the hem so that the knot is securely inside.

6 Starting at the edge of the fabric, wrap the working thread round the first two threads of the border, make a hem stitch into the fold of the hem as for regular hemming, then overcast the next two threads of the border. Continue in this way, overcasting the threads of the border and hemming the fold alternately for the length of the border, always picking up the same number of threads each time.

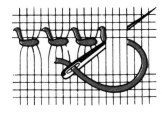

7 To strengthen the opposite edge of the border, work along it in a similar way, overcasting the same pairs of threads and

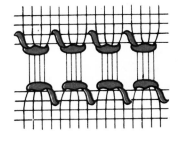

overcasting the edge of the fabric to match the hemmed side.

Four sided borders

When working a border round all four sides of a cloth, the threads are withdrawn in a slightly different way.

1 Calculate the total depth of the hem as for a simple border. Measure in this amount from both directions in each corner and mark the point where they meet with a pin or coloured tack to indicate the outer corners of the border. *Threads must not be withdrawn beyond this point.*

2 Cut the first thread of the border 2.5cm (1 inch) away from the marked point at both ends. Pull out the cut ends as far as the point and leave them hanging. Pull out the remaining portion of thread from the middle completely.

3 Continue to withdraw threads in this way all round the border for the required depth.

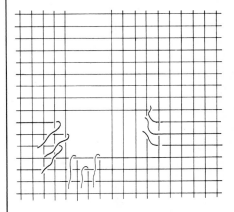

4 The strongest and tidiest way of securing the loose threads at the corners is to turn them back into the hem and enclose them when the hem is stitched. Alternatively, on a very fine and firmly woven linen the threads can be cut close to the edge and secured by buttonhole stitch.

5 Turn up the hem, mitring the corners, and slip stitch the diagonal fold neatly.

6 Work the hem stitching as for a simple border.

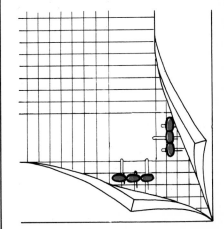

Drawn thread insertions and borders

These insertions can all be used for table linen, to decorate the hems of curtains and, if worked in a heavier thread, for garments. Most drawn thread insertions are first hem stitched along both edges, thus securing the hem if the insertions are used as a border, strengthening the edges when used as plain insertions, and also tying the threads together for the final decorative stitches.

Twisted border

In this insertion, the tied threads are twisted together into bunches of two or three. For wide insertions, two or three rows of twisting can be worked. Beads can also be picked up on the needle between each twisting to make an attractive variation.

1 Using a heavier or contrasting thread to the one used for hemstitching, anchor it to the middle of the outside edge of the corner square of the border.

2 Pass the needle over the space to form one spoke of the spider's web filling to be completed later (see below).

3 Take the needle over the first two tied groups of threads, then back under the second group and over the first group. Pull the thread taut so that the groups twist.

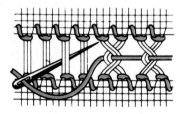

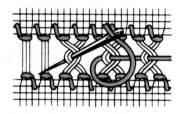

4 Repeat this process along the whole border, take the thread across to the opposite side of the corner space and fasten off on the wrong side.

5 Continue like this on each side of the border.

6 Add four extra crossing threads to the four already formed on each corner space and complete the wheel or web as shown in an earlier chapter.

Coral stitch twisted border

This is worked in a similar way, but coral stitch is used to tie the groups together.

Lattice border

The groups of threads are drawn together with a binding stitch, by taking the thread alternately above and below the groups.

1 Pass the needle over the first two groups, bring the needle round the second group, pass it over the second and third group, round the third group and over the third and fourth group.

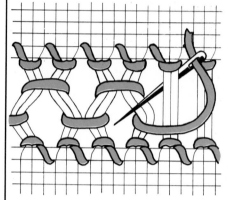

2 Continue in this way, binding the bunches above and below as shown, passing the needle behind the bars from right to left and keeping the working thread above the needle for the upper bars and below the needle for the lower bars.

Needleweaving border

This can be very effective when worked on a heavy slubbed linen with toning and/or contrasting threads.

1 Work the hem-stitching along each edge, tying the threads into bunches of four.

2 Run the working thread into the hem or edge above the starting point, leaving about 2.5cm (1 inch) to be darned in when the needle weaving is finished.

3 Bring the needle through the hem or edge and pass it over the first four threads to the right, bring the needle up again at the starting point and pass it over and under the first two threads to the left.

4 Working on these four threads, weave over and under until you are halfway down the block of withdrawn threads.

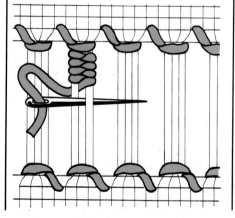

5 Pass the needle to the next four threads to the right and continue weaving over this block until you reach the opposite edge of the insertion.

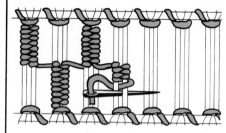

6 Carry the working thread inside this completed block of weaving until you reach the starting point of the block in the middle of the border.

7 Start weaving upwards on the next group of four threads to the right to the top of the border.

8 Continue to weave upwards and downwards on the groups, carrying the needle through the woven blocks to the next position.

9 When you reach the end of the insertion, return to the beginning and weave on the remaining threads in each block to complete the insertion. Fasten the thread securely and thread it back through the last block of weaving to neaten the work. The weaving should be as neat on the back as on the front of the work.

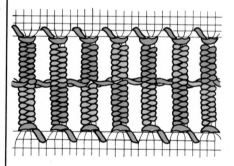

Finishing the corners

Where the withdrawn threads meet at the corners of a border a small square space is formed which should be strengthened and filled with stitchery, such as a woven spider's web. This should be worked after the hem stitching and additional stitchery is worked.

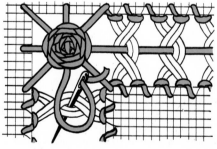

Pulled thread work

Pulled thread work is a method of creating a pattern of holes, spaces or shapes on an even-weave fabric with embroidery stitches which are pulled tightly.

This type of embroidery is ideal for making all kinds of table linen and for lampshades, borders on garments, curtains, bedspreads and cushions.

Sometimes known as drawn fabric work, it is of European peasant origin and developed through the use of embroidery on loosely woven muslins and calicos. To prevent the thread from lying loosely over the fabric the stitches were pulled tightly and it was discovered that this could create attractive patterns.

Pulled thread work should not be confused with drawn thread work, in which the pattern is created by actually withdrawing threads from the fabric and stitching on those remaining.

The fabric

Pulled thread work is a form of counted thread embroidery where the stitches are worked over a specific number of threads. For this reason the fabric should be of an even-weave (one with an equal number of warp and weft threads to the same measurement) and the threads should be large enough to count easily.

Several kinds of fabric are suitable: linen in various weights, from heavy furnishing linen to linen scrim as used for window cleaning; cotton in many weights and colours; even-weave wools; Moygashel dress fabrics and synthetic furnishing fabrics.

The thread

Generally the thread used for the stitchery should be of equal thickness to a withdrawn thread of the fabric, with the addition of thicker or thinner threads to vary the texture and pattern. If the fabric is a good one and will unravel easily, it is possible to remove threads from an unused end and work the embroidery in these.

Other suitable threads include Perlé cotton and crochet cottons in all weights, coton à broder, which is available in a good range of colours, linen threads and lace threads, available from bobbin lace suppliers.

Stranded embroidery cottons and mercerized sewing cottons are not suitable for this type of work as they tend to fray and break. Pure silk buttonhole thread can be used where you need a fine thread of silky texture. Traditionally the embroidery was worked in thread of the same colour as the fabric, but nowadays a contrasting colour is often used.

Needles

Always use a tapestry needle for pulled thread work as this will not split the threads of the fabric. Normally the needle should be of a suitable weight for the fabric so it passes between the threads easily. But when you are working a border or edging in a progressive stitch such as three-sided or four-sided stitch, you may find it easier to use a larger needle than for the rest of the work.

Frames

Always use a frame for this type of work as it will keep it at an even tension, prevent the fabric from pulling out of shape and enable the threads to be counted easily. The only exception to this rule should be when working an edging.

The stitches

The stitches used in pulled thread embroidery are some of the easiest to work and many are based on satin stitch, worked in lines or blocks at an even tension or pulled tightly. When these two methods are combined, a pattern is produced which can be varied at will. A combination of only two stitches, such as four-sided stitch and satin stitch, can produce a number of patterns when the tension and stitch order are varied. Honeycomb stitch and three-sided stitch are other stitches used. (Border stitches are covered in the next chapter).

Before you start a project, it is advisable to practise some of the stitches, working each separately and then in combinations, using both thin and thick threads (such as a fine crochet cotton and a heavier Perlé cotton).

To begin stitching do not use a knot but bring the thread through the fabric some distance away from the stitching point and make a small back stitch to anchor it. Continue until the thread is finished then return to the starting point and darn in the surplus thread through the stitching line. Alternatively, hold the end of the thread under the stitching line for a short way and work over it.

To finish stitching darn in the end of the thread to the stitchery on the back of the work, making a small back stitch to secure it. Pulled thread work should be as neat on the back of the fabric as on the front, particularly for table linen and lampshades.

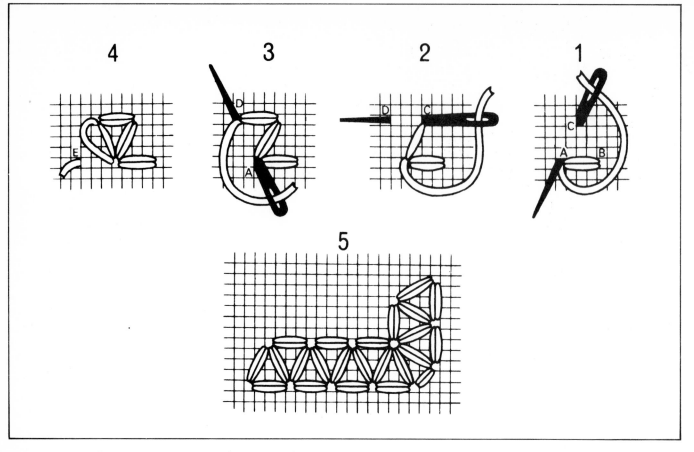

Three-sided stitch

This stitch is worked from right to left. Figure 1. Bring the thread through at A and make two stitches from A to B over four threads of fabric. Bring the needle through at A and take two stitches to C. Figure 2. Bring the needle through at D and take two stitches from D to C. Figure 3. Take two stitches from D to A. Figure 4. Bring the needle through at E. Figure 5. Turning a corner.

Honeycomb filling stitch

This stitch is worked from the top down. Figure 1. Bring the needle through at the arrow and insert at A. Bring through at B and insert at A. Bring through at B and insert at C. Bring through at D, insert again at C and bring through at D. Continue in this way for the row. Figure 2. Where rows connect, the vertical stitches are worked into the same holes.

Four-sided stitch

This stitch is worked from right to left. Figure 1. Bring the thread through at the arrow, insert it at A and bring it through at B.
Figure 2. Insert at the arrow and bring out at C.
Figure 3. Insert at A and bring out at B. Continue like this for a row or close the end for a single stitch.

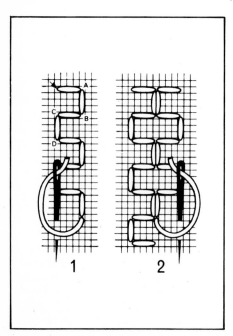

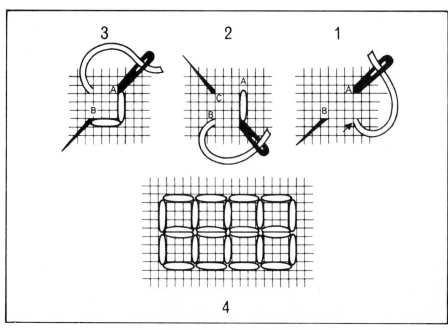

Edgings and borders

One of the most attractive uses for the techniques of pulled thread work is to combine them to form simple yet decorative borders on household linens and tableware.

Four-sided and satin stitch border

This border is suitable for table linen or to decorate the panels of a lampshade. It combines a repeating pattern of seven satin stitches worked over eight threads with a block of four four-sided stitches worked over four threads. The satin stitch is pulled tightly and the four-sided stitch is worked at normal tension.

1 Using a thread similar in weight to the fabric, work seven satin stitches over eight threads of the fabric. Follow this by four four-sided stitches worked over the centre four threads of the eight. Repeat to the end of the row.

2 Repeat this row two or three times to form a border of the required width (you will normally need a wider border for a lampshade than for a place mat, for example).

3 Start the next row with four four-sided stitches worked over the centre four threads of a block of eight. Continue with seven satin stitches over all the eight threads. Repeat to the end of the row.

4 Repeat this row until you have the same number of rows as the first pattern. The satin stitches should alternate with the four-sided stitches every two or three rows, depending on the width of the pattern required. The pattern can be varied further by changing the stitch sequence in alternate rows.

Honeycomb and satin stitch border

This border can be worked vertically as shown in the previous chapter to decorate the panels of a lampshade, or it can be worked horizontally for table linen. Follow the diagram for honeycomb stitch, but incorporate eight satin stitches pulled tightly, followed by one back stitch and eight more satin stitches from each back stitch section of honeycomb stitch.

1 Bring the needle through at the arrow.

2 Insert the needle four threads to the right.

3 Bring the needle through four threads down at B.

4 Insert the needle again at A and bring through two threads below.

5 Work eight satin stitches pulled tightly over these two threads.

6 Work one back stitch pulled tightly over four threads and bring the needle through two threads below the first row of satin stitches.

7 Work eight satin stitches pulled tightly below the first row.

8 Proceed to the next honeycomb stitch and repeat as before.

9 When the line of stitching is the required length, turn the work and repeat the honeycomb and satin stitch combination until the border is complete.

Incorporating beads into the work

The honeycomb and satin stitch border can be made more decorative by adding a pearl or china bead of the right size in the centre space which is formed between the two rows of honeycomb stitching. Use a strong thread and secure the bead with two stitches before passing on to the next space. Carry the thread from space to space along the back of the work and finish off with a secure overcasting stitch on the back of the work.

Eyelets

These are also simple to work and effective, either singly or in groups. They consist of a number of straight stitches worked into a central hole, usually over a square of eight threads of fabric. They can be arranged in groups to form a pattern, or worked singly as squares or rectangles. Some of the most useful are square eyelet, single cross eyelet and back-stitched eyelet. These can all be worked as rectangles instead of squares, and they can also be grouped irregularly together, leaving part of the eyelet unworked.

Square eyelet

This is worked over a square of eight threads.

1 Begin in the centre of one side and take a straight stitch over four threads into the centre hole.

2 Bring the needle up in the next space to the right and take a straight stitch over four threads into the centre hole. Repeat round the square until the eyelet is complete.

Single cross eyelet

Work in a similar way over eight threads as for the square eyelet, but leave one

thread between each quarter.

Back stitched eyelet

This is also worked over eight threads.

1 Begin in the centre of one side and work one straight stitch over four threads into the centre hole.

2 Bring the needle out two threads beyond the straight stitch and make a back stitch into it, then work one straight stitch over four threads into the centre hole. Continue round the sides of the square until the eyelet is complete.

Pulled fabric edgings

One of the features of pulled thread embroidery is that it can be worked round the edge of the fabric and incorporate the hem. The three following edgings are all suitable for most types of table linen.

Edging 1

This is a very simple edging and consists of two rows of four-sided stitch, one of which is worked through a fold or double thickness of fabric.

1 On the right side of the fabric count 10 or 12 threads up from the raw edge and work one row of four-sided stitch over four threads for the required distance.

2 Fold the fabric to the wrong side so that the fold is level with the outer edge of the stitching. Tack in place.

3 On the right side of the fabric work the second row of four-sided stitch through the double thickness of fabric.

4 Remove the tacking and trim the surplus edge back to the line of stitching.

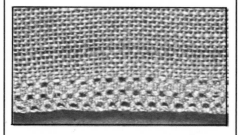

Edging 2

This is worked in the same way as the first edging with the addition of two rows of buttonhole stitch. Work the buttonhole stitch in a fine and firmly twisted thread to produce a hard-wearing edging and use a slightly larger tapestry needle than usual for the four-sided stitch to make the buttonhole stitch easier to work.

1 Count 10 or 12 threads in from the raw edge and work one row of four-sided stitch over four threads as before.

2 Turn the raw edge on to the wrong side and work the second row of four-sided stitch through the double fabric.

3 Using a small tapestry needle, on the right side of the fabric and over the folded

edge, work five buttonhole stitches into each hole made by the first row of four-sided stitch.

4 Work a second row of buttonhole stitch into the holes formed by the second row of four-sided stitch.

5 For a deeper border, the rows of four-sided stitch can be increased. The edging will be further defined if you work the buttonholing in a thread of a slightly darker tone.

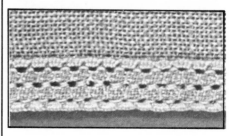

Edging 3

This combines four-sided, three-sided and buttonhole stitch.

1 Count 10 threads in from the raw edge of the fabric and fold the fabric over to the wrong side along this thread. Tack in place.

2 Count three threads in from the fold and work a row of three-sided stitch over the next four threads on the right side of the fabric.

3 Work one row of four-sided stitch above the three-sided stitch.

4 Cut the surplus fabric back to the second line of stitching.

5 Work five buttonhole stitches into each stitch hole formed by the four-sided stitch.

6 To finish the edging, work five buttonhole stitches over the three threads along the folded edge and into the holes formed by the three-sided stitch.

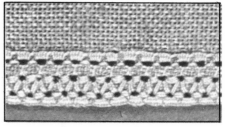

Turning corners

To turn a corner using four-sided stitch, count the threads and check that the number is divisible by four.

To turn a corner using three-sided stitch, count the threads as you near the corner and adjust the fold of the hem so that the stitch can be worked over four threads across the corner.

The corner can also be turned by working one-third of three-sided stitch, known as eyelet filling stitch. The base of the three-sided stitch used for this should come across the corner to be turned.

Pulled fabric runner

This elegant pulled fabric table runner will fit in with any decor, traditional or modern. The three stitches used, satin stitch, ringed back stitch and honeycomb filling are simple to work. Make the runner longer or shorter if you wish, to fit your own furniture.

Size
90cm (*35 inches*) by 31cm (*12 inches*)

Fabric required
0.35m (⅜ *yard*) off-white evenweave fabric, 21 threads to 2.5cm (*1 inch*), 150cm (*59 inches*) wide

☐ Anchor Stranded Cotton, 15 skeins 0375 snuff brown.

The design
1 Cut a piece from the fabric measuring 34.5cm (*13½ inches*) by 95cm (*37½ inches*). Mark the centre of the fabric lengthwise with a line of tacking stitches. This acts as a guide when placing the design. The working chart shows a section of the design, with the centre marked by a blank arrow which should coincide with the line of tacking stitches.

2 Each stitch must be pulled firmly, except the satin stitch triangles which are worked with normal tension.

3 Use six strands of thread for satin stitch and three strands for the rest of the embroidery.

4 With the long side of the fabric facing, begin working the design with ringed back stitch, 5cm (*1¼ inches*) from the narrow edge of the fabric. Continue until the embroidery measures 86.5cm (*34 inches*). Work the rest of the embroidery outwards from this central band. Repeat the three outer lines of satin stitch 7.5cm (*3 inches*) from the central band of embroidery.

Ringed back stitch
This stitch is worked from right to left and can be used as a border or as a filling. It is worked in two stages as shown in the diagrams. Figure 1: bring the thread through at the arrow; insert the needle at A (2 threads down), bring it through at B (4 threads up and 2 threads to the left); insert at arrow, bring it through at C (2 threads up and 4 threads to the left); insert the needle at B, bring it through at D (2 threads down and 4 to the left); insert it at C, bring it through at E (4 threads down and 2 to the left). Continue making half rings of back stitch for the required length. Figure 2: turn the fabric

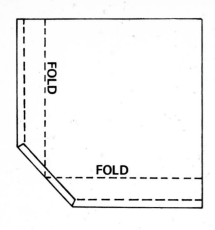

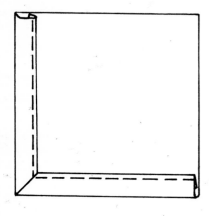

Mitring the corners

round and work back in the same way to complete the rings. All connecting stitches are worked in the same holes.

Honeycomb filling stitch

This stitch is worked from the top downwards, again in two stages. Figure 1: bring the thread through at the arrow; insert the needle at A (2 threads to the right), bring it through at B (2 threads down); insert again at A, bring through at B; insert at C (2 threads to the left), bring through at D (2 threads down); insert again at C and bring through at D. Continue in this way for the required length. Turn the fabric round and work back in the same way. Figure 2 shows the work turned ready for the second row. Figure 3 shows the completed stitch. Pull each stitch firmly.

Finishing off

Press the embroidery on the wrong side. Turn back 1.5cm ($\frac{1}{2}$ inch) hems. Mitre the corners and slip stitch. Press the runner again on the wrong side.

The chart shows a section of the design, indicating the position of the stitches.

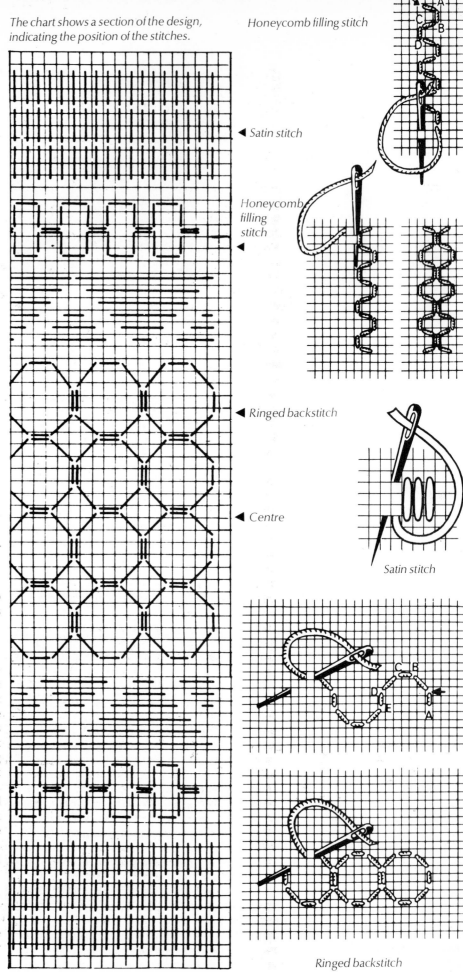

◀ Satin stitch

◀ Honeycomb filling stitch

◀ Ringed backstitch

◀ Centre

Honeycomb filling stitch

Satin stitch

Ringed backstitch

HARDANGER WORK

Hardanger work, sometimes called Norwegian embroidery, originated from a district of the same name in western Norway where the local inhabitants were famous for their fine work.

It is a form of drawn thread work which is quick and easy. It is geometric in design with an overall heavy openwork appearance, and is popular in Scandinavia for adorning traditional dress and household linens.

The main characteristic of this type of embroidery is the rectangular grouping of satin stitch, known as kloster blocks, arranged to outline the spaces and build up the basic portion of the design.

Fabric and threads

Hardanger embroidery requires a fabric with a very regular weave in which the warp and weft threads are equal, or special Hardanger linen or canvas which is woven with double warp and weft threads so that it is extremely strong and does not fray in cutting.

This embroidery is traditionally worked on white or natural linen with self-coloured threads but the work can be very effective if a dark thread is used on a light ground and vice versa.

The working threads should be slightly coarser than the threads of the fabric for the satin stitch blocks which form the basis of the design, and slightly finer for the fillings of the open work spaces. Coton à broder and pearl cotton are both suitable for more traditional work.

However, provided the fabrics are of suitable weight and even weave, you could break with tradition and use synthetic or wool fabrics and threads to create your own exciting and contemporary designs for wall hangings, lampshades, cushion covers, dress insertions and accessories. The tools required are tapestry needles and a pair of very sharp pointed embroidery scissors.

The design

By its very nature the design has to be geometrical in form, with squares, triangles, diamonds or oblongs.

The main outlines of the design should be kept as simple as possible and the basic shapes and their relationship to each other in forming a pattern can easily be worked out on graph paper. The design can be developed by building up small shapes around and within the larger shapes, and adding surface stitchery.

Working the design

It is essential throughout the work that both the threads and stitches are counted with great accuracy and that the fabric is carefully cut because any irregularity would spoil the general effect. It is much easier to achieve this and to keep the embroidery at an even tension if a frame is used.

There are four stages in working Hardanger embroidery.

1 Outlining the spaces and design with Kloster blocks.
2 Working any surface embroidery.
3 Cutting and drawing the threads for the open spaces.
4 Decorating the bars of the larger spaces and adding the lace stitch fillings.

Kloster blocks

A kloster block is made up of an irregular number of stitches enclosing a regular number of fabric threads. Five stitches to a block is the usual size, but this can vary from nine stitches enclosing eight threads to three stitches enclosing two. The blocks may be grouped vertically or horizontally to outline the space.

To make a vertical line across the fabric to outline a diamond or triangle the blocks should be worked in steps following the weave of the fabric. If you wish to accentuate certain shapes the blocks may be varied in height as well as length. The head of the stitch should always face the cut space to protect the ends of the fabric and prevent them from fraying.

Surface stitchery

In addition to the outlining blocks, decorative surface stitchery is added to create interest and enrich the design. It should correspond to the general pattern and principle of following the weave of fabric and a variety of stitches can be used, such as back-stitch, star-stitch, herringbone, eyelets, back-stitched or woven wheels, four-sided and interlacing stitches.

Cutting the threads

In Hardanger work the embroidery is half complete before the work is cut, unlike other drawn thread work where the threads are removed first and then the decorative stitchery applied.

Using very sharp scissors, cut the threads in the spaces enclosed by the blocks close to the stitches. Complete one motif at a time, removing either all the horizontal threads or the vertical threads, but do not mix these two stages.

When the cutting is complete it will have created an open mesh of geometric shapes within the outline of the blocks. These now need to be strengthened and decorated.

Decorating the bars

The bars of the threads left in the spaces can be strengthened by overcasting or needleweaving, but it is advisable not to mix the two methods.

At this stage decide if you want to incorporate lace stitch fillings to add to the delicacy of the work as these are made as a series of twists or loops while the bars are being covered.

On articles not subject to wear, you could leave the bars without weaving or overcasting and just add a filling or interlocking lace stitch. An attractive filling for a larger space can be a back-stitched or woven wheel, worked over an even number of anchoring threads.

1 Work the overcasting diagonally across a group of threads, making each stitch firm and covering each bar completely. When one bar is complete, carry the thread behind the work to the next bar, leaving a small square of fabric visible between the bars at the intersections.

2 Work the needleweaving over the bars, following the method given in the section on page 65. At this stage if you are not adding a lace stitch filling, you could incorporate small picots.

3 Place the picots on each side of the bar in the middle, twisting the thread round the needle to make the picot on one side and then moving to the other side and repeating the process.

Hardanger work tablecloth

Size

127cm (*50 inches*) square

Fabric required

1.40 metres (*1½ yards*) of 132cm (*52 inch*) wide medium weight linen with 29 threads to 2.5cm (*1 inch*)

You will also need

☐ Clark's Anchor Pearl cotton No.5 (10 grm ball): 3 balls white 0402
☐ Clark's Anchor Pearl cotton No.8 (10grm ball): 1 ball white 0402
☐ Tapestry needles, 1 each No.20 and No.24

Preparing the fabric

Trim the fabric so that it is an exact square. Mark the centre in both directions with lines of tacking.

The design

This tablecloth uses the techniques of Hardanger embroidery.
The layout diagram shows the placing of the design for one quarter of the cloth and this is repeated on the remaining three-quarters. The broken lines correspond to the tacked lines across the centre of the fabric, the numerals indicate the number of threads, and the shaded area is the section given in figure 1.
Figure 1 shows the stitches in a section of the design and how they are arranged on the threads. Follow figure 1 and the number key for the actual embroidery, and the layout diagram for the placing of the design. Work all parts similar to the numbered parts in the same stitch.

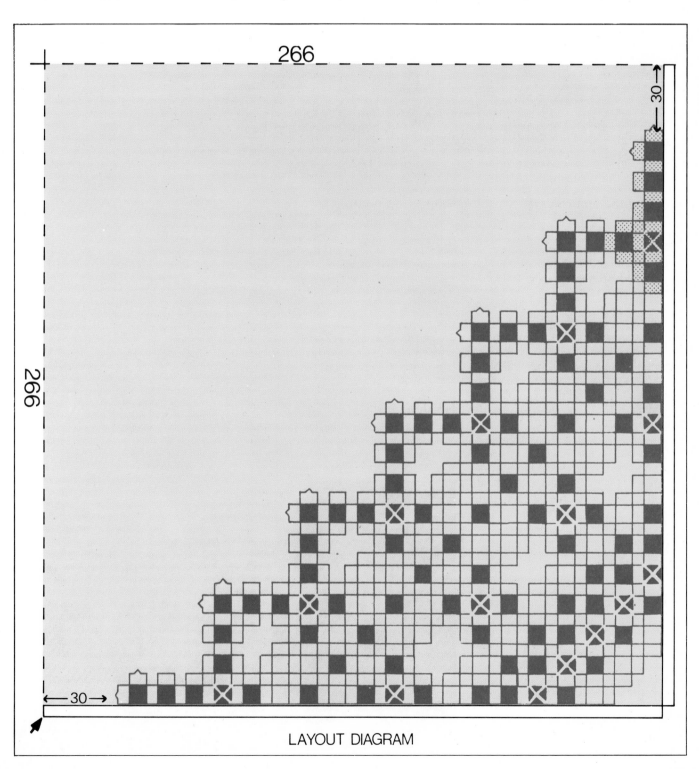

266

266

30

30

LAYOUT DIAGRAM

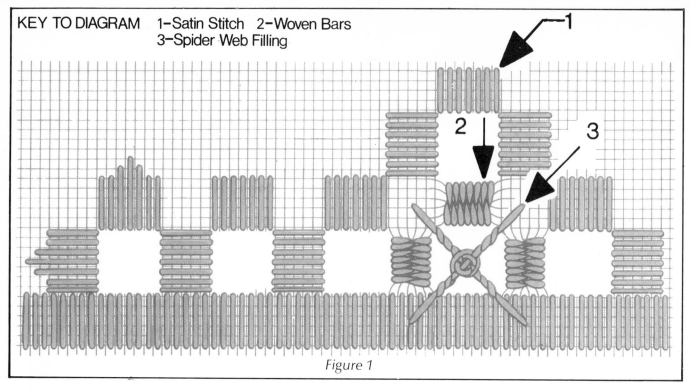

KEY TO DIAGRAM 1–Satin Stitch 2–Woven Bars
3–Spider Web Filling

Figure 1

Working the embroidery

1 Using the No.5 Pearl cotton and the No.20 tapestry needle, start the embroidery at the black arrow shown in the layout diagram, 266 threads down from the crossed tacking threads. Work the section given.

2 When all the satin stitch blocks are complete, cut away the threads shown in the black squares on the layout diagram and blank on figure 1.

3 Using the No.8 Pearl cotton and No.24 tapestry needle, work the woven bars and fillings (see below) and then complete the remaining sections of the cloth in the same way.

Woven bars

Withdraw an even number of threads from the areas shown in figure 1 and separate the remaining threads into bars with three threads in each by weaving over and under them until the threads are completely covered.

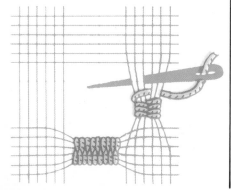

Spider's web filling

1 Work one twisted bar by carrying the thread diagonally across the space. Enter the fabric as shown, twist the thread over the first thread and return to the starting point.

2 Work another twisted bar in the opposite direction but twist the thread back to the centre only.

3 Pass the thread over and under the crossed bars twice and then under and over twice. Complete the twisting of the second bar.

Finishing off

Press the embroidery on the wrong side. Make 2.5cm (*1 inch*) hems all round, mitring the corners.

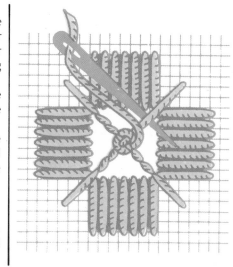

NEEDLEWEAVING

Needleweaving is an ancient craft dating back over three thousand years. Most of the early examples are Coptic and they are known today as loom embroideries as it is thought they were incorporated in the main weaving process of the fabric. Needleweaving is a form of drawn thread work and consists of a decorative pattern worked in weaving or darning stitch upon warp or weft threads after some of the crosswise threads have been withdrawn.

The fabric
Needleweaving is usually worked on a foundation of evenly woven fabric from which threads can be easily removed. Hessians, heavy linens, cottons, woollens and tweeds as well as some acrylic curtain fabrics are all suitable.

The threads
The choice of threads is limitless provided that they are of a similar weight or slightly heavier than the withdrawn threads of the fabric. If the threads supporting the weaving are sufficiently open and strong, you can incorporate a variety of threads, such as carpet thrums, chenille, raffia, heavy nubbly wools and even string, leather thongs, ribbon and thin strips of nylon. Beads, rings and metal washers can all be added as the weaving progresses to add interest and texture.

Needles
You will need an assortment of heavy tapestry needles in various sizes to take the threads you are using. If you are planning to incorporate fine ribbon or thonging an elastic threader or bodkin is also useful.

The design
If you want a fairly free design, the simplest way is to choose a fabric and some interesting threads and begin work without spending time on working out the design first – some of the most exciting results with needleweaving can be created spontaneously.

If the needleweaving is for a specific purpose, such as a border with a geometric pattern or in the form of repeating motifs arranged symmetrically to fill a given space, you should first chart out the design on graph paper showing how the motifs are linked and the colours to be used.

Preparing the fabric
If the needleweaving is for a border, prepare the fabric by withdrawing the threads in the same way as for drawn thread work (see the chapter on drawn thread work). If you weave a simple repeating pattern it can be helpful to hem-stitch the threads into even groups of threads at the top and bottom of the border as this helps in the counting of threads during the weaving process. If you are working on a heavy, loosely woven fabric where the threads are easily counted, this step is not necessary.

The stitch
Weaving or darning stitch is worked by passing the needle over one thread, under the next thread and so on. If you prefer, you can divide the threads into blocks of two, three or four and pass the needle over and under each block.

To start weaving, insert the needle about 2.5cm (1 inch) above the first block of weaving and pull through leaving a length of thread to be darned in later. Begin weaving between the first and second group of threads, working from left to right. Continue weaving between the threads for the required amount, making sure that each row of stitches lies closely to the preceding one and is not pulled too tightly.

To pass to the next block of threads, slip your needle up the side of the block to the top and then work over the next block. You can also pass from one block of weaving to the next by darning the working thread through the back of the work. If you are using several different types of thread, take care to maintain an even tension.

More open effects
You can vary the solid effect of needle-weaving with single bars of overcasting with satin stitch. Work needleweaving over the first block of threads for four or six rows, return to the beginning of the block and overcast with satin stitch the first two threads. Slip the needle up the side of the overcast threads and start to weave over the next block. If you wish, the overcast bars can be woven over in the middle of the border.

Needlewoven belt
This belt can be made in wool as shown in the photograph or you could make it in an evenweave cotton or linen, using soft embroidery or stranded cotton threads.

Size
7.5cm (3 inches) wide, to fit any waist size

Fabric required
0.25cm (¼ yard) fabric × the length of belt required + 5cm (2 inches), with approximately 14 threads to 2.5cm (1 inch)

You will also need
☐ Coats Anchor Tapisserie wool: 4 skeins black (0403); 3 skeins each chestnut 0347, 0348; 1 skein chestnut 0351
☐ 7.5cm (3 inches) × the length of belt of non-woven interfacing
☐ Buckle
☐ Tapestry needle No.18

The design
The design is a repeating pattern which can be adjusted to make a belt to your own measurements. The diagram below gives a section of the design with the colours used for each area.

Preparing the fabric
With one long side of the fabric facing you, withdraw 26 lengthwise threads centrally to within 5cm (2 inches) from each end. Darn in the ends neatly.

Working the needleweaving
1 With one long side facing, start the needleweaving at the left-hand edge and work the section given following diagram 1 and the letter key for the colours. Diagram 2 shows how the needleweaving is worked over four threads of fabric and how the connecting stitch is worked over and under the start of a new block.
2 Repeat the section until all the loose threads are woven.

Making up the belt
1 Trim the fabric to within 6.5cm (2½ inches) on the long sides of the belt and to within 2cm (¾ inch) on the short ends.
2 Sew the interfacing lightly in place centrally on the wrong side of the embroidery.
3 Fold one long side of fabric over the interfacing and tack. Turn under the seam allowance of 1.3cm (½ inch) on the other side and hem in place along the centre of the wrong side of the belt. Turn under the seam allowance at each short end and sew. Sew the buckle to one short end of the belt.

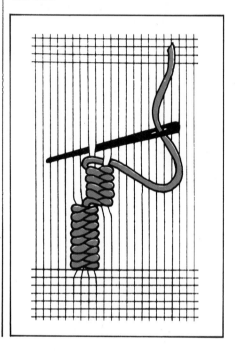

0347   0348   0351   0403

CUT WORK
Simple techniques

Cut work is the name given to open-work methods of embroidery where portions of the background are cut away and, in the more elaborate forms, re-embroidered. Cut work is basically the link between embroidery and needlemade lace and should not be confused with the counted thread methods, Hardanger and Hedebo.

Types of cut work
There are four main types of cut work, varying from simple cut spaces to larger and more elaborately filled spaces.

In simple cut work (see below), the cut spaces are quite small. In Renaissance work they grow larger, while in Richelieu work the addition of bars and picots gives a more decorative appearance. Reticella work has the largest cut spaces with intricate fillings, giving a lace-like quality to the embroidery. These more elaborate and highly decorative methods are covered in later chapters.

Uses of cut work
Cut work is suitable for all types of household linen and can also be successfully used as dress decoration, provided the design is planned as an integral part of the dress and is not just added as an afterthought.

Fabric and threads
As the main interest of cut work lies in the variation of texture produced by the cut spaces – either as open shapes or decorated with bars, picots, spider's web or woven wheels and needlepoint fillings – colour is of secondary importance. Most of the charm of cut work lies in it being self-coloured although colour used tonally with simple cut work can be effective. It is important to avoid colour contrasts with the more elaborate forms.

Only a firm, evenly woven linen or very strong cotton should be used for cut work because other fabrics fray when the spaces are cut. Choose a linen or fine pearl cotton or coton à broder in a weight to suit the fabric. Linen lace thread may also be used, although this is available in creamy shades only. Do not use stranded cotton because the strands are not strong enough when divided and would not withstand friction through wear and washing.

Needles
Fine crewel needles are suitable for simple cut work although sharps are normally best for working the lace-like fillings of the other forms of cut work. Choose the size according to the weight of the thread being used. You may also need tapestry needles in various sizes to work the hems and finish the edges.

You should also have a pair of very sharp, finely pointed embroidery scissors.

Designs for cut work
Traditional cut work designs are nearly always floral and the more intricate fillings of Reticella work are similar to old lace patterns.

Simple cut work has no bars or picots and consists solely of a design of simple shapes worked in buttonhole stitch and the background area around the motif cut away, thus throwing the main part of the design into relief.

All cut work, however elaborate, may be designed initially by arranging cut paper shapes, either as a repetitive border or as a single motif or design, to fit a given shape. Whatever the function, the pattern of the cut shapes should balance with the more solid parts of the design.

When planning or adapting a design, check that all the shapes tie up at vital points of the structure or they will hang loosely when the background is cut away. Draw all the main outlines of the design in double lines to act as a guide for the running stitch which is worked within them to act as padding for the buttonhole stitch. A design of curved or circular shapes is much easier to work in this method than a geometric design with sharp angles.

Transfer the design to the fabric using dressmaker's carbon or the prick and pounce method (see the chapter on Transferring designs).

The stitches
1 Start by working several rows of running stitch round the motifs inside the double lines. These form a foundation for the buttonholing and enable a firm edge to be worked. The running stitches should lie very evenly in the fabric – if pulled too tightly the work will pucker.

2 Work the buttonholing close together with the looped edge of the stitches facing the space which is to be cut away.

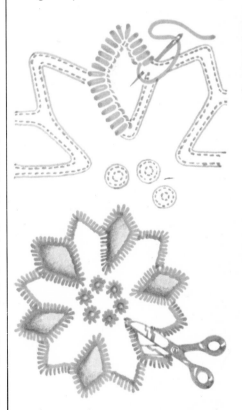

3 Using very sharp scissors, cut away the fabric close to the buttonholing. Cut cleanly, using the points of the scissors so that the edge will not fluff.

Do not be tempted to cut away part of the work before all the stitching is complete or the work will pull out of shape.

Renaissance and Richelieu cut work

Renaissance and Richelieu cut work are more complicated than the simple cut work illustrated in the previous chapter because the cut spaces are larger and need the addition of bars across the spaces to strengthen and hold together the main parts of the design.

The design

As the bars are the most decorative feature of Renaissance cut work, their symmetrical placing is most important. Where there are larger cut spaces than can be adequately filled with a single straight bar, the bar may be branched. These branched bars show to best advantage if they balance the solid parts of the work, but the cut spaces should not be too large and clumsy. Where a number of bars intersect they can be further enriched by a spider's web filling or woven wheel or by a buttonhole ring.

Fabric and threads

Use the same kinds of fabric and thread as for simple cut work and prepare the embroidery in a similar way.

Working the embroidery

1 When the design has been traced or painted on to the fabric, start the embroidery by working the outer row of the padding running stitches. When you reach the position of the first bar, take the thread across the space and make a tiny stitch within the double lines on that side. Return the thread to the starting point of

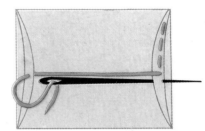

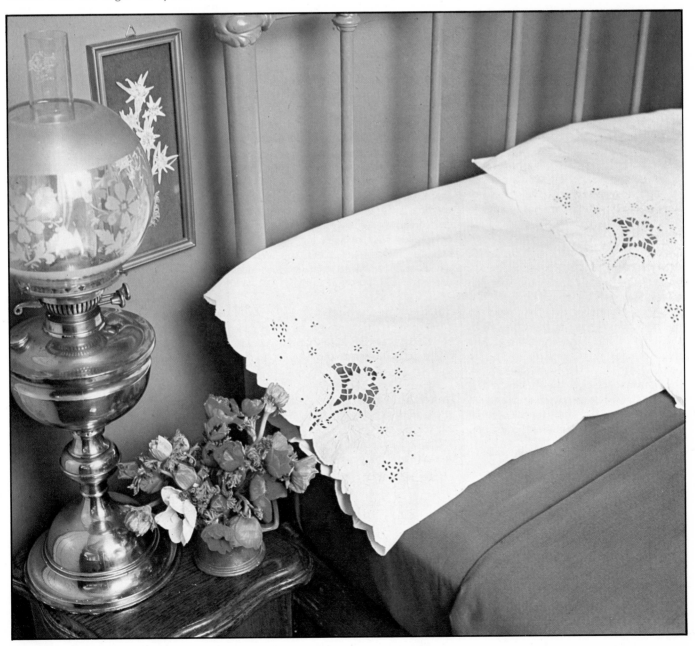

the bar and take another small stitch, go across the space again.

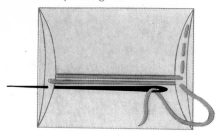

2 Cover the three threads of the bar with close buttonholing, keeping the bar firm and taking care not to let the needle penetrate the fabric below.

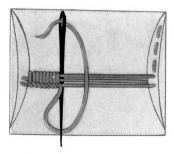

3 Continue with the running stitches around the shape until you reach the next bar and work it in the same way. When all the bars have been worked, complete the second row of padding running stitch.
4 Finish the shape by working close buttonholing over the padding as for simple cut work. Take care not to cut the bars when cutting away the background fabric.

Branched bars

1 Carry the threads across the space in the same way as for a single bar.
2 Work buttonholing over the threads to the point where the bar branches. From this point work the second bar, laying three threads across the space to the point where it joins the double lines. Work the buttonholing over the threads of the second bar back to where it branched from the first bar and then continue working the remaining part of the first bar.

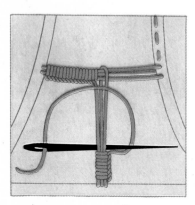

A three or four-branch bar is worked in the same way.

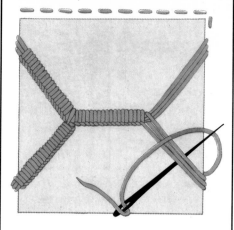

Spider's web filling

If you are filling a large cut space which needs more than a few branched bars, a spider's web filling makes a good alternative. The filling can be placed in the centre or deliberately off-centre by altering the angle at which the twists are made.
1 Carry a single thread across the shape from top to bottom, take a tiny stitch between the double lines and take the thread back to the centre of the space, twisting the thread around the needle.
2 From the centre, take another thread across to the side, twist back to the centre and so on, until you have divided the shape into five sections. Before completing the final twist (over the last half of the first thread worked), work a woven wheel or spider's web by weaving under and over the five threads. Keep the web or wheel fairly small so that it does not detract from the twisted spokes.

Back-stitched wheel

If the space is large enough, six twists can be worked across it, either at regular or irregular intervals, and then a back-stitched wheel worked over them.

Buttonhole ring

This is another decorative filling for a larger cut shape.
1 Wind a fine thread five or six times round a small pencil. Slip the ring off the pencil

and cover it closely all round with buttonholing.
2 Break off the thread and pin the ring in position on the fabric. To secure the ring to the space, work four or five twisted bars at intervals from the ring to the double lines of the design. To carry the thread to the next twist, work a few running stitches along the double lines to avoid spoiling the ring itself.

Richelieu cut work

This is similar to Renaissance cut work although the cut spaces are a little larger and the bars are decorated with picots.
Looped picots. Work the buttonholing over the bar to the centre from left to right. Insert a pin into the fabric beneath the bar and pass the working thread under the head of the pin from left to right, then up over the bar and out under the bar to the right of the pin. Pass the needle through the loop on the pin and the thread beyond it. Pull the working thread tightly to make the picot and continue buttonholing to the end of the bar.

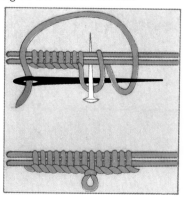

Bullion picots. These are worked on the same principle although they are a little more elaborate. Work close buttonholing to the centre of the bar, make a bullion stitch from the looped edge of the last stitch by twisting the thread four or five times round the needle and pulling the thread through the twists to make a firm twisted loop. To secure the picot, work the next buttonhole stitch close to the previous stitch.

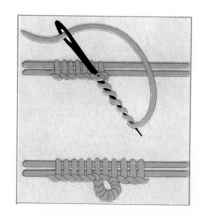

Reticella cut work

This is the most elaborate and lacy form of cut work and bears a strong resemblance to reticella lace. The types of fabric and working threads are the same as for the simple cut work forms and Renaissance and Richelieu work.

The design

The main part of the design for reticella cut work is formed by the stitchery worked within cut squares or geometric shapes. The various fillings are based on a button-holing or weaving stitch.

While few people today have the time to make large pieces of reticella cut work, small motifs can be made and used to decorate table linen and various types of dress. These motifs can look most effective but do not require the heavy surface stitchery which traditional examples often contained.

A modern pattern or design can be built up by arranging a series of small squares.

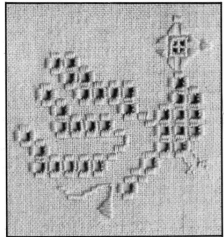

each containing a different filling. The squares can be cut out completely or a number of threads may be left for a basis on which to work the filling stitchery.

Preparing the squares

1 Start by marking the position of the squares accurately and outlining them with several rows of running stitch to strengthen the cut area. If you are planning to leave threads within the square, count them and check that there is an even number. Leave the threads in pairs both horizontally and vertically. It often helps to tack a piece of firm white paper behind the squares as this gives a firmer foundation than the fabric alone, although the stitches are not worked into the paper.

2 Cut the threads to be removed to within three threads of the running stitch. On fine and firm fabrics, turn the cut edges onto the back of the work, overcast the edge and cut away the surplus. On heavier fabrics, work buttonholing over the edge to prevent the filling stitches from pulling away.

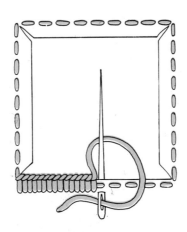

Filling open squares

The fillings on an open square are used to build up small solid shapes, such as tri-angles, arcs and semi-circles, within a framework of bars worked in buttonholing.

1 Start at the widest part of the shape and take a double thread across from one corner of the square to the other. Work a row of buttonholing on this double thread.

2 Work each following row into the looped edge of the previous row, reducing the number of stitches to form the shape which is anchored to the fabric on the opposite side.

Filling other squares

1 To strengthen the threads left in squares, either cover them with weaving or close

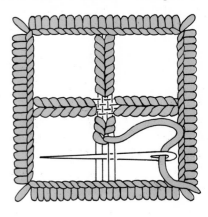

buttonhole stitch. If you add further decoration with picots, check that these do not come at a point where you will be working further bars.

2 To work diagonal lines, take a long stitch from the centre to the corner of the square and back again, and fasten off at the back of the centre. Cover the diagonal threads by overcasting or buttonholing to the position of the first bar or arc.

3 To form the bar or arc, take a double thread across for the foundation, cover it with overcasting or buttonholing and then complete the diagonal line to the centre of the square. The bars or arcs can be decorated with picots.

4 Alternatively a solid triangular shape can be worked in detached buttonhole stitch from the bar which dissects the diagonal line.

5 On fine fabrics the centre of the square can be decorated by working a small back-stitched spider's web over the junction of the threads.

Finishing off

Finish off with a simple hem-stitched border. For something more elaborate, work several rows of hemstitching and twist the threads into bundles (see bead weaving later).

Broderie anglaise

Broderie anglaise is a form of embroidery which consists of eyelets of different shapes and sizes, additional surface embroidery and scalloped edging.

During the 18th and 19th centuries when broderie anglaise was worked in its original form (Ayrshire work) it was composed of much elaborate, floral surface stitchery, eyelets and larger cut spaces with needle-made lace or drawn thread fillings.

The intricacy of the work gave it a very delicate appearance which was ideal for the beautiful christening robes and bonnets made in that period. Traditionally it was worked in white thread on white fabric such as cambric, cotton or fine linen, lawn and muslin.

Later the method became simpler, using less surface stitchery with more emphasis on eyelets and cut shapes and it became known as broderie anglaise or 'Madeira work', after the island where it became a cottage industry. It was used to decorate dress, lingerie, baby wear and household linen, as it still is today.

The design

Broderie anglaise need not be confined to white embroidery, but if colour is chosen it is best to use matching or toning threads rather than contrasting ones. Traditional broderie anglaise was always elaborately floral in design. A contemporary design may be made for a simple border by using a geometric arrangement of circles and ovals of various sizes with a little surface stitchery and scalloping. Both floor and wall tiles can give ideas for this type of design.

The fabrics and threads

Although much broderie anglaise is made by machine nowadays, it is still worth making your own by hand for the beautiful delicate results which can be achieved and the range of fabrics, threads and designs which can be used.

Choose a firm and fine fabric which will not fray with washing, and match the working thread in quality, texture and colour (it can be a different tone). On cotton or linen, use a cotton or fine linen mercerized thread and on silk fabrics, a fine twisted silk.

Stitches and equipment

Only four basic stitches are used in broderie anglaise – running, overcasting, button-holing and satin stitch.

To make the eyelets you will need a pair of really sharp embroidery scissors and a stiletto or steel knitting needle.

Making eyelets

1 To make round eyelets, outline the circle with small running stitches.

2 If the circles are less than 0.6cm ($\frac{1}{4}$ *inch*) in diameter, pierce the centre with the stiletto or knitting needle and then cover the edge with fine overcasting.

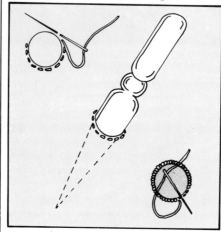

3 For larger circles snip from the centre, vertically and horizontally, out to the running stitch. Turn the points of fabric under to the back of the work with the needle and overcast the edge taking the stitches over the folded edge and the running stitch. Cut away the surplus fabric close to the stitching.

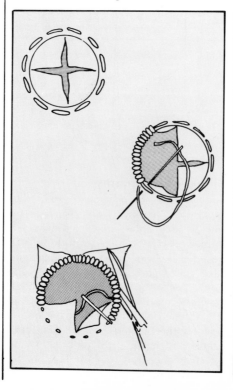

4 If several eyelets run close together, so that they almost touch, work the running stitch along the lower edge of the first hole, cross to the top of the second hole and so on alternately and complete the circles on the return journey. This helps to prevent the work from tearing during working and in wear later on.

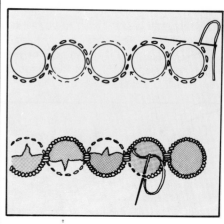

5 To give a heavier effect, or to make the circles thicker on one side, work several rows of running stitch to pad the area and raise it. Then overcast all round the eyelet, grading the length of the overcasting over the padded area.

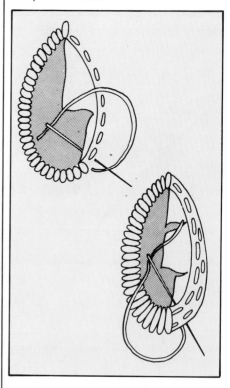

6 To make oval and triangular eyelets, work in the same way as for round ones, taking care that the shapes are kept accurate and do not become distorted.

7 When making a slot for ribbon, mark the slot and work around it before cutting the opening in order to avoid pulling it into a shapeless hole during working.

The surface embroidery

This is usually worked in satin or stem stitch. If you want solid padded shapes to give emphasis or detail to the design, they should be padded by working horizontal satin stitch across the shape just inside the outline, with vertical satin stitch to cover the padding stitches.

Scalloping

This is one of the main features of broderie anglaise and is used to decorate and finish the work.

1 To make a simple scalloped edge, draw the shapes round a coin or small saucer 1.3cm ($\frac{1}{2}$ inch) from the raw edge, or more if the fabric frays badly.

2 Pad the edge by working several rows of running stitch along the outline, graduating the distance between the stitches in the points of the scallops.

For a more solid or raised effect, use chain stitch for the padding instead of running stitch.

3 Cover the padding with closely worked buttonholing, working from left to right and with the looped edge of the stitch to the outside. Keep the stitches as even in tension as possible and do not pull the working thread too tight or the work will pucker. Make the stitches quite small in the points of the scallops, increasing in size round the curves to emphasise their symmetry.

4 To finish off a length of thread, take a few running stitches through the padding on the unworked section and fasten off. Join on the new length in a similar way, bringing the needle up through the loop of the last buttonhole stitch.

5 When all the buttonholing is worked, cut away the surplus fabric close to the stitches with very sharp scissors.

6 To make a more elaborate scalloped edge, draw a pattern of the shape, including about three repeats and then cut it out of cardboard. You can then use this as a template to draw the shapes along the entire edge.

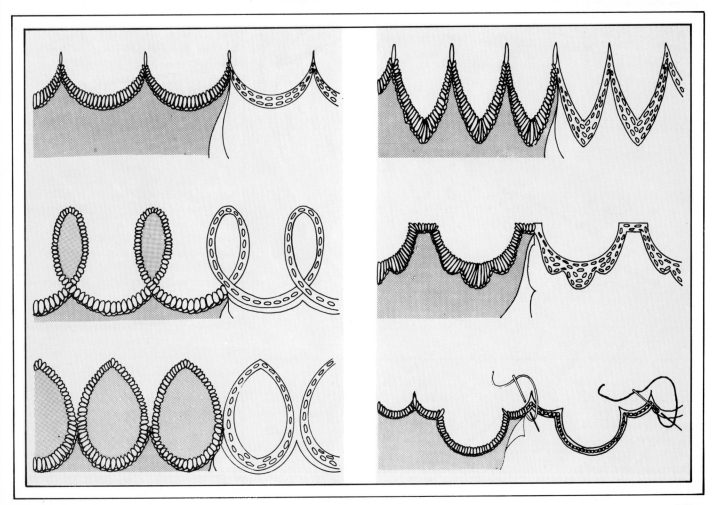

HEDEBO

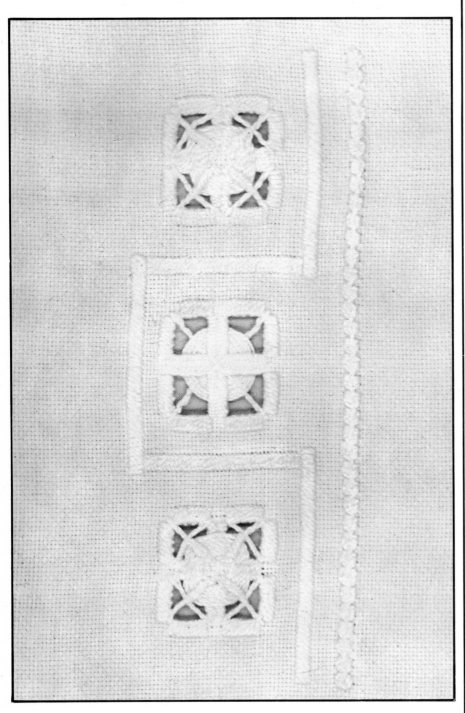

Hedebo is a form of white embroidery of Danish origin. It dates from the 16th century when the peasant women of Heden, a flat part of Denmark, used to decorate their homespun linens with it.

Types of Hedebo

There are three basic types of Hedebo.

The oldest and most traditional was adapted from wood carvings and usually consisted of formal floral shapes combining surface embroidery with a few open and drawn thread fillings. Most of the surface embroidery was in chain stitch and the finished effect was soft. and graceful.

The second type of Hedebo evolved around 1840 when the original floral shapes and cut work were somewhat restrained and the embroidery lost some of its original character. Further cut and drawn thread work was added, usually in squares, making the whole design more formal and geometric.

The third type of Hedebo dates from about 1850 when it became quite popular and gradually lost its peasant-like quality. In modern Hedebo shapes became more conventional and the spaces were cut instead of drawn and cut, and they were filled with more elaborate lace stitchery.

Designs for old Hedebo

Old Hedebo is traditionally worked on a close handwoven linen in a medium weight linen thread.

The main open shapes are formed by cutting and leaving two threads alternately, both vertically and horizontally, from the back of the work. The edge of the shape is then made firm by overcasting which is worked in groups of two over the horizontal and vertical bars. The spaces are enriched with more decorative stitches and the shapes are outlined with a double row of small close chain stitches.

The working method for the second form of Hedebo is very similar, with the open drawn squares being arranged in diagonal lines to form a diamond pattern, often interspersed with floral-type surface embroidery.

Designs for Modern Hedebo

Design for modern Hedebo usually consists of an arrangement or pattern of circular, oval or lozenge-shaped cut spaces which are strengthened and then outlined with buttonhole stitch.

Choose a fine, firm linen for the work with a matching linen thread. If a linen thread is unobtainable, use a fine coton à broder or pearl cotton.

The shapes are filled with a variety of lace stitches which are looped, twisted or buttonholed into the foundation row of buttonholing. Buttonholed pyramids are a feature of this type of work and these can be incorporated into the larger shapes or used as edgings to decorate the work. Satin stitch and eyelets, rather like broderie anglaise, can be added and the work can be finished with a needlepoint lace edging. This form of Hedebo is often used for the decoration of collars and cuffs.

1 Transfer the design on to the fabric either by tacking round an arrangement of cut paper shapes or by using a very finely pointed pencil and outlining the shapes with minute dots.

2 Work a double row of running stitches

around the outlines.

3 Cut away the fabric within the shape, leaving a margin of about 0.6cm ($\frac{1}{4}$ *inch*) or 0.3cm ($\frac{1}{8}$ *inch*) for smaller spaces. Clip into this margin and turn it on to the wrong side. Outline the space with Hedebo buttonhole stitch (see below), making sure that the fabric is turned under the needle and that the stitch is worked through both layers. Trim away the surplus fabric close to the stitches.

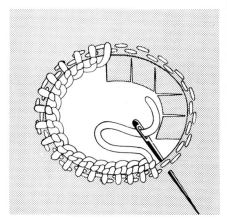

4 Fill the spaces and then add the surface embroidery.
5 Finish the work with a narrow hem-stitched edge or needlepoint lace, constructed of Hedebo buttonholing to form loops, pyramids or small rings.

Hedebo buttonholing

The buttonholing used for outlining the shapes is slightly different from regular buttonholing in that it is worked in two separate movements.
1 Hold the fabric so that the edge to be worked is away from you and insert the needle into the fabric from underneath. Draw the thread through until a small loop remains.
2 Slip the needle through the loop and pull both stitch and loop tight.

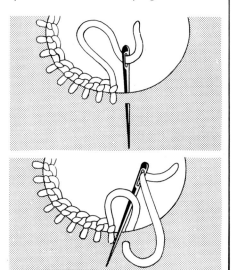

3 To join in a new thread, slip it under the last loop of thread worked and place it alongside the first thread. Work six or seven stitches over both threads and then cut off the remainder of the first thread.

Filling stitches
Circles

1 Work an inner circle of Hedebo buttonholing loosely inside the first circle, placing one stitch into every third stitch of the first circle. To obtain a loose effect, omit the final sharp pull to each stitch.
2 When the inner circle is complete, overcast or whip the looped edges.

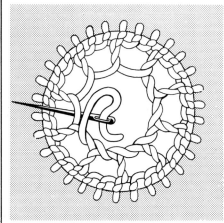

3 Fill the centre of the circle by working a woven or back-stitched wheel over four or six threads anchored into the last row of buttonholing.

Circles and lozenge shapes

Fill circles and lozenge shapes by constructing a number of bars with two or three threads across the shape. Cover these with close Hedebo buttonhole stitch.

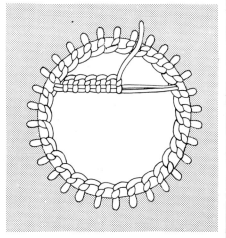

Pyramids

These are a characteristic feature of modern Hedebo and are constructed of Hedebo buttonholing stitches in increasing or decreasing rows. They can be worked singly to fill a small space or in groups of four to fill an oval or pear-shaped space.

1 Prepare the edge with a foundation row of buttonholing.
2 Start the pyramid by working from left to right, working one stitch less at the ends of each row.
3 Continue in this way until the top of the pyramid is reached, then slip the needle down the right side to start the next pyramid.

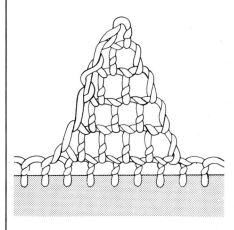

Six-pointed star

This is worked as a separate motif for insertion.
1 Wrap the thread round a pencil several times and secure the circle with a stitch.
2 Remove the circle from the pencil and buttonhole over it. This forms the foundation circle.
3 Work a further round of buttonholing, counting the stitches carefully to make a multiple of six.
4 Work a pyramid on to each multiple number of buttonhole stitches, making six points in all.
5 Secure the shape in position with a single stitch at each point.

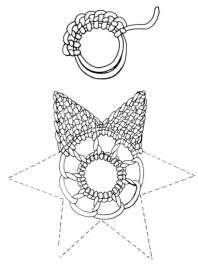

FAGGOTING

Tablemats
Size
40.5cm (15¾ inches) × 32cm (12½ inches)

Fabric required
For four mats:
0.70 metre (¾ yard) firm cotton or linen, 91cm (36 inches) wide (alternatively, you can use fabric remnants and cut the panels in sizes to suit the fabric available).

You will also need
☐ Stranded embroidery cotton or pearl cotton to match the fabric
☐ Matching sewing thread
☐ Crewel embroidery needle
☐ Four strips of firm paper, 32cm (12½ inches) × 4cm (1½ inches)

Preparing the fabric
1 Cut the fabric across the width to make two pieces 35cm (13½ inches) × 91cm (36 inches). Cut these pieces in half down the length to make four pieces, each 35cm (13½ inches) × 45.5cm (18 inches).
2 Cut each of the four pieces into three, with two sections 9cm (3½ inches) wide and one section 27.5cm (11 inches) wide.
3 Turn under 1.5cm (½ inch) on the wrong side round the edge of all the pieces and make narrow hems with mitred corners. Hem by hand two opposite sides of the large sections and one long side and two short sides of the smaller sections. Leave the remaining edges tacked in position.
4 For each mat, place the tacked hem of one small section on to the edge of the strip of firm paper so that it overlaps slightly. Tack in place. Overlap the tacked hem of the larger section on to the opposite edge of the paper and tack down, leaving a gap of 1.5cm (½ inch). Repeat this process with the opposite edge of the larger section and the second smaller section.

Working the faggoting
1 Mount the fabric into a frame.
2 Work the faggoting between the tacked edges, following one of the stitch patterns shown in the diagram. Make sure that the stitches worked into the edges of the fabric catch the hems securely.
3 When all the faggoting is complete, press the finished mats with a warm iron.

Faggoting is an attractive method of joining two pieces of fabric in an open-work design. It is particularly useful for tableware for which you do not necessarily need the strength of a regular seam and where a seam line would spoil the effect.

If you are making a tablecloth from 91cm (36 inch) wide dress fabric or 122cm (48 inch) wide furnishing fabric for example, and need to join panels to make it the right width for your table, you could join the panels with faggoting. The panels need not be confined to long strips but could be cut to make an attractive feature. Faggoting can be used for both square and round shapes, providing the edges to

be joined lie along the grain of the fabric – if you try to work them on the bias grain they will not lie flat.

Many of the stitches used in faggoting are common embroidery stitches but, although they are simple to work, their success depends on keeping their size and the spaces between the edges absolutely even, so it is worth mounting the work into a frame.

Faggoting can be worked in most kinds of embroidery thread of a weight to suit the fabric you are working on. You could also use a fine crochet cotton. The instructions given below are for making the mat shown in the photograph but they can easily be adapted for a tablecloth.

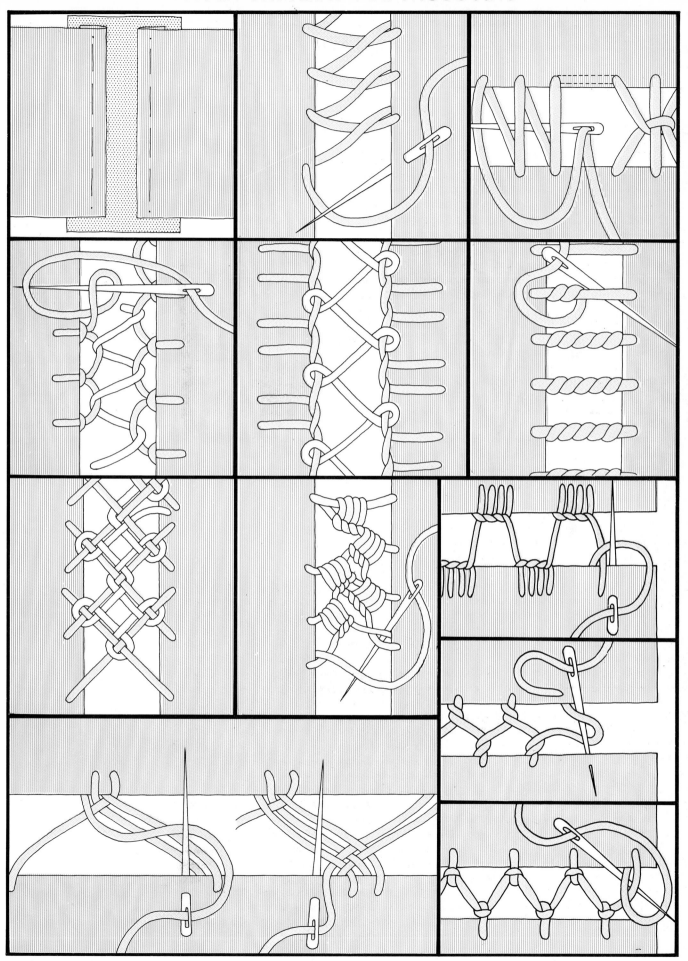

NEEDLEMADE LACE

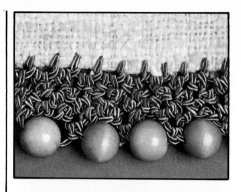

Lace-making using a needle is quite different from lace made with an implement, such as crochet or tatting, and it should not be confused with bobbin lace made on a pillow, sometimes called pillow lace. Needlemade lace is an old craft which was popular in all European countries in the mid-fifteenth and sixteenth centuries. It is directly derived from the elaborate cut and drawn work of the fifteenth century which was often used for ecclesiastical purposes and to decorate the household articles and fashionable garments of the nobility.

The stitches

The Italian name for needlemade lace is *Punto in aria*, meaning stitches in the air and the lace itself is made with nothing more than a foundation, a needle and thread.

The stitches involved are merely variations of simple embroidery stitches and the main stitches used are buttonhole (or blanket) stitch in one of its various forms, and a number of knotted stitches.

The threads

The thread should be suitable in weight for the fabric on which the edging is to be placed. If you are working on linen, use a linen thread, coton à broder, pearl cotton or crochet thread. If the fabric is heavy, such as a tweed, a heavier corded thread or heavy wool would be suitable. For working the edgings use a tapestry needle of a suitable size.

First method

This method could be used for narrow borders to decorate table linen, lampshades or a dress. It is worked directly on the folded edge of the fabric.

1 Join your thread into the side of the edge to be decorated and take a tiny stitch into the fold about 1cm ($\frac{3}{8}$ inch) further along (point A), leaving a small loop.

2 Go back to the starting point and make another stitch. Go to point A again, make another stitch, keeping the loops the same size. Return to the starting point again. You now have four equal loops, forming a small scallop.

3 Work over the scallop in close buttonhole stitch.

4 Make a second loop in exactly the same way and then lay the threads for a third scallop but work only halfway across in buttonhole stitch.

5 Make a loop from the centre of the third scallop to the centre of the second one and then from the centre of the second one to the centre of the first one. Repeat this until there are three loops in each of these two scallops thus forming a second row.

6 Work over the first loop and halfway over the second loop in the second row.

7 Make a loop from the middle of the second scallop in the second row into the middle of the first one. Repeat until there are three loops in the scallop and then work over them in buttonhole stitch and over the half loops left in the first and second rows.

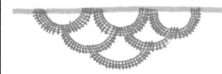

Second method

This border can be worked into a hem or on to a foundation of buttonholing. Work all rows from left to right and fasten off the thread at the end of each row.

1 Start by working a row of spaced double knotted buttonhole stitch into the edge of the fabric.

2 For the second row, work the same stitch putting each one into a loop between the knots of the first row.

3 For the third row, work two double knotted stitches into the first loop, an ordinary single buttonhole stitch into the next loop, and so on alternately to the end of the row.

4 For the last row, work two ordinary buttonhole stitches into the loop on each side of the single stitch in the third row and with two double knotted stitches into each space between the double knots.

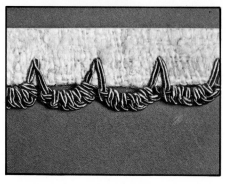

Working a separate strip

If you prefer to make the lace in a separate strip and then sew it on later (this would be more convenient on a large or heavy item), use a piece of stiff linen or bookbinding cloth as a foundation. The strip should be the same length as the required piece of lace and about 5cm (2 inches) wider.

1 Rule a line along the strip about 1.3cm ($\frac{1}{2}$ inch) from the top edge.

2 Couch a double thread of crochet cotton or other firm thread along the line (using a contrasting colour for the stitches to hold the thread will make it easier to remove).

3 Work the lace on to the couched thread and remove the small stitches holding the thread when the lace is complete.

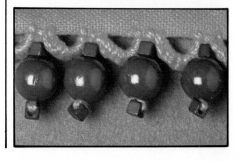

VENETIAN LACE

Make a border with stars or buttonhole pyramids to form a circle.

Venetian lace is the oldest type of needle-made lace. The motifs are geometric in design and, like the narrow edgings described in the previous chapter on needle-made edgings, they are made with fine, closely worked buttonhole stitches and knotted stitches.

They are worked on to couched threads, which are held with temporary stitches on a firm foundation, while the lace is being made.

The finished motifs, depending on the weight of the thread used, could be stitched on to lingerie, blouses and dresses, and on to sheets, pillowcases and table linen.

The threads and equipment

Linen thread is usually the best for working most types of lace, although fine crochet cotton, pearl cotton, and coton à broder are suitable.

For the couching, use a linen thread or mercerized crochet cotton, and for the final padding, a soft thread such as Sylko Size 5.

You will also need fine tapestry and crewel needles to suit the weight of the thread and a pair of finely pointed embroidery scissors.

For marking the design and for the foundation you will need either white paint and strong black paper with a matt texture, or Indian ink or a black felt-tipped pen and tracing paper. Both kinds of foundation should be backed with strong muslin or book-binding cloth. Alternatively you can use book binding cloth alone as the foundation.

Marking the design

1 Start by planning a well-balanced geometric design on graph paper, and consider how the lines are to be joined and the spaces filled. One way of doing this is to draw parts of the design in close double lines which separate and then rejoin. The spaces can be filled with bars or bridges.

2 Draw the design accurately on to the foundation.

Tracing the design

1 Trace over the design by outlining it with couched threads. Keep the threads as continuous as possible and, where they are double, lying evenly side by side. Where one line branches to another, divide the thread and couch it as far as

necessary and then double back to the starting point. Where one line touches another, thread the couching under and back again so that the pattern is joined.

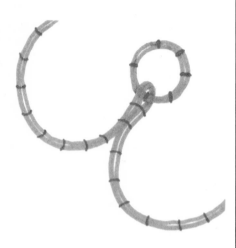

2 Secure the couching on to the foundation with small temporary stitches. These stitches can be in a contrasting colour to make them easier to remove, but if the lace is being worked in white this is best avoided if possible as the colour may leave a trace.

Filling in the design

1 Fill in the various spaces of the design by using one of the buttonhole stitches given below. Be as inventive as you like, for it is the variety of the stitches which give this type of lace its character.
2 When the filling is complete, make the final bars or bridges to link those lines which do not touch each other. These can be worked by buttonholing or by overcasting.
3 Start by laying several threads evenly across the space to be filled by taking small stitches into the outline threads on each side. Cover these threads with buttonholing or overcasting.

4 If you want a wider bar, work buttonhole stitch along both edges and decorate the bar with rings, picots or other bars.

Outlining the design

This is the stage which gives the final touch to the lace. The whole design is outlined in close buttonholing using a fine thread to bring it to life.
To give it dimension and emphasis on various parts work over a couple of strands of soft padding thread. Where one part appears to pass over another, work the under part first.
When joining in and fastening off threads, take a few neat overcast stitches into the part of the outlining nearest to you. These stitches will also get worked in with the final outlining which should cover them completely and also help strengthen the lace.

Finishing off

The last and most exciting stage is the removal of the lace from the foundation, which is done quite simply by cutting and removing the stitches which hold down the couched thread.

The stitches

These are just a few of the basic stitches which can be used to create needlemade lace. You can also invent numerous patterns by the interplay of the various stitches and the spaces created by them. You can also embellish them with picots and loops to give greater dexterity to the work. Basic buttonhole stitch, single and double knot stitch and bullion stitch were all described in the previous chapter on needlemade lace edgings.
Knotted buttonhole stitch
1 Work a row of buttonhole stitches from left to right over the couched thread.
2 Work a second row, from right to left, reversing the stitch into the loop made by

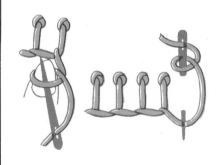

the first stitch. Work each stitch at a slight angle, pulling tight each knot thus formed before continuing on to the next stitch. Two or three buttonhole stitches can often be drawn together by working this stitch over a whole group at once.
Corded buttonhole stitch
1 Work a row of spaced buttonhole stitch from right to left.

2 Work a row of overcasting from left to right over the loops of the previous row.
3 Repeat these rows alternately for the required amount. When working the third row, check that you stitch into the loop of the buttonholing, not the overcasting.
Twisted stitches
These give a light and airy appearance to the work. It is important to keep the tension as even as possible and the stitches themselves carefully spaced. They are capable of great variety. One method is to overcast the loops, as for corded buttonhole stitch. Alternatively, they can be built up into a pyramid formation, each row having one less twisted stitch than the previous one.

Picots
1 To work a picot, make a second buttonhole stitch into the loop of the last stitch worked and then insert the needle into the loop of this second stitch just made.
2 Twist the working thread round the needle, draw up the knot and pass the needle through the loop of the original buttonhole stitch, ready to continue the row of buttonholing. The knots should twist and form into a small circle.

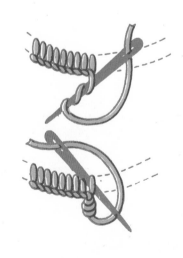

SHADOW WORK

Shadow work

Shadow work is a type of embroidery which relies for effect on a filling stitch, worked on the wrong side of a transparent fabric so that the colour of the working thread shows through to the right side of the work in a subdued tint.

It is usually worked on a very fine fabric such as organdie, organza, fine linen lawn, cotton lawn, muslin and crepe de chine in a soft shade.

Until this century it was always worked in white or a white fabric with double back stitch (a variation of herringbone). The threads of the stitches cross on the back of the work to give an opaque quality on the right side.

In more modern work the introduction of colour has changed the effect to produce an opalescence, and this type of work lends itself well to such articles as baby clothes, lingerie, party dresses and aprons as well as on the more delicate table linen and lampshades.

The design

Designs for shadow work should consist of narrow shapes which have simple outlines. Traditionally the work was always floral in design with the addition of a little surface stitchery but nowadays abstract shapes of suitable proportions can be used.

The shapes are nevertheless restricted in width by the double back stitch or herringbone stitch which fills and outlines them. To transfer the design on to the fabric, simply place the fabric over the design with the right side facing down and trace the design with a fine pencil.

Threads and needles

Choose a fine thread – either pure silk, stranded cotton or fine coton à broder – in a darker or brighter colour than the fabric so that you can achieve the desired finished effect.

Use fine crewel or betweens needles.

The working method

When the design has been traced on to the wrong side of the fabric, work all the main areas in close herringbone stitch (or double back stitch). Extra wide shapes can be filled in with two rows of herringbone, but this is best avoided.

Close herringbone stitch is worked in the same way as ordinary herringbone but with the stitches touching each other at the top and bottom, thus building up two parallel lines of back stitch on the front of the work with the opaque area between them.

Form the stitches as evenly as possible, following the outline of the shapes and working into all the corners and points in order to complete the outline accurately on the right side.

Work the stitches slightly smaller and closer together on the inside of curves and slightly larger on the outside. Take care that the stitches do not slope and always remain perpendicular to the base line.

When all the main areas are filled in, any additional stitchery such as linear detail, eyelets and spider's web wheels can be worked on the right side.

Because the fabric is transparent, take care to conceal all ends of threads.

Do not use knots but darn all ends back into the work securely and neatly.

French shadow work

This is extremely easy to work and produces quick and attractive results.

The motif most normally used is the square, which is marked on to the fabric by drawing a thread from side to side to ensure an accurate outline.

The squares are first worked one way and then the other, taking up an equal number of threads each time. The threads must be counted carefully so that the blocks of stitches are perfectly even.

Several variations of the square can be developed and the Greek fret design is always a good stand-by. The addition of eyelet holes adds variation to this type of design.

Indian shadow work

This has almost the same effect as traditional shadow work but a slightly different working method is used.

Instead of the stitches crossing on the back of the work they are taken from side to side, picking up a small amount of fabric each time and zig-zagging between the lines of the design.

Take care to pick up a small stitch each time or the threads will be too openly spaced on the back of the work, thus spoiling the shadow effect on the front.

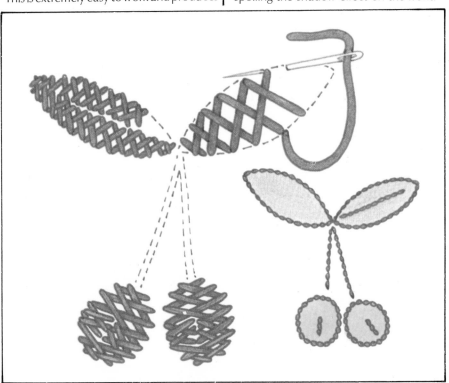

Shadow work for sheers

Fabric required

Length of fine pale green nylon or organdie to fit window, plus 3.5cm (1½ *inch*) turnings at top and bottom and 0.5cm (¼ *inch*) turnings at side.

You will need

☐ Required length of lightweight Rufflette nylon curtain tape.

☐ Anchor Stranded Cotton in the following colours and quantities (to work 8 motifs): 2 skeins each 0210 laurel green and 0402 white; 1 skein 036 blossom pink.

☐ Alternatively, Anchor Pearl Cotton No. 8: one 10 grm ball each 025 carnation, 0243 grass green, 0402 white.

☐ Circular embroidery frame to keep the fabric taut while working

☐ Tracing paper

☐ Milward 'Gold Seal' crewel needle No. 7

Transferring the motif

Two complete motifs are illustrated to size in the trace pattern. Trace the motifs and transfer them to the fabric either with dressmakers' carbon paper or by outlining with small tacking stitches.

Alternate the motifs evenly along the edge of the fabric, placing them above the final hem turning.

The design

1 No special skill is required for shadow work but it is important to work neatly so that the double lines of back stitch lie closely together. This will be easier to do if the work is held taut in a circular embroidery frame.

2 Using 3 strands of cotton throughout, follow the working chart as a guide to the colours and stitches used for each part of the motif.

3 Double back stitch, or closed herringbone stitch, can be worked either from the right or the wrong side of the fabric. Figure 1 shows how a small back stitch is worked alternately on each side of the traced double lines. The dotted lines on the diagram show the formation of the thread on the wrong side of the fabric, with the colour showing delicately through.

4 Figure 2 shows closed herringbone stitch worked on the wrong side of the fabric with no spaces left between the stitches. Both methods achieve the same results. But whichever method you choose, take care that the work is as neat on the back as on the front as the curtain will be seen from both sides.

5 To finish off, press the embroidery on the wrong side, turn up the side and bottom hems and sew on the curtain tape at the top.

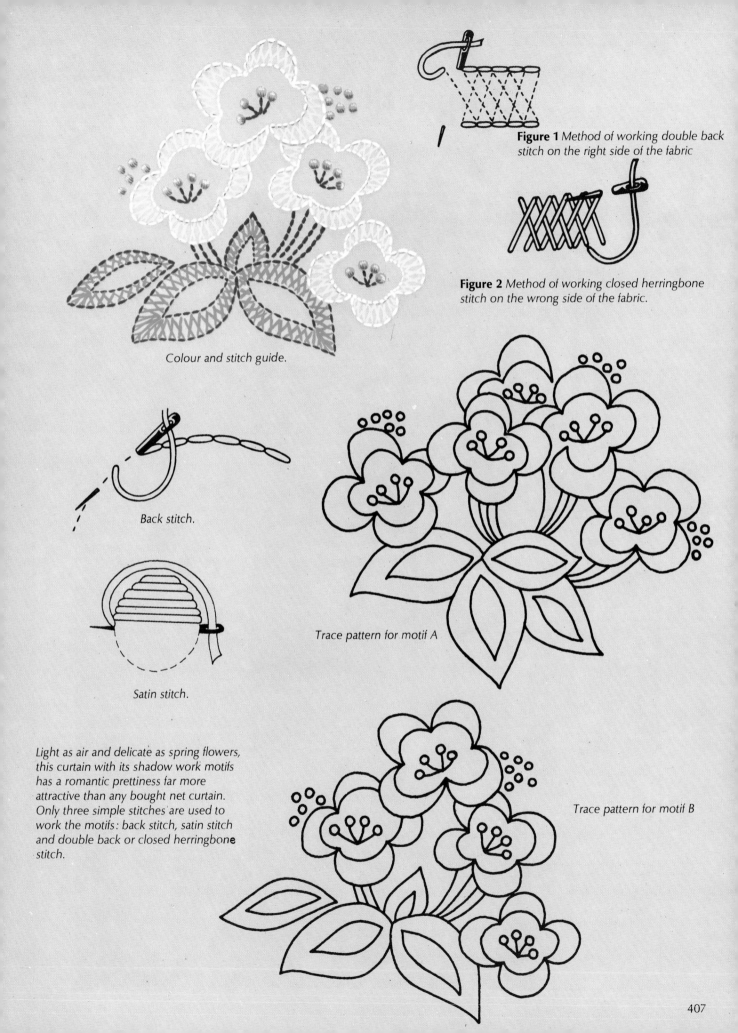

Colour and stitch guide.

Figure 1 *Method of working double back stitch on the right side of the fabric*

Figure 2 *Method of working closed herringbone stitch on the wrong side of the fabric.*

Back stitch.

Satin stitch.

Trace pattern for motif A

Light as air and delicate as spring flowers, this curtain with its shadow work motifs has a romantic prettiness far more attractive than any bought net curtain. Only three simple stitches are used to work the motifs: back stitch, satin stitch and double back or closed herringbone stitch.

Trace pattern for motif B

Organdie apron

Size

The length can be adjusted to fit the size you require.

Fabric required

1.15 metres ($1\frac{1}{4}$ yards) cotton organdie, 112cm (*44 inches*) wide

You will also need

- [ ] Matching pure silk thread
- [ ] Stranded embroidery cotton in a darker and lighter shade of main colour
- [ ] Pearl cotton embroidery thread in a lighter shade of main colour
- [ ] Fine crewel needle
- [ ] Fine tapestry needle

Cutting out

Fold the fabric in half lengthways placing the selvedges together. Cut out the pieces as shown in the chart.

Making up

1 Place the facing strip to the bottom edge of the main section and tack together all round the edge. This now forms the wrong side of the apron.

2 Using a sharp pencil and a small plate or saucer as a guide, draw a scalloped edge on the wrong side of the fabric along the top edge of the facing. Start from the centre-front and work outwards to the sides so that the scallops are balanced.

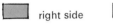

■ right side   □ wrong side

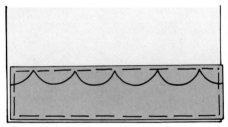

3 With the tapestry needle and pure silk thread, work pin stitching along the scalloped line on the wrong side of the fabric. Use sharp embroidery scissors to trim the excess fabric back to the stitching line.

4 Place the fabric, wrong side facing up, over the motif and trace it, placing one motif above each scallop as shown.

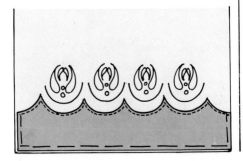

5 Still working on the wrong side, fill in the two inner shapes in herringbone stitch, using the darker shade of stranded cotton and the fine crewel needle. Keep the top and bottom of the stitch equal in width so that the work will be even on the right side.

6 Work the two outer shapes in the same way, using the lighter shade of the stranded cotton.

7 Using the fine pearl cotton complete the surface stitchery on the right side of the work.

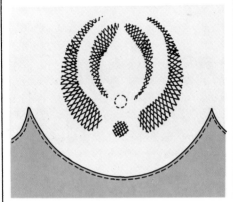

Work a back-stitch spider's web in the middle.

8 For the stitching enclosing the bottom of the motif, work a graduating line of fine satin stitch, 0.3cm ($\frac{1}{8}$ *inch*) apart, starting with a very small stitch and gradually getting wider then tapering off to a very small stitch at the beginning of the line.

9 On the satin stitch line work a row of raised chain band, making it a double row where the line thickens in the centre and tapering it by starting and finishing with several stem or split stitches.

Work a motif on to the pocket in the same way.

The frill

10 Finish each side of the apron with a 1.3cm ($\frac{1}{2}$ *inch*) hem.

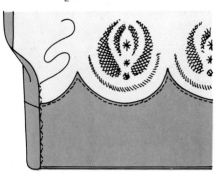

Join the pieces for the frill along the narrow edge with a French seam.

Make a narrow hem along the short ends and bottom edge of the frill. Work a row of gathering along the top edge.

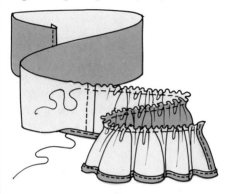

11 Remove the tacking thread from the bottom edge of the apron. With right sides together tack the top edge of the frill to the bottom of the apron, arranging the gathers evenly and leaving the edge of the facing free. Machine stitch, taking 1.3cm ($\frac{1}{2}$ *inch*) turnings.

12 Press the turnings upwards, turn under the edge of the facing and place the fold to the stitch line. Hem into place.

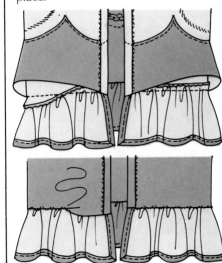

The pocket

13 Prepare the pocket frill in the same way as for the main frill.
Place the frill, wrong side down, on the right side of the pocket so that the raw edges are level along the top. Arrange the gathers evenly and tack in position.

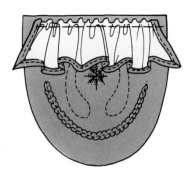

14 Work a very narrow hem along one long edge of the pocket facing. Place the facing on to the top of the pocket so that the raw edges are level along the top and sides. Tack and machine stitch along the top and sides, taking 1.3cm ($\frac{1}{2}$ inch) turnings. Turn the facing on to the wrong side of the pocket and press.

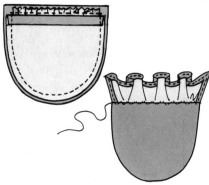

15 Turn under the remaining sides of the pocket. Place the pocket in position on to the apron. Tack and machine stitch.

The waistband

16 Fold under the short ends of the waistband for 1.3cm ($\frac{1}{2}$ inch) on to the wrong side and tack. Fold the waistband in half lengthways.

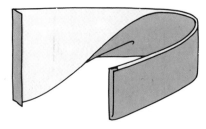

17 Try on the apron for length and adjust it at the top edge if necessary. Work a row of gathering along the top edge. With right sides together, pin the gathered edge to one long side of the waistband, arranging the gathers evenly. Tack in place.

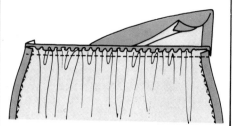

18 Make narrow hems along the two long sides and one short side of the apron ties. Place the fourth side to the ends of the waistband, gathering the fullness as shown.

19 Stitch, taking 1.3cm ($\frac{1}{2}$ inch) turnings from the left edge at the top of the tie, across the front and over the tie at the right edge.
Fold under the remaining edges of the waistband and hem to the stitch line.

Cutting layout for apron

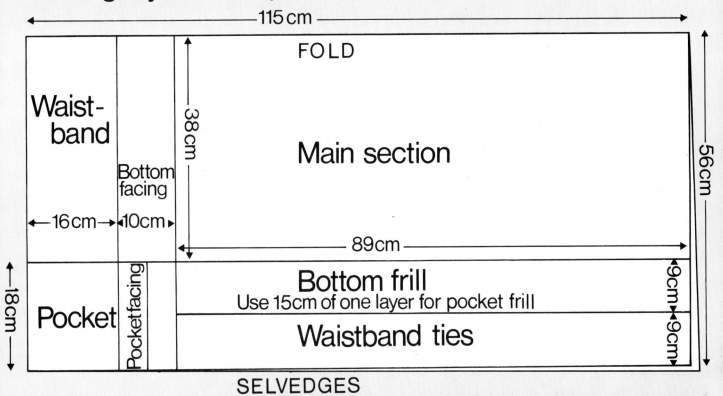

115 cm

FOLD

Waist-band

Bottom facing

16 cm — 10 cm

38 cm

Main section

89 cm

56 cm

18 cm

Pocket

Pocketfacing

Bottom frill
Use 15cm of one layer for pocket frill

Waistband ties

9cm — 9cm

SELVEDGES

Trace pattern for embroidery

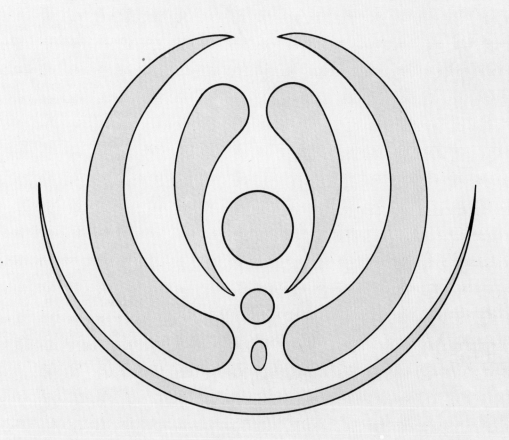

Stitching a sampler

For centuries the sampler was an essential part of every girl's education. Many survive today as beautiful examples of fine needlework. Now you can work your own sampler in the traditional manner. Nearly 20 different stitches, including drawn thread work, are included to make this sampler a technical exercise for the experienced needlewoman as well as the beginner. Add your name and the date of completion at top or bottom for a really authentic touch.

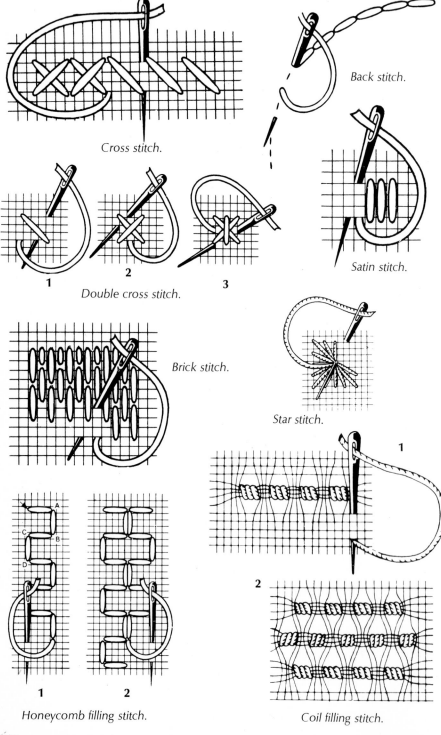

Cross stitch.

Back stitch.

Double cross stitch.

Satin stitch.

Brick stitch.

Star stitch.

Honeycomb filling stitch.

Coil filling stitch.

Fabric required

90cm (*36 inches*) beige medium weight evenweave fabric, 21 threads to 2.5cm (*1 inch*), 150cm (*59 inches*) wide

You will also need

☐ Anchor Stranded Cotton in the following colours and quantities: 2 skeins tapestry shade 0905, 2 skeins each tapestry shades 0843, 0845, 0887; 1 skein each tapestry shades 0848, 0850, 0851, 0885, 0888 geranium 06, 010 and 013.

☐ Picture frame with mounting board or cardboard to fit embroidery

☐ Milward 'Gold Seal' tapestry needles Nos. 20 and 24 for 6 and 3 strands respectively

The design

1 Cut a piece from the fabric to measure 90cm (*36 inches*) square. Mark the centres both ways with a line of tacking stitches.

2 Diagram I gives slightly more than half the design with the centre indicated by black arrows. Each background square on the diagram represents 2 threads of the fabric.

3 Use 6 strands of thread and needle size 20 for Swedish darning, satin stitch, couching and oblique loop stitch. Use 3 strands and needle size 24 for the rest of the embroidery.

4 Diagram 2 shows the Swedish darning and satin stitch tree. The background lines on this diagram indicate the threads of the fabric.

5 Begin working the sampler centrally with four sided stitch filling, 2 threads down and 6 threads to the right of the crossed tacking stitches. Follow Diagram 1 and the stitch and colour key for the main part of the design. Repeat in reverse from the lower black arrow to complete the second half of the sampler.

6 Couching is worked horizontally between satin stitch C9 on the diagram.

7 Once the embroidery for Diagram 1 has been completed, work Diagram 2 in the position indicated, following the key for the design and stitches used. The four drawn thread borders are worked one on each side of the completed design, linked by woven bars and oblique loop stitch as shown in the photograph.

Finishing off the sampler

Press the completed sampler on the wrong side. Place it centrally over the mounting board, fold the surplus fabric to the back of the board and secure it all round with pins stuck into the edge of the board. Lace the fabric across the back both ways with strong thread. Remove the pins and mount the sampler in a frame.

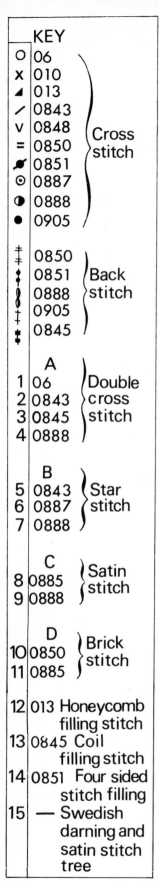

KEY

O	06	
X	010	
◢	013	
/	0843	
v	0848	Cross
=	0850	stitch
◗	0851	
⊙	0887	
◖	0888	
●	0905	

‡	0850	
⁝	0851	Back
◖	0888	stitch
†	0905	
✚	0845	

	A	Double
1	06	cross
2	0843	stitch
3	0845	
4	0888	

	B	
5	0843	Star
6	0887	stitch
7	0888	

	C	Satin
8	0885	stitch
9	0888	

	D	Brick
10	0850	stitch
11	0885	

12	013 Honeycomb filling stitch
13	0845 Coil filling stitch
14	0851 Four sided stitch filling
15	— Swedish darning and satin stitch tree

DIAGRAM 1 ▶

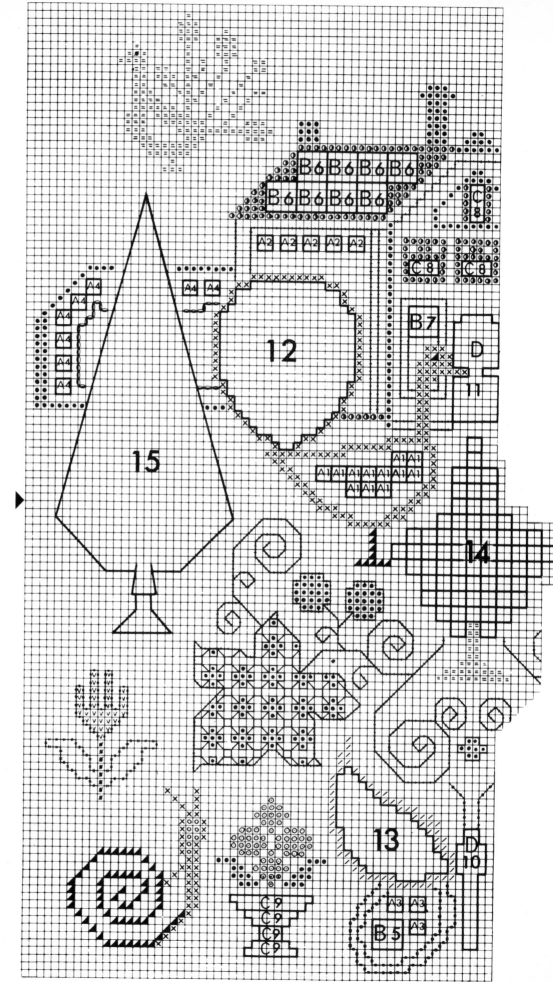

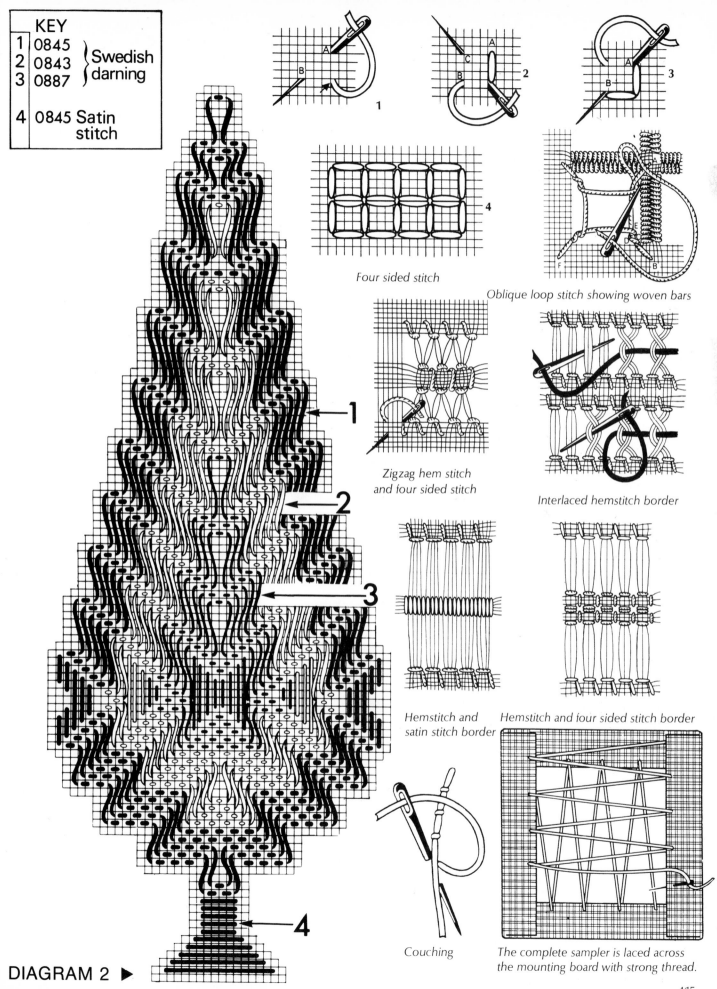

KEY

1	0845	} Swedish darning
2	0843	
3	0887	
4	0845	Satin stitch

Four sided stitch

Oblique loop stitch showing woven bars

Zigzag hem stitch
and four sided stitch

Interlaced hemstitch border

Hemstitch and
satin stitch border

Hemstitch and four sided stitch border

Couching

The complete sampler is laced across
the mounting board with strong thread.

DIAGRAM 2 ▶

CANVAS WORK
Basic equipment

Canvas work

Canvas work is a relaxing form of embroidery. It requires little mental effort and can be most effective when worked in one stitch. Carried out on a stiff, open-weave fabric, it is hard-wearing for use in the home as chair seat covers, stool tops, cushions, lamp bases, etc. It can also be made into exciting and useful accessories, such as belts, bags and slippers. Its use for clothes, however, is more restricted because of its stiffness although it could be made up into a simple garment such as a waistcoat. Canvas work is often known as needlepoint or – mistakenly – tapestry work. Tapestry is the name given to a form of weaving, usually of a pictorial kind and this has led to the canvases sold with the design ready painted also being called tapestries.

The equipment

Canvas work can be done without a frame if you are able to maintain an even tension throughout, but it frequently does become distorted as the heat of the hands affects the stiffening in the threads of the canvas. This usually results in the work having to be pinned and stretched over layers of damp blotting paper to restore it to its former shape.

It is much better to use a slate frame or a canvas work frame to prevent this and also to protect the canvas from being creased or crumpled while working as this affects the rigidity that keeps the stitches in place.

Types of canvas frame

There are two types of canvas frame, the flat bar and the screw bar. The flat bar frame is more suitable for large pieces of work using conventional stitches and threads because the canvas is rolled up as the work progresses. It is not so suitable for more adventurous designs using wooden beads, rings, plastic or leather shapes, because these additions prevent the work rolling smoothly.

The screw bar frame has adjustable side pieces which fit into rollers at both ends. This sort of frame has to be large enough to take the fully extended canvas because it cannot be rolled.

An old picture frame or artist's painting stretcher can be used successfully as a substitute frame. To attach the canvas to it, machine-stitch wide tape over the edge

of the canvas to strengthen it and then fix firmly to the frame with drawing pins placed at 1.3cm ($\frac{1}{2}$ inch) intervals.

A circular or tambour frame is suitable only for small pieces of work where the part of canvas enclosed by the rings will be cut off as it will have become distorted from the pressure.

The canvas

Canvas is made from linen, hemp and cotton. Single canvas has the threads interwoven singly and is the variety most often used because all types of stitches can be worked without difficulty.

Double canvas has the threads woven in pairs and is normally used when fine

detail and small stitching is wanted in the design. The stitches are mostly worked over the pair of threads for the background of the design and over one thread of the pair for the detailed sections.

The number of the mesh indicates the number of threads to the centimetre or inch.

Good quality hessian or wide-meshed linen scrim can be used instead of canvas where you want a more pliable effect and these can be worked with all the usual canvas work stitches (see the following chapter) but often with much more expressive results.

Fine wire mesh and wire gauze have also been used for experimental canvas work.

The needles

Tapestry needles, which are blunt-ended with a large eye to enable the thread to be pulled through easily, are sold in a variety of sizes to suit the canvas and thread used. Before threading a needle with wool, hold the wool up to the light to see the direction of the fibres (drawing the thread through your fingers will show you if the fibres are lying in the right direction). Thread the wool into the needle so that the fibres are lying away from the threaded end. In this way the fibres will be stroked downwards when pulled through the canvas, thus reducing tension on the wool and ensuring a smoother finish to the work.

You will also need two pairs of good scissors, one for cutting the canvas and paper for designs, and another small sharp-pointed pair for cutting threads. A pair of tweezers can be very useful if you have to unpick any stitches.

The designs

In Victorian times canvas work was used for elaborate pictorial designs such as wreaths of full-blown roses, baskets and fruit and other still-life scenes, usually worked in tent stitch or cross stitch. Nowadays, however, canvas work is at its most attractive when used for geometric designs which allow a variety of textures, threads and stitches to be used.

Cut paper shapes arranged in a geometric pattern are perhaps the easiest form of designing for a beginner.

Squared paper or graph paper is best for drawing the final designs for canvas work because each square of paper can be used to denote one stitch worked over two threads of the canvas. It is often possible to buy the graph paper with squares corresponding to those of the canvas which enables intricate designs to be worked out in detail.

A useful economy is to copy the design on to greaseproof or tracing paper and to place this over the graph paper to redraw and 'square off'. In this way the graph paper can be re-used several times.

To transfer the design on to the canvas, tack the tracing to the canvas round the edges and then tack along each line of the design using a coloured tacking thread and small stitches.

An alternative method is to outline the tracing with black poster paint, Indian ink or felt tipped pen. The canvas is then centred over the design and the outline traced on to the canvas with waterproof Indian ink. It is advisable to mark the centre of each side of both the tracing and the canvas so that they can be matched accurately and to secure the tracing with drawing pins if you are using this method.

The threads

It is extremely important that the yarns and threads used for canvas work should match the mesh of the canvas so that the stitches cover the canvas completely. A large mesh canvas is obviously unsuitable for fine yarn and vice versa.

The type of thread depends largely on the nature of the work and how it will be used. Wool is the traditional thread for canvas work and is the most hardwearing Crewel wool is sold specially for canvas work and can be used with two or three strands to suit the mesh. Knitting wool can also be used if crewel wool is unobtainable.

There is an almost unlimited choice of other threads which can be used – pearl cotton in various weights, stranded cotton, twisted silks, tapisserie wool, coton à broder, soft cotton, lurex and even raffia and string.

Canvas work stitches

Key to Chart
1 Padded satin stitch
2 Hungarian stitch
3 Large cross stitch worked alternately with Hungarian
4 Long-legged cross stitch
5 Brick stitch
6 Long-legged cross stitch
7 Norwich stitch
8 Large cross stitch and straight cross stitch
9 Paris stitch
10 Eye stitch
Background: tent stitch

There are a great number of canvas work stitches, many of which are similar to those used in regular embroidery. Here are a few of the most useful stitches.

Smyrna or double cross
This is double cross stitch worked in two directions. Work cross stitch over four threads and then complete each stitch by

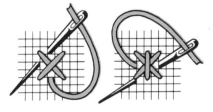

working another cross stitch vertically over the first stitch as shown.

Long-legged cross
This is a useful stitch because it can be worked in horizontal rows from left to right and from right to left, or in vertical rows from the top down and from the bottom up. Work as shown in the diagram, always beginning and ending each row with a regular cross stitch. If used to fill in a background, the rows can be worked

alternately in each direction. The long-legged cross stitch can also be combined with the tent stitch in alternate rows.

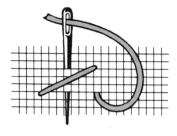

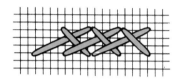

Tent stitch

This looks similar to a half cross-stitch but is so worked to give more coverage on the back of the canvas. It can be worked from right to left, in vertical rows or diagonal rows. It is a good background stitch and throws into relief more chunky stitches.

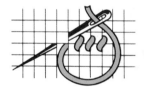

Knot stitch

This is another variation of cross stitch with one of the obliques worked over three threads and the other oblique worked over one thread to tie it. It is a useful filling stitch giving a good texture for backgrounds.

Rice stitch

This is a development of cross stitch. Work the crosses in a thick yarn over four threads. Then using a finer thread in a contrasting colour or texture work a single oblique over each corner. Work these stitches in two horizontal rows, tying down the two upper corners of each cross in the first row and the two lower corners in the second row.

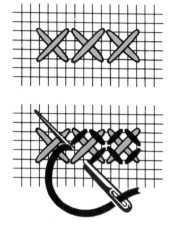

Hungarian stitch

This is a simple stitch which is more effective when worked in two colours or two textures. It consists of straight stitches worked in groups of three. For the first row, work the first stitch over two threads, the second over four threads and the third over two threads. Leave two threads and repeat to the end of the row. Work the second row as for the first, fitting the longer stitches into the spaces left by the previous row as shown.

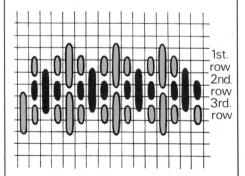

Paris stitch

This is a good background filling stitch made by working alternately over one and then over three threads of the canvas in alternate rows from left to right and right

to left. The short stitches in the second row fit in under the long stitches of the rows on each side.

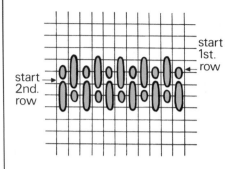

Eye stitch

This consists of 16 stitches worked over eight threads, all radiating from the same centre hole.

Norwich stitch

This is not as complicated as it appears. It can be worked over any size square, providing that the square consists of an uneven number of threads. Start at point 1 and take a straight stitch to point 2. Go to the opposite corner and take a stitch from point 3 to point 4. Continue in this way round the square, taking stitches between the points shown on the diagram, thus giving the effect of a square on the diagonal.

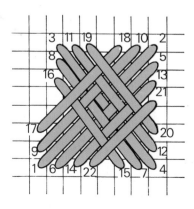

Canvas work sampler

This cushion can be worked as a sampler to practise many different stitches making up an interesting collection of textures. The simple use of one colour also emphasises the variation of stitches, although other colours may be used to complement the subtle variety of stitches.

Size

43cm (17 inches) square

Fabric required

Cream fabric for backing, 48.5cm (19 inches) square

You will also need

- ☐ Anchor Tapisserie Wool: 43 skeins 0386 cream
- ☐ 0.60m ($\frac{5}{8}$ yard) single thread tapestry canvas, 68.5cm (27 inches) wide, 18 threads to 2.5cm (1 inch)
- ☐ Cushion pad to fit
- ☐ Tapestry frame with 68.5cm (27 inches) tapes
- ☐ Milward 'Gold Seal' tapestry needle No. 18

The design

1 Mark the centre of the canvas along a line of holes in both directions with tacking stitches. Mount the canvas in the frame, with the raw edges to the tapes. When working fern stitch turn the frame on its side to allow the stitches to be worked in the correct direction, as indicated by the black arrows on the working chart. The working chart gives a section of the complete design. Blank arrows indicate the centre of the design, which should coincide with the tacking stitches.

2 Follow the working chart using the stitch key for the design. Each background square represents two threads of the canvas. Detailed stitch diagrams are given showing the number of threads over which the stitches are worked. When working cross stitch it is important that the crosses cross in the same direction.

3 Begin the design at the small black arrow 6 threads down and 14 threads to the left of the crossed tacking stitches in the centre of the canvas, and work the section as given on the working chart. Omit the centre section and repeat the stitches in reverse from the blank arrow to complete one quarter of the design. Work the other three quarters to correspond. The completed canvaswork should be dampened, then pinned and stretched to the correct shape, on a clean dry board with rustless drawing pins and left to dry naturally.

To work velvet stitch

This stitch resembles the pile of an oriental carpet. It is worked from left to right in rows working from the bottom upwards. Follow the stitch diagram, bringing the thread out at the arrow and insert the needle at A (2 threads up and 2 threads to the right), then bring it out again at the arrow. Re-insert the needle at A, leaving a loop of thread at the bottom, bring the needle out at B (2 threads down). Insert at C (2 threads up and 2 threads to the left), bringing the needle out again at B in readiness for the next stitch. To maintain a regular length to the loops they can be worked over a thick knitting needle. After all the rows have been worked, cut the loops and trim them evenly, taking care not to trim the tufts too short.

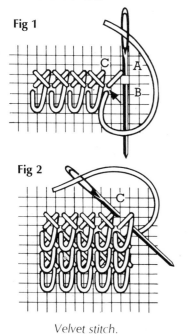

Fig 1

Fig 2

Velvet stitch.

To work brick stitch

This stitch is worked in rows alternately from left to right or from right to left. The first row consists of long and short stitches into which are fitted rows of even satin stitch, giving a 'brick' formation. The whole filling must be worked very regularly, making each satin stitch of even length and all exactly parallel.

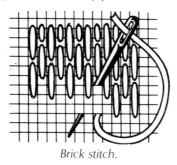

Brick stitch.

To work cross stitch and upright cross stitch

1 Work the required number of cross stitches over 4 threads, then work upright cross stitch between each cross stitch, working diagonally from the lower right to the top left corner in the following way.

2 Figure 1 – bring the thread out at the arrow; insert the needle at A (2 threads up), then bring it out at B (2 threads to the left). Continue in this way to the end of the row.

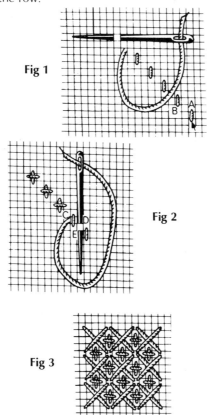

Fig 1

Fig 2

Fig 3

Cross stitch and upright cross stitch.

3 Figure 2 – after completing the last stitch, bring the needle through as shown at C. Insert the needle at D (2 threads to the right), and bring it though at E. Continue in this way to the end of the row. Figure 3 shows the finished effect.

To work fern stitch

Pull the thread through at the arrow and insert the needle 2 threads down and 4 threads to the right bringing it out 2 threads to the left. Then insert the needle 2 threads to the right. Bring it out 2 threads down and 4 threads to the left in readiness for the next stitch. The diagram also shows the direction of the two rows of fern stitch as they have been worked on the cushion.

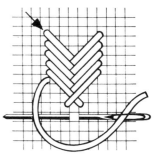

Fern stitch.

To work eye stitch

This stitch is worked in the same way as star stitch, to form a square over 8 horizontal and 8 vertical threads of canvas. It consists of 16 straight stitches all taken into the same central hole but with their outer ends arranged over a square of eight threads. Finish off the square with an outline of back stitch worked over 2 canvas threads, shown in Figure 2.

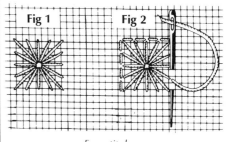

Fig 1   **Fig 2**

Eye stitch

To work gobelin stitch

Work a trammed stitch from left to right, then pull the needle through 1 thread down and 1 thread to the left, inserting

Straight gobelin stitch.

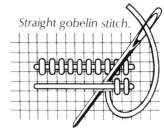

again 2 threads above. Pull the needle through 2 threads down and 1 thread to the left in readiness for the next stitch.

To work the cord

Measure off six 13.75m (15 yard) lengths of wool. With another person to help you, double the pieces of wool in half to make a length of 6.90m (7½ yards), then knot the loose ends together and insert a pencil at each end. Pull the threads and, keeping them taut, turn the pencils round in opposite directions following the natural twist of the wool. Continue until the cord is sufficiently tight and begins to curl. Still keeping the cord tight, place another pencil in the centre and double the cord over it until both ends meet, making a length of 3m (3¼ yards). Next twist the cord in the opposite direction, until it begins to curl naturally. Set the cord by exerting a steady pull at both ends which will cause it to stretch slightly and so retain its twist permanently.

To make the tassels

For one tassel, wind 2 skeins of wool neatly round a piece of card 7.5cm (3 inches) wide Tie them together with a piece of matching wool at one end, cut the wool at the opposite end, and then remove the card. Now take another piece of wool, about ¼ skein, and wind this round the tied ends near the top to form a head, then fasten off securely. If the wool does not lie properly when the tassel is completed, hold it for a few minutes in the steam from a kettle, or press with a cool iron.

To make up

Trim the canvas, leaving a 2.5cm (1 inch) border of unworked canvas all round. Place the canvaswork and backing fabric right sides together and sew close to the embroidery round three sides. Turn back to the right sides, insert the cushion pad, and slip stitch along the opening. Stitch the cord in position around the edge of the cushion and attach the tassels securely to the corners.

KEY

1 Velvet stitch
2 Cross stitch
3 Satin stitch
3a Satin stitch (horizontal)
4 Brick stitch
5 Cross stitch and upright cross stitch (variation)
6 Fern stitch
7 Eye stitch
☐ Petit point
☐ Straight gobelin stitch

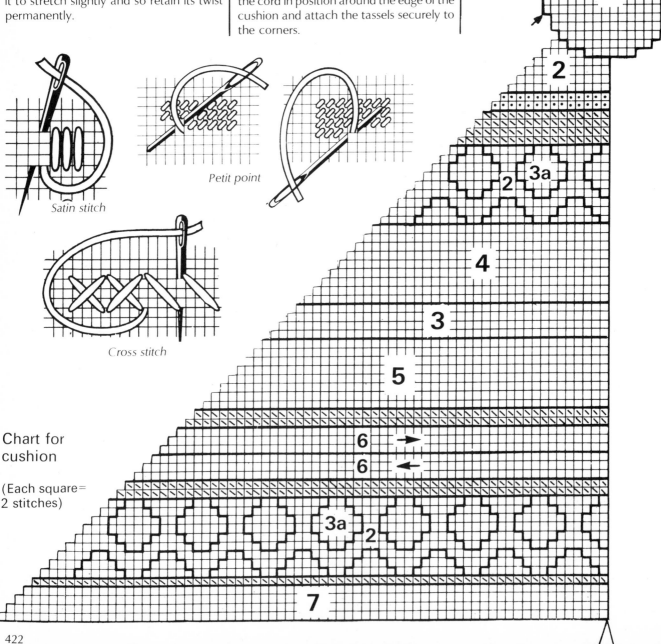

Satin stitch

Petit point

Cross stitch

Chart for cushion

(Each square = 2 stitches)

Quillwork desk set

For your desk

This smart desk set was inspired by the quillwork embroidery of North American Indian tribes. The colours, ochre, indigo and rust, are similar to those produced by natural dyes. The embroidery is worked throughout in variations of satin stitch. The simple basic design can easily be adapted to make the pieces of the set larger or smaller if you wish.

Fabric required

0.65m (⅔ yard) single thread canvas, 16 threads to 2.5cm (1 inch), 59cm (23 inches) wide 0.25cm (¼ yard) felt, 1.85m (72 inches) wide to match one of the main colours

You will also need

☐ Anchor Tapisserie Wool in the following colours and quantities: 8 skeins 0850 indigo, 7 skeins 0412 rust, 5 skeins 0315 ochre, 4 skeins 0848 light blue.
☐ Hardback address book, 12.5cm by 20.5cm (5 inches by 8 inches)
☐ 29grm (10½ ounce) soup tin, 10cm (4 inches) high, for pen holder
☐ Piece of heavy cardboard, thin plywood or plastic sheet 40.5cm by 59cm (16 inches by 23 inches)
☐ Milward 'Gold Seal' tapestry needle No. 22
☐ Sewing needle
☐ Thread to match felt

The design

1 Tape the raw edges of the canvas and, following the working charts, work the parts of the desk set. Do not cut the canvas, but leave a 5cm (2 inch) border of unworked canvas around each piece of embroidery. The embroidery is worked in satin stitch of various lengths.
2 The completed canvaswork should be dampened, then pinned and stretched to the correct shape on a clean board, and left to dry naturally.

Pen holder

Trim the canvas to 2cm (¾ inch) all round. Fold the canvas round to form a ring, trim the top layer of unworked canvas down to 4 threads. Work satin stitch, using indigo thread, over the 4 threads as shown, joining the two layers of unworked canvas. Cut a strip of felt 10cm by 2cm (4 inches by 9 inches) and sew the short ends together. Turn under the border of unworked canvas round top and bottom, slip the felt inside the canvas and slip stitch together round top and bottom. Fit the completed cover over the tin.

Address book cover

Trim the canvas all round to 2cm (¾ inch). Mitre the corners and fold down the

borders of unworked canvas. Cut a strip of felt 28cm by 21cm (11 inches by 8¼ inches). Stitch one short end of the felt to the canvas as shown in the diagram. Cut another piece of felt 10.5cm by 21cm (4¼ inches by 7¼ inches), sew this to the remaining 3 sides of the canvas. Slide the embroidery onto the front cover of the book, fold the rest of the felt around the book and inside the back cover. Slip stitch at top and bottom.

Blotter

Trim the canvas to 2cm (¾ inch) all round. Cut a piece of felt as shown in the diagram. Turn under the unworked borders of canvas and sew the two embroidered end pieces onto the felt as shown. Lay the top of the felt and fold the end pieces round to the front. Fold the excess felt at top and bottom to the back of the board and stitch down. Insert blotting paper.

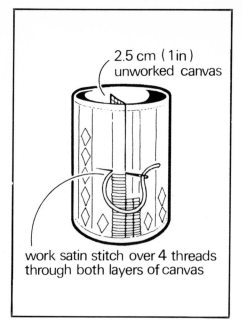

Sewing the pen holder cover.

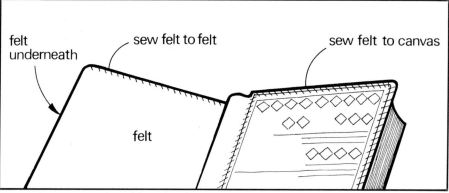

Fitting the cover on the address book.   *Cutting felt for the blotter.*

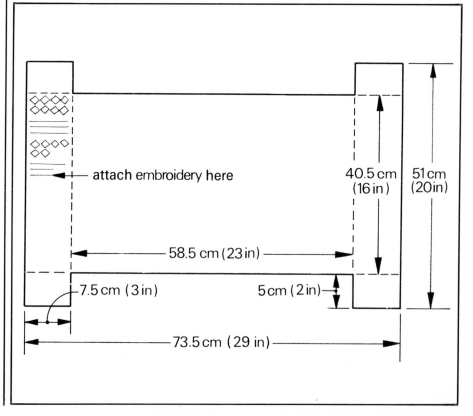

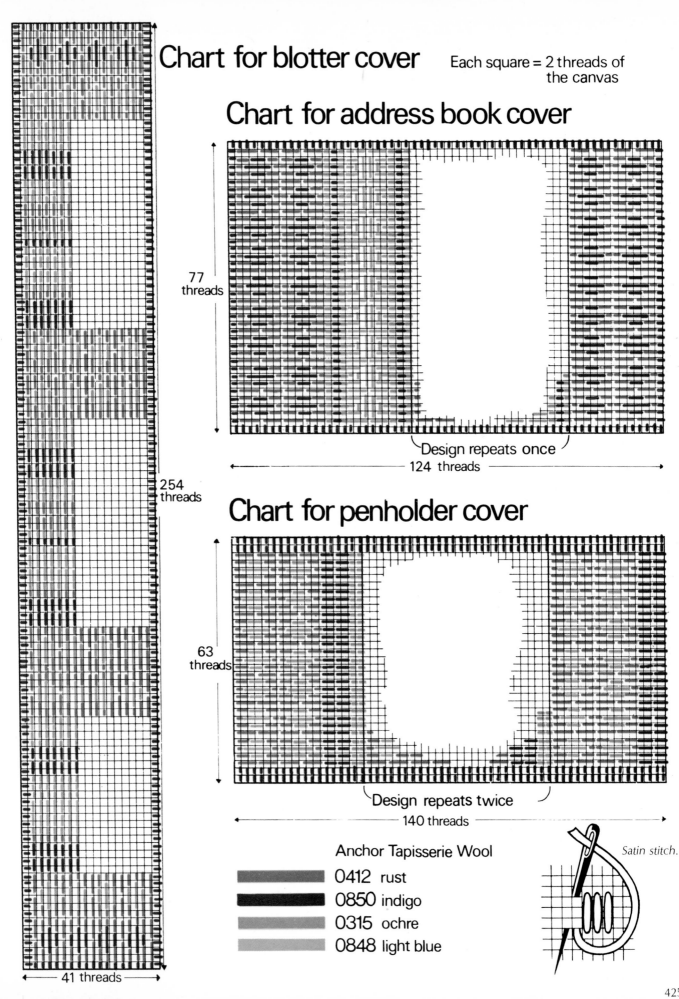

Chart for blotter cover

Each square = 2 threads of the canvas

Chart for address book cover

77 threads

254 threads

Design repeats once

124 threads

Chart for penholder cover

63 threads

Design repeats twice

140 threads

41 threads

Anchor Tapisserie Wool

0412 rust
0850 indigo
0315 ochre
0848 light blue

Satin stitch.

FLORENTINE EMBROIDERY

Florentine canvas work dates back as far as the thirteenth century and is thought to be of Hungarian origin.

It is also known as Bargello, which is probably a corruption of Jagiello, the family name of the Polish King Vladislaw who married a young Hungarian princess. She incorporated the arms of Hungary and Poland in a bishop's cope which she worked in the stitch now known as Florentine.

It became known as Florentine work in the fifteenth century when one of the Medici family married a Hungarian bride who taught the art to the ladies of the Florentine court. Other names for Florentine work include Hungarian point, 'Fiamma' or flame stitch.

There is a great difference between the Florentine work of the past and that of today. The main characteristic of the work is the shading and blending of colour, but while the early work was subtle with carefully arranged colour tints, modern work is bolder and more striking.

Traditionally Florentine work was used for upholstery on stool tops, chair seats and bed drapes but it can also be made into smaller articles such as accessories like bags and purses.

Choosing the colours

As a general rule, it is advisable to use two or three basic colours with as many intermediate shades of these colours as you like. Each successive line is worked in a lighter or darker tint to the previous line, so shading gradually from one tone to another. When you are working in shades which are very close, grade and number the skeins before starting.

Materials

Use single thread canvas with yarn in the correct thickness to match the mesh and completely cover the canvas. Tapestry and crewel wools are the most frequently used being specially designed to suit a wide range of different sized canvases. Both are sold in a good colour range. Knitting wool can also be used and it is possible to incorporate silk threads on a fine mesh canvas.

Estimating the amount of yarn

1 Cut a 45cm (*18 inch*) length of yarn. Stitch as much of the pattern repeat as this length will allow and then count up the number worked. Multiply by the yarn length to calculate how much you need for a complete row and then multiply by the number of rows worked in each colour.

2 Calculate from the amount specified by the manufacturer how many skeins of each colour you will need.

Needles

Use tapestry needles of a suitable thickness for the canvas and yarn.

Frames

Technically this form of canvas work can be evenly stitched whether held in the hand or mounted in a frame so it is a matter of personal preference.

Preparing the canvas

Tack the centre lines both vertically and horizontally on the canvas and any other guide lines necessary. Count and mark the high points of any pattern where the repeat is the same throughout.

The stitch

Only one type of stitch is used for Florentine work. It is a vertical stitch usually covering an even number of threads, such as four, six or eight, and moving either upwards or downwards over one or more threads depending on the pattern.

Patterns are constructed by working blocks of stitches side by side, then moving higher or lower to make another block, and so on.

Zig zag stitch

This is the most commonly used Florentine stitch and is worked by passing each stitch over four threads and back under two. The easiest way to vary it is to take it over six threads and back under one. To avoid monotony in the pattern, vary the height of the pinnacles formed or make the slopes more gradual, perhaps by making two stitches over the same number of threads.

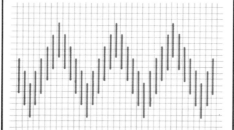

Flame stitch

This is worked over four threads and back under one and produces a flame-like effect. It is important to start in the centre of the canvas with the apex of the stitch at the highest point. Both flame stitch and Florentine stitch can be the basis of more complex designs using squares, diamonds or trellises.

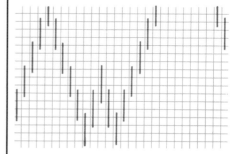

Curves

You can form the illusion of a curve by working blocks of stitches over the same number of threads by varying the rate of progression. Thus stitches or blocks of stitches worked on the 6/1, 5/1 and 4/1 principle will produce steeper curves than those worked on the 6/3 and 4/2 principle.

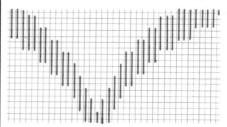

Medallion pattern

This is a popular repeating pattern where each stitch is taken over four threads and back under two, starting with four single stitches, followed by one block of two stitches, then three blocks of three stitches to form the top of the pattern.

Progress downwards, repeating the same number of stitches. This forms the outline of the pattern which can be repeated for the whole work. The spaces formed between the medallions can be filled with contrasting yarns.

The foundation row

All Florentine patterns depend on an accurate first row and in some patterns the embroidery is worked either above or below this row. In others each section is filled in from one outer foundation row or grid. When working this foundation row it is extremely important to count the threads accurately – if you make a mistake, cut it out rather than trying to unpick it which takes too long and frays the wool so badly that it is unusable again.

For patterns where symmetry is important, begin at the marked centre line of the canvas and stitch the first row from the centre outwards. The following rows can be worked from side to side in the normal way, following the pattern established by the first row.

Starting and finishing

Use a length of yarn about 38cm (15 inches) long and knot one end. Thread the needle with the other end and pass the needle through the canvas from the front about 5cm (2 inches) from the position of the first stitch. Bring the needle up in the position for the first stitch, work several stitches and then cut off the knot, leaving the tail.

Thread the tail through to the back of the canvas and work it in through the back of the stitches. Finish off by working a short length through the stitches on the back in the same way. Always avoid starting and finishing in the same place so that the work has an even finish and darn in the ends as they occur to avoid matting and tangling on the back of the work.

Florentine clutch bag
Size

19cm (7½ inches) × 30cm (11¾ inches) × 5cm (2 inches)

Fabric required

0.35cm (⅜ yard) single thread tapestry canvas, 68.5cm (27 inches) wide 14 threads to 2.5cm (1 inch)
Small skin of suede for back of bag and gussets
1 × felt square, 61cm × 61cm (24 inches × 24 inches)

You will also need

☐ Coats Anchor Tapisserie wool: 4 skeins Raspberry 071, 2 skeins each Raspberry 067, 068, 069; 1 skein grey 0398
☐ Clark's Anchor Stranded Cotton: 3 skeins rose pink 048, 2 skeins each white 0402, grey 0397. Use six strands throughout.
☐ Tapestry frame with 68.5cm (27 inch) tapes
☐ Adhesive

The design

This design is worked in Florentine canvas embroidery.

The photograph gives a section of the design with the double row of three straight stitches forming the centre.

Working the embroidery

1 Mount the canvas into the frame. Mark the centre of the canvas widthwise with a line of tacking.

2 Start the embroidery in the centre of the canvas with the double row of three straight stitches. Work the motifs on each side and repeat to the sides and above and below to the required size. Grade the colours according to the photograph showing a detail of the bag.

Most stitches are worked over six threads of canvas with some stitches over three threads to complete the design.

Making up

1 Cut out pieces of suede measuring 21.5cm (8½ inches × 32.5cm (12¾ inches) for the front; 18cm (7 inches) × 32.5cm (12¾ inches) for the back, and two pieces, 7.5cm (3 inches) × 37cm (14½ inches) for the gusset.

2 With right sides together stitch the gusset pieces along their short edges taking 1.3cm (½ inch) turnings. Press the turnings open with your fingers.

3 With right sides together stitch the Florentine flap to one long edge of the suede back. Press the seam open. Working from the right side top-stitch the suede close to the seam line.

4 Cut out pieces of felt the same size as the suede for the front and gusset and 32.5cm (12¾ inches) × 40.5cm (16 inches) for the flap and back. Stitch the gusset sections as for the suede.

5 With right sides together, stitch the felt back and flap piece to the Florentine flap as far as the fold line which is 4cm (1½ inches) from the seam.

Clip across corners, turn through to the right side and press. Clip seam allowance at the fold line.

6 Place the remaining felt pieces on to the wrong side of the corresponding pieces of suede and treat them as one piece.

7 To neaten the top edge of the front, fold under the turnings for 1.3cm (½ inch), place together and glue with adhesive. Top-stitch close to the edge.

8 With right sides together, stitch the front to the gusset, clipping the gusset turning at the corners. Repeat with the back. Trim seams and turn right side out. Top-stitch the seams through all thicknesses 0.6cm (¼ inch) from the edge.

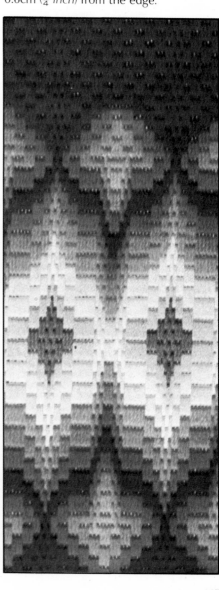

Florentine chair seat

The quantities and instructions are given for a dining chair with a larger than average drop-in seat but they can easily be adapted to fit your own chairs or even worked for the top of a foot stool or for a cushion cover.

Materials required
- [ ] Coats Anchor Tapisserie wool: 5 skeins each Tangerine 0311, 0313, 0315, Chestnut 0350, Black 0403, 2 skeins Flame 0334
- [ ] 0.70 metre (¾ yard) single thread tapestry canvas, 7 threads to 1cm (18 threads to 1 inch) 68.5cm (27 inches) wide
- [ ] Tapestry frame (optional)
- [ ] Tapestry needle No. 18
- [ ] Paper for making template of chair seat
- [ ] Upholstery tacks, 1cm (⅜ inch) long
- [ ] Tack hammer
- [ ] Wood plane (if necessary)

KEY TO DIAGRAM

- Foundation row 0403
- **2** – 0311
- **3** – 0313
- **4** – 0315
- **5** – 0350
- – 0334

TAPISSERIE WOOL

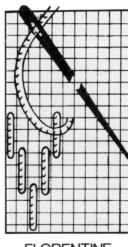

FLORENTINE STITCH

Making the template

1 Remove the seat from the chair, place it on to the paper and draw round.

2 Draw a second line 2.5cm (*1 inch*) outside the first line to allow for the depth of the padding. Draw 2.5cm (*1 inch*) squares in each corner for mitred corners. The stitching should not be worked in these squares. Cut along the outside line.

3 Pin the template on to the canvas and draw round the edge using waterproof ink. Allow at least 2.5cm (*1 inch*) unworked canvas all round so that it can be attached to the under-side of the seat.

Marking the design

1 Mark the centre of the canvas in both directions with tacking.

2 Following the chart, mark the pattern on to the canvas starting at the centre (indicated by the arrows) and working outwards. Repeat the design until you reach the outside edges.

3 Mount the canvas on to a tapestry frame if you are using one.

Working the design

1 The design is worked in Florentine stitch and satin stitch over four threads of the canvas. Work the foundation row first in the colour shown on the chart, starting at the centre and going out to the sides in both directions.

2 Work the next row below the foundation row in the colour shown on the chart. The tops of the stitches in this row should be worked into the same holes as the bottom of the stitches in the foundation row.

3 Work the following rows in the same way.

4 When the colour sequence is complete, start again with the foundation row and continue as before, working to the outline shape.

5 To complete the design work the horizontal straight stitches.

Attaching the canvas

1 Place the canvas on to the seat and fold the excess on to the underside. Try the seat in position on the chair.

2 If the canvas is too thick for the seat to fit back into the chair, remove the tacks holding the original fabric. Plane the sides of the frame by the required amount and carefully re-tack the fabric back on to the seat.

3 Mitre the corners of the canvas and attach the canvas centrally to the seat as for the cover fabric.

4 Replace the seat on the chair.

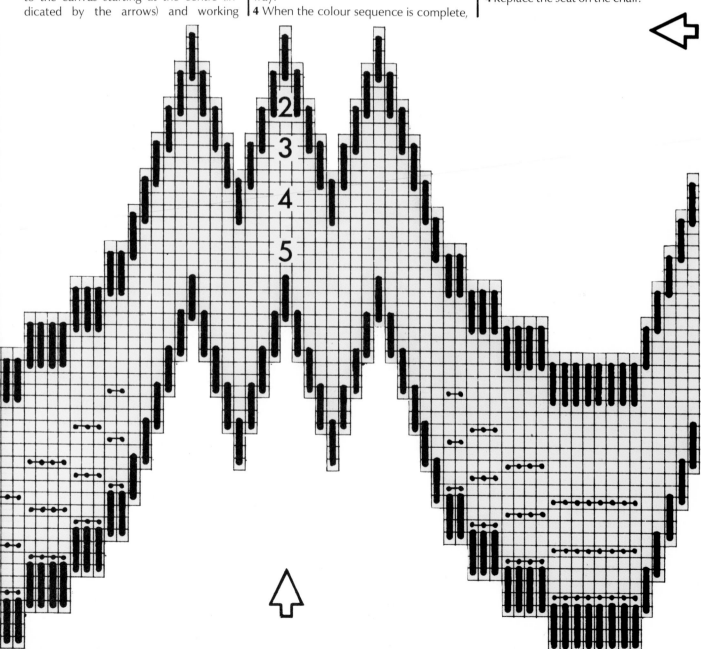

BEADWORK
Simple techniques

Beads have been used as decoration for thousands of years and have been made of many different materials such as pebbles, bone, teeth, seeds, glass and even paper. During the 19th century, embroidery with beads reached its peak when clothes and household articles were often heavily beaded; Berlin woolwork, a form of canvas embroidery incorporating beads, is a good example of this.

Today, beads – wooden, plastic and glass – are used in many ways. They can be combined with stitchery in cut work, canvas work, smocking, quilting, drawn and pulled fabric embroidery and they can be used without stitchery to decorate any number of things.

Types of beads

There are wide varieties of beads, sequins and acetate shapes, and can be obtained in many sizes. Jumble sales and junk shops often prove a good source as fragments of old beaded clothes, bags and lampshades will often yield very interesting beads which can be washed and re-used. A bag of 'sweepings' from a workroom will often provide sufficient beads and sequins for many pieces of embroidery. When choosing beads for clothes or articles which need to be washed or dry-cleaned, check that they are durable because some acetate shapes will not stand laundering or a hot iron. Most sequins can be washed with care although you should avoid touching them with a hot iron.

Designing with beads

Choose the beads to enhance the background fabric, not necessarily to contrast with it. Often the best effect can be obtained by creating a subtle contrast rather than an obvious one. Always try to avoid crude or over bright effects.

A geometric pattern is probably the easiest way of building up a pattern which can be repeated on a bag, belt or garment, and the simplest starting point is with a square. Start by placing a square acetate bead on a piece of felt and surround it with a row of medium size square or round beads and surround these with a row of flat sequins which might be oval or boat shaped. These could be followed by a small quantity of fine piping cord, securely couched on to the background fabric and covered with succeeding rows of small beads. If you prefer a circular motif, use the same principle but start with a large jewel or circular domed sequin. Another way that beaded and sequinned motifs can be used successfully is to place them on a geometrically patterned fabric, building up a pattern on the design of the fabric.

Whether you decide to build up a geometric pattern or to work out a less formal idea, the design should fill the space intended or it will look thin and meagre. Try to ensure that different parts of the design balance. A large solid shape should be balanced with several smaller ones. If you are interpreting a design based on cut paper shapes, consider the spaces formed in between the shapes as they are just as important as the shapes themselves.

Frames

It is important to use a square or rectangular frame for bead embroidery. A tambour frame is not suitable except for an isolated motif because you will often need both hands free and it does not provide sufficient tension on the fabric. When embroidering a section of a garment, mount the whole piece into the frame, complete the bead embroidery, remove from the frame and then make up the garment.

Fabric

Any type of fabric can be enhanced with

beads which are suitable for the weight and texture – naturally small glass beads would be unsuitable for a heavy tweed when large wooden or china beads would give the best effect.

It is advisable to back the fabric to be embroidered. If it is heavily beaded, a firm non-woven interfacing will support the beads on a bag or a belt. For a garment use a firm lightweight cotton or lawn as a backing for the beaded part only. Cut away the surplus before making up that part of the garment.

Thread

The thread you use will depend on the size and type of fabric and beads. Never use a polyester thread because it will stretch too much. The beads should lie on the fabric without being too loose or puckering it. Pure sewing silk is the most satisfactory – choose a colour to match the bead or sequin. Always wax the thread with beeswax to strengthen it and prevent the beads – particularly bugle beads – from cutting it.

Needles

Use special beading needles which are long and pliable and are available in sizes 12–18. Choose the size to slip through the beads easily.

Attaching beads

Beads, depending on their size, can be attached to fabric in one of four ways.

1 They can be sewn on to the background fabric with a straight stab stitch. The thread is brought through the fabric, the bead is threaded onto the needle and the needle is passed through the fabric again. The bead will then lie on its side.

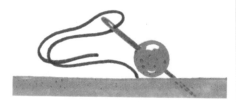

2 The bead, if large enough, can be secured by two or four stitches through the centre hole so that it will then lie with the hole upwards.

Square beads are more effective when used in this way but it will depend on the effect you are trying to produce.

3 Beads can be sewn on with a back stitch or several beads can be threaded on to a needle and couched down to follow a line of the design.

4 A large bead can be sewn on by bringing the threads through the fabric, sliding on the large bead and then one small toning or contrasting bead. The needle and thread then re-enter the large bead and the fabric. This secures the large bead so that it is free-standing.

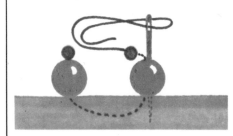

It is advisable to fasten the thread off after sewing on each heavy bead, rather than carry the thread on the back of the work from bead to bead.

Attaching sequins

Sequins are available in flat and cupped shapes in a number of sizes. They can be attached as for beads or jewels when used as isolated units or they can be sewn on in line so that they overlap.

1 Bring the needle up through the fabric and through the hole in the centre of the first sequin. Pass the needle back through the fabric at the edge of the sequin and bring it up again immediately next to the point that it entered.

2 Thread on the next sequin making sure that cupped sequins all lie in the same direction with the domed side uppermost. Continue in this way for the whole line. Each sequin should evenly overlap the preceding one.

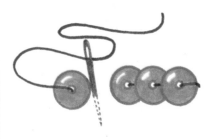

Sewing beads over cord

Piping cord can be used as a base and can be dyed to show through glass beads.

To attach the cord, place it on the line of the design and secure it with three over-casting stitches at each end and with three straight stitches from the fabric to the centre of the cord alternately each side. To cover the cord with beads, bring up the thread at the side of the cord, slide on enough beads to cover the cord from side to side and insert the needle into the fabric on the opposite side of the cord. Repeat this over the entire length of the cord, keeping the beading tightly packed and with the same number of beads for each stitch.

Attaching bugle beads

Bugle beads can be sewn flat, arranged in regular numbers to produce a repeat pattern. For example three or four beads could be placed vertically followed by the same number placed horizontally. Or they could be arranged in blocks in a brick pattern.

Some beads are set in metal mounts which have channels through which the thread passes or they might have a hole in the centre or at either end. Both kinds can be attached as for heavy beads.

Fastening on and off

Never use a knot for fastening on and off. Work all ends in securely on the back of the work, keeping it as neat as possible.

A touch of luxury

Add a touch of exclusive luxury to your clothes with this spray motif of beads and paillettes. For a very individual look, beading has been worked here onto the patterned velvet bodice of a smock dress. Tiny pearls and beads in shades of brown and gold subtly pick up the colours of the fabric. Paillettes and feather stitch trim give the dress an exotic air.

To work the embroidery

1 If the beading is to be worked on a garment you are making yourself, do it before sewing the seams. Outline the shape of the pattern piece, then position and trace the outline of the motif, either with tacking stitches or light chalk lines.

Attaching the beads

2 On a casual dress which will receive more wear than a special occasion dress, the beads should be attached as securely as possible. Thread used for beading should be the finest and strongest silk or cotton available and should match the background fabric. Use the thread double and draw it across a piece of beeswax for extra strength. Special beading needles, long and very fine, are available in sizes 10–13. To sew the beads on, fasten the thread securely on the underside of the fabric. Bring the beading needle to the front of the work and slide one bead along the needle and onto the thread. Pick up a tiny piece of fabric, the length of the bead along the design line. Draw the needle through the fabric and place the bead in position. Pick up the second bead.

Attaching the paillettes

1 Use stranded cotton, either matching or in direct contrast to the colour of the paillettes and fabric. The web of stitchery circling the paillette is attractive enough to be a feature of the design. Work with 3 strands of cotton in the needle. Hold the paillette in place with your left thumb and take a stitch across it four times (Figure A). Make a small stitch over the crossed threads at each of the four corners (Figure B).

2 Place the needle at right angles to the square of thread and pick up a small piece of fabric just outside the edge of the paillette, keeping the thread to the right and under the needlepoint. Draw the thread through, keeping the stitch flat (Figure C). Still with the thread to the right, push the needle under the thread forming the square and over the thread emerging from the fabric (Figure D). Repeat the last two steps, working clockwise round the paillette until the circle is complete and the foundation threads covered.

Ideas for using the motif

Work the spray motif as a bold contrast or as a subtle highlight on a dress bodice, a wide waistband, or on the flap of a velvet bag. Try making up your own motif; this one is the simplest possible arrangement of curving lines. Play around with simple flowing shapes, place beads on a scrap of fabric, move them around and see how they look.

Beware of enthusiatically over-beading. A simple motif has impact, while too many beads, especially on a printed fabric, can look unattractive.

Chart for position of beads and paillettes

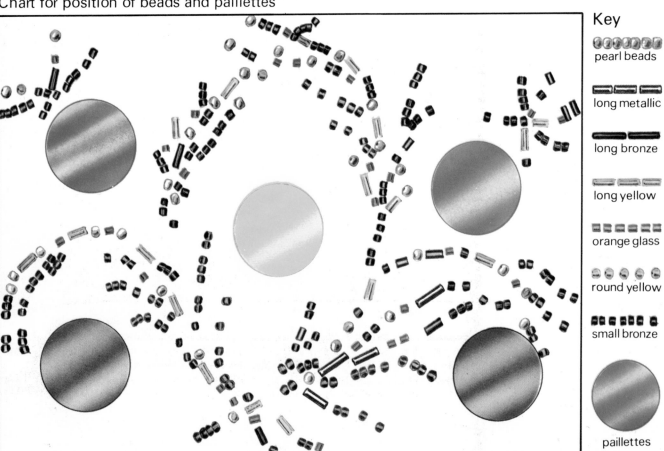

Key

pearl beads

long metallic

long bronze

long yellow

orange glass

round yellow

small bronze

paillettes

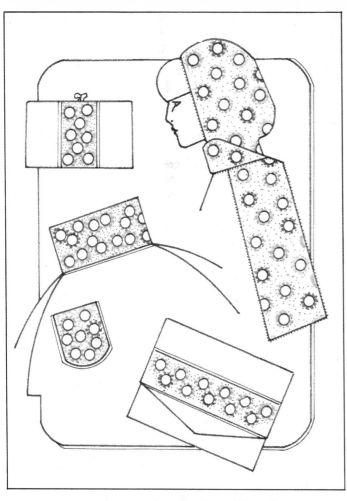

Other ideas for using the bead motif

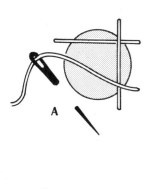

A

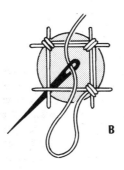

B

Attaching the paillettes

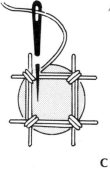

C

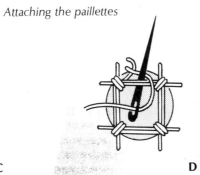

D

Feather stitch

BEAD WEAVING

Bead weaving is an ancient craft used to make a garment, jewellery or a wall decoration. Traditionally it has been a craft associated with South America. Bead weaving is used to decorate parts of some national costumes, and has developed into a highly decorative and sophisticated art form. Egyptians also used bead weaving and traces of it have been found in tombs dating back over 3,000 years.

The equipment

Little equipment is needed for bead weaving apart from a beading loom and beading needles. The looms are inexpensive to buy or you could construct one from a wooden or cardboard box by cutting notches along the edge or by hammering tacks along the edge for small pieces of work. The notches or tacks hold the warp threads and the spaces between them should be equal to the length of the beads.

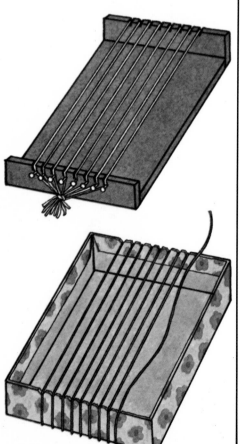

The beads

Any type of bead can be used, although glass, ceramic, wooden or plastic ones are the easiest to work with. Choose beads of equal size for an even piece of weaving.

Needles and thread

Both the beading needle and thread must be fine enough to pass twice through the bead. Depending on the size of the beads, pure silk, linen, cotton, or carpet threads can be used. Do not use a synthetic thread because this tends to stretch. All threads should be waxed with beeswax to strengthen them and make the beads slide on easily.

The pattern

The finished bead weaving can be used for a belt, an evening bag, cuffs and collar for a dress, or a piece of jewellery such as a bracelet or necklace.

It is easiest to work from a chart which you can draft out for yourself on graph paper, with each square representing one bead of the design. Colouring the chart with ink or crayon in shades to represent the colours of the beads being used, enables the chart to be read easily while you are working.

A geometric pattern will often produce the most effective pieces of bead weaving, and is easiest to follow if you intend to build up your own pattern. Alternatively, charts for canvas embroidery or cross-stitch can be used and adapted so that one bead represents each stitch marked on the chart.

Setting up the loom

The vertical threads of the design are known as the warp, and these fit into the grooves cut into the combs or bridges on the loom. The beads lie between the warp threads so you should decide how far apart to position the threads and set up the loom accordingly. There should always be one more warp thread than there are beads in the width of the pattern. The weaving is strengthened when you are using fine threads if the two outer warp threads are made double. To set up the loom:

1 Cut the warp threads to the length of the beading you require plus 15cm (*6 inches*).
2 Knot the warp threads into small equal

bunches, pass them over the roller at the end of the loom and tie them securely to the nail or hook supplied on the roller.
3 Stretch the warp threads tightly across both combs or bridges on the loom making sure that each warp thread lies in the correct groove. If you are using small beads, the warp threads should lie closely together. With larger beads they should be spaced further apart so that the beads will fit easily between them.
4 Wind the surplus warp thread around the pegs or nails at the opposite end of the loom, making sure that they are evenly taut to give a good tension to the weaving.

Starting to weave

1 Thread the needle with the working thread and attach it securely with a knot to the double thread on the left of the warp threads. If you are using very fine beads, you can give a firm edge to the weaving by working a few rows of darning stitch under and over the warp threads before starting to use the beads.
2 Thread the required number of beads on to the needle for the first row of the pattern, working from left to right.
3 Place the string of beads under the warp threads and position each bead between two warp threads. Press the string of beads up between the warp threads with the fingers of your left hand.

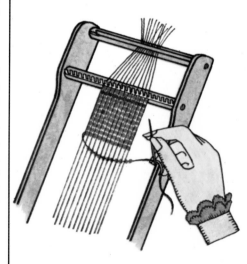

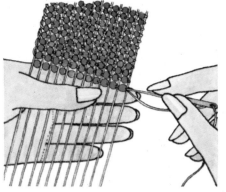

4 Bring the needle out round the last warp threads and pass it back from right to left over the warp threads and through the hole of each bead, thus securing the beads in position. Keep the tension as even as possible to avoid distorting the edge of the weaving.

5 Work the remaining rows of the pattern in the same way.

6 When the work is the required length, work a row, or two of darning stitch if you are using fine small beads, and then take the working thread back through the last but one row of beads and cut the end. Lift the warp threads from the loom and darn each thread back through the beads or in and out of the thread between the beads. Cut the thread, making sure you leave no loose ends.

7 If you are making a long length of weaving, work over the warp threads on the loom, then loosen them, wind the weaving round the roller and stretch the unwoven warp threads into the correct position for weaving. Tighten the roller by re-positioning the pin which secures it.

SMOCKING:
Basic techniques

No other form of embroidery is quite so simple or so effective as smocking. Through the combined devices of gathering into pleats and subsequent decorative stitching, the appearance of the surface of a fabric and of a whole garment is altered in the most attractive way.

The history of smocking

The initial purpose of smocking was utilitarian; it was found to be an effective method of controlling fullness in an English labourer's garment. By the eighteenth century, the popular 'smock frock' had become decorative as well as durable and, in the next century, this garment reached its peak in elaboration. Ultimately the smocked area was combined with a variety of embroidered patterns, the pattern chosen depending on the trade of the wearer. This embroidery usually adorned the 'box', an area on either side of the smocking, and sometimes the collar and cuffs. Many surviving smocks are identifiable as having belonged to gardeners, shepherds and milkmaids, by the pattern of flowers, staffs, hearts and other similar forms on each.

The designs worked on these hardwearing linen smock frocks were seldom drawn on to the fabric before working, as the needlewomen who worked them developed a keen eye for following the thread of the fabric. The most frequently used fabric was heavy weight linen, often in a natural, unbleached colour, with the embroidery worked in a twisted linen thread. Both materials were sturdy enough for a garment which had to accommodate activity and ease of movement.

There were no curves at all in the design of the basic smock; it was, instead, entirely a composition of squares and rectangles. One popular style was reversible, with a square opening for the head, and another had a wide embroidered collar. Although all the working in the smocked area was traditionally a variation of stem or outline stitches, a number of stitches were used for other decorative embroidery on a garment. Among these stitches were feather stitch, chain stitch, stem stitch, satin stitch and faggot stitch. As in smocking today, the success of these smocks depend upon accuracy and even tension in smocking, as well as a carefully executed choice of stitches.

Smocking today

Over the years, the range of uses for smocking has widened to include an attractive variety of garments for children and adults. Children's clothes, women's nightdresses, blouses and dresses are all particularly suited to the texture and shape which smocking gives.

Fabric

Among the materials suitable for smocking are linen, cotton, nylon, voile and velvet. Any fabric that can be easily gathered is ideal for this purpose. The garment itself will determine the most suitable weight for the fabric to be used. Be sure to allow adequate width for the smocking – about three times the finished width is a general

Surface honeycomb stitch reduces fullness at waist and upper sleeve.

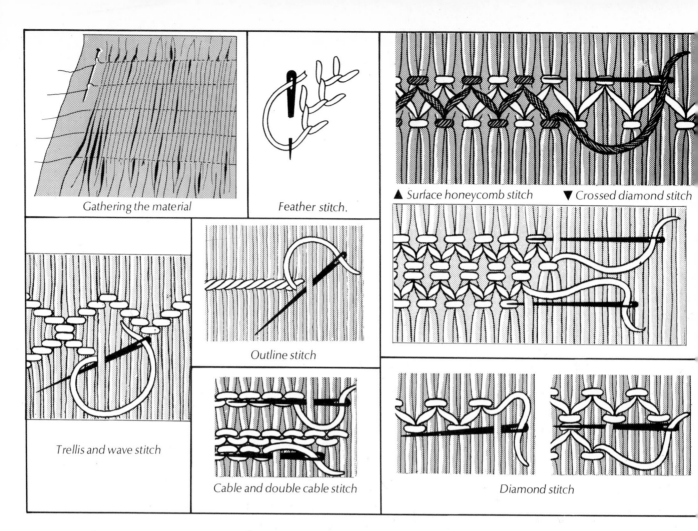

Gathering the material

Feather stitch.

▲ *Surface honeycomb stitch*　▼ *Crossed diamond stitch*

Outline stitch

Trellis and wave stitch

Cable and double cable stitch

Diamond stitch

rule, although this depends upon the tension and elasticity of the stitches, the weight of the fabric used and the depth of the gathers.

Colour possibilities

As the decorative value of smocking does not depend on the colour – too much colour actually detracts from the effect of the stitching – plan ahead to make quite certain that the colour scheme is kept simple. There are three possibilities to consider when smocking: one may use threads in the same colour as the background fabric, threads in a contrasting colour, or threads of various colours. The effectiveness of matching threads is exemplified by the blouse illustrated. On this blouse a little colour has been introduced with some floral embroidery on the bodice, whereas the smocking itself is merely a part of the textured backdrop.

Thread

It is most important that the thread used for the smocking is suitable for the fabric on which it is being worked. Traditionally, a linen thread was used on linen fabric and cotton thread on cotton or similar fabric. In fact, most kinds of embroidery thread are suitable but, for most work, coton à

broder or pearl cotton may be used in a medium sized crewel or embroidery needle. Always work the smocking before a garment is made up. Mark the area to be smocked with a tacking stitch following the thread of the material.

Smocking transfers

Ideally, transfers should not be used for smocking, as they are rarely evenly printed and it is difficult to follow the thread of the fabric. If, however, a smocking transfer is used, the spacings between the dots should be determined by the weight of the fabric (a coarse material requiring more widely spaced dots than a fine material). Iron the dots on to the wrong side of the material, aligning them with the weave of the material as accurately as possible. An alternative method of using a transfer is to mark the dots on the fabric with a sharp pencil and a ruler. This is, in most cases a more accurate way of aligning the dots on the fabric.

Gathering up the fabric

To gather up each row, use a strong thread with a secure knot at one end. Begin on the right side of the first row of dots and pick up a few threads at each one. At the end of the row, leave the thread unknotted.

Then, after running across the second row of dots, tie the two loose ends together. Continue in this way, tying each pair of threads together along the left hand side of the work. Remember, too, that when it is worked, smocking is flat on the surface but has a certain amount of bulk underneath.

The gathered lines should be pulled up so that the folds in the fabric become a series of close, parallel tubes. After drawing up all the rows of gathers, turn the fabric over and begin to smock.

Smocking stitches

Feather stitch, honeycomb and similar stitches are a modern innovation in smocking; the original smock frocks were worked only in variations of stem or outline stitch. Most smocking stitches are worked from left to right with two notable exceptions, which are worked from right to left. It is particularly important to remember that the only knot in the stitchery must be at the beginning of the row; remember, therefore, to have enough thread in the needle at the beginning of a row to complete that row. After completing the work, remove the tacking threads and discover the elasticity of the stitchery on the garment.

Smocking on heavy fabrics

A mixture of stem, wave and straight stitches ideal for working on heavy fabrics.

Smocking can be just as attractive when worked on heavier fabrics as on traditional fine lawns and cottons.

Many of the same stitches can be used, although the fabric should be prepared in a slightly different way. The stitch used here is particularly suitable for heavy fabric.

Preparing the fabric

Because of the extra bulk when using heavy fabrics for smocking, allow only twice the required final width before gathering instead of the more usual three widths. If the fabric is spotted, striped or checked, the gathers can be worked using the pattern as a grid. If you are working on corduroy or needlecord the gathers can be worked by picking up alternate ribs, unless it has widely spaced ribs in which case a stitch should be worked on each one. If you are buying commercially printed dot transfers or are marking the grid yourself, they should be fairly widely spaced – approximately 1.3cm ($\frac{1}{2}$ inch) apart or even more for very heavy fabrics. If you are unsure, it is advisable to make some trial gathers on a small piece of spare fabric to see how tightly gathered it should be. The fabric should look well pleated and there should be no need to stroke the gathers down as they should lie in flat and even folds.

If you are smocking a definite pattern, count the number of rows and gathers required to complete the pattern accurately, and work the gathering to allow for this. This is particularly important with wide patterns such as open diamond, feather stitch and chevron.

The threads

Use pearl cotton, coton à broder, stranded cotton (use all six strands) or pure silk twist when smocking on heavy fabrics. It is possible to use a fine string or carpet thread on hessian and linen scrim.

The design

Plan the smocking design carefully before you start work as it could be spoilt unless a good balance is worked out with the

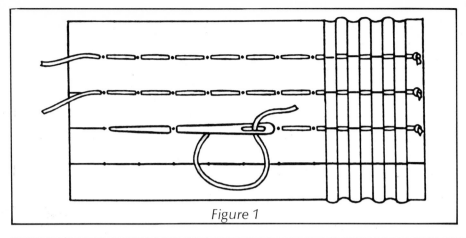

Figure 1

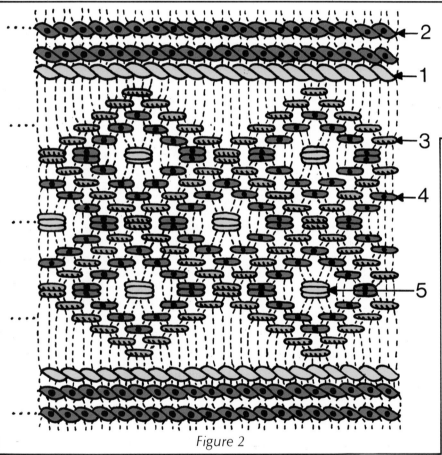

Figure 2

not pull too tightly as the finished garment must have elasticity.

Figure 2 indicates a section of the design repeated across the fabric. The dotted lines at the left hand side indicate the lines of gathers and the placing of stitches in relation to the rows. The vertical broken lines indicate the pleats.

Stem stitch Working from left to right, fasten the thread on the wrong side and bring the needle up through the first pleat. Pick up the top of the next pleat inserting the needle at a slight angle with the thread below the needle. Always work

Key

1–0303	**Stem stitch**
2–0352	
3–0309	**Wave stitch**
4–0352	
5–0303	**3 straight stitches**

the thread over two pleats but pick up only one (figure 3).

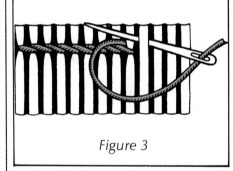

Figure 3

Wave stitch Working from left to right fasten the thread on the wrong side and bring the needle through to the left of the first pleat. Take a stitch through the second pleat on the same level with the thread below the needle. Take a stitch on the third pleat slightly higher than the previous pleat with the thread still below the needle. Continue in this way for five stitches finishing the top stitch with the thread above the needle. This completes the upward slope. Work in the same way on the downward slope except with the thread above the needle (figure 4).

Figure 4

various patterns. The fundamental smocking stitch is stem or outline stitch and this should be used at the beginning of the work along the edges of the border to give it a firm foundation. The modern introductions of feather stitch and herringbone stitch are better used sparingly as they tend to mask the pleated background which is such an important characteristic of smocking.

The pattern shown in the photograph is a simple design using stem stitch and wave stitch and it can easily be adjusted for garments made from heavy fabrics.

Stem stitch and wave stitch pattern

Mark the areas to be embroidered on the wrong side of pieces to be smocked within the rectangles already marked. Use a soft pencil or tailor's chalk for this and draw fine parallel lines 1.3cm ($\frac{1}{2}$ *inch*) apart. Using the horizontal lines as a guide, work five rows of gathering stitches, making sure that the stitches correspond exactly on each line (figure 1). Pick up a small thread only at regular intervals and leave a loose thread at the end of each row.

Pull up the lines of gathering, easing gently to form pleats. Do not pull up too tightly as the pleats must be flexible enough to work the stitches over. Tie the loose ends together in pairs close to the last pleat.

When working the smocking stitches, do

Honeycomb smocked bedspread

Fabric required

Cotton gingham with 2.5cm (1 inch) checks. To calculate the amount of fabric needed, measure the width and the length of the bed. Add 1.3cm ($\frac{1}{2}$ inch) for turnings and 10cm (4 inches) for the pillows.

For the gathered flounce, measure from the edge of the bed to the floor and, to allow fullness and a half for the gathering, multiply the length of the bed by 3 and the width by $1\frac{1}{2}$.

You will also need

- ☐ 6–7 skeins stranded embroidery cotton to match the gingham
- ☐ Crewel embroidery needle
- ☐ Regular sewing thread

Making up

1 Mount each piece of gingham with a plain piece of fabric. Tack all round the edge.

2 Join the pieces for the flounce, matching the checks of the gingham carefully. Press the turnings open.

Working the smocking

The smocking is different from regular smocking in that the fabric is not gathered first. The stitches are worked on the corners of the gingham squares and form a honeycomb pattern.

1 Working from right to left on the right side of the fabric, leave a complete gingham square along the top and right hand edge of the flounce. Using three strands of embroidery thread, knot the end of the cotton and make a small stitch at the bottom right hand corner of the first square.

2 Pass the thread along the front of the fabric and make another small stitch at the bottom right hand corner of the next square. Pull the thread tight, thus drawing the first and second stitches together. Make another half back stitch and pass the needle on to the wrong side of the

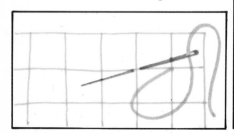

fabric. This completes the first honeycomb stitch.

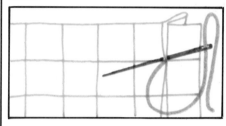

3 Still with the needle on the wrong side, bring it out at the corner of the next square.

4 Keep the fabric flat between the previous stitch and this point and make a small back stitch to secure the thread. Then pass the needle along the front of the fabric and make a small stitch at the corner of the next square.

Pull the thread tight to draw the third and fourth squares together.

5 Continue like this until six honeycomb stitches have been made.

6 Move to the row below and work five honeycomb stitches in the alternate

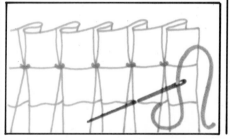

spaces to the row above so you are joining the second square to the third, the fourth to the fifth and so on.

7 Work four honeycomb stitches centrally in the third row so you are omitting the first and sixth stitches of the first row.

8 Work three honeycomb stitches in the fourth row, two stitches in the fifth row and one stitch in the sixth row to complete the V shape.

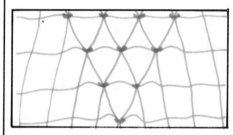

9 Work the next blocks of stitches in the same way all along the length of the flounce. You will now see how the space between the blocks forms an inverted 'V' shape.

Attaching the flounce

1 When all the smocking has been worked, it will form into pleats automatically along the top edge of the flounce. Pin these down and secure with tacking.

2 Make narrow hems along the side edges of the flounce.

3 Pin the top edge of the flounce round the edge of the main section of the bedspread and machine stitch taking 1.3cm ($\frac{1}{2}$ inch) turnings. Neaten the turnings and press them on to the main section.

4 Make a hem along the top edge of the main section.

5 Try the bedspread on to the bed and mark the hem line so that it just clears the floor.

6 Stitch the hem and press the finished bedspread.

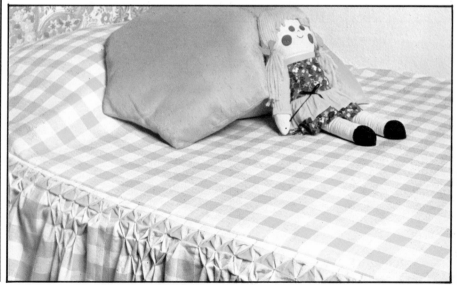

Pleated smocked cushions

Sizes

Square cushion: 38cm (*15 inches*) square
Round cushion: 40.5cm (*16 inches*) diameter, 10cm (*4 inches*) thick

Fabric required

For square cushion:
61cm (*24 inches*) lightweight furnishing velvet, 122cm (*48 inches*) wide
For round cushion:
90cm (*36 inches*) lightweight furnishing velvet, 122cm (*48 inches*) wide

You will also need

☐ Buttonhole thread to match velvet
☐ Graph paper for making pattern
☐ Tacking thread in different colours
☐ 2 button moulds, 2.5cm (*1 inch*) diameter
☐ Cushion pads in the same sizes as the finished covers
☐ Transfer pencil (optional)

The smocking

This sort of smocking is different from conventional smocking in that the stitches are all worked on the wrong side of the fabric and do not show on the right side. The fullness is not reduced by gathering but simply by drawing points of fabric together to give a decorative pleated finish on the right side.

Although velvet has been used for the cushions in the photograph, this method of smocking is also very attractive on satin or gingham.

The pattern

Each line of smocking is worked over three vertical rows of dots, spaced 2.5cm (*1 inch*) apart. It is possible to buy transfers of the dots which can be ironed on to the fabric but it is quite simple and much less expensive – particularly if you are making several cushions – to draw your own pattern and transfer the dots to the fabric with tailor's tacks. Alternatively, you could mark the dots on the pattern with a transfer pencil and then iron on to the fabric with a cool iron.

Making the pattern

Using graph paper, draw the pattern for the cushion shape you are making to scale. One square = 2.54cm square (*1 inch square*). If you are making the square cushion, mark the dots for each line of smocking in different colours as shown so you can easily see where the rows overlap. Repeat rows two and three until you have ten rows in all.

The square cushion
Cutting out

Cut the fabric in half to make two pieces, 61cm square (*24 inches square*). Place the pieces together and pin pattern centrally to them. Mark the dots with tailor's tacks, using different coloured thread for the rows as indicated on the pattern. Unpin the pattern, cut through the tacks and open out the fabric. Work the smocking on each piece separately.

Working the smocking

For ease of working the dots are numbered to show the order of the stitches. It may seem very confusing as you start but after the first few smocked pleats are formed you will soon get into the rhythm.

1 With the wrong side of the fabric facing up, start at dot 1 in the top left hand corner. Using a long length of buttonhole thread, knot the end and make a small stitch at dot 1. Pass the thread along the fabric and make another small stitch at dot 2 in the line of dots to the left.

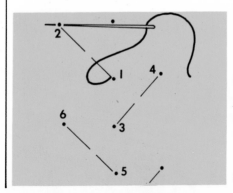

2 Go back to dot 1, make another small stitch over the one already there and then pull dots 1 and 2 together. Knot them tightly by making a loop of the thread above the stitches and passing the needle under the stitches and through the loop. Be careful not to catch the fabric as you do this or the stitch will show on the right side.

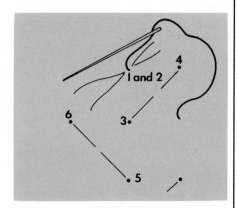

3 Pass the thread along the fabric to dot 3 and make a small stitch. Keep the fabric completely flat between dots 1 and 3, make a loop of the thread above dot 3 and slip the needle under the thread between the dots and above the loop to make another knot. Do not draw up the thread between the dots.

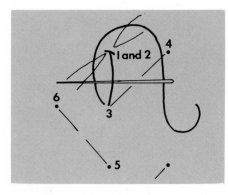

4 Pass the thread along the fabric to dot 4, make a small stitch, go back to dot 3 and make another small stitch. Pull dots 3 and 4 together and knot them as for dots 1 and 2.

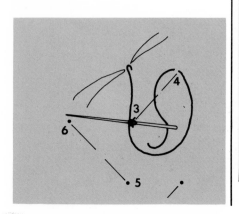

5 Move down to dot 5 and knot the thread keeping the fabric flat, as at dot 3. Pick up a small stitch at dot 6 and join it to dot 5 in the same way as before.

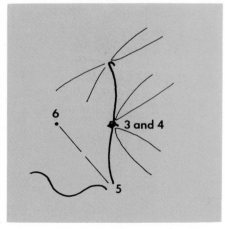

6 Continue down the whole line in this way, picking up a dot on the left, moving down to the next dot in the middle row and then picking up a dot on the right.
7 Work all the lines of smocking in the same way, and then smock the other side of the cushion cover.

Finishing off

1 When the smocking is complete, you will find that pleats have formed all round the edge. Pin these down evenly and tack in position, checking that each side of cover measures 38cm (15 inches). Pin the pleats on the other side of the cover in a similar way, but with the pleats facing the opposite direction so that when the sides of the cover are put together the pleats will match.
2 Place the sides of the cover together and tack and machine stitch round three sides, taking 1.3cm (½ inch) turnings.
3 Insert the cushion pad, fold under the turnings of the opening and slip-stitch the folds together.

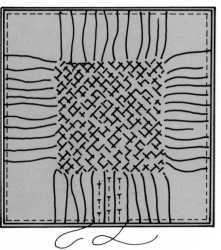

The round cushion
Cutting out

Cut the fabric in half to make two pieces, 90cm × 61cm (36 inches × 24 inches). Join the pieces along the longer edges, taking 1.3cm (½ inch) turnings and making sure that the pile runs the same way on both pieces. Trim the length of the fabric to 178cm × 53cm (70 inches × 21 inches) and use the spare piece to cover the button moulds.
Fold the fabric right side out along the seam line. Place on the pattern with the line indicated to the fold. Mark all the dots with tailor's tacks. Unpin the pattern, cut through the tacks and open out the fabric.

Working the smocking

1 Join the short ends of the fabric, taking 1.3cm (½ inch) turnings. The smocking is then worked in a continuous round.
2 Work the smocking in a similar way as for the square cushion. The finished effect will be less tightly plaited than the square cushion because the lines are spaced apart.

Finishing off

1 Using strong thread, attach the end securely 0.6cm (¼ inch) from the edge of the fabric.
2 Form the nearest pleat with your fingers and make a small stitch through the fold. Draw up the thread tightly.

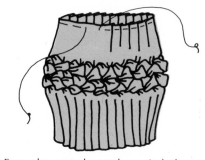

3 Form the next pleat, take a stitch through the fold and pull it up to meet the first pleat. Continue all round the cushion.
4 Insert Pad. Repeat on other side.
5 Sew the covered buttons to the centre of each side of the cushion.

Graph for square cushion
1 Square = 2·5cm (1 inch)

Graph for round cushion
1 Square = 2·5cm (1 inch)

Square cushion grid — columns headed ROW 1, ROW 2, ROW 3

ROW 1		ROW 2		ROW 3	
2		2		2	
	1	4	1	4	1
6	3	6	3	6	3
	5	8	5	8	5
10	7	10	7	10	7
	9	12	9	12	9
14	11	14	11	14	11
	13	16	13	16	13
18	15	18	15	18	15
	17	20	17	20	17
22	19	22	19	22	19
	21	24	21	24	21
26	23	26	23	26	23
	25	28	25	28	25
30	27	30	27	30	27
	29	32	29	32	29
34	31	34	31	34	31
	33	36	33	36	33
38	35	38	35	38	35
	37	40	37	40	37
	39		39		39

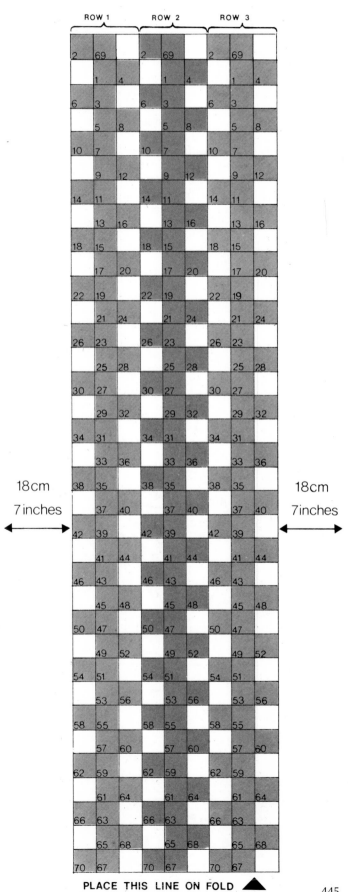

18cm / 7 inches

18cm / 7 inches

PLACE THIS LINE ON FOLD ▲

445

CANDLEWICKING

Candlewick originated in the United States in early Colonial days when, with a severe shortage of sewing materials of all kinds, women settlers used the thick cotton wick intended for candlemaking as an embroidery thread, working it into knotted and tufted designs on bedspreads. For many years the use of candlewick was restricted to bedspreads, but it looks effective in many other forms and can be used for cushions, rugs and bath mats as well as for warm garments such as dressing gowns.

Materials for candlewick

There are two kinds of candlewicking, tufted and smooth, but for both types it is essential that the material on which the embroidery is worked should shrink on the first washing to secure the candlewick in the fabric.

Usually, unbleached calico is used for candlewick, but linen can also be used. It is important to choose a weave which will take two thicknesses of the candlewick cotton.

The trace design given in this chapter is adaptable for almost any use and builds up extremely well, placing the motifs as linking squares. It can be used for both tufted and smooth types of candlewicking and parts of the design might be adapted for a matching border motif.

Yarn

Strutts Candlewick Cotton is used for candlewick and is sold in skeins, available in a variety of colours. Skeins can be cut into 122cm (48 inch) lengths or wind the yarn into a ball and use as required.

Needles

A special candlewick needle is used; this is fairly large with a flattened, curved point and a big eye.

Scissors

It is essential to have scissors which are extremely sharp for cutting the loops. A blunt pair will drag and pull the tufts out of the fabric.

Designs

Designs for candlewick are most effective when based on geometric shapes, but flowing designs can also be used if they are large sized. Small, intricate patterns are difficult to work and the shapes become distorted with the tufting. The candlewick can follow the outlines of the design, can fill in some areas, or cover the background completely as an all over design, giving a solid area of pile texture.

Tufted candlewick

In some early examples of candlewick French knots and backstitch were used, but in modern embroidery the stitch mainly used is running stitch worked 0.6cm to 1.3cm ($\frac{1}{4}$ to $\frac{1}{2}$ inch) apart along the line of the design, leaving a small loop between each stitch. To keep the loops of even length place a pencil under the cotton as each loop is made. The candlewick yarn is used double. Cut a length twice as long as is required and thread it through the needle until the ends are level. It is not necessary to finish off the ends when starting or finishing – begin on the right side of the fabric, leaving an end equal to the size of the completed tuft and end in the same way.

When all the design is completely worked cut the loops evenly with a very sharp pair of scissors.

Smooth candlewick

This type of candlewick is worked simply in running stitch. One double length of cotton is used in the needle as for tufted candlewick and the stitches are worked about 0.6cm ($\frac{1}{4}$ inch) long and 0.6cm ($\frac{1}{4}$ inch) apart. This results in a bead-like stitch giving a beautifully raised, sculptured effect. This type of candlewick is at its best worked in geometric designs built up into solid shapes and covering the entire area of the fabric.

Finishing candlewick

The completed work should be washed

A trace design for working in either tufted or smooth candlewicking.

A detail of the design above worked in tufted stitch and showing the reverse.

Smooth candlewick in a modern bedspread.

so that the fabric shrinks to fix the tufts more securely and to fluff them up. If a washing machine is used, wash for at least 20 minutes in warm soapy water. If washing by hand let the work soak for three to four hours. Do not wring or squeeze, just shake out.

Dry the work out of doors in a strong breeze and shake it frequently whilst drying to eliminate creasing and to make the tufts fluffier. Brush the tufts lightly with a soft brush before they are quite dry to fluff them up.

It is best to avoid ironing candlewick as this will flatten the tufts.

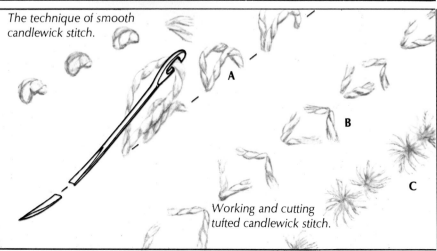

The technique of smooth candlewick stitch.

A

B

C

Working and cutting tufted candlewick stitch.

MACHINE EMBROIDERY
BASIC EQUIPMENT

Although the sewing machine is a standard piece of equipment in so many homes, it is seldom used for embroidery and many people are not even aware of its decorative potential. In these chapters we introduce you to the simpler aspects of machine embroidery and a whole new range of decorative effects and stitches, many of which can be created with even the simplest straight stitch machine.

Machine embroidery is not only a quick method of decorating clothes and furnishings. It can be as delicate as traditional hand embroidery or as bold and chunky as a rug or a heavy woven wall hanging. The possibilities are endless. The other important aspect of the craft is the use of the machine to hold applied fabrics, braids, wool, weaving yarn or even string to the background. In this case the machining may be nearly invisible or used to supplement the texture of the applied material.

Basic Equipment

The only equipment needed for machine embroidery is a sewing machine, fabric, thread, a frame and tracing paper.

Your Machine

It is a common misapprehension that a special sewing machine is needed for machine embroidery. This is not so. There is a great deal you can do on a straight stitch machine and if your machine does even a simple zig-zag you can do a great deal more, whilst the effects with an automatic machine are unlimited.

Most modern machines have a drop feed, that is a control to lower the feed for darning and embroidery while others require a plate which will fit over the feed. To adapt a machine, when it is not possible to obtain a plate, the throat plate may be removed and small washers inserted under it before returning the screws. This raises the throat plate to the level of the teeth at their highest point.

Whichever machine you use it is essential that it is in perfect working order as it receives far more wear during embroidery than dressmaking due to the speed at which it is worked. The machine must be cleaned and oiled regularly. Oil before use rather than after as fine oil tends to evaporate. Run the threaded machine over a spare piece of fabric before starting your work to remove the excess oil. Check foot controls and motors occasionally for overheating and if this occurs have your machine serviced.

Fabrics

Many fabrics are suitable for machine embroidery. It is important however that the fabric being worked should be firmly woven so avoid stretch and knitted fabrics such as jersey or crepe which pull out of shape when framed. Embroidery will not give with these fabrics. However, for a technique such as appliqué work, where the individual shapes need not necessarily be held in a frame, this elasticity is in fact an advantage.

As framing is so important, and practice is needed to get the fabric into the rings tightly without tearing, the beginner should choose to work on medium weight fabrics such as sailcloth or dress-weight linens. With more experience exciting and varied effects can be achieved using net, and fine fabrics such as cotton organdie and even plastics and leather.

Thread

Machine embroidery thread is supplied in two thicknesses, 50 and 30. The 50 is the finer of the two while 30 is comparable in weight to ordinary machine dressmaking thread. 50 should always be used in the

spool unless a thicker thread is needed for special effect. 40 and 50 sewing cotton are needed for variety in the weight of stitching and for whip-stitch, while a collection of wool and hand embroidery thread is always useful.

Invisible thread is invaluable to the more experienced embroiderer. It is available in light and dark tones and is useful for sewing on fabric pieces when an exact colour match cannot be made. It gives a rich glint to the work when used for free embroidery and is best used with machine embroidery thread in the spool partly to provide colour interest and partly because it will not stand a warm iron. Therefore work should be pressed from the back.

Glitter threads are also available and handicraft shops will provide a variety of textured threads for appliqué work.

Frames

The frame comprising of two interlocking frames with an adjustable screw is an essential piece of equipment. A 20.5cm – 25.5cm (8 inch – 9 inch) frame is ideal for beginners. The more experienced embroiderer may prefer a 30.5cm (12 inch) frame. A very small frame is useful for eyelets and working in corners. The most satisfactory frames are made of wood, are narrow enough in depth to pass under the raised machine needle and have a screw adjustment for extra tightening. Plastic frames are not as good as they do not grip the fabric so well, particularly if it is slippery, although covering the inner ring with tape or bias binding may help. Metal frames have the disadvantage of being too deep to slide easily under the needle on most machines and need complete screw adjustment every time the frame is moved on the fabric.

Tracing paper

For marking out designs use dressmaking tracing paper. It can be pricked and pounced as for hand embroidery (see the chapter on Transferring designs). If the structure of the design is in a straight stitch the main lines may be transferred to the cloth by machining over the paper with the presser foot down, then tearing the paper away. If the design is heavily drawn on the paper with felt tip pen, it is possible

to trace it directly on to the fabric by taping the paper to a window with the fabric over it. Use a tailors chalk pencil for a dark fabric and a sharp, hard pencil for a light fabric, making a dotted rather than a solid line.

This striking fish design is an example of machine embroidery used to great effect on the table mats shown above.

STITCHES
Automatic stitches

Automatic stitches can be used for a wide variety of pleasing designs on clothes and furnishings. They can be used to good effect with applied pieces of fabric, braid or ribbon, for border patterns and decorative motifs for casual wear, for children's clothes and to give the most ordinary household linens a luxury look. Automatic stitches must be used selectively; if too many stitches are combined in one design, the results can be confused and un-attractive.

Many machines only make stitches based on the side to side throw of the needle, but some combine this with a backwards and forwards motion of the feed thus making a much wider range of stitches available.

Automatic stitching is normally worked using the presser foot in the usual way without framing the fabric. Worked freely in the frame they completely lose their effect unless you have acquired the skill of moving the frame smoothly with your left hand while operating the stitch lever with your right hand. This will come with practice. Free machine embroidery will be described in more detail later in this section.

The stitching can be done with 30 or 50 machine embroidery cotton which gives a smoother and more lustrous effect than sewing cotton or with a thicker thread to give a bolder effect. To prevent the thread fraying, it is essential that the needle is large enough for the thread to pass easily down the groove and through the eye. If a very thick thread is used it must be put in the spool, a technique which will be more fully described in a later chapter. The stitch should always be tested on spare fabric before you begin your design. The space between the stitches should be adjusted to achieve the desired stitch density according to the thickness of thread.

Some degree of tension is essential on upper and lower threads but swing needle work tends to pull up the fabric more than straight stitching. To counteract this, the upper tension should be slackened as much as possible without affecting the even appearance of the stitching. The

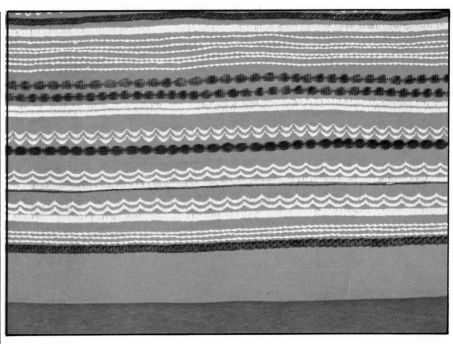

lower tension may also be loosened but in the absence of a numbered dial remember to memorise the pull of the thread and the position of the screw groove in relation to its socket. In this way the tension may be easily reset for normal sewing. It is often necessary to back the fabric to prevent it pulling up when the needle swings, or stretching when machining on the bias. The finer the fabric the more important it is to back it. The ideal backing is vanishing muslin which tears away easily after stitching but medium weight paper is a good substitute. Vilene should only be used if a permanent stiffness is required. The fabrics should be firmly tacked to whatever backing is used.

Automatic patterns need not be limited to straight lines of stitching along the straight grain of the fabric. It is not difficult to follow gently curving lines using the right hand to open and close the stitch width lever to give further variety. It is also possible to put the fabric into an embroidery frame, replacing the presser foot when the frame is under the needle. This method is suitable for a series of small shapes or a design with short lines radiating out from the centre. Check that your frame is small enough in diameter to pass

completely round the needle while resting on the throat plate of your machine. Framing will be described in more detail later in this section.

These patterns may be made even more exciting if shaded threads are used. An interesting effect is sometimes achieved by using different coloured threads above and below and tightening the upper tension or loosening the lower tension to give the stitch spool coloured edges.

You could use any simple smock pattern with plain square yoke and cap sleeves. The design, embroidered in two colours, uses twin needles for the double patterns such as the scallops and a stretch stitch for the heavy lines. The satin stitch is used to stabilize the whole design. Automatic stitches will differ from machine to machine but similar effects can be achieved on most machines.

The design is worked before the smock is made up. Be sure to cut out the pattern pieces allowing approximately 5cm (2 inches) all round to make handling easier during embroidery. Allow extra when buying your fabric. Mark each pattern piece and the design areas with tailors chalk or tacking and work each piece starting at its lowest edge.

Design using free machine embroidery

It is in free machine embroidery that skill and imagination can come fully into play. The sewing machine is a very sensitive drawing instrument and while mastery of this craft takes practice it can be very rewarding. Even a beginner can soon produce spontaneous designs of great freshness and originality.

Consult your machine manual to find out how to convert your machine. If it is an old model the instructions may come under the heading of darning. The feed will either be covered with a special plate or will be retractable (see the opening chapter on Machine Embroidery).

Frame your work carefully. To do this lay the outer ring on a flat, level surface, lay your fabric right side up across it and press the inner into the outer ring. The screw should have been adjusted so that relatively heavy pressure is required to achieve this. Tighten the fabric by pulling it upwards and inwards to prevent the rings dislodging and taking care not to distort the threads. If there is any tendency for the fabric to slip back when pulled, the screw on the frame should be tightened and the pulling up process repeated until the fabric is stretched to its limit. It cannot be overstressed that the success of all kinds of free stitching depends on careful framing. If the work is loose it will tend to lift when the needle passes through it and the machine will miss stitches which may cause the thread to break. The tautness of the work is the only way in which the tension on the machine cotton is counteracted. Badly stretched work will not lie flat when removed from the frame and no amount of steam pressing will flatten it. Remove the presser foot and with the needle at its highest point slide the frame under. Draw the lower thread up through the fabric and lower the presser foot bar to re-set the tension on the upper thread. The stitch length lever should be set at 0. The size of the stitch is decided by the combination of the speed of the motor in conjunction with the speed at which you move the frame. Turn the stitch width lever to 0. Hold the frame to guide the fabric under the needle. With practice you will find the most comfortable position for your hands. The work is done mainly by the right hand which should swing from the shoulder to move the frame. Control will be greater if thumb and little finger are outside the frame and the remainder inside, being careful not to get them too close to the needle. The left hand should be flat on the work to hold the work down while steadying it. The little finger braced against the edge gives greater control. If the frame is 20.5cm (*8 inches*) or less it is probably safer to have both hands positioned on the frame. The left elbow should rest on the table. The fabric should not lift while stitching but the larger the frame the more likely it is to do so.

Hold both threads under your left forefinger while you start, to prevent them getting pulled down into the race and tangling. Run the machine fairly fast and move the frame smoothly. As a safety measure do not put your foot on to the foot control unit until you are ready to stitch and train yourself to remove it every time you stop. Aim to make 20 – 30 stitches to 2.5cm (*1 inch*) using a large sharp needle. Anything finer than a 14/90 needle is too flexible and may be broken on the edge of the plate. A 14/90 needle will take up to a 40 sewing cotton but anything thicker, such as buttonhole twist, will need the largest needle.

Although you may not have to alter your tension with some threads, if you use 50 machine embroidery cotton for instance, it is wise to loosen the tension by a couple of numbers. If the cotton snaps, loosen it until this no longer happens. If this results in a bad stitch, loosen the lower tension as well. However, the effect you get with a tighter top tension when your spool colour will show on top may be just the one you want. If you do loosen the lower tension be sure to memorize the normal pull and only adjust the screw by a quarter turn at a time.

When moving from one part of a frame to another raise the needle to its highest point, lift the presser foot bar to release the tension from the needle, move the frame to the new position, dip the needle down, lower the presser foot bar and continue. If at the end of a line of stitching you move your frame slowly to make small stitches which won't unravel, your ends can be cut off close to the work. If the back is to be visible, trim after the front but not so closely.

Apart from meticulous drawing, interesting filling textures can be made by running the machine at top speed and moving the frame backwards and forwards or in a small continuous circular movement. If the machine is set for zig-zag a heavy line can be made by moving the frame slowly. When the frame is moved from side to side with the needle swinging, large stitches can be made up to 1.3cm ($\frac{1}{2}$ *inch*) in length. These long stitches catch the light giving a quite different effect to the same movement done with a straight stitch. Always begin and end satin stitch with a few straight stitches or take the ends through and tie them.

The embroidered cloth

The circular, linen tablecloth illustrated is 122cm (*48 inches*) in diameter and divided into 8 sections. The motifs are worked using appliquéd fabric and eyelets (to be described in a later chapter) and free running stitch.

The design for each section was drawn on paper and tacked to the wrong side of the tablecloth. The fabric to be appliquéd was tacked to the right side and stitched in position from the wrong side using straight stitch and the presser foot. The excess appliquéd fabric was then cut away and satin stitch was used round the edges of the shapes. The paper was then torn away and the eyelets and free machining were worked from the right side in the frame.

The edges should be neatened with zig-zag stitch, turned to the wrong side and slip-stitched. Decorative stitching may then be used on the right side to conceal the hem.

Whip stitch

When embroidering by machine you can forget all the rules for normal sewing. For it is by using different colours and thicknesses of thread through the needle and through the spool and experimenting with different tensions that varied and original effects will be discovered.

One of the most effective variations of free running stitch is whip stitch. This stitch lends itself well to small curving designs and looks particularily striking when shaded thread is used in the spool. Use 50 machine embroidery cotton in the spool for best results and a 40 cotton on top. Tighten the upper tension 2 or 3 numbers above normal, run the machine fast and move the frame slowly. If the top thread breaks it may be necessary to loosen both tensions.

The top thread should be flat on the fabric pulling the spool thread up. The stitches should be close enough together to enclose the top thread, giving a raised, corded appearance. If the frame is moved quickly so that the stitches are separated the top thread is visible. Different coloured upper and lower threads produce a speckled line, but if you move the frame slowly again a solid line will result. A most attractive graded line can be obtained by smoothly increasing and decreasing the speed at which you move the frame. If the upper tension is not tightened enough the top thread will appear at uneven intervals producing a pleasing textural line. Side to side and circular textures are very effective using whip stitch settings.

Whip stitch ends should be taken to the back of the work and fastened, so lines should be continuous wherever possible. If the upper tension is set to its tightest and the lower tension very loose or the spool spring completely removed, a feather stitch is obtained. This is because the tight upper tension causes a loop of the spool thread to be pulled through to the right side with each stitch. This stitch should be worked in a continuous clockwise or anti-clockwise movement. If it is worked in a straight line the result is merely a series of untidy loops.

Remember that whenever the upper tension is slightly tighter than the lower tension, the top colour will be affected by the

colour in the spool and can be purposely deepened or lightened. Experiment by using a range of different colours in the spool and by varying the length of stitch. Whenever you change the direction of the frame movement there will be a concentration of the spool colour at the point of change and if you run the machine at full speed and move the frame in a series of pauses and jerks a dotted texture is obtained. This effect can be used to give tinted edges to filled in shapes.

With a tighter upper tension and the needle swinging, a satin stitch with spool coloured edges is obtained. If the frame is moved from side to side (full speed essential) in a series of pauses and jerks, crisp satin stitch bars will occur. Do not move the frame until each bar is of the required density.

These bars can be used freely or more formally by stopping the machine after each one to position the frame accurately for the next. If the needle stops on the wrong side to lead on to the next bar, turn the balance wheel by hand.

These bars could be used to make an attractive decoration for the centre of a self covered button or the centre of an embroidered flower. Being raised they catch the light and give a rich beaded look but are best worked with a stitch width of 2 or more.

To avoid unravelling never cut the threads between the bars. You may if you wish, conceal the connecting threads with straight free machining round the bars.

The panel illustrated is worked entirely in whip stitch using shaded thread on the spool and moving the frame slowly so that the needle thread is concealed.

Cable stitch

Cable stitch is a useful means of introducing heavy lines and textures into a design. It is often used with the presser foot for decorative top stitching but can also be used freely in the frame. The design is worked from the wrong side. Cable stitch is hard wearing and as such is particularly appropriate for articles which will be in constant use.

With cable stitch the top thread passing round the thick thread with each stitch protects it from the chafing it may receive if the thread is applied by stitching along its length.

The thick thread must be wound on the spool either by hand or on the spool winder. You should create slight tension with your fingers to ensure the thread winds evenly. The thread should be smooth enough not to clog the tension spring. The tension should be loosened so that the pull of the thread feels the same as for normal sewing and the stitch appears even. If you are embroidering an article which will receive a lot of wear use 30 machine embroidery cotton or ordinary sewing cotton on top. Should you have difficulty getting the thick thread through

the fabric when you dip the needle, pierce a hole with a bodkin. Some machines have a separate spool case and the tension screw and spring may be completely removed. Without the tension spring, threads the thickness of soft hand embroidery cotton can be used. Textured yarns can be used provided they are fine enough to pass easily through the hole in the side of the spool case. Be sure when replacing the spring to insert the end into the slot in the spool case before replacing the screw.

It is a good idea to wind several spools at once if you are working a lot of cable stitch as the thick thread runs out quickly. If the spool colour is being changed frequently it is a good idea to change the top cotton as well so that the shape of each colour area can be seen on the wrong side (the side from which you are working). This is a good method of producing very rich and varied textures. If the lower tension is released completely and you are using a fairly fine thread it will tend to be released too quickly from the spool making a pleasing, textural looped line.

Unless you are completely familiar with the reactions of your machine always work a test sample. Set the upper tension just tight enough to grip the heavy thread firmly. If it is very tight it can pull a fine to medium thickness thread through a loosely woven fabric to the wrong side giving a moss-like texture which can be used on the right side by reversing your fabric.

With some machines it is possible to get an effect like heavy whip stitch by greatly increasing the lower tension and moving the frame slowly so that the spool thread is encased by the top thread. Even if you cannot manage to entirely conceal the thick thread it is a very interesting way of working the more solid areas of a design and looks particularly effective if shaded thread is used on top.

Cable stitching and its variations are especially useful for dress embroidery as the design may be marked on the wrong side. When the cable stitching is completed it should give enough guidance for free stitching or other work on the right side without further marking.

The sample shows a freely drawn motif worked in cable stitch and free running stitch. To achieve the bobbled effect on the cable stitch, the tension screw and spring on the spool are completely removed. Silky hand embroidery thread is used on the spool and sewing cotton through the needle. Machine embroidery cotton is used on the spool and through the needle for the free running stitch which is worked after the cable stitch from the right side.

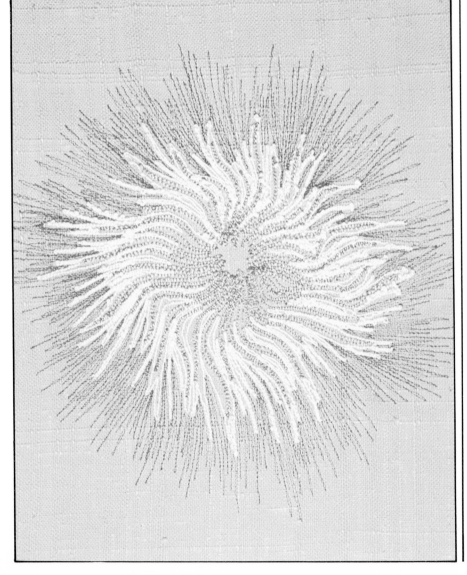

DECORATIVE EFFECTS
Shapes and appliqué

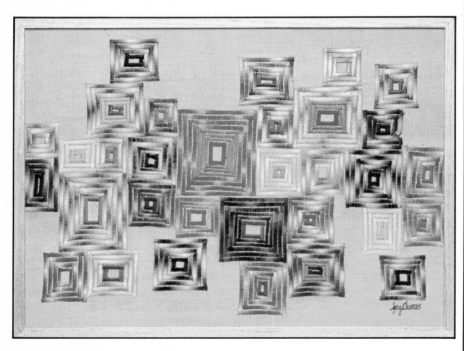

Decorative effects using the presser foot and satin stitch

With a little imagination decorative effects can be worked with the presser foot, without using a frame. Lines and sharp angles are easily incorporated. Sharp curves are more difficult to negotiate but are made easier by use of the quilting foot with its shorter length, rather than the presser foot, and a shorter than normal stitch length. Geometric designs should be marked out with a series of pencil dots which show on a dark or a light fabric. With more experience you will be able to machine straight between dots spaced further apart. Because the threads at each end of a line should be taken through to the back and tied, lines should be continuous wherever possible. Straight stitch effects can be worked on a reasonably firm fabric such as sailcloth without a backing.

Heavier effects can be achieved by working a zig-zag or satin stitch over an applied thread. There may be a special hole through the embroidery foot to guide a fine thread under the needle. An Elna foot is designed to apply any number of threads the thickness of pearl cotton side by side which can be held down with the serpentine (multiple zig-zag) or other automatic stitch. This foot can be used on some other machines. On a straight stitch machine it is possible with practice to guide a thick thread under the needle so that it is stitched accurately down the centre. These suggestions can be used in conjunction with applied braids and ribbons for border patterns. Ends of ribbons and braids should have their edges turned in unless they go to the edge of the fabric or are enclosed in a seam. Heavy threads must be passed to the back. When a shape rather than a line is to be worked it is wise to take the thread through the back of the fabric before starting to stitch. This will avoid the thread obscuring your work as you machine and also helps prevent tangling. Always work the heaviest stitching in a design first forming the main structure to which finer straight stitching or free machine embroidery may be added. On a fully automatic machine the stretch stitch makes a heavy line which can be used decoratively on the right side of the fabric. The twin needle can be used to make freely shaped pin-tucks either on the background fabric or on fabric to be applied. If a transparent fabric is used a coloured wool or embroidery thread can be laid under the needle to give a shadowed effect. Buttonhole twist can be used through the needle (largest size for your machine) to give a thick line on the right side. Thicker threads must be used in the spool and the lower tension should be released until it feels the same as for normal sewing. The work must be wrong side uppermost. This is called cable stitch. This technique was described in the previous chapter.

Always work a sample on the fabric to be used to check tensions and stitch length. Only use closely woven fabric or the satin stitch will have irregular edges. Work with tensions as light as possible and take care there is no weight on the fabric passing under the foot which might distort the fabric. If any pulling up of fabric occurs either back the fabric with vanishing muslin or stretch the work in a frame. If a lengthening of the stitch is required as well as variation of width this is best achieved by pulling the work gently through the machine. It is not possible to alter both stitch width and length at the same time. Ends should be taken through to the back and tied.

The panel is worked in satin stitch using the presser foot. 50 machine embroidery cotton in shaded colours is used throughout. The area of each square in the design is marked on the background with light pencil dots and the shapes are filled in from the outside towards the centre.

Table mats

These table mats were illustrated in the first chapter on Machine Embroidery. They are made of washable linen/cotton furnishing fabric. The fish design is worked before the mats are cut out.

The heavy line, designed to be continuous wherever possible, is marked on paper, transferred to the fabric (also explained in the earlier chapter) and worked by applying a medium weight embroidery thread with a zig-zag stitch using the presser foot. 50 machine embroidery cotton is used on the spool and through the needle. The design is then framed and free machining is worked in different colours to build up areas of texture.

The fringed edges of the mats are finished with a machine hemming stitch.

Embroidered and applied shapes on fine fabrics

One of the greatest attractions of machine embroidery is that intricate and delicate designs may be completed in a comparatively short time.

With a little experience it is possible to frame and embroider very fine fabrics but the utmost care must be taken when stretching them in the frame, as the tension necessary for good results could easily cause the fabric to split. To avoid this adjust the screw on the frame until it is just tight enough to grip the fabric, alternatively tighten the screw and gently pull up the fabric making sure you grip it along the width of both palms, spreading the strain as evenly as possible. This needs great patience but if you pull up the fabric between thumb and forefingers the fabric will almost certainly split.

Cotton organdie is a particularly attractive fabric to embroider but as it creases easily it is best used in a design where it will be covered with embroidery. Subtle effects may be obtained by applying pieces of organdie to an organdie background or by placing coloured fabric on the wrong side of the background for a shadow effect. Embroidered tablemats can be particularly successful when worked on cotton organdie as it looks well placed over most colours.

Fine fabrics such as organza, cotton organdie or chiffon can be applied to net for evening dresses, or wedding dresses and veils. The fabric to be applied can be mounted on the net and then framed together and tightened securely.

Using free running stitch, outline the edges of all the shapes two or three times. Pull the work clear of the machine, cut away the excess applied fabric and finish the raw edges with further lines of machining or some fine texture. The shapes should be worked far enough apart to be able to insert the points of the scissors between them.

If the shapes to be applied are very small they may be cut out separately, laid in position and held with the fingers whilst they are stitched. With more experience you will not be afraid of putting your fingers close to the needle and it is a great advantage to be able to do so. This method is easier to work and there is no danger of damaging the net during the cutting away process. If you are applying pieces of net to net use the second method whatever the size but if the shapes are very large use a presser foot.

Do not attempt to do anything other than straight stitch techniques on fragile fabrics. Satin stitch may pull up the fabric so that it is not possible to press your work flat and also fine threads may get dislodged spoiling the effect of the stitch unless its purpose is purely textural.

Embroidery worked on an open fabric gives a completely different effect to that worked on a closely woven fabric as with an open fabric both upper and lower threads are visible so the stitching appears heavier. All weights of net can be embroidered from the heavy net used for ballet tutus to a fine dress net. Shapes may be embroidered on net then cut out and applied to, or inserted into, another fabric. If you are applying net shapes to a solid background either turn the edges under, making a clearly defined edge which can be secured with hemming or zig-zag stitch. Alternatively leave 1.3cm ($\frac{1}{2}$ *inch*) outside the stitching on each shape and attach it with free machine embroidery which will soften the edge and blend it into the background.

This method of machine embroidery is very good for decorating clothes as the minimal amount of stitching on the background will not impair its draping qualities. Use soft dress net for the embroidered shapes which may be applied with some shapes in a more closely woven fabric for contrast, overlapping the net shapes on the others for even greater variety.

Use your imagination when choosing your background fabric. Plastic mesh vegetable bags can make interesting backgrounds for panels. Satin stitch can be used but generally straight running stitch is most effective used in a very textural way with contrasting spool colours to build up subtle shaded areas. Some cotton vegetable bags have a very open weave and, once washed, are very rewarding to use. The threads can be dislodged to make large holes and spaces contrasting with heavily worked areas. They are ideal for lampshades mounted over a fabric fine enough to allow the light to pass through.

The motif illustrated is worked in the frame. The organdie shapes are applied to the background with free running stitch using 50 machine embroidery cotton on the spool and through the needle. The edges of each shape are trimmed after stitching and emphasised with more running stitch. An eyelet is worked in the centre of the motif (see the following chapter in this section) and a free running texture worked round it. The leaves are then worked in free running stitch using sewing cotton.

The delicate art of eyelet embroidery and openwork

Eyelets are simple to work and extremely effective used on their own, or in combination with other free stitching effects and they make an interesting focal point in a design.

The attachments for eyelets are not supplied with the machine but can be bought in two or three sizes. When working eyelets the smaller you make your central hole, the wider your stitching can be and vice versa.

The work must be framed using a frame small enough to completely revolve around the needle and the eyelets should be positioned within the frame so that they do not hamper this movement.

Follow the machine manufacturers instructions for fitting the eyelet plate. For best results use 50 machine embroidery cotton. When piercing the hole using the awl supplied with the attachment, be careful not to make the hole too large. Set your machine for satin stitch, place the work in position on the eyelet plate, (you may have to remove and replace the needle), position the needle to the left and draw the thread up through the hole. Hold both thread ends when starting and run the machine fast revolving the frame evenly. It is better to turn the frame twice quickly rather than once slowly, although a delicate effect can be achieved by spacing the stitches so that the fabric remains visible between them.

When the eyelet is complete the ends of the stitching should be tied on the wrong side of the fabric. If a number of eyelets are to be worked this can be avoided by making the eyelets touch each other or else designing the work so that the linking threads may be concealed by further textural stitching. Another way of finishing is to position the needle to the right and work another row of small straight stitching round the circumference of the eyelet. The threads can then be cut close to the work and the stitching gives an added finish.

A further textural variation can be given to eyelets by working with a different colour through the needle to that on the spool and with the upper tension tighter than the lower so that the bobbin colour shows round the edges. Loosen the lower tension as well if necessary.

Openwork may be described as a decorative version of darning. It is the technique either of inserting a delicate web-like pattern of machine stitching into specially prepared holes and spaces, or, working over the spaces so solidly that they become as heavy as the background fabric. If this technique is to be used for dress embroidery the shapes should be well filled if they are large. If the shapes are small they may be left more open but are best worked where there is no likelihood of damage from such things as buckles, handbags or bracelets.

Generally with openwork the same thickness of thread is used through the needle and on the spool. It is important to use a thread which will stand up to wear and washing so choose a thread thicker than 50 machine embroidery cotton. Cable stitch is a good choice of stitch to work as it fills in the space quickly. The tensions should always be set as for normal sewing. For best results use a closely woven fabric of any weight such as linen sailcloth, cotton lawn or organdie. Frame the work and outline the shapes with three or four lines of free running stitch which lie either on top of each other or touching. This will prevent the edges of the shape from stretching. Remove the work from the machine and cut out the shapes close to the stitching. Work a few stitches round the edge to secure the threads, then machine backwards and forwards across the space carrying the stitching round the edge to the next line if necessary until a framework has been made. The focal points may then be built up by machining continuously round any area where lines intersect without necessarily continuing the stitching to the edge. If you change colours during your design either secure the ends by close stitching or else take them through to the wrong side and tie them.

The edges of the hole may be finished with satin stitch, either freely if you are sufficiently skilled or else using the presser foot. Whichever method you use the work should remain stretched in a frame small enough to pass easily round the needle. A softer edge is obtained by working a whipstitch or free running texture over the edge of the hole which blends it into the background. It is a good idea on a swing needle machine to use a throat plate with a needle hole rather than a slit. If it is necessary to reframe the work to complete your design avoid the edge of the frame crossing the stitching if possible. If this cannot be avoided see that the main bulk of stitching is at right angles to the edge of the frame to minimise the risk of damage and tighten the work from the opposite side.

For purely decorative designs, such as wall hangings and panels, holes of any size up to the size of the frame can be filled. The holes should be rounded rather than crescent shaped as the lack of edge tension on the latter causes too many difficulties in working.

Openwork can look particularly exciting if different fabrics are laid underneath the shapes such as leather, foil or metallic fabrics but you should bear in mind the function of the finished article.

For permanent objects such as mobiles, lampshade rings or millinery wire may be used to give the edges of the shape support. Millinery wire should be cut long enough to go round the circumference twice with the ends touching each other. Conceal the join with thread tied over it. To secure each line of stitching as you work wired shapes, you should stop your machine each time you reach the wire and work four stitches backwards and forwards over it, (finishing the fourth stitch inside), turning the balance wheel by hand. You should also try to make the basic structure of wide angles to prevent the threads of your embroidery slipping. To also help avoid this, it is a good idea, having completed a horizontal line of stitching in your shape, to work the fourth stitch over the wire so that the stitch finishes inside the wire and above that line of embroidery. This means that when you work the vertical line, the first stitch is worked over the horizontal line so pulling the stitches over the wire close together helping to anchor them. Satin stitch can be worked over the wire or ring to conceal it using the widest needle throw to lessen the risk of the needle catching on the wire and breaking. Shapes may be worked on stiff wire, which can be bent into more complex shapes. To join the wire, cross the ends and wind an elastic band round them. When the shape is complete, it can be laid in position on a background and fastened with a few running stitches inside the wire at each point. Then cut the wire at intervals, carefully remove each section, and further strengthen the points of the shape with stitching or conceal them with satin stitch or applied thread. Never cut the loops which result when the wire is removed.

Several of these shapes can make a pleasing arrangement for a panel but should only be used when the completed work will be stretched, or the effect will be lost. This particular aspect of openwork therefore is unsuitable for dress embroidery.

The sample shows a motif worked with eyelets and a variation of whip stitch. 40 sewing cotton is used through the needle and 50 machine embroidery cotton on the spool throughout.

Embroidered At Home Dress

This embroidery can be used on any dress with a plain yoke, such as the one illustrated. It is worked on the front bodice before the dress is made up. When you cut out the front bodice piece make sure you allow extra fabric all round to enable you to frame your work.

The free shapes are worked in the frame using running stitch and cable stitch. Because you are working across spaces the cable stitch can be worked from the right side. Pure silk thread is used through the needle throughout and silky hand embroidery thread is wound on the spool. A free running texture is used round the edge of the shape to conceal the raw edges and soften them into the background.

The front bodice is cut out in lining tacked in position on the wrong side of the front bodice matching notches. The pattern piece is then treated as one layer during making up.

QUILTING
Basic techniques

From the small fragments found in early Egyptian tombs, quilting is known to have been used as a means of padding garments and bed covers for warmth and as decoration from the very earliest times. Later, quilting was worn instead of armour in battle and it was also worn under metal armour to prevent chafing.

As well as bed covers and household furnishings, quilting of garments of all kinds for warmth and decoration was universal during the 16th to mid 19th centuries. In the 19th century, which was the heyday of decorative sewing, quilting was practised on a scale similar to patchwork and the two crafts became closely allied. In America, where patchwork was an economy measure with the early settlers, it was customary to make the patchwork quilt tops during the winter and hold a neighbourhood quilting party in the spring to complete the quilts, so the two crafts progressed together to an equal degree of technical expertise.

Types of quilting

Nowadays five different types of quilting are practised in embroidery. These are English quilting, Italian quilting, Trapunto quilting, and the delicate shadow quilting.

Of these, English quilting is the most popular and is the only one which provides real extra warmth because it incorporates all-over padding, although the other methods can give added weight and substance to fabrics as well as decoration. All five methods can be used for bedcovers, quilts, cushions, tea and coffee pot covers, jackets, housecoats and other similar garments.

English quilting

This is the method of sandwiching padding between a top cover and muslin backing or fabric lining and then securing the three layers together by over-all running stitching. The decoration comes from the patterns worked by the stitching and the attractive texture produced.

Quilting in Britain is particularly associated with North West England and South Wales, and many of the designs have local names, such as the Welsh heart and Weardale chain. Most of them are based on simple shapes of leaves, feathers, circles, scissors, spectacles, etc., and it is worth obtaining templates of these basic shapes which can be increased or reduced in size according to the size of the article being made.

Alternatively, some designs used on Continental ceramic tiles might give ideas for patterns. When planning the design for a piece of English quilting, the pattern should traditionally consist of principal motifs and a background filling pattern which throws into relief the main areas of the design. The filling pattern can be a lattice of squares or diamonds or a series of lozenge shapes.

Italian quilting

This is worked through two thicknesses of fabric only, a top cover and a muslin or lawn backing. The stitching is worked in double lines, 0.6cm – 1cm ($\frac{1}{4}$ *inch* – $\frac{3}{8}$ *inch*) apart to form channels which are threaded with soft wool, known as quilting wool, to give a raised design on the front of the work.

The designs for Italian quilting should be linear and preferably continuous. The scroll patterns on wrought-iron work and the interlaced forms of Celtic decorative lettering are often suitable as the basis for designs.

Trapunto quilting

This is also worked on a top fabric and muslin backing but differs from Italian quilting in that the stitching is worked in single lines which completely encircle shapes which are then raised by padding them with a stuffing of soft wool or wadding.

Shadow quilting

This is a variation of both Italian and Trapunto quilting. The stitching is worked on a transparent fabric such as organdie or organza with a backing of a similar fabric

or muslin. The areas to be raised are stuffed and threaded with a coloured quilting wool or soft thick knitting wool.

Fabrics for all quilting

Because it is the design which is all-important in quilting rather than the stitches which are worked in a colour to match the fabric, the top cover fabric should be one which really shows the texture formed. For this reason if you are using satin, it should be the dull sort rather than the shiny surfaced one. Other suitable fabrics are fine silk, shantung, rayon, glazed cotton, fine wool, Viyellas, cotton poplin and closely woven linen.

Thread and needles

Pure silk thread in a colour to match the fabric is the most satisfactory, although cotton or fine linen thread can be used. For stitching use a No.7, 8, or 9 betweens needle, according to the weight of the fabric. For marking the design for English quilting, you will also need a yarn or rug needle. For threading the quilting wool in Italian quilting, you will need a large blunt needle, such as a tapestry needle.

The stitches

Running stitch is used for all methods of quilting except for English which is sewn in either back, running or chain stitch.

Working English quilting

In the past carded sheep's wool or cotton wadding was used for padding, but nowadays it is best to use nylon or Terylene wadding as these can be washed easily (cotton wadding tends to become lumpy

with wear and washing). The backing fabric can be muslin or soft cotton if you are lining the article separately, or a toning rayon lining fabric if a separate lining is not required.

1 Tack the layers together, sandwiching the padding between the top fabric and backing. Work a line of tacking across the centre of the fabric in both directions.

2 Mount the triple layer of fabric on to a traditional frame, with top fabric facing up.

3 Cut a template of the principal motif, keeping its size in proportion to the article. Place in position on the fabric, using the centre tacking lines as a guide.

4 To transfer the design to the fabric, mark round the edge of the template with a large needle held at an angle to the work. The point of the needle will leave an impression on the fabric which is easy to follow with running stitch.

5 Work the main areas of the design first in even running stitch. Start stitching with a small knot on the back of the work which buries itself in the wadding and finish with a small back stitch.

6 When the main areas have been worked, mark the filling background pattern with a flat ruler and yarn needle. Work along the lines in running stitch.

7 When all the quilting has been worked, take the work off the frame and finish the article as required. If you are making something like a bed cover or quilt, one of the best finishes is a piping in the same fabric as the top cover.

8 To attach the piping, make up the casing and enclose the cord in the standard way.

9 If you are having a separate lining, attach

the piping round the edges of the article on the right side and stitch through all layers. Cut the lining fabric to the required size and place it on the quilting with right sides together and edges matching. Stitch on the piping line, leaving an opening in one side. Turn right side out and close the opening with neat hemming.

10 If the lining is not separate, un-do the tacking joining the layers together and stitch the piping to the top cover and wadding only. Turn under the edges of the lining and slip-stitch neatly to the piping line.

Working Italian quilting

Traditionally the design was marked on the muslin backing and the stitching worked on this side. However, you may find it easier to keep the running stitches even if you work on the top fabric, in which case the design should be marked by the prick and pounce method (see Transferring designs earlier) and not by tracing or drawing which would still show when the work is finished.

1 Tack the fabric and backing round the edges and mount them as one on to a frame, with the working side facing up.

2 Trace your design on to the fabric and work along the double lines in running stitch. If you like, some parts of the design can be emphasised by working in chain or back stitch on the right side of the fabric instead of running stitch.

3 Thread a large blunt needle with the quilting wool and insert it along the channels formed by the double lines of stitching. Where there is an angle, break or intersection in the design, bring the wool to the surface on the muslin and reinsert the needle leaving a small loop. This allows for even tension and a small amount of shrinkage if the quilting is washed or dry cleaned.

Working Trapunto quilting

This is worked in a similar way to Italian quilting, with the main exception that the design is marked in single lines which enclose the area to be raised or padded. The method of padding, however, is different and also applies to shadow quilting.

1 When the stitching is complete, make an incision through the muslin into the areas to be stuffed, with a blunt needle, or knitting needle if the area is large.

2 Remove the top skin of wadding and tease the wadding into small amounts which can easily be inserted through the incision. The amount of stuffing you use depends on the effect your require.

3 When enough padding is inserted, close the opening with overcasting stitches before moving on to the next area.

Quilted cushion

This simple design for quilting can be modified and used to decorate various objects of home furnishings.

The directions are given for a pillow 40.5cm (*16 inches*) × 30.5cm (*12 inches*), but the quilting can be adapted for a larger pillow by spacing out the motifs or for a small square pillow by omitting the small leaf shapes.

Fabric required

0.70 metre ($\frac{3}{4}$ *yard*) rayon kafka, or a not too shiny pure silk, or a dull satin, 91cm (*36 inches*) wide

You will also need

- □ 0.45 metre ($\frac{1}{2}$ *yard*) thin cotton fabric, 91cm (*36 inches*) wide for backing the quilting
- □ 0.45 metre ($\frac{1}{2}$ *yard*) synthetic wadding
- □ 1.60 metres ($1\frac{3}{4}$ *yards*) cotton piping cord, no. 2 size
- □ 1 reel pure sewing silk to match the fabric
- □ 1 reel mercerized sewing cotton
- □ Tracing paper
- □ Thin white card for the templates
- □ 1 large fine-pointed darning needle
- □ Sewing needles (fine crewels or betweens) for quilting
- □ Cushion pad to fit pillowcase

Making the templates

1 Trace the heart and leaf motifs for the quilting on to the quilting paper.
2 Place the tracing on to the card, pin or stick in position and cut round.

Working the quilting

1 Cut the quilting fabric to the size of the finished pillow, plus 1.3cm ($\frac{1}{2}$ *inch*) all round for turnings. Cut the wadding and the cotton backing fabric to the same size.
2 Tack the three layers together, sandwiching the wadding between the fabrics.
3 Mark the centre lines of the fabric with tacking diagonally from corner to corner.
4 Mount the fabric into the embroidery frame (see Embroidery frames, earlier).
5 Lay the mounted fabric (in the frame) right side up on a folded blanket on a firm surface.
6 Position the heart template in the four positions as shown in the diagram. Holding the large needle at an angle, trace round the card shape firmly to leave a sharp impression on the fabric. Take care not to cut the fabric with the needle point if your fabric is thin. Trace round the leaf shape at each end of the cushion. Place the smaller shape inside the heart and trace round.
7 Start to quilt the fabric, using the matching silk and working in small even running stitch.
8 When the main motifs are complete, draw in the background diamond shapes using a ruler and large needle. Draw in the lines, working from each corner and keeping them 2cm ($\frac{3}{4}$ *inch*) apart. Quilt along the lines.
9 When all the quilting is complete,

remove it from the frame and fasten off all ends neatly.

Making up the pillow case

1 From the surplus fabric, cut a piece the same size as the quilting for the back of the pillowcase and then cut bias strips 4cm (1½ *inches*) wide for the piping casing. Make up the piping casing.

2 Pin the piping in position round the edge of the quilting and tack. Place the two sides of the pillowcase together with right sides facing. Tack and machine stitch using the mercerized sewing cotton along the piping line. Leave one side of the pillowcase open and turn it right side out.

3 Insert a zip fastener into the open side and then insert the cushion pad, or insert the pad first and slip-stitch the sides of the opening together.

Travelling slippers and case
Fabric required

0.45 metre (½ *yard*) fabric for quilting, 91cm (*36 inches*) wide

0.45 metre (½ *yard*) cotton fabric, 91cm (*36 inches*) wide, for the backing

0.45 metre (½ *yard*) rayon lining fabric, 91cm (*36 inches*) wide

You will also need

☐ 0.45 metre (½ *yard*) synthetic wadding
☐ One pair of foam rubber inner soles in required size
☐ Felt, to cover foam soles
☐ PVC, to cover bottom of slippers
☐ Adhesive
☐ Quilting equipment as for pillowcase

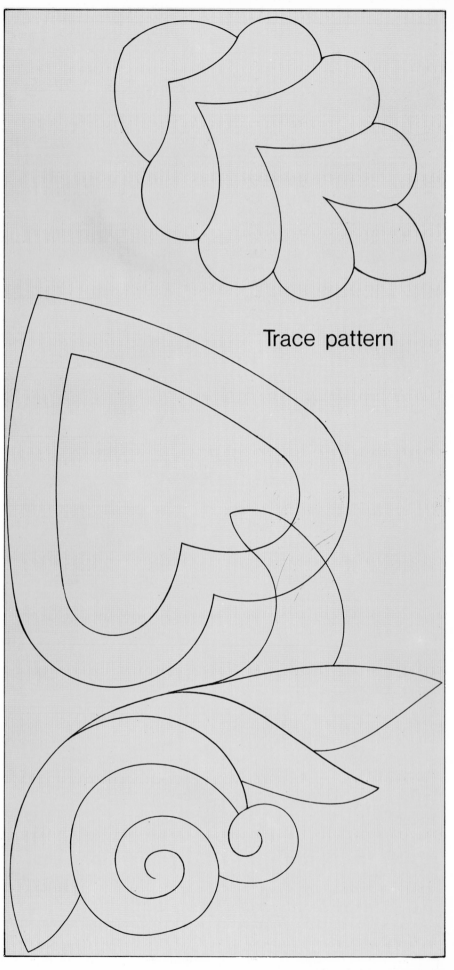

Trace pattern

Working the quilting

1 Trace the shapes for the slipper fronts and case and tack the shapes on to the quilting fabric, allowing at least 2.5cm (1 inch) between each one.

2 Sandwich the wadding between the quilting fabric and cotton backing and tack the layers together. Mount them into an embroidery frame.

3 Mark the quilting shapes, using the leaf for the slippers and the scroll for the case. Work the quilting.

4 Mark the background diamond pattern, placing the lines 1.3cm (½ inch) apart.

Making up the slippers

1 Cut round the tacked shapes of the slippers, leaving 2.5cm (1 inch) for turnings. Cut out linings for the slippers to the same size.

2 Cut bias strips and make up piping about 12.5cm (5 inches) long for each slipper. Tack in place along each top edge. Place the lining on to the slipper front with right sides together and stitch close to the piping. Turn right side out and tack the lining and quilting together round the remaining edge.

3 Place the foam inner soles on to the felt and draw round, leaving 1.3cm (½ inch) turnings.

4 Clip into the turnings of the felt, place on to the foam inner soles and stick the turnings down on the underside.

5 Place the slipper fronts right side up on to the felt side of the soles, fold the turnings on to the underside and pin in position. Try on the slippers and adjust the size of the turnings if necessary. Stick in position with adhesive.

6 Cut out two shapes of the soles from the PVC and stick in position on the under-side to cover the raw edges of the quilting and felt.

Making up the slipper case

1 Cut out the lining to the same size as the quilting.

2 Place the quilting and lining together with right sides facing and tack and machine stitch along the top curved edge, taking 0.6cm (¼ inch) turnings. Clip into the angle and turn right side out.

3 Tack along the top seam so that no lining shows on the quilted side of the case. Press.

4 Fold the case in half so that the curved edges match and the quilted side is inside. Tack and machine stitch down the side and bottom edge, taking 0.6cm (¼ inch) turnings. Neaten the edges by overcasting or zig-zag stitching. Turn the finished case right side out.

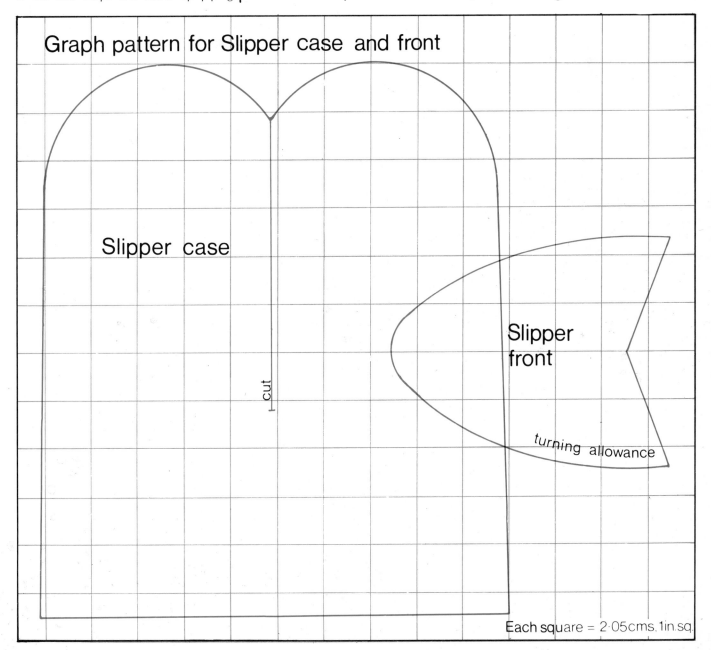

Graph pattern for Slipper case and front

Slipper case

cut

Slipper front

turning allowance

Each square = 2·05cms. 1 in.sq.

QUILTING BY MACHINE

The cording foot and quilting

Most machines have a cording or braiding foot as an extra attachment. This foot guides a thick thread or cord under the needle. It can be straight stitched down the centre, zig-zagged or enclosed with satin stitch. This is an effective way of working solid shapes.

The shapes can be worked directly on to the article or on separate pieces of fabric which are then applied to give a more raised effect. The edges of the applied shapes can then be turned under and hem stitched so they are not visible or the application may become part of the design and can be satin stitched for instance, or concealed with free embroidery. Whichever of these methods you choose the shapes should be worked from the outside towards the centre or the shape may become distorted.

If the fabric is a fine one it will be necessary to back the shape with paper. Iron-on interfacing is excellent for dress embroidery providing the work does not have to drape.

A test sample should always be worked to make sure that the cord used is fine enough to be gripped firmly by the foot. A thicker cord might cause subsequent lines to be uneven and the groove on the underside of the foot, which allows for the passage of the thick thread, may catch on an adjacent line dislodging the work. However, if you wish to use a thicker cord, this difficulty can be overcome by changing to the presser foot after the first round has been completed. To make stitching easier use soft yarns which flatten under the presser foot. Textured yarns may be used and generally look best if a matching thread is used to attach them. In the absence of a good match use transparent thread on top and the nearest colour match in the spool.

Quilting can be used on its own or combined with areas of free embroidery or any other stitch effects already described. It can be worked in the usual way using the quilting foot and guide, and also in the frame making it possible to sew smaller and more intricate shapes. For the best effect the work should not be too tightly stretched in the frame and only a limited amount of wadding can be used to allow it to fit into the frame at all. For this reason it is better not to use a frame with the inner ring bound. If, with the thickness of the work, the machine tends to miss stitches, use the darning foot and work with looser tensions. Quilting by this method could provide a decorative yoke and hem, or collar and cuffs for a dress.

Cotton, Terylene or thin foam make good

fillers for quilting and the latter two have the advantage of being washable. Fine soft fabric should be used for the backing. Cotton lawn is excellent. Italian quilting is particularly attractive for garment embroidery. Two parallel lines of stitching are worked holding two fabrics together and thick wool is inserted by hand from the back between the fabrics. The distance between the two lines is governed by the thickness of the wool. If a fine fabric is used on top an attractive shadow effect is achieved. An openweave fabric should be used for the backing to facilitate the wool insertion.

Quilting may be worked in cable stitch in which case the design can be marked on tissue paper, tacked to and worked from the wrong side, then torn away. Alternatively, the design may be drawn with tailors chalk and worked from the right side by applying a fine embroidery thread with a zig-zag stitch.

Work from the centre of a design outwards allowing plenty of extra fabric for the seam allowances. Do not trim the edges of cut-out pattern sections until the quilting has been completed.

The flower-shaped motif shown is worked freely in the frame and the geometric motif is worked with the quilting foot. The design for the floral motif is marked on paper first and tacked to the wrong side of the fabric. Cable stitch is worked from the wrong side using a silky hand embroidery thread on the spool and sewing cotton through the needle.

Pure silk thread is used for the straight machining which is worked from the right side. The upper and lower tensions are balanced.

The quilted waistcoat

The pattern for the waistcoat, illustrated opposite, is ideal for a geometric quilted pattern. Adapt a similar pattern to fasten edge to edge at the centre-front and omit the interfacing. This waistcoat is lined in self fabric. The pattern pieces are cut in 2oz. washable quilting, the dart shapes are cut out and the edges overstitched together by hand. The lining is made up and the darts are worked on each remaining pattern piece. The quilting is then tacked very firmly on the wrong side of those pieces.

The embroidery is worked using the quilting foot. The thread and tensions used are the same as those described for the motifs.

When the embroidery is complete the waistcoat is made up according to the instructions with the pattern. Hooks and eyes may be sewn at centre-front if required.

A GUIDE TO FABRICS AND THREADS

As more people experiment all the time with ever-increasing number of materials available, the days when a particular embroidery method was worked only on one specific type of fabric are past, but this chart endeavours to give both traditional methods and threads and suggestions for progressive embroidery.

| Type of Embroidery | Traditional Use | | Contemporary Use | |
	Fabrics	Threads	Fabrics	Threads
Basic stitchery	Linen (samplers) Cotton	Linen Silk	Any type of material from hessian to organdie	Threads of wool, silk, cotton, tricel, nylon, chenille, cords, nylon string
Quilting Traditional English padding – carded sheep's wool, cotton wadding, or flannel	Fine silk Fine linen Dull satin Fine wool	Pure silk Fine linen, silk, Sylko Silk	Shantung satin, nylon, tricel, glazed cotton, poplin, Viyella, fine wool	Pure silk Pure silk Molnlycke (similar to Sylko) Pure silk Pure silk
English Padding now synthetic wadding	As above	As above	As above	As above
Italian (soft quilting wool for padding – Traditional method, coloured wool and heavy cord for articles not requiring laundering	As above	As above	As above	As above
Trapunto Padding traditionally quilting wool and wadding, now is synthetic wadding	As above	As above	As above	As above

Counted thread Embroidery	Traditional Method Fabrics	Threads	Contemporary Method Fabrics	Threads
Drawn(or pulled) fabric	Linen of various weights with matching threads (even weave)		Cotton, wool, linen, synthetic even-weave fabrics	Coton perlé Coton à broder Wool and linen
Drawn thread	As above		As above	As above
Blackwork	As above		As above	As above
Hardanger Hedebo Assisi Cross stitch	Even-weave cotton and linen		As above, plus wool tweed, hessian, flannel, many linen, cotton and rayon dress fabrics	Variety of threads in cotton, silk, wool to contrast in weight and texture
Canvas work Florentine	Single and double canvas and linen worked with crewel wool		Hessian, single and double canvas and linen	Crewel wools, knitting wools, stranded cotton, silk and crochet threads
Shadow work	Traditionally worked in fine white threads on translucent white material, organdie and muslin		White and coloured organdie, organza, chiffon, nylon	Pure silk, sewing silk for applied areas. Silk, wool and stranded cotton for shadow embroidery
Smocking	Muslin, fine cotton, georgette, crepe de chine, silk, fine wool and chiffon, fine linen	Silk, cotton and linen threads (threads generally should be slightly heavier than fabric)	Chiffon, cotton, wool synthetics, some types P.V.C. needlecord, flannel and dress tweed	Crochet cotton, knitting wools, Raffene, silk, buttonhole twist, linen embroidery threads
Ayrshire work and Broderie Anglaise, (white work)	Fine linen, linen lawn fine cotton, muslin, organdie (always white)	Matching fine threads in cotton and linen (cotton floche and coton à broder)	Cotton, organdie, linen lawn, Swiss cotton and muslin organza	Matching threads in cotton, silk and linen
Cutwork Simple (stranded cotton is unsuitable for working threads)	White or natural linen with matching threads of linen, cotton or mercerised threads		Coloured linen, strong cotton, dress tweed, furnishing fabrics if firm woven	Matching threads (in linen and cotton)
Renaissance embroidery	As above		As above	As above
Richelieu embroidery	As above		As above	Also fine crochet threads
Reticella embroidery	As above		As above	As above
Needleweaving	Loosley woven linen, linen crash, huckaback, furnishing fabrics	Threads should be slightly thicker than withdrawn thread	Hessian, canvas, heavy linens, linen scrim, dress tweeds	Linen thread of different sizes

A DICTIONARY OF STITCHES

This alphabet of free style embroidery stitches includes outline, flat, looped, chained, knotted, couching, filling and composite stitches. Diagrams and step-by-step instructions make the alphabet a useful source of reference material for both a beginner and the more experienced embroiderer.

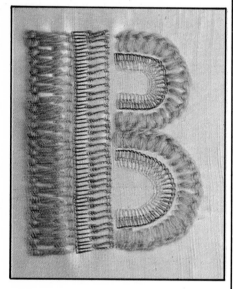

Back stitch

Bring the thread through on the stitch line, then take a small backward stitch through the fabric. Bring the needle through again a little in front of the first stitch and take another stitch, inserting the needle at the point where it first came through.

Blanket stitch and buttonhole stitch

These stitches are worked in the same way – the difference being that in buttonhole stitch the stitches are close together. Bring the thread out on the lower line, insert the needle in position in the upper line, taking a straight downward stitch with the thread under the needle point.
Pull up the stitch to form a loop and repeat.

This stitch may also be worked on even-weave fabric.

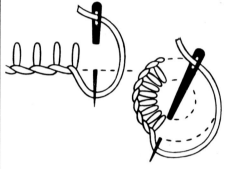

Bokhara couching

This stitch is useful and ornamental for filling in shapes of leaves and petals of flowers. It is worked in the same way as Roumanian stitch, but the small tying stitches are set at regular intervals over the laid thread to form pattern lines across the shape. The tying stitches should be pulled tight, leaving the laid thread slightly loose between.

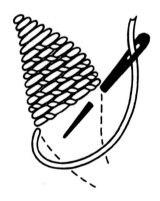

Bullion stitch

Pick up a back stitch, the size of the bullion stitch required, bring the needle point out where it first emerged. Do not pull the needle right through the fabric. Twist the thread round the needle point as many times as required to equal the space of the

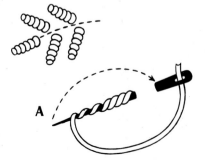

back stitch. Hold the left thumb on the coiled thread and pull the needle through; still holding the coiled thread, turn the needle back to where it was inserted (see arrow) and insert in the same place (A). Pull the thread through until the bullion stitch lies flat. Use a needle with a small eye to allow the thread to pass through the coils easily.

Buttonhole stitch bars and double buttonhole stitch bars

These bars are used in cut-work and Richelieu work. Make a row of running stitch between the double lines of the design as a padding for the buttonhole stitch. Where a single line bar occurs, take a thread across the space and back, securing with a small stitch and buttonhole stitch picking up any of the fabric (A). Buttonhole stitch round the shape, keeping the looped edge of the stitch to the inside, then cut away the fabric from behind the bar and round the inside of the shape. Where a double line or a broad bar is required between shapes or for stems of flowers, when the fabric is to be cut away on each side, make a row of running stitch along one side, spacing the stitches slightly. Buttonhole stitch along the other side into the spaces left by the first row. The fabric is then cut away close to the buttonhole stitch, leaving a strong, broad bar (B).

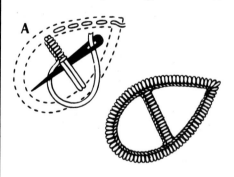

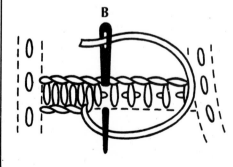

Buttonhole insertion stitch

This insertion stitch consists of groups of four buttonhole stitches worked alternately on each piece of fabric to be joined. The upper row is worked as in ordinary buttonhole stitch. The diagram shows the method of working the groups on the lower row.

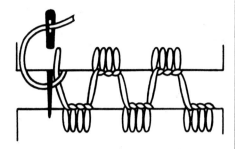

Buttonhole stitch and picot

Work as for ordinary buttonhole stitch until a picot is required, then hold the thread down with the left thumb and twist the needle three times round the thread (A). Still holding the thread securely, pull the working thread until the twisted threads are close to the buttonhole stitch, then make a buttonhole stitch into the last loop (B).

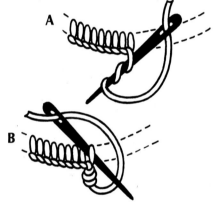

Cable stitch

This stitch is worked from left to right. Bring the thread through on the line of the design. Insert the needle a little to the right on the line and bring the needle out to the left midway between the length of the stitch, with the thread below the needle (Figure A). Work the next stitch in the same way but with the thread above the needle. Continue in this way, alternating the position of the thread. This stitch may also be worked on evenweave fabric (Figure B).

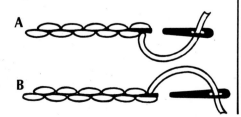

Cable chain stitch

Bring the thread through at A and hold it down with the left thumb. Pass the needle from right to left under the working thread, then twist the needle back over the working thread to the right and, still keeping the thread under the thumb, take a stitch of the required length. Pull the thread through.

Chain stitch

Bring the thread out at the top of the line and hold down with left thumb. Insert the needle where it last emerged and bring the point out a short distance away. Pull the thread through, keeping the working thread under the needle point.

Chained feather stitch

Working between two parallel lines, bring the thread through at A and make a slanting chain stitch, tying down the stitch at B. Take a second slanting chain stitch from the right at C, tying it down at D. The tying stitches must form a regular zig-zag pattern.

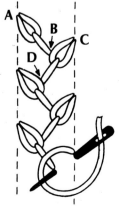

Chequered chain stitch

This stitch is worked in the same way as chain stitch, but with two contrasting threads in the needle at the same time. When making the loops, pass one colour under the needle point and let the other colour lie on top. Pull through both threads. Work the next loop with the other colour under the needle point.

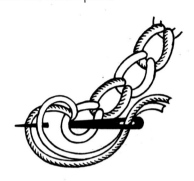

Chevron stitch

Bring the thread through on the lower line at the left side, insert the needle a little to the right on the same line and take a small stitch to the left, emerging halfway between the stitch being made. Next, insert the needle on the upper line a little to the right and take a small stitch to the left as at A. Insert the needle again on the same line a little to the right and take a small stitch to the left, emerging at the centre as at B. Work in this way alternately on the upper and lower lines. This stitch may also be worked on evenweave fabric.

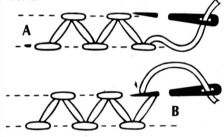

Closed buttonhole stitch

The stitches are made in pairs forming triangles. Bring the thread through at A, insert the needle at B and, with the thread under the needle, bring it through at C. Insert the needle again at B and bring it through at D. This stitch may also be worked on evenweave fabric.

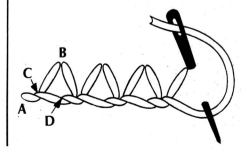

Closed feather stitch

This stitch is worked along two parallel lines. Bring the thread through at A and with the thread under the needle, take a stitch from B to C. Swing the thread over to the left and, with the thread under the needle, take a stitch from D to E. Repeat these two stitches.

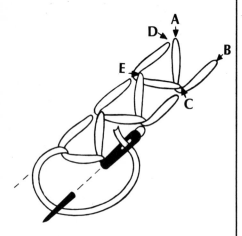

Coral stitch

Bring the thread out at the right end of the line, lay the thread along the line of the design and hold it down with the left thumb. Take a small stitch under the line and the thread and pull through, bringing the needle over the lower thread as in the diagram.

Couching

Lay a thread along the line of the design and, with another thread, tie it down at even intervals with a small stitch into the fabric. The tying stitch can be in a colour which contrasts with the laid thread if desired.

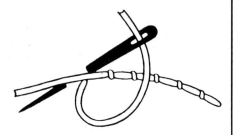

Cretan stitch

Bring the needle through centrally at the left-hand side, taking a small stitch on the lower line, needle pointing inwards and with thread under the needle point, as shown at A. Take a stitch on the upper line and thread under the needle as shown at B. Continue in this way until shape is filled.

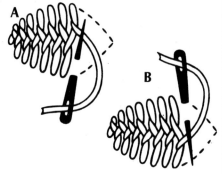

Cross stitch

Bring the needle through on the lower right line of the cross and insert at the top of the same line, taking a stitch through the fabric to the lower left line (Figure A). Con-

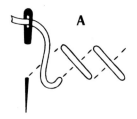

tinue to the end of the row in this way. Complete the other half of the cross (Figure B). It is important that the upper half of each stitch lies in the same direction.

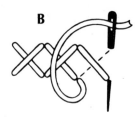

Double back stitch or closed herringbone stitch

This stitch is used for shadow work on fine, transparent fabric and can be worked on the right side of the fabric as at A – a small back stitch worked alternatively on each side of the traced double lines (the dotted lines on the diagram show the formation of the thread on the wrong side of the

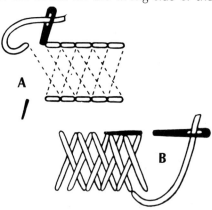

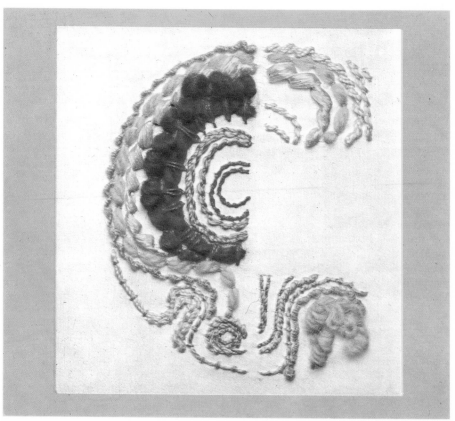

fabric). The colour of the thread appears delicately through the fabric. Figure B shows the stitch worked on the wrong side of the fabric as a closed herringbone stitch with no spaces left between the stitches. Both methods achieve the same result.

Daisy or detached chain stitch

Work in the same way as chain stitch (A), but fasten each loop at the foot with a small stitch (B). Daisy stitch may be worked singly or in groups to form flower petals.

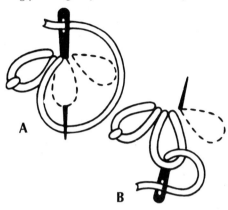

Double knot stitch

Bring the thread through at A. Take a small stitch across the line at B. Pass the needle downwards under the surface stitch just made, without piercing the fabric, as at C. With the thread under the needle, pass the needle again under the first stitch at D. Pull the thread through to

form a knot. The knots should be spaced evenly and closely to obtain a beaded effect.

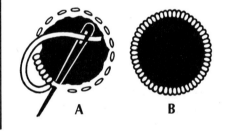

Eyelet holes

Figure A. Work a row of small running stitches round the circle. Pierce the centre with a stiletto and fold back the ragged edge. Closely overcast the folded edge with running stitch. Trim away any ragged edges at the back. Figure B shows the appearance of the finished eyelet hole. Instead of piercing with a stiletto, larger circles or longer eyelet holes may be cut across the centre both ways and the cut ends folded back.

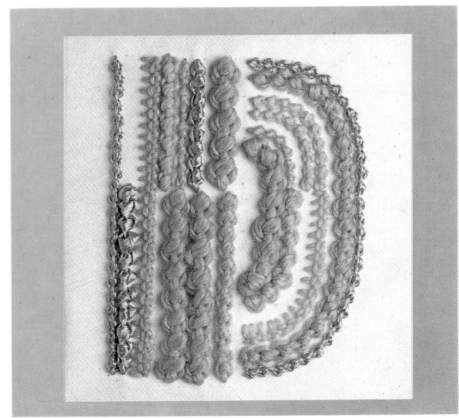

Feather stitch

Figure A. Bring the needle out at the top centre, hold the thread down with the left thumb, insert the needle a little to the right on the same level and take a small stitch down to the centre, keeping the thread under the needle point. Next, insert the needle a little to the left on the same level and take a stitch to centre, keeping the thread under the needle point. Work these two movements alternately. Figure B shows double feather stitch, in which two stitches are taken to the right and left alternately.

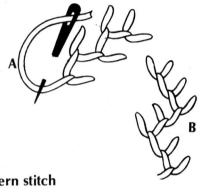

Fern stitch

This stitch consists of three straight stitches of equal length radiating from the same central point, A. Bring the thread through at A and make a straight stitch to B. Bring the thread through again at A and make another straight stitch to C. Repeat once more to D and bring the thread through at E to commence the next three radiating stitches. The central stitch follows the line of the design. This stitch may also be worked on evenweave fabric.

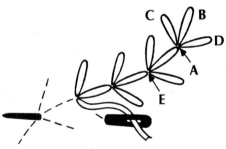

Fishbone stitch

This stitch is useful for filling small shapes. Bring the thread through at A and make a small straight stitch along the centre line of the shape. Bring the thread through

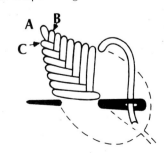

again at B and make a sloping stitch across the central line at the base of the first stitch. Bring the thread through at C and make a similar sloping stitch to overlap the previous stitch. Continue working alternately on each side until the shape is filled.

Flat stitch

Take a small stitch alternately on each side of the shape to be filled, with the point of the needle always emerging on the outside line of the shape. Two lines may be drawn down the centre of the shape as a guide for the size of the stitch. The stitches should be close together and fold into one another.

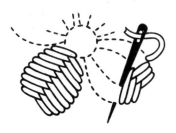

Fly stitch

Bring the thread through at the top left, hold it down with the left thumb, insert the needle to the right on the same level, a little distance from where the thread first emerged and take a small stitch downwards to the centre with the thread below the needle. Pull through and insert the needle again below the stitch at the centre (A) and bring it through in position for the next stitch. This stitch may be worked singly or in horizontal rows (A) or vertically (B).

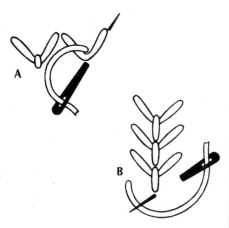

French knots

Bring the thread out at the required position, hold it down with the left thumb and encircle the thread twice with the needle as at A. Still holding the thread firmly, twist the needle back to the starting point and insert it close to where the thread first emerged (see arrow). Pull the

thread through to the back and secure for a single French knot or pass on to the position of the next stitch as at B.

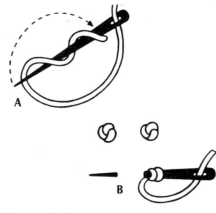

Heavy chain stitch

Bring the thread through at A and make a small vertical stitch. Bring the thread through again at B and pass the needle under the vertical stitch, without piercing the fabric, and insert it again at B. Bring the thread through at C and again pass the needle under the vertical stitch and insert

it at C. The third and all following stitches are made in exactly the same way, except that the needle always passes under the two preceding loops.

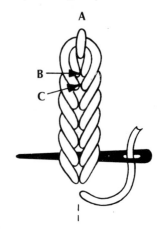

Herringbone stitch

Bring the needle out on the lower line at the left side and insert on the upper line a little to the right, taking a small stitch to the left with the thread below the needle. Next, insert the needle on the lower line

a little to the right and take a small stitch to the left with the thread above the needle. These two movements are worked throughout. For the best effect, the fabric lifted by the needle and the space between the stitches should be of equal size. This stitch can be laced with a matching or contrasting thread. Use a round pointed needle for lacing and do not pick up any of the fabric. Herringbone stitch may also be worked on evenweave fabric.

Interlaced band

This stitch is composed of two rows of back stitch with an interlacing. Work two parallel rows of back stitch (as shown at the top of the diagram) having the rows approximately 1.5–2.0cm ($\frac{1}{2}$–$\frac{3}{4}$ inch) apart, with the stitches worked as on the diagram, i.e., the end of one stitch is directly in line with the centre of the opposite stitch. Bring a matching or contrasting thread through at A and, follow the diagram, interlace it through every stitch.

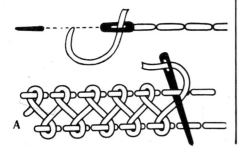

Interlacing stitch

The foundation of the border stitch is a double row of herringbone stitch worked in two journeys, with the stitches intertwined in a certain way. The first row of herringbone stitch is shown in medium tone on the diagram. In working the rows of herringbone stitch for the interlacing, there is a slight change in the usual method. In the top stitch the needle is passed under the working thread in each case instead of over it, and attention should be paid to the alternate crossing of the threads when working the second row. Do not work this foundation tightly, as the interlacing thread tends to draw the stitches together. When the rows of herringbone stitch are worked, bring the thread for the surface interlacing through at A and follow the diagram closely. When the end of the row is reached, lace the thread round the last cross in the centre and work back in a similar fashion along the lower half of the foundation. The last two crosses on the diagram have been left unlaced so that the construction of the herringbone stitch may be seen clearly.

Jacobean couching or trellis

This stitch makes an attractive filling stitch for the centres of flowers or shapes where an open effect is required. It consists of long evenly spaced stitches (laid threads) taken across the space horizontally and vertically (A) or diagonally (B). The crossed threads are then tied down at all intersecting points. The tying or couching stitch can be a small slanting stitch or cross stitch.

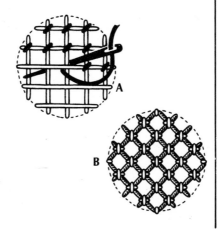

Knot stitch edging or Antwerp edging

Bring the thread through from the back of the fabric and work a single buttonhole stitch. Pass the needle behind the loop of the stitch and over the working thread as shown in the diagram. Space the stitches about 0.5cm ($\frac{1}{4}$ inch) apart. This edging is very useful for handkerchiefs or lingerie. Several rows, using a different colour for each row, make a lacy edging. The stitches of the second and following rows are worked over the loops between the stitches of the previous row.

Knotted buttonhole stitch

Make a loop from right to left over the left thumb. Insert the needle, point upwards, under the loop as at A. Slip the loop onto the needle and, with the loop still round the needle, take a stitch into the fabric as at B. Before drawing the needle through, tighten the loop round the head of the needle by pulling the working thread.

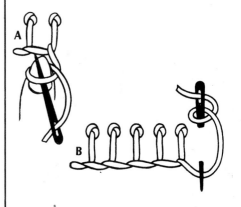

Knotted buttonhole filling stitch

Make an outline of back stitch or close running stitches, then work the detached filling as shown in the diagram. The link with the edging stitches is exaggeratedly large for clarity.

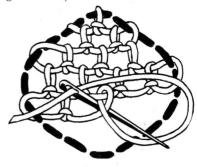

Knotted cable chain stitch

This stitch is worked from right to left. Bring the thread through at A and place it along the line of the design; then, with the thread under the needle, take a stitch at B, which is a coral knot. Then pass the needle under the stitch between A and B without piercing the fabric, as shown at C. With the thread under the needle, take a slanting stitch across the line at D, close to the coral knot. Pull the thread through to form a chain stitch.

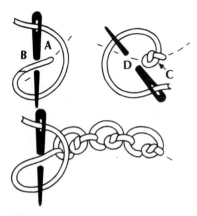

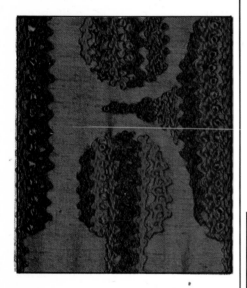

Knotted insertion stitch

This stitch is similar to knot stitch (or Antwerp stitch) edging, except that the stitches are made alternately on each piece of fabric to the joined. A small buttonhole stitch is worked into the edge of the fabric and a second stitch worked over the loops as shown in the figure.

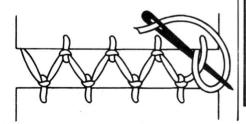

Laced running stitch

Running stitch can be laced with a contrasting colour to form a decorative border. Use a round pointed needle for lacing and do not pick up any of the fabric.

Ladder stitch

This stitch may be used to fill shapes of varying widths, but it is shown worked between parallel lines. Bring the thread through at A, insert the needle at B and bring it out at C. Insert the needle again at D and bring out at E. Pass the needle under the first stitch at F and through the double stitch at G. Continue in this way, the needle passing under two stitches at each side to form the plaited edge.

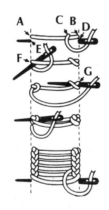

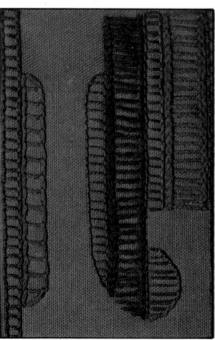

Leaf stitch

Bring the thread through at A and make a sloping stitch to B. Bring the thread through at C and make a sloping stitch to D. Bring the thread through at E, then continue working alternate stitches on each side in this way until the shape is lightly filled. This stitch is generally finished with an outline worked in stem stitch or chain stitch.

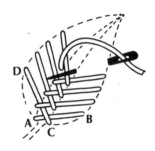

Long and short stitch

This form of satin stitch is so named because all the stitches are of varying lengths. It is often used to fill a shape which is too large or too irregular to be covered by ordinary satin stitch. It is also used to achieve a shaded effect. In the first row the stitches are alternately long and short and closely follow the outline of the shape. The stitches in the following rows are worked to achieve a smooth appearance. The figure shows how a shaded effect may be obtained.

Loop stitch

This stitch is worked from right to left. Bring the thread through at A and insert the needle at B. Bring it though again at C immediately below B. With the thread to the left and under the needle, pass the needle under the first stitch without piercing the fabric.

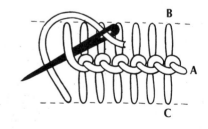

Maltese cross

This decorative motif is worked in a similar way to interlacing stitch. The intertwining of the herringbone stitch must be worked accurately, otherwise the interlacing cannot be achieved. Bring the thread through at A and take a stitch from B to C. Carry the thread from C to D and take a stitch from D to E. Continue in this way following Figure 1 until the foundation is complete. Figure 2 shows the method of interlacing, which commences at F. Figure 3 shows the complete motif.

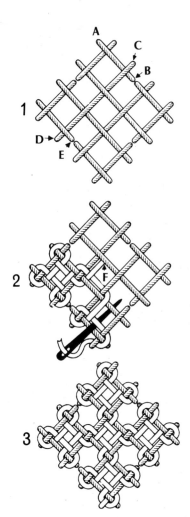

Open chain stitch

This stitch is shown worked on two parallel lines, but it may be used for shapes which vary in width. Bring the thread through at A and, holding the thread down with the

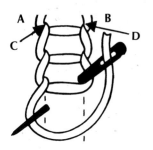

left thumb, insert the needle at B. Bring the needle through at C, the required depth of the stitch. Leave the loop thus formed slightly loose. Insert the needle at D and, with the thread under the needle point, bring it through in readiness for the next stitch. Secure the last loop with a small stitch at each side.

Open Cretan stitch

Bring the thread through at A and, with the thread above the needle, insert the needle at B and bring it through at C. With the thread below the needle, insert the needle at D and bring it through at E. All stitches lie at right angles to the guiding lines as shown in the diagram and are spaced at regular intervals. This is a useful stitch for borders.

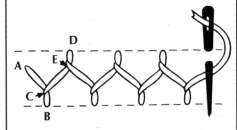

Open fishbone stitch

Bring the thread through at A and make a sloping stitch to B. Bring the thread through again at C and make another sloping stitch to D. Bring the thread through at E, continue in this way until the shape is filled.

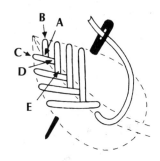

Overcast stitch (or trailing)

Bring the laid threads through at A and hold with the left thumb, then bring through the working thread at A and work small satin stitches closely over the laid threads, following the line of the design.

The laid threads are taken through to the back of the fabric to finish. This stitch resembles a fine cord and is useful for embroidering delicate stems and outlines.

Pekinese stitch

Work back stitch in the usual way, then interlace with a thread to tone or a thread of a different colour. The stitch is shown open in the diagram but the loops should be pulled slightly tighter when working.

Portuguese border stitch

Work the required number of foundation bars, which are evenly spaced horizontal straight stitches. Bring the thread through at A, with the working thread to the left of the needle. Carry it over and under the first two bars and under the second bar only without piercing the fabric. The thread is now in position at B to commence the second pair of stitches. Continue working in the same way to the top of the row. Bring a new thread through at C and proceed in exactly the same way, but with the working thread to the right of the needle. Do not pull the surface stitches tightly.

Portuguese stem stitch

Figure A, begin as for ordinary stem stitch. Figure B, pull the thread through and pass the needle under the stitch just made, without entering the fabric. Figure C, pass the needle under the same stitch below the first coil. Figure D, make another stem stitch. Figure E, pass the needle twice under the stitch just made and under the previous stitch. Figure F, a section showing the formation of the stitch.

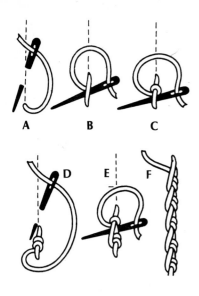

Punch stitch

This stitch can be used as a filling stitch in free embroidery – that is, over a tracing of squares or spots. A punch needle is used for the traced design to make the holes. The stitches are pulled firmly. Bring the thread through and take a stitch directly above, bringing the needle out where the thread first emerged (A). Insert the needle into the same hole above and bring out the same distance to the left on the lower line (B). Work along the row in this way, two stitches into the same place in each case (C). Turn the work upside down for each following row and continue in the same way until all vertical rows are complete (D). Turn the work sideways and repeat the process to complete the squares (E).

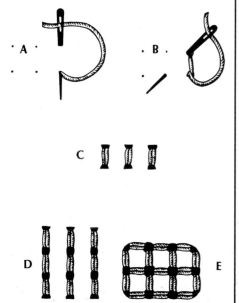

Raised chain band

Work the required number of foundation bars, which are fairly closely spaced horizontal straight stitches. Bring the thread through at A, then pass the needle upwards under the centre of the first bar and to the left of A. With the thread under the needle, pass the needle downwards to the right of A and pull up the chain loop thus formed.

Rosette chain stitch

Bring the thread through at the right end of the upper line, pass the thread across to the left side and hold down with the left thumb. Insert the needle into the upper line a short distance from where the thread emerged and bring it out just above the lower line, passing the thread under the needle point (A). Draw the needle through and then pass the needle under the top thread (B) without picking up any of the fabric. This stitch can be used for small flowers if worked round in a circle or for borders when worked straight.

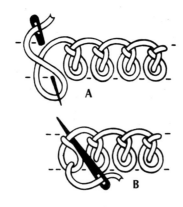

Roumanian couching

This form of couching is useful for filling in large spaces in which a flat, indefinate background is required. Bring the thread through on the left, carry the thread across the space to be filled and take a

small stitch on the right with the thread above the needle (A). Take small stitches along the line at intervals, as in B and C, to the end of the laid thread, emerging in position for the next stitch (D).

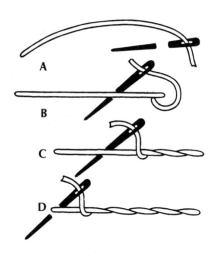

Roumanian stitch

Figure A, bring the thread through at the top left of the shape, carry the thread across and take a stitch on the right side of the shape with the thread below the needle. Figure B, take a stitch at the left side, thread above the needle. These two movements are worked until the shape is filled. Keep the stitches close together. The size of the centre crossing stitch can be varied to make a longer oblique stitch or a small straight stitch.

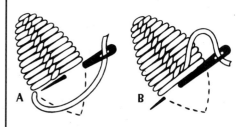

Running stitch

Pass the needle over and under the fabric, making the upper stitches of equal length. The under stitches should also be of equal length, but half the size or less of the upper stitches.

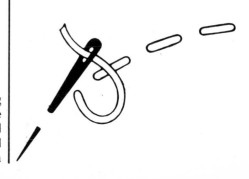

Satin stitch

Proceed with straight stitches worked closely together across the shape, as shown in the diagram. If desired, running stitch or chain stitch may be worked first to form a padding underneath; this gives a raised effect. Care must be taken to keep a good edge. Do not make the stitches too long, as this makes them liable to be pulled out of position. To keep a neat edge outline the shape first in chain or split stitch.

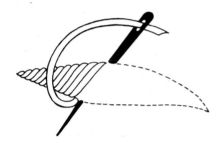

Scroll stitch

This stitch is worked from left to right. The working thread is looped to the right then back to the left on the fabric. Inside this loop the needle takes a small slanting stitch to the left under the line of the design, with the thread of the loop under the needle point. The thread is then pulled through. The stitches should be evenly spaced. This stitch forms an attractive border.

Seeding

This simple filling stitch is composed of small straight stitches of equal length placed at random over the surface, as shown in the figure.

Sheaf stitch

This is an attractive filling stitch consisting of three vertical satin stitches tied across the centre with two horizontal overcasting stitches. The overcasting stitches are worked round the satin stitches; the needle only enters the fabric to pass on to the next sheaf. The sheaves may be worked in alternate rows as shown, or in close horizontal rows directly below each other.

Spanish knotted feather stitch

Bring the thread through and hold down to the left with the left thumb. Take a slanting stitch to the left through the fabric under the laid thread and pull through with the needle point over the working thread as shown at A. Pass the thread over to the right and back to the left to form a loop and hold down, then take a slanting stitch to the right under the laid thread and pull through with the needle over the working thread B. Take a stitch in the same way to the left C. Repeat B and C to the end of the line, then fasten off with a small stitch as shown at D.

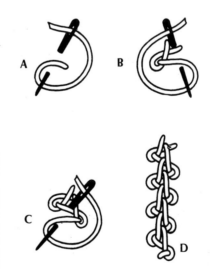

Spider's web filling

Commence with a fly stitch to the centre of the circle as shown in A. Then work two straight stitches, one on each side of the fly stitch tail, into the centre of the circle. This divides the circle into five equal sections and the 'spokes' form the foundation of the web. Weave over and under the 'spokes' until the circle is filled as at B. In drawn thread embroidery the 'spokes' are not completely covered by the weaving; only half the circle is filled, which gives the filling an open, lacy appearance.

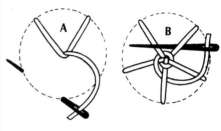

Split stitch

Bring the thread through at A and make a small stitch over the line of the design, piercing the working thread with the needle as shown in the figure. Split stitch may be used as a filling where a fine flat surface is required.

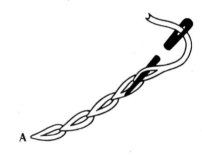

Stem stitch

Work from left to right, taking regular, slightly slanting, stitches along the line of the design. The thread always emerges on the left side of the previous stitch. This stitch is used for flower stems, outlines, etc. It can also be used as a filling, where rows of stem stitch are worked closely together within a shape until it is filled completely.

Straight stitch or single satin stitch

This is shown as single spaced stitches worked either in a regular or irregular manner. Sometimes the stitches are of varying size. The stitches should be neither too long nor too loose. This stitch may also be worked on evenweave fabric.

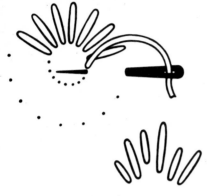

Striped woven band

Work the required number of foundation bars which are evenly spaced horizontal straight stitches. Thread two needles with contrasting threads and bring them through the fabric to lie side by side at A, the light thread on the left side. Pass the light thread under the first straight stitch and leave it lying. Take the dark thread over the first straight stitch and under the second straight stitch and also under the light thread. Leave the dark thread lying and pass the light thread over the second straight stitch, under the third straight stitch and also under the dark thread. Continue to the end of the border. Begin each following row from the top. By altering the sequence of the contrasting threads, various patterns may be achieved.

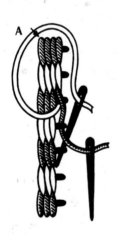

Twisted chain stitch

Commence as for ordinary chain stitch, but instead of inserting the needle into the place from where it emerged, insert it close to the last loop and take a small slanting stitch, coming out on the line of the design. Pull the thread through. The loops of this stitch should be worked closely together to give the correct effect.

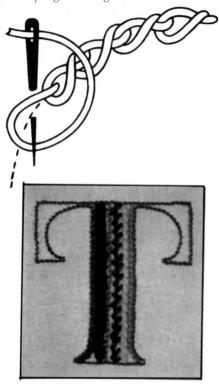

Twisted insertion stitch

A small stitch is taken alternately on each piece of fabric to be joined. The needle always enters the fabric from beneath and is twisted once round the thread before entering the fabric for the opposite stitch.

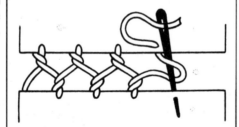

Up and down buttonhole stitch

Figure A. Commence as for ordinary buttonhole stitch and pull thread through. Figure B. Insert the needle on the bottom line and take a straight upward stitch with the thread under the needle point. Pull the thread through first in an upward move-

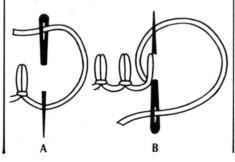

A   B

ment, then downwards to continue. This stitch may also be worked on evenweave fabric.

Vandyke stitch

Bring the thread through at A. Take a small horizontal stitch at B and insert the needle at C. Bring the thread through at D. Without piercing the fabric, pass the needle under the crossed threads at B and insert at E. Do not pull the stitches too tightly, otherwise the regularity of the centre plait will be lost.

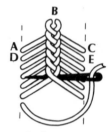

Wheatear stitch

Work two straight stitches at A and B. Bring the thread through below these stitches at C and pass the needle under the two straight stitches without entering the fabric. Insert the needle at C and bring it through at D.

Zigzag cable chain stitch

This stitch is a variation of ordinary cable chain stitch, each stitch being taken at a right angle to the previous stitch. Pull the twisted thread firmly round the needle before drawing the needle through the fabric.

480

INDEX

APPENDIX

Metrication of knitting needles

As with the measurements of most materials and tools, knitting needles are being converted to metric sizes. The designs in this book have been worked on the existing British sizes but when purchasing new needles, it is essential to check that you obtain the correct size. In order to allow you to become familiar with the new sizes, new needles will bear both the metric sizes in millimetres and the old British number. The following conversion chart has been issued by The Needlemakers' Association and from this you will see that, for example, what is now the new No. 4mm is the old No. 8, and should not be confused with the old No. 4.

English	Metric
14	2mm
13	$2\frac{1}{4}$mm
12	$2\frac{3}{4}$mm
11	3mm
10	$3\frac{1}{4}$mm
9	$3\frac{3}{4}$mm
8	4mm
7	$4\frac{1}{2}$mm
6	5mm
5	$5\frac{1}{2}$mm
4	6mm
3	$6\frac{1}{2}$mm
2	7mm
1	$7\frac{1}{2}$mm
0	8mm
00	9mm
000	10mm

Knitting and crochet abbreviations

alt	alternate(ly)
approx	approximate(ly)
beg	begin(ning)
ch	chain(s)
cm	centimetre(s)
cont	continu(e)(ing)
dec	decrease
dc	double crochet
dtr	double treble
foll	follow(ing)
g st	garter stitch, every row knit
grm	gramme(s)
gr(s)	group(s)
htr	half treble
in	inch(es)
inc	increase
K	knit
K up	pick up and knit
K-wise	knitwise
No.	number
psso	pass slipped stitch over
patt	pattern
P	purl
P up	pick up and purl
P-wise	purlwise
rem	remain(ing)
rep	repeat
RS	right side
sl	slip
sl st	slip stitch in knitting
ss	slip stitch in crochet
sp	space(s)
st(s)	stitch(es)
st st	stocking stitch, 1 row knit, 1 row purl
tbl	through back of loop
tog	together
tr	treble
tr tr	triple treble
WS	wrong side
yd(s)	yard(s)
ydk	yarn back
yfwd	yarn forward
yon	yarn over needle
yrh	yarn round hook
yrn	yarn round needle

Tension – this is the most important factor in successful knitting and crochet. Unless you obtain the tension given for these designs, you will not obtain satisfactory results.

To avoid confusion it is recommended that you decide whether to use metric or imperial measurements when beginning any pattern and adhere to the same method throughout. Note that when converting inches to centimetres, tension samples will be given to the nearest exact equivalent i.e. 10cm = 3.9in.

Symbols

An asterisk, *, shown in a pattern row denotes that the stitches shown after this sign must be repeated from that point. Square brackets, [ ], denote instructions for larger sizes in the pattern. Round brackets, ( ), denote that this section of the pattern is to be worked for all sizes. Crochet hooks have been standardized into an International Size Range, (ISR), and these sizes will be used throughout these instructions.

Picture credits:
American Museum in Britain 323
Beta pictures 350
Camera Press 168B, 193, 325, 328, 329, 343, 347, 356, 436
Cooper Bridgeman 331
100 Idees de Marie Claire 168T, 332
PAF International 334, 335, 336
Transworld 349
Ulster Folk and Transport Museum 163
Pictures page 3 by courtesy of the Victoria and Albert Museum, London.

Photographers: Steve Bicknell, Stuart Brown, John Carter, Roger Charity, Monty Coles, Richard Dunkley, Alan Duns, David Finch, Jean Paul Froget, John Garrett, Melvin Grey, Peter Heinz, Graham Henderson, Tony Horth, Jeany, Peter Kibbles, Trevor Lawrence, Chris Lewis, Sandra Lousada, Dick Millar, Julian Nieman, Kjell Nilsson, Tony Page, Roger Phillips, Peter Pugh-Cook, Iain Reid, John Ryan, Jill Smyth, John Swannell, Jerry Tubby, Jean Claude Volpeliere, Rupert Watts, Paul Williams.